AMERICAN
JOURNALISM
HISTORY

AMERICAN JOURNALISM HISTORY

An Annotated Bibliography

Compiled by
Wm. David Sloan

Bibliographies and Indexes in Mass Media and Communications,
Number 1

GREENWOOD PRESS
New York • Westport, Connecticut • London

Library of Congress Cataloging-in-Publication Data

Sloan, W. David (William David), 1947-
    American journalism history.

    (Bibliographies and indexes in mass media and
communications, ISSN 1041-8350 ; no. 1)
    Includes index.
    1. Journalism—United States—History—Bibliography.
I. Title. II. Series.
Z6951.S54 1989 [PN4731]   016.071'3   88-35800
ISBN 0-313-26350-7 (lib. bdg. : alk. paper)

British Library Cataloguing in Publication Data is available.

Library of Congress Catalog Card Number: 88-35800
ISBN: 0-313-26350-7
ISSN: 1041-8350

First published in 1989

Greenwood Press, Inc.
88 Post Road West, Westport, Connecticut 06881

Printed in the United States of America

The paper used in this book complies with the
Permanent Paper Standard issued by the National
Information Standards Organization (Z39.48-1984).

10 9 8 7 6 5 4 3 2

To Joanne

Contents

Preface

A number of individuals over the years have helped me in compiling this bibliography. Without their help, I never would have finished it. At the risk of forgetting some, I especially would mention the following. Hiley Ward, editor of *Media History Digest*, and Tom Reilly, founding editor of *Journalism History*, were particularly gracious in providing back issues of their journals. For help in locating works on the frontier press, I appreciate the assistance of Bill Huntzicker, who provided me bibliographical lists he had compiled for use in his research.

At the University of Alabama, a number of staff members and students spent innumerable hours assisting in locating and photocopying material and in the time-consuming production chores required in bibliographical work. Had they not been so generous and energetic, I might have stopped working several years ago. I especially appreciate the assistance given by Martha Mills, Julie Barnett, Dai Minxiang, Vanessa Murphree, Chris Roberts, Penny Poole, Christine Thompson, Li Xiaojia, and Yu Yang Chou.

Finally, as anyone knows who has spent years on a project, without a considerate and supportive family, such work would be intolerable. I owe a special debt to my children, Cheryl and Christopher, and to my patient wife, Joanne.

Guide to Journal Abbreviations

AA	American Archivist
AAAPS	Annals of the American Academy of Political Science
AASP	American Antiquarian Society Proceedings
ABAJ	American Bar Association Journal
AC	American Collector
AF	American Film
AgH	Agricultural History
AGR	American-German Review
AH	American Heritage
AHB	Atlanta Historical Bulletin
AHL	American History Illustrated
AHQ	Arkansas Historical Quarterly
AHR	American Historical Review
AI	Annals of Iowa
AJ	American Journalism
AJES	American Journal of Economics and Sociology
AJH	American Jewish History
AJLH	American Journal of Legal History
AL	American Literature
AlR	Alabama Review
AM	Atlantic Monthly
AmM	American Mercury
AmSp	American Speech
AmW	American West
APSP	American Philosophical Society, Proceedings
AQ	American Quarterly
A R	Antioch Review
ArHR	Arizona Historical Review
ARR	American Review of Reviews
AS	American Studies
ASc	American Scholar
ASp	American Spectator
AW	Arizona and the West
AWy	Annals of Wyoming
BAASB	British Association for American Studies Bulletin
BF	Book Forum

BHE	Black Hills Engineer
BHR	Business History Review
BHSP	Buffalo Historical Society Publications
BPLQ	Boston Public Library Quarterly
BSP	Bostonian Society, Proceedings
CA	Christian Advocate
CBAA	Current Bibliography of African Affairs
CCJ	Community College Journalist
CH	California History
CHQ	California History Quarterly
CHSM	Chronicles of the Historical Society of Michigan
CHSQ	California Historical Society Quarterly
CHSR	Columbia Historical Society Records
CJR	Columbia Journalism Review
CLAJ	CLA Journal
CM	Colorado Magazine
CO	Chronicles of Oklahoma
CQ	Communication Quarterly
CR	Communication Research
CSMC	Critical Studies in Mass Communication
CSMP	Colonial Society of Massachusetts Publications
CSMT	Colonial Society of Massachusetts Transactions
CuH	Current History
CWH	Civil War History
DAB	Dictionary of American Biography
DH	Delaware History
DLQ	Drexel Library Quarterly
EMCH	Essays and Monographs in Colorado History
EP	Editor and Publisher
FC	Film Comment
FCHQ	Filson Club History Quarterly
FCL	Federal Communications Law
FHQ	Florida Historical Quarterly
FLR	Fordham Law Review
FM	Frontier and Midland
GE	Grassroots Editor
GHQ	Georgia Historical Quarterly
GLJ	Georgetown Law Journal
HJFRT	Historical Journal of Film, Radio, and Television
HHJ	Hayes Historical Journal
HLQ	Huntington Library Quarterly
HM	Historical Magazine
HNMM	Harper's New Mothly Magazine
HP	History of Philosophy
HW	Harper's Weekly

IH	Indian Historian
IHB	Indiana History Bulletin
IHJ	Illinois Historical Journal
IMH	Indiana Magazine of History
JA	Journal of Advertising
JAC	Journal of American Culture
JAH	Journal of Arizona History
JAS	Journal of American Studies
JC	Journal of Communication
JCH	Journal of Contemporary History
JCI	Journal of Communication Inquiry
JE	Journalism Educator
JER	Journal of the Early Republic
JH	Journalism History
JISHS	Journal of the Illinois State Historical Society
JM	Journalism Monographs
JNH	Journal of Negro History
JOB	Journal of Broadcasting and Electronic Media
JPC	Journal of Popular Culture
JPFT	Journal of Popular Film and Television
JPH	Journal of Presbyterian History
JQ	Journalism Quarterly
JSH	Journal of Southern History
JW	Journal of the West
KH	Kansas History
KHQ	Kansas Historical Quarterly
KQ	Kansas Quarterly
LaH	Louisiana History
LH	Labor History
LMM	Lippincott's Monthly Magazine
LT	Library Trends
MAH	Magazine of American History
MCR	Mass Communication Review
MCRJ	Midwest Communications Research Journal
MHD	Media History Digest
MHM	Maryland History Magazine
MHR	Missouri Historical Review
MHSB	Missouri Historical Society Bulletin
MHSC	Massachusetts Historical Society Collections
MHSP	Massachusetts Historical Society Proceedings
MiHSC	Missouri Historical Society Collections
MJR	Montana Journalism Review
MLR	Michigan Law Review
MVHR	Mississippi Valley Historical Review
NAR	North American Review

NCHR   North Carolina Hstorical Review
ND   Negro Digest
NDH   North Dakota History
NEHGR   New England History and Genealogical Record
NEQ   New England Quarterly
NHB   Negro History Bulletin
NHSB   Newport Historical Society, Bulletin
NJHSP   New Jersey History Society Proceedings
NM   National Magazine
NMHR   New Mexico Historical Review
NOQ   Northwest Ohio Quarterly
NR   Nieman Reports
NYH   New York History
NYPLB   New York Public Library Bulletin
NYHSQ   New York Historical Society Quarterly
NYSHA   New York State Historical Association Proceedings
NYULR   New York University Law Review
OH   Ohio History
OHQ   Oregon Historical Quarterly
OHSQ   Oregon History Society Quarterly
PAH   Perspectives in American History
PBSA   Papers of the Bibliographical Society of America
PC   Printer's Circular
PeM   Pearson's Magazine
PH   Pennsylvania History
PHi   Pacific Historian
PHR   Pacific Historical Review
PI   Printing Impressions
PM   Pennsylvania Magazine
PMHB   Pennsylvania Magazine of History and Biography
PNLH   Pacfic Northwest Labor History
PNQ   Pacific Northwest Quarterly
POQ   Public Opinion Quarterly
PP   Pacific Printer
PR   Princeton Review
PRR   Public Relations Review
PSQ   Political Science Quarterly
PTR   Public Telecommunication Review
QJLC   Quarterly Journal of the Library of Congress
QRFS   Quarterly Review of Film Studies
RIH   Rhode Island History
RKHS   Register of the Kentucky Historical Society
RMLR   Rocky Mountain Law Review
RP   Review of Politics
SAPD   Studies in American Political Development

SAQ	South Atlantic Quarterly
SCQ	Southern California Quarterly
SDHC	South Dakota Historical Collections
SDLR	South Dakota Law Review
SE	Social Education
SHQ	Southwestern Historical Quarterly
SJMC	Studies in Journalism and Mass Communication
SLR	Syracuse Law Review
SMM	Scribner's Monthly Magazine
SR	Southern Review
SS	Social Science
SSH	Social Science History
SSJ	Social Science Journal
SWMCJ	Southwestern Mass Communication Journal
TC	Technology and Culture
THQ	Tennessee Historical Quarterly
UHQ	Utah Historical Quarterly
UQGR	Universalist Quarterly and General Review
VH	Vermont History
VMHB	Virginia Magazine of History and Biography
VQR	Virginia Quarterly Review
WHSP	Wisconsin Historical Society Proceedings
WJR	Washington Journalism Review
WLR	Wayne Law Review
WMH	Wisconsin Magazine of History
WMQ	William and Mary Quarterly
WPHM	Western Pennsylvania Historical Magazine
WTHA	West Texas Historical Association
WVH	West Virginia History

AMERICAN
JOURNALISM
HISTORY

Introduction

Americans have been writing about the history of their news media for more than 175 years. When Isaiah Thomas published *The History of Printing in America* in 1810, he initiated the most enduring form of study of mass communication. Since then, journalists, professors, sociologists, psychologists, lawyers, and other researchers have devised new disciplines to examine the media, but history has remained. While other methods have been introduced and some of them have passed away, history continues to offer a dynamic as well as fascinating means of considering American journalism. For the scholar, it provides a vital method of examining the past for the knowledge it will yield, not only about itself but about our own times also. For the layman, if book sales and popular articles are any indication, it holds more interest than any other area of the mass media except perhaps entertainment.

That such should be true is not surprising. History is one of the oldest forms of study in Western civilization. It pre-dates behavioral and social sciences, the areas popular among communication researchers today, not just by centuries but by millennia. Herodotus and Thucydides, those eminent Greek historians, were writing narratives of their nation's past more than 2,000 years before there were ever such specialists as psychologists and sociologists. History is the most universal and oldest form of study for an educated people. That Americans should turn first to history to study their nation's news media is, therefore, to be expected.

The pervasiveness of Americans' interest in journalism history is attested to by the wide range of people who have written history. In the nineteenth century, media history writing attracted its share of journalists, as one would expect; but popular writers and serious historians likewise took journalism as their subject. In the twentieth century, journalism history has become the domain principally of the college journalism professor, but professional journalists still write many of the books and articles every year, as do popular writers unconnected to either teaching or the journalism profession. No other area of study of journalism attracts such a diverse group of researchers and writers.

If anyone should wonder whether interest in history is on the decline, one needs only to look at the number of articles and books published every year. In the nineteenth century when history was the only form of media study, the number of works totaled only a few hundred. Today, more are being published than at any time in the past. Journals specializing in media history publish scores of articles each year, along with numerous articles in professional magazines and non-media journals, while the number of books has never been greater. This bibliography, which is intended primarily for the serious historian, includes only books and, for the most part, serious scholarly articles, but they total more than 2,500. Had every popular article and every article in every state and regional journal been included, the number of entries probably would be double that.

The primary purpose of this book is to assist historians in their bibliographical searches. Thorough searches are fundamental to sound historical research. The historian must be aware of the body of writing on a topic and must recognize how the historian's own work fits into that body. Today, much writing in journalism history has been undertaken with the researcher having no more than a cursory knowledge of other works. As a result, it is not uncommon for readers to find conference papers and journal manuscripts referring to general survey textbooks as the authoritative works on a topic, when in fact several specialized articles or books may have been published. This bibliography should help the researcher avoid that problem and make the task of finding specialized studies much less demanding. One will find the most important articles and books included in the following pages. Yet, no claim is made that this bibliography is exhaustive. The historian should recognize that there may be other articles and books that should be examined before research into original sources is started. In the search for those works, the historian will find other bibliographies on specialized topics useful. They should be consulted, along with the shorter bibliographies included in articles and books on the topic under study. After, and only after, the historian has become familiar with the literature on the topic, will he or she be ready to undertake research.

With so many works, the historian needs a way to keep them sorted and to comprehend them. This bibliography is intended not only to serve as a reference in the historical researcher's search for relevant studies, but also to provide a concise description of a work's approach or explanation of its theme. Even so, the person using this bibliography will gain a deeper insight into each work if that person is familiar with the schools from which journalism history has been written. By "school," we mean the general perspective the historian used. After examining hundreds of pieces of historical writing, one begins to recognize certain characteristics of groups of historians and their underlying points of view. Recognizing the school to which the historian belongs helps the reader gain a fuller understanding of the work and why the historian provides a particular assessment of the subject of the work. The following outline sketches the contours of the most common schools of journalism historians.

The writing of journalism history has gone through several periods and perspectives. The schools accounting for most of the work are the following: (1) Nationalist, (2) Romantic, (3) Developmental, (4) Progressive, (5) Consensus, (6) Cultural, and (7) Libertarian. Although we should bear in mind that some historians have written from a Marxist perspective or "Business History" approach or have studied "Intellectual History" or have attempted to apply psychoanalysis to historical subjects or have approached history from other perspectives, by far the greatest output has come from historians in the first seven schools. Understanding these schools will help the researcher grasp a wide range of the material that journalism historians have written. When attempting to understand historians' perspectives, one needs to recognize also that some historians have combined approaches from more than one school.

The earliest writing on media history, including Isaiah Thomas' *The History of Printing in America,* was done by *Nationalist* historians. They believed that the essential story of journalism history was the progress of freedom within an overall story of the developing liberty of mankind and, in particular, of the American people. In that story, America was the nation chosen to lead to the eventual liberty of all of mankind, and the press was a central feature. These historians typically were journalists or were gentlemen from New England's socially elite families who tended to favor conservatism. Most of the works they produced, like Theodore Sedgewick's *A Collection of the Political Writing of William Leggett* (1840) and Pliny White's *The Life and Services of Matthew Lyon* (1858), were predominantly political in tone, with most attention devoted to the press against a panorama of national politics. While Nationalist historians usually approached their subjects from a partisan point of view, most of them, regardless of their political leanings, were strongly nationalistic and considered the history of America as the advancing revelation of the nation's leadership in mankind's improvement. They viewed the American press as highly influential and as one of the primary factors in the advance. For Nationalist historians, journalists had been honorable men of high character and motives who fulfilled the American ideal of achievement that could be made in a society of opportunity and individualism.

The *Romantic* historians who followed shared many of the characteristics of their Nationalist predecessors. They, too, were for the most part well-to-do gentlemen from the Northeast. Indeed, such a background was essential for the historian of the nineteenth century. With public libraries a thing of the future and research libraries and archives for the collection of private papers non-existent, the historian needed some other source of material. Only those people who could afford their own libraries -- or who had acquaintances among printers and editors on whom they could rely for information -- had available the materials necessary for studying history. The historian also found it useful to have acquired some wealth; the occupation of historian was not a lucrative one. There were few people who could afford to practice it.

Romantic historians also shared the view of history as the story of the progress of liberty, civilization, and especially the American nation. They began writing about journalism history in the middle of the nineteenth century, a time when pride in American progress and achievements was popular. Like the Nationalist historians, they usually were from respectable, conservative families and tended to favor journalists from the Northeast who were patriotic and who were for the progress of mankind and liberty but not disrespectful toward established values and traditions.

The most conspicuous difference between the approach of Romantic historians and that of Nationalists was the structure of their writings. Whereas Nationalist historians tended to tell journalism history within the bigger picture of American history and institutions, Romantic historians usually placed their studies within the framework of narrative biographies. That was the result of the influence of Romanticism on literature and the arts, exalting the individual and the story-telling nature of historical composition. The Romantic historians' works, whether published as books or as articles in periodicals such as *Harper's New Monthly Magazine*, were aimed at the popular audience. The premier Romantic historian was James Parton, author of such works as *Life of Horace Greeley* (1855) and *Life and Times of Benjamin Franklin* (1864). As in those books, biographies and autobiographies accounted for approximately one-third of the works on journalism history published in the second half of the nineteenth century.

It was during the last decades of that century that the publication of journalism studies received a major boost. In the 1870s -- and increasingly in the 1880s -- history began to be taught in universities, ushering in the period of the professional historian, that scholar trained in the study of history and making a living by teaching it. The increased emphasis on history resulted in the appearance of several publications devoted exclusively to the field, such as the *Magazine of American History* and *Pennsylvania Magazine of History and Biography*. The former undertook one of the most ambitious journal projects on journalism history with the publication in 1887 of a three-part series of articles on editors from colonial times to the early 1800s. While book-length biographies continued as the primary outlet for historical writing, journals such as these were beginning to play a more prominent part.

Yet, a change had taken place in journalism even before then, and it was eventually to alter the study of history as well. In 1833 Benjamin Day had begun publication of the New York *Sun*, the first successful "penny" newspaper. It was oriented not toward politics but toward entertaining and informing the general public. By the end of the Civil War, with the stunning success of such papers as the *Sun*, Horace Greeley's New York *Tribune*, James Gordon Bennett's New York *Herald*, and Henry Raymond's New York *Times*, many people had come to think of such newspapers in the Northeastern metropolises as the proper sort of journalism and of the old partisan newspapers as aberrations. Some journalists began to think of themselves as members of a journalism profession. History seemed to them to be the story of how journalism had originated and how it had progressed to reach the successful, proper stage that the penny press had ushered in.

The first and, in many ways, most important of these *Developmental* historians was Frederic Hudson. Not only was he the managing editor of the New York *Herald*, the *news* paper *par excellence*, but he also was the author of the first book since the appearance of the penny press surveying the overall history of American journalism, *Journalism in the United States, from 1690 to 1872* (published in 1873). Many journalism historians since Hudson have drawn on his interpretation and his information. With his news-oriented background, he viewed the history of journalism as the origin and continuing evolution of journalistic techniques. His approach emphasized narratives of various episodes and biographical profiles of leading journalists, those which had contributed to journalism's progress. He explained the colonial period in terms of the beginnings of newspaper practices and the first attempts to gain freedom of the press. The revolutionary period was important not only for the colonies' fight for independence but for the press freedom it brought. The period of the party press was a negative one from the standpoint of journalistic progress, for politicians controlled the press and therefore prevented it from developing professional standards. True journalism, Hudson concluded, emerged only with the appearance of the penny press.

As the field of journalism expanded in the late 1800s, interest in the history of the profession began to grow. As a result, historical studies of the press increased in number. Although differing on a few particulars, they largely echoed Hudson's themes. As journalism in the twentieth century became more and more sophisticated as a profession, it developed more standards considered appropriate and proper for the press. Historians, most of whom had a background in the profession, began to apply the concept of professional development ever more widely, so that, except for the works of the historians in the Progressive school, the Developmental interpretation pervaded most historical studies. Many works were devoted entirely to chronicling the development of particular aspects of journalism such as the editorial function and news gathering, and others provided biographies of the individuals who had contributed to the advance of journalism, while others were based implicitly on the assumption of development.

In the early 1900s, there occurred a major development which led not only to greater reliance on the Developmental interpretation, but which resulted in a surge in writing on journalism history. That was the appearance of journalism education at the college level. Following the lead of such early programs as those at Columbia University and the universities of Illinois, Wisconsin, and Missouri, colleges around the nation began to add journalism to their curricula. By 1920, there were 131 universities offering instruction in journalism. History was one of the earliest scholarly research concerns of professors at those schools. Trained in the occupation of journalism, most professors who wrote about history approached it with the perspective of professional journalism. The Developmental interpretation then had a pervasive impact on historical assumptions because most textbooks for college courses in journalism history were cast in terms of the professional framework. With early textbooks such as James Melvin Lee's *History of American Journalism*, published in 1917, and Willard G. Bleyer's *Main Currents in the History of American Journalism*, published just ten years later, the Developmental interpretation became entrenched in historical thinking. Bleyer's was the most widely used of the early textbooks, and its successor in the 1940s,

Frank Luther Mott's *American Journalism*, continued the Developmental influence on thinking. Used as a textbook for more than thirty years, Mott's work provided the apex of the Developmental interpretation, and historians ever since have worked in his shadow. Studied by generations of students and future historians of journalism, the textbooks tended to reinforce the explanation that the history of American journalism was the story of how the press evolved in its professional characteristics.

After World War II, changing conditions in journalism encouraged changing attitudes among a new generation of Developmental historians. Several events contributed to the expansion of the professional concept that the press ideally should be autonomous from outside authority and independent of other parts of society. Influenced much by journalism's role in such episodes as the civil rights movement of the 1950s and 1960s, the Vietnam war, and the Watergate political scandal, historians sometimes viewed history as a clash between the press and established institutions such as government, religion, the military, big business, and the white racial majority. Thus, while some earlier historians had emphasized the press as a means of working within society to achieve social and political change, Developmental historians tended to emphasize such historical topics as press freedom and press-government relations in which the press confronted other units of society. Recent Developmental historians often appeared anti-nationalist. The devotion of the press, they suggested, should be to journalistic ideals rather than to a nation. Thus, they showed considerable concern with such issues as the press' autonomy in the area of national security, press freedom during wartime, and the press as a safeguard against government propaganda.

The rise of journalism education in the early 1900s also resulted in one other fundamental change in the writing of journalism history. In 1912 educators formed the American Association of Teachers of Journalism (now the Association for Education in Journalism and Mass Communication). In 1924 the AATJ, responding to the concern that the field needed its own academic journal, began publication of *Journalism Bulletin* (now *Journalism Quarterly*). It was the first journal to provide a specific outlet for historical works devoted to journalism history, and it therefore encouraged a number of professors to do historical study. Over the years, *Journalism Quarterly* has published more works on journalism history than any other publication. In 1974, however, responding to an increasing interest in history among journalism professors and a concern that the nature of *Journalism Quarterly* was too narrow for historical study, there appeared the journal *Journalism History*. It was followed in 1983 by *American Journalism*. Those two journals today publish the bulk of scholarly articles in the field. They are supplemented by *Media History Digest*, a magazine supported by the trade journal *Editor and Publisher* and aimed at a general audience.

Even during the period of journalism education and the growing dominance of the Developmental interpretation, a number of other approaches have exercised considerable influence. Next to the Developmental interpretation, the *Progressive* school has been most important. Beginning in the early 1900s, many reform-oriented journalism historians -- influenced by the ideas of such Progressive American historians as Charles A. Beard and Vernon Parrington -- began to view the past in terms of conflict between social classes. Their interpretation, clearly ideological in nature, may be summarized this way. The story of the past is that of a struggle in which editors, reporters, and some publishers were pitted on the side of freedom, liberty, civil reform, democracy, and equality against the powerful forces of wealth, class, and conservatism. The primary purpose of the press was to crusade for liberal social and economic causes, to fight on the side of the masses of common, working people against the entrenched interests in American business and government. The fulfillment of the American ideal required a struggle against those individuals and groups which had blocked the achievement of a fully democratic system. Progressive historians often placed the conflict in economic terms, with the wealthy class attempting to control the press for its own use.

Considering history to be an evolutionary progression to better conditions, Progressive historians thought of the press as an influential force in helping assure a better future.

They wrote in such a way as to show the media as tools for social change, progress, and democracy. They explained the past in cycles of democratic and journalistic advance. The latter occurred when the press improved in serving the masses in America. Progressive historians praised journalists and episodes which had contributed to greater democracy, and they criticized those favoring an elitist society and political system. Their ultimate intent was to use history in a way to influence conditions of their own time and eventually to bring about changes from the conservative status quo.

The Progressive approach was strongest before World War II, but it continues to influence writing today. Works by historians such as Oswald Garrison Villard, George Seldes, and Harold Ickes in the 1920s and 1930s provided some of the harshest attacks that have been made on the conservative press. They claimed, among other things, that newspaper owners' primary interest in making profits prevented their papers from leading much needed crusades, that self-serving owners hoped to destroy the democratic foundation of the American political system, and that owners had made newspapers into private profit-seeking businesses rather than public-spirited crusaders. Progressive historians continued such attacks after World War II, but they changed their main target from newspaper owners to conservative forces in general. The greatest threat to the press and to society, they argued, came from what they considered to be reactionary government leaders and other members of the "establishment." The main objective of the press, they believed, had to be opposition to those forces.

Similar views often were expressed by Developmental historians, who in recent years have given a distinctly liberal color to what they consider to be the proper practices of journalism. Thus, when one analyzes works by historians from the two schools, it is sometimes difficult to distinguish the particular school in which a historian fits. The clue is that Developmental historians consider liberal stands (such as support of minority groups and opposition to the government) to be part of proper journalistic practices, while Progressive historians consider such practices to be valuable within the context of liberal social and political progress.

The Progressives' emphasis on class and social differences and on economic motivations was challenged by *Consensus* historians. Reacting against the explanation of the press as an agent in a conflict between groups over social and economic structures, these historians argued that even though Americans in the past may have disagreed on isolated issues, their differences took place within a broader realm of agreement on underlying principles. Consensus historians also generally assumed that the nation as a whole was more important than one of its individual institutions, the press. They therefore favored journalistic philosophies and activities which they believed worked for the good of the nation.

The Consensus interpretation emerged as the United States faced the international threats of World War II. In the face of the threats, historians reasoned that America's past was marked more by general agreement than by conflict and that Americans, rather than being sundered by class differences, tended to be more united than divided. While Americans from time to time might disagree on particulars, their differences existed within a larger framework -- such as a belief in democracy, human freedom, and constitutional government -- that overshadowed their differences. Generally, Consensus historians claimed that American history was not marked by extreme differences among groups; and in their hands the Progressives' villains such as industrialists, businessmen, and big media owners were molded into less evil people who made constructive contributions to America. At the same time, they painted Progressives' heroes such as reformers and the labor press as less idealistic and more egocentered. Forsaking the critical attitude which had characterized much Progressive writing, Consensus historians tended to emphasize the achievements of America and its press, with the intent of showing Americans' agreement on basic principles.

The Consensus outlook had a major impact on the interpretation of numerous aspects of journalism. Historians argued, for example, that the American Revolution and the press' role in it were primarily democratic rather than economic or social. While sometimes acknowledging that muckrakers had served admirably in bringing about some much-needed reforms, some Consensus historians claimed that muckrakers frequently were amateurish in their understanding of problems and business conditions and at times aimed their darts at targets that did not deserve attack. On the other hand, in response to liberal historians' attacks on muckrakers for being conservative, some Consensus historians argued that such conservatism was a source of positive achievements. Muckrakers, they argued, comprised a constructive force precisely because they did advocate traditional moral and political principles and shunned radical changes in a social and political structure that essentially was good. Consensus historians explained the press' role in America's entry into World Wars I and II in terms of the general agreement among Americans that involvement was necessary. They viewed press performance during the wars positively, crediting the press and government information agencies for providing adequate information to the public. They concluded that the press performed responsibly in dealing with social issues and problems during the 1920s and 1930s, while criticizing extremism in radical and labor publications for its narrow perspective perspective and ineffectiveness. In general, they approached journalism history from the viewpoint that the press should work with the public and government to solve problems rather than create divisions by emphasizing problems and conflicts.

Like Consensus historians, those of the *Cultural* school considered the press a part of society, rather than a separate institution, as Developmental historians had thought of it. As an integral part of society, the press therefore was influenced by various features of its surroundings. Cultural historians were concerned primarily with how such forces as economics, politics, technology, and culture acted on and influenced the press. Thus, such questions as what factors were responsible for the founding of newspapers and under what financial conditions newspapers operated began to interest them.

The impetus for the Cultural interpretation may be traced to a 1925 work on urban sociology by Robert E. Park, one of the members of the prestigious school of sociology at the University of Chicago. In "The Natural History of the Newspaper" he suggested that the evolution of American journalism was a result of its interaction with its environment. The primary factors in determining the nature of the newspaper, he stated, were not great individual journalists but the conditions of the society and the system in which the press operated. He explained the party press of the early 1800s, for example, as a natural development from American journalism's earlier involvement with the political system. In a partisan environment, newspapers ceased to be carriers of gossip and became journals of opinion whose role was to be party mouthpieces.

In the wake of Park's essay, historians began to give more consideration to factors outside journalism itself which affected the press. Their works normally dealt with the nature and cultural role of the press, and they found that journalism usually was a mirror of society and that social, political, cultural, and economic factors greatly influenced its character. The most prolific writer in the Cultural school was Sidney Kobre. In a number of works he attempted to explain journalism as "a product of environment." His ideas typify those of the Cultural school. The nature of the press at any time in history, he believed, could be explained in large measure by the sociological influences acting on it. In *The Development of the Colonial Newspaper* (1944), for example, he attempted to show how "the changing character of the American people and their dynamic social situation produced and conditioned the colonial newspaper." The first American newspapers were products of various influences, including city growth, the public's desire for political and commercial news, and the need of business for an advertising medium. The public's and printers' ideas about political self-determination, a new American philosophy taking shape during the colonial period, greatly affected the character of the newspaper.

In 1974 James Carey published an article in which he proposed that journalism history be approached from a "cultural" perspective, and since then a number of theory-oriented historians have attempted to apply the concept. Carey's proposal should not be confused, however, with what Cultural history generally has been understood to be. A philosopher of communication rather than a historian, Carey previously had popularized a "cultural" approach to understanding the role of present-day communication. He argued that mass communication plays an essential part in people's understanding of the world about them. In studying journalism history, he said, historians should be concerned primarily about the "idea of the report," that is, what media content means to the audience. Historians who have used Carey's approach frequently have employed the phrase "symbolic meaning" of media content to express the same concept. Their studies have been marked by an emphasis on this "grand theory" to reduce the diversity of history to a single cause, and they have tended to rely on the theory, selected facts, and secondary sources rather than on rigorous research. Their primary activity has been in essays and panel discussions at academic conferences rather than in documented historical studies.

The seventh school to be discussed here, the *Libertarian* school, is as old as historical study of the American press. It also has been pervasive among journalism historians, most of whom have favored freedom of the press and have believed that Americans likewise historically have favored it. A strain of libertarianism can be detected in almost every work on journalism history. The major challenge to the Libertarian interpretation was mounted by Leonard Levy in his 1960 book *Legacy of Suppression*. There he contended that the theory of freedom of expression in early America was narrow, that the First Amendment was not intended to supersede the existing common law against seditious libel, and that it was not until the debates over the Alien and Sedition Acts in 1798-1800 that a libertarian concept of freedom of expression got a solid foothold. Levy's work has been one of the most important ever produced in influencing understanding of journalism history.

While the number of works that have been written about journalism history is vast, one does find that most studies have focused on specific underlying questions. Keeping these questions in mind will help the researcher understand the basic assumptions of historians and recognize the historiographical context of each work. The most fundamental issues addressed by historians on the various chapters in American journalism history may be stated as the following:

The Colonial Press, 1690-1765: Were America's first journalists mirrors of colonial society, advocates of their country's independence and of liberty, or the originators of modern journalism?

The Revolutionary Press, 1765-1783: Were printers ideological radicals or conservatives, and how much influence did they exercise on the American Revolution?

The Party Press, 1783-1833: Were partisan editors sycophants of politicians, central figures in the political system, or journalists who abrogated their responsibilities as independent reporters and writers?

Freedom of the Press, 1690-1800: Were early American attitudes libertarian or narrow?

The Penny Press, 1833-1861: Were journalists the founders of true journalism or the voices of the masses.

The Civil War Press, 1827-1865: Were editors effective advocates of antislavery or reluctant reformers, or were they journalists who did a professional job covering the war?

The Industrial Press, 1865-1883: Were editors advocates of progressive change, or were they reactionary; were they refining the techniques of professional journalism; or were they simply the pawns of great urban forces?

The Age of New Journalism, 1883-1900: Were people such as Joseph Pulitzer and William Randolph Hearst social reformers, reactionaries, or media giants?

The Sectional and Frontier Press, 1800-1900: Were journalists the result of the unique influences of their environment, or were they individualists who brought a unique vitality to their newspapers?

The Modern Media, 1900-1945: Was journalism a working profession, big business, an agency of reform or reactionaryism, or the outcome of huge modern economic/industrial forces?

The Media and the Age of Reform, 1900-1917: Were muckrakers concerned about liberal reform or about their own social status; and how effective were they in bringing about reform?

The Media and National Crises, 1917-1945: During the critical period bounded by the two world wars, did journalists act primarily as propagandists, responsible patriots, or professional newspeople?

Broadcasting, 1920-present: Are the electronic media best understood as traditional journalism, the result of revolutionary technology, or as a distinctive influence on American society; as primarily entertainment, business, or a democratizer of society?

The Contemporary Media, 1945-present: Are the news media today public servants, profiteering businesses, or professional journalism organizations?

In each of these questions, one sees that the essential inquiry is about the fundamental nature of American journalism. Historians have been trying to answer that question since 1810. As the recent vitality of historical study is demonstrating, they will continue to do so for many more years.

1

General History of Journalism, 1690–Present

NOTE: This section includes works that overlap two or more periods.

1. Abrams, Alan E., ed. *Journalist Biographies Master Index*. Detroit: Gale, 1979. "A guide to 90,000 references to historical and contemporary journalists in 200 biographical directories and other sources."

2. Ajami, Joseph G. "The Arabic Press in the United States Since 1892: Socio-Historical Study." Ph.D. dissertation, Ohio University, 1987. The "early ethnic press of Arab Americans played a significant role in the Arab community between 1892 and 1930. It guided the immigrants, informed them, and served as a link between them and their countrymen here and abroad....The 'new' press...reflects the characteristics of recent immigrants, noted for their high skills, mixed backgrounds, education, political awareness, and nationalistic orientation."

3. Altschull, J. Herbert. *Agents of Power: The Role of News Media in Human Affairs*. New York: Longman, 1984. History of THE American press until 1917, when the U.S. became a world power. While the press can be influential, it has been the agent of powerful political and economic forces and has operated under their control.

4. Andrews, J. Cutler. *Pittsburgh's Post-Gazette*. Boston: Chapman and Grimes, 1936. History of the *Gazette*, founded in 1786, through its 150 years. The *Gazette* began as a small paper in a sparsely-populated settlement. It played an integral role in the growth of the community into a major city. Of key interest to the paper throughout most of its existence was politics, in which it was originally Federalist, then anti-Masonic, Whig, and Republican.

5.   Angelo, Frank. *On Guard: A History of The Detroit Free Press*. Detroit: Detroit Free Press, 1981. Uncritical, in-house history on the 150th anniversary of the *Free Press*, whose author served as managing editor and associate editor for 40 years. It tells the developmental story of the *Free Press* as a *news* paper in the 1800s which broke with the opinion-oriented tradition in newspaeprs. John S. Knight took over as publisher in 1940 and took a relatively moderate stance, and the newspaper changed with the city, focusing at various times on such issues as labor, blacks, and economic and social problems.

6.   Arndt, Karl J.R., and May E. Olson, eds. *The German Language Press of the Americas*, 3 vols. Munich, Germany: K.G. Saur, 1980. Collection of 24 essays, reprinted from other publications.

7.   Arndt, Karl J.R., and May E. Olson. *German-American Newspapers and Periodicals, 1732-1955*. Heidelberg, Germany: Quelle & Meyer, 1961.

8.   Ashley, Perry J., ed. *Dictionary of Literary Biography: American Newspaper Journalists 1690-1872*. Detroit: Gale Research Co., 1985. Collection of biographies of various prominent journalists.

9.   Ashley, Perry J., ed. *Dictionary of Literary Biography: American Newspaper Journalists 1873-1900*. Detroit: Gale Research Co., 1983. Collection of biographies of various prominent journalists.

10. Baehr, Harry W., Jr. *The New York Tribune Since the Civil War*. New York: Dodd, 1936. Narrative of the newspaper institution from the Civil War through its political battles with Boss Platte, purchase of the *Herald*, and development in the 20th century.

11. Baker, Thomas Harrison. *The Memphis Commercial Appeal: The History of a Southern Newspaper*. Baton Rouge: Louisiana State University Press, 1971.

12. Bartow, Edith Merwin. *News and These United States*. New York: Funk and Wagnalls, 1952. Developmental, sociological, progressive approach to the history of news. The development of modern concepts of news was influenced by the wishes and interests of the public.

13. Beasley, Maurine, and Shelia Silver. *Women in Media: A Documentary Sourcebook*. Washington: Women's Institute for Freedom of Press, 1977. Women have been important in journalism history but often have had to battle male opposition to their participation in journalism. Compilation of excerpts from more than 30 significant documents that reflect the activities of women in the media from 1790 to the present.

14. Beckham, Raymond E. "One Hundred Years of Journalism in Provo, Utah: A History of the *Daily Herald* and Its Predecessors from 1872 to 1972." Ph.D. dissertation, Southern Illinois University, 1972. Chronological narrative of the newspaper from its early days as a Mormon paper to a member of the Scripps chain.

15. Belford, Barbara. *Brilliant Bylines: A Biographical Anthology of Notable Newspaper Women in America*. New York: Columbia University Press, 1986. Twenty-four biographies with selections from each woman's writing. The purpose is to show how "personal and economic necessity,... parents, siblings, friends, teachers, husbands, lovers...mentors," and editors influenced the women's work.

16. Bell, Earl, and Kenneth Crabbe. *The Augusta Chronicle.* Athens: University of Georgia Press, 1960. The evolution of the *Chronicle* went hand-in-hand with the evolution of American journalism, 1785-1960. Written by two Georgia newspapermen.

17. Bent, Silas. *Newspaper Crusaders: a Neglected Story.* Freeport, N.Y.: 1939. The purpose of this history, covering colonial times to the 1930s, is to bring attention to the crusade, an "immensely important function of the daily press." During the historical development of the press, crusading has been a chief element. The press is "our most powerful single agency of information, opinion, and reform." It has served "as a medium of political ideas...since its beginning in this country....[A]t times its work in this area has assumed the aspect of a crusade." (viii-ix) "As champions of reforms, as defenders of individuals," papers had "important" influence. (3)

18. Berger, Meyer. *The Story of the New York Times, 1851-1951.* New York: Simon & Schuster, 1951. Emphasizes 1896-1951. Adolph Ochs succeeded because he was bold in his business ventures, ambitious, aggressive, and persistent. Because of him and Sulzberger, the *Times* is America's pre-eminent newspaper. Gives special attention the *Times'* coverage of great news events such as the Titanic, world wars, and Peary and Byrd expeditions which *Times* subsidized.

19. Berman, Barbara Ann Portnoy. "Environmental Impact on the Ideology of a Social Movement Organization: The Jewish Daily Forward 1887-1966." Ph.D. dissertation, University of Michigan, 1972.

20. Bishop, Robert L., et al. "Determinants of Newspaper Circulation: A Pooled Cross-Section Time-Series Study in the United States, 1850-1970." *CR* 7, 1 (1980): 3-22. Price has been the most consistent variable explaining circulation.

21. Blanchard, Margaret A. "Beyond Original Intent: Exploring a Broader Meaning of Freedom of Expression." *JH* 14 (1987): 2-7. The meaning of the First Amendment should be derived from various American experiences with freedom of expression, including academic freedom, censorship, the rights of aliens, labor's right to organize, and wartime dissent.

22. Blanton, Lynne. "The Agrarian Myth in Eighteenth and Nineteenth-Century American Magazines." Ph.D. dissertation, University of Illinois, 1979. While "the traditional rhetoric praising the farmer continued almost unabated [in magazines], there was a steady erosion of the foundations of the agrarian myth beginning...[as early as] Jefferson's day."

23. Bleyer, Willard Grosvenor. *Main Currents in the History of American Journalism.* Boston: Houghton Mifflin, 1927. One of the best survey histories of American journalism emphasizes the importance that the press has exercised in democracy, public enlightenment, and social and civic improvement. The history of journalism is the story of the continuing progress and development of professional standards in the betterment of society and democracy, even though occasional setbacks, especially during periods of sensationalism, marred the progress. The press should operate responsibly and with a proper respect for propriety in order to best fulfill its responsibilities to society.

24. Brasch, Walter M. *Black English and the Mass Media.* Lanham, Md.: University Press of America, 1984. Superficial historical theorizing that the amount of Black English appearing in the media runs in cycles.

25. Brasch, Walter M., and Dana R. Ulloth. *The Press and the State: Sociohistorical and Contemporary Interpretations.* Lanham, Md.: University Press of America, 1986. Summarizes 5,000 years of the tension that exists between the press and government, with political philosophy and freedom of the press being major components. The first 35 chapters of this thick book deal with history, while the remaining 16 are written by various authors and cover a range of topics.

26. Brigham, Clarence S. "Bibliography of American Newspapers, 1690-1820." *AASP* 27-28 (1923-1924). Series of articles which "attempts to present a historical sketch of every newspaper printed in the United States from 1690 to 1820;...to locate all files found in the various libraries of the country; and...to give a complete check list of the issues in the library of the American Antiquarian Society." An excellent reference source.

27. Brod, Donald F. "Church, State, and Press: Twentieth-Century Episodes in the United States." Ph.D. dissertation, University of Minnesota, 1969. Newspapers generally did a good job covering four events, from the Scopes trial to the 1960 presidential campaign, related to the "separation of church and state."

28. Brown, Karen Fitzgerald. "The Black Press of Tennessee: 1865-1980." Ph.D. dissertation, University of Tennessee, 1982. Survey history chronicling the number of papers, prominent editors, and notable papers.

29. Buchstein, Frederick D. "The Anarchist Press in American Journalism." *JH* 1 (1974): 43-45, 66. Brief overview since the first anarchist newspaper was founded in 1833. The anarchist press has advocated liberty and the improvement of conditions for the poor; but some writers have irresponsibly advocated violence, leading to public intolerance of the anarchist press in general.

30. Bullard, Frederic Lauriston. *Famous War Correspondents.* Boston: Little, Brown, 1914. Story of the rise and professionalization of war correspondents, told in one overview chapter, twelve biographies, and two chapters on the Civil War and Spanish-American War.

31. Bullock, Penelope L. *The Afro-American Periodical Press, 1838-1909.* Baton Rouge: Louisiana State University Press, 1981.

    Brief narrative histories of 97 magazines accompanied by sketches of their editors and publishers. They campaigned for emancipation, integration, and education in an attempt to improve the conditions of black Americans. They serve as valuable sources of information on Afro-American history and culture.

32. Bullock, Penelope L. "The Negro Periodical Press in the United States, 1838-1909." Ph.D. dissertation, University of Michigan, 1971. See previous entry.

33. Burgess, Claudia F. "Editors/Reporters Who Became Novelists." *MHD* 3, 1 (1983): 34-41, 59. Sketches include Americans Stephen Crane, Ernest Heminghway, Harriet Beecher Stowe, Richard Harding Davis, William Allen White, Jack London, Damon Runyon, Sinclair Lews, Dorothy Thompson, and Mark Twain. "First hand experiences, facts mixed with imagination and insight -- these were the stuff of creative reporters and novelists whom history calls great." (59)

34. Burks, Mary Fair. "A Survey of Black Literary Magazines in the United States, 1859-1940." Ed.D. dissertation, Columbia University Teachers College, 1975.

35. Byrnes, Garrett D., and Charles H. Spilman. *The Providence Journal: 150 Years*. Providence, R.I.: Providence Journal Co., 1980. A poorly edited coffee-table book published by the *Journal*, founded in 1829, celebrating its sesquicentennial. Although the paper was integrally linked to partisan politics until the end of the nineteenth century, the authors maintain that it based its success on faithfully reporting the news, high principles, and excellent staffs.

36. Cappon, Lester J. *Virginia Newspapers: A Bibliography with Historical Introduction and Notes*. New York: D. Appleton-Century, 1936. Lists daily and weekly papers from 1821-1935, along with facts about editors. Introduction gives a history of Virginia journalism, emphasizing relationships between the press and social, political, and economic movements. Covers ownership influences, the effectiveness of the press with public opinion, methods of news gathering, and problems of newspaper economy.

37. Carter, Hodding. *Their Words Were Bullets: The Southern Press in War, Reconstruction and Peace*. Athens: University of Georgia Press, 1970. Collection of four lecture essays covering the late 1700s to the present, including the author's efforts on behalf of racial tolerance for which he won the Pulitzer Prize for editorial writing while editor of the *Delta Democrat-Times* in Greenville, Miss.

38. Caudill, Charles Edward. "The Evolution of an Idea: Darwin in the American Press 1860-1925." Ph.D. dissertation, University of North Carolina, 1986. Conflict was a major theme in press coverage of Darwin's theory of biological evolution and the reaction to it. Although the theory "did conflict with existing ideas about natural science in 1860 and with literal interpretations of the Bible...the...conflict may have been magnified by the nature of the press and its reliance on actions and reaction, whether in events or ideas....The press was not always a reliable conveyor of complex ideas."

39. Chamberlin, Joseph E. *The Boston Transcript*. Boston: Houghton Mifflin, 1930. Centennial narrative focusing on the newspaper's personnel, content, and role in Boston and its coverage of events.

40. Chambers, Lenoir, and Joseph E. Shank. *Salt Water and Printers Ink: Norfolk and Its Newspapers, 1865-1965*. Chapel Hill: University of North Carolina Press, 1967. Centennial narrative of the origins and growth of journalism in Norfolk, Va., told by two former editors of the *Virginian-Pilot*, emphasizes journalistic practices, colorful people, interesting events, crusades, stunts, newpaper mergers, financing, and other details about the inner workings of the town's newspapers.

41. Chielens, Edward E., ed. *American Literary Magazines: The Eighteenth and Nineteenth Centuries*. New York: Greenwood, 1986. Introductory essay provides an overview of 1774-1900, followed by vignettes of 92 magazines written by various professors of literature.

42. Churchill, Ward, Norbert Hill, and Mary Ann Hill. "Media Stereotyping and Native Response: An Historical Overview." *IH* 11 (December 1978): 46-56, 63. The mass media have stereotyped American Indians since the late 19th century. In the 1960s, however, a changing social climate led to the creation of "a forum for nonstereotypical

Native entertainers" in popular music and to a lesser degree in film and television.

43. Claiborne, Jack. *The Charlotte Observer, Its Time and Place, 1869-1986.* Chapel Hill: University of North Carolina Press, 1986. Narrative history written by an associate editor of the newspaper, emphasizing its stands on social and political issues, its growth, and its relationship to its city.

44. Conrad, Will C., Kathleen F. Wilson, and Dale Wilson. *The Milwaukee Journal: The First Eighty Years.* Madison and Milwaukee: University of Wisconsin Press, 1964. Laudatory narrative, written by three members of the *Journal's* staff, recounts the successful efforts of publishers Lucius W. Nieman, who founded the paper in 1882, and Harry J. Grant. The paper's success has been based on integrity, concern for the public good, tolerance for diverse ideas and freedom of thought, and its emphasis on news..

45. Cope, Neil B. "A History of the Memphis *Commercial Appeal.*" Ph.D. dissertation, University of Missouri, 1969. Narrative history with emphasis on the newspaper's notable achievements.

46. Covington, Jess Baker. "A History of the *Shreveport Times.* Ph.D. dissertation, University of Missouri, 1964. Narrative history of a "great, modern newspaper that has been a recognized leader for more than 90 years in Northwest Louisiana, Northeast Texas, and Southwest Arkansas."

47. Culp, D.W., ed. *Twentieth Century Negro Literature.* Atlanta: J.S. Nichols, 1902. Includes biographies of journalists.

48. Czitrom, Daniel J. *Media and the American Mind: From Morse to McLuhan.* Chapel Hill: University of North Carolina Press, 1982. How Americans' attempts "to comprehend the impact of modern communication" have evolved since the mid-1800s and how these efforts figure in "the larger realm of American social thought." Examines contemporary responses to the telegraph, motion picture, and radio. The telegraph served to modernize the press and commercial systems. Motion pictures "challenged the received notions of culture itself" and had a major impact on everyday life. Radio and advertising were wed and served to "commercialize" aspects of American culture. Examines philosophers/scholars' attempts to explain the role of the media. While media technologies have offered the opportunity for promoting progress, unfortunately they have been used for dominance and exploitation. Especially in broadcasting, advertising has promoted the "consumption ethic as the supreme virtue," although it is also true that broadcasting (radio) has helped to carry ideas across cultural and racial lines, thus helping to promote an integration and leveling of society.

49. Dabney, Thomas E. *One Hundred Great Years: The Story of the Times-Picayune from Its Founding to 1940.* Baton Rouge: Louisiana State University, 1944. Favorable institutional narrative written by a former New Orleans newspaperman, emphasizing the history of the city and times as revealed in the *Times-Picayune's* columns.

50. Daniel, Walter C., ed. *Black Journals of the United States.* Westport, Conn: Greenwood, 1982. Contains profiles of various publications.

51. Daniels, Jonathan. *They Will Be Heard: America's Crusading Newspaper Editors.* New York: McGraw-Hill, 1965. Editors who fought for improvements served as leaders in the "continuing American crusade." This history of crusaders, which favors a

liberal ideology, covers the colonial period to the 20th century and is built around brief biographies of journalists (including, among others, John Peter Zenger, William Duane, Francis Blair, Elijah Lovejoy, Horace Greeley, George Jones, and William Allen White) and narratives of episodes. Generally, the journalists have been on the side of the average person against the aristocratic and rich, the democratic against the monarchic, the liberal against the conservative, "the rights of the people" against "strict social order and profitable economic stability." (44)

52. Danky, James P., Maureen E. Hady, and Richard Joseph Harris, eds.. *Native American Press in Wisconsin and the Nation*. Madison: University of Wisconsin Library School, 1982. Proceedings of a 1982 conference, including papers on the history of American Indian journalism.

53. Dann, Martin, ed. *The Black Press (1827-1890)*. New York: G.P. Putnam, 1971. Anthology of articles by black writers in black newspapers as part of the quest for black national identity.

54. Davis, Elmer. *History of the New York Times, 1851-1921*. New York: New York Times, 1921. Focuses most attention on the years after 1896, favorably portraying Adolph Ochs as an indefatigable publisher who resurrected the *Times* through his keen business sense, sound management, and fair news and editorial policy.

55. Dennis, Everette E., and Melvin L. Dennis. "Political Cartoonists: Honing a Fine Edge." *MHD* 5, 4 (1985): 17-22, 49. Survey from Thomas Nast to the present, with emphasis on the Great Depression. "[E]ditorial cartoonists of the 1930s concerned themselves with cartoons of immediate impact, which provided a clear presentation of an editorial idea. These cartoons were simply drawn....Personal caricature diminished and cartoons seem to have lost their sting." (17)

56. Desmond, Robert W. *The Information Process: World News Reporting to the Twentieth Century*. Ames: Iowa State University Press, 1978. Survey history of world news reporting from Acta Diurna in 131 B.C. to the end of the 19th century, along with the social, political, economic, and technological background. Most of the book covers British and American correspondents, agencies, and technology in the last half of the 19th century.

57. Detweiler, Frederick G. *The Negro Press in the United States*. Chicago: University of Chicago Press, 1922. General survey history covering the previous 100 years. The treatment of antebellum history is weak. The treatment of the content of the press is adequate, but the explanation of why the press took on the characteristics it did is superficial.

58. Dill, William A. *Growth of Newspapers in the United States*. Lawrence: University of Kansas Bulletin, 1928. General survey history.

59. Drewry, John E. "A Study of *New Yorker* Profiles of Famous Journalists." *JQ* 23 (1946): 370-80. Lists journalists who have been profiled in the *New Yorker* magazine.

60. Edelman, Hendrik. *The Dutch Language Press in America: Two Centuries of Printing, Publishing and Bookselling*. Nieuwkoop, The Netherlands: De Graff, 1986. Introduction provides a survey history, followed by a bibliography covering 1693 to 1948.

61. *Editor & Publisher 100th Anniversary 1884-1984. EP* Sec. 2 (March 31, 1984): 370ff. Articles survey various aspects of journalism during *Editor & Publisher's* century of publication.

62. El Dabbas, Maida M. "Historical Overview of Arab-American Newspapers." *MHD* 5, 2 (1985): 53-56. "Arab-Americans have played a significant role in the development of the press in the United States with their establishment and maintenance of Arabic newspapers and journals." (53)

63. Ely, Margaret. *Some Great American Newspaper Editors*. New York: 1916.

64. Emery, Edwin, ed. *The Story of America as Reported by Its Newspapers from 1690-1965*. New York: Simon and Schuster, 1965. Reproductions of newspaper front pages covering the major and sensational events in American and newspaper history. Reproductions are arranged chronologically and accompanied by summary histories of each period.

65. Emery, Edwin, and Henry Ladd Smith. *The Press and America: An Interpretative History of the Mass Media*. Englewood Cliffs, N.J.: Prentice-Hall, 1954. (Revised five times; later editions are co-authored by Edwin Emery and Michael Emery). This survey history, written from a black-and-white Progressive ideological perspective, has been widely used as a textbook. History is the story of how the press supported the rights of the common people against the powerful and wealthy. The great journalists have been liberal ones. The press should challenge the "establishment" and must defend its rights against attacks from government and from conservative groups.

66. Evans, Harold. *Front Page History: Events of Our Century That Shook the World*. London: Quiller Press/Photo Source, 1984. Summarizes major stories, 1900 to 1984, from newspapers in the United States, England, and Canada.

67. Fairbanks, Merwin G. "A History of Newspaper Journalism in Alton, Illinois, from 1836 to 1962, as Represented by the Alton *Evening Telegraph* and Its Predecessors." Ph.D. dissertation, Southern Illinois University, 1973. Narrative history of the editors and events.

68. Farrar, Ronald T., and John D. Stevens, eds. *Mass Media and the National Experience: Essays in Communications History*. New York: Harper & Row, 1971. Collection of original essays by eleven authors exploring various aspects of journalism history in an attempt to propose new approaches to such topics as press freedom, quantitative methods in historical research, media and government, and communication technology. Essays are the following: "Mass Communication History: A Myriad of Approaches" (Ron Farrar); "Freedom of Expression: New Dimensions" (Stevens); "Politics, Economics, and the Mass Media" (William Ames and Dwight Teeter); "Technology: Freedom for What?" (Donald Shaw); "The Challenge of Regionalism" (Richard Hixon); "Black Journalism: Neglected No Longer" (Stevens); "The Journalist as Social Critic" (John Harrison); "Photographic Communication: An Evolving Historical Discipline" (R. Smith Schuneman); "Broadcast History: Some Unresolved Issues" (Richard Burke); "Local Newspapers and Local History" (William Taft); and "Behavioral Concepts and Tools: The Historian as Quantifier" (Robert Thorp).

69. Finnegan, Owen E. "An Historical and Metaphysical Study of Natural Law Theory Applied to Questions of Freedom of Expression in the United States." Ph.D.

dissertation, Michigan State University, 1965. An attempt "to develop through empirical investigation and historical study an ethic of the media of mass communication proper to the American political philosophy rooted as this is in natural law theory."

70. Fishkin, Shelly Fisher. *From Facts to Fiction: Journalism and Imaginative Writing in America.* Baltimore: Johns Hopkins University Press, 1985. The journalistic work of five American writers -- Walt Whitman, Mark Twain, Theodore Dreiser, Ernest Hemingway, and John Dos Passos -- provided the material for subjects and the style for their best fictional writing.

71. Ford, Edwin. *Readings in the History of American Journalism.* Minneapolis: University of Minnesota, 1939.

72. Ford, Edwin, and Edwin Emery. *Highlights in the History of the American Press.* Minneapolis: University of Minnesota Press, 1954. Reprint of 27 historical articles on major episodes.

73. Forsyth, David P. *The Business Press in America, 1750-1865.* Philadelphia: Chilton Books, 1964. Specialized business publications, through their relationship to business and industry, wielded an extensive influence on the nation's economy.

74. Forsyth, David P. "The Rise of the Business Press in the United States, 1750-1865." Ph.D. dissertation, Northwestern University, 1962. See previous entry.

75. Francke, Warren. "Sensationalism and the Development of 19th-Century Reporting: The Broom Sweeps Sensory Details." *JH* 12 (1985): 80-85. Such journalistic devices as court reports, interviews, and eyewitness reporting lent themselves to sensationalized coverage from the 1830s to the 1890s.

76. Garistina, Concetta A. "The Imaginary World of Pen Names." *MHD* 7, 1 (1987): 49-53. How some famous journalistic pen names originated.

77. Giffin, Joseph. *History of the Press of Maine.* 1872.

78. Gleason, Timothy W. "The Origins of the Watchdog Concept of Freedom of the Press: The Influence of Nineteenth Century Common Law." Ph.d. dissertation, University of Washington, 1986. "[P]ublishers in the 19th century used the watchdog concept [i.e., that of the press protecting the public's rights] in attempts to fashion a legal defense for the publication of false facts within the common law of libel." Most courts did not accept their argument.

79. Gleason, Timothy W. "19th-Century Legal Practice and Freedom of the Press: An Introduction to Unfamiliar Terrain." *JH* 14 (1987): 26-33. Examination of "the common law, the teaching and scholarship of law, and judicial use of common law to protect majoritarian interests" (27) suggests "that 19th-Century judges did not view freedom of the press through the same libertarian prism used in the 20th Century and that the law did not reflect the broad libertarian view of freedom of the press attributed to the founding fathers." (26)

80. Good, Howard. "The Image of Journalism in American Poetry." *AJ* 4 (1987): 123-32. "Distinguished American poets of the past century and a half have portrayed journalism

either ambivalently or negatively. Their view of the press, particularly of the mass-circulation newspaper and television, has been anything but unbiased. As their voices
have been increasingly drowned out by shrill headlines and fast-talking newscasters,
and as they have felt their cultural authority eroding, they have grown increasingly dis-
traught and resentful. Poetry and journalism have seemed to most of them to occupy
opposite ends of the spectrum." (123)

81.   Good, Howard. "The Image of War Correspondents in Anglo-American Fiction." *JM*
      97 (1986). Novels and short stories suggest "that the reporters are frauds and thrill
      freaks; that they callously profit from the misery of others; that they cannot continue in
      their jobs without losing their essential humanity....The war correspondent of contem-
      porary fiction doubts the sanity and morality of his role even as he rushes off to the lat-
      est flashpoint. War for him is less and less an adventure or a crusade and more and
      more an unalleviated disaster." (20-21)

82.   Gordon, George N. *The Communications Revolution: A History of Mass Media in the
      United States*. New York: Hastings House, 1977. Sketchy survey history of print and
      broadcast media, emphasizing the 20th century and the Northeast and focusing on de-
      velopments.

83.   Gore, George W., Jr. *Negro Journalism: An Essay on the History and Present Condi-
      tions of the Negro Press*. Greencastle, Ind.: DePauw University, 1922. Brief overview
      expanded from an undergraduate term research paper.

84.   Gottlieb, Robert, and Irene Wolt. *Thinking Big: The Story of the Los Angeles Times,
      Its Publishers and Their Influence on Southern California*. New York: Putnam's, 1977.
      The *Times* under the Chandler family grew as Los Angeles expanded. The owners
      were the arbiters of business and culture in the city, and the paper typified the nation's
      growing trend toward metropolitan newspaper monopoly.

85.   Gramling, Oliver. *AP: The Story of News*. New York: Farrar and Rinehart, 1940. Ac-
      count of the beginning, growth, and progress of the Associated Press written by an AP
      staff member. From its founding in 1848, the AP has played a large role in the growth
      of objective reporting, telegraphy, the inverted-pyramid story form, etc.

86.   Griffith, Louis T., and John E. Talmadge. *Georgia Journalism, 1763-1950*. Athens:
      University of Georgia Press, 1951. Journalists were motivated by their distinctive
      Georgia heritage and surroundings.

87.   Grose, Charles William. "A Century of Black Newspapers in Texas, 1868-1969."
      Ph.D. dissertation, University of Texas, 1972. "Operating as a supplement to white
      newspapers...black newspapers...played a significant role in the black man's civil
      rights struggle. Black unity, loyalty and advancement were among the emphases of the
      papers."

88.   Gutierrez, Felix. "Spanish-Language Media in America: Background, Resources, His-
      tory.' *JH* 4 (1977): 34-41. Favorable survey history emphasizing the achievements of
      the Latino press and calling for improvements in historians' study of it.

89.   Hart, Jack Robert. "The Information Empire: A History of the Los Angeles *Times* from
      the Era of Personal Journalism to the Advent of the Multi-Media Communications Cor-
      poration." Ph.D. dissertation, University of Wisconsin, 1975. From its founding in

1881 by Harrison Gray Otis, the *Times* was conservative in politics. In the 1960s Otis Chandler began to reduce the influence of ideology on news coverage, and the *Times* became one of the best papers in the nation.

90. Hart, Jack. *The Information Empire: The Rise of the Los Angeles Times and the Times Mirror Corporation.* Washington: University Press of America, 1981. See previous entry.

91. Hart, Jim Allee. "An Historical Study of the St. Louis *Globe-Democrat*, 1852-1958." Ph.D. dissertation, University of Missouri, 1959. Since its founding, the newspaper has been a solid, respectable one that has shunned sensationalism. It is a "typical" daily.

92. Hart, Jim Allee. *A History of the St. Louis Globe Democrat.* Columbia: University of Missouri Press, 1961. See previous entry.

93. Hart, Jim A. "The Other Newspaper in St. Louis." *JQ* 39 (1962): 324-32. Overview history of the *Globe-Democrat.* See previous entry.

94. Hart, Jim Allee. *Views on the News: The Developing Editorial Syndrome, 1500-1800.* Carbondale: Southern Illinois University Press, 1970. History of the development of the editorial function. It was during the period of the party press in the 1780s and '90s that the editorial separate from the news columns developed.

95. Hess, Stephen, and Milton Kaplan. *The Ungentlemanly Art: A History of American Political Cartoons.* New York: Macmillan, 1968, 1975.

Includes 300 cartoons from previous two centuries.

96. Hoe & Co., R. *A Short History of the Printing Press and of the Improvements in Printing Machinery from the Time of Gutenburg up to the Present Day.* New York: R. Hoe, 1902. History of technological improvements compiled and published by the leading manufacturer of printing presses.

97. Hohenberg, John *The Pulitzer Prizes: A History of the Awards.* New York: Columbia University Press, 1974. Account of the various winners of the Pulitzer, along with inside information about the administration of the awards, written by the Pulitzer Prize administrator and told from a favorble viewpoint.

98. Hooker, Richard. *The Story of an Independent Newspaper: One Hundred Years of the Springfield Republican, 1824-1924.* New York: Macmillan, 1924. The paper rejected "the lure of greater financial returns, to be had for the paper through the practice of other ways." (ix) It was born as a partisan voice. This history provides a favorable account of the paper as an opponent of aristocratic politics and an advocate of democracy. Its founder, Samuel Bowles, "recognized the need of a determined direction for the new paper, which was to be 'a genuine democratic press' representing the Republicans." (7) (Hooker was a member of the paper's staff.)

99. Hower, Ralph M. *The History of an Advertising Agency: N.W. Ayer and Son at Work, 1869-1949.* Cambridge, Mass.: Harvard University Press, 1949. Business history of the newspaper ad agency.

100. Howey, Walter, ed. *Fighting Editors*. Philadelphia: David McKey Co., 1948. Collection of stories originally appearing in the *American Weekly* of brave editors and reporters in crusades for truth in reporting. Editors were more interested in serving the people than in gaining something themselves. Progressive/developmental popular account including such topics as Zenger, the Miami *Herald*, Henry Grady, the Ku Klux Klan, Hazel Brannon Smith, World War I, etc.

101. Hudson, Frederic. *Journalism in the United States, From 1690 to 1872*. New York: Harper & Row, 1873. The first survey journalism history written after the appearance of the penny press, Hudson's is a Developmental history told from the perspective of the penny press as being true journalism. Many journalism histories since Hudson's have used his perspective and much of the material in this work. The narrative is detailed with character profiles of journalists and various episodes involving papers. Hudson had been a staff member of the New York *Herald*, a paper which emphasized news over opinion more than did other papers of the mid-1800s.

102. Hudson, Robert V. *Mass Media: A Chronological Encyclopedia of Television, Radio, Motion Pictures, Magazines, Newspapers, and Books in the United States*. New York: Garland, 1987. Lists events from 1638 to 1985 with a brief summary of each.

103. Hughes, Helen M. "A Geneology of Human Interest Stories." *JQ* 14 (1937): 1-6. See next entry.

104. Hughes, Helen M. "The Human Interest Story: A Study of Popular Literature." Ph. D. dissertation, University of Chicago, 1936. Survey history and definition of the "human interest" news story, which appeals to human curiousity to understand the experiences of people like oneself.

105. Ingelhart, Louis Edward. *Press Freedoms: A Descriptive Calendar of Concepts, Interpretations, Events, and Court Actions, from 4000 B. C. to the Present*. Westport, Conn.: Greenwood Press, 1987. Encyclopedia of events and quotations about freedom of the press arranged in chronological order.

106. Isaacs, George A. *The Story of the Newspaper Printing Press*. London: Co-operative Printing Society, 1931. Detailed account of the developments from the Gutenberg press to the high-speed presses of the 20th century, with considerable attention to mechanics.

107. Johnson, Allen, and Dumas Malone, eds. *Dictionary of American Biography*, 21 vols. New York: Scribners, 1928-1937. Contains biographies of many journalists.

108. Johnson, Charles S. "The Rise of the Negro Magazine." *JNH* 13 (January 1928): 7-21. The "shifting and intangible circumstances of Negro status" have been the most important element in determining the nature of black magazines. From the first black publication (*Freedom's Journal*, 1827), the problems facing magazines have been "in essence the same....Increasing literacy, economic improvement, and the shifting facets of such general social questions as temperance, religion and morals, have determined largely the changes." (7)

109. Johnson, Gerald, et.al. *The Sunpapers of Baltimore, 1837-1937*. New York: Knopf, 1937. The Baltimore *Sun* started out as penny newspaper modeled after the New York penny press. This favorable centenniel, authorized history was written by members and former members of the *Sun's* staff.

110. Jones, Robert W. *Journalism in the United States.* New York: Dutton, 1947. Survey history placing the press against its social and economic background, with particular interest in journalism outside the metropolitan east.

111. Kaminski, Thomas H. "Congress, Correspondents and Confidentiality in the 19th Century: A Preliminary Study." *JH* 4 (1977): 83-87, 92. In four cases in the 1800s, newspaper reporters refused to divulge the sources of information in their stories. The reporters considered "confidentiality as one of their profession's settled principles." (83)

112. "The Kansas City Star: The First 100 Years -- A Man, a Newspaper, and a City." Kansas City *Star*, special centennial section (Sept. 18, 1980).

113. Kauffmann, Samuel H. *The Evening Star (1852-1952): A Century at the Nation's Capital.* Washington: Newcimen Society, 1952. Authorized centennial history.

114. Kessler, Lauren. *The Dissident Press: Alternative Journalism in American History.* Beverly Hills, Calif.: Sage, 1984. America has had a long tradition of alternative journalism. This survey from the 1800s to the present focuses on journalism of six "fringe groups -- political, social, and cultural -- who, denied access to the mainstream media marketplace, started marketplaces of their own...: Black Americans; utopians and communitarians; feminists; non-English-speaking immigrants; Populists, anarchists, socialists, communists, and the splinter groups; and pacifists, noninterventionists, and resisters during World War I, World War II, and Vietnam." (15-16)

115. Kessler, Lauren. "Up the Creek without a Paddle." *Quill* (November 1984): 40-44. Brief, favorable survey of dissident and underground newspapers, which served as important "forums for unpopular political, social, cultural, and religious beliefs" (40) and in so doing helped protect Constitutional rights.

116. King, William L. *The Newspaper Press of Charleston, S.C.: A Chronological and Biographical History, Embracing a Period of One Hundred and Forty Years.* Charleston: Edward Perry, 1872.

117. Kinsley, Philip. *The Chicago Tribune: Its First Hundred Years.* 5 vols. New York: Knopf; Chicago: Chicago Tribune, 1943-1946. Institutional, disjointed history covering the *Tribune's* staff, coverage, views, growth, and success from the paper's founding in 1847 (written by a member of the paper's staff).

118. Kleisch, Ralph E. "History and Operations of the McGraw-Hill World News Service." Ph.D. dissertation, University of Minnesota, 1968. Narrative history of an international news-gathering service as "one minor, but important, aspect of the American business press."

119. Kluger, Richard. *The Paper: The Life and Death of the New York Herald Tribune.* New York: Knopf, 1986. History from the founding of the *Herald* in 1835 and of the *Tribune* in 1841 until after the *Herald Tribune's* death in 1966. The *Tribune's* owners, from Horace Greeley to John Hay Whitney, always had been concerned about quality. The paper set trends in writing, subject matter, and typographic appearance. Its death was due to the baneful influence of corporate chain journalism.

120. Kobre, Sidney. *Development of American Journalism.* Dubuque: Wm. C. Brown,

1969. Lengthy, detailed survey history, attempting to place journalism within the context of its cultural, sociological, political, and economic environment, demonstrating "how American journalism as a social institution evolved. The interest is not only in painting in the historical background of the great press periods, but in showing the interaction of the press with changing social forces. This sociological approach gives coherence to a multitude of complex facts about the press."

121. Kobre, Sidney. *Foundations of American Journalism*. Tallahassee: Institute of Media Research, School of Journalism, Florida State University, 1958. Survey history from colonial period through the Civil War.

122. Kraus, Andrew Read. "Editors Who Ran for President." *MHD* 1,1 (1980): 8-16. Sketches of five: James Birney, Horace Greeley, Robert La Follette, Warren Harding, and Henry Wallace. "With the exception of Harding, they were all third party candidates whose papers served as mouthpieces for their own philosophies. For the most part, their impact was likely greater than the votes indicate, as each fought earnestly for a cause and leavened the ingredients of the American process and dream." (16)

123. La Brie, Hank, III. "Black Newspapers: The Roots are 150 Years Deep." *JH* 4 (1977): 110-113. Brief overview of the history of black American newspapers from the founding of the first, *Freedom's Journal*, in 1827 through their 150th anniversary. The "black press has served to light the way toward freedom and more importantly, chronicle the events and personalities of black America." (111)

124. La Brie, Henry G., III. *Perspectives on the Black Press*. Kennebunkport, Me.: Mercer House, 1974.

125. Lawson, Gregg. "Jailhouse Journalism: History of Prison Papers." *MHD* 5, 2 (1985): 28-31, 40. Survey history of a handful of newspapers produced by inmates. They have made positive contributions to prison life.

126. Lee, Alfred McClung. *The Daily Newspaper in America: The Evolution of a Social Instrument*. New York: Macmillan, 1937. Study of the press from sociological, economic, and liberal political points of view. The topical arrangement emphasizes that impersonal sociological influences, rather than great individuals, determined the course of history. The development of newspapers was a natural result of "technological changes, raw material conditions, labor difficulties, financial relationships, circulation arrangements, advertising practices, newsgathering methods, legal considerations and editorial policies." (vii) Newspapers went through an evolutionary growth (similar to changes as posited in the biological theory of evolution) marked throughout history by a process of invention or of variation from methods, selective elimination of less effective methods, and transmission of the effective methods to other newspapers.

127. Lee, James Melvin. *History of American Journalism*. Boston: Houghton Mifflin, 1917 (rev. ed., 1923) Disjointed, antiquarian survey history emphasizing the development and progress of journalism, written from the favorable perspective of professional journalism.

128. Lent, John A. "The Wild, Wild Names of Newspapers." *MHD* 6, 1 (1986): 36-39. Stories behind some strange newspaper names, especially those of the frontier west.

129. Leonard, Thomas G. *The Power of the Press: The Birth of American Political*

Reporting. New York: Oxford University Press, 1986. The news media have served as a common means for Americans to participate in the political system. Narrative concentrates on seven episodes from the Boston inoculation controversy in the 1720s to muckraking in the early 1900s.

130. Levy, Sheldon G. "Distance of Politically Violent Events From Newspaper Source over 150 Years." *JQ* 51 (1974): 28-32. The nature of violent events, rather than their distance from the newspaper, appears to be the main consideration in the nature of news coverage by the *National Intelligencer* and New York *Times*.

131. Lipper, Mark. "Comic Caricatures in Early American Newspapers as Representations of the National Character." Ph.D. dissertation, Southern Illinois University, 1973. From the colonial period to 1860, "newspaper caricatures entered the popular culture not because they reflected the character and custom of the nation, but because they served as effective vehicles for social and political satire and had the broad appeal that is necessary in the popular arts of a middle-class, democratic and capitalistic society."

132. Lippy, Charles H., ed. *Religious Periodicals in the United States.* Westport, Conn.: Greenwood, 1986. Contains profiles of various publications.

133. Littlefield, Daniel F., Jr., and James W. Parins. *American Indian and Alaska Native Newspapers and Periodicals, 1826-1924.* Westport, Conn.: Greenwood, 1984. Contains profiles of more than 200 publications, along with references, bibliography, and other research information.

134. Long, David F. "The New York News, 1855-1906: Spokesman for the Underprivileged." Ph.D. dissertation, Columbia University, 1950.

135. Loomis, Carl Floyd. "Monoserif: An Historical Review of the Technical Developments Affecting the Designing of Typefaces." Ph.D. dissertation, Syracuse University, 1974. Overview of various mechanical, "technical developments in the manufacture of type and the effect they had on...type designers."

136. Lutz, William W. *The News of Detroit: How a Newspaper and a City Grew Together.* Boston: Little, Brown, 1973.

137. Lyons, Louis M. *Newspaper Story: One Hundred Years of the Boston Globe.* Cambridge, Mass.: Harvard University Press, 1971. Centennial chronology written by a former reporter (1919-1946) for the *Globe*, with an emphasis on its internal workings and personnel.

138. Magyar, Linda Feinfeld. "The Evolution of Presidential Press Secretaries." *MHD* 5, 2 (1985): 2-9. Chronology of activities that led to institution of the position, emphasizing developments from McKinley to Hoover.

139. Malmquist, O. N. *The First 100 Years: A History of the Salt Lake Tribune 1871-1971.* Salt Lake City: Utah State Historical Society, 1971. The *Tribune* was founded as an opponent of Brigham Young and with the goal of reforming the Mormon Church. Much of its first half-century was marked by struggles about the role of the church in Utah. In the 20th century, it came under the direction of Thomas Kearns, whose political ambitions necessitated that he moderate the *Tribune's* stand on church issues, and then Kearns' personal secretary, John Fitzpatrick, who emphasized an objective,

detached approach. Under Kearns and Fitzpatrick, especially the latter, the *Tribune* became a solid, stable newspaper.

140. Marbut, Frederick B. "Congress and the Standing Committee of Correspondents." *JQ* 38 (1961): 52-58. Since its founding in 1877, the committee of journalists has worked to provide accommodations and rules of procedure for reporters covering the U.S. Congress.

141. Marbut, Frederick B. *News from the Capital. The Story of Washington Reporting.* Carbondale and Edwardsville: Southern Illinois Press, 1971. This history of the press coverage of Washington from 1806 to 1971 emphasizes the importance of the coverage to the development of the American democratic system.

142. Marzolf, Marion Tuttle. "The Danish-Language Press in America." Ph.D. dissertation, University of Michigan, 1972. In the hundred years since the first Danish-language newspaper was founded in 1862, the press' "major impact...was as an aid to the immigrants' assimilation."

143. Marzolf, Marion. "The Literature of Women in Journalism History: A Supplement." *JH* 3 (1976): 116-20. Continuation of next entry.

144. Marzolf, Marion, Romona R. Rush, and Darlene Stern, comps. "The Literature of Women in Journalism History." *JH* 1 (1974): 117-28. Useful bibliography covering works about the general topic and about particular female journalists.

145. Marzolf, Marion. *Up From the Footnote: A History of Women Journalists.* New York: Hastings House, 1977. Women journalists have been discriminated against. They have been important in journalism history, even though they've had to battle the opposition of men. They have progressed from the society page to other parts of the paper.

146. Marzolf, Marion. "The Woman Journalist: Colonial Printer to City Desk." *JH* 1 (1974): 100-07, 146. Survey history from colonial times to the 1970s with favorable biographies of a number of women. Based on secondary rather than primary sources.

147. Matheson, John M. "Steam Packet to Magic Lantern: A History of Election-Returns Coverage in Newspapers of Four Illinois Cities, 1836-1928." Ph.D. dissertation, Southern Illinois University, 1967. "[S]peedy collection and dissemination of election returns depended not only upon development of technology, but on organization capable of utilizing that technology to maximum advantage....[A] concept of 'unofficial returns' has become institutionalized and...the press...provides non-governmental agencies to audit the outcome of elections."

148. Mathews, Joseph J. *Reporting the Wars.* Minneapolis: University of Minnesota Press, 1957. Survey history of war coverage from the Crimean War to the Korean.

149. McNulty, John Bard. *Older Than the Nation.* Stonington, Conn.: Pequot Press, 1964. Bicentennial history of the Hartford (Conn.) *Courant* from 1764 to 1964.

150. McPhaul, John J. *Deadlines & Monkeyshines: The Fabled World of Chicago Journalism.* Englewood Cliffs, N.J.: Prentice-Hall, 1962. Entertaining, well-documented account of the antics of Chicago reporters and editors since 1833.

151. McWilliams, Carey. "One Hundred Years of 'The Nation.'" *JQ* (1965): 189-97. Centennial history written by *The Nation's* editor argues that the writings of Godkin, Villard, and other editors "exerted a significant, demonstrable impact on the course of events." (189) The magazine "has always stood...[for] idealism." (197)

152. Meyer, Katherine, John Seidler, Timothy Curry, and Adrian Aveni. "Women in July Fourth Cartoons: A 100-Year Look." *JC* 30 (Winter 1980): 21-30. Political cartoons "reflect women's place in American culture without specifically intending that theme." Five newspapers' Fourth of July cartoons between 1870 and 1976 show "a continual decline in the percentage of cartoons portraying women, a distancing of female images via stylization, and an increased subtlety of subordination" to men. Men have remained dominant over women throughout the entire period.

153. Miller, Sally M. ed. *The Ethnic Press in the United States: A Historical Analysis and Handbook*. Westport, Conn.: Greenwood, 1987. Includes essays by various authors discussing the newspapers of 28 ethnic groups, their histories, and their relevance to their community. The main purposes of the ethnic press have been preservation of ethnic culture and assimilation into American society.

154. Moore, Roberta June. "The Beginning and Development of Protestant Journalism in the United States, 1743-1850." Ph.D. dissertation, Syracuse University, 1966. Describes how 400 periodicals "portrayed and affected movements and controversies in American Protestant churches."

155. Morison, Bradley L. *Sunlight on Your Doorstep: The Minneapolis Tribune's First Hundred Years*. Minneapolis: Ross & Haynes, 1966. Centennial history, commissioned by the *Tribune* and written by a retired member of its staff, details the paper's editorial positions, its influence on the city, and the important roles played by such publishers as William Murphy and John Cowles and by its editors.

156. Morris, James M. "Journalism Behind Bars." *QJLC* 40 (Spring 1983): 150-61. Survey history of newspapers produced by prisoners since the first American one began in 1800. The writers and editors have tried to educate the public about prison conditions and "focus attention on what they consider the many injustices of the system." (161)

157. Mosco, Vincent, and Janest Easko, eds. *Critical Communications Review, Volume 1: Labor, the Working Class, and the Media*. Norwood, N.J.: Ablex, 1983.

Examines the historical relationship between the media, labor, and industry. Concern primarily is contemporary and activist.

158. Mott, Frank Luther. *American Journalism: A History of Newspapers in the United States Through 250 Years, 1690 to 1940*. New York: Macmillan, 1941. Survey history written with a "sympathetic admiration for American journalism" which, in revised editions, for many years served as the standard textbook. Views history from the professional perspective of the present as the origin, development, and perfection of journalism: emphasis on news, press freedom, political independence, mass circulation, support of the common people, and journalism as a profession. This book serves as a standard source on journalism history.

159. Mott, Frank Luther. *A History of American Magazines*, 5 vols. New York: D. Appleton; Cambridge: Harvard University Press, 1930-1968. Exhaustive survey covering

1741 to 1930s which won both the Pulitzer and the Bancroft prizes for history. Each volume chronicles selected magazines, discusses various aspects of their publishing practices, and places them within their social, economic, and literary environment. Of all works published on journalism history, this is the most authoritative. It covers the general development of American magazines, including types of writing, relations to politics, arts and sciences, publishing problems of finance and advertising, and the editing, management, distribution and contents of magazines.

160. Mott, Frank Luther, and Ralph O. Casey, eds. *Interpretations of Journalism*. New York: F.S. Crofts, 1937. Collection of 64 notable articles about the press and about journalism history.

161. Moyes, Norman Barr. "Major Photographers and the Development of Still Photography in Major American Wars." Ph.D. dissertation, Syracuse University, 1966. Study of "the most notable combat photographers" from the Civil War to the Vietnam war, including "their problems, equipment and training....Trends have included the recognition of the role of the combat photographer, the emphasis on the photo journalist,...the advent of the miniature cameras," and increased emphasis on human-interest photographs.

162. Murphy, James E., and Sharon M. Murphy. *Let My People Know: American Indian Journalism*. Norman: University of Oklahoma Press, 1981. Descriptive chronicle covering 1828 to 1878. Indian newspapers, laboring in meager financial conditions, have attempted to preserve the Indians' heritage and to fight for their rights in society.

163. Nelson, William. *Notes Toward a History of the American Newspaper*. New York: Charles F. Heartman, 1918. Histories of newspapers of 30 states in alphabetical order. Incomplete: one of two intended volumes.

164. Nevins, Allan. *American Press Opinion, Washington to Coolidge*. New York: Heath, 1928. Extensive anthology of newspaper editorials from the 1780s to the 1920s. Introductory essays for the various periods are well-informed, lucid narratives.

165. Nevins, Allan. *The Evening Post: A Century of Journalism*. New York: Boni & Liverwright, 1922. Perhaps the best history of an individual newspaper. The *Evening Post* was founded in 1801 as a vehicle for the expression of Alexander Hamilton's views during the Federalists' bleakest hour, right after Jefferson's election. Nevins describes the paper not as a scurrilous one but as one interested in accurate news on many subjects and in well-reasoned opinion. It was a superior newspaper under William Coleman, William Cullen Bryant, and successive editors.

166. Nevins, Allan, and Frank Weitenkampf. *A Century of Political Cartoons*. New York: Scribner's, 1944. Collection of 100 cartoons published in the 19th century. The best cartoonists provided artistic craftsmanship, interpretation, and satire.

167. *New York Sun: One Hundredth Anniversary, 1833-1933*. New York: The Sun, 1933. In-house centennial history.

168. North, S.N.D. *History and Present Condition of the Newspapers and Periodical Press of the United States*. Washington: Government Printing Office, 1884. A publication of the 10th census, containing extensive statistical tables.

169. O'Brien, Frank M. *The Story of the Sun*. New York: Appleton, 1919, 1928. Favorable narrative, institutional history of the first successful penny newspaper, emphasizing its founding in 1833 and early success and its years under Charles Dana, when it became the "newspaperman's newspaper."

170. O'Kelly, Charlotte G. "Black Newspapers and the Black Protest Movement: Their Historical Relationship, 1827-1945." *Phylon* 43 (Spring 1982): 1-14. "The black press has been closely related to the black protest movement and to racial issues in general. Black owned and operated newspapers began in relation to the abolitionist movement and continued to operate within the context of the general social movement protesting treatment of blacks in the United States....A strong tradition of protest and activism thus developed during the earliest years of the black press." (14)

171. O'Kelly, Charlotte G. "The Black Press: Conservative or Radical Reformist or Revolutionary?" *JH* 4 (1977): 114-7. Historiographical essay on how historians and other writers have explained the nature of the black press. Suggests that "how militant or conservative the black papers have been may be...irrelevant. From a wider point of view, the content of the black press may be more fruitfully viewed as a reaction to white society." (115)

172. *One Hundred Years of Famous Pages from the New York Times, 1851-1951*. New York: Simon & Schuster, 1951. Fascimile reproductions of 100 pages covering notable events.

173. Oswald, John Clyde. *A History of Printing: Its Development Through Five Hundred Years*. New York: Appleton, 1928. Narrative, encyclopedic account of printing after 1450, with the bulk of attention devoted to Europe.

174. Park, Robert E. "The Natural History of the Newspaper." 80-98 in Park, Ernest W. Burgess and Robert D. McKenzie, *The City*. Chicago: University of Chicago Press, 1925. This sociological approach to explaining the development of the modern newspaper has been widely quoted by historians. "The press, as it exists, is...the outcome of a historic process in which many individuals participated without foreseeing what the ultimate produce of their labors was to be. The newspaper, like the modern city, is not wholly a rational product. No one sought to make it just what it is. In spite of all the efforts of individual men and generations of men to control it and make it something after their own heart, it has continued to grow and change in its own incalculable ways." (80)

175. Payne, George Henry. *History of Journalism in the United States*. New York: Appleton, 1920. Survey history, written from a Progressive perspective, emphasizing the importance of journalism to democracy, freedom, and political advance throughout American history. The leading journalists have been crusading reformers.

176. Pember, Don. *Mass Media History*. Chicago: Science Research Associates, 1984. Survey history covering more than 500 years, from the invention of movable type to the present, showing the changes in media as societies changed from agricultural to industrial and to post-industrial.

177. Penn, Garland I. *The Afro-American Press and Its Editors*. Springfield, Mass.: Wiley, 1891. Editors attempted to improve the status of black Americans by removing stereotypes and advocating changes in political policies and economic conditions.

Because of the low economic status of black readers, newspapers had financial difficulty.

178. Perkin, Robert L. *The First Hundred Years: An Informal History of Denver and the Rocky Mountain News, 1859-1959*. Garden City, N.Y.: Doubleday, 1959.

179. Perry, Edwin A. *The Boston Herald and Its History*. Boston: 1878.

180. Petersen, William J. *The Pageant of the Press: A Survey of 125 Years of Iowa Journalism 1836-1961*. Iowa City: State Historical Society of Iowa, 1962. Collection of facsimile reproductions of newspaper pages, preceded by a short introductory historical essay on the state's pioneer press, the Des Moines *Register*, and recent recipients of the state press association's "Master Editor-Publisher Award."

181. Peterson, Paul Vanard. "The *Omaha Daily World* and *World-Herald*, 1885-1964." Ph.D. dissertation, University of Minnesota, 1966. The newspaper succeeded because its staff was tenacious, it gave readers more and better news than its competitors did, and it aligned with the surging Democratic party. Emphasis is on 1885 to World War I.

182. Pickett, Calder M. *Voices of the Past: Key Documents in the History of American Journalism*. Columbus, Ohio: Grid, 1977. Useful anthology of newspaper articles from colonial times to the present.

183. Pilgrim, Tim A. "Privacy and American Journalism: An Economic Connection." *JH* 14 (1987): 18-24. In the 19th century, privacy "may have been threatened by journalists who were willing to pry information from people and write that information in a sensational way. Many reporters...practiced aggressive and sensationalistic writing...because ...the news system...placed reporters into intense competition with one another and rewarded them economically depending largely on whether or not the resulting story was published....Thus...any drive by reporters to invade privacy has an economic connection -- a connection running parallel to economic elements dominating development of the mass press." (24)

184. Pollard, James E. *The Presidents and the Press*. New York: Macmillan, 1947. A useful compendium of quotes about the press found in presidents' correspondence, in effect a chronology of presidential statements in regard to journalism. The author makes little attempt at interpretation, categorization, or explanation. Some presidents acted differently toward the press than did others, and there was no typical model.

185. Press, Charles. *The Political Cartoon*. East Brunswick, N.J.: Associated University Press, 1981. During a history of 250 years, the cultural, social, and political environment and the cartoonist's art have been instrumental in determining the nature of the cartoon.

186. Preston, Dickson J. *Newspapers of Maryland's Eastern Shore*. Queenstown, Md.: Queen Anne Press; and Centreville, Md.: Tidewater Publishers, 1986. Popular history filled with anecdotes on papers from the early 1800s to the 1980s. Early papers were more concerned with political causes than with making money. Since the Civil War, they have been primarily interested in events of their local area rather than in national affairs.

187. Price, Warren Charles. "The Eugene Register-Guard: Citizen of Its Community, 1867-1967." Ph.D. dissertation, University of Minnesota, 1967. Favorable "centennial history [which] traces both the growth of newspaper journalism in...Eugene and the changing patterns of life in the community itself." The paper campaigned for the welfare of its community and for civil liberties.

188. Price, Warren C. *The Eugene Register-Guard: Citizen of Its Community.* Vol. 1. Portland, Ore.: Binford & Mort, 1976. See previous entry. Price died before completing the manuscript, which detailed the history only through the 1950s, thus accounting for the "Vol. 1" designation.

189. Pride, Armistead S. "A Register and History of Negro Newspapers in the United States 1827-1950." Ph.D. dissertation, Northwestern University, 1956.

190. Prior, Granville T. "A History of the Charleston *Mercury*, 1822-52." Ph.D. dissertation, Harvard University, 1947.

191. Reilly, Mary Lonan. "A History of the Catholic Press Association 1911-1968." Ph.D. dissertation, Notre Dame University, 1970.

192. Rice, William B. *The Los Angeles Star 1851-1864.* Berkeley: University of California Press, 1947. Narrative history of the policies, growth, staff, and role of the newspaper in its community.

193. Riley, Sam G. *Index to Southern Periodicals.* Westport, Conn.: Greenwood, 1986. A companion reference work to the following entry.

194. Riley, Sam G. *Magazines of the American South.* Westport, Conn.: Greenwood, 1986. Profiles 89 magazines from 1764 to 1984.

195. Roberts, Chalmers M. *The Washington Post, The First 100 Years.* Boston: Houghton Mifflin, 1977. Centennial, authorized, in-house history written by a *Post* reporter and emphasizing the newspaper's content.

196. Roff, Sandra Shoiock. "A Feminist Expression: Ladies' Periodicals in the New-York Historical Society Collection." *JH* 9 (1982): 92-99. Survey of the characteristics of 19th-century women's magazines found in the Society's collection. The magazines provided "an important outlet for feminine expression and together probably had some influence on trends in manners, morals and literature." (98)

197. Rosenberg, Norman L. *Protecting the Best Men: An Interpretive History of the Law of Libel.* Chapel Hill: University of North Carolina Press, 1985. Libel law has varied from colonial times to the present because of differing conditions in such things as social values, newspaper practices, constitutional interpretation, and legal doctrines. In the 1800s, when defamed political figures could rely on partisan newspapers to defend them, there was little interest in legal protection against libel. Around 1900, with the influx of poorly educated immigrants and the emergence of newspapers independent of political parties, political officials began to forge libel laws for protection. From then until the *Times v. Sullivan* case in 1964, libel was not considered to be protected by the First Amendment.

198. Rosewater, Victor. *History of Cooperative News-Gathering in the United States.* New

York: Appleton, 1930. Favorable account of the origin, development, and progress of news-gathering agencies, told by a former newspaperman. The first cooperative effort was New York's association of morning newspapers in 1820s. Emphasizes the Associated Press.

199. Rutland, Robert. *The Newsmongers: Journalism in the Life of the Nation 1690-1972.* New York: Dial Press, 1973. General survey history.

200. Saalberg, Harvey. "*Westliche Post* of St. Louis: A Daily Newspaper for German-Americans, 1857-1938." Ph.D. dissertation, University of Missouri, 1967. "Although primarily serving the German immigrant, whose number was large in St. Louis, the *Westliche Post* played an active part in the affairs of St. Louis and Missouri, as it guided the political direction of German-Americans to some extent."

201. Saalberg, Harvey. "The *Westliche Post* of St. Louis: German-Language Daily, 1857-1938." *JQ* 45 (1968): 452-6. See previous entry.

202. Sass, Herbert Rovenel. *Outspoken: 150 Years of the News & Courier.* Columbia: University of South Carolina Press, 1953. A history, not especially well done, published on the occasion of the sesquicentennial of the Charleston newspaper.

203. Scharf, J. Thomas, and Thompson Westcott. "The Press of Philadelphia," in *History of Philadelphia*, Vol. II. Philadelphia: L. H. Everts & Co., 1884. Encyclopedic survey history.

204. Schiller, Dan. "An Historical Approach to Objectivity and Professionalism in American News Reporting." *JC* 29, 4 (1979): 46-57. Objectivity was "the fundamental contribution of a thoroughly commercial newspaper press arising in the middle decades of the nineteenth century." This brief survey examines how and why it developed and how journalists learned its implicit rules. By 1900 objectivity no longer "served to balance the commercial newspaper's apparent concern for public good with its own private interest, and with concerns of its major sources." Objectivity, therefore, was threatened and then became part of the "professional" and ethical codes of journalism. (See Schiller entry in the "Penny Press" chapter of this bibliography.)

205. Schilpp, Madelon Golden, and Sharon M. Murphy. *Great Women of the Press.* Carbondale. Southern Illinois University Press, 1983. Collection of essays on 18 journalists, all of whom were pioneers in various areas, and their contributions to the press. Their family backgrounds and environments were important to their newspaper careers.

206. Schroth, Raymond A. *The Eagle and Brooklyn: A Community Newspaper 1841-1955.* Westport, Conn.: Greenwood, 1979. From its founding until about 1920, the *Eagle* was one of America's best newspapers, despite the fact that it had not always acted with integrity. It was a promoter of Brooklyn's success and the city's controlling economic and political groups. As Brooklyn became an economically, religiously, and racially mixed urban area in the 20th century and as Manhattan superseded it, the *Eagle* continued with the same unrealistic "chamber of commerce" and elitist approaches it had used in the 19th century in promoting Brooklyn. Eventually the *Eagle*, out of touch with modern reality, ceased publication, leaving one of the U.S.'s largest urban centers without a newspaper.

207. Schudson, Michael. *Discovering the News: A Social History of American Newspapers*. New York. Basic Books, 1978. Interpretive explanation of the rise and fall of objectivity in news coverage, 1830s-1970s. Objectivity did not emerge with the wire services, as some historians argued, but in the 1920s and 1930s in response to the general loss of faith in facts and the spread of subjectivity following World War I. (Research relies primarily on secondary sources.)

208. Schwarzlose, Richard Allen. "The American Wire Services: A Study of Their Development as a Social Institution." Ph.D. dissertation, University of Illinois, 1965. "The major American wire services...have developed as a central component in the process of mass social communication." Before the 1890s, a central aspect of their history was the attempt to bring stability to the field. Since then, "the drive for stability has been replaced...by market-oriented, geographical and technological expansion."

209. Scott, Frank W. "Newspapers, 1775-1860," 176-95 in *The Cambridge History of American Literature*, Vol. 2. New York: Putnam, 1918. Brief survey chronicling the conditions and development of the press. Uses outstanding examples to demonstrate influence, politics, writing style, new practices, social conditions and their effects, etc.

210. Scott, Frank W. "Newspapers Since 1860," pp. 319-36 in *The Cambridge History of American Literature*, Vol. 3. New York: Putnam, 1921. Journalism grew and advanced in news-gathering techniques after 1860. "[I]ts desire and ability to serve...the best public interests are on the whole remarkable." (336)

211. Scroggins, Albert W. "History of the *Missouri Intelligencer*. Ph.D. dissertation, University of Missouri, 1960.

212. Shaw, Archer H. *The Plain Dealer: One Hundred Years in Cleveland*. New York: Knopf, 1942.

213. Shaw, Donald Lewis. "Bias in the News: A Study of National Presidential Campaign Coverage in the Wisconsin English Daily Press, 1852-1916." Ph. D. dissertation, University of Wisconsin, 1966. Bias declined, primarily because of the increased use of wire service material.

214. Shaw, Donald L. "The Nature of Campaign News in the Wisconsin Press 1852-1916." *JQ* 45 (1968): 326-29. Over time, Wisconsin newspapers' use of telegraph stories on presidential campaigns increased, both in number and the percentage of the news hole they filled. See previous entry.

215. Shaw, Donald L. "News Bias and the Telegraph: A Story of Historical Change." *JQ* 44 (1967): 3-12. Bias in campaign news stories in Wisconsin newspapers declined in the 1880s because of increased use of telegraph news. See previous entry.

216. Sloan, Wm. David. "Great American Editorials." *Masthead* (1978-1988). Continuing series on editorials selected for their historical significance or stylistic quality.

217. Sloan, Wm. David, ed. *Pulitzer Prize Editorials: America's Best Editorial Writing, 1917-1979*. Ames: Iowa State University Press, 1980. Anthology containing one editorial from each winner of the prize.

218. Sloan, Wm. David, Valarie McCrary, and Johanna Cleary, eds. *The Best of Pulitzer*

Prize News Writing. Columbus, Ohio: Publishing Horizons, 1986. Anthology of 71 articles from 1916 to 1982, with selection based on writing quality.

219. Smiley, Nixon. *Knights of the Fourth Estate: The Story of the Miami Herald*. Miami: Seeman, 1974. Admiring narrative, with ample background on Miami and Florida history, about the development of the *Herald* into an outstanding modern newspaper.

220. Smith, Anthony. *The Newspaper: An International History*. London: Thames & Hudson, 1979. Economics, technological, social, and cultural factors determined the history of the press.

221. Smith, J. E. *One Hundred Years of Hartford's Courant: From Colonial Times through the Civil War*. New Haven, Conn.: Yale University Press, 1949. The *Courant* sought to be on the side of substantial benefits for large numbers of people.

222. Smythe, Ted Curtis. "A History of the Minneapolis *Journal*, 1878-1939." Ph.D. dissertation, University of Minnesota, 1967. Chronological history "with emphasis on changes [in technology, content, and responsibility] brought by men and time."

223. Sneed, Stephanie. "Hoaxes." *MHD* 1, 2 (1981): 58-60. Brief details of a handful of faked newspaper stories.

224. Stensaas, Harlan S. "The Objective News Report: A Content Analysis of Selected Daily Newspapers for 1865 to 1954." Ph.D. dissertation, University of Southern Mississippi, 1986. Objectivity continually increased from 1865 to 1954. "It was apparently not influenced by the introduction of the telegraph and wire services, and there is no apparent difference between reports between New York City newspapers and those of other cities....[The] possible 'cause' [was] a basic shift in Western culture and thought which may be labeled 'Secularization.'"

225. Stevens, George Edward. "A History of the Cincinnati Post." Ph.D. dissertation, University of Minnesota, 1969. Chronology of the paper's success under Scripps ownership.

226. Stewart, Kenneth, and John Tebbel. *Makers of Modern Journalism*. Englewood Cliffs, N.J.: Prentice-Hall, 1952. Survey history, beginning with colonial journalism, told in the context of outstanding journalists and based on the theme that the main characteristic of the press has been the effort to gain freedom and its main purpose to safeguard the people from the government. "The newspapers of America began as the voice of revolution, and in little more than two centuries they have accomplished the full swing from radical revolt to solid conservatism. In the process, however, they have retained the single dominant quality which has always distinguished the press in this country: a freedom of thought and action unsurpassed anywhere else in the world. [Journalists] have been considered dangerous men by those who crave absolute power and authority." (3-4)

227. Stonecipher, Harry. "Editorial Role-Playing in History." *GE* 16 (March-April 1975): 18-24; 16 (May-June 1975): 18-22. This brief survey views at the role of the editor as a crusader, guardian of the public trust, persuader, interpretor, and news communicator from colonial times to the present. James Franklin was the first American editor to crusade and to question the authority of the church in everyday life. The colonial editor was not a newsman but a publisher of material submitted by others.

Editors play roles shaped by their experience and society.

228. Suggs, Henry Lewis. *The Black Press in the South 1865-1979. Contributions in Afro-American and African Studies*. No. 74. Westport, Conn.: Greenwood, 1983. Historical essays on 12 states. White papers did not cover blacks, making it necessary for blacks to have their own papers. Low literacy rates and little advertising, however, limited the quality that the papers could attain.

229. Summerlin, Claude W. "A History of Southern Baptist State Newspapers." Ph.D. dissertation, University of Missouri, 1968. Analytical narrative history (1802-1967) detailing purposes, financing, content, editorial stands on social and political issues, and role in denominational affairs.

230. Taft, William H. *Encyclopedia of Twentieth Century Journalists*. New York and London: Garland, 1986. Brief biographical sketches of more than 750 journalists, most after World War II.

231. Taft, William H. "The Toledo Blade: Its First One Hundred Years, 1835-1935." Ph.D. dissertation, Western Reserve University.

232. Talley, Robert. *One Hundred Years of The Commercial Appeal*. Memphis: Memphis Publishing Co., 1940. Centennial, institutional, in-house history of the Memphis newspaper.

233. Tebbel, John. *An American Dynasty: The Story of the McCormicks, Medills, and Pattersons*. New York: Doubleday, 1947; Westport, Conn.: Greenwood, 1968. The dynasty owed its growth and success to "the stubborn, aggressive, eccentric McCormicks; the willful, aristocratic, domineering Medills; and the religiously dogmatic Pattersons." Covers the New York *Daily News* and Washington *Times-Herald*, with emphasis on Col. Robert McCormick and the Chicago *Tribune*.

234. Tebbel, John *The Compact History of the American Newspaper*. New York: Hawthorn Books, 1963 (rev. 1969). Brief narrative survey written from a liberal professional perspective. During the first 50 years of the history of U.S. newspapers, "the broad outlines of a great struggle were clearly laid down, one which continues to the present day. For the history of the American newspaper is a record of the Establishment's effort to control the news and of private individuals to disclose it without restriction." (11) People such as Benjamin Harris, James Franklin, and John Peter Zenger were heroes who "were quite naturally in revolt against the Establishment....The pioneer was James Franklin, ...who became the first real newspaper editor in America, and whose *New England Courant* was the first American newspaper worthy of the name." (16-17)

235. Tebbel, John. *The Media in America*. New York: Crowell, 1975. This narrative survey history, focusing mainly on print media, is intended for a general audience and explains the past in terms of parallels with the present. It explains newspapering as both journalistic and political. The underlying theme in media history has been the struggle to define the idea of a free press and make it a reality, to free the press from government regulation.

236. Thomas, Isaiah. *The History of Printing in America*. Albany, N.Y: Munsell, 1810. Newspapers played an important role in the creation of the American nation and the

liberties of its citizens. One of the central features in their history was gaining freedom from British authority. The colonial press was "not entirely free from restraint. The rulers in the colony of Virginia in the seventeenth Century, judged it best not to permit public schools, not to allow the use of the press, and thus, by keeping the people in ignorance, they thought to render them more obedient to the laws, to prevent them from libelling the government, and to impede the growth of heresy, etc. The press had become free some years previous to the commencement of the revolution; but it continued for a long time only to discriminate between liberty and licentiousness." (7)

237. Thomas, Dana L. *The Media Moguls*. New York: Putnam: 1981. Anecdotal, critical treatment of the most prominent newspaper publishers and other media owners from the late 19th century to the present.

238. Van Meter, Andy. *Always My Friend: A History of the State Journal-Register*. Springfield, Ill.: Copley Press, 1981. Institutional history of the Springfield paper since its founding in 1836.

239. Ward, Hiley Henry. "Ninety Years of the National Newspaper Association: The Mind and Dynamics of Grassroots Journalism in Shaping America." Ph.D. dissertation, University of Minnesota, 1977. Study of "the themes and controversies that united the [small-town] editors in the changing, troubled years of the tightening of the frontier and cessation of ideas of progress and the ebbing of the dream of a redeemer nation."

240. Waxman, Meyer. "Survey of the American Jewish Press," pp. 1279-1305 in *A History of Jewish Literature*, Vol. 4: 2. New York: 1960. Overview history of the Yiddish, Hebrew, and Anglo-Jewish press.

241. Weisberger, Bernard A. *The American Newspaperman*. Chicago: University of Chicago Press, 1961. Brief narrative overview of the general history of journalism from colonial times to the present, as one of the volumes in the "Chicago History of American Civilization Series," edited by Daniel Boorstin.

242. Weissberger, S.J. "The Rise and Decline of the Yiddish-American Press." Ph.D. dissertation, Syracuse University, 1972. The "evolution of the Yiddish press" is traced "from its beginning in 1870, through various periods of development, growth, and significant influence, to its present state of decline."

243. Wells, Robert W. *The Milwaukee Journal: Its First 100 Years*. Milwaukee: Journal Co., 1981. Centennial in-house history.

244. Wendt, Lloyd. *The Chicago Tribune: The Rise of a Great American Newspaper*. Chicago: Rand McNally, 1979. Voluminous history detailing the personnel, politics, relationship of Chicago, and development of the *Tribune*, which for many years called itself "The World's Greatest Newspaper," from its founding in 1847 through its intense political conservatism to its responsible journalism in 1977.

245. Westmoreland, Reginald Conway. "A History of the Dallas (Tex.) *Times Herald*. Ph.D. dissertation, University of Missouri, 1961. The paper, founded in 1879, has had "a colorful and energetic background." Narrative focuses on the "leadership and influence" of various editors and publishers.

246. Whitfield, Stephen J. "The Jewish Contribution to American Journalism." *AJ* 3

(1986): 99-112. Survey history of Jews who have been notable American journalists. They have played a role whose significance is disproportionate to their number in American society possibly because of their cosmopolitan outlook.

247. Wilds, John. *Afternoon Story: The History of the New Orleans States-Item*. Baton Rouge: Louisiana State University Press, 1976. Narrative, institutional centennial history of the *Item*, founded in 1880 and merged with the *States* in 1958.

248. Willis, Paul G. "Political Libel in the United States, 1607-1949." Ph.D. dissertation, Indiana University, 1949.

249. Wilson, Charles. *First with the News: A History at W.H. Smith and Son Since 1792-1972*." Garden City, N.Y.: Doubleday, 1986. History of a British distributor of periodicals.

250. Wittke, Carl. *The German-Language Press in America*. Lexington: University of Kentucky Press, 1957. Survey history covering 1732 to 1957.

251. Wolseley, Roland E. *The Black Press, U.S.A.* Ames: Iowa State University Press, 1971. Contemporary survey includes three historical chapters listing the outstanding journalists and newspapers.

2

The Colonial Press, 1690–1765

252. Abbott, Jacob. "Early and Private Life of Benjamin Franklin." *HNMM* 4 (1852): 145-65. Romantic biography includes some material on Benjamin Franklin's internship to his brother James.

253. Abbott, Jacob. "Public Life of Benjamin Franklin." *HNMM* 4 (1852): 289-309. Part two of Jacob's biography of Franklin.

254. Aldridge, A. Owen. "Benjamin Franklin and the Pennsylvania Gazette." *APSP* 106 (1962): 77-81. "[N]o works are more significant in Franklin's literary career than his contribution to his newspaper, the *Pennsylvania Gazette*." (77) In colonial newspapers, news was the most important content, especially news from Europe. Essays and literary material were fillers. Franklin often made his news humorous or bawdy to get reader interest. Catalog and analysis of *Pennsylvania Gazette's* content.

255. Baker, Ira. L. "Elizabeth Timothy: America's First Woman Editor." *JQ* 54 (1977): 280-85. Elizabeth Timothy was the widow of Lewis Timothy (editor of the *South Carolina Gazette)* and succeeded him as editor on his death in 1738, a pattern followed by later female editors. Biographical narrative of how she handled business content, opinion, literary content, etc. Although she was not exceptional, she "exercised shrewd business ingenuity in her tenure as editor and publisher." (285)

256. Berthold, Arthur Benedict. *American Colonial Printing as Determined by Contemporary Cultural Forces 1639-1763*. New York: Burt Franklin, 1934. Concerns "itself mostly with the relationship which existed between the trends of thought and events

that animated the colonial mind and the expression which they found through the medium of the colonial press."

257. Bond, Donovan H., and W. Reynolds McLeod, eds. *Colonial Newsletters to Newspapers: Eighteenth-Century Journalism*. Morgantown, W.V.: School of Journalism, West Virginia University, 1977. Collection of papers presented at an academic conference. The unifying theme is the development of journalism and its emergence as a profession. (See chapters below.)

258. Botein, Stephen. "'Meer Mechanics' and an Open Press: The Business and Political Strategies of Colonial American Printers." *PAH* 9: 127-225.

259. Brigham, Clarence S. *Journals and Journeymen: Contributions to the History of Early American Newspapers*. Philadelphia: University of Pennsylvania Press, 1950. Surveys miscellaneous characteristics of newspapers and their operation, 1690-1830. Series of brief, disconnected chapters on the development of early American journalism, including circulation, subscription worries, advertising, crude illustrations, slowness of travel and communication, time-lag in the printing of news, women as publishers, newspaper distribution, etc.

260. Brigham, Clarence S. *A History and Bibliography of American Newspapers, 1690-1820*. Worcester, Mass.: American Antiquarian Society, 1947. Compilation of names, dates, etc., of newspapers. "The mortality in newspapers before 1821 was notable."

261. Brigham, Clarence S. "James Franklin and the Beginnings of Printing in Rhode Island." *MHSP* 65 (1936): 536-44. Narrative emphasizing the development of printing. Franklin could not get along with Boston authorities and "decided to seek the more free-thinking atmosphere of Rhode Island." He established the first print shop at Newport in 1727 and continued it until 1733 and published the *Rhode Island Gazette* (1732-1733), the first newspaper in New England outside Massachusetts. It was the most important part of his printing, although not very successful: it had little advertising and little news and usually included only two pages.

262. Burlingame, Roger. *Benjamin Franklin, Envoy Extraordinary*. New York: Coward-McCann, 1967. Favorable treatment of Franklin as a personable, winning ambassador to Europe.

263. Cappon, Lester J., and Stella F. Duff. *Virginia Gazette Index, 1736-1780*, 2 vols. Williamsburg, Va.: Institute of Early American History and Culture, 1950. Index of the contents of the *Gazette*.

264. Carden, Robert. "American Magazines That Predate the U.S." *MHD* 1, 1 (1980): 38-43. Brief narrative of eight magazines published between 1741 and 1776.

265. Chapin, Howard M. "Ann Franklin, Printer." *AC* 2 (1926): 461ff.

266. Chapin, Howard M. "James Franklin, Jr., Newport Printer." *AC* 2 (1926): 326ff.

267. Chudacoff, Nancy Fisher. "Woman in the News 1762-1770 -- Sarah Updike Goddard." *RIH* 32-33 (Fall 1973): 98-105. Although Sarah Goddard was an important printer in Providence, she considered her role as a wife and mother her main duty.

268. Cohen, Hennig. *The South Carolina Gazette 1732-1775*. Columbia: University of South Carolina Press, 1953. Collection of items from the *Gazette* about colonial life, describing "some of the major facets of the cultural life of the colonial South as they are revealed in this newspaper." (vii)

269. Cook, Elizabeth Christine. "Colonial Newspapers and Magazines." Ch. 7 in *The Cambridge History of American Literature*, Vol. I. New York: 1917.

270. Cook, Elizabeth. *Literary Influences in Colonial Newspapers, 1704-1750*. New York: Columbia University Press, 1912. Survey of literary material that appeared in papers. The weekly paper was the most important source in the dissemination of non-sectarian literature in the colonies and was to a large extent a non-news, non-political news, literary journal featuring essays, poetry, and prose.

271. Crane, Verner Winslow. *Benjamin Franklin and a Rising People*. Boston: Little, Brown, 1954. Biography, intended for the general reading public, contains no new material. Franklin was completely an American. He viewed printing as a means to an end. He was a literary figure, politician, colonial agent, diplomat, and statesmen who was concerned with the unity and liberty of the colonies.

272. Crane, Verner Winslow. *Benjamin Franklin, Englishman and American*. Baltimore: Williams and Wilkins, 1936. Focuses on Franklin's social philosophies and political theories. After 1725-26, he was concerned with resolving practical problems and conducted a persistent search for a solution to the major problem of the time: reconciling colonial autonomy with imperial authority. He was far ahead of contemporaries in planning federal union. He rejected British authority over America by 1776, although he favored reconciliation.

273. Demeter, Richard L. *Primer, Presses and Composing Sticks: Women Printers of the Colonial Period*. Hicksville, N.Y.: Exposition Press, 1979. Contains a chapter on each of nine female printers. Their role was socially acceptable, and they were influential as printers and newspaper publishers through dissemination of ideas and information, with increasing concern for politics as the Revolution approached. They helped create the public frame of mind that helped bring about the Revolution.

274. De Armond, Anna Janney. *Andrew Bradford: Colonial Journalist*. Newark: University of Delaware Press, 1949. Bradford published the *American Mercury* from 1719 to 1742. It was a representative colonial paper. Timeliness was the key and obstacle of the paper; its emphasis was on news, as up to date as possible. It got its news from other papers. Although it carried inter-colonial news, foreign news (especially British) predominated, and personalities were emphasized. Bradford was conservative and had few controversies. Like other editors, he published no editorial page and placed his emphasis on news. He was especially concerned, even apologetic, when conditions (such as bad weather) delayed or reduced the amount of news he published.

275. Eberhard, Wallace B. "Press and Post Office in Eighteenth-Century America: Origin of a Public Policy," in Bond and McLeod, 145-54. "The American newspaper industry was nourished by an effective, economical means of disseminating its products -- the Post Office. In turn, the Eighteenth-Century development of the postal system was encouraged, guided and frequently supervised by men who were also editors, printers or publishers." (145) If it had not been for the postal system, newspapers might have been unable to survive. Article outlines and examines the development of the press-post

office relationship and discusses the roles played by a few major figures in that relationship. "There is little doubt that the Eighteenth-Century growth of the post office and the newspaper publishing industry were related. They shared common interests, goals and functions as the nation's need for speedy communication of messages and news grew. Both served the new nation, flourishing as they did so." (151)

276. Fames, Wilberforce. "The Antigua Press and Benjamin Mecom, 1748-1765." *AASP* 38 (October 1928): 303-48.

277. Faris, John Thomson. "The History of Three Bradfords, Colonial Publishers and Printers," pp. 34-62 in Faris, *The Romance of Forgotten Men*. New York: Harper, 1928. Narrative profiles of the Philadelphia family members.

278. Farrar, Frederic B. "Wallpaper and Wood: Odd Newspapers." *MHD* 3, 1 (1983): 2-5, 44. Describes unusual newspapers, from formats to material used for printing.

279. Fogel, Howard H. "Colonial Theocracy and a Secular Press." *JQ* 37 (1960): 525-32. The colonial press won its freedom from interference by religious authorities in a gradual process as a byproduct of the larger issue of freedom of expression. James Franklin and William Bradford were highlights in the process.

280. Ford, Edwin H. "Colonial Pamphleteers." *JQ* 13 (1936): 24-36. The colonial pamphlet, especially that by editorial writers, was important in the development of public opinion. It "played no small part in the American pre-newspaper era by establishing the precedent of sound, intelligent comment on public affairs by men who were leaders in national and civic life." (24) The pamphlets "may reasonably be considered the colonial progenitors of the modern American editorial."(25) By the 1770s, the "day of the pamphleteer had passed, but the tradition of independent and fearless expression of opinion which he had handed down was to set the pattern for generations of future American editors." (36)

281. Ford, Paul L. "History of a Newspaper: The Pennsylvania Gazette." *MAH* 15 (1886): 452-56. Narrative history of the paper to 1821. Samuel Keimer stole Benjamin Franklin's idea for a paper; Franklin then injured the new paper by writing a series of "Busy-Body" articles for Bradford's *Mercury*, which drew attention away from Keimer's paper. Keimer then sold the paper cheap to Franklin, who improved it. One of the first papers in America, it helped inaugurate a rich tradition of American journalism.

282. Ford, W.C. "Benjamin Harris, Printer and Bookseller." *MHSP* 57 (1923-4): 34-68.

283. Ford, W.C. "Franklin's New England Courant." *MHSP* 57 (1924): 336-53.

284. Frasca, Ralph. "Benjamin Franklin's Printing Network." *AJ* 5 (1988): 145-58. Franklin made arrangements with apprentices and fellow printers under which he offered financial and other means of support and received part of the profits.

285. Garcia, Hazel. "Of Punctilios Among the Fair Sex: Colonial American Magazines, 1741-1776." *JH* 3 (1976): 48-52, 63. Five per cent of the content of 19 magazines was about women, but less than one per cent was written by women. Most of the material written by men dealt with love and marriage, but that written by women show them asserting themselves.

286. Haig, Robert L. "*The Gazetteer*, 1735-1797." Ph.D. dissertation, Indiana University, 1954.

287. Henry, Susan. "Ann Franklin: Rhode Island's Woman Printer," in Bond and McLeod, 129-144. As the wife of James, Ann Franklin learned printing, and after his death she ran the printing business alone and in partnership with her son and Samuel Hall. How should she be evaluated by historians? "Ironically, she both began and ended her career as a printer out of necessity rather than choice. Throughout her almost thirty years of work, she proved a competent printer -- if not an extraordinary one -- whose major accomplishments were in the business area. She demonstrated economic astuteness and a control of the practicalities of printing which, more than the quality of the work produced, accounted for the firm's eventual prosperity. And most important, she persevered and endured." (138)

288. Henry, Susan. "Colonial Woman Printer as Prototype: Toward a Model for the Study of Minorities." *JH* 3 (1976): 20-24. Suggests ways to give more study to women in journalism history. Female printers have received little historical attention because most historians have been white males and traditionally historical study has dealt with the most prominent people. "Not only did women printers perform a demanding and important service, but they were also typical of a type of person vital to the American 18th Century economy: The businesswoman." (20)

289. Henry, Susan Jane. "Notes Toward the Liberation of Journalism History: A Study of Five Women Printers in Colonial America." Ph.D. dissertation, Syracuse University, 1976. Describes the professional and personal lives of Ann Franklin of Newport, R.I.; Sara Goddard of Providence, R.I.; Margaret Draper of Boston; Hannah Watson of Hartford, Conn.; and Mary Crouch of Charleston, S.C., and Salem, Mass. They were "capable, determined and intelligent women who deserve far more historical attention than they have previously received."

290. Henry, Susan. "Sarah Goddard, Gentlewoman Printer." *JQ* 57 (1980): 23-30. As operator of a printing business from 1765 to 1768 in Providence, R.I., Goddard "not only transformed a failing business into a profitable one through her superior financial skills, but also demonstrated a commitment to printing as a community service which surpassed her more-famous son's [William Goddard]." (23)

291. Hester, Al, Susan Parker Humes, and Christopher Bickers. "Foreign News in Colonial North American Newspapers, 1764-1775. *JQ* 57 (1980): 18-22, 44. As indicated by a content analysis, three newspapers used "a preponderance of news from Western Europe, especially from Great Britain, with only very minor amounts of news from other parts of the globe. Three subjects -- domestic government-politics, war-defense, and foreign relations -- accounted for two-thirds of the foreign stories." (22)

292. Hildeburn, Charles Swift Riche. *A Century of Printing. The Issue of the Press in Pennsylvania, 1685-1784*, Vol. I: 1685-1763. Philadelphia: Matlocks and Harvey, 1885-86. Reference work with titles of books, pamphlets, broadsides, etc. Almanacs, publications with descriptions of the country designed to encourage immigration, religious and political tracts, and reproductions of English works predominated during the colonial period.

293. Hildeburn, Charles R. *Sketches of Printing in Colonial New York*. New York: Dodd, Mead, 1895. Biography of each printer in New York from 1693-1784. Political tracts

were numerous, whereas in Boston and Philadelphia theological ones predominated. Nearly all Tory literature came from New York. Series of political arguments (including essays by various writers) printed by Zenger (1734-38) and Rivington (1774-75) were the two ablest series before the Revolution.

294. Hoffman, Ronald. "The Press in Mercantile Maryland: A Question of Utility." *JQ* 46 (1969): 536-44. The press was not vital to the development of the upper Chesapeake region from 1760 to 1785. It was helpful, convenient, and useful, but not essential to the prospering of Maryland's economy or merchant community.

295. Hooper, Leonard. "Women printers in America's colonial times." *JE* 29, 1 (1974): 24-27. "In colonial America, many women worked as printers and newspaper publishers, often getting into the business because they were widows of printers. When a printer-husband died, the need to support children was urgent. There were no laws or public opinion against employment of women. Necessity generally forced the decision."(24) "A colonial newspaper publisher invariably was an important person in the community. Some education was required, even if it was self-education or apprenticeship, and with so few schools, a woman could be as well educated as her husband or brother. Because the colonial printer frequently could not find and keep enough journeymen, his wife and female relatives often assisted at the type cases and in other occupations of the shop. These colonial women served successfully as competent managers of print shops left untended by the extended absence or death of the male printer." (27)

296. Hudson, Robert V. "The English Roots of Benjamin Franklin's Journalism." *JH* 3 (1976): 76-79. "The English roots of journalism in the United States are nowhere more clearly exemplified than in the early career of Benjamin Franklin, whose working years during the first half of his life were devoted to newspaper, magazine and book publishing. British influences on his writing, printing and editing directly contributed to his prominence and success as a publisher. "In many ways, North American colonial journalism was British journalism transplanted." (76)

297. Hudak, Leona M. *Early American Women Printers and Publishers: 1639-1820.* Metuchen, N.J.: Scarecrow Press, 1978. Reference work, listing works printed by America's earliest women printers, accompanied by brief biographies. Women were important in the early American trade of printing, working "alongside men in the endless effort to disseminate information, and by so doing, earn a living, and even, in certain instances, a place of their own in the sun." Feminist history: Women today are placed in sex roles, but there is no historical justification for it. The colonial period proved the exception to the rule of sex roles.

298. Hudson, Robert V. "Non-Indigenous Influences on Benjamin Franklin's Journalism," in Bond and McLeod, 119-28. "It might be mistakenly assumed that his [Franklin's] writing was a purely and totally American (or colonial) product, that it was formed and influenced exclusively or at least primarily by local influences. Yet a study of his printing, writing, editing, and publishing, especially in reference to the *Pennsylvania Gazette*, as well as to other of his works of the first forty-two years of his life (the period in which he was primarily a journalist), suggests many non-indigenous influences. This paper emphasizes those ideas and practices which influenced his writing directly from abroad, without modification by the colonial environment." (119) Franklin's style was influenced by books he read (such as *Pilgrim's Progress*), English journalism and philosophers (such as Locke, Swift, and Addison), his teenage life in England, London newspapers, etc. Franklin's journalism was more the product of modified-British,

colonial influences than of purely foreign ones. But his European roots warrant recognition as an important, integral aspect of his extremely successful journalistic career." (126)

299. Isaacs, George A. *The Story of the Newspaper Printing Press*. London: Co-operative Printing Society, 1931. The history of mechanical developments in the press.

300. Jorgenson, Chester E. "A Brand Flung at Colonial Orthodoxy: Samuel Keimer's Universal Instructor in All Arts and Sciences." *JQ* 12 (1935): 272-77. Keimer's paper was the "dawn of the emergence of a liberal spirit suggestive of English deism." He emphasized science and rationalism (reason).

301. Jones, Haratio Gates. *Andrew Bradford*. Philadelphia: 1869.

302. Kiessel, W.C. "The Green Family, a Dynasty of Printers." *NEHGR* 104 (1950): 81-93. Genealogical account (1600s to 1800s) of Samuel Green of Cambridge, Mass., and his descendants, whose "distinguished work...in spreading the typographic arts through Massachusetts, Connecticut, Canada, Vermont, New Hampshire, Maryland, and Virginia is unprecedented and unequalled." (91)

303. King, Marion Reynold. "One Link in the First Newspaper Chain, the South Carolina Gazette." *JQ* 9 (1932): 257-68. Narrative covering Benjamin Franklin's partnership (1731-37) in the Charleston paper with Thomas Whitemarsh and later with Lewis Timothy, then with his widow, Elizabeth Timothy.

304. Kobre, Sidney. *The Development of the Colonial Newspaper*. Pittsburgh: Colonial Press, 1944. One of the few works covering the entire colonial period, divided into sections covering 1690-1725, 1725-1750, and 1750-1783. "[T]he changing character of the American people and their dynamic social situation produced and conditioned the colonial newspaper." Publishers "altered the character of their products to conform to...transformations in society....Expensive machinery, large personnel and extensive office building and plants were not necessary. Given these economic and technological conditions, a free press was easily secured for the people. It would automatically result, the colonists thought, as long as publishers were freed from political control."

305. Kobre, Sidney. "The First American Newspaper: A Product of Environment." *JQ* 17 (1940): 335-45. The first American papers (as evidenced by Boston's *Publick Occurrences* and *News-Letter*) were greatly influenced by economic, social, and cultural conditions -- including city growth, the desire for political and commercial news, and the need for an advertising medium.

306. Larson, Cedric. "Patent Medicine Advertising and the Early American Press." *JQ* 14 (1937): 333-41. Examines the "evolution" of patent medicine advertising from 1720 "until the press had come of age toward the middle part of the nineteenth century." (333) Widespread advertising campaigns made patent medicine a highly complex industry. Colonists had simple faith in the claims of advertisers.

307. Lathem, Edward Connery. *Chronological Tables of American Newspapers 1680-1820*. Barre, Mass: American Antiquarian Society and Barre Publishers, 1972.

308. Lemay, J.A. Leo. *A Calendar of American Poetry in Colonial Newspapers and Magazines and in the Major English Magazines through 1765*. Worcester: American

Antiquarian Society, 1972. Reference work, listing over 2,000 poems.

309. Lent, John. "Newsboys Begging Broadsides in Pennsylvania." *MHD* 2 (1982): 45-49. Beginning in 1741, newsboys on New Year's Day solicited small gifts from customers by reciting verses of rhyme. The practice originated in Philadelphia. Describes the verses used through the Jacksonian period.

310. Lipper, Mark. "Franklin's 'Silence Dogood' as an Eighteenth-Century Censor Morum," in Bond and McLeod, 73-84. As the concepts of divine right and ordained authority began to disappear in the 1700s, the "censor morum" appeared, created by the period's journalism and giving guidance on proper morals and manners for society. Franklin's "Silence Dogood" letters in the *New-England Courant* normally have been thought of as imitations of the more serious Spectator essays of Addison and Steele. Actually, they "were intended to be more parody than imitation, more political satire than social commentary."(73) The articles "may have had little influence on the manners and morals of Boston society, but they could not have failed to provoke laughter. And possibly behind the laughter some thought was given to the anti-authoritarianism and egalitarian themes of the satire -- themes that later were to reappear in the Declaration of Independence and in the writing of the revolution."(80)

311. Littlefield, George Emory. *The Early Massachusetts Press, 1678-1711*. Philadelphia: 1907.

312. McAnear, Beverly. "James Parker versus John Holt." *NJHSP* 59 (1941): 77-95. Narrative of the career, business conditions, and tribulations of a printer. (See next two entries also.)

313. McAnear, Beverly. "James Parker versus New York Province." *NYH* 22 (1941): 7ff.

314. McAnear, Beverly. "James Parker versus William Weyman." *NJHSP* 59 (1941): 5-23.

315. McMurtrie, Douglas C. *The Beginnings of the American Newspaper*. Chicago: Black Cat Press, 1935. Brief history of the newspaper in Boston, tracing the careers of early Cambridge and Boston printers. Offers nothing not found in standard histories.

316. McMurtrie, Douglas C. *The Beginnings of Printing in Virginia*. Lexington, Va.: Washington and Lee Press, 1935. History and development of the early printing press after the first printing press appeared in Virginia in 1682. Colonial laws against printing were repressive. William Porless started the first newspaper, the *Virginia Gazette* in Williamsburg, in 1736. In 1766 a rival printing shop was encouraged by people such as Jefferson who were tired of government domination of the press. Norfolk in 1774 was the second town to have a press. Presses spread quickly after that.

317. McMurtrie, Douglas C. *A History of Printing in the United States*. New York: Bowker, 1936. Intended as four volumes, the first one published being Vol II. Vol. I, which was never published, was to cover the introduction of printing in New England and the methods of the pioneer printer in general. Vol II (which is factual rather than interpretive, often merely a recital of names, dates, and places) is about the introduction of printing into the original colonies south of New England and tells the story of the press' "influence during the pioneer period of each state" until 1810. The spread of printing, although often of real consequence and against great odds, was not spectacular. The early printers almost invariably started newspapers to make work for the print

shop. After newspapers, the bulk of the printing was for legislative proceedings, digests of laws, magazines, and literary works.

318. Matthews, Albert. "America's First Newspaper?" *CSMP* 10, 2 (1906): 318-19. Refutes claim made by William Green Shillaber in 1902 that a 1689 publication, "The Present State of New English Affairs," was America's first newspaper. "[T]he sheet of 1689 is a broadside, but is not a newspaper."

319. Miller, Clarence William. *Benjamin Franklin's Philadelphia Printing, 1728-1766*. Philadelphia: American Philosophical Society, 1974. Bibliography with short narrative biography of Franklin as a printer.

320. Miller, Daniel A. *Early German-American Newspapers*. Lancaster, Pa.: 1911.

321. Miller, Perry. *The New-England Courant*. Boston: American Academy of Arts and Science, 1956. Fascimile reproduction of first issues of the *Courant*. Introduction: James Franklin should be respected historically for his work primarily as an editor rather than printer. While his foreign news was typical of colonial papers, domestic news on controversial issues in Boston was of primary importance. He had the temerity to oppose governmental and religious authorities and ultimately raised the question of press freedom, in which he was "our first, and most unjustly forgotten, martyr to the cause."

322. Mitchell, Edward Page. "Colonial Journalism in New York." *NYSHA Proceedings* 16 (1917).

323. Morse, Jarvis Means. *Connecticut Newspapers in the Eighteenth Century*. New Haven: Yale University Press, 1935.

324. Mott, Frank Luther. "The First Sunday Paper: A Footnote to History." *JQ* 35 (1958): 443-46. Article interested in "firsts": details several papers which seem to have been first in publishing on Sunday.

325. Mott, Frank Luther. "What is the Oldest Newspaper?" *JQ* 40 (1963): 95-98. Provides details on the history of several newspapers which might be among the oldest surviving ones in America.

326. Mott, Frank Luther, and Chester E. Jorgenson. *Benjamin Franklin: A Representative Selection*. New York: American Books, 1936 (rev. 1962). "Franklin, the American Voltaire -- always reasonable if not intuitive, encyclopedic if not sublimely profound, humane if not saintly -- is best explained with reference to the age of the Enlightenment, of which he was the completest colonial representative." (XIII)

327. Muddiman, J.G. "Benjamin Harris, the First American Journalist." *Notes and Queries* 163 (1932): 129-33, 147-50, 166-70, 223, 273-74. Detailed narrative of Harris' life. In England he got into trouble because of his scandalous attacks on authority. In America, he was a partisan who brought trouble on his head because of his printing of "False News."

328. Nelson, William. "The American Newspapers of the Eighteenth Century as Sources of History." American Historical Association *Annual Report* 1 (1910). Reference work.

329. Nelson, William. *Some Account of American Newspapers, Particularly of the 18th Century, and Libraries in Which They Are Found.* New Jersey Archives, 1st series, Vols. 11, 12, and 19. Paterson, N.J.: 1894-1897. Reference work.

330. Nelson, William. "Some New Jersey Printers and Printing in the Eighteenth Century." *AASP* 21 (1911, n.s.): 15-56. Development of printing from 1702 to 1805. "The ruling powers in England had always a jealous dread of the influence of the press, which in times of political excitement was wont to pour forth a torrent of virulent pamphlets, loading with obloquy the person attacked." (15) Printers often were young men who were optimistic and had a vision of the future, and "advocated opinions that blazed the way for many a change in the body politic. They contributed to the unification of the country." They believed in freedom of the press, were opposed to tradition, were "a power in the land....they were the pioneers who laid the foundations, broad and deep, for that mighty structure which...in this country has aspired to be the voice of public opinion. Surely, the present generation is largely indebted to these gallant young printers of the eighteenth century." (56)

331. Nordin, Kenneth. "The Entertaining Press: Sensationalism in Eighteenth-Century Boston Newspaper." *CR* 6 (1979): 295-320. Newspaper content (especially sensationalism) catering to the masses began in the 1700s, not with the penny press in the 1830s. The colonial press was the origin of American newspapers' pandering to popular taste.

332. "Old Virginia Editors." *WMQ* 7 (ser. 1) (1899): 9-17. Chronological biographies of the successive editors of the *Virginia Gazette*, founded in 1736 by William Parks.

333. Oldham, Ellen M. "Early Women Printers of America." *BPLQ* 10 (January 1958): 6-26; (April 1958): 78-92; (July 1958): 141-153. Biographies of Dinah Nuthead, Ann Franklin, Cornelia Bradford, Elizabeth Timothy, Anna Zenger, Sarah Updike Goddard, Anne Green, Clementina Rind, Margaret Draper, Mary Crouch, and Mary Katharine Goddard. Their common characteristic "was the necessity of supporting themselves, and in most cases their children upon the death of their husbands, good printers all!" (6) "All eleven women must have had unusual forcefulness of character" (7) to have been able to operate successfully "in the days before the emancipation of women." (6)

334. Oswald, John C. *Benjamin Franklin, Printer.* Garden City, N. Y.: Doubleday, Page, 1917. Emphasizes Franklin as a printer and entrepreneur (printing, editing, publishing, advertising) because the fact that he was first a printer has too often been obscured by the emphasis on Franklin as a patriot, diplomat, and statesman. Oswald was a hobbyist interested in Franklin rather than an historian.

335. Oswald, John Clyde. *Printing in the Americas.* New York: Gregg Publishing, 1937. Sketches of famous printers, printing families, women, colonial printshop equipment, bookmaking, trade organization, etc., in every state. Based on secondary sources, hurriedly done, more a compilation of data than a history.

336. Paltsits, Victor Hugo. "New Light on 'Publick Occurrences.'" *AASP* 5 (1949): 75-88. Narrative of America's first paper. Cotton Mather favored continuation of the paper.

337. Partington, Wilfred. "The First American Newspaper and the 'New England Primer.'" *Bookman* 76 (January 1933): 103-04. This brief account of Benjamin Harris is a

summary of Muddiman's work (above). Tries to answer the question, Did Harris print the first American newspaper and first American book?

338. Parton, James. *Life and Times of Benjamin Franklin*. New York: 1864. James Franklin's *Courant* was the "most spirited, witty, and daring" colonial newspaper. Bostonians were accustomed to dullness in papers, and the *Courant* excited interest as America's "first sensation newspaper." (78) It was marked by sarcasm and ridicule of the established civil and religious authority. It was a success. As owner of the *Pennsylvania Gazette*, Benjamin Franklin was a very competent businessman and editor, making the *Gazette* "imcomparably the best newspaper published in the colonies." (218)

339. Richardson, Lyon F. *A History of Early American Magazines, 1741-89*. New York: Thomas Nelson and Sons, 1931. Analysis of magazine content and the circumstances of their publication. Some of the 37 magazines, although they lasted for only short periods because of lack of support, were important as a center for the expression of opinion and as a forum for discussion. Author's aim is "to present the period in all its phases of thought and emotion as preserved in the miscellanies."

340. Ringwalt, Jessie E. "Early Female Printers in America." *PC* 7 (October 1872): 284-85.

341. Sappenfield, James A. *A Sweet Instruction: Franklin's Journalism as a Literary Apprenticeship*. Carbondale: Southern Illinois University Press, 1973. Literary analysis by an English professor of Benjamin Franklin's journalistic writings which, written over a 25-year period, influenced his later writings. Although the research is sketchy, this study traces the progress of Franklin's writing and devotes major attention to the Silence Dogood essays in the *New-England Courant* (1722), the Busy-Body essays in Philadelphia's *American Weekly Mercury* (1729), Poor Richard's Almanacs, and his autobiography. Through his journalistic writing, Franklin learned tactics, self-control, and how to create fictionalized characters and make them speak as though they were alive. His journalistic writing showed conscious self-training, imaginative experimentation, and creation of character.

342. Shaaber, Matthews. "Forerunners of the Newspaper in America." *JQ* 11 (1934): 339-47. Before the first newspaper, printers interested in serving a cause or making some profit published pamphlets and broadsides containing news. Before 1665, because there was no private commercial press, most published information came in official printed statements from the government. The private, occasional pamphlets and broadsides issued later usually were published on the occasion of some event such as the death in 1685 of Charles II of England. Little domestic news was printed. "[J]ournalism -- the printing and sale of news for the information of the public or for the profit of the publisher or for both reasons -- is older in America than the newspaper by nearly forty years at least. If comparatively little news was printed before 1704, the reasons were rather that presses were few, the authorities strict, and publishers unenterprising than that there was no way of making news public in print." (346-47)

343. Simpson, Lewis P. "The Printer as a Man of Letters: Franklin and the Symbolism of the Third Realm," 3-20 in J.A Leo Lemay, ed., *The Oldest Revolutionary: Essays on Benjamin Franklin*. Philadelphia: University of Pennsylvania Press, 1976. Although Franklin spoke of himself as a printer, he really was a literary man and an enlightenment thinker.

344. Smith, Albert Henry. "Franklin as a Printer." *Independent* (Jan. 11, 1906). Through-out his life, Franklin "was chiefly interested in the art of printing."

345. Steele, Ian K. *The English Atlantic 1675-1740: An Exploration of Communication and Community.* New York: Oxford University Press, 1986. News traveled by merchant ships crossing the Atlantic.

346. Steffens, Pete. "Franklin's Early Attack on Racism: An Essay Against a Massacre of Indians." *JH* 5 (1978): 8-12, 31. "As an astonishing early outcry against racism, the work [a pamphlet by Benjamin Franklin against the murder of Indians] merits the attention of journalism historians, especially those interested in appreciating and as-sessing Franklin, the 1760s and colonial pamphleteering as combative journalism. Franklin's skill as a reporter, commentator and writer -- as well as of an advocate and polemicist -- come alive in this publication."(8) The pamphlet "still stands out as a bracing, early moral statement in our nation's struggle against racism." (31)

347. Van Doren, Carl. *Benjamin Franklin.* New York: Viking, 1938. Emphasizes Franklin's individuality less than his typicality. Relies greatly on Franklin's accounts of himself and is flattering. He was a man of letters who was versatile and knowledgeable in many areas.

348. Weeks, Lyman H., and Edwin M. Bacon. *An Historical Digest of the Provincial Press.* Boston: Society for America, Inc., 1911. Collation of material on American affairs printed in newspapers from 1689 to 1783.

349. White, William. "The *Maryland Gazette*: America's Oldest Newspaper?" *JQ* 35 (1958): 439-42. As of 1957, the *Gazette* was not the oldest continuous American newspaper. Article deals solely with the question stated in title.

350. Winship, George Parker. "Newport Newspapers of the Eighteenth Century." *NHSB* 14 (1914): 3ff.

351. Wolf, Edwin. *Franklin's Way to Wealth as a Printer.* Philadelphia: 1951.

352. Wright, Esmond. *Franklin of Philadelphia.* Cambridge, Mass.: Belknap Press of Har-vard University, 1986. Chronological biography of the printer, writer, inventor, and statesman.

353. Wroth, Lawrence. *The Colonial Printer.* Portland, Me.: Southworth-Anthoensen Press, 1938. Emphasizes mechanics of printing: what the colonial press used for paper, how ink was made, profits, great printers, cost of printing, how books were manufactured, etc.

354. Wroth, Lawrence. "The First Press in Providence." *AASP* 51 (October 1941): 351-83. Study of the social and political role of the press in colonial society, emphasizing the influence of the press on conditions and changes, including preparing the way for the Revolution. An inquiry into "the degree and kind of alteration brought about in the life of a community...by the operations of a printing press within its bounds." (352) When William Goddard set up a printing operation in 1762, 300 years after Gutenburg, printing still was considered "ingenious." Goddard's press was looked on by the com-munity as a means of helping the town achieve its ambition of becoming prosperous. It printed blank forms, an almanac, and newspaper. The newspaper was important in "the

formation of opinion on public questions." (365) The *Providence Gazette and Country Journal* (founded in 1762) provided an outlet for literature and leadership in local town affairs and political controversy, industrial development, and the development and independence of the nation.

355. Wroth, Lawrence C. *History of Printing in Colonial Maryland, 1686-1776.* Baltimore: Typathetac of Baltimore, 1922. Annotated bibliography of books, broadsides, and newspapers printed in Maryland, 1686-1776. In the historical development of printing, the livelihood of early presses was the printing of colonial laws and government documents.

356. Wroth, Lawrence C. *William Parks, Printer and Journalist of England and Colonial America.* Richmond, Va.: Appeals Press, 1926. Parks was the "father of journalism in Maryland and Virginia," founder of the *Maryland Gazette* in 1727 and the *Virginia Gazette* in 1736.

357. Yodelis, Mary Ann. "Who Paid the Piper? Publishing Economics in Boston, 1763-1775." *JM* 38 (1975). Religious publications provided more revenue for printers than government printing did. Government printing was not necessary for a successful printing business, and government therefore could exercise little financial coersion.

3

The Revolutionary Press, 1765–1783

358. Adams, Willi Paul. "The Colonial German-language Press and the American Revolution," in Bailyn and Hench (see below), 151-228. In contrast to Mott's description of the German-language newspapers as primarily religious, Adams contends that they were thoroughly secular.

359. Alden, J. E. "John Mein: Scourge of Patriots." *CSMP* 34 (1937-1942): 571-99.

360. Aldridge, A. Owen. *Thomas Paine's American Ideology*. Newark: University of Delaware Press, 1984. Payne believed in American moral superiority and that America had a providential mission to bring freedom to mankind. His writings fell into three categories of ideas: (1) America should be separated and isolated from Europe, (2) people were equal, with moral character more important than individual rank resulting from birth, and (3) people of all nations comprised a brotherhood made "as the work of one creator": a "circle of civilization...a universal society."

361. Bailyn, Bernard, ed. *Pamphlets of the American Revolution, 1750-1776*. Cambridge, Mass.: Harvard University Press, 1965. Introduction, "The Transforming Radicalism of the American Revolution," analyzes the relationship between ideas and the Revolution and evaluates the revolutionary nature of the Revolution. The ideas in the pamphlets became the determinants in the history of the period by causing the colonists to change their beliefs and attitudes. The ideas were based on the tradition of England's Commonwealthmen, such as Trenchard and Gordon, who had advocated radicalism on behalf of religious dissenters, social radicals, and opposition politicians. Americans believed that a sinister plot had developed in England to deprive citizens of English

liberties.

362. Bailyn, Bernard, and John B. Hench, eds. *The Press and the American Revolution*. Worcester, Mass.: American Antiquarian Society, 1980. Collection of essays by various historians. (See entries on Botein, Weir, Adams, Potter and Calhoon, Langford, and Tanselle in this section.)

363. Bengamin, S.G.W. "A Group of Pre-Revolutionary Editors. Beginnings of Journalism in America." *MAH* 17 (January 1887): 1-28. Narrative biographies of printers through the Revolution. The press helped bring about the Revolution. The "rise and progress of the American newspaper press...was directed by men of character and ability, who understood their opportunity, and made the quill and the printing press scarcely less potential [sic] in asserting and securing the liberties than the forum and the field. If the utterances of the colonial press were often acrimonious and severe, we must remember that the life of a nation was at stake." (28)

364. Berger, Carl. *Broadsides and Bayonets: The Propaganda War of the American Revolution*. Philadelphia: University of Pennsylvania Press, 1961. Study of British and American efforts (largely unsuccessful) during the war itself to convert, persuade, or intimidate people who seemed vulnerable. Both American and British propagandists were ineffective. Events and real conditions were more persuasive than words. By 1777, at the latest, most minds were made up. Despite actions aimed at such things as subverting the Hessian allies of Britain, fomenting slave insurrection, and winning the support of Indians, most attempts were ineffective. Real events had more impact than propaganda. Thus, for example, Canada was saved for Britain by force, Indians stayed neutral or took sides as they were impelled by solid economic or political motives, and the provocation of slave insurrection by Britain merely embittered and fortified the slaveholders. The greatest impact came not from propagandists such as Franklin but simply from the news of the war (such as American victory at Saratoga). Neither persuasive appeals, nor threats, nor tricks could compare in influence with military victories or political or economic factors.

365. Botein, Stephen. "Printers and the American Revolution," in Bailyn and Hench, 11-58. Printers were traditionally neutral and impartial, but their attitudes were often determined by political conditions. In periods of political unrest, they found it profitable to be partisan; in quieter times they could afford to open their presses to diverse opinions. Objectivity and neutrality were principles of the trade.

366. Brown, R.A. "New Hampshire Editors Win the War." *RIH* (1939): 35-51. Study of the contents of New Jersey newspapers of 1775-1784 and of the approaches used to persuade. "Whig leaders...were as appreciative of the importance of propaganda, and as adept at its use, as are any political and business leaders of this period." (35-36) It is impossible to measure the effect newspaper propaganda had on readers, but several writers were prominent state leaders.

367. Brown, R.A. "The Newport Gazette, Tory Newssheet." *RIH* 13 (1954): 97-108; and 14 (1955): 11-20. Analysis of types of propaganda John Howes used in his Rhode Island paper from 1777 to 1779 and its relation to the conduct of the war. The possibility of a French-American war, possible peace proposals, war news, rebel cruelty stories, attacks on the currency of the new states, and "what appear to be conscious efforts to create the impression among the rank and file of the Whig adherents that their leaders were self-interested, tyrannical individuals, seeking to gain wealth and position at the

expense of their followers" (98) were some of the major types of propaganda. "[W]hether consciously or unconsciously selected they must have had some effect on the people who read them, especially on that large class of Americans who wavered with the changing tide of victory." (20).

368. Brown, R.A. "The Pennsylvania Ledger: Tory News Sheet." *PH* 9 (1942): 161-75.

369. Calkin, Homer L. "Pamphlets and Public Opinion During the American Revolution." *PMHB* 64 (1940): 22-42. Study of the influence of pamphlets: "Unquestionably, the pamphlet was considered of prime importance in forming and shaping the minds of the people....[It] must be considered in a study of the American Revolution because of the place it occupied in presenting and forming the ideas and theories of the two sides in the many controversial questions which arose from 1763 to 1783." (41-42)

370. Canfield, Cass. *Sam Adams' Revolution 1765-1776.* New York: Harper & Row, 1976. "[I]t was primarily Adams who fanned the flame of rebellion and...he did so more effectively than any other major American leader. Without him...American independence could not have been declared in 1776." [xiii] Adams was a tenacious and uncompromising leader of the independence movement, an agitator, mass organizer, political manipulator, and master propagandist. He was effective in employing mass demonstrations and economic boycotts and in creating an infrastructure for the revolutionary movement.

371. Conway, Moncure D. *Life of Thomas Paine.* New York: 1892. First full-scale biography of Paine intended to rescue Paine from the opprobrium heaped on him by an ungrateful America. Conway was as radical as Paine. Born into antebellum aristocracy in the South, Conway later was influenced by Emerson and entered the Unitarian ministry. For the rest of his life he was a gadfly, pricking the conscience of smug Victorian society.

372. Conway, Moncure D., ed. *The Writings of Thomas Paine.* Anthology with an introduction favorable of Paine's attitudes and influence.

373. Crane, Verner W. "Benjamin Franklin and the Stamp Act." *CSMT* 32 (1937): 56-77. Franklin's opinion of the act.

374. Crane, Verner W. *Franklin's Letters to the Press, 1758-1775.* Chapel Hill: University of North Carolina Press, 1950. Franklin was a press agent and propagandist writing under pseudonyms. This collection of approximately 90 essays which he wrote for newspapers emphasizes 1765-1775, when Franklin was the chief American advocate in England. He was skillful at explaining the American frame of mind, using satire, exposition, etc., writing industriously in the interest of his countrymen using irony and shrewdness. He sought to influence public opinion in England and America and was successful.

375. Cullen, Maurice R. "Benjamin Edes: Scourge of Tories." *JQ* 51 (1974): 213-18. Edes played a major role in the formation of the Sons of Liberty and kept his paper in the forefront of anti-British activity. He deserved as much credit for the revolutionary movement as did other Boston leaders such as John and Sam Adams and James Otis.

376. Cullen, Maurice R. "The Boston *Gazette:* A Community Newspaper." *JQ* 36 (1959): 204-08. Aside from its Patriot, partisan content, the fiery *Gazette* was a hometown

paper -- running much non-political news from America and abroad that was of interest to the general reader. It served well as a community paper (although partisan content filled a majority of its space).

377. Cullen, Maurice R. "Middle-Class Democracy and the Press in Colonial America." *JQ* 46 (1969): 531-35. An examination of the public's economic opportunity, extent of political democracy, and literacy leads to the conclusion that the Revolution was not a class struggle but a fight for democracy, with the press itself seeking political separation from England.

378. Davidson, Phillip. *Propaganda in the American Revolution, 1763-1783*. Chapel Hill: University of North Carolina Press, 1941. Propagandists were effective: "Without their works independence would not have been declared in 1776 nor recognized in 1783....The propagandists thus gave expression to ideas that had been germinating for years." People were pre-disposed to accept propagandists' arguments. Churches, schools, clubs, mechanics' organization, and other groups helped propagandize. Success depended on the volume of output, ability to distribute material, and ability to suppress or censor the propaganda of the opposition. The failures of the Tories seems natural since they were unable to compete with the Patriots in these activities. Hate and aspersions on Tories were some of the primary approaches used by patriots. "The struggle, said the propagandists, was one between a young, hopeful, and virile nation of high ideals, and an older, effete civilization of low standards and debased morals." Americans who disagreed with Patriots were branded as unpatriotic and immoral. A large number of ideas, which were idealist, were devised to justify the course in politics advocated by Patriots.

379. Dicken Garcia, Hazel. "Letters Tell the News (Not 'Fit to Print'?) About the Kentucky Frontier." *JH* 7 (1980): 49-53. 1769-1784. Study of the differences in information about the Kentucky frontier provided to the East by newspapers and newsletters. Newsletters "fulfilled many functions later associated with newspapers: What now are called background, interpretation, follow-up and especially local news....[S]uch differences seem to represent a transition in the historical evolution from newsletter to newspaper."

380. Dickerson, Oliver Morton. *Boston Under Military Rule*. Boston: Chapman and Grimes, 1936. Compilation of material from the Boston *Evening Post* and New York *Journal* in 1768 and 1769 chronicling the British occupation of Boston.

381. Dickerson, Oliver Morton. "British Control of American Newspapers on the Eve of the Revolution." *NEQ* (1951): 453-68. Study of financial methods by which British authorities supported editors after passage of the Townshend Acts. Before 1765, "newspapers were relatively unimportant as agencies for molding or reporting public opinion." Because printing was a business, printers normally printed material favorable to authorities who awarded them government contracts. Such editors as John Mein and James Rivington, therefore, were government advocates.

382. Duff, Stella. "The Case Against the King: The Virginia Gazettes Indict George III." *WMQ* (ser. 3), 6 (1949): 381-97. Criticisms of George during 1766-1776 by various colonial leaders were chronicled by the papers so well that conflicts became well-known issues and thus helped prepare the way "for the vicious attacks on the king in the Declaration of Independence." (397)

383. Edwards, Samuel. *Rebel: A Biography of Tom Paine*. New York: Praeger, 1974. Average, popularized biography based on secondary sources.

384. Eliot, John. "A Narrative of Newspapers Printed in New-England." *MHSC* 6 (ser. 1, 1799): 73ff.

385. Fast, Howard. *Citizen Tom Paine*. New York: Duell, Sloan, Pearce, 1943.

An historical *novel*. Paine's pen was as mighty as a general's sword. "Common Sense" (Jan. 10, 1776) was a turning point in American history and established Paine with Cobbett and Defoe as one of the greatest pamphleteers, and he had greater impact than either of the others. It was widely read (120,000 copies printed in three months) and dissolved doubt and conservatism. It changed people's minds about independence and war, and its exposition of the merits of democracy helped radicalize American thinking. He was a fighter for democracy and a champion of universal enlightenment and reform.

386. Fast, Howard, ed. *The Selected Works of Thomas Paine Set in the Framework of His Life*. New York: Duell, Sloan, Pearce, 1945. Collection of Paine's better-known works. Introduction is superficial, biased in Paine's favor, and is more concerned about literary flair than historical accuracy.

387. Foner, Eric. *Tom Paine and Revolutionary America*. New York: Oxford University Press, 1976. Places Paine's ideology in the context of the artisan/craftsman background of America. Industrial/capitalist changes created social divisions. Paine was critical of British intentions in America and of American slavery. He opposed hereditary authority and favored representative government. His ideas were not new. "What was brilliantly innovative was the way Paine combined them into a single comprehensive argument and related them to the common experiences of Americans." He believed in the importance of property and wealth, but not in hereditary privilege or gain, and in egalitarianism. He was an important contributor to liberal, democratic philosophy, and his main goal was to eliminate inequalities and abuses and lay the foundation for an orderly, democratic world. From an impoverished background himself, he wished to help the downtrodden. In America, he advocated the rights of the common people and separation from England in order to help them. His writings helped hesitant colonists decide in favor of independence.

388. Ford, Paul Leicester. "The Authorship of 'Plain Truth.'" *PMHB* 12 (1888-89): 421-24. William Smith was the author of the pamphlet written in refutation of Paine's "Common Sense."

389. Ford, Paul L., ed. *The Journals of Hugh Gaine, Printer*, 2 vols. New York: 1902. Collection of the Tory publisher's private papers, introduced by a biographical sketch.

390. Frank, Willard C. "Error, Distortion and Bias in the *Virginia Gazette*, 1773-74." *JQ* 49 (1972): 729-39. The Williamsburg printers changed their emphasis from a collection of miscellany to playing the role of conscious editors of powerful journals of opinion. Reports were slanted or distorted and yet were probably believed by radicals, thus playing a large role in urging Virginians to rebel (since the *Gazettes* was the only widely-read newspaper available).

391. Granger, Bruce I. "Franklin as Press Agent in England," 21-32 in J.A. Leo Lemay, ed. *The Oldest Revolutionary: Essays on Benjamin Franklin*. Philadelphia: University of

Pennsylvania Press, 1976. During the years Franklin was in England (1757-1762, 1764-1775) he contributed more than 100 essays to the press. The letters "reveal him as a political moderate who, in language more homespun than legalistic, put the welfare of America ahead of that of England whenever the interests of the two clashed." (21) He exhibited real writing ability (clarity, vigor, humor) in arguing that America should be granted dominion status in the British Empire.

392. Harlan, Robert D. "David Hall and the Stamp Act." *PBSA* 61 (1967): 13-37. Since most historical works on the Stamp Act and the press have dealt with the press in general, this work is an attempt to present a more detailed and personal account "of the effect of the Stamp Act crisis on an American printer's career." (13) "Aware even before the passage of the Stamp Act that in hard times he must rely more upon his newspaper than on the bookshop for an income, Hall allowed his editorial and personal policies to conform more and more, after September 1765, to those of the radical party and the popular opinion which it directed, for it was soon apparent to him that the chief cause of the substantial decline in *Pennsylvania Gazette* subscriptions was the unpopularity of his former policy of non-alignment. Hall was also aware that unless he reversed the policy, he was in danger of losing his newspaper. While Hall's conversion, which was occasioned as much by financial as by political considerations, cannot be said to have been totally voluntary, neither was it insincere. By 1766, it was finally fixed, and in a formerly loyal subject the British government now had an enemy." (36-37).

393. Harlow, R.V. *Samuel Adams; Promoter of the American Revolution: A Study in Psychology and Politics.* New York: Henry Holt, 1923. Suggests that Adams imposed his opinions on the community but does not explain how he did it. Attempts to psychoanalyze Adams to explain his revolutionary attitudes. Adams was neurotic and irrational and thus saw in standard government practices a "subjective creation" of British tyranny. "His political activity was the product not of his reason, but of his emotions, and his behavior in politics was on that account always irrational." [143]

394. Harrison, John M. "The War of Words: The Role of Our First Editorial Writers in Making a Revolution," in Bond and McLeod, 207-18. In the period just preceding the Revolution, "the power of the press in this country was firmly established." (207) Develops Schlesinger's thesis that "the impassioned arguments and virtual unanimity of opinion represented in the writings of editors of the newspapers of the period, and those of their numerous contributors, were a major force in the making of a revolution. It is my purpose to expand those arguments by suggesting that these men represent the first editorial writers in the American press, establishing one of the primary functions of newspapers as they were to develop in the United States, and providing a significant example of how news media are used to influence opinion and to precipitate action." (207) "In varying degree, this can be said of all these Patriot editors. Some of them may have been irresponsible in their manipulation of the materials at hand to stir a generally lethargic public to action. But, in demonstrating the potential of the press to inform the public and to move it to action, these men were significant beyond the time in which they lived. Of Isaiah Thomas, of Samuel Adams, of Thomas Paine, and of many others, it can be said that they not only helped to make a revolution but established standards which continue to represent a challenge to succeeding generations of American journalists." (216)

395. Hebert, Elsie Mae Stallworth. "Press Coverage of Louisiana's Shifting Role During the American Revolutionary Period, 1763-1783." Ph.D. dissertation, University of Texas, 1977. Analysis "of news reports concerning events that affected Louisiana" in selected

newspapers of the American colonies, England, France, and Spain.

396. Henry, Susan. "Margaret Draper: Colonial Printer Who Challenge the Patriots." *JH* 1 (1974): 141-44. As publisher of the *Massachusetts Gazette and Boston News-Letter* from 1774 to 1776 following the death of her husband, Draper supported the Tory cause. "Ironically," however, in a period during which women were not fully appreciated, " -- and undoubtedly like countless other women in history -- her own considerable contribution to a political cause was quickly subsumed beneath her husband's (which, it can be argued, was less substantial)." (143)

397. Hixson, Richard F. "Founding of New Jersey's First Permanent Newspaper." *JQ* 40 (1963): 233-35. The *New-Jersey Gazette* was established through the efforts of officials to aid the Patriot cause. "The *New-Jersey Gazette*, endorsed by the governor and subsidized by the legislature, came into being only a few months after the decisive winter of 1776-77 as the struggle for independence reached a major crisis....As the Revolution progressed and the patriot cause suffered many setbacks, several of the out-of-state papers ceased publication, others moved to distant points, paper became more scarce, and delivery by postriders became uncertain. And as the war drew on into 1777, with New Jersey the 'cockpit of the revolution,' it became apparent that the state needed its own publication." (233) Isaac Collins was encouraged to start a paper with an offer to become official printer. He was a sound businessman and a libertarian on freedom of the press.

398. Hixson, Richard F. *Isaac Collins: A Quaker Printer in 18th Century America*. New Brunswick, N.J.: Rutgers University Press, 1968. Concerned primarily with Collins' printed products and his business operations. He "was an individualist and an astute businessman at a time when nearly as many printers failed as succeeded in business." He was frugal, meticulous, stern and a dignified printer, retailer, editor, and publisher "who would not willingly compromise on matters of truth or principle or the high professional standards he set himself." He started New Jersey's first newspaper, the *Gazette*, in 1777 and ran it as a pro-Patriot paper. Most of his problems during the Revolution were related to business operations: getting paper, collecting from subscribers, etc. He was a champion of freedom of the press. He was primarily a printer, running a newspaper for only seven years, and the book is primarily a history of printing. He ran his printing business for 40 years and died in 1817.

399. Hixson, Richard F. "Literature for Trying Times: Some Pamphlet Writers and the Revolution." *JH* 3 (1976): 7-10. Pamphlets were important as a medium for arguing the Patriot cause, and some of the best arguments of the time were in pamphlets. Study assumes the arguments exerted influence in helping bring about the Revolution. Includes narratives of some pamphlet writers.

400. Humphrey, Carol Sue. "Producers of the 'Popular Engine': New England's Revolutionary Newspaper Printers." *AJ* 4 (1987): 97-117. Description of characteristics of printers: "The average...printer...was a hard worker who had learned his professin through an apprenticeship to a master in the trade and then had established his position by opening his own business, more often than not in his early thirties....[He] was increasingly conscious that printing was a vocation with standards and ethics to uphold....[He] supported the American side in the quarrel with Great Britain and used his newspaper to further the goals of the American Revolution. He eventually held some sort of political office....While not financially successful on a grand scale, he did manage to make a comfortable living and died with a fairly sizable estate to leave to his

family." (111)

401. Kern, John. "Boston Press Coverage of Anglo-Massachusetts Militancy in the 1730s," in Bond and McLeod, 57-72. The "use of American newspapers as political engines or as weapons of warfare did not suddenly originate during the Stamp Act crisis [as Schlesinger argued]....[I]nstead...the Revolutionary press drew some of its strength from earlier exercise, and...at least in Boston some of the political influence of Eighteenth-Century journalism antedated the Revolution." (57) Argues that the press was influential in affecting American attitudes, based on a study of the Boston *News-Letter* reports on militant actions of resistance in Great Britain and Massachusetts from 1733 to 1741. The paper's stories "contributed to a growing political awareness among the people of Massachusetts, and provided them with examples of political opposition, and urged them to further political actions." (57-58).

402. Kobre, Sidney. "The Revolutionary Colonial Press -- A Social Interpretation." *JQ* 20 (1943): 193-204. "...between 1750 and 1775 the newspaper entered into a new and distinct period, characterized especially by rapid expansion and growth and widespread influence." (193-94) Article attempts to "trace the sociological causes for this growth and to show, incidentally, how closely the newspaper depended upon and was related to its social and economic environment....Perhaps the most significant change in the newspapers was their transition from weak, inconsequential organs, with several hundred circulation each, to powerful agencies of propaganda, in some instances having as many as 3,000 readers. Newspapers were increasingly recognized by the Patriots as effective hammers to weld the nation together, so that action could be taken against the common foe....Without over-estimating the importance of the press, it may be safely said that it was the only agency of a national character which could act as a channel of news and persuasion." (194) Newspapers also multiplied in number because of the increase in population, growth of business and agricultural, improvement in transportation and communication system, increase in freedom of press, educational and cultural advances, desire for inter-colonial news, and tension created by the Revolution.

403. Langford, Paul. "British Correspondence in the Colonial Press, 1763-1775: A Study in Anglo-American Misunderstanding before the American Revolution," in Bailyn and Hench, 273-314. Challenges the view that between 1763 and 1775 "the press was increasingly expressing a preoccupation with specifically American concerns." Colonial papers carried content similar to provincial English papers, and colonists found London news more interesting than local news.

404. Lawson, John L. "The 'Remarkable Mystery' of James Rivington, 'Spy.'" *JQ* 35 (1958): 317-23, 394. The myth that Rivington was a spy for George Washington is false. His being able to remain in America after the war was a result of Americans' respect for freedom of the press.

405. Lee, Alfred McClung. "Dunlap and Claypoole: Printers and News-Merchants of the Revolution." *JQ* 11 (1934): 160-78. History of the *Pennsylvania Packet and Daily Advertiser*. Although Dunlap and Claypoole have been overlooked by historians, they were among the most important of the printers of the period.

406. Lorenz, Alfred Lawrence. "Hugh Gaine: A Colonial Printer-Editor, 1752-1783." Ph.D. dissertation, Southern Illinois University, 1968. See next entry.

407. Lorenz, Alfred L. *Hugh Gaine: A Colonial Printer-Editor's Odyssey to Loyalism.* Car-

bondale: Southern Illinois University Press, 1972. Gaine successfully straddled the fence to gain financially. He never became a major figure because he insisted on fairness when partisanship was expected. He contributed more than other more famous printer-editors to the modern/later business-oriented, objective journalism. He was primarily oriented toward business and did whatever was necessary to prosper.

408. Marble, Annie R. *From 'Prentice to Patron: The Life Story of Isaiah Thomas.* New York: Appleton-Century, 1935. Narrative collection of data rather than interpretive history. As a printer, Thomas had initiative, courage, a sharp writing style, determination, and great business acumen. He was inclined to restlessness and liberalism but still managed to gain the respect and admiration of a conventional and conservative society. In pre-Revolutionary America the *Massachusetts Spy* was notable because of its political radicalism and the adaptation of a style popular with a large constituency. Thomas was active-minded, acquisitive, and public-spirited. Book has been criticized for Marble's shortage of knowledge of the period.

409. Matthews, Albert. "Bibliographical Notes on Boston Newspapers, 1704-1780." *CSMP* 9 (1907): 430-32, 470-71, 484-93.

410. Matthews, Albert. "The Snake Devices, 1754-1776, and the Constitutional Courant, 1765." *CSMP* 11 (1906-07).

411. McMurtrie, Douglas C. "The Green Family of Printers." *Americana* 26 (1932): 364-75. Genealogical narrative of the growth and development of the family of printers established by Samuel Green in Massachusetts and spread to Maryland.

412. Miller, John C. *Samuel Adams, Pioneer Propagandist.* Boston: Little, Brown, 1936. Adams was the radical leader of the common people of Boston, and through his efforts to bring about a confrontation between them and the British he was able to engineer the start of the Revolution. He capitalized on authorities' errors and blunders to reach his goal. When opponents failed to provide such errors, he colored and created facts. He was so important that there may not have been a revolution without him. Massachusetts conservatives had failed to consider the common people, whereas Adams recognized how to appeal to them. Book sometimes fails to substantiate claims.

413. Miner, Ward F. *William Goddard, Newspaperman.* Durham, N.C.: Duke University Press, 1962. Goddard, although a pro-Patriot printer, insisted on freedom to print material from both sides of the conflict and would not withhold news even though Patriot mobs tried to intimidate him. He was an ardent defender of freedom of the press. He was the creator of the postal system organized by the Second Continental Congress to help the delivery of news and papers. He was a successful journalist who published some of the colonies' most popular and successful papers, the *Pennsylvania Chronicle* and *Maryland Journal.* He was competent but quarrelsome and got into trouble with Patriots because of his insistence on being impartial. The book has been criticized by reviewers for historical errors.

414. Morgan, Edmund Sears, and Helen Morgan. *The Stamp Act Crisis: Prologue to Revolution.* Chapel Hill: University of North Carolina Press, 1953. Focuses primarily on areas other than journalistic aspects of the act. Most American leaders denied to Parliament the right to levy external taxes for revenue as well as internal taxes in 1764 and 1765, long before Charles Townshend sought to impose his ill-considered duties. "[T]he significance of the Stamp Act crisis lies in the emergence, not of leaders and

methods and organization, but of well defined constitutional principles. The resolutions of the colonial and inter-colonial assemblies in 1765 laid down the line on which Americans stood until they cut their connections with England. Consistently from 1765 to 1776 they denied the authority of Parliament to tax them externally or internally; consistently they affirmed their willingness to submit to whatever legislation Parliament should enact for the supervision of the empire as a whole." (295).

415. Mott, Frank Luther. "The Newspaper Coverage of Lexington and Concord." *NEQ* 17 (1944): 489-505. Evaluation and description of newspapers' coverage in order "to study the American newspaper of these times" when "their coverage was conditioned by the primitive techniques of eighteenth-century news-gathering, by such facilities of communication as existed, and by the stage of development at which the newspaper had arrived." (489) Most newspaper information was not first-hand or timely.

416. Murphy, Layton Barnes. "John Holt, Patriot Printer and Publisher." Ph.D. dissertation, University of Michigan, 1965.

417. "Old Virginia Editors." *WMQ* 7 (1899): 9-17. Antiquarian, genealogical account of editors of the *Virginia Gazette* from 1736 (beginning with William Parks) to 1779.

418. Ours, Robert M. "James Rivington: Another Viewpoint," in Bond and McLeod, 219-34. Rivington, who was the most hated Tory editor during the Revolution because he was accused of distorting and slanting facts, actually acted as he had promised he would: "impartial and neutral....[F]reedom of the press dictated that he, as a printer, open his columns to all viewpoints. That he attempted to do this seems clear upon a close inspection of his newspaper in the period 1773 to late April, 1775." (219) "Rivington's direct legacy to American journalism was virtually nil -- largely because of his reputation as a Tory liar. That was unfortunate, because his newspaper was one of the better ones in the colonies in the early months of its existence. James Rivington had an excellent pattern to offer journalists in his policies regarding impartiality and freedom of the press. The evidence is strong that he tried to adhere to his announced policies. That he failed in the long run was largely the result of wartime pressures and polarization." (230)

419. Paltsits, Victor Hugo. "John Holt, Printer and Postmaster: Some Facts and Documents Relating to His Career." *NYPLB* 24 (1920): 483-99.

420. Parker, Peter J. "The Philadelphia Printer: A Study of an 18th Century Businessman." *BHR* 40 (Spring 1966): 24-46. Printing changed between 1758 and 1800. Before the Revolution, the printer was an artisan and merchant. The Revolution accelerated the growth of his business. By 1800, he thought of his business apart from himself. He no longer was an artisan, but a "fledgling capitalist." (46)

421. Pomerantz, Sidney I. "Newspaper Humor in the War for Independence." *JQ* 21 (1944): 311-17. Collection of humorous quotes and entertaining content. Humor was employed to keep up "morale in the fight for freedom." (311)

422. Pomerantz, Sidney I. "The Patriot Newspaper and the American Revolution," 305-31 in R. B. Morris, ed., *The Era of the American Revolution*. New York: Columbia University Press, 1939. The New York and New Jersey press had high standards of news reporting. Editors did commendable jobs in accuracy, moderate tone, literary standards, independence of mind, adherence to principle, open-mindedness, and avoidance of

personal abuse.

423. Potter, Janice, and Robert M. Calhoon. "The Character and Coherence of the Loyalist Press," in Bailyn and Hench, 229-72. Analysis of the intellectual and ideological content and character of newspaper essays that supported Britain. The most common themes were disaffection, petulance, ingratitude, and disloyalty. The loyalist press did not succeed in communicating a fully developed alternative ideology or political creed, but it did exhibit a profound "moral estrangement from the values that the Revolutionaries claimed for themselves."

424. Randolph, J. Ralph. "The End of Impartiality: *South Carolina Gazette*, 1763-75." *JQ* 49 (1972): 702-09, 720. Peter Timothy, printer of the *Gazette*, changed to editorial partiality because of the Anglo-American crisis, although as a general rule he believed in press impartiality.

425. Robbins, Peggy. "Benjamin Franklin and His Son, a Tory." *AHL* 14 (November 1980): 38-46. Franklin was estranged from his son William over ideological differences.

426. Schlesinger, Arthur M. "Colonial Newspapers and the Stamp Act." *NEQ* 8 (March 1935): 63-83. Newspapers played a "significant role" during the Stamp Act crisis. "When the American colonists began to feel the tightening grip of imperial control after 1763, they naturally resorted to the printing press to disseminate their views and consolidate a favorable public support." (63) Papers were an important medium of propaganda. "The newspaper propaganda against the act began the journalistic warfare which eventually led to revolution and independence." Editors viewed the tax as a threat to press freedom, and defiance was widespread.

427. Schlesinger, Arthur M. "Politics, Propaganda, and the Philadelphia Press, 1767-1770." *PMHB* 60 (1936): 309-22. The combined efforts of the *Journal*, *Gazette*, and *Chronicle* raised concerted public opposition to the Townshend Acts.

428. Schlesinger, Arthur M. *Prelude to Independence: The Newspaper War on Great Britain, 1764-1776*. New York: Knopf, 1958. Study of the "real American Revolution": the "radical change in the principles, opinions, sentiments, and affections of the people" which preceded the Revolution. The press was effective in bringing about the war. (The book's theme is summarized on p. 280.) Because printer/editors had moved around and lived in various colonies and had ties throughout the colonies, they were continental minded rather than provincial, seeing things only from the view of individual colonies. The repeal of the Stamp Act, legislation which was unwise because it affected printers, was a tremendous victory for the press. Boston journalists, who were the leaders of the patriot movement in the press, helped raise a public uproar against the Tea Act of 1773. The independence movement could hardly have succeeded "without an ever alert and dedicated press."

429. Schlesinger, Arthur M. "Propaganda and the Boston Newspaper Press, 1767-1770." *CSMP* 32 (1937): 396ff. See previous entry.

430. Schneider, Norma. "Clementina Rind: 'Editor, Daughter, Mother, Wife.'" *JH* 1 (1974): 137-40. As editor and publisher of the Williamsburg *Virginia Gazette* in 1773-1774, following the death of her husband, Rind played a "demanding role...as the editor of an important...newspaper and head of a large family during a time of tremendous

political upheaval in Colonial America." (137)

431. Shipton, Clifford. *Isaiah Thomas: Printer, Patriot, Philanthropist, 1749-1831*. Rochester, N.Y.: Printing House of Leo Hart, 1948. Admiring narrative of Thomas' contributions to the field of printing and to other aspects of American life. Thomas was the "father of the modern American printing and publishing business." (xi)

432. Siebert, F.S. "The Confiscated Revolutionary Press." *JQ* 13 (1936): 179-81. Narrative of what happened to the *Virginia Gazette's* printing press after it was confiscated.

433. Skaggs, David C. "Editorial Policies of the *Maryland Gazette, 1765-1783.*" *MHM* 59 (1964): 341-49. Attempts to analyze a local institution to determine what ideas made "men of [the Revolutionary] age to stand as the architects of modern liberty....On the Chesapeake Tidewater one of the most significant institutions influencing the change of colonial ideals from dependence to independence, and at the same time leaving such concepts as freedom of religion, speech, and press ingrained in the revolutionary mind, was the Annapolis journal operated by Jonas Green, his wife, and his sons. Throughout the period from the passage of the Stamp Act to the signing of the Treaty of Paris, the *Maryland Gazette's* weekly issues both influenced and reflected local thought." (341) Annapolis had many business, political, and social leaders. The *Gazette* reflected their views and politics, but "in turn it influenced those who read its pages. Thus the Greens' weekly helped construct American democracy." (349)

434. Smith, J. Eugene. *One Hundred Years of Hartford's Courant: From Colonial Times through the Civil War*. New Haven, Conn.: Yale University Press, 1949. The newspaper was both a news medium and a factor in shaping public opinion. It was also influenced by its culture, by what readers wanted. Founded in 1764 by Thomas Green as the *Connecticut Courant*, it survived the Revolution and several changes of ownership. It was identified with parties and partisan groups; but except for its interest in anti-slavery and prohibition, it was not a crusading newspaper in the 1800s, probably because for most of its life it had been owned by practical printers interested as much in mechanical aspects as in editorials.

435. Smith, Robert W. "What Came After?: News Diffusion and Significance of the Boston Massacre, 1770-1775." *JH* 3 (1976): 71-75, 85. The massacre was not universally viewed by American newspapers as a significant event. Local conditions dictated the manner in which it was perceived.

436. Spaulding, E. Wilder. "The *Connecticut Courant*, A Representative Newspaper in the Eighteenth Century." *NEQ* 3 (1930): 443-63. Cultural narrative of 1764-1800. "The *Connecticut Courant* appeared upon the Hartford scene at a fortunate moment. The American newspaper of 1764 was still the drab, unpretentious by-product of the tiny print-shop. But the French War, followed by new ministerial policies, set America to thinking and talking as never before. She wanted only opportunity for putting her ideas on paper. And as a medium for agitation the prosaic little American newspaper had as yet no rival in book or magazine printing. Its only rivals, the broadsides and the pamphlet, it was to overtake and pass by the end of the Revolution, making of itself the most effective mirror of the life and thought of its community. Of such journals none reflected more accurately the ideals, the heart-throbs, and the disappointments of its neighborhood than did the venerable *Courant*." (443) As a rebel colonial paper, it supported liberty and the patriot side; in the 1780s it became conservative and Federalist,"reflecting Hartford's own lapse into staid respectability." It "was always a remark-

ably accurate mirror of the city's ways of thinking."

437. Steirer, William F. Jr. "A Study in Prudence: Philadelphia's 'Revolutionary' Journalists." *JH* 3 (1976): 16-19. On the issue of the role black people were to play in the colony and the state, Philadelphia's journalists had only a few moments when they spoke out boldly for reform. "To act otherwise would be to flirt with financial troubles that no small printer/businessman needed." In general they were not dedicated to reforming society; "prudence and caution, not bravery and idealism, dominated" their behavior. They were small businessmen protecting their investments.

438. Stone, F.D. "How the Landing of Tea Was Opposed in Philadelphia by Colonel William Bradford and Others." *PMHB* 15 (1891-1892): 385-93. Reprint of contemporary newspaper accounts of opposition in Philadelphia to the tea tax. Not primarily journalism history.

439. Stoudt, John J. "The German Press in Pennsylvania and the American Revolution." *PMHB* 59 (1935): 74-90. German printer/editors were important in the Revolutionary period, and "[i]n the final analysis the positive influence of the German press in Pennsylvania on the American Revolution resolves itself almost wholly to that of one paper: *Der Woechentliche Philadelphische Staatsbote* of Henry Miller, printer. This paper was the medium of expression for the German liberals in the complex maneuverings preceding the American Revolution." (90)

440. Tanselle, G. Thomas. "Some Statistics on American Printing, 1764-1783," in Bailyn and Hench, 315-64. Survey of the types of subject matter printed between 1764 and 1783, the geographical distribution, and how various areas compared with others. Theology was the most popular subject, but during the early war years political science, history, and law became dominant themes.

441. Tapley, Harriet Silvester. *Salem Imprints, 1768-1825: History of the First Fifty Years of Printing in Salem, Massachusetts.* Salem: Essex Institute, 1928. Narrative and bibliography of printing and library holdings.

442. Teeter, Dwight L. "John Dunlap: The Political Economy of a Printer's Success." *JQ* 52 (1975): 3-8, 55. "This study traces the economic fortunes of John Dunlap as he picked his way through the War for Independence, consistently bettering his position during a conflict which was financially damaging if not ruinous to several of his competitors. One key to Dunlap's success was business related to politics, or, as 18th century Americans might have said, 'political economy.'" (3-4) "His *Packet* and his other ventures suggest that Dunlap was the quintessence of the successful 18th-century printer-businessman who used his ties to government to assist in building a fortune....He was doubtless what many enterprising printers of the 18th century hoped to become: rich." (55)

443. Thomas, C.M. "The Publication of Newspapers during the American Revolution." *JQ* 9 (1932): 358-73. Narratives of John Holt (Patriot); James Rivington (Loyalist); and Hugh Gaine (Turncoat). It was Patriot printers who became "the fathers of American journalism." (373) "A printing press was difficult to move, yet many were moved during the Revolutionary War. Those that were not shipped from town to town often saw their editors change sides as quickly as a chameleon changes color. The well known influence of colonial papers in the struggle with England was equalled only by the influence which the war later had on the newspapers themselves. The very nature of the

printer's business made neutrality in a civil struggle impossible for him. The ordinary inhabitant, even though he favored one side and had no desire to be neutral, could remain in a city and conduct his business regardless of the fortunes of war if he was willing to remain quiet; but the editor of a newspaper could not remain quiet. The few who tried to remain neutral soon discovered such a course to be impossible....The editors of some colonial newspapers remained loyal to England throughout the war, while a third group changed loyalties as often as was necessary and possible. The purpose of this article is to show the services and experiences of each group." (358)

444. "Tom Paine's First Appearance in America." *Atlantic Monthly* 4 (November 1859): 565-75. Favorable narrative of Paine during 1774-1787, emphasizing his writing ability, originality, good and pleasant character, and important support of liberty and civil government.

445. Walett, Francis G. "The Impact of the Stamp Act on the Colonial Press," in Bond and McLeod, 157-70. "Historians generally agree with the statement of Dr. David Ramsay in 1789 that 'In establishing American independence, the pen and the press had a merit equal to that of the sword.' [*The History of the American Revolution.* Philadelphia: 1789, II p. 319] Evidence sustains Ramsay's judgment with reference to the press in general, but particularly in the case of colonial newspapers, a fact which is the more remarkable when one views the weak and puerile condition of American newspapers at the beginning of the dispute with Britain. Examination of the newspapers and other sources (both printed and unprinted) reveals that the new British colonial policy of the 1760s -- especially the Stamp Act -- greatly aroused not only the generality of colonists, but also printers and publishers. Several very important results of this turbulence can be noted: the press played a vital role in colonial agitation; newspapers (which grew in numbers, strength and independence) gained much power; with their wider circulation and new-found power they were influential in forging a greater degree of united feeling and organized resistance among the colonists than had existed before; and the controversy was a major step at the start of a revolution in American journalism itself." (157) As a result of the battle over the Stamp Act, "newspapers, once described as petty, dingy and languid, had risen up in a crisis to defy British authority successfully. They could and would do so again in future conflicts." (167)

446. Walett, Francis G. *Massachusetts Newspapers and the Revolutionary Crisis, 1763-1776.* Boston: Massachuesetts Bicentennial Commission, 1974. After 1765, the press became strong in opposition to British authorities. The leading American newspapers were in Boston. The press -- through news and propaganda -- "played an unusually large part in the movement toward American independence." (44)

447. Walett, Francis G. *Patriots, Loyalists, and Printers.* Worcester, Mass: American Antiquarian Society, 1976. Collection of 64 newspaper articles about the Revolution written in 1975-1976 by the author.

448. Wallace, John W. *An Old Philadelphian, Colonel William Bradford of 1776.* Philadelphia: 1884.

449. Wax, Harold D. "The Image of the Negro in the *Maryland Gazette*, 1745-1775." *JQ* 46 (1969): 73-80, 86. What were the origins of present-day attitudes about race? The *Gazette* presented "the image of the Negro as property and hence subject to further exchange." (75) Yet it also "offered its readers a Negro whose total image was many-sided and complex, an image which saw the Negro as property but which also revealed

his human qualities." (86) Stories in the *Gazette* pointed out blacks' "distaste for slavery and potential for violence" (76) and that they were "criminally inclined," (77) infantile, comic, etc. Today's "patterns of race prejudice and discrimination are deeply set in the nation's past." (86)

450. Weir, Robert M. "The Role of the Newspaper Press in the Southern Colonies on the Eve of the Revolution: An Interpretation," in Bailyn and Hench, 99-150. The Southern press was more attached to the upper class and the government than the Northern press was. It was more dependent upon the establishment and tended to reinforce rather than undermine the position of local leaders. As politics replaced religion as the chief concern of the intelligentsia, the press became the equivalent of secular Bibles.

451. Wells, William V. *Life and Services of Samuel Adams*. Boston: 1865.

452. Wheeler, J. Towne. *The Maryland Press, 1777-1790*. Baltimore: Maryland Historical Society, 1938. Sociological study shows printers in relation to their times.

453. Woodward, W. E. *Tom Paine, America's Godfather*. New York: Dutton, 1945. Admiring biography. "Paine was a saint in the cause of truth and freedom." He believed ardently in the cause of freedom of all men. However, because of his ideas such as deism, which was viewed as atheism, he eventually was ostracized in America; but like Washington, Jefferson, John Adams, and others, he was one of "the founders of the Republic." (12)

454. Yodelis, Mary Ann. "Genteel Rooms, Umbrilloes and Velvet Corks: Advertising in the Boston Press, 1763-1775." *JH* 3 (1976): 40-47. Advertising was an important source of revenue for many newspapers, but there is little evidence that partisanship and advertising were related. "The press was fairly free of economic coercion from advertisers." (47)

455. Yodelis, Mary Ann. "The Press in Wartime: Portable and Penurious." *JH* 3 (1976): 2-6, 10. "At best, wartime publishing was a hazardous and risky venture," but many printers were able to make some income outside their newspaper activities, with the result that "a free press generally was economically possible during the war."

456. Zall, Paul M. *Comical Spirit of Seventy-Six: The Humor of Francis Hopkinson*. San Marino, Calif: Huntington Library, 1976. Collection of Hopkinson's newspaper propaganda, indicating his humor, literary style, politics, and good-natured observations. Introductory essay: "In the crucial period between the convening of the first Continental Congress in 1774 and the ratification of the Constitution in 1789, Hopkinson played the role later to be assumed by such national jesters as Will Rogers and Art Buchwald -- relieving the tensions of an anxious age with an effervescent mixture of tomfoolery and common sense. While his contemporary writers argued for revolution and federalism with sermons or harsh satires, Hopkinson used fantasy and good humor that appealed alike to radicals, conservatives, and the vast undecided majority in between whose support proved decisive in the end....[His words] inspired his countrymen to go on with a war they thought would never end. And when at last the war did end, his good humor and good sense lightened the darkest hours of the emerging nation." (1)

457. Zimmerman, John J. "Benjamin Franklin and the *Pennsylvania Chronicle*." *PMHB* 1 (1957): 351-64. William Goddard published in the *Chronicle* Franklin's letters in an effort to show that Franklin was an opponent of the Stamp Act, after he had been

charged by political opponents with favoring the Act. The relationship between Goddard and Franklin helped elevate Franklin from a position of leader of a divided Quaker
party to spokesman of all Pennsylvania in asserting American rights.

4

The Party Press,
1783–1833

458. Allen, Eric. "Economic Changes and Editorial Influence." *JQ* 8 (1931): 342-59. Study of the business arrangements for operating newspapers, the effects they have on editorial autonomy, and how the types of arrangements have changed over time, from 1801 to 20th century. The purpose of the party press was success for a political faction or party. "[A] newspaper was not so much a separate profession, as one of the necessary ingredients in the career in the public life of any man who did not spring from the landed aristocracy." (345) A favorable but not very substantial or well documented work on the nature of the newspaper and its political purpose.

459. Ambler, Charles Henry. *Thomas Ritchie: A Study in Virginia Politics.* Richmond: Bell Book and Stationary, 1913. Favorable biography. Ritchie tried to run the Richmond *Enquirer* on a high moral plane. "To Ritchie more than to any one of his contemporaries the press of to-day owes a debt of gratitude for the high ethical conceptions which he brought to and made a part of his profession." (293)

460. Ames, William E. "Federal Patronage and the Washington D.C. Press." *JQ* 9 (1972): 22-30. Federal printing contracts were awarded to papers in Washington as rewards for or encouragement of press partisanship. The historical view that cooperation between government and the press reflects "disrepute on the latter...generally ignores the more than 60 years of this nation's history during which the federal government was intimately tied to the press through a well-developed patronage system." (22) "By today's standards the patronage press lacked much. These papers failed to provide a diversity of subject matter, an entertaining style, breadth in coverage, interesting makeup and objective news. They did provide, however, able coverage of the national gov-

ernment, depth analysis of the key political issues and a strong leadership function.." (30)

461. Ames, William E. *A History of the National Intelligencer.* Chapel Hill: University of North Carolina Press, 1972. History of a leading political organ during the first half of the 19th century, providing one of the first attempts to refute the "dark ages" concept of the party press: "[P]olitical journalism...offered a higher quality information and interpretation of American society than at any other time in American history." (ix) Ames based his evaluation of partisan journalism on one paper, the *National Intelligencer,* which he concluded was more interested in news reporting than vituperative political opinion, and assumed that the *National Intelligencer* was a "good" paper because it was different from other party papers.

462. Ames, William E. "A History of the *National Intelligencer,* 1800-1869." Ph.D. dissertation, University of Minnesota, 1962. See previous entry.

463. Ames, William E. "Samuel Harrison Smith Founds the *National Intelligencer.*" *JQ* 42 (1965): 389-96. Based on research used for Ames' book. Recounting of the difficulties -- access to Congress, financial stability, etc. -- faced by Smith in founding the *National Intelligencer.* The financial rewards of getting printing contracts from Congress and being the recognized spokesman of Jefferson were considered worth the risks. Views Smith more as an entrepreneur and neutral information officer than as a devoted Jefferson partisan.

464. Ames, William E., and Dean S. Olson. "Washington's Political Press and the Election of 1824." *JQ* 40 (1963): 343-50. The press was an important and probably influential factor in the 1824 presidential election, when papers were the "sole means of communication of the candidates to the voters." (344) The party caucus had broken down, the campaign was waged on personality rather than issues, personal campaigning was frowned on -- all factors contributing to the importance of the role played by the press. "[T]he campaign was waged largely through the newspapers...[which] responded to the need of the times and the candidates, even though they served a party or a man, not a community or a nation." (350)

465. Ames, William E., and Dwight L. Teeter. "Politics, Economics, and the Mass Media," 38-63 in Ronald T. Farrar and John D. Stevens, eds., *Mass Media and the National Experience.* New York: Harper & Row, 1971. Sociological study challenging the developmental concept and focusing on the political/economic influences on the press. Political patronage had positive benefits, and the party press (as exemplified by such Washington papers as the *National Intelligencer*) performed well in a number of areas. Some papers were independent, covered news in the national capital, analyzed issues, provided diverse opinion on political issues, and helped make national policy. Patronage freed papers from pressures possible from advertising and mass reader interest.

466. Ammon, Harry. "The Fifth President and the Press: Monroe." *MHD* 3, 2 (1983): 22-28. General overview of the relations between Monroe and newspapers.

467. Austin, Aleine. *Mathew Lyon: "New Man" of the Democratic Revolution, 1749-1822.* University Park: Pennsylvania State University Press, 1981. Progressive, sympathetic yet critical biography places Lyon in the context of the Enlightenment, viewing him as one of the Americans who embraced both the right of property and the right to pursuit of happiness. Shows him as a case of the times making the man. Takes an in-depth

look at events that affected and were affected by this "new man" of the American Democratic Revolution.

468. Avery, Donald R. "American Over European Community? Newspaper Content Changes, 1808-1812." *JQ* 63 (1986): 311-14. Prior to the War of 1812, despite the fact that foreign news was available, American newspapers began to give more attention to domestic than foreign news, indicating that "American interests...were changing in the early years of the nineteenth century." (311)

469. Avery, Donald R. "The Emerging American Newspaper: Discovering the Home Front." *AJ* 1, 2 (1984): 51-66. Content analysis reveals that "American newspapers began giving less attention to matters foreign and more attention to domestic news in the years just prior to the War of 1812. Far from occurring during the war, as has been suggested by historians, the trend appears to have begun in earnest as early as 1810." (62)

470. Avery, Donald R. "The Evolution of the American Newspaper in the Pre-War of 1812 Period: A Shift from Foreign to Domestic News Content." *SJMC* 1 (1982): 35-43. Content analysis shows that American newspapers emphasized domestic news prior to the War of 1812. (See previous entry.)

471. Axelrod, Jacob. *Philip Freneau: Champion of Democracy.* Austin: University of Texas Press, 1967. Argues that Freneau helped arouse public interest in the early national period's political issues, but it places more emphasis on Freneau as a literary figure than on his historical role as a "champion of democracy."

472. Baldasty, Gerald J. "The Boston Press and Politics in Jacksonian America." *JH* 7 (1980): 104-08. Refutes the "dark ages" concept. The leaders of the second party system in Boston were editors. "The political editor was much more than a scurrilous pen-for-hire....Some editors...gained national recognition as political analysts, debaters and even as important advisers to politicians and statesmen....These political editors were more than writers, for they served in elective office, as party spokesmen, and as campaign organizers." (104, 108)

473. Baldasty, Gerald J. "The Charleston, South Carolina, Press and National News, 1808-47." *JQ* 55 (1978): 519-26. Newspapers throughout the nation relied on those in Washington, D.C., for news. Modes of transportation played an important role in news distribution.

474. Baldasty, Gerald J. "The New York State Political Press and Antimasonry." *NYH* 64 (July 1983): 261-79. In the rapid growth of the Antimasonic party in the late 1820s, "[t]he key ...device...clearly was the newspaper; the establishment of party presses was deemed absolutely essential to any hope of victory at the polls. Editors consequently emerged as the major organizers and tacticians in the new party both on the state and county levels." (279)

475. Baldasty, Gerald J. "The Political Press in the Second American Party System: The 1832 Election." Ph.D. dissertation, University of Washington, 1978. "The leaders of the second American party system, as exemplified by the election of 1832, were partisan newspaper editors. These...editors were much more than party scribblers or public relations agents for the Jacksonian or National Republican parties. Rather, they were the major agents of the new party system." Analyzes ways in which editors served as

party leaders.

476. Baldasty, Gerald J. "The Press and Politics in the Age of Jackson." *JM* 89 (1984). The press provided "a forum for public opinion...but its role in American political society was far more extensive. In particular, editors formed the nucleus of political organization in the 1820s and 1830s, and thus were central to the dramatic growth in partisan activity that characterized the age of Jackson." (2)

477. Baldasty, Gerald J. "The Washington D.C. Political Press in the Age of Jackson." *JH* 10 (1983): 3-4, 50-53, 68-71. Editors served as organizers and leaders of parties, and newspapers played a critical role in the political system.

478. Beasley, Maurine. "The Curious Career of Anne Royall." *JH* 3 (1976): 98-102, 136. Anne Royall, a political journalist, "left a 'profile in courage,' the picture of a woman, paranoid or not, who was willing to pursue a man's career and turn into a town freak rather than shrivel up mentally and physically just because convention called upon her to remain quiet." (136)

479. Benjamin, G. G. W. "Notable Editors between 1776 and 1800. Influence of the Early American Press." *MAH* 17 (February 1887): 97-127. There is "strong evidence of the power of the press." (97) Views the history of the party press against important and fierce political strife. Romantic/Nationalist narrative based on concern for how the press contributed to the progress of the nation's political system. The "press influenced the destinies of the republic." (127) Biographical sketches of "a few of the more prominent editors who through the press influenced the destinies of the republic." (127) Editors were influential in the "fight for liberty" (97) and were very important to the debate over the nation's political structure that followed the Revolution until 1800.

480. Bigelow, John. *William Cullen Bryant*. Boston: Houghton Mifflin, 1890. This biography was written by Bryant's co-worker.

481. Boston, Ray. "The Impact of 'Foreign Liars' on the American Press (1790-1800)." *JQ* 50 (1973): 722-30. The research could have been more substantial, and the leap from sketchy biographies of editors to his conclusions more fully justified, but Boston did provide an interpretation of the Republican press which deserves attention. He attributed the effectiveness of the Republican press to a group of foreign-born journalists who came to America with common radical political opinions. In a narrative of these editors and some of their political writings, he assumed that the press was important and played a significant role in Jefferson's election, although he made no attempt to analyze the political roles of the editors. He included some sketchy pieces of information, set generally in the framework of biographies of editors, and concluded, "[H]ad the foreign exiles merely accommodated themselves to the deferential style of newspaper journalism which they found on their arrival instead of actively engaging in transforming it into a fighting, propagandistic instrument, there might have been no Jeffersonian Revolution -- which, after all, is their finest epitaph." (73)

482. Bowen, Marjorie. *Peter Porcupine: A Study of William Cobbett, 1762-1835*. New York: Longmans, Green, 1935. This study adds little fact or interpretation to Cole's biography and does not attempt to evaluate Cobbett's role in American journalism. However, it does present a thesis worthy of consideration: Cobbett was the typical 18th-century peasant suddenly made articulate through the new, outspoken journalism. It gives limited treatment to Cobbett's American career.

483. Bowers, Thomas A. "'Precision Journalism' in North Carolina in the 1800s." *JQ* 53 (1976): 738-40. "The journalistic origins of survey research may go back further than originally thought....In fact, a rudimentary form of survey research was used by the Raleigh, N.C., *Star* as early as 1810." (739) The survey was sent to men in various counties, seeking information about each county, through 21 questions on a question-naire.

484. Bradsher, E. L. *Mathew Carey, Editor, Author and Publisher.* New York: Columbia University Press, 1912. Narrative of Carey's career as editor, the conditions in publishing, and Carey's work to free America from journalistic dependence on Europe.

485. Brigham, Clarence S. "Daniel Hewitt's List of Newspapers and Periodicals in the United States in 1828." *AASP* 44 (October 1934): 381-82.

486. Brown, Charles H. *William Cullen Bryant.* New York: Scribner's, 1971. Definitive general biography of Bryant, focusing on his journalism and literary work. After joining the New York *Evening Post* in the late 1820s, Bryant became a major figure in the city and, for awhile, a leading supporter of Andrew Jackson. The *Evening Post* was New York's best paper. He became an advocate of the Free Soil movement and then the Republican party in the 1840s. In the Civil War he was one of Lincoln's leading supporters. In later years he was New York's most famous citizen and its official speaker at city functions. "Bryant was the first of the great personal editors. The *Evening Post* was a responsible, respected newspaper, and Bryant was a champion of liberty.

487. Buckingham, Joseph Tinker. *Personal Memoirs and Recollections of Editorial Life,* 2 vols. Boston: Ticknor, Reed and Fields, 1852. Buckingham founded the Boston *Courier* in 1824 and served as its editor until 1848. During that time, he knew many notable figures in journalism. They are recounted in this personalized narrative.

488. Buckingham, Joseph T. *Specimens of Newspaper Literature, 1179-1861, With Personal Memoirs, Anecdotes, and Reminiscences,* 2 vols. Boston: Redding and Co., 1882. Descriptive anecdotal autobiographical narrative combines history with biography with an emphasis on New England papers. Based largely on Isaiah Thomas' work, with expanded biographies and extracts from papers.

489. Chambers, W. N. "Thomas Hart Benton: Editor." *MHR* 46 (July 1952): 335-45. Although best known as a Missouri politician, Benton was also "the driving, broad-thinking, capable editor of the second newspaper west of the Mississippi River," the St. Louis *Enquirer,* from 1818 to 1820 (335).

490. Clark, Allen Cullen. *William Duane.* Washington: 1905. See also *CHSR* 9 (1906): 14-62. Biography of the Republican editor of the *Aurora.*

491. Clark, Mary Elizabeth. *Peter Porcupine in America: The Career of William Cobbett, 1792-1800.* Philadelphia: University of Pennsylvania/Times & News Publishing Co., 1939. The only book-length work on Cobbett's journalistic career in America. Others emphasize his career in England. Clark gives a favorable treatment of the Federalist editor's role in politics but concludes that although he attempted to help his party, his vituperation actually swayed the nation toward Republicanism. (This is a difficult thesis to accept, since most other editors -- including Republicans -- also were vituperative.)

492. Cole, G. D. H. *The Life of William Cobbett.* New York: Harcourt, Brace, 1924. The standard work on the life of Cobbett, an English pamphleteer and reformer who stirred up public opinion in England and America. Favorable evaluation of Cobbett as a prophet of democracy. Devotes few pages to Cobbett's life in America, however.

493. Coll, Gary. "Noah Webster: Journalist, 1783-1803." Ph.D. dissertation, Southern Illinois University, 1971. Story of Webster with an emphasis on his journalistic abilities. "Webster played a solid part in the growth of American journalism." He was motivated by a desire for America to develop as a distinctive nation and culture.

494. Coll, Gary. "Noah Webster, Journalist: 1783-1803," in Bond and McLeod, 303-18. See previous entry.

495. Congleton, Betty C. "The Louisville Journal: Its Origin and Early Years." *RKHS* 62 (April 1964): 87-103. Friends of Henry Clay promoted a new newspaper to support his candidacy for the U.S. presidency in 1832. However, George D. Prentice, the editor, was especially concerned about its financial success. The *Journal* succeeded through his ability to appeal to readers and build circulation.

496. Crouthamel, James L. "Did the Second Bank of the United States Bribe the Press?" *JQ* 36 (1959): 35-44. Most editors, including Duff Green and the partnership of James Watson Webb and Mordecai Noah (who reversed their editorial opinions to favorable ones on rechartering the bank), were not influenced by loans from the bank. There is little evidence to suggest that Green, Webb, or Noah was bribed or subsidized by loans from the bank, a charge that was sometimes made.

497. Crouthamel, James L. *James Watson Webb, a Biography.* Middletown, Conn.: Wesleyan University Press, 1969. Webb, editor of the New York *Courier and Enquirer,* 1827-1861, improved news-gathering methods and worked for political and social reform in New York City. He was deeply involved in New York state and national politics.

498. Crouthamel, James L. "James Watson Webb and the New York *Courier and Enquirer,* 1827-1861. Ph.D. dissertation, University of Rochester, 1958. See previous entry.

499. Cunningham, Noble E., Jr. *The Jeffersonian Republicans: The Formation of Party Organization, 1789-1801.* Chapel Hill: University of North Carolina Press, 1957. See next entry.

500. Cunningham, Noble E., Jr. *The Jeffersonian Republicans in Power: Party Operations 1801-1809.* Chapel Hill: University of North Carolina Press, 1963. Cunningham provided the most fully organized discussion of the party press in any non-journalism history. In his two volumes he made the point that the Republicans considered the press important in helping the party gain and maintain power. His discussion of the press was primarily narrative, but he noted that the Republican party encouraged a partisan press because of press influence on public opinion and assumed that the party "expected to look to the party press to support and advance the Republican administration." (236)

501. Dennis, Everette E. "Stolen Treaties and the Press: Two Case Studies." *JH* 2 (1975): 6-14. Discussion of two cases which dealt with government information as property. The notion arose of public property which was owned and open to the public. Gov-

ernment was viewed in light of a private person who cannot restrict this "public property." Judges' decisions affirmed that government has secrets to which people have no access.

502. Dowling, Ruth Naomi Apking. "William Cobbett, His Trials and Tribulations as an Alien Journalist, 1794-1800." Ph.D. dissertation, Southern Illinois University, 1972. Political opponents instituted a number of legal actions against Cobbett.

503. Eberhard, Wallace B. "Sara Porter Hillhouse: Setting the Record Straight." *JH* 1 (1974): 133-36. Shows the development of the first woman editor and printer and the impact of her close family and community ties.

504. Elliott, Chuck. "Conscience of England: The Unknown Side of William Cobbett."*MHD* 2 (Summer 1982): 57-64. Narrative history of William Cobbett as an influential journalist whose strong writings had great political and journalistic effect.

505. Elliott, Robert Neal, Jr. *The Raleigh Register, 1799-1863*. Chapel Hill: University of North Carolina Press, 1955. Study is concerned principally with the *Register's* support of Jeffersonian Republicans, Whig politics, and efforts to preserve the Union. Joseph Gales, its first editor, was a liberal and progressive leader of Southern journalism. The *Register* started as an ardent supporter of Jefferson and gradually changed into an extremely conservative paper. Elliott does not deeply analyze the reasons for the change. Gales' paper was devoted largely to national politics. It had great influence, and its editors played a prominent public role. Gales was an effective champion of progressive policies, freedom of thought, internal improvements, education, libraries, agricultural and industrial development, and penal reform. He was more moderate in his editorial writing than were most other writers.

506. Ellis, Harold Milton. *Joseph Dennie and His Circle: A Study in American Literature from 1792 to 1812*. Austin: Bulletin of the University of Texas, no. 40 (1915). Romantic, chronological biography of a man "once esteemed the finest writer in America." (iii)

507. Ericksson, Erik McKinley. *Official Newspaper Organs and the Presidential Elections of 1828, 1832, and 1836*. Nashville: 1927. See also *Tennessee Historical Magazine*, Vols. 8-9.

508. Ershkowitz, Herbert. "Andrew Jackson: Seventh President and the Press." *MHD* 5, 2 (1985): 10-16, 40. During Jackson's presidency, the press was transformed into "an agent of political parties." (40)

509. Ewing, Gretchen Garst. "Duff Green, Independent Editor of a Party Press." *JQ* 54 (1977): 733-39. Favorable biography of the editor/owner of the *United States Telegraph*. "Duff Green epitomized the bombastic, vitriolic and highly personal style of journalism that characterized partisan newspapers during the first few decades of the 19th century....As editor of the primary organ for promoting the election of Andrew Jackson, Green encountered numerous problems...[such as the need for capital and differences among Democrats which] made editorial independence difficult. Despite these adversities, Green maintained financial and editorial control of the *Telegraph* and expanded the role of partisan journalism." (733) He "guided the paper to the pinacle of journalistic success during the campaign of 1828. In less than three years, the *Telegraph* had grown from an uncertain and tottering beginning to be the most widely read

paper of the day." It also was financially prosperous. "Green had received financial and editorial assistance from...[Democratic] congressmen, yet he maintained command of the paper, bore the ultimate responsibility for its success or failure, and exerted a fierce editorial independence. His aggressive leadership and willingness to take personal risks kept the *Telegraph* operational and focused on its primary goal -- the election of Aandrew Jackson and John Calhoun to the presidency and vice-presidency in 1828. This success of the *Telegraph* is a testimony to the man behind the paper. The image of partisan journalist reflected the political vigor of both the time and the man himself." (739)

510. Farrar, Frederic. "Constitution Era Newspapers: Fourteen Survive." *MHD* 7, 1 (1987): 43-47. Brief geneology of the newspapers published in the late 1700s which are still publishing today.

511. Fassett, Frederick Gardiner, Jr. *A History of Newspapers in the District of Maine 1785-1820*. Orono: University of Maine, 1932. Useful state study of the activities of journalists outside the major cities on the eastern seaboard and the conditions under which they operated.

512. Fay, Bernard. "Benjamin Franklin Bache, A Democratic Leader of the Eighteenth Century." *AASP* 40 (October 1930): 277-304. A distillation of Fay's 1933 book on Bache.

513. Fay, Bernard. *Notes on the American Press at the End of the Eighteenth Century*. New York: Grolier Club, 1927. Study of the role of the press from 1775 to 1800 and the sources from which the press derived its information.

514. Fay, Bernard. *The Two Franklins: Fathers of American Democracy*. Boston: Little, Brown, 1933. Of the biographies of party editors, this is the one with the most provocative thesis. In a fairly glowing account, Fay contended that Bache was the most important of the men who brought about America's political changes between 1790 and 1800. Bache formulated Republican strategy and directed its attack and was "the man who first gave...form to radical opinion in the United States and fashioned the Democratic Party." (361) Fay's thesis is weakened, however, through too many unvalidated assumptions and because of the reputations other men such as Madison and Jefferson had for formulating a democratic ideology.

515. Foik, Paul J. *Pioneer Catholic Journalism*. New York: United States Catholic Historical Society, 1930. Narratives of periodicals published between 1809 and 1840.

516. Ford, Emily E. F. *Notes on the Life of Noah Webster*. New York: 1912. Two volumes, privately printed, narrating the life of the Federalist editor and lexicographer.

517. Ford, Paul L. "Freneau's National Gazette." *Nation* 60 (Feb. 21, 1895): 13-44.

518. Ford, Worthington C. "Jefferson and the Newspaper, 1785-1830." *CHSR* 8 (1905): 78-111. Clearly anti-Jefferson, although Ford's animosity toward Jefferson was produced by no admiration for the press. Writing from a pro-Federalist viewpoint which typified much non-journalism history of the 19th century, Ford based his evaluation of Jefferson's relationship with the press on his opposition to Jefferson, who he believed was indecisive and weak in cultivating the press. Generally critical also of the Republican press which supported Jefferson.

519. Ford, Worthington C. *Thomas Jefferson and James Thomson Callender, 1798-1802*. Brooklyn: Historical Printing Club, 1897. An anthology of the correspondence between Jefferson and Callender and with others in regard to their relationship. Offers no interpretation of the episode.

520. Garrison, Bruce L. "Robert Walsh's American Review: America's First Quarterly." *JH* 8 (1981): 14-17. Favorable treatment of Walsh as a strong, progressive editor.

521. Glicksberg, Charles I. "William Cullen Bryant and the American Press." *JQ* 16 (1939): 356-65, 370. Study of Bryant's attitude toward newspapers and his work, at a time when vituperative partisan journalism "was all part of the snarling temper that characterized American journalism during the first half of the nineteenth century." (358) Favorable view of Bryant, who -- although practicing partisan journalism -- would have preferred that newspapers be conducted on a higher plane.

522. Glicksberg, Charles I. "William Leggett, Neglected Figure of American Literary History." *JQ* 25 (1948): 52-58. An attempt to improve Leggett's literary reputation, because he "has been unjustly neglected by the historians of American letters...[p]artly because journalism for a long time was held in disrepute." (58) Leggett was sincere in his convictions and an excellent writer. Study is critical of the journalistic times in which Leggett worked: "Journalism in the first part of the 19th century was neither dignified nor restrained. It was, for the most part, a vehement and envenomed feud, seething with personal controversies and partisan prejudices. Passion ran high and the ethics of the profession sank correspondingly low." (53) This study, however, praises Leggett for those characteristics the author criticizes in other journalists: "Invariably sincere and outspoken in his opinions, he naturally created many enemies." (54)

523. Goddard, Delano A. *Newspapers and Newspaper Writers in New England, 1787-1815*. Boston: A. Williams, 1880. Reprint of a narrative, biographical paper read before the New England Historic Genealogical Society.

524. Godwin, Parke. *A Biography of William Cullen Bryant*. New York: Appleton, 1883. Favorable biography written by Bryant's co-worker.

525. Goldberg, Isaac. *Major Noah, American-Jewish Pioneer*. Philadelphia: Jewish Publication Society of America, 1936. Biography of Mordecai Noah, Republican editor.

526. Goldsborough, Reid. "Debate in the Press." *MHD* 7, (1987): 18-21. Newspapers had much to say about the issue of adoption of a U.S.Constitution. The debate was "freewheeling and often bitter." (21)

527. Goldsmith, Adolph O. "The Roaring Lyon of Vermont." *JQ* 39 (1962): 179-86. Lyon was strongly opposed to anything which seemed opposed to full popular democracy, was so vigorous that he received the nickname "roaring Lyon," "made life miserable for John Adams and the Federalists, and was responsible in a large measure for the swing of public opinion away from Adams to Jefferson and the Republicans in the presidential election of 1800." (179)

528. Granato, Leonard A. "Freneau, Jefferson and Genet: Independent Journalism in the Partisan Press," in Bond and McLeod, 291-302.

529. Green, Fletcher M. "Duff Green, Militant Journalist of the Old School." *AHR* 52

(January 1947): 247-64. Green, editor of the *United States Telegraph*, was an effective supporter of Andrew Jackson, motivated by ideology and not by money. He believed strongly in the South but also in the unity of the nation. He championed a free and independent press.

530.   Guertler, John Thomas. "Hezekiah Niles: Wilmington Printer and Editor." *DH* 17 (Spring-Summer 1976): 37-53. Examines the early life of Hezekiah Niles, who between 1811 and 1826 published an anomoly in American journalism of the times: a national news magazine which attempted to report the news accurately, factually, and in an unbiased manner. How the publisher of *Niles' Weekly Register* came to undertake such a task is described through an examination of his early printing experience and his editing of a weekly literary magazine called the *Apollo*.

531.   Hage, George S. "Anti-Intellectualism in Newspaper Comment on the Elections of 1828 and 1952." Ph.D. dissertation, University of Minnesota, 1956. See next entry.

532.   Hage, George S. "Anti-Intellectualism in Press Comment: 1828 and 1952." *JQ* 36 (1959): 439-46. Content analysis suggests that anti-intellectualism in the Adams-Jackson campaign was at least as pronounced as it was in the Eisenhower-Stevenson campaign, indicating that anti-intellectualism in America was nothing new in 1952.

533.   Hartung, Barbara W. "America's Era of Many Opinions: 1790-1830." *PRR* 6, 2 (1980): 3-10. Politicians, parties, and the press were closely related.

534.   Havas, John M. "Commerce and Calvinism: The *Journal of Commerce*, 1827-1865." *JQ* 38 (1961): 84-86. Arthur Tappan's "twin objectives" were "publishing a daily newspaper of general interest for businessmen and spreading moral enlightenment." (85) But the New York paper failed because it "submerged moral arguments under commercial ones," and, despite claims that there was a "higher law," "recognized no law higher than the constitution for public officials to obey, even after secession." (86)

535.   Hench, John B. "The Newspaper in a Republic: Boston's 'Centinel' and 'Chronicle,' 1784-1801." Ph.D. dissertation, Clark University, 1979.

536.   Herbert, William. "Jackson, the Bank, and the Press." Ph.D. dissertation, University of Missouri, 1975. In arguing the issue of the Second Bank of the United States, newspapers, many of which "did not...even try to be objective and fair," influenced "events by fanning controversy to which perceptive politicians were attentive."

537.   Hofstadter, Richard. "William Leggett, Spokesman of Jacksonian Democracy." *PSQ* 58 (1950): 581-94. The associate editor of the New York *Evening Post* championed the democratization of America's "economic life. [He] proposed that the humble savings of the plain people should be given access to the great sources of profit and the great avenues of opportunity." (594)

538.   Hooper, Leonard John. "Decade of Debate: The Polemical, Political Press in Illinois, 1814-1824." Ph.D. dissertation, Southern Illinois University, 1964. Illinois' first five newspapers were more concerned with politics, law, and literature "than with the prompt reporting of the latest occurrences." They did a crude job of gathering news, and they printed much personal attack. It is difficult to determine if they had any influence in politics.

539. Horward, Donald D., and William Warren Rogers. "The American Press and the Death of Napoleon." *JQ* 43 (1966): 715-21. Narrative of how U.S. newspapers responded to Napoleon's death. Editors "displayed various reactions to the passing of Napoleon: neutral, hostile, favorable and objective." (721) "No distinct political or geographical patterns of opposition or praise emerged. The French leader had admirers and detractors throughout the country who professed a variety of political persuasions." (715)

540. Humphrey, Carol Sue. "'Little Ado About Something': Philadelphia Newspapers and the Constitutional Convention." *AJ* 5 (1988): 63-80. Newspapers agreed with the members of the convention that the proceedings should be conducted in closed session so that deliberation and debate among the delegates would be free and candid, and the newspapers therefore published little about the proceedings.

541. Jackson, George. *Uncommon Scold: The Story of Anne Royall*. Boston: Bruce Humphries, 1937. Biography of the "first woman journalist." Special emphasis on the early portions of her life. Deals to a large extent with her personality and character, as well as her writing -- comparing her to various landmark individuals.

542. Jellison, Charles A. "That Scoundrel Callender." *VMHB* 67 (1959): 295-306. Study of Callender's political journalism and his relationship with Jefferson. Takes a middle-of-the-road approach, placing less blame on Callender as a completely scurrilous journalist than other historians have done.

543. Kielbowicz, Richard B. "Party Press Cohesiveness: Jacksonian Newspapers." *JQ* 60 (1983): 518-20. Although the Washington *Globe*, the leading national Jackson paper, provided "direction to the smaller papers on the complex issue of the U.S. Bank," on most other issues, editors provided a mix of stories from various sources. Newspapers, therefore, were not "regimented" as much as historians have assumed. (521)

544. Kielbowicz, Richard B. "The Press, Post Office, and Flow of News in the Early Republic." *JER* 3 (1983): 255-80. When Congress approved postal privileges for newspapers in the 1790s, it "committed the nation's resources to forge, through a joint venture with private publishers, a system of mass communication indispensable for a growing nation....Both Federalists and Republicans believed that the same policy -- low newspaper postage -- advanced their political goals." (255) During the following quarter-century, newspapers not only provided important economic information but contributed to the nation's political cohesion.

545. Knudson, Jerry W. "The Case of Albert Gallatin and Jeffersonian Patronage." *WPHM* 52 (July 1969): 241-50. Newspapers argued over Jefferson's appointments when he first became president. The appointees causing the most uproar was Gallatin, secretary of the treasury. Federalist opposition was based on nativism and politics (Jefferson's spoils system), while Republicans argued that the president had the right to appoint whomever he wanted. (Based on Knudson's dissertation.)

546. Knudson, Jerry W. "Jefferson the Father of Slave Children? One View of the Book Reviewers." *JH* 3 (1976): 56-58. Criticizes the poor historical methods used in Fawn M. Brodie's *Thomas Jefferson, An Intimate History* (1974) and some of the book critics who gave it favorable reviews.

547. Knudson, Jerry W. "The Jefferson Years: Response by the Press, 1801-1809." Ph.D.

dissertation, University of Virginia, 1974. Compilation of newspaper opinion detailing the reactions of four Republican and four Federalist papers to the administrations of Jefferson on seven major issues. The papers were intensely partisan. Secondarily, this dissertation attempts to detail the development of techniques, such as the editorial, which the party press used.

548. Knudson, Jerry W. "The Jeffersonian Assault on the Federalist Judiciary, 1802-1805: Political Forces and Press Reaction." *AJLH* 14 (January 1970): 55-75. Federalist papers contended that Jefferson's attempt to repeal the Judiciary Act of 1801 was not intended to improve the judicial system but to give the Republicans partisan control over the system. Republicans argued that the act had been intended to give Federalist such control. Similar partisan arguing occurred over the impeachment of Supreme Court Justice Samuel Chase. (Based on Knudson dissertation.)

549. Knudson, Jerry W. "Newspaper Reaction to the Louisiana Purchase, 'This New, Immense, Unbounded World.'" *MHR* 63 (January 1969): 182-213. Federalist newspapers, especially in New England, objected to the purchase because of the potential political strength of the states that would be carved out of the area and because politically the region would be aligned with Virginia and the southeast. They also criticized the purchase of a "wilderness" and claimed it was "visionary." Republican papers defended the purchase because of the relatively low cost for such a large area and because it so greatly expanded the nation. Federalists claimed the cost could not be afforded by the U.S. (From Knudson dissertation.) Implicit in Knudson's articles is the vitality with which newspapers participated in public debates and the fact that apparently newspapers were considered the primary forums for the public discussion of national issues.

550. Knudson, Jerry W. "Political Journalism in the Age of Jefferson." *JH* 1 (1974): 20-23. Partisan journalism, as evidenced by brief biographies of leading editors, was going strong during the time of the first party system. The *Aurora*, and not the *National Intelligencer*, was the leading Republican paper. Article touches on the development of editorial comment, the "watchdog" function, vilification, press reaction to major issues, Jefferson's poor relations even with the Republican press, and the effectiveness of the Republican press. "Yet partisan journalism was costly for the prestige of the institution of the press." (23) Article is a distillation of Knudson's dissertation, which detailed the editorial reaction of four Republican and four Federalist papers to the administrations of Jefferson, 1801-1809. "[T]he fury of partisan journalism continued unabated during the presidency of Thomas Jefferson." (20)

551. Knudson, Jerry W. "The Rage Around Tom Paine, Newspaper Reaction to His Homecoming in 1802." *NYHSQ* 53 (January 1969): 34-63. Federalist papers were vehement in their opposition to Paine's 1802 return from France, using vicious language to attack his atheism and participation in the violent French revolution. Republican papers attempted, although unsuccessfully, to defend Jefferson's part in Paine's return. The debate over his return was purely partisan, the return being simply a cause celebre for political warfare. Federalists were victors in the argument. (Based on Knudson dissertation.)

552. Knudson, Jerry W. "Thomas Jefferson and James Thomson Callender, The Myth of 'Black Sally.'" *NHB* 32 (November 1969): 15-22. It was Callender's hatred of Jefferson, caused by his inability to persuade Jefferson to give him either money or a postmastership, which prompted him to devise the story of Jefferson's mistress. Al-

though the story has occasionally been accepted by historians, it was a myth created by Callender and repeated by Federalist newspapers.

553. Kobre, Sidney. "The Editor Who Freed Hostages." *MHD* 1, 2 (1981): 55-57, 60. Mordecai Noah, U.S. consul to Tunisia, negotiated the release of American seamen captured by the Barbary Coast pirates.

554. Kropf, C.R. "The Accounts of Samuel Harrison Smith, Philadelphia Printer." *PBSA* 74, 1 (1980): 13-25. Weekly records of income and expenditures are contained in three of Smith's account books from 1794 to 1796.

555. Lanman, Charles. "The 'National Intelligencer' and Its Editors." *AM* 6 (October 1860): 470-81. Favorable biography of Joseph Gales (the father) a man of "good sense and probity of purpose," temperateness, and moderation. "[A]midst all the heats of faction, he never fell into violence." (471) He was a successful editor with "both reputation and many friends....By the constant merit of his journal [*Raleigh Register*], its sober sense, its moderation, and its integrity, he won and invariably maintained the confidence of all on that side of politics with which he concurred...and scarcely less conciliated the respect of his opponents." (474) Similarly glowing accounts of Joseph Gales Jr., Samuel H. Smith, W.W. Seaton, the *National Intelligencer*, etc. All conducted journalism on a high plane. These men were Lanman's "distinguished friends" and "are universally respected and beloved by those who know them." (481)

556. Lee, Robert Edson. "Timothy Dwight and the Boston *Palladium*." NEQ 35 (1962): 229-39. Dwight, a frequent contributor to the *Palladium*, and "other leading Federalists" tried "to influence all of New England through a subsidized, religious-political newspaper," the *Palladium*. (229) Dwight, the president of Yale College, 1795-1817, had great influence, exercised partially through the *Palladium*, which he subsidized. Although his fight was primarily against "irreligion," he "incidentally propagated the Federalist system of politics." (238)

557. Lerche, Charles O., Jr. "Jefferson and the Election of 1800: A Case Study in the Political Smear." *WMQ* 5, 3rd series (1948): 467-91. Study of the various smear tactics used in the 1800 campaign, including those (especially personal vilification) used in newspapers. Jefferson was viciously denounced for his alleged atheism, philosophy, pro-French and revolutionary leanings, attachment to democracy (a scare word meaning mob rule), and opposition to federalism.

558. Levermore, Charles H. "The Rise of Metropolitan Journalism, 1800-1840." *AHR* 6 (1901): 446-65. Survey of the importance of the press to democracy and the effects democracy has on the press. The party press, though important to the political system, was limited in influence because of its attachment to parties. It was not until the advent of the penny press in the 1830s that the press attained the real power it could exert by reaching large numbers of readers. Influence in a democracy depended on a press aimed at the democratic masses. Details reasons for the success of James Gordon Bennett, editor of the penny New York *Herald*.

559. List, Karen K. "Magazine Portrayals of Women's Role in the New Republic." *JH* 13 (1986): 64-70. Three magazines which were studied in the 1790s "were preservers of the status quo, not challengers of it." Despite the intense partisanship of the period, the magazines did not portray women in a politically active way. Instead, they stated that "women's place was in the home, where the primary goal was to be amiable and com-

pliant." (69)

560. List, Karen K. "The Role of William Cobbett in Philadelphia's Party Press, 1794-1799." Ph.D. dissertation, University of Wisconsin, 1980. Rather than a Federalist, Cobbett was a Tory. "Some of Cobbett's contemporaries write that Cobbett harmed the Federalist cause because of his abusiveness, his Britishness and his editorial policy. Cobbett probably would have shrugged off this criticism because his efforts were devoted not to promoting the Federalist party, but to promoting England and his English ideal."

561. List, Karen K. "The Role of William Cobbett in Philadelphia's Party Press, 1794-1799." *JM* 82 (May 1983). See previous entry.

562. List, Karen K. "Two Party Papers' Political Coverage of Women in the New Republic." *CSMC* 2, 2 (1985): 152-65. Examines the *Aurora's* and *Porcupine's Gazette's* contributions to the inclusion of women in politics.

563. List, Karen K. "William Cobbett in Philadelphia, 1794-1799." JH 5 (1978): 80-83, 104. Cobbett was a major journalistic figure in party politics. Generally, however, he was not decent, lacked wide perspective, used his publications for personal vendettas, and criticized cruelty and injustice only when it suited his purposes to do so. "His American experience [however] did allow him to make a name for himself, develop his skill as a political pamphleteer and pave the way for his career in England." (104)

564. Luxon, Norval Neil. *Niles' Weekly Register: News Magazine of the Nineteenth Century*. Baton Rouge: Louisiana State University Press, 1947. Until 1832, the *Register* took strong editorial positions in favor of a protective tariff, aid to western development, Clay's American System, etc. It was propagandistic without denying space and fair treatment to the opposition.

565. Lyle, Cornelius R. "New Hampshire's Sentinel: The Editorial Life of John Prentiss, 1799-1846." Ph.D. dissertation, Northwestern University, 1972. "This work attempts a close study of editorial points of view expressed by a...weekly publisher..., set against the backdrop of community, state and nation. The aim is to obtain greater understanding of community journalism in gaining and keeping reader trust...[Prentiss] was an ordinary man in an ordinary town, much like many editors and towns then and now."

566. Marbut, Frederick B. "Decline of the Official Press in Washington." *JQ* 33 (1956): 335-41. Intra-party bickering and competitive Washington reporting spelled the end of the official party paper in Washington. Details the characteristics of the official papers, including being spokesmen of the president. Narrates political attempts to control the awarding of federal printing contracts to 1893 and discusses the political role of the press and the importance accorded to the role of official newspapers.

567. Marbut, Frederick B. "Early Washington Correspondents: Some Neglected Pioneers." *JQ* 25 (1948): 369-74, 400. Narrates the biographies of early correspondents (after 1808) in an attempt to determine who the first one was.

568. Marsh, Philip M. "Freneau and Jefferson: The Poet-Editor Speaks for Himself about the 'National Gazette' Episode." *AL* 8 (May 1936): 180-89. Accepting Freneau's credibility and at face value his explanation of the founding and operation of the *Na-*

tional Gazette, Marsh concludes that Jefferson did not control or influence Freneau in editing the paper. Attempts to refute the charge made by Hamilton and accepted by some historians as a black mark against Freneau that he was subservient to Jefferson, who used the *National Gazette* as his publicity outlet.

569. Martin, Benjamin Ellis. "Transition Period of the American Press -- Leading Editors in This Century." *MAH*, 17 (April 1887): 273-94. A collection of narrative biographies of political editors from the 1790s through the 1820s. The partisan press was unique for "its coarseness and cruelty, its venemous vigor of invective, its contempt for all that should be sacred in political warfare and in private life." (273)

570. McFarland, C. K., and Robert L. Thistlethwaite. "20 Years of a Successful Labor Paper: The Working Man's Advocate, 1829-1849." *JQ* 60 (1983): 35-40. The paper reflected the concerns of the working class during Jacksonian democracy. The labor press' "goals and reforms were surprisingly liberal even by some of the standards of the 20th Century. It identified and defined issues and called for an end to intolerable social and economic conditions through the exercise of political power." (35)

571. McLaughlin, J. Fairfax. *Matthew Lyon: The Hampden of Congress*. New York: Wynkoop Hallenbeck Crawford, 1900. Biography of the Republican editor, the "roaring Lyon of Vermont."

572. McNally, Brendan C. "Coverage and Attitudes of the United States Press Relative to the Independence Movements in the Spanish Americas, 1810-1825." Ph.D. dissertation, St. Louis University, 1949.

573. Melton, Baxter F. "Amos Kendall in Kentucky, 1814-1829: The Journalistic Beginnings of the 'Master Mind' of Andrew Jackson's 'Kitchen Cabinet.'" Ph.D. dissertation, Southern Illinois University, 1977. The editor of the *Argus* was partisan, "vitriolic and abrasive." He switched his support from Henry Clay to Jackson because he believed Clay played a role in the *Argus'* losing both its national and state printing contracts.

574. Melville, Lewis. *The Life and Letters of William Cobbett in England and America*. Vol. I. London: John Lane, 1913.

575. Middleton, Kent R. "The Partisan Press and the Rejection of a Chief Justice." *JQ* 53 (1976): 106-10. Narrative of the *Columbian Centinel's* and *Aurora's* coverage of Congress' rejection of Federalist John Rutledge for Chief Justice in 1795. The Federalist *Centinel* opposed him, while the Republican *Aurora* supported him, an anomolous situation. Article never suggests, however, what significance this interesting situation had and is disappointing in its absence of explanation.

576. Miller, Alan R. "America's First Political Satirist: Seba Smith of Maine." *JQ* 47 (1970): 488-92. "Smith was the pioneer of political satire in U. S. newspapers and became the forerunner of...[later] homespun political philosophers." (488) "His contribution to American journalism was made when he introduced the American newspaper reader to gentle, subtle, political satire. Its merit was evidenced by the copyists who tried to follow his example during the mid 1800s, and the development of the art of political satire in the media." (492)

577. Murphy, Lawrence W. "John Dunlap's 'Packet' and Its Competitors." *JQ* 28 (1951):

58-62. Dunlap was Philadelphia's best editor. This narrative of the competition he faced from other editors from 1784 to 1796 provides a favorable view of Dunlap, "for he set the pace of early dailies in many cities after 1784 and his ideas were carried over into dailies of other times." (58) Dunlap met each competitor by operating on the principle that "all that buyers have ever asked" is that "a paper should be the best among its competitors." (60)

578. Murphy, Lawrence W. "A Monopoly Daily of 1785 Looks at Its Obligations." *JQ* 26 (1949): 202-03. Reprint of a 1785 article from Dunlap's *Pennsylvania Packet and Daily Advertiser*. The paper believed itself obligated to print both sides of controversies. Brief, inconsequential article.

579. Murphy, Lawrence W. "A New Sidelight on Benjamin Franklin Bache." *JQ* 30 (1953): 501-02. Bache was unethical in trying to charge members of Congress more than the normal rate for subscriptions to the *Aurora*. The paper was not popular and thus suffered financially.

580. Nord, David Paul. "The Evangelical Origins of Mass Media in America, 1815-1835." *JM* 88 (1984). The distribution of religious material by the American Bible Society and the American Tract Society "helped to lay the foundation for mass media in America through their pioneering work in mass printing and mass distribution of the written word....Perhaps more than anything else, the missionary impulse...lay at the foundation of the popularization of print in the 19th century." (2)

581. Osborne, John W. *William Cobbett: His Thought and His Times*. New Brunswick: Rutgers University Press, 1966. Negative evaluation of Cobbett's periodical writing in England. Cobbett was "a failure in politics, a dunce regarding most economic matters, out of touch with the changing society, and of very limited influence in his lifetime." Much of his vehemence came from bafflement. The more complex the problem, the more furious his writing.

582. Parker, Peter J. "The Revival of the Aurora: A Letter to Tench Coxe." *PMHB* 96 (1972): 524-25. After Bache's death, correspondence between his widow and Coxe indicates that the politician provided funding for the continuation of the *Aurora*.

583. Pearl, Morris Leonard. *William Cobbett: A Bibliographical Account of His Life and Times*. London: Oxford University Press, 1953. Includes a 232-page annotated bibliography of Cobbett's works, preceded by a brief, sketchy biography.

584. Phillips, Harry. "The *Courant's* Long and Eventful Life." *PI* 12 (June 1969): 15ff.

585. Potter, J. "Cobbett in North America." *BAASB* (March 1961): 16ff.

586. Prince, Carl E. "The Federalist Party and the Creation of a Court Press, 1789-1801." *JQ* (1976): 238-41. Federalists used as their main instrument of patronage the appointment of printers and editors as postmasters to develop a partisan press, thus contributing to the rapid expansion of the press and to the role of the federal government in consciously nurturing party newspapers.

587. Read, Allen Walker. "Noah Webster's Project in 1801 for a History of American Newspapers." *JQ* 11 (1934): 258-75. In 1801 Webster toyed with the idea of compiling a history but did not. His interest indicates that journalists were interested in the

occupation of journalism.

588. Read, Arthur L. "Asa Greene, New England Publisher, New York Editor and Humorist, 1789-1838." Ph.D. dissertation, University of Minnesota, 1954.

589. Reitzel, William. "William Cobbett and Philadelphia Journalism: 1794-1800." *PMHB* 59 (1935): 223-44. "Cobbett was not creating his own audience or defying the foul fiend in a lonely and heroic way; but...he was fitting himself into a place that circumstances had made for him." (224) The cultural/political atmosphere was favorable for his style of partisan journalism. He was oriented toward the past and tradition and thus attacked radical Republicanism.

590. Robinson, Elwyn Burns. "The Dynamics of American Journalism from 1787 to 1865." *PMHB* 61 (1937): 435-45. Political parties and business depended on public favor. Newspapers were motivated by selfish economic reasons more than by editorial integrity and were willing to aid parties and business in persuading the public.

591. Rollins, Richard M. *The Long Journey of Noah Webster*. Philadelphia: University of Pennsylvania Press, 1980. Psycho-history (based frequently on incomplete analysis and superficial assumptions) of Webster's change from a radical revolutionary to a conservative evangelical. Webster psychologically was trying to establish a place of importance for himself in American society, but he became concerned about the problems created by mass democracy and reacted by embracing the need for authority and social control.

592. Rosemont, Henry P. "Benjamin Franklin and the Philadelphia Typographical Strikers of 1786." *LH* 22 (1981): 398-429. Franklin had a "rapport for these militants, workers who dared combine against employers who had combined against them."

593. Rosemont, Victor. "The Constitutional Convention in the Colonial Press." *JQ* 14 (1937): 364-66. The convention was held in secrecy, and "the right to detailed reports on the Convention was something of which editors hardly dreamed, much less demanded as they would today." (364)

594. Rutland, Robert A. "Madison, The Fourth President and the Press." *MHD* 3, 1 (1983): 21-25. Of the Founding Fathers, none had a better conception of the role the press should play in the country than Madison.

595. Sarna, Jonathan D. *Jacksonian Jew: The Two Worlds of Mordecai Noah*. New York: Homes & Meier, 1981. Noah attempted to harmonize minority identity and national allegiance. He had political aspirations, but he failed. Primarily religious factors prevented him from being a great political editor.

596. Schulz, Constance. "'Of Bigotry in Politics and Religion': Jefferson's Religion, the Federalist Press, and the Syllabus." *VMHBm*, 91 (1983): 73-91. In response to Federalist newspaper accusations from 1800 to 1803, Jefferson wrote an explanation to state the rationality of his deist creed and to reassure "his family and friends that he was not the heretical atheist so graphically depicted by the Federalist press." (90)

597. Scudder, Horace E. *Noah Webster*. Boston: Houghton Mifflin, 1883. Chronological, descriptive biography (based largely on Webster's diary) set against the background of Federalist-Republican contentions with emphasis on Webster as a literary "man of let-

ters." He "liked to think that he had a hand in pretty much every important measure in the political and literary history of the country." (6) He was for Federalists, "democracy," freedom, and the nation. His main concerns were the nation and patriotism.

598. Seaton, Josephine. *William Winston Seaton of the National Intelligencer: A Biographical Sketch with Passing Notices of His Associates and Friends.* Boston: James R. Osgood, 1871. Superficial, romantic portrait of Seaton.

599. Sedgwick, Theodore, Jr. *A Collection of the Political Writing of William Leggett.* New York: Taylor and Dodd, 1840. Anthology of work by the assistant editor of the New York *Evening Post.*

600. Shaw, Peter. "The Second President and the Press." *MHD* 1, 2 (1981): 12-15, 30. John Adams was a believer in the power of the press and frequently wrote for newspapers. Even though he believed in freedom of expression, his support of the Alien and Sedition Laws identified him as an opponent of press freedom, which became one of the primary causes for his defeat in the presidential election of 1800.

601. Singletary, Michael W. "The New Editorial Voice for Andrew Jackson: Happenstance or Plan?" *JQ* 53 (1976): 672-78. Examines the historical assumptions of how Francis Blair was selected to edit the Washington *Globe*. Challenges the widely held assumption that Andrew Jackson alone was responsible for originating the *Globe* and that Blair's selection was made impulsively. Instead, a number of members of the administration, primarily the Kitchen Cabinet, suggested Blair's selection, Blair having been known by Jackson confidants for years.

602. Sloan, Wm. David. "The Early Party Press: The Newspaper Role in American Politics, 1788-1812." *JH* 9 (1982): 18-24. The party press played a central role in the first American party system. Its accepted purpose was to be partisan, and newspapers fulfilled their role through a number of specific practices.

603. Sloan, Wm. David. "Examining the 'Dark Ages' Concept: The Federalist-Republican Press as a Model." *JCI* 2 (1982): 105-19. Argues that historians' designation of the party press era as a meaningless one in journalism history is based on fallacious assumptions about history.

604. Sloan, Wm. David. "The Federalist-Republican Press: Newspaper Functions in America's First Party System, 1789-1916." *SJMC* 1 (Spring 1982): 13-22. Examines the political-journalistic methods of party newspapers.

605. Sloan, Wm. David. "The Party Press: The Newspaper Role in National Politics, 1789-1816." Ph.D. dissertation, University of Texas, 1981. Newspapers were expected to be partisan, and "the press was a major instrument in the Federalists' and Republicans' attempts to gain political dominance." Argues that the dominant, critical view among historians has been based on later journalistic standards and not on the conditions that existed in 1789-1816.

606. Sloan, Wm. David. "Scurrility and the Party Press, 1789-1816." *AJ* 5 (1988): 97-112. The press' scurrility was natural for the times, and politicians often encouraged it.

607. Smith, Culver H. *The Press, Politics, and Patronage: The American Government's Use of Newspapers, 1789-1875.* Athens: University of Georgia Press, 1977. Devotes primary attention to the Jacksonian period. Emphasizes patronage and how newspapers were selected to publish the laws and receive government printing contracts. Editors eagerly sought patronage and became servile and vituperatively partisan. Quotes a Kentucky Whig: the Democratic press was "prostituted, polluted, mercenary."

608. Smith, Culver H. "The Washington Press in the Jackson Period." Ph.D. dissertation, Duke University, 1933.

609. Smith, Elbert B. *Francis Preston Blair.* New York: Free Press, 1980. The editor Blair was a politician. Emphasis on his relations with presidents Jackson, Van Buren, Lincoln, and Johnson as well as with the political dynasty he helped establish and on the politics of which he was a part.

610. Smith, Henry Ladd. "The Two Major Downings: Rivalry in Political Satire." *JQ* 41 (1964): 74-78, 127. Writing under the "Jack Downing" byline in the 1830s, Seba Smith and Charles Augustus Davis "helped to establish the tradition of the...critic of political and social issues who appears to the broad base of the public by use of humor in the vernacular." (74)

611. Smith, William E. "Francis P. Blair, Pen-Executive of Andrew Jackson." *MVHR* 17 (1931): 543-56. Blair was "the greatest partisan journalist and defender of Jacksonian democracy....Jackson ruled for the people and appealed to them for support. His party journalist, who was of the people and had lasting faith in them, effectually convinced the multitudes of the good intents and purposes of his master." Blair's influence was "tremendous."

612. Smith, William E. *The Francis Preston Blair Family in Politics,* 2 vols. New York: Macmillan, 1933. Under Blair, the Washington *Globe* was the nation's most influential Democratic journal. With the Civil War, however, he and his two sons (Montgomery and Francis Jr.) joined the radical Republicans. Personal ambition and intense political strife marked their careers, and they were intimately involved in the dynamic politics of ante-bellum America.

613. Snapp, Elizabeth. "Government Patronage of the Press in St. Louis, Missouri: 1829-1832." *MHR* 24 (1980): 190-216. The St. Louis *Beacon* received patronage from local, state, and national government and played a central role in politics. It "contributed to a more vigorous political debate and enabled a broader segment of the American people to receive a more balanced understanding of the major issues."

614. Spargo, John. *Anthony Haswell, Printer, Patriot, Ballader.* Rutland, Vt.: Tuttle, 1925.

615. Steirer, William F., Jr. "Riding 'Everyman's Hobby Horse'; Journalism in Philadelphia, 1764-1794," 263-76 in Bond and McLeod. Describes the change from earlier patterns and habits of papers after the end of the Revolution. Journalists began to take control, making each newspaper different and beginning many of the basic principles and practices used in papers today.

616. Stewart, Donald H. *The Opposition Press of the Federalist Period.* Albany: State University of New York Press, 1969. Primarily a collection of newspaper quotes. Gener-

ally negative of the tone and methods of the press, pointing up the excesses of the press. Most papers were committed to the political fight and worked with vitality. Assumes that the role of the press was to influence opinion and that the press was successful. Provides little analysis.

617. Stewart, Donald H. "The Press and Political Corruption during the Federalist Administrations." *PSQ* 67 (1959): 426-46. Provides an insightful conclusion about one of the methods of the Republican press: "[T]he incessant newspaper emphasis on betrayal and corruption, in a political party [Federalists] which had become entrenched in power, did much to further the development of our first opposition party....[T]hese reiterated accusations were powerful in bringing the Federalist regime to an inglorious end." (446)

618. Stewart, Robert K. "The Exchange System and the Development of American Politics in the 1820s." *AJ* 4 (1987): 30-42. Through the exchange of newspaper subscriptions and the information that newspapers contained, Jacksonian newspapers and party leaders "nurtured a budding party apparatus that enabled the systematic waging of a war of words and ideas from the largest cities to the most remote outposts of the country." (31)

619. Tagg, James D. "Benjamin Franklin Bache and the Philadelphia Aurora." Ph.D. dissertation, Wayne State University, 1973.

620. Tankard, James W., Jr. "Public Opinion Polling by Newspapers in the Presidential Election Campaign of 1824." *JQ* 49 (1972): 361-65. "The earliest forerunners of the modern public opinion poll appear to be tallies of voter preference reported by the" Raleigh *Star* and Wilmington *American Watchman* in 1824. They were crude, not attempting to poll a representative sample since usually their polls were partisan, although the *Watchman* did carry some results contrary to its preference.

621. Tebbel, John. "Van Buren: The 'Little Magician' and the Press." *MHD* 6, 1 (1986): 40-45. "More than any president who preceded him, Van Buren appeared to have a natural understanding of the relationship between press and public, and he was the first who knew how to manipulate the press in somewhat the same style that is commonplace today." (41)

622. Thornton, Mary Lindsay. "Public Printing in North Carolina, 1749-1815." *NCHR* 21 (July 1944): 181-202. Public printing contracts greatly influenced the press. Patronage caused papers to become partisan. Editors were manipulated by politicians, whose use of "the newspapers as a medium of party expression made editors take part in party battles." (191)

623. Ward, Harry M. "The First President and the Press." *MHD* 1, 1 (1980): 2-7, 64. Even Washington, who had been seen as a national hero, had strong critics -- especially Bache -- among the press because of differences on partisan issues. Criticism got so harsh that Washington hated the Republican press.

624. Ward, Harry M. "George Washington and the Media." *MHD* 7, 2 (1987): 22-27, 35. Reprint of previous entry.

625. Weed, Thurlow. *Life of Thurlow Weed, Including His Autobiography and a Memoir*, 2 vols. Harriet A. Weed and Thurlow Weed Barnes, eds. Boston: Houghton Mifflin,

1883-1884. Weed's account of his experiences as a Whig and Republican editor-politician.

626. White, Pliny H. *The Life and Services of Matthew Lyon.* Burlington, Vt.: 1858.

627. White, Shane. "Impious Prayers: Elite and Popular Attitudes Toward Blacks and Slavery in the Middle-Atlantic States, 1783-1810." *NYH* 67 (July 1986): 262-83. Newspapers, magazines, and almanacs presented a view of black people that "was not stylized or sentimentalized but matter of fact and direct, suggesting that popular racial attitudes...were surprisingly benign." (283)

628. Williams, John Camp. *An Oneida County Printer.* New York: 1906. William Williams was an influential printer, publisher, and editor in Utica, N.Y., from 1803 to 1838.

629. Worton, Stanley N. "William Leggett, Political Journalist (1801-1839)." Ph.D. dissertation, Columbia University, 1954.

630. Wyman, Mary Alice. *Two American Pioneers, Seba Smith and Elizabeth Oakes Smith.* New York: Columbia University Press, 1927.

631. Zimmer, Roxanne. "The Urban Daily Press: Baltimore, 1797-1816. Ph.D. dissertation, University of Iowa, 1982. Four daily papers were primarily interested in commercial affairs rather than politics or other types of news.

5

Freedom of the Press, 1690–1800

632. Allis, Frederick S., Jr. "Boston and the Alien and Sedition Laws." *BSP* (1951): 25-51. The reaction of Federalists in Massachusetts to the Kentucky and Virginia resolutions against the Sedition Act showed "little sympathy for this Republican nonsense." They favored strict enforcement. In the only Sedition Act case tried in Massachusetts, David Brown was sentenced to 18 months in prison for erecting a liberty pole in Dedham, the home of Federalist Fisher Ames. Thomas and Abijah Adams, proprietors of Boston's *Independent Chronicle*, were arrested for seditious libel under Massachusetts law rather than the Sedition Act. Thomas was too ill to stand trial, but Abijah was given a 30-day sentence. The presiding judge refused to allow the defense to present a legal argument based on broad freedom of the press.

633. Anderson, David A. "The Origins of the Press Clause." *UCLA Law Review* 30 (February 1983): 455-537. "[M]ost of the Framers [of the U. S. Constitution] perceived, however dimly, naively, or incompletely, that freedom of the press was inextricably related to the new republican form of government and would have to be protected if their vision of government by the people was to succeed." (537)

634. Anderson, Frank M. "Contemporary View of the Virginia and Kentucky Resolutions." *AHR* 4 (October 1899): 545-63; 5 (July 1900): 225-52. Contemporary newspaper commentary on the resolutions condemning the Alien and Sedition Acts. The resolutions were "designed primarily as a protest against the infringement" of complete freedom of expression made by the Alien and Sedition Acts. (45) They were supported strongly by some people and opposed strongly by others.

635. Anderson, Frank M. "The Enforcement of the Alien and Sedition Laws." *Annual Report of the American Historical Association* (1912): 113-26. Washington: AHA, 1914. Study of how the Alien and Sedition Acts were enforced. High Federal officials were energetic in enforcing the laws. Republican charges of unfairness were numerous. Juries were packed, judges' interpreted the acts favorably in accord with Federalist intent, and the deportment of some judges was questionable.

636. Baldasty, Gerald J. "Flirting with Social Science: Methodology and Virginia Newspapers, 1785-86." *JH* 1 (1974): 86-88. "No uniform agreement existed on the meaning of press freedom in Virginia newspapers 1785-6, but apparently citizens could comment on and discuss political issues. No indications appear that Virginians felt the strictures on discussion inherent in Levy's definition of seditious libel, although negative evidence leaves much to be desired." (86)

637. Baldasty, Gerald J. "Toward an Understanding of the First Amendment: Boston Newspapers, 1782-1791." *JH* 3 (1976): 25-30, 32. Attempts "to clarify the discussion on press freedom through examination of popular thought in newspapers before the adoption of the First Amendment." (25) Concentrates on (1) the concept of press freedom developed by Boston newspaper printers and writers and (2) the concept of legal constraints on the press, especially defamation law. Concludes "that a theory of press freedom may have been emerging in the decade before the adoption of the First Amendment. This theory may not have been well conceptualized or coherently stated. But press freedom as expressed by printers and newspaper writers included freedom from excessive taxation, protection from the central government through constitutional guarantees, and the right to discuss public measures and to scrutinize the conduct of officials as long as personal characters were not attacked...Printers do not appear to have suffered from fears of government prosecution, nor does the legislation appear to have been a major threat to the press." (32) The term "seditious libel" is too vague to apply to press freedom for any useful purpose. "[G]eneral criticism of government and officials was quite common." (32) Argues that Levy exaggerated the "reception of common law [of seditious libel] from England into the new nation." (32)

638. Berns, Walter. "Freedom of the Press and the Alien and Sedition Laws: A Reappraisal," 109-59 in *Supreme Court Reports*, 1970. Chicago: University of Chicago Press, 1970. Challenges historians who claimed that a "broad libertarian theory" emerged with opposition to the Sedition Act. The opposition as expressed in the Virginia and Kentucky Resolutions was based not on libertarian arguments of civil liberties "but the doctrine of states' rights, or nullification, or disunion. The men principally responsible for the development of liberal law of free speech and press -- for fashioning a remedy for the deprivation of the constitutional rights of freedom of speech and press -- were the Federalists Alexander Hamilton and James Kent who were able to do this because, unlike Jefferson and his colleagues and successors, they were not inhibited by an attachment to the institution of slavery."

639. Bleyer, Willard G. "The Beginnings of the Franklins' *New-England Courant*." *JQ* 4, 2 (1927): 1-5. History of the *Courant* during its first year. It was the first American paper to challenge authority. Unlike the *News-Letter* and Boston *Gazette*, the *Courant* "from its first issue was an open challenge to those in authority, civil and ecclesiastical. Never before had the puritan leaders been so openly flouted....From the point of view of the development of journalism the *Courant* is significant as the first American newspaper to question the authority of the church in matters of everyday life. The inoculation issue merely furnished the occasion for the revolt. That the publisher of the

Courant should be called to account for his temerity was inevitable. Although the question of the freedom of the press was not decided in the case of the *Courant*, as was the case with Zenger and his *New-York Weekly Journal*. Franklin raised the question of the right of a newspaper to criticize outspokenly those in authority. The course of the *Courant*, therefore, marks the beginning of the great struggle for the liberty of the press." (5)

640. Brant, Irving. *The Bill of Rights: Its Origin and Meaning*. Indianapolis: Bobbs-Merrill, 1965. A collection of historical incidents related to the Bill of Rights, viewing the Alien and Sedition Acts as a "perversion of the Constitution" passed in a time of "super-patriotic jingoism." (248, 247) They were enforced only against political opponents and with as little regard for justice as the passage of the laws had shown for constitutional rights. The first part of the book traces the English background of the concept of freedom of the press. Part two discusses the background of the Bill of Rights, especially the First Amendment, the Sedition Act of 1798, and Supreme Court interpretations of the First Amendment in the 20th century. Argues that the intention of the writers of the First Amendment was libertarian.

641. Brant, Irving. "Seditious Libel: Myth and Reality." *NYULR* 39 (January 1964): 1-19. See previous entry. The writers of the First Amendment intended to reject the British common law on seditious libel. The Sedition Act provided a "balancing test." Such a test has been used occasionally by those who do not believe in absolute freedom of expression.

642. Brown, Stuart G. "Politics and Mr. Crosskey's Constitution, II. The Constitution in the Debates on the Alien and Sedition Acts." *SLR* 7 (Fall 1955): 27-37. Challenges William W. Crosskey's *Politics and the Constitution in the History of the United States* interpretation of the political issues in the debate over the Alien and Sedition Acts. Contends that the Federalists turned to the Sedition Act as the most effective means of stifling Republican opposition. They preferred federal to state action to get around Republican governors.

643. Buel, Richard, Jr. "Freedom of the Press in Revolutionary America: The Evolution of Libertarianism, 1760-1820," in Bailyn and Hench, 59-98. As opposed to Levy's interpretation, Buel maintains that colonial and revolutionary printers "made a tremendous stride toward formulating and implementing those libertarian ideals concerning freedom of the press that we embrace today." Although there were many obstacles to absolute freedom, early Americans viewed freedom as a good ideology. But their ideology included that freedom should be used for the public good. Thus, after the Revolution, Federalists' views on restricted freedom were not inconsistent with their belief that licentiousness would endanger the nation.

644. Buranelli, Vincent. "The Myth of Anna Zenger." *WMQ*, 3rd series, 13 (1956): 157-68. Refutes Cooper's thesis: "To call her the 'Mother of Freedom' is to abandon history for romance." (168)

645. Buranelli, Vincent. "Peter Zenger's Editor." *AQ* 7 (Summer 1955): 174-81. The lawyer James Alexander played a key role in the New York *Weekly Journal* and the Zenger trial. Zenger's fame rightfully "grows with the years." (174) The *Weekly Journal*, directed and edited by Alexander, was "the great spokesman for freedom, attempting to educate its readers into the meaning of the concept, and at the same time giving a practical demonstration of the concept in action." (175)

646. Buranelli, Vincent, ed. *The Trial of Peter Zenger*. New York: New York University Press, 1957. The introduction views the issues in black-and-white terms, good vs. evil, followed by an edited version of the trial. Adds little new and is fairly simplistic. The trial and verdict were "something to be referred to whenever the liberties of its subject were endangered."

647. Carroll, Thomas F. "The Evolution of the Theory of Freedom of Speech and of the Press." *GLJ* 11 (November 1922): 27-48. Examines the concept of press freedom at the time the First Amendment was adopted; the early controversy over its meaning; the interpretations of Alexander Hamilton, Blackstone, Thomas M. Cooley; and Oliver W. Holmes; and how each interpretation was modified by later writers and court decisions. Concludes that press freedom has been an expanding concept.

648. Carroll, Thomas F. "Freedom of Speech and the Press in the Federalist Period: The Sedition Act." *MLR* 18 (1920): 615-51. The First Amendment does not prohibit Congress from passing laws that are necessary and proper. It was this concept that Federalists used to pass the Sedition Act. They believed Congress had the right to prohibit publications that interfered with the government in the exercise of its constitutional duties. The Sedition Act was no more severe than the common law of libels.

649. Chamberlin, Bill F. "Freedom of Expression in Eighteenth-Century Connecticut," in Bond and McLeod, 247-62. Examines the relationship between Connecticut newspapers and the state government from 1782-1791 to consider the possibility of informal restraints on expression and look at the nature of press feedom in the late 18th century. The Connecticut legislature exercised power to penalize an unruly press.

650. Chaplin, George. "Jefferson and the Press." *NR* 25, 2 (1971): 3-8. A philosophical essay on freedom of expression, giving Jefferson credit for libertarian ideas about freedom of expression. Jefferson's understanding of the necessity of a free press for the preservation of democracy is as sorely needed now as it was in his day. "We are able in this country to speak freely and print freely because of Jefferson. More than any other of his era, he recognized that popular government is built on the freest flow of information." (3) "We live in a world far more complex than Jefferson's but he holds aloft the torch of liberty, still stirs minds and hearts of men with his belief in human dignity and equality of rights. His standard is one which all of us in journalism may pursue with honor and devotion and hope." (8) The article is the text of the 1971 Jefferson Fellowship Lecture delivered to the Jefferson Fellows at the University of Hawaii.

651. Chenery, William L. *Freedom of the Press*. New York: Harcourt, 1955 (rev.ed., Westport, Conn.: Greenwood Press, 1977). The tradition in early America was one of freedom of expression, with the people fighting against conservative, repressive government to attain and maintain freedom. Uses history of freedom to argue for freedom in the 1950s. Covers major episodes such as the Zenger trial, Alien and Sedition Acts, Jefferson's writings, etc.

652. Cheslau, Irving G. *John Peter Zenger and "The New-York Weekly Journal"; A Historical Study*. New York: Zenger Memorial Fund, 1952. In the trial the "defense made an eloquent plea for freedom of the press and anticipated the modern laws of libel by three-quarters of a century," but the trial, although a milestone in American freedom, did not establish a legal precedent and "did not sweep out the rigors of the common law" of libel.

653. Cheyney, Edward P. "Freedom and Restraint: A Short History." *AAAPS* 200 (November 1938): 1-12. Freedom of expression has been cherished in American tradition, but it has sometimes been interfered with at difficult times, as when the Alien and Sedition Acts were invoked during the threat of war with France, although at such times "the claims of freedom have even more constantly asserted themselves." (4) This article was written as a response to the danger posed to freedom of expression in the 1930s by totalitarian government.

654. Cooper, Kent. *Anna Zenger, Mother of Freedom.* New York: Farrar, Strauss, 1946. Fictionalized, quasi-biographical novel with the thesis that Anna Zenger was the prime mover in the Zenger episode.

655. Covert, Cathy. "Passion Is Ye Prevailing Motive: The Feud Behind the Zenger Case." *JQ* 50 (1973): 3-10. Zenger was simply the printer for James Alexander, who developed his ideas of press freedom because of his feud with Gov. William Cosby. He saw the press as a political weapon, and his concepts of press freedom -- which became important to the American ideology of press freedom -- were developed for their usefulness in political battle.

656. Crane, Verner W. "Benjamin Franklin and the Stamp Act." *CSMT* 32 (1937): 56-77. Although seemingly equivocal on the Stamp Act, Franklin attempted to dissuade Grenville from adopting the scheme. After the measure was adopted, he philosophically accepted the measure but pleaded for the removal of the tax in a hearing before the House of Commons.

657. Crosman, Ralph L. "The Legal and Journalistic Significance of the Trial of John Peter Zenger." *RMLR* 10 (January 1938): 258-68. The Zenger trial was important legally and journalistically. It established the basic principles later incorporated into laws of libel.

658. Downs, Robert B. "Freedom of Speech and Press: Development of a Concept." *LT* 19 (July 1970): 8-18. Brief overview of various events from colonial to recent times. The events, such as the Sedition Act and efforts to prohibit the use of the mails for abolitionist material, show that Americans' right to freedom of expression is fragile. It must be constantly guarded.

659. Duniway, Clyde A. *The Development of Freedom of the Press in Massachusetts.* New York: Longmans, Green, 1906. During the period from 1638 to 1827, freedom of the press was primarily an attempt to open government proceedings to public view. By 1827 the press, after a gradual and continuing battle, had gained its complete freedom with passage of a more liberal libel law. The evolution of press freedom included such episodes as the institution of royal control over the colonial press, the struggle of editors against executive and legislative restrictions and against the stamp act, the development of constitutional guarantees, persecutions under the Sedition Act, and passage of the 1827 libel law, which was just and reasonable. During colonial times, Massachusetts had a tendency to place restrictions on freedom of expression, and control over the press was arbitrarily exercised. Until 1730 the law specified careful supervision of the press, but supervision gradually diminished and more and more publications were issued without license. After 1730 the colonial governor was not required to maintain censorship, but criminal prosecutions for seditious libel were relied on to check the press. During the revolutionary period, papers opposed to the crown were arbitrarily suppressed. Under the state constitution, unrestricted but undefined freedom

became a part of the organized law.

660. Farber, Alan J. "Reflections on the Sedition Act of 1798." *AABJ* 62 (March 1976): 324-28. Because the Sedition Act (or any other later prosecution for seditious libel) was never tried by the Supreme Court, the possibility of prosecution still remains a part of our legal system.

661. Fisher, Joshua Francis. "Andrew Hamilton, Esq., of Pennsylvania." *PMHB* 16 (1892): 1-27 (originally published in *HM* [August 1868]). Hamilton was "one of the earliest and boldest asserters of the liberty of Speech and Writing" and was pre-eminent "in the enunciation of the now universally accepted doctrine of the law of libel." (1)

662. Heming, Thomas J. "A Scandalous, Malicious and Seditious Libel." *AH* 19, 1 (December 1967): 22-27, 100-06. Narrative of the Croswell case.

663. Fogel, Howard H. "Colonial Theocracy and a Secular Press." *JQ* 37 (1960): 525-33. "The American colonial press won its freedom from interference by religious authorities in a gradual process, highlighted by the experiences of William Bradford in Pennsylvania and James Franklin in Massachusetts."

664. Forkosch, Morris D. "Freedom of the Press: Croswell's Case." *FLR* 33 (March 1965): 415-48. Analysis of the 1804 libel case.

665. Gault, Tom. *Peter Zenger, Fighter for Freedom.* New York: Crowel, 1951. Fictionalized account of Zenger and his trial.

666. Gavin, Clark. *Foul, False and Infamous; Famous Libel and Slander Cases of History.* New York: Abelard, 1950. Popular, simplistic book includes Zenger and Thomas Cooper. Zenger "refused to compromise with political tyranny in colonial New York. The stand he took then created freedom of the press as we know it today, and it has rightfully been called 'the foundation stone of American liberty.'" Cooper refused to compromise in his right to criticize the government. His stand was one of the causes for voiding the Alien and Sedition Acts.

667. Goodell, A.C., Jr. "Remarks on the censorship of the press in Massachusetts." *MHSP* 8, 2nd ser. (1892-1894): 271-73. Brief survey.

668. Goodwin, Maud W. "The Zenger Trial," 193-205 in *The Dutch and English on the Hudson: A Chronicle of Colonial New York.* New Haven, Conn.: Yale University Press, 1919. Romantic account intended for a popular audience, includes the social background of colonial New York and the founding and settlement of the colony.

669. Grotta, Gerald L. "Phillip Freneau's Crusade for Open Sessions of the U.S. Senate." *JQ* 48 (1971): 667-71. Although the final vote to provide "suitable gallaries" came the year after the death of the *National Gazette*, Freneau played a major role in forcing open the doors of the Senate. "One of the early battles for an 'open meeting law' was fought nearly 180 years ago by poet-journalist Phillip Freneau, who crusaded for the right of newsmen (and the general public) to attend sessions of the United States Senate." (667) "Although there were to be future battles over access to governmental meetings and records -- battles which continue today -- an important victory had been won in the Senate's vote in 1794." (671)

670. Hall, Fredrick T. *Decisive Battles of the Law; Narrative Studies of Eight Legal Contests Affecting the History of the United States between the Years 1800 and 1886.* New York: Harper, 1906. Includes an account of James Callender, who was convicted for seditious libel.

671. Hanson, Lawrence. *Government and the Press: 1695-1763.* New York: Oxford University Press, 1936. Newspapers were used as an important tool in politics, and political groups used various methods to suppress and direct them. Ultimately, however, the government failed to prevent newspapers from "encroaching" into politics or to control its effects.

672. Harlow, Alvin F. "Martyr for a Free Press." *AH* 6, 6 (October 1955): 42-47. Popular, superficial account of Matthew Lyon and how he was tried and imprisoned under the Sedition Act.

673. Hudon, Edward G. *Freedom of Speech and Press in America.* Washington: Public Affairs Press, 1963. This study is a Libertarian attempt to establish an historical basis for today's libertarian belief in the need for freedom of expression in a complex society. It is a well-documented study of "the British law of speech and press as it existed in England and colonial America prior to the revolution, and also into the theories of law and sovereignty which permitted this English and Colonial law to follow the course that it did." The Alien and Sedition laws were a threat to freedom. Attempts to analyze and place in proper perspective "the natural law environment from which the constitution and the Amendment arose....The speech and press guarantees of the First Amendment were intended as more than instruments of political expediency. Their purpose was to protect the rights of the minority from any whims of the majority." (ix) The First Amendment was intended to break away from the repressive concepts of British law and fulfill the Declaration of Independence statement that "all men are created equal, that they are endowed by their creator with certain inalienable rights." (168)

674. Humphrey, Carol Sue. "'That Bulwark of Our Liberty': Massachusetts Printers and the Issue of a Free Press, 1783-1788." *JH* 14 (1987): 34-38. In the face of attempts by the state government to limit freedom of the press, Massachusetts printers "praised the benefits of a free press and supported the removal of all restrictions." (34) They "voiced a belief in a libertarian view of a free press -- that one could publish without fear of censorship or reprisal." (37)

675. Huxford, Gary. "The English Libertarian Tradition in the Colonial Newspaper." *JQ* 45 (1968): 677-86. Traces the influence of "Cato" (John Trenchard and Thomas Gordon) and other British Libertarian writers, through the first half of 18th century, on American writers. The libertarian ideas of England's "commonwealth men" influenced American editors, who promoted the ideas of freedom, equality, and autonomy in the colonies. The editors "found in the natural rights doctrine of the Old Whigs their [political] arguments."

676. Hynes, Terry. "A Conversation with Leonard Levy." *JH* 7 (1980): 96-103. Interview with the controversial historian.

677. Kahane, Dennis S. "Colonial Origins of Our Free Press." *ABAJ* 62 (February 1976): 202-06. Popular, descriptive libertarian account.

678. Kaminiski, Thomas H. "Congress, Correspondents and Confidentiality in the 19th

Century: A Preliminary Study." *JH* 4 (1976): 83-87, 92. In the 1800s journalists exerted a right of confidentiality of sources, so that by 1848 "confidentiality had become a settled principle." (83) Provides a history of the right of confidentiality from 1812 to the 1890s, foreshadowing such a right today. The emphasis is after 1840, but the idea of confidentiality first had been argued around 1812.

679. Konkle, Burton A. *The Life of Andrew Hamilton, 1676-1741, "The Day-Star of the American Revolution."* Philadelphia: National Publishing Co., 1941. Chapters 11-14 focus on the Zenger trial. For his service to press freedom, Gouverneur Morris called Hamilton "the day-star of the American Revolution."

680. Kunstler, William M. "Andrew Hamilton," 17-45 in the *The Case for Courage.* New York: Morrow, 1962. Hamilton was a courageous lawyer who defended Zenger. His interpretations of the law of criminal libel have been accepted by the English-speaking world.

681. Lawrence, Eugene. "The Freedom of the Press in New York in 1733-35; an Epoch in American Journalism." *NM* 18 (July-August 1893): 113-27. Narrative of the Zenger case and its contributions to American freedom of the press.

682. Lawson, Elizabeth. *The Reign of Witches: The Struggle Against the Alien and Sedition Laws, 1798-1800.* New York: Civil Rights Congress, 1952. Popular account, written in light of the Smith and McCarran Acts of 1950s.

683. Leder, Lawrence H. "The Role of Newspapers in Early America: 'In Defense of Their Own Liberty.'" *HLQ* 30 (November 1966): 1-16. Examination of the attitudes of American editors from 1690 to 1762 toward press freedom. Speculation on press freedom did not appear in the first 30 years, and later only as newspapers tried to break a press monopoly.

684. Levy, Leonard W. "Did the Zenger Case Really Matter?" *WMQ* 17 (3rd ser.) (January 1960): 35-50. The verdict in the Zenger case revealed more about the ability of his lawyer, Andrew Hamilton, than it did about changes toward more liberal law on seditious libel. "The Zenger case at best gave the press the freedom to print the 'truth' but only if the truth were directed away from the assembly....No cause was more honored by rhetorical denunciation and dishonored in practice than that of freedom of expression during the revolutionary period, from the 1760's through the War of Independence."

685. Levy, Leonard. *Emergence of a Free Press.* New York: Oxford University Press, 1985. Slightly revises Levy's early concept of limited freedom of the press. Examines Revolutionary papers and pamphlets, which showed an editorial daring.

686. Levy, Leonard W., ed. "Freedom in Turmoil, Era of the Sedition Act: The Crisis of 1797-1800," 188-262 in *Major Crises in American History: Documentary Problems, Vol. I (1689-1861).* New York: Harcourt, Brace, 1962. Collection of documents.

687. Levy, Leonard W. *Freedom of the Press from Zenger to Jefferson.* Indianapolis: Bobbs-Merrill, 1966. Anthology of statements on freedom of the press. The introduction, covering 1690-1804, propounds the same theme as *Legacy of Suppression.* The First Amendment was not the gift of freedom-loving Founding Fathers but the legacy of "new libertarians," who in response to the Sedition Act cast off Blackstonian

concepts to forge a more libertarian view. The book is useful primarily as an anthology of leading statements on freedom of the press from Andrew Hamilton's arguments in the Zenger trial of 1735 to Alexander Hamilton's arguments in the Croswell trial of 1804. The documentary evidence supports the thesis that Levy proposed in *Legacy of Suppression.*

688. Levy, Leonard. *Jefferson and Civil Liberties: The Darker Side.* Cambridge, Mass.: Belknap Press of Harvard University Press, 1963. A frankly critical, debunking treatment of Jefferson. Argues that Jefferson was restrictive rather than libertarian and that, while Jefferson at times talked liberty, in practice he cared little for it. Liberty in Jefferson's view was only for those ideas that agreed with his. Jefferson, considered the leading exponent of American liberty, "did not directly apply to practical political problems a libertarian creed to which he adhered consistently." There was "a strong pattern of unlibertarian, even antilibertarian thought throughout Jefferson's long career."

689. Levy, Leonard W. *Legacy of Suppression.* Cambridge, Mass: Belknap Press of Harvard University Press, 1960. This book is one of the most influential ever published in journalism history. It exercised a major influence on historians' thinking about and approaches to the issue of the concept of freedom of the press in early America. The concept of freedom of the press, Levy argued, was limited in early America, meaning no more than freedom from prior restraint. It was not until the Sedition Act that the concept developed to attack the crime of sedition. The restrictions that the Alien and Sedition Acts placed on freedom of expression in regard to seditious libel were acceptable according to the prevailing philosophy. The First Amendment was not intended to supersede common law -- as the passage of the Sedition Act evidenced -- and even after adoption of the First Amendment, government retained the power to punish criticism. As measured against the libertarian approach to freedom of expression, the attitude of Americans in the 1790s fell short. It was the debates over the Alien and Sedition Acts that finally crystallized the libertarian view in America.

690. Levy, Leonard. "Liberty and the First Amendment: 1790-1800." *AHR* 68 (October 1962): 22-37. A "sudden break-through in American libertarian thought on freedom of speech and press" occurred in 1798 with the debates over the Sedition Act. Advocates of a libertarian approach to freedom of expression challenged Blackstone's concept that press freedom simply meant freedom from prior restraint. This new libertarian approach originated as an "expedience of self-defense on the part of a besieged political minority." It "established virtually all at once and in nearly perfect form a theory justifying the rights of individual expression and of opposition parties."

691. Levy, Leonard. "The Third President and the Press." *MHD* 2 (Summer 1982): 18-26, 54. Extract from *Jefferson and Civil Liberties.*

692. Lewis, Walker. "The Right to Complain: The Trial of John Peter Zenger." *ABAJ* 46 (January 1960): 27-30, 108-111. Retelling of the trial, emphasizing Hamilton's arguments.

693. "Liberty of the Press; Seditious Law of 1798." *SR* 3 (May 1829): 450-67. An 1829 U.S. House of Representatives resolution (providing for restoration of fines levied under the Sedition Act) was needed to prohibit punishment of political libels in the future.

694. Lossing, Benson J. "Freedom of the Press Vindicated." *HNMM* 57 (July 1878): 293-98. The Zenger case "was a notable struggle in the province of New York for the maintenance of the liberty of the press. Considered in all its bearings, social, political, and historical, that struggle constituted one of the most important events in the early annals of the state." The controversy revolved around two factions, one supporting "royalty and its prerogative; the other...sovereignty of the people and freedom of thought and of speech." (293) The case involved "the great principles enunciated in the Magna Charta and the Bill of Rights. It raised the question of the right of the subject to criticize the conduct of a ruler, the liberty of speech, and the freedom of the press." Contemporaries viewed it as the beginning of American liberty, revealing the "philosophy of freedom both of thought and speech as an inborn human right." (295)

695. MacCracken, Henry N. *Prologue to Independence: The Trials of James Alexander, 1715-1756.* New York: James H. Heineman, 1964. Chapters 7 and 8 cover Alexander's role in the Zenger trial.

696. Malone, Dumas. *The Public Life of Thomas Cooper, 1783-1839.* New Haven, Conn.: Yale University Press, 1926. Cooper was a defender of press freedom, and his "Treatise on the Law of Libel and the Liberty of the Press" (1830) was one of the earliest attempts to formulate a libertarian doctrine of press freedom. He was an agitator attempting to influence statesmen by speeches, pamphlets, and newspaper articles. His most firmly held belief was man's right to express himself freely. In his early years, he was idealistic, individualistic, even radical in his views on the rights of man, although as he grew older (1820s on) he grew more conservative.

697. McCormick, Robert R. *The Freedom of the Press.* New York: Appleton-Century, 1936. Popular account. Tyrants in authority have a history of trying to suppress the press. American colonists, however, believed strongly in freedom of expression. The Zenger case was a victory for freedom, and the Stamp Act -- because it was aimed at press freedom -- was the immediate cause of the Revolution. The Alien and Sedition Acts were so unpopular that their authors were considered odius, and the Acts were the cause of the Federalists' downfall. One-fourth of book covers history up to the 1804 Croswell case; most of remainder is about contemporary conditions.

698. McCoy, Ralph E. *Freedom of the Press: An Annotated Bibliography.* Carbondale: Southern Illiois University Press, 1968. Extensive bibliography not only of press freedom but of the broad area of freedom of expression. Contains many works on journalism history other than those dealing exclusively with freedom of the press.

699. McCoy, Ralph E. *Freedom of the Press: A Bibliocyclopedia, Ten Year Supplement (1967-1977).* Carbondale: Southern Illinois University Press, 1979. Continuation of previous entry.

700. McCullough, Dan H. "The History of the First Amendment and the Acts of September 24, 1789, and March 2, 1831." *SDLR* 12 (Spring 1967): 171-257. Narrative of the development of law of contempt of court. The Judiciary Act of 1789 established the English common law doctrine that courts have the inherent power to punish as contempt all conduct which would tend to influence or prejudice judicial proceedings.

701. McMaster, John B. "A Free Press in the Middle Colonies." *PR* 61 (January 1886): 78-90. William Bradford was "the first man in America to stand up boldly for unlicensed printing." After being censored for book publication in Philadelphia, he moved to New

York in 1693 and established a press. It was six years before Pennsylvania had another press, and it was placed under the censorship of a committee.

702. Middleton, Kent R. "Commercial Speech in the Eighteenth Century," in Bond and McLeod, 277-90. Looks at the attitudes of the framers of the Constitution toward freedom and protection of commercial expression. Commercial speech was possibly intended to be covered under the First Amendment, but courts today do not usually follow the feelings of the 1790s in their decisions.

703. Miller, Helen H. "Freedom of the Press," 26-66 in *The Case for Liberty*. Chapel Hill: University of North Carolina Press, 1965. Events in the colonies were more important than the precedents of British law in shaping the guarantees of individual rights in state constitutions and the U.S. Bill of Rights.

704. Miller, John C. *Crisis in Freedom: The Alien and Sedition Acts*. Boston: Little, Brown, 1951. Similar in theme but less expansive in scope and detail than James Smith's book *Freedom's Fetters*. The Alien and Sedition Acts were political in intent and were enacted during a time of perceived national crisis (an impending war with France) and were not in accord with the dominant American attitude toward freedom of expression. Federalists, who were authoritarian in nature, were not oriented toward freedom and democracy and enacted the acts contrary to prevailing ideas. In a period of histeria brought on by the French revolution, the Federalists enacted the Alien and Sedition laws to protect their administration from criticism.

705. Montagno, George L. "Federalist Retaliation: The Sedition Trial of Matthew Lyon." *VH* 26 (January 1958): 3-16. Narrative of the trial, conviction, imprisonment, and political martyrdom of Lyon. He was attacked under the Sedition Act because he championed radical democratic ideas and attacked conservatism.

706. Morris, Richard. "The Case for the Palatine Printer: Zenger's Fight for Free Press," 69-95 in *Fair Trial*. New York: Knopf, 1953. The long-standing freedom to criticize public officials "goes back to the courageous battle put up against the Royal Government in America by a New York printer named John Peter Zenger. The Zenger case destroyed once and for all the notion that government officials were entitled to unqualified allegiance and support and that they were untouchables immune from criticism."

707. Mott, Frank Luther. *Jefferson and the Press*. Baton Rouge: Louisiana State University Press, 1943. A very favorable view of Jefferson as a libertarian philosopher who could do little wrong despite the fact that journalists treated him harshly and unfairly.

708. Murphy, Lawrence W. "Thomas Maule: The Neglected Quaker." *JQ* 29 (1952): 171-74. Maule is a little-known but important figure in the fight for freedom of expression. His was the first case in the Salem, Mass., area in which a jury sided with the accused against the colonial authorities in a matter involving printing and authorship.

709. Neilson, Winthrop, and Frances Neilson. *Verdict for the Doctor*. New York: Hastings House, 1958. Narrative of Dr. Benjamin Rush's Philadelphia libel case against William Cobbett. The unprecedented decision ruled in favor of Rush, showing that an action for libel could be won even in Pennsylvania, where freedom of press roots ran deep. The book attempts to illustrate the virulence of party strife and the liberty the press enjoyed.

710. Nelson, Harold L., ed. *Freedom of the Press from Hamilton to the Warren Court.* Indianapolis: Bobbs-Merrill, 1966. An anthology of documents with a 29-page introduction. The lapse of the Alien and Sedition Acts under Jefferson virtually ended prior restraint until the slavery issue popped up, and the Croswell case resulted in greater freedom from libel prosecutions, establishing truth as a defense and vitiating the argument that libels tend to cause breaches of the peace by libelled people seeking revenge.

711. Nelson, Harold L. "Seditious Libel in Colonial America." *AJLH* 3 (April 1959): 160-172. After the Zenger trial, legislatures or governors' councils, rather than courts, disciplined printers. The colonial assembly became the major force in limiting the press and freedom.

712. "New York and the 'Liberty of the Press.'" *HW* 38 (July 28, 1894): 703ff.

713. Oliver, L. Stauffer. "A Famous Colonial Lawyer and the Zenger Trial." *Historical Publications of the Society of Colonial Wars in the Commonwealth of Pennsylvania.* 5, 3 (1939): 13-17. Biographical sketch of Andrew Hamilton.

714. Plasterer, Nicholas N. "The Croswell Case: Paradox of History?" *JQ* 44 (1967): 125-29. An attempt to establish the historical importance of the Croswell case. It was an important trial "which apparently had a direct and important causal relationship with our present libel laws." (125)

715. Plopper, Bruce Loren. "Political Unconsciousness and the Sedition Act: A Case Study" in *Graduate Communication Studies.* Carbondale: School of Journalism, Southern Illinois University, 1977. This article, one in a collection of five historical studies by Southern Illinois University graduate students, examines statements in three Boston Federalist newspapers in 1798 for evidence about the beliefs and attitudes of Boston Federalist leaders toward the Sedition Act.

716. Price, Warren C. "Reflections on the Trial of John Peter Zenger." *JQ* 32 (1955): 161-68. The background to the Zenger case was political, not that of press freedom. The situation of Zenger gained public support probably because of the unpopularity of the corrupt Gov. Cosby. The case did not set a legal precedent.

717. Rivera, Clark. "Ideals, Interests and Civil Liberty: The Colonial Press and Freedom, 1735-76." *JQ* 55 (1978): 47-53, 124. Colonial freedom of the press was libertarian. It "did surpass what the law allowed, it was in general less restricted than in other contemporary cultures, and it did foster and utilize broadminded conceptions of freedom which foreshadowed those of today." (124)

718. Robbins, Jan C. "Jefferson and the Press: The Resolution of an Antimony." *JQ* 48 (1971): 421-30, 465. Jefferson's attitudes toward freedom of expression, sometimes thought contradictory by historians, sprang from the same philosophy. He believed self-preservation -- expressed ultimately in the power of the nation to preserve itself -- to be a right of more ultimate importance than freedom of expression, for if the nation should be destroyed, so would its freedoms. The laws of self-preservation were higher than written guarantees; the government might rightly suppress "evil" expression to preserve itself.

719. Royster, Vermont. *The American Press and the Revolutionary Tradition.* Washington, D.C.: American Enterprise Institute for Policy Research, 1974. The brief text of

Royster's presentation in the Distinguished Lecture Series on the Bicentennial traces the development of the concept of press freedom from English common law to the adoption of the First Amendment. "Among the many revolutionary ideas to emerge from the American Revolution, none proved more revolutionary than the idea of freedom of press. None has proved more durable, for it has withstood two centuries of assault." Today, however, the press oversteps proper bounds under the defense of "freedom of the press." Despite abuses, freedom of the press must be maintained because freedom is so important in the American democracy.

720. Rutherford, Livingston. *John Peter Zenger, His Press, His Trial, and a Bibliography of Zenger Imprints*. New York: Dodd, Mead, 1904. The standard biography of Zenger, with a bibliography of works on his trial, issues of the *Journal*, and publications by Zenger. The trial "first established in North America the principle that in prosecution for libel the jury were the judges of both the law and the facts. The liberty of the press was secure from assault and the people became equipped with the most powerful weapon for successfully combatting arbitrary power: the right of freely criticizing the conduct of public men....[T]he result of the trial had imbued the people with a new spirit; henceforth they were united in the struggle against governmental oppression." (131)

721. Rutland, Robert Allen. *The Birth of the Bill of Rights, 1776-1791*. Chapel Hill: University of North Carolina Press, 1955. "The story of how Americans came to rely on legal guarantees for their personal freedom." In the minds of the American people, the rights guaranteed in the Bill of Rights were inviolable. At the same time, opponents of the Bill of Rights often were advocates of democracy who believed that having the rights specified in written form would lead to their being interpreted too narrowly. In the minds of the people, these rights were extremely important and inviolable by government. The concept of natural law was prevalent.

722. Schuyler, Robert Livingston. *The Liberty of the Press in the American Colonies Before the Revolutionary War*. New York: Thomas Whitaker, 1905. Colonists in Massachusetts, Pennsylvania, and New York argued that they had "constitutional" rights as Englishmen and, according to Lockean theory, natural rights as individuals. They wanted to safeguard individual liberty from the government.

723. Shumate, T. Daniel, ed. *The First Amendment: The Legacy of George Mason*. Fairfax, Va.: George Mason University Press, 1985. Collection of four conference papers by various authors, with only Robert Rutland's "George Mason and the First Amendment" discussing press freedom. Mason and his contemporaries "thought the real purpose of the first amendment was to preserve our political -- and not our personal -- freedom." Shumate's introduction provides an overview of Mason's role in formulating the First Amendment.

724. Sloan, Wm. David. "The Party Press and Freedom of the Press, 1798-1808." *AJ* 4 (1987): 82-96. Refutes claims of most other historians that American attitudes about freedom of expression in the early 1800s were libertarian. "[W]hile claiming freedom for themselves, politically passionate Americans urged that their opponents' freedom be restricted. Each side in the partisan politics believed itself alone to be right. Political ardor outweighed any desire for broad freedom of expression." (84)

725. Sloan, Wm. David, and Thomas A. Schwartz. "Historians and Freedom of the Press, 1690-1801: Libertarian or Limited?" *AJ* 5 (1988): 159-78. Historiographical essay on

historians' perspectives and explanations about press freedom, focusing on their disagreement about whether early American attitudes were libertarian. This essay is a
good starting point for the researcher wanting to understand historical study of press
freedom.

726. Smelser, Marshall. "George Washington and the Alien and Sedition Acts." *AHR* 59
(January 1954): 322-34. Washington was exasperated by the many and bitter attacks
on him and his administration by editors, and he mistrusted the politics of immigrants,
particularly of a French conspiracy. Washington approved and defended the Alien and
Sedition Acts.

727. Smelser, Marshall. "The Jacobin Frenzy: Federalism and the Menace of Liberty,
Equality, and Fraternity." *RP* 13 (1951): 457-82. During strained American relations
with France, many Federalists thought America was endangered by mismanagement of
foreign relations. Aristocratic Federalists, because of "distaste for having their acts and
motives minutely reviewed by the vulgar mass" began to show symptoms of "social
paranoia." Repressive legislation seemed the defense. Out of this climate came the
Sedition Act.

728. Smith, James M. "Alexander Hamilton, the Alien Law, and Seditious Libel." *RP* 16
(July 1954): 305-33. Hamilton should not be given credit for the clause in the Sedition
Act providing that truth be a defense and that the jury should determine both the law
and the facts.

729. Smith, James M. "The Aurora and the Sedition Laws." *PMHB* 77 (January 1953): 3-
23; 77 (April 1953): 123-55. Benjamin Franklin Bache and William Duane, editors of
the *Aurora*, were both subjected to the Sedition Act. Original version of *Freedom's
Fetters* chapter.

730. Smith, James M. *Freedom's Fetters: The Alien and Sedition Laws and American Civil
Liberties*. Ithaca: Cornell University Press, 1956. This is the most thorough historical
work on the Alien and Sedition Acts. It focuses on the "enactment and enforcement of
the Federalist measures of 1798 and attempts to assess their influence in shaping the
development of the political process of republicanism, with its dual goals of majority
rule and individual rights." The acts were politically motivated attempts to silence the
Federalists' opposition and were a logical development of the Federalists' authoritarian
approach. The book provides a detailed history of the debates on the bills and of enforcement of the laws, which showed that enforcement was political in nature. It includes detailed narratives of the all the cases prosecuted under the acts.

731. Smith, James M. "President John Adams, Thomas Cooper, and Sedition: A Case
Study in Suppression." *MVHR* 42 (1955): 438-65. Original version of *Freedom's
Fetters* chapter.

732. Smith, James M. "Sedition in the Old Dominion: James T. Callender and *The Prospect
Before Us*." *JSH* 20 (May 1954): 157-82. Original version of *Freedom's Fetters*
chapter.

733. Smith, James M. "The Sedition Law, Free Speech, and the American Political Process." *WMQ*, 3rd. series, 9 (1952): 497-511. "The Alien and Sedition Laws played a
prominent role in shaping the American tradition of civil liberties. Based on the concept that the government was master, these laws provoked a public response which

clearly demonstrated that the people occupied that position." (310)

734. Smith, Jeffery A. "Freedom of Expression and the Marketplace of Ideas Concept from Milton to Jefferson." *JCI* 7, 1 (1981): 47-63. Jefferson and Paine were the leading American advocates of the "marketplace" concept. The concept was widely used by people to justify their assaults on authority. It "gradually began establishing itself as the basis for freedom of expression. No longer were opinions only to be offered when allowed by authority, but rather, they could be given in spite of it." Ultimately, contemporaries believed, the concept was the "soundest approach to carrying on the business of religion and government." (59)

735. Smith, Jeffery Alan. "Printers and Press Freedom: The Ideology of Early American Journalism." Ph.D. dissertation, University of Wisconsin, 1984. Attempts to refute Levy's claim that freedom of expression in early America was not a libertarian one. The libertarian theory was "remarkably lucid and clear," standing on three foundations: rejection of the controls of the press exercised in England, acceptance of the "marketplace of ideas" concept to protect attacks upon authority, and agreement with the Enlightenment ideas of social progress and political structure.

736. Smith, Jeffery A. *Printers and Press Freedom: The Ideology of Early American Journalism*. New York: Oxford University Press, 1988. See previous entry.

737. Smith, Jeffery A. "Public Opinion and the Press Clause." *JH* 14 (1987): 8-17. "More than a century of demonstrations of popular support for freedom of expression preceded the press clause of the Constitution. Public demands were responsible for the drafting and ratification of the First Amendment. Still, American political theorists saw a need to shield rights such as liberty of the press from the public. The principle of journalistic freedom was easy to advocate for oneself, but sometimes difficult to uphold for opponents in the course of partisan confrontation." (15)

738. Steiner, Bernard C. "Andrew Hamilton and John Peter Zenger." *PM* 20 (1896): 405-08. Biographies of Hamilton and Zenger -- containing no thesis on freedom of the press.

739. Stevens, John W. "Congressional History of the 1798 Sedition Law." *JQ* 43 (1966): 247-56. Narrative of the congressional debates over the Sedition Act and its provisions. "The sedition law has a significant, if only negative, role in the development of the concept of freedom of the press. When Republicans found that the procedural safeguards which had been the essence of libertarian thought up until that time were worthless in the hands of political enemies, they championed a broader definition. Second, the law left such a bad taste that the United States did not pass another national sedition law for 116 years. Third, and perhaps most important, the debate on the sedition law opened a dialogue on the role of free expression within a democracy (particularly at a time of crisis) which has continued to this day." (256)

740. Taylor, Telford. *Two Studies in Constitutional Interpretation*. Columbus: Ohio State University Press, 1969. Essays trace the legal history of search and seizure from its use in Britain and America to reveal seditious publications to present-day views.

741. Teeter, Dwight L. "Decent Animadversions: Notes Toward a History of Free Press Theory," in Bond and McLeod, 237-46. Oswald and Bailey, rival printers in Philadelphia in the late 1700s, considered free press the right to publish whatever the printer

wished. Their activities were part of the development of freedom of expression in America.

742. Teeter, Dwight L. "King Sears, the Mob and Freedom of the Press in New York, 1765-75." *JQ* 41 (1964): 539-44. Isaac Sears, a hot-headed patriot, and his mobs intimidated journalists who expressed Tory views. Free expression was reserved for printers who shared the patriots' view.

743. Teeter, Dwight Leland. "A Legacy of Expression: Philadelphia Newspapers and Congress During the War for Independence, 1775-1783." Ph. D. dissertation, University of Wisconsin, 1966. Attempts to refute Levy's argument that America's legacy of press freedom was one of suppression. Freedom grew out of political battles, in which factions defended the liberty of printers on their own side.

744. Teeter, Dwight L. "Press Freedom and the Public Printing: Pennsylvania, 1775-83." *JQ* 45 (1968): 445-51. Philadelphia journalists, though getting financial support through government printing, still criticized government. They were protected by the maneuverings of political factions and were free from excessive reliance on government's economic support; they also were free spirits who believed that newspapers should carry conflicting opinions and that criticism of government served the public good.

745. Teeter, Dwight L. "The Printer and the Chief Justice: Seditious Libel in 1782-82." *JQ* 45 (1968): 235-42, 260. Although Eleazer Oswald's arguments for press freedom "sprang more from practical politics and the desire to avoid punishment than from libertarian principle...by asserting a right to criticize government and government officials, the *Gazetteer* attacked the core of seditious libel. By struggling for a one-sided freedom -- his own -- Oswald anticipated, in part, the broader freedom which the Jeffersonians helped create during their struggle against the Sedition Law of 1798." (260)

746. Terwillings, W. Bird. "William Goddard, Victory for Freedom of the Press." *MHM* 36 (June 1941): 139-49. In 1777 Goddard withstood the vigilante pressures of a local Whig Club and refused to reveal the name of the author of an article in the *Maryland Journal*. He received the support of the Committee of Grievances of the Maryland House of Delegates to whom he referred the case.

747. Van Alstyne, William W. *Interpretations of the First Amendment*. Durham, N.C.: Duke University Press, 1984. History and theories of the First Amendment, with primary concern about the recent past. The press should not receive special privileges because such privileges can lead to regulation.

748. Van Vechten, Veeder. "The History of the Law of Defamation." *Select Essays in Anglo-American Legal History* 3 (1909): 446-73.

749. Wiggins, James Russell. "Afterword: The Legacy of the Press in the American Revolution," in Bailyn and Hench, 365-72. Our concept of freedom of the press is, in large part, the handiwork of the colonial and revolutionary journalists.

750. Wills, Elbert V. "Case of Doctor Cooper." *SAQ* 18 (January 1919): 6-14. Thomas Cooper was convicted under the Sedition Act for libel of President Adams and was sentenced to six months in jail and fined $400. He was fearless in defying the Alien and Sedition Acts.

751. Wilson, C. Edward. "The Boston Inoculation Controversy: A Revisionist Interpretation." *JH* 7 (1980): 16-9, 40. James Franklin's *Courant* does not deserve the historical credit for conducting the first crusade or as being the first newspaper publishing without government authority. The press debate over inoculation was already going before the *Courant* began publication, the people of Boston generally shared Franklin's anti-inoculation position, and "the colonial government was either neutral or impotent in respect to newspapers at the time." (16) Neither was Franklin a defiant, bold advocate for press freedom. He seemed uncertain of his views and tended to waver and backpedal.

752. Witten, Manley. "Andrew Hamilton: Light on the Horizon." *MHD* 2 (Summer 1982): 42-44. A brief outline of the professional career of Andrew Hamilton, beginning with his defense of Zenger. He gained a reputation as a defender of press freedom, as evidenced by what his peers said of him.

753. Worton, Stanley N. *Freedom of Speech and Press*. Rochelle Parks, N.J.: Hayden, 1975. Collection of documents on various episodes involving freedom and law. One chapter, "Dissent Is Not Treason: Zenger Trial and Alien and Sedition Acts, 1798," is on early freedom of the press.

754. Yodelis, Mary Ann. "Boston's First Major Newspaper War: A 'Great Awakening' of Freedom." *JQ* 51 (1974): 207-12. Disputes Levy's thesis. The Boston printer Thomas Fleet "repeatedly expressed some generally libertarian attitudes during Boston's first major newspaper war in the 1740s." (207) He made "strong and fearless statements on press freedom and the right to criticize governing authority in both civil and religious matters....[His] libertarian concept of the role of a free press in the religious disputes...and his confrontations with government must have served as some kind of a model for the attitudes with which some printers...faced their task of informing the colonists about the political struggles during the revolution....[He] demonstrated that the newspaper publishers of the time...were dedicated to principles of civil and religious liberty." (212) Fleet's defiance of religious authority was equivalent to defiance of government authority.

755. Yodelis, Mary Ann Patricia. "Boston's Second Major Paper War: Economics, Politics, and the Theory and Practice of Political Expression in the Press, 1763-1775." Ph.D. dissertation, University of Wisconsin, 1971. Despite partisanship and coercion, "a basic concept of a free press was developing in revolutionary Boston," a belief that "lively and free political debate is essential to constitutional government and that government and its political opposition...should be criticized."

756. Yodelis, Mary A. "Courts, Counting Houses and Streets: Attempts at Press Control, 1763-1775." *JH* 1 (1974): 11-15. Summary of the "constraints exercised against all the Boston newspapers and publishers: legal, economic, violent, symbolic, and rhetorical." Documents "the widening gap between the law of seditious libel in theory and the law in fact." (11) "The press in revolutionary Boston remained relatively free, often in spite of bitter partisanship. In fact, freedom may have developed from such partisanship....Threats from government, except for an occasional loss of appointments, were perceived as unenforceable. There was no successful court prosecution for seditious libel. The assembly would not censure popular party publishers. When the council did act against writers or publishers, the reprimands were mild and without teeth or penalty. It was a law in theory, but not in fact. The force of public opinion, extra-legal action and economic constraints were clearly more effective controls on

the press... [Neutral editors] seldom were intimidated, attesting to the theory that more than the press was free in revolutionary Boston. It may be speculated that press freedom may have been strengthened and the basis for later First Amendment theory developed through these conflicts before the War for Independence." (14)

6

The Penny Press, 1833–1860

757. Baskette, Floyd K. "Reporting the Webster Case, America's Classic Murder." *JQ* 24 (1947): 250-56. Newspapers sensationally covered the trial and catered to mass readership.

758. Behrens, John. "New York Times Pentagon Papers Case Similar to Investigation of the New York Herald in 1848." *NR* 26 (1972): 23-25. John Nugent, Washington correspondent for the *Herald*, was "subpoenaed to appear in the Senate chamber...when his paper...published the peace treaty and related correspondence between the United States and Mexico." (23) His case had many parallels to that of the New York *Times'* correspondent, Neil Sheehan, involved in the "Pentagon Papers" incident.

759. Bergman, Herbert. "The Influence of Whitman's Journalism on *Leaves of Grass*." *American Literary Realism 1870-1910,* 3 (1970): 399-404.

760. Bergman, Herbert. "Walt Whitman as a Journalist, 1831-January, 1848." *JQ* 48 (1971): 195-204. "By January 1848...Whitman had edited six newspapers, had helped edit two, and had written for six others -- truly an enviable journalistic record for one only 28." (204)

761. Bergman, Herbert. "Walt Whitman as a Journalist, March 1848-1892." *JQ* 48 (1971): 431-37. Chronicle of Whitman's newspaper career after being dismissed from the Brooklyn *Eagle*. His "journalistic writing was good, competent, serious work, not highly distinguished, but not pedestrian hack work either. It is significant for the light

it throws on Whitman's mind and art and for the picture it gives of his period." (437)

762. Bergman, Herbert. "Whitman on Editing, Newspapers and Journalism." *JQ* 48 (1971): 345-48. Collection of quotes from Whitman dealing with the practices of journalism.

763. Bigelow, John. *Life of William Cullen Bryant*. Boston: Houghton Mifflin, 1890.

764. Bodson, Robert Louis. "A Description of the United States Occupation of Mexico as Reported by American Newspapers in Vera Cruz, Pueblo, and Mexico City, September 14, 1847, to July 31, 1848." Ed.D. dissertation, Ball State University, 1971.

765. Borden, Morton. "Five Letters of Charles A. Dana to Karl Marx." *JQ* 36 (1959): 314-16. Brief article contains the texts of the letters, uncovered after Borden's 1957 article (next entry).

766. Borden, Morton. "Some Notes on Horace Greeley, Charles Dana and Karl Marx." *JQ* (1957): 457-65. The *Tribune's* publication of Marx's writings provided him with a needed salary and helped increase the paper's readership. His works were published anonymously. Although Dana received credit for many of them, Marx appreciated the wide circulation the *Tribune* had given his views. Greeley and Dana sympathized with socialistic ideas.

767. Bradshaw, James Stanford. "A Forgotten Firebrand: George W. Wisner." *CHSM* 19, 3 (1986): 2-11. After leaving the New York *Sun*, Wisner became a politician and partisan editor in Michigan.

768. Bradshaw, James Stanford. "George W. Wisner and the New York *Sun*." *JH* 6 (1979): 112, 117-21. Biography covering the New York *Sun* years of Wisner, who "helped establish the first truly mass circulation newspaper in the United States, as well as a pattern for future journalists." Wisner ran the *Sun's* news operation.

769. Bradshaw, James Stanford. "'To Correspondents' -- Horace Greeley." *JQ* 58 (1981): 644-46, 673. As editor of the *New Yorker*, Greeley was interested in literature. Brief article details his relations with writers.

770. Brasher, Thomas L. *Whitman as Editor of the Brooklyn Daily Eagle*. Detroit: Wayne State University Press, 1970. While famous as a poet, Whitman exhibited a "zest" for journalism and took his job seriously. He based much of his poetry on the observations of people he made as a journalist.

771. Brinley, Francis. *Life of William T. Porter*. New York: Appleton, 1860. Porter edited New York's *Spirit of the Times* from 1831 to 1856.

772. Brockway, Beman. *Fifty Years in Journalism*. Watertown, N.Y.: Daily Times, 1891. Autobiographical account of the mid-19th century by a journalist.

773. Brodwin, Stanley, Michael D'Innocenzo, and Joseph G. Astman, eds. *William Cullen Bryant and His America*. New York: AMS Press, 1983. Fifteen essays deal primarily with Bryant as a man of letters, although D'Innocenzo's "William Cullen Bryant and the Newspapers of New York" (39-50) focuses on Bryant's career as editor of the *Evening Post*.

774. Brown, Charles H. "Young Editor Whitman: An Individualist in Journalism." *JQ* 27 (1950): 141-48. As editor of the New York *Aurora* for two months in 1842, Whitman "was, almost above all, an individualist objecting strongly to the encroachments of government on human liberty." (148)

775. Brown, Ernest Francis. *Raymond of the Times*. New York: Norton, 1951. Favorable, detailed biography of the founder and editor of the New York Times. Raymond was a brilliant journalist and politician, but he was handicapped by being too impartial. While his contemporaries in politics and journalism were intensely partisan, he treated both sides in issues fairly.

776. Bryant, William Cullen II, and Thomas G. Voss. eds. *The Letters of William Cullen Bryant*, 3 vols. New York: Fordham University Press, 1978-1981. Collection of Bryant's correspondence.

777. Buddenbaum, Judith. "The Religion Journalism of James Gordon Bennett." *JH* 14 (1986).

778. Carlson, Oliver. *The Man Who Made News*. New York: Duell, Sloan & Pearce, 1942. James Gordon Bennett led the way in the development of news as an instrument to sell papers. Circulation, though, was not Bennett's only consideration. He believed news was important to readers and newspapers were obligated to report fully, promptly, and objectively. He also was concerned, though, about his circulation and profit.

779. Commons, John R. "Horace Greeley and the Working Class Origins of the Republican Party." *PSQ* 24 (1909): 468-88. Greeley was an idealistic thinker who put together a constructive program for improving the conditions of the working class and providing land for farmers. His ideas helped form the Republican party, which "was not an anti-slavery party...[but] a homestead party." (488)

780. Copeland, Fayette. *Kendall of the Picayune, Being His Adventures in New Orleans, on the Texas Santa Fe Expedition, in the Mexican War, and in the Colonization of the Texas Frontier*. Norman: University of Oklahoma Press, 1943. George W. Kendall was founder of the New Orleans *Picayune*, "the first representative in the South of the vigorous, rollicking 'penny press.'" Through Kendall's work as editor and as "the first modern war correspondent," the paper became recognized as the authoritative source for news in Texas and Mexico in the 1840s.

781. Crouthamel, James L. "James Gordon Bennett, the *New York Herald*, and the Development of Newspaper Sensationalism." *NYH* 54 (July 1973): 294-316. Sensationalism began with the penny press, not the yellow journalism of the 1890s. James Gordon Bennett, to whom "most of the credit should go" (294) for its development, relied on it for the New York *Herald's* financial success.

782. Crouthamel, James L. "The Newspaper Revolution in New York 1830-1860." *NYH* 45 (April 1964): 91-113. From its rudimentary beginnings in the 1830s, the penny press had matured by the 1850s and was providing better news than the mercantile press.

783. Dana, Charles A. "Greeley as a Journalist," pp. 78-95 in Vol. VII of Edmund C. Stedman and Ellen M. Hutchinson, ed., *A Library of American Literature*. New York:

W.E. Benjamin, 1889.

784. Delano, Sterling F. *"The Harbinger" and New England Transcendentalism: A Portrait of Associationism in America*. Rutherford, N.J.: Fairleigh Dickinson University Press, 1983. The magazine promoted social reform and exercised a major influence on American thought and social and political movements.

785. Dickerson, O.M. "Letters of Horace Greeley to Nathaniel C. Meeker." *CM* 19 (March 1942): 50-62; (May 1942): 102-10.

786. Dyer, Carolyn Stewart. "Census Manuscripts and Circulation Data for Mid-19th Century Newspapers." *JH* 7 (1980): 47-48. U.S. census data probably give a fairly accurate count of newspaper circulation.

787. Eberhard, Wallace B. "Mr. Bennett Covers a Murder Trial." *JQ* 47 (1970): 457-63. As a reporter for the New York *Courier and Enquirer*, James Gordon Bennett challenged the contempt power of the court trying a murder case in Salem, Mass. Bennett's work demonstrated his audacity and his "deep dedication" to the profession of journalism.

788. Egan, Betty. "Baseball Meets the Press." *MHD* 5, 2 (1985): 60-64. Newspapers became interested in baseball only slowly, probably because baseball itself developed slowly.

789. Entrikin, Isabelle Webb. *Sarah Josepha Hale and Godey's Lady's Book*. Lancaster, Pa.: Lancaster Press/Entrikin, 1946. As editor of *Ladies' Magazine* and *Godey's Lady's Book*, Hale made a number of contributions to journalism, magazine editing, and American literature. She was especially concerned about improving social and cultural conditions.

790. Estes, David C. "The Rival Sporting Weeklies of William T. Porter and Thomas Bangs Thorpe." *AJ* 2 (1985): 135-43. In the 1840s Porter's *American Sporting Chronicle* and Thorpe's *Southern Sportsman* helped liberate American sports from British dominance, but the two owner-editors had a heated rivalry based on business interests and egotism.

791. Fern, Fanny. *Ruth Hall and Other Writings*. Joyce W. Warren, ed. New Brunswick, N.J.: Rutgers University Press, 1986. Collection of Fern's writings from 1851 to 1872, most of which appeared in her popular column in the New York *Ledger*. Book is part of the American Women Writers Series.

792. Finley, Ruth E. *The Lady of Godey's: Sarah Josepha Hale*. Philadelphia: Lippincott, 1931. Hale edited *Godey's Lady's Book* for forty years. She was especially interested in education for women.

793. Ford, Edwin H. "Walt Whitman -- Sublimated Editorial Writer." *JQ* 17 (1940): 39-43. Whitman, while an outstanding journalist, gained more lasting fame than others because he "sublimated his consciousness of contemporary phenomena and expressed it with a creative vitality." (39) The moral is this: journalists are concerned with the ephemeral; poets, with the eternal.

794. Fox, Louis H. "New York City Newspapers, 1820-1850, a Bibliography." *PBSA* 21 (1928): 1-7. Brief essay precedes a list of all news publications published in New

York City during the period.

795. Fulcher, James. "Murder Reports: Formulaic Narrative and Cultural Context." *JPC* 18 (Spring 1985): 31-42. The New York *Daily-Times'* stories of murders in 1851 and 1856 followed a formula and suggested that immigrants were the main criminals. Behind the stories were American ideas of freedom, progress, and community.

796. Fuller, Landon E. "The *United States Magazine and Democratic Review,* 1837-59: A Study of Its History, Contents, and Significance." Ph.D. dissertation, University of North Carolina, 1948.

797. Gambee, Budd Leslie, Jr. *Frank Leslie and His Illustrated Newspaper, 1855-1860.* Ann Arbor: University of Michigan Department of Library Science, 1964.

798. Greeley, Horace. *Recollections of a Busy Life.* New York: J.B. Ford, 1868. Autobiography.

799. Hale, William Harlan. *Horace Greeley, Voice of the People.* New York: Harper, 1950. Greeley was an "oracle" heard from one end of the country to the other. He "not only wished to inform and entertain the mass of his friends, the people. He wished to convert...[and] uplift and reform the entire world." His special quality lay in his relationship with his readers; he talked earnestly to them. He is explained by the fact that he was a popular editor and a "searching popular moralist." (iv-v)

800. Hauck, Richard Boyd. "The Literary Content of the New York *Spirit of the Times,* 1831-1856." Ph.D. dissertation, University of Illinois, 1965.

801. Hoover, Merle M. *Park Benjamin: Poet and Editor.* New York: Columbia University Press, 1948. As editor of the *New England* magazine and of the weekly *New World* (1839-1845), Benjamin influenced American literature.

802. Hudspeth, Robert N., ed. *The Letters of Margaret Fuller,* 3 vols. Ithaca, N.Y.: Cornell University Press, 1984. Collection of the correspondence of Fuller, who was the editor of the *Dial,* the transcendentalist quarterly, and book reviewer for Horace Greeley's New York *Tribune.*

803. Ingersoll, Lurton D. *The Life of Horace Greeley, Founder of the New York Tribune.* Chicago: Union, 1873. Commemorative biography written at the time of Greeley's death.

804. Isely, Jeter Allen. *Horace Greeley and the Republican Party, 1853-1861: A Study of the New York Tribune.* Princeton, N.J.: Princeton University Press, 1947. Political biography of the *Tribune* editor.

805. Jacobs, Robert D. *Poe: Journalist and Critic.* Baton Rouge: Louisiana State University Press, 1969. Among Poe's concerns as a critic was the aesthetic education of the general public. Publishers sometimes inhibited his ability to perform as he desired as a critic.

806. Jones, Charlotte D. "The Penny Press and the Origins of Journalistic Objectivity: The Problem of Authority in Liberal America." Ph.D. dissertation, University of Iowa, 1985. "[T]he ideology of objectivity must be understood as a legacy of the American

political culture. The modern newspaper, in the form of the penny press, surfaced as a direct reaction to a strain of press criticism that saw rampant factionalism threatening the republican experiment."

807. Kielbowicz, Richard B. "News Gathering by Mail in the Age of the Telegraph: Adapting to a New Technology." *TC* 28 (1987): 26-41.

808. Kielbowiez, Richard B. "Speeding the News by Postal Express 1825-1861: The Public Policy of Privileges for the Press." *SSJ* 22 (January 1985): 49-63.

809. Linn, William Alexander. *Horace Greeley, Founder and Editor of the New York Tribune*. New York: Appleton, 1903. "A gawky country lad, with a limited education and a slight acquaintance with the printer's trade, comes to the principal city of the land with a few dollars in his pocket and a single suit of clothes, and fights a fight the result of which is the founding of the most influential newspaper of his day, and the acquirement of a reputation as its editor which secures for him a nomination for the presidency of the United States." (5)

810. Lunde, Erik S. *Horace Greeley*. Boston: Twayne, 1981. Brief biography examines Greeley's ideas on such issues as slavery, labor, and utopianism within the cultural, intellectual context of his times.

811. Mackey, Philip English, ed. *A Gentleman of Much Promise: The Diary of Isaac Mickle, 1837-1845,* 2 vols. 1978. Born in 1823, Mickel was, among other occupations, a journalist while still a teenager and, later, editor of the Camden (N.J.) *Eagle*.

812. Marbut, Frederick B. "The History of Washington Newspaper Correspondence to 1861." Ph.D. dissertation, Harvard University.

813. Marbut, Frederick B. "The United States Senate and the Press, 1838-41." *JQ* 28 (1951): 342-50. Narrative of James Gordon Bennett's successful effort to persuade the Senate to open its sessions to newspaper reporters.

814. Martin, Lawrence. "The Genesis of Godey's Lady's Book." *NEQ* 1 (January 1928): 41-70. The magazine's purpose was "'to carry onward and upward the spirit of moral and intellectual excellence in [women], till their influence shall bless as well as beautify civil society. These principles we shall guard with scrupulous care, and watch that nothing be introduced to undermine those sacred relations of domestic life, in which the Creator has placed the sceptre of woman's empire.'" (70)

815. Maverick, Augustus. *Henry J. Raymond and New York Press for Thirty Years*. Hartford, Conn.: A. S. Hale, 1870. Biography of the New York *Times'* editor written by a contemporary.

816. McFarland, C.K., and Robert Thistlethwaite. "20 Years of a Successful Labor Paper: The Working Man's Advocate, 1829-49." *JQ* 60 (1983): 35-41. The New York newspaper "was dedicated to goals and reforms that were surprisingly liberal even by some of the standards of the 20th Century. It...called for an end to intolerable social and economic conditions through the exercise of political power." (35)

817. McPherson, Elizabeth Gregory. "The History of Reporting the Debates and Proceedings of Congress." Ph.D. dissertation, University of North Carolina, 1941. Focus is

on stenographers, whose notes were printed in journals.

818. Merriam, George S. *Life and Times of Samuel Bowles,* 2 vols. New York: Century, 1885. Biography of Samuel Bowles II of the Springfield (Mass.) *Republican,* emphasizing 1844-78. He was an important figure in journalism (which was an important aspect of American society) and exercised a wide influence. Covering both his public and private life, this biography details the growth of a man as a sincere and bold individual. He had the ambition for great achievement and a character to bring it about. Emphasizes the progress of mankind and journalism: the old partisan style of journalism was replaced by a "new journalism," the penny press.

819. Mott, Frank Luther. "The Beginnings of Artemus Ward." *JQ* 18 (1941): 146-52. Charles F. Brown, later the humorist "Artemus Ward," established his early following as a writer of "locals" for the Cleveland *Plain Dealer.* He succeeded because of his comic ability and the fact the he "came into American journalism at a time when local reporting -- not yet conventionalized in an arbitrary pattern -- lent itself to such play of fancy as could create a great comic character." (152)

820. Mott, Frank Luther. "Facetious News Writing, 1833-1883." *MVHR* 29 (June 1942): 35-54. The penny press brought with it a new concept of news and "began to break down the established rule of dull seriousness in the news columns." (35) By the 1880s, however, "the increasing respect for the accuracy of the news...[had] resulted in separating humor and news....[I]t is doubtless a good rule that humorists ought not to tamper with what may be called news *qua* news." (54)

821. Nelson, Anna Kasten. "Secret Agents and Security Leaks: President Polk and the Mexican War." *JQ* 52 (1975): 9-14, 98. Polk was a secretive man, and press leaks frustrated him during the war.

822. Nerone, John C. "The Mythology of the Penny Press." *CSMC* 4 (December 1987).

823. Nevins, Allan. "The Effects of Greeley on Dana." *JQ* 5, 2 (1928): 1-5. It was during the 15 years Dana served as Greeley's managing editor that he changed from an idealist to a cynic. He became a disillusioned idealist, in part because Greeley (a supreme idealist) was an impractical visionary lacking in critical judgment. Dana rebelled and became hardheaded.

824. *"The New York Herald,* from 1835 to 1866." *NAR* 102 (April 1866): 373-419. Despite the paper's mercurial, superficial, irresponsible editorial policy and its reliance on sensationalism, it was the leading American newspaper because of its great emphasis on providing news. Bennett was one of the most disreputable and least respected public men in the nation. (The author of this disdainful article perhaps was James Parton.)

825. Nilsson, Nils Gunnar. "The Origin of the Interview." *JQ* 48 (1971): 707-13. In the 1830s, penny press reporters, led by James Gordon Bennett, began using question-and-answer story forms and placing an emphasis on human interest material. "From there the step to the interview was very short." (713)

826. Olasky, Marvin. "Advertising Abortion During the 1830s and 1840s: Madame Restell Builds a Business." *JH* 13 (1986): 49-55. Some advertising in the penny press, as Restell's ads demonstrated, was motivated by the desire for profit, not by morals. Even though abortion was against the law and the ads made it clear what service they

were offering, the New York *Sun* and New York *Herald* did not control the advertising. It is possible that the advertising influenced them not to criticize abortion editorially.

827. Olasky, Marvin. "Shocking Ads, News in Early Abortion Wars." *MHD* 7, 1 (1987): 20-24, 28. While some newspapers in the mid-1800s ran abortion ads without misgivings, others exposed abortion practices. Eventually, public sentiment turned against the abortionists.

828. Oliva, Jay L. "America Meets Russia: 1854." *JQ* 40 (1963): 65-69. At the beginning of the Crimean War, despite the general American sympathy for Russia, American newspaper content was anti-Russian because newspapers relied on European sources for their news.

829. Parton, James. *Life of Horace Greeley*. New York: Mason Brothers, 1855. Masterful Romantic biography of a leader in national politics and journalism, written by the "father of American biography."

830. Pickett, Calder M. "Technology and the New York Press in the 19th Century." *JQ* 37 (1960): 398-407. For newspapers to survive, they had to adopt the new technology, but the degree of acceptance -- and the vigorous role played by individual editors -- demonstrates that response to technology was not uniform.

831. Poore, Ben Perley. *Perley's Reminiscences of Sixty Years in the National Metropolis*, 2 vols. Philadelphia: Hubbard Brothers, 1886. Autobiographical account of Washington, D.C., by a capital correspondent for the Boston *Journal*.

832. Pray, Isaac C. *Memoirs of James Gordon Bennett and His Times*. New York: Stringer and Townsend, 1855. Admiring biography written by a Bennett employee.

833. Reed, Barbara Straus. "A History and Content Analysis of the Pioneer American Jewish Periodical Press (1823-1858)." Ph.D. dissertation, Ohio University, 1987. "[A]s the only Jewish intercommunal agency in existence...the press sought unity; it cried out in pain against assimilationist practices and indifference....The press demonstrated there was no need to conform to an Anglo-Saxon mold, to join in a melting pot only to emerge as a Super American or to become part of an orchestra of cultural pluralism."

834. Reid, Whitelaw. *Horace Greeley*. New York: 1879. Laudatory biography written by one of Greeley's closest associates.

835. Reilly, Thomas William. "American Reporters and the Mexican War, 1846-1848." Ph.D. dissertation, University of Minnesota, 1975. The war was extensively reported. Study looks at various types of correspondents, individual reporters, their attitudes, the role of the New Orleans press, military suppression of the news, use of the telegraph, and other topics.

836. Reilly, Tom. "Jane McManus Storms: Letters from the Mexican War 1846-1848." *SHQ* 85 (July 1981): 21-44.

837. Reilly, Tom. "Newspaper Suppression During the Mexican War." *JQ* 54 (1977): 262-70, 349. The military censored or suppressed a number of American-operated and

Mexican newspapers when "military authorities felt they were...a threat to local military control." (270)

838. Reilly, Tom. "'The War Press of New Orleans': 1846-1848." *JH* 13 (1986): 86-95. By energetically covering the Mexican War, New Orleans newspapers enlarged their national reputations, provided most of the news that other American newspapers used about the war, and did a comparatively good job of covering the news.

839. Rickels, Milton. *Thomas Bangs Thorpe: Humorist of the Old Southwest.* Baton Rouge: Louisiana State University Press, 1962. In the 1840s, Thorpe wrote popular journalism for newspapers such as New York's *Spirit of the Times.*

840. Robbins, R.M. "Horace Greeley: Land Reform and Unemployment, 1837-1862." *AgH* 7 (1933).

841. Robinson, Elwyn B. "The *Public Ledger:* An Independent Newspaper." *PMHB* 64 (1940): 43-55. In Philadelphia, the penny newspaper pursued a political course not tied to parties and a "civic-minded editorial policy...combined from the outset [with] unusual enterprise in securing news of important events at the earliest possible moment." (44)

842. Rogers, Sherbrooke. *Sarah Josepha Hale: A New England Pioneer 1788-1879.* Grantham, N.H.: Tompson & Rutter, 1985. Editor of *Godey's Lady's Book*, Hale worked for education for women and for social reform.

843. Ross, Earle D. "Horace Greeley and the South, 1865-1872." *SAQ* 16 (1917): 324-38. Greeley's travels made him a medium for the exchange of regional ideas and experiences.

844. Ross, Earle D. "Horace Greeley and the West." *MVHR* 20 (1933): 63-74. During a period of intense, bitter controversies between the eastern and western sections of the United States, "Greeley with his national outlook, based upon an intimate knowledge of the material interests and popular psychology of both sections, was in the best position to be a continuing moderator and mediator." (74)

845. Russo, David J. "The Origins of Local News in the U.S. Country Press, 1840s-1870s." *JM* 65 (1980). "[R]egular local news columns...became a standard part of American newspapers only gradually over a long period of time, appearing here and there in the 1840s, somewhat more regularly in the 1850s, and typically by the 1860s and 1870s." (4) "Why this was so is not clear." (34) Possible factors included eastern newspapers publishing "news from home" for subscribers who had moved west and country weeklies then emulating the practice.

846. Saalberg, Harvey. "Bennett and Greeley, Professional Rivals, Had Much in Common." *JQ* 49 (1972): 538-46, 550. Greeley and Bennett "championed personal journalism and innovated journalistic practices that survive to this day." Bennett was "the innovator of modern news gathering and reporting," and Greeley developed "the editorial page in its modern American character."

847. Scheidenhelm, Richard. "James Fenimore Cooper and the Law of Libel in New York." *AJ* 4 (1987): 19-29. Cooper's libel suits against New York newspapers in the 1840s and editors' responses to them, by encouraging changes in procedural rules in

trials, "helped facilitate the defense of truth as justification." (19)

848. Schiller, Daniel T. *Objectivity and the News: The Public and The Rise of Commercial Journalism*. Philadelphia. University of Pennsylvania Press, 1981. Objectivity sprang from the social, commercial, and political environment during the 1830s, when the penny press orginated and identified with the mass public. Penny editors believed that the elite should not control news, and they began to publish objective information as a means of making political and economic knowledge available to the masses.

849. Schwarzlose, Richard A. "Early Telegraphic News Dispatches: Forerunner of the AP." *JQ* 51 (1974): 595-601. There is "evidence that some form of news broker operation existed in New York City" as early as June 1846 "as the city's earliest telegraphic lines were being completed." (601)

850. Schwarzlose, Richard. "The Foreign Connection: Transatlantic Newspapers in the 1840s." *JH* 10 (1983): 44-49, 67. American newspapers got much of their news from British newspapers which were published timed with the departure of transatlantic steamers. Before the transatlantic cable, they were the main source of European news.

851. Schwarzlose, Richard A. "Harbor News Association: The Formal Origin of the AP." *JQ* 45 (68): 253-60. Argues that the correct date for the formal origin of the AP was Jan. 11, 1849, when owners of five New York papers signed a partnership agreement forming a Harbor News Association.

852. Schwarzlose, Richard A. "The Nation's First Wire Service: Evidence Supporting a Footnote." *JQ* 57 (1980): 555-62. Supports Alfred McClung Lee's statement in *The Newspaper in America...* that the New York State Associated Press, rather than the Associated Press, was the nation's first wire service.

853. Seitz, Don C. *Artemus Ward: A Biography and Bibliography*. New York: Harper, 1919. Narrative life story of the humorist, along with a list of writings by and about him.

854. Seitz, Don C. *Horace Greeley: Founder of the New York Tribune*. Indianapolis: Bobbs-Merrill, 1926. Greeley was influential yet contradictory, earnest and honest, courageous yet lacking deep insight.

855. Seitz, Don C. *The James Gordon Bennetts; Father and Son; Proprietors of the New York Herald*. Indianapolis: Bobbs-Merrill, 1928. Narrative biography of the Bennetts, who ran the *Herald* from 1835 to 1918 and formed "the longest newspaper dynasty we Americans have known."

856. Shaw, Donald Lewis. "At The Crossroads: Change and Continuity in American Press News 1820-1860." *JH* 8 (1981): 38-50. Content analysis of 3,000 newspaper stories shows that newspapers in 1860 continued to emphasize politics, although they became "more social," devoting more attention to the activities of ordinary people. However, there was not the sudden revolution in news which historians traditionally have associated with the emergence of the penny press. Newspapers also began to run more stories written by reporters rather than clipped from other papers. The author explains the methods used for this research in "Some Notes on Methodology...," which follows the article.

857. Shaw, Donald L. "In the Eye of the Beholder? Sensationalism in American Press News, 1820-1860." *JH* 12 (1985): 86-91. Sensationalism made up only a small part of newspaper content after the advent of the penny press, contrary to what historians have said.

858. Sheppard, Carol. "The Blighted Life of the Writer, Circa 1840." *AH* (August-September 1986): 102-05. Descriptive narrative of *The New Mirror* in New York City revealed that writers' "urge to create literature was as strong in the mid-1800s as it is today, but rejections were brutal and the pay was even worse." (102)

859. Sloan, Wm. David. "George W. Wisner: Michigan Editor and Politician." *JH* 6 (1979): 113-16. Wisner, editor of the New York *Sun*, played an important role in politics and partisan journalism in Michigan after departing from the Sun.

860. Smith, Henry Ladd. "The Beauteous Jennie June: Pioneer Woman Journalist." *JQ* 40 (1963): 169-74. As a member of the New York *Herald* staff, Jane Cunningham Croly was a superior journalist and a leader in the feminist movement. She had a number of significant accomplishments and "firsts."

861. Sotheran, Charles. *Horace Greeley and Other Pioneers of American Socialism*. New York: 1892.

862. Spell, Lota M. "The Anglo-Saxon Press in Mexico, 1846-1848." *AHR* 38 (October 1932): 20-31.

863. Stearns, Bertha-Monica. "Reform Periodicals and Female Reformers 1830-1860." *AHR* 37 (1932): 678-99. Prior to the 1830s, periodicals did not address women seriously on reform issues. Between 1830 and 1860, however, "a group of periodicals definitely addressed to women, and very largely edited by women, clamored loudly for some Right, or agitated vigorously against some Abuse." (678)

864. Stoddard, Henry L. *Horace Greeley: Printer, Editor, Crusader*. New York: Putnam, 1946. Narrative biography showing Greeley as brilliant, independent, generous, resolute, and industrious, yet changeable, profane, lonely, and unhappy. He supported various serious reforms but also was inclined to fads.

865. Taylor, Sally. "Marx and Greeley on Slavery and Labor." *JH* 6 (1979): 103-06. Greeley and Marx agreed, at least superficially, on social issues (including slavery and labor), but Greeley's increasing inflexibility on wider issues and Marx's increasing attacks on the capitalist system eventually led to Marx's dismissal as a *Tribune* writer. Marx was a revolutionary, Greeley an idealist. Marx believed the *Tribune's* support of real reform was superficial. Greeley was optimistic that social improvement could be attained; Marx pessimistic.

866. Theus, Kathryn T. "From Orthodoxy to Reform: Assimilation and the Jewish-English Press of Mid-Nineteenth Century America." *AJ* 1, 2 (1984): 15-26. Jewish-English newspapers (1855-1859) were "powerful instruments for advancing Reform ideology and assimilation." (15) They "fostered feelings of solidarity and interdependence among Jews throughout the world..., supported active participation in political life by providing insight on how to manipulate the American political system...[and] provided information on matters of importance to Jews, which helped to fill in knowledge gaps inevitable in an immigrant population." (26)

867. Thompson, Robert L. "Wiring a Continent: The History of the Telegraphy Industry in the United States, 1832-66." Ph.D. dissertation, Columbia University, 1948.

868. Tinling, Marion. "Hermione Day and the Hesperian." *CH* 59 (Winter 1980/81): 282-89. Day successfully edited the literary magazine for women from 1858 to 1862 in San Francisco. It specialized in women's rights, biographies, botany, and birds.

869. Turnbull, George. "Some Notes on the History of the Interview." *JQ* 13 (1936): 272-79. Greeley, not Bennett, created the newspaper interview. His interview of Mormon leader Brigham Young in 1859 was the first published in an American newspaper.

870. Van Deusen, Glyndon Garlock. *Horace Greeley: Nineteenth Century Crusader.* New York: Hill and Wang, 1953. The *Tribune,* a national institution, mirrored the age, as indicated by its stands on such issues as nationalism, reform and Whig/Republican policies, and party warfare. Greeley was a symbol of the age.

871. Van Deusen, Glyndon G. *Thurlow Weed: Wizard of the Lobby.* Boston: Little, Brown, 1947. Biography focuses on Weed, who started as a printer and editor, in his role as a political boss.

872. Warner, Richard Fay. "Godey's Lady's Book." *AmM* 2 (August 1924): 399-405. From its founding in 1830 until 1876, *Godey's* "never printed an immoral thought or a profane word. It was...'the guiding star of female education, the beacon light of refined taste, pure morals and practical wisdom,' and a whole generation of American women took color from it." (399)

873. Whitby, Gary Lamar. "The New York Penny Press and the American Romantic Movement." Ph.D. dissertation, University of Iowa, 1984. "American romanticism affected the development of the penny press in such areas as content, style, social reform, and the overall mission of the penny papers."

874. Worth, Gorham A., et al. *Sketches of the Character of the New York Press.* New York: 1844.

875. Yates, Norris W. *William T. Porter and the "Spirit of the Times".* Baton Rouge: Louisiana State University Press, 1957. Porter was editor of the literary antebellum newspaper which printed the works of a number of notable authors.

876. Zabriskie, Francis N. *Horace Greeley, the Editor.* New York: Funk & Wagnalls, 1890.

7

The Antebellum and Civil War Press, 1820–1865

NOTE: This section includes historical works about not the only the press and the Civil War but also those about the press and the various issues that led to the war.

877. Andrews, J. Cutler. *The North Reports the Civil War*. Pittsburgh: University of Pittsburgh Press, 1955. This is the most thoroughly documented, authoritative history on Civil War reporting of the several books that have been published. The war was extensively covered by reporters. Despite various obstacles, they performed well. They sometimes gave erroneous reports, but their intentions were to provide accurate information to readers.

878. Andrews, J. Cutler. "The Pennsylvania Press During the Civil War." *PH* 9 (January 1942): 22ff.

879. Andrews, J. Cutler. *The South Reports the Civil War*. Princeton, N.J.: Princeton University Press, 1970. Well documented narrative of southern reporters in their attempts to cover the battles of the war. The final chapter provides a useful summary of the book's findings.

880. "Arms and the Press." Special section of *AH* (June–July 1985). Includes articles on various aspects of the press during the Civil War.

881. Aubrey, Cullen B. *Reflections of a Newsboy in the Army of the Potomac*. Milwaukee: 1904.

882. Babcock, Havilah. "The Press and the Civil War." *JQ* 6, 1 (1929): 1-5. The northern press was energetic, but the Civil War had a damaging effect on southern newspapers.

883. Barrow, Lionel C., Jr. "'Our Own Cause': *Freedom's Journal* and the Beginnings of the Black Press." *JH* 4 (1977): 118-22. *Freedom's Journal*, founded in 1827, the first black American newspaper, "gave blacks a voice of their own and an opportunity not only to answer the attacks printed in the white press but to read articles on black accomplishments, marriages, deaths, that the white press of the day ignored." (122)

884. Beasley, Maurine. "Pens and Petticoats: Early Women Washington Correspondents." *JH* 1 (1974): 112-15, 136. "During the turbulent decades before and after the Civil War, women journalists established national reputations for columns of social and political commentary written from the nation's capital. Frequently using pen names, [they] contributed to some of the most influential publications of their day. Their careers illustrated that the Civil War social climate permitted women a foothold in the masculine field of Washington reporting in spite of cultural conflicts between their roles as women and as journalists." (112)

885. Benton, J., ed. *Greeley on Lincoln: with Mr. Greeley's Letters to Charles A. Dana and a Lady Friend*. New York: 1873.

886. Blackmon, Robert E. "Noah Brooks: Reporter in the White House." *JQ* 32 (1955): 301-10, 374. The Washington correspondent for the Sacramento *Union* was an able reporter and a confidant of Lincoln and provided "'inside' coverage of the White House unmatched in the history of the American press." (301)

887. Blair, Cecil C. "The Chicago Democratic Press and the Civil War." Ph.D. dissertation, University of Chicago, 1948.

888. Blassingame, John W., Mae G. Henderson, and Jessica M. Dunn, eds. *Antislavery Newspapers and Periodicals*, 5 vols. Boston: G.K. Hall, 1980-1984. Index to the contents of the publications.

889. Bloch, J. M. "The Rise of the *New York World* During the Civil War Decade." Ph.D. dissertation, Harvard University, 1941.

890. Bond, Donovan H. "How the Wheeling Intelligencer Became a Republican Organ." *WVH* 11 (April 1950): 160-84. During 1856-1858 the Virginia newspaper advocated "free speech for all" and had a "policy of letting all parties express their views in its columns." These approaches "did not fit well with the practices of its orthodox Southern and Democratic contemporaries." (160) They therefore identified the *Intelligencer* as a Republican newspaper. Its editor, A.W. Campbell, then began to champion the Republican party, his city, and his western region of Virginia, and he became a leading spokesman for separating from Virginia and forming the new state of West Virginia.

891. Bontemps, Arna. *Free at Last: The Life of Frederick Douglass*. New York: Dodd, Mead, 1971. Ordinary narrative biography of the noted black editor of the *North Star*.

892. Brad, David R. "Gamaliel Bailey and the National Era: A Conservative Antislavery Editor in the Crisis Years, 1847-1859." Ph.D. dissertation, University of Maine, 1974.

893. Braithwaite, William Stanley. "Negro America's First Magazine. *ND* 6 (December 1947): 21-26. Short narrative of the *Colored American Magazine*.

894. Brantley, Rabun Lee. *Georgia Journalism of the Civil War Period*. Nashville: George Peabody, 1929.

895. Brantley, Rabun Lee. "A Southern Paper and the Civil War." *JQ* 2, 2 (1925): 23-28. The Macon *Telegraph*, although thinking secession unwise, optimistically supported the war effort throughout the conflict.

896. Brewer, William M. "John B. Russwurm." *JNH* 13 (1928): 413-22. Biography of the editor of *Freedom's Journal*, America's first black newspaper, and advocate of colonization of former slaves.

897. Bryan, Carter R. "Negro Journalism in America Before Emancipation." *JM* 12 (1969). Brief narrative survey of the newspapers and "forgotten editors who labored in the cause of freedom." (foreword) They were "devoted to the cause of freedom, the elevation of the moral and intellectual level of free Negroes and better understanding between the white and Negro races." (1)

898. Burke, Ronald K. "*The Impartial Citizen* of Samuel Ringgold Ward." *JQ* 49 (1972): 759-60. Brief physical description of the black abolitionist newspaper published in New York City, 1849-1850.

899. Burks, Mary Fair. "The First Black Literary Magazine in American Letters." *CLAJ* 19 (March 1976): 318-21. The *Anglo-African Magazine*, founded in 1859 in New York, "succeeded in creating a tradition of *belles lettres* among blacks and in establishing a nascent countermovement...to assimilationist literature, which often was no more than an imitation of a white culture, unknown to millions of blacks....[F]or generations to follow it became a model of the black literary journal." (321)

900. Bussel, Alan. "The Atlanta *Daily Intelligencer* Covers Sherman's March." *JQ* 51 (1974): 405-10. As Union troops approached, the *Intelligencer* remained unrealistically optimistic about final Confederate victory. There was "disparity between the events of 1864 and the *Intelligencer's* reports...but...the paper was giving its readers a Southern viewpoint of the war....As in the case with most newspapers...[it] both reflected and tried to mold public opinion. To war-weary Southerners, its optimism may have been heartening." (410)

901. Cappon, Lester J. "The Yankee Press in Virginia, 1861-1865." *WMQ* 15 (January 1935): 81-88. Union troops published as many as a dozen newspapers in occupied Virginia territory. "Most of these crudely printed sheets served as a means of relaxation for the soldier as well as an expression of his ego. To the civilian they were a source of irritation, although, in most instances, they were not intended as such....[although they contained] obvious prejudice and antagonism." (88)

902. Chalfant, Edward. *Both Sides of the Ocean. A Biography of Henry Adams, His First Life 1838-1862*. Hamden, Conn.: Archon Books of the Shoe String Press, 1982. In

1861-1862, Adams, while with his father, Charles Francis Adams, the U.S. ambassador to Great Britain, wrote correspondence anonymously for the New York *Times* and tried to influence British-Union relations.

903.   Chiasson, Lloyd. "A Newspaper Analysis of the John Brown Raid." *AJ* 2 (1985): 22-36. The New Orleans *Picayune* "tried to calm the fears of a region apparently frightened of those persons in the North who might try to reduce southern rights through violence....The New York *Tribune's* opinions were squarely opposite those held by the [*Picayune*], and the *Tribune's* intentions in reporting the John Brown episode appear clear. It wanted to lead public opinion, not to follow it. In attempting to do so, [it] in large part relinquished its role as informer for one as anti-slavery propagandist." (33)

904.   Chu, James C.Y. "Horace White: His Association with Abraham Lincoln, 1854-60." *JQ* 49 (1972): 51-59. The correspondent for the Chicago *Press and Tribune* had a close, friendly relationship with Lincoln. He attributed it to their mutual opposition to slavery and their political accord within the Republican party.

905.   Coffin, Charles Carleton. *Boys of '61*. Boston: 1881. Coffin, the war correspondent for the Boston *Journal,* was a keen observer and prolific writer, although he wrote in a routine style. During the war, he wrote three books for juveniles (e.g., *My Days and Nights on the Battlefield*, 1864), followed by four books after the war ended. Based on Coffin's first-hand observations, the later books are useful for historians of both the Civil War and journalism.

906.   Congdon, Charles T. *Reminiscences of a Journalist*. Boston: James R. Osgood, 1880. Autobiography of the New York *Tribune* reporter.

907.   Congdon, Charles T. *Tribune Essays: Leading Articles Contributed to the New York Tribune from 1857 to 1863*. New York: J.S. Redfield, 1869. Anthology of Congdon's writing.

908.   Congleton, Betty C. "George D. Prentice: Nineteenth Century Southern Editor." *RKHS* 62 (April 1964): 87-103.

909.   Cornish, Lori L. "Samuel Cornish: Co-founder of Nation's First Black Newspaper." *MHD* 7, 1 (1987): 25-28. Cornish published *Freedom's Journal* with meager financial support and advocated self-help and education for blacks.

910.   Coulter, Ellis M. *William G. Brownlow: Fighting Parson of the Southern Highlands*. Chapel Hill: University of North Carolina Press, 1937. Well researched and interestingly written biography of the zealous Tennessee editor, preacher, and politician. He lived a fiery life, first as a Methodist attacking Baptists and Presbyterians, then as an ardent abolitionist and anti-secessionist. As Reconstruction governor of Tennessee he ran a particularly harsh administration.

911.   Crozier, Emmet. *Yankee Reporters, 1861-65*. New York: Oxford University Press, 1956. Chronicles reporters' coverage of battles.

912.   Cullen, Maurice R., Jr. "William Gilmore Simms, Southern Journalist." *JQ* (1961): 298-302, 412. In addition to being "the recognized leader of Southern literary endeavor in the period spanning the American Civil War," the South Carolinian also

"was a dedicated journalist who, in several instances, placed his life in jeopardy in order to tell in print what he felt *had* to be told." Although he originally had been pro-Union, with the Civil War he "emerged as a fire-eating editor." (298)

913. Curry, Roy Watson. "The Newspaper Press and the Civil War." *WVH* 6 (January 1945): 226-64. "Colorful and proficient editors characterize the journalism of the Civil War period. Such men as Horace Greeley, James Gordon Bennett, and William Cullen Bryant, of the New York press, were national figures; and their papers were magnified expressions of their personalities. Speaking forth in robust and picturesque language, these men were of great force in American life. Provincial papers were likewise organs of outspoken men as romantic in character as any who have appeared on the American scene." (226) West Virginia suffered from the ravages of the Civil War. "Free soil, free labor and a new state had been achieved in the struggle. For much of the new state success she could thank the Union press." (263)

914. Dana, Charles A. *Recollections of the Civil War*. New York: Appleton, 1898. Narrative of Dana's activities and personal experiences while serving as an observer of the military campaigns and then as the United States' Assistant Secretary of War from 1863 to 1865. In those roles he made many visits to the battlefields and military field headquarters and reported back to Lincoln and Secretary Stanton.

915. Del Porto, Joseph A. "A Study of American Anti-Slavery Journals." Ph.D. dissertation, Michigan State University, 1954.

916. Dillon, Merton L. *Elijah P. Lovejoy, Abolitionist Editor*. Urbana: University of Illinois Press, 1961. Sympathetic biography of the martyr-editor from Alton, Ill. In advocating emancipation, Lovejoy was motivated by religious zeal.

917. Dumond, Dwight L., ed. *Southern Editorials on Secession*. New York: Century, 1931. Anthology of 183 editorials selected from 72 newspapers, "showing the variety, conflict, and concurrence of opinion in the southern states during and shortly before the crisis of secession."

918. Endres, Kathleen L. "The Women's Press in the Civil War: A Portrait of Patriotism, Propaganda, and Prodding." *CWH* 30 (March 1984): 31-53. Most women's publications during the Civil War period can be classified as either "reform" or "mainstream." Although the two types had various differences, editors agreed "that the women's press had a responsibility to build up the spirits of their readers." (53)

919. Engbring, Robert W. "The Waukesha Freeman: A Study of Its Editorial Defense of Civil Rights from Its Founding March 29, 1859, to April, 1863, Three Months after the Emancipation Proclamation." Ph.D. dissertation, Marquette University, 1971. A "survey of the news and editorial objectives and accomplishments" of a weekly newspaper near Milwaukee,

920. Fahrney, Ralph Ray. *Horace Greeley and the Tribune in the Civil War*. Cedar Rapids, Iowa: Torch, 1936. Greeley and the *Tribune* exercised a powerful influence, although the editor was inconsistent, sometimes even enigmatic, in his stands.

921. Floan, Howard R. "The New York *Evening Post* and the Ante-bellum South." *AQ* 8 (Fall 1956): 243-53. William Cullen Bryant, *Evening Post* editor, in the 1830s attempted to play down divisive issues. As differences between the North and South

worsened, however, he grew stronger in his condemnation of southern attitudes and actions. Having a first-hand knowledge of the South, he understood, "[u]nlike many of his contemporaries in the North,...that the fight was not against a...villain in the likeness of Simon Legree. It was perhaps this knowledge of the variety of Southern life and character that inflamed his rancor against Southern leadership, for he saw it as a betrayal not only of America but also of the South." (253)

922. Foner, Phillip S. *Life and Writings of Frederick Douglass,* 5 vols. New York: International Publishers, 1963. Collection of the works by the noted freed slave and editor.

923. Garrison, Wendell Phillips, and Francis J. Garrison. *William Lloyd Garrison, 1805-1879: The Story of His Life Told by His Children,* 4 vols. New York: Century, 1885-1889.

924. George, Joseph, Jr. "'A Catholic Family Newspaper Views the Lincoln Administration: John Mullaly's Copperhead Weekly." *CWH* 24 (June 1978): 112-32. Narrative of the pro-slavery activities of the *Metropolitan Record* in New York.

925. Gill, John. *Tide without Turning: Elijah P. Lovejoy and Freedom of the Press.* Boston: Beacon, 1958. Not only was Lovejoy a martyr to the anti-slavery cause, but he staunchly advocated the First Amendment guarantee of press freedom. He died because he was willing to exercise that freedom.

926. Goldfarb, Joel. "The Life of Gamaliel Bailey Prior to the Founding of the National Era: The Orientation of a Practical Abolitionist." Ph.D. dissertation, University of California, 1958.

927. Goldsmith, Adolph O. "Reporting the Civil War: Union Army Press Relations." *JQ* 33 (1956): 478-87. "Restrictions on handling of war news...were extremely loose as a general rule, but unnecessarily tight in specific instances. The haphazardness of controls resulted in more damage to the war effort than if there had been no controls at all....Uninformed newspaper criticism of Lincoln's conduct of the war prodded generals into striking before they were ready...and at other times fostered a feeling of defeatism not conducive to the most effective prosecution of a war." (487)

928. Greenwood, Grace. "An American Salon." *Cosmopolitan,* 8 (1890): 437-47. Memorial tribute to the anti-slavery editor Gamaliel Bailey, who "realized the national iniquity and disgrace of slavery." (437)

929. Gross, Bella. "Freedom's Journal and the Rights of All." *JNH* 17 (July 1932): 241-86. The most complete early scholarly narrative of the two early black newspapers.

930. Guback, Thomas H. "General Sherman's War on the Press." *JQ* 36 (1959): 171-76. "Throughout the Civil War, there were many conflicts between the Northern press and the military. The trouble was widespread and nearly every general...had his share. But [Sherman]...was plagued mercilessly by the press during the entire war." He "hated" the press because he felt it treated him unfairly. (171) This article provides a narrative of Sherman's unsuccessful attempt to get Thomas Knox of the New York *Herald* executed as a spy.

931. Hall, Martin Hardwick. "*The Mesilla Times*: A Journal of Confederate Arizona." *AW*

5 (1963): 337-51. The *Times* was a staunch advocate of the Confederacy. Although forced to suspend publication after only a brief life (1860-1862) when Federal troops occupied Mesilla, it "nevertheless performed a valuable public service in keeping its readers abreast of local, national, and international events." (351)

932.   Hardt, Hanno R.E. "A German-American Editor Supports the Union, 1860-61." *JQ* 42 (1975): 457-60. Franz Grimm, editor of the *Belleviller Zeitung* in southern Illinois, "played a major role in the interpretation of the [Civil] war to the 'hyphenated' American." He was a "German radical liberal who became an ardent Republican" who believed in "liberty and freedom for all people." (457)

933.   Harper, Robert S. *Lincoln and the Press*. New York: McGraw-Hill, 1951. Lincoln was tolerant and patient with the press despite the difficulties and complexities of the Civil War, many of which the press created, with the Copperhead newspapers especially troublesome. He allowed some censorship, but it was lenient considering the circumstances.

934.   Harrold, Stanley. "Gamaliel Bailey, Abolitionist and Free Soiler." Ph.D. dissertation, Kent State University, 1975. See next entry.

935.   Harrold, Stanley. *Gamaliel Bailey and Antislavery Union*. Kent, Ohio: Kent State University Press, 1986. Through the *Philanthropist*, the organ of the Ohio Anti-Slavery Society, and the *National Era* in Washington, D.C., Bailey played a central role in the abolitionist movement.

936.   Hart, Jim A. "The Missouri Democrat, 1852-1860." *MHR* 55 (January 1961): 127-41. In St. Louis, which was "the focal point in Missouri for the struggle of free labor versus slave labor," the *Democrat* "became the mouthpiece for the emerging Republican party...[and] instigated and led the fight to keep Missouri from seceding from the Union." (127)

937.   Harwell, Richard B. "Atlanta Publications of the Civil War." *AHB* 6 (July 1941): 165-200.

938.   Harwell, Richard B. "The Creed of a Propagandist: Letters from a Confederate Editor." *JQ* 28 (1951): 213-18. Henry Hotze, propaganda agent of the Confederacy in England, published a newspaper, the *Index*, to promote the Confederate cause and worked effectively to get other British newspapers to run favorable articles.

939.   Hesseltine, William B., ed. *Three Against Lincoln: Murat Halstead Reports the Caucuses of 1860*. Baton Rouge: Louisiana State University Press, 1960. Anthology of Halstead's Cincinnati *Commercial* articles covering the 1860 national political conventions.

940.   Holmes, J. Welfred. "Some Antislavery Editors at Work: Lundy, Bailey, and Douglass." *CLAJ* 7 (1963): 48-55. "These three men of diverse talents and viewpoints, while editing their papers in a highly individual manner, struck telling blows against slavery....Despite the human failings that all displayed at times in their journals, these three men were as one in urging their countrymen to move faster toward the ideals upon which the nation was founded." (55)

941.   Holzer, Harold, Gabor S. Boritt, and Mark E. Neely, Jr. *The Lincoln Image:*

Abraham Lincoln and the Popular Print. New York: Scribner's, 1984. Photographs and other published likenesses helped make Lincoln familiar to Americans, helped him win the 1860 presidential election, and informed the public of his official actions. They were important to his political career and public image.

942. Horan, James D. *Matthew Brady: Historian with a Camera.* New York: Crown, 1955. Collection of 500 photographs by Brady, who believed that photographs should serve as an historical record, thus making him a reporter of first rank.

943. Horner, Harlan H. *Lincoln and Greeley.* Urbana: University of Illinois Press, 1953. Study of the relationship between two men who played critical roles in America from 1860 to 1865. Lincoln and Greeley had similar backgrounds and attitudes, but Lincoln was more compassionate and Greeley egotistical.

944. Houzeau, Jean-Charles. *My Passage at the New Orleans Tribune: A Memoir of the Civil War Era.* Baton Rouge: Louisiana State University Press, 1984. Houzeau was a Belgian scientist and liberal polemicist who passed as a Negro and served as chief editor of the black, anti-slavery *Tribune.* It advocated racial justice and equality. This book is a compilation of two journal articles he wrote in 1870, preceded by an introduction by the book's editor.

945. Incitti, Michael A. "Henry Villard: Reporter Who Knew Lincoln Best." *MHD* 6, 2 (1986): 38-44, 61. Villard's thorough coverage of Lincoln after the 1860 election "provided the American people an incisive portrait of the man who would lead them through the crisis of civil war." (38)

946. Jensen, Oliver. "War Correspondent: 1864. The Sketchbooks of James E. Taylor." *AH* 31 (August/September 1980): 48-64. Taylor, an artist, covered the Civil War for *Frank Leslie's Illustrated Newspaper,* providing the combination of words and pictures that readers craved about the battlefront.

947. Johnson, Curtiss S. *Politics and a Belly-Full: The Journalistic Career of William Cullen Bryant, Civil War Editor of the New York Evening Post.* New York: Vantage, 1962. Progressive interpretation of Bryant as a liberal who believed fully in humanitarianism and human freedom. Notable was "Bryant's open-mindedness -- without a trace of intransigence -- the mark of a genuine liberal." He was not so much concerned with the news role of newspapers as with their editorial role, and he was a pioneer in establishing "the meaningful editorial page." His views on freedom were espically evident on the slavery issue, and for his time he was considered "radical" on many leading social, political, and economic issues. But history has proved his view right.

948. Johnson, David W. "Freesoilers for God: Kansas Newspaper Editors and the Anti-slavery Crusade." *KH* 2 (Summer 1979): 74-85. In the 1850s fight for a free Kansas, editorials emphasized slavery as a violation of the Bible and God's principles.

949. Johnson, Oliver. *William Lloyd Garrison and His Times, or Sketches of the Anti-Slavery Movement in America, and of the Man Who Was Its Founder and Moral Leader.* Boston: Houghton Mifflin, 1880.

950. Kendall, John C. "The New York City Press and Anti-Canadianism: A New

Perspective on the Civil War Years." *JQ* 53 (1975): 522-30. Daily newspapers' criticism of Canada was not as responsible for Canada's anti-North attitude as historians have assumed.

951. Kobre, Sidney. "Anti-Slavery Editor Elijah Lovejoy: Press Martyr." *MHD* 6, 2 (1986): 63-64. Brief summary biography of the publisher of the Alton (Ill.) *Observer* who was killed in 1837.

952. Kraditor, Aileen S. *Means and Ends in American Abolitionism: Garrison and His Critics on Strategy and Tactics, 1834-1850.* New York: Random House, 1967. Analysis of the ideas of abolitionists argues that Garrison was a realistic, successful abolitionist and social thinker rather than an irrational zealot. "The unrealism was not the abolitionists' for feeling guilty [about slavery] but their neighbors' for not feeling guilty."

953. Krumm, Tahlman, Jr. "The Gethsemane Factor: A Historical Portrait of Samuel Medary of Ohio and Analysis of the Rhetorical Dilemma of His *Crisis* Years, 1861-1864." Ph.D. dissertation, Ohio State University, 1978. "During a long, influential career in journalism, Medary promoted a host of social, economic, and political causes...especially the interests of the Democratic party....[He] also represented the embodiment of two sociopolitical themes that have persisted throughout the American experience -- racism and populism."

954. Langley, Peter, III. "Pessimism-Optimism of Civil War Military News: June 1863-March 1865." *JQ* 49 (1972): 74-78. In reporting the major battles of the Civil War, the New York *Times* and Richmond *Dispatch* "exhibited, for the most part, a creditable level of news-sense and objectivity." (74)

955. Larsen, Robin Fisher. "Cooper Union Speech: New York Media Launch a Candidate." *MHD* 6, 2 (1986): 2-7. The glowing praise in New York newspapers following Lincoln's speech in early 1860 brought favorable public attention to Lincoln.

956. Leiter, Bernard Kelly. "A Study of the Relationship between General Ulysses S. Grant and Various Illinois Newspapers Covering the Period March, 1864, to November, 1868." Ph.D. dissertation, Southern Illinois University, 1970. The news stories and editorials of four papers were influential in Grant's career as a general and presidential candidate.

957. Malone, Henry T. "Atlanta Journalism During the Confederacy." *GHQ* 37 (September 1953): 219ff.

958. Malone, Henry Thompson. "The Charleston *Daily Courier*: Standard Bearer of the Confederacy." *JQ* 29 (1952): 307-15. The *Courier* remained a consistent and enthusiastic supporter of Jefferson Davis and of the Confederacy throughout the Civil War.

959. Malone, Henry T. "The Weekly Atlanta Intelligencer as a Secessionist Journal." *GHQ* 37 (December 1953): 278-86. With the secessionist crisis of 1860-1861, the *Intelligencer* "became defiantly pro-Southern. For the period between Lincoln's election and the fall of Fort Sumter, the *Intelligencer* offers an interesting and representative picture of Atlanta journalism during critical times." (278) It served readers by "facing the issues squarely, striving for accuracy, and, withal, offering an interesting

newspaper." (286)

960.   Marks, Bayly Ellen, and Mark Norton Schatz, eds. *Between North and South: A Maryland Journalist Views the Civil War: The Narrative of William Wilkins Glenn, 1861-1869.* Rutherford, N.J.: Fairleigh Dickinson University Press, 1978. The diary of Glenn, a Baltimore newspaper publisher, focusing primarily on the non-journalistic aspects of his life.

961.   Marszalek, John F. *Sherman's Other War: The General and the Civil War Press.* Memphis: Memphis State University Press, 1981. Sherman's "anti-press attitude was based on personal biases rather than on a cogent philosophy of putting the constitution aside during war." (109) Yet, Sherman and journalists, with little precedent to follow, developed a relatively open working relationship.

962.   Martin, Asa Earl. "Pioneer Anti-Slavery Press." *MVHR* 3 (March 1916): 509-28. Between 1800 and 1830, journals (published primarily in the border states) "kept alive the anti-slavery sentiment, organized it and formulated definite plans of operation....They were the pioneers of the movement, struggling almost single-handed against the numerous difficulties that threatened to overwhelm them; yet out of chaos they brought an organization, a well defined purpose and a unity of action that made possible the success of the efforts of those who were to follow them." (528)

963.   Meredith, Roy. *Mr. Lincoln's Camera Man, Mathew S. Brady.* New York: Scribner's, 1946. First book-length, though superficial, biography of Mathew Brady, containing 400 photographs. Brady's motivation was to provide a photographic record of notable Americans and of the Civil War.

964.   Mitgang, Herbert. "From New Salem to the White House: Friend of the Press." *MHD* 6, 2 (198): 9-12. Recognizing the importance of the press in informing the public, Lincoln cultivated supporters among editors.

965.   Mitgang, Herbert, ed. *Lincoln As They Saw Him.* New York: Rinehart, 1956. (Republished as *Abraham Lincoln: A Press Portrait*; Chicago: Quadrangle Books, 1971). Anthology of periodical opinion articles on Lincoln from 1832 to 1865. Acrimonious, villifying articles predominated during his presidency.

966.   Muehl, Siegmar. "Edward Muehl: 1800-1854: Missouri Editor, Religious Free-Thinker and Fighter for Human Rights." *MHR* 81 (1987): 18-36. "Although not a major historical figure in Missouri history, Muehl pioneered as a German-American publisher in the state. His 'free-thinking' views as expressed in his editorials and speeches stirred interest and sometimes controversy....His early [1843] and out-spoken antislavery stand, in the midst of slaveholding neighbors, required considerable courage." (19)

967.   Nord, David Paul. "Tocqueville, Garrison and the Perfection of Journalism." *JH* 13 (1986): 56-63. Garrison's *Liberator*, rather than the penny newspapers, embodied Tocqueville's concept of a democratic press. The "1830s marked a lush first flowering of democratic journalism in America -- participatory journalism of the sort that Tocqueville heralded. But this flush of democracy in journalism had nothing to do with the rise of the penny press, as standard journalism histories take for granted; in fact, the penny press was inherently inimical to it....[P]ersonal, even fanatical, editorship [as embodied in the *Liberator*] was [central] to the democratic function of

journalism." (56)

968. Nordin, Kenneth D. "In Search of Black Unity: An Interpretation of the Content and Function of 'Freedom's Journal.'" *JH* 4 (1977): 123-28. *Freedom's Journal*, founded in 1827, the first black American newspaper, "was more than a reforming abolitionist newspaper. It tried to establish a sense of fraternity among blacks and chart the course people of color should take to improve their positions in American society. It tried also to provide its readers with a sense of culture and to furnish them with the significant news of the day." (128)

969. Norton, L. Wesley. "The Religious Press and the Compromise of 1850: A Study of the Relationship of the Methodist, Baptist, and Presbyterian Press to the Slavery Controversy 1846-1851." Ph.D. dissertation, University of Illinois, 1959.

970. Nye, Russel B. "Freedom of the Press and the Antislavery Controversy." *JQ* 22 (1945): 1-11. "Abolition provided the first really important issue in the struggle for a free press that the nation had seen since the founding of the republic." (11) Southern states abridged freedom with the argument that freedom did not allow the distribution of obnoxious doctrines. Northern legislatures refused to abridge press freedom, and abolitionists quickly recognized the relationship between their cause and constitutional liberty.

971. O'Brien, Eleanor L. "Michigan War Correspondent -- Civil War Style." *Chronicle*, 18 (Winter 1982): 4-8.

972. Page, Charles Anderson. *Letters of a War Correspondent*. James R. Gilmore, ed. Boston: L.C. Page, 1899. Anthology of dispatches by the New York *Tribune* reporter covering the Army of the Potomac, giving considerable insight into the daily routine and adventures of Civil War correspondents.

973. Perkins, Howard C., ed. *Northern Editorials on Secession,* 2 vols. New York: Appleton-Century, 1942. Anthology of editorials during the crisis of 1860-1861, preceded by an introduction describing the general characteristics of the period's newspapers.

974. Perry, P. Dolores Brewington. "Frederick Douglass: Editor and Journalist." Ph.D. dissertation, University of North Carolina, 1972.

975. Perry, Patsy Brewington. "The Literary Content of *Frederick Douglass' Paper* through 1860." *CLAJ* 17 (December 1973): 214-29. Douglass was "an arbiter of cultural and literary taste....[He] provided rich literary fare for his readers -- ...he was, in fact, a champion of belles lettres." (214)

976. Potter, David M. "Horace Greeley and Peaceable Secession." *JSH* 7 (1941): 145-59. Greeley's argument that the southern states should be allowed to secede peaceably was impractical and illusory. It "obscured the clarity of the true alternatives -- compromise and war." (159) His tone was like that of other prominent Republicans: "generally either blustering or vacillating, and, in either case, unrealistic." (145)

977. Pride, Armistead S. "'Rights of All': Second Step in Development of Black Journalism." *JH* 4 (1977): 129-31. Brief chronology of the six-month life of *Rights of All*, founded in 1829 by Samuel Cornish, the second black American newspaper.

978.   Quarles, Benjamin. *Frederick Douglass*. Washington, D.C.: Associated Publishers, 1948. Biography of the freed slave and editor.

979.   Randall, James G. "Federal Generals and a Good Press." *AHR* 39 (1934): 284-97. "[I]n specific instances unnecessary battles were fought and men killed because of the premature disclosure of the movements of troops." The confidential correspondence of James Gordon Bennett of the New York *Herald* indicates, however, that the problem "was not always the fault of journalists alone, for ambitious generals were anxious to see their feats, actual or alleged, duly celebrated, in order that their chances of preferment over rivals might be improved." Additionally, federal government officials, "anxious to guard themselves and their departments against newspaper attack, were ready to purchase immunity by entrusting important secrets to influential journalists." (284)

980.   Randall, James G. "The Newspaper Problem in Its Bearing upon Military Secrecy During the Civil War." *AHR* 23 (January 1918): 303-23. For years, this article was considered the leading authority on press freedom during the Civil War. "Acting under no effective governmental restraint, the newspapers of the North...undoubtedly did the national cause serious injury by continually revealing military information, undermining confidence in the management of public affairs, and giving undue publicity to the virtues of ambitious generals and the sensational features of the war." (303) "[T]he actual governmental interference with the freedom of the press was comparatively slight, and...voluntary restraint or popular pressure had far greater effect in keeping improper material out of newspapers than official repression....There was during the war no real suppression of opinion." (323)

981.   Raper, Horace W. *William W. Holden: North Carolina's Political Enigma*. Chapel Hill: University of North Carolina Press, 1985. Holden, journalist and governor during Reconstruction, "[m]ore than any other North Carolinian of his era...shaped the state's political, social, and economic development as he worked unceasingly for the betterment of his fellowman." Eventually, however, his opponents, including the plantation aristocracy and the Ku Klux Klan, gained political control of the state.

982.   Raymond, Henry J. "Extracts from the Journal of Henry J. Raymond." *SMM* 19 (November 1879; January and March 1880). Memoirs of the New York *Times* editor during the Civil War.

983.   Reilly, Tom. "Early Coverage of a President-Elect: Lincoln at Springfield 1860." *JQ* 49 (1972): 469-79. "During the three months at Springfield and the trip Eastward the President-elect changed from a relatively unknown regional politician into a nationally known figure who commanded the public's interest and growing support. Most of the change in his public status was due to the ever-increasing coverage on the part of the Northern newspapers," especially the work by Henry Villard, who "maintained a good working relationship with his ssources in order to obtain the news...[and thus] broke historical ground for the many President reporters who were to follow him." (479)

984.   Reilly, Tom. "Lincoln-Douglas Debates of 1858 Forced New Role on the Press." *JQ* 56 (1979): 734-43, 752. "[T]he function of political reporters and the inter-relationship between the press and the politicians were sharpened somewhat by the intensity and importance of the 1858 [U.S. senatorial] campaign [in Illinois]. The journalists and their papers argued for better reporting conditions and recognition of their role

and right to report the debates. It was to be 'a new style of journalism'....The previous ties between the candidates, their parties and the press were still close, but the 1858 campaign provided indications that the old relationships were changing....[Newspapers'] detailed accounts aided the public's understanding of the people, events and issues." (752)

985. Reilly, Tom. "A Spanish-Language Voice of Dissent in Antebellum New Orleans." *LaH* 23 (1983): 325-39. In opposing American intervention in Cuba in 1851 and the Mexican War, *La Union* stood up against prevailing sentiment among the Anglo-American populace of New Orleans.

986. Reynolds, Donald. *Editors Make War: Southern Newspapers in the Secession Crisis.* Nashville: Vanderbilt University Press, 1970. Southern newspapers, which tended to favor union in early 1860, strongly advocated secession by 1861 and had considerable influence on southern opinion.

987. Richardson, Abby Sage, ed. *Garnered Sheaves: From the Writings of Albert D. Richardson.* Hartford, Conn.: 1871. Anthology of writings by the New York *Tribune's* noted war correspondent.

988. Richardson, Albert Deane. *Secret Service; the Field, the Dungeon and the Escape.* Hartford: American, 1865. The reporter tells his personal account of his capture by the Confederate army, imprisonment, and dramatic escape to the North.

989. Robinson, Elwyn Burns. "The *Pennsylvanian*: Organ of Democracy." *PMHB* 62 (1938): 350-60. In ante-bellum Philadelphia, the *Pennsylvanian* received patronage from Democratic politicians and supported Democratic, southern interests in slavery and secession.

990. Robinson, John W. "A California Copperhead: Henry Hamilton and the Los Angeles *Star*." *AW* 23 (Autumn 1981): 213-30. In frontier California in the 1850s and 1860s, Hamilton was a "relentless critic of...Lincoln..., a negrophobe, and a vocal supporter of the Confederacy....[He] openly rallied local Southern Democrats, gloated over Union defeats..., [and] survived arrest....[His] passions and pronouncements typified a young frontier society in transition." (230)

991. Rowan, Steven, ed. *Germans for a Free Missouri: Translations from the St. Louis Radical Press, 1857-1862.* Columbia: University of Missouri Press, 1983. Collection of articles from the *Anzeiger des Westerns* and *Westliche Post*, which strongly argued the abolitionist stance.

992. Schafer, Judith Kelleher. "New Orleans Slavery in 1850 as Seen in Advertisements." *JSH* 47 (February 1981): 33-55. An analysis of advertisements in nine New Orleans newspapers indicates "a booming slave trade in which the equivalent of one in five of the bondsmen in New Orleans were sold annually." (33) While "slaves in New Orleans in 1850 might have been declining in numbers, the peculiar institution was nevertheless firmly entrenched in the city's society and economy." (56)

993. Schurz, Carl. *The Reminiscences of Carl Schurz*, 3 vols. New York: McClure, 1907-1908. Recollections of Schurz's journalism career, which began during the Civil War and extended beyond Reconstruction.

994. Scott, Frank W. "Newspapers Since 1860," 319-336 in *The Cambridge History of American Literture,* Vol. 3. New York: Putman's, 1921. General survey history emphasizing the progress and developments in American journalism.

995. Sears, Stephen W. "The First News Blackout." *AH* (June-July 1985): 24-31. "The Civil War ignited the basic conflict between a free press and the need for military security. By war's end, the hard-won compromises between soldiers and newspapermen may not have provided all the answers, but they had raised all the modern questions." (24)

996. Shaw, Donald L., and Stephen W. Brauer. "Press Freedom and War Constraints: Case Testing Siebert's Proposition II." *JQ* 46 (1969): 243-54. "Analysis of the threats against a North Carolina Civil War editor [William W. Holden] proves the proposition that official and unofficial pressures on press freedom increase in times of governmental stress." (243)

997. Shilobod, Marlene. "Winslow Homer: Illustrator of Sea and War." *MHD* 5, 4 (1985): 52-55. For *Harper's Weekly* during the Civil War, Homer's illustrations documented soldiers' routine, especially camp life and leisure time,

998. Shivers, Lynne. "Why Mary Lincoln Got Such a 'Bad Press.'" *MHD* 6, 2 (1986): 13-22. Newspapers portrayed Mrs. Lincoln unfairly by exaggerating her weaknesses.

999. Shuford, Thomas Eugene. "Three Texas Unionist Editors Face the Secession Crisis: A Case Study on Freedom of the Press." Ph.D. dissertation, University of Texas, 1979. Press freedom was restricted in Texas. Secessionists attempted to silence opponents through non-governmental efforts, but "personal and political character...allowed three Texas editors (A.B. Norton, Ferdinand Flake, and James P. Newcomb) to outlast many of their journalistic peers in their advocacy of unionism."

1000. Siegel, Alan A. *For the Glory of the Union: Myth, Reality and the Media in Civil War New Jersey.* Rutherford, N.J.: Fairleigh Dickinson University Press, 1984. Study of editorials, reporting, and newspapers' effect on public opinion. Three of Newark's newspapers differed in the ways they covered a story involving the 26th Regiment from New Jersey.

1001. Simon, Paul. *Lovejoy, Martyr to Freedom.* St. Louis: Concordia Publishing House, 1964. Readable popular biography that presents nothing new about Elijah Lovejoy, the antislavery editor killed by a mob in Alton, Ill., in 1837. He was a model of moral courage. Following a religious conversion, he slowly became an abolitionist. (The author, an Illinois state senator, later became a U.S. Senator.)

1002. Skidmore, Joe. "The Copperhead Press and the Civil War." *JQ* 16 (1939): 345-55. The Copperhead press in the North was "vigorous and fearless in the face of official suppressions and unofficial mobbings and lootings." By "crying loudly for peace in a hysterical country at war, [newspapers] occupied significant roles....In tactical maneuvering and in dissemination of its doctrine, [the press'] methodology commands respect even [today]." (345)

1003. Smart, James G., ed. *A Radical View: The "Agate" Dispatches of Whitelaw Reid, 1861-1865,* 2 vols. Memphis: Memphis State University Press, 1978. Collection of the Radical-Republican Civil War correspondent's articles for the Cincinnati *Gazette*. He reported the war thoroughly.

1004. Snodgrass, James E. "A Pioneer Editor." *AM* 17 (June 1866): 743-51. "Subjected as Dr. [Gamaliel] Bailey was so frequently to the fury of mobs, and the pressure of social opposition and pecuniary want, he led the hosts of Anti-slavery Reform into the very stronghold [Washington, D.C.] of the enemy's country; and...he maintained his position with integrity and success....As a writer he was clear and logical to an uncommon degree, carrying certainconviction to the mind, wherever it was at all open to the truth; and with the rare habit of stating fairly the position of his opponent, he never failed of winning his respect and confidence." (750-51)

1005. Snorgrass, J. William. "The Black Press in the San Francisco Bay Area 1850-1900." *CH* 60 (Winter 1981-82): 306-17. The seven newspapers founded in the Bay Area had two objectives: "to provide a platform from which blacks could express their views and combat racial prejudice and discrimination in the United States." (306)

1006. Starr, Louis M. *Bohemian Brigade: Civil War Newsmen in Action.* New York: Knopf, 1954. Entertaining story of how reporters from the North, especially New York City, contributed to the development of journalism through their reporting of the Civil War. Through their reports, they helped satisfy the public's thirst for news; and by the end of the war, news had gained preeminence over editorials. The "Bohemians" were colorful, personalized reporters who defied "censors, generals, the elements, and often their own common sense....[They] established the right to report as one that was recognized, however grudgingly, as vital to the democratic process."

1007. Stedman, Edmund Clarence. *Life and Letters of Edmund C. Stedman.* Laura Stedman and George M. Gould, eds. New York: 1910. Stedman's diary and letters to his family draw a portrait of a war correspondent and the Civil War period.

1008. Steen, Ralph W. "Texas Newspapers and Lincoln." *SHQ* 51 (January 1948): 199-212. Newspaper attitudes toward Lincoln changed between 1860 and 1946. "The Texas press accepted Lincoln's election in 1860 as a tragedy and his assassination as a major blessing." (199) Since 1909, the centennial of his birth, he "has been made into a legendary character with all good attributes and no faults." (212)

1009. Stewart, James B. "The Aims and Impact of Garrisonian Abolitionism, 1840-1860." *CWH* 15 (1969): 197-209. The radical "Garrisonian approach to northern politics was not nearly as unsophisticated and unproductive as historians have assumed." (197) Radical abolitionism was politically acute and practical, and "the secession crisis represented the culmination of radical impact in the politics of antebellum America." (209)

1110. Sullivan, Julie. "How Frederick Douglass Saw the Great Emancipator." *MHD* 6, 2 (1986): 56-61. To the editor of *The Douglass Monthly*, "Lincoln was at once a spokesman for the underprivileged and at the same time a vanguard of the white race." (57) Douglass "vacillated...between awe and mistrust" (61) of Lincoln.

1111. Sutherland, Daniel E. "'Altamont' of the *Tribune:* John Williamson Palmer in the Civil War." *MHN* 78 (Spring 1983): 54-66. Palmer, war correspondent for the New York *Tribune*, was one of the "new breed of reporter -- tenacious, resourceful, and innovative." His scoops, human-interest writing style, and "uncompromising standards of honesty and integrity" contributed to the revolution in reporting. (54)

1112. Swett, Herbert E. "AP Coverage of the Lincoln Assissination." *JQ* 47 (1970): 157-59. Brief chronological narrative indicating that the Associated Press of New York "reported the murder of...Lincoln and related events promptly and with reasonable accuracy and thoroughness." (157)

1113. Tarbell, Ida M. *A Reporter for Lincoln: The Story of Henry W. Wing, Soldier and Newspaperman.* New York: Macmillan, 1927. The adventures during the last year of the Civil War of a cub reporter for the New York *Tribune* who was on close terms with Lincoln.

1114. Tenney, Craig D. "Major General Ambrose E. Burnside and the First Amendment: A Case Study in Civil War Freedom of Expression." Ph.D. dissertation, Indiana University, 1977. Burnside suppressed press freedom in a number of instances. Lincoln "provided the general with ample precedent -- even encouragement -- for suppression of speech and press."

1115. Tenney, Craig. "To Suppress or Not to Suppress: Abraham Lincoln and the Chicago *Times*." *CWH* 27 (September 1981): 248-59. See previous entry. Even though Lincoln rescinded Burnside's order to suppress the *Times,* he did so out of political motives rather than for concern for First Amendment principles.

1116. Thomas, Benjamin P., ed. *Three Years with Grant, as Recalled by War Correspondent Sylvanus Cadwallader*. New York: Knopf, 1955. Recollections of a newspaper reporter in the field during the Civil War.

1117. Thorp, Robert K. "The Copperhead Days of Dennis Mahoney." *JQ* 43 (1966): 680-86, 696. "A Democratic Iowa editor,...Mahoney was a persistent critic of Abraham Lincoln and the Union war effort. But his Copperhead stand was in reality a conservative's attempt to hold back change." (680)

1118. Trexler, Harrison A. "The Davis Administration and the Richmond Press." *JSH* 16 (May 1950): 177-95.

1119. Truman, Ben C. "Old Time Editors and Newspapers I Have Known." *PP* 6 (December 1911): 338ff.

1120. Vallandigham, James L. *A Life of Clement L. Vallandigham.* Baltimore: 1872. Favorable biography of the Ohio Copperhead editor.

1121. Vartorella, William Frederick. "The Other 'Peculiar Institution': The Free Thought and Free Love Reform Press in Ohio during Rebellion and Reconstruction, 1861-1877." Ph.D. dissertation, Ohio University, 1977. "The present investigation attempts to place these obscure, though significant, reform publications and their editors...within the contexts of an anti-slavery, anti-colonization impetus and the futile search by utopians for the millennium."

1122. Villard, Harold G., and Oswald Garrison Villard, eds. *Lincoln on the Eve of '61: A Journalist's Story.* New York: Knopf, 1941. Collection of New York *Herald* articles and a first-hand account by reporter Henry Villard of Lincoln's daily life between the times of his election and inauguration.

1123. Villard, Henry. "Army Correspondence: Its History." *The Nation*, 1 (July 20, July 27, Aug. 3, 1865), 79ff, 114ff, 144ff.. By providing news about the Civil War, the press exercised a profound influence on public opinion. Unfortunately, it exhibited little "moral force" because by the end of 1862 correspondents as a whole "possessed neither intelligence, nor education, nor character in a degree which fitted them to represent journalism. With them a deterioration commenced in the quality of special reports for the press from the field, that continued and became more unmistakable from campaign to campaign."

1124. Villard, Henry. *Memoirs of Henry Villard: Journalist and Financier, 1835-1900*, 2 vols. Boston: Houghton Mifflin, 1904. First-hand account by the correspondent takes a realistic look at Civil War journalism, providing a more serious view than that of the colorful "Bohemian" reporters.

1125. Walsh, Justin E. *To Print the News and Raise Hell*. Chapel Hill: University of North Carolina Press, 1968. As editor of the Chicago *Times*, Storey (1838-1884) opposed the rights of blacks, arguing that abolitionists "fostered miscegenation...and treason." He practiced a raucous, sensational, and controversial style of journalism. It brought him curses, infamy, circulation, and money.

1126. Walsh, Justin E. "To Print the News and Raise Hell: Wilbur F. Storey's Chicago *Times*." *JQ* 40 (1963): 497-510. See previous entry.

1127. Washburn, Israel. "Gamaliel Bailey." *UQGR* 5 (July 1868): 298-302.

1128. Weisberger, Bernard A. "McClellan and the Press." *SAQ* 51 (July 1952): 383-92. When Lincoln removed George McClellan as commanding general of the Army of the Potomac, the press, which idolized McClellan, subjected Lincoln to intense editorial criticism. It continued to support McClellan through his unsuccessful 1864 campaign for the presidency.

1129. Weisberger, Bernard A. *Reporters for the Union*. Boston: Little, Brown, 1953. During the Civil War, the status of the reporter advanced from that of an inferior newspaper staff member to that of a prominent public figure and professional journalist. Reporters also helped to influence public opinion and government policy. Politically biased, they frequently meddled in government and military affairs.

1130. Weldy, Margaret. *George Dennison Prentice*. New York: Columbia University, 1929. Brief biography of the editor of the Louisville *Journal* editor.

1131. Wert, Jaffery D. "The Great Civil War Gold Hoax." *AHL* 14 (April 1980): 20-24. John Howard, city editor of the Brooklyn *Eagle*, fabricated a news story containing a proclamation from Lincoln hoping "that the business community's reaction to...dire news would send the price of gold upward." (22)

1132. White, Laura A. *Robert Barnwell Rhett: Father of Secession*. New York: Century, 1931. The definitive biography of the fire-eating editor of the Charleston (S.C.) *Mercury*. He argued for secession as early as 1850 and remained a staunch advocate of slavery and southern extremism throughout the Civil War.

1133. Wilkie, Franc Bangs. *Personal Reminiscences of Thirty-five Years of Journalism.* Chicago: F.J. Schulte, 1891. Observations by the war correspondent for the New York *Times* and Chicago *Times*.

1134. Wilkie, Franc Bangs. *"Walks About Chicago" and Army and Miscellaneous Sketches.* Chicago: Church, Goodman and Donnelley, 1869. Anthology of Wilkie's Chicago *Times* articles.

1135. Willis, Landon. "Clay, the 'True American.'" *GE* 24, 2 (1983): 3-6. Routine narrative of Cassius Clay's abolitionist Kentucky newspaper.

1136. Wilson, James Harrison. *The Life of Charles A. Dana.* New York: Harper, 1907. Admiring, authorized biography devoted primarily to Dana's Civil War career.

1137. Wilson, Quintus C. "The Confederate Press Association: A Pioneer News Agency." *JQ* 26 (1949): 160-66. Narrative of the founding and operation of the CPA, a cooperative newsgathering service. One of the major problems it faced was military censorship.

1138. Wilson, Quintus C. "Voluntary Press Censorship During the Civil War." *JQ* 19 (1942): 251-61. Both military and voluntary censorship was practiced. "Washington correspondents of the early months of the Civil War are to be credited with the first voluntary effort to prevent circulation of information that would give 'aid and comfort to the enemy.'" (251) Both the North and the South had occasional problems with censorship and with newspapers revealing information, but "Union generals...suffered more than their Confederate opponents due to the zealous handling of news by competing papers in the large cities of the North." (261)

1139. Wing, Henry Ebenezer. "Stories of a War Correspondent." *CA* 88-90 (Feb. 6, March 27, May 22, Oct. 2, Oct. 30, Nov. 27, 1913; April 2, May 21, Oct. 1, 1914). Recollections of the New York *Tribune* reporter.

1140. Young, John Russell. *Men and Memories: Personal Reminiscenses.* New York: Neely, 1901. The distinguished managing editor of the Philadelphia *Press* provides recollections of Philadelphia newspapermen during the Civil War period.

8

The Press of the Industrial Age, 1865–1883

1141. Abbot, Willis J. "Chicago Newspapers and Their Makers." *ARR* 11 (1895): 640-65.

1142. Abramoske, Donald J. "The Chicago Daily News: A Business History, 1875-1901." Ph.D. dissertation, University of Chicago, 1963.

1143. Abramoske, Donald J. "The Founding of the *Chicago Daily News*." *JISHS* 59 (1966): 341-53. "The history of the *Chicago Daily News* begins in the mind of one man -- Melville E. Stone. From the first day of publication, on December 23, 1875, until his retirement in 1888, the *Daily News* was his creation," (341) although it was modeled after Dana's New York *Sun*.

1144. Abramoske, Donald J. "Victor Lawson and the Chicago *Weekly News*: A Defeat." *JQ* 43 (1966): 43-48. Lawson attempted to publish a weekly edition of the *Daily News* from 1878 to 1895. "Almost from the beginning," however, it "was to prove an annoying burden, distracting Lawson from the profitable business of managing his daily." (43)

1145. Armstrong, William M. "E.L. Godkin and American Foreign Policy, 1865-1900." Ph.D. dissertation, Stanford University, 1954.

1146. Armstrong, William M., ed. *The Gilded Age Letters of E.L. Godkin*. Albany: State University of New York Press, 1974. Collection of personal correspondence written by the New York *Evening Post* and *Nation* editor between 1851 and 1902.

1147. Austin, James C. *Petroleum V. Nasby*. New York: Twayne, 1965. Short descriptive biography of David Ross Locke, the author of the "Nasby" columns, emphasizing his "journalistic career, his satire and reforming interests" and his influence on public issues.

1148. Bard, David R., and William J. Baker. "The American Newspaper Response to the Jamaican Riots of 1865." *JQ* 51 (1974): 659-63. The race riots intensified the press argument over the nature of Reconstruction and the status of freed slaves in the American South.

1149. Beasley, Maurine H. "Mary Clemmer Ames: A Victorian Woman Journalist." *HHJ* (Spring 1978): 57-63.

1150. Bisland, Elizabeth. *The Life and Letters of Lafcadio Hearn*, 2 vols. Boston: Houghton Mifflin, 1906. Romantic biography of the New Orleans editor known for his luminous editorials and fiction.

1151. Bradshaw, James Stanford. "The 'Detroit Free Press' in England." *JH* 5 (1978): 4-7. From 1881 to 1899 the *Free Press* published a successful weekly humor/feature paper in London, the first time an American paper had published a British edition.

1152. Brakeman, Mark. "Thomas Nast: Pen With Power." *MHD* 5, 4 (1985): 23-27, 48-49. General narrative biography briefly summarizing the cartoonist's career.

1153. Braly, Earl B. "William Dean Howells, Author and Journalist." *JQ* 32 (1955): 456-62. The novelist "was proud of his journalistic experiences; he owed much to them. He constantly tried to refine the ephemeral stuff of journalism into the more durable essence of literature." (462) Because of his genius, however, he probably would have succeeded as a novelist even if he had never worked in journalism.

1154. Brown, Warren. "Social Change and the Negro Press, 1860-1880." Ph.D. dissertation, New School for Social Research, 1950.

1155. Bryan, Carter R. "Carl Schurz: Journalist and Liberal Propagandist." *JQ* 40 (1963): 207-12. Schurz was a liberal spokesman in the cause of freedom, especially promoting the view that America offered and should offer a great amount of freedom. His writings were influential in affecting public opinion and politics.

1156. Clayton, Charles G. *Little Mack: Joseph B. McCullagh of the St. Louis Globe-Democrat*. Carbondale: Southern Illinois University Press, 1969. McCullagh successfully combined the news emphasis of Bennett with the editorial ability of Greeley. He emphasized ethics and good writing.

1157. Cooper, John Milton, Jr. *Walter Hines Page: The Southerner as American 1855-1918*. Chapel Hill: University of North Carolina Press, 1977. U.S. ambassador to Great Britain, Page was also a journalist who, as owner of *Forum*, originated the investigatory magazine article. He also ran *Atlantic* and founded *World's Work*.

1158. Cortissoz, Royal. *The Life of Whitelaw Reid*, 2 vols. New York: Scribner, 1921. Favorable, one-sided political biography of the editor-owner of the New York *Tribune* written by a member of the *Tribune* staff. Reid was an insider in the Republican party and the American ambassador to both France and England.

1159. Davis, Stephen. "'A Matter of Sensational Interest': The *Century* 'Battles and Leaders' Series." *CWH* 27 (1981): 338-49. In the 1880s *Century* magazine published a series of articles on the Civil War. The series, which now has considerable value as a historiographical source, was begun primarily from commercial motivations.

1160. Dennis, Charles H. *Victor Lawson: His Time and His Work*. Chicago: University of Chicago Press, 1935. An uncritical, house biography by a friend of Lawson during his years with the Chicago *Daily News*, 1876-1925. Lawson was a humanitarian. With the emergence of newspapers into businesses, Lawson -- although making personal profits -- remained honest, independent, and clean. He was an innovator of a number of newspaper techniques such as the women's department. He stood for fair news and against sensationalism and made the *Daily News* into one of the best and most profitable newspapers in the country.

1161. Dennis, Everette E., and Christopher Allen. "*Puck*, the Comic Weekly." *JH* 6 (1979): 2-7, 13. *Puck* (1877-1918) was the "first and most important" (2) comic magazine in the late 19th century. This study examines the reasons for its success.

1162. Dornfield, A.A. *Behind the Front Page: The Story of the City News Bureau of Chicago*. Chicago: Academy Chicago, 1983. Narrative history of the Bureau from the time of its founding in the late 19th century, written by a veteran of the staff.

1163. Duncan, Bingham. *Whitelaw Reid: Journalist, Politician, Diplomat*. Athens: University of Georgia Press, 1975. Reid, who had been a Civil War correspondent, succeeded Greeley as publisher of the New York *Tribune*, served as U.S. ambassador to France, and ran for the U.S. vice-presidency.

1164. Edson, J.M. *History of the A.N. Kellogg Newspaper Company*. Chicago: 1890.

1165. Eide, Richard B. *North Star Editor*. New York: King's Crown Press, 1944. For Joseph A. Wheelock, editor of the St. Paul *Pioneer Press*, "the ideal journal was the newspaper that was conservative yet progressive, crusading yet fair, critical yet tolerant. It catered to no class, feared no power, and lived up to its obligations as a public trust."

1166. Endres, Kathleen L. "Strictly Confidential: Birth Control Advertising in a 19th-Century City." *JQ* 63 (1986): 748-51. Birth-control advertisers used carefully worded classifieds in Cleveland newspapers. However, advertising fell victim to state anti-abortion legislation and the anti-obscenity campaign in the 1870s.

1167. Fedler, Fred. "Mrs. O'Leary's Cow and Other Newspaper Tales About the Chicago Fire of 1871." *AJ* 3 (1986): 24-38. Erroneous reports were picked up and reprinted by other newspapers. The tale of Mrs. O'Leary's cow starting the Chicago fire "seems to have been created by a reporter who wanted to make his story about the fire more interesting. It was a fanciful tale, much more interesting than the truth. Other journalists copied it, and the public believed and remembered it." (24)

1168. Fenton, Alfred H. *Dana of the Sun*. New York: Farrar & Rinehart, 1941. Narrative biography intended for a teenage audience.

1169. Francke, Warren T. "W.T. Stead: The First New Journalist?" *JH* 1 (1974): 36, 63-66. The author of newspaper expose`s and the 1894 book *If Christ Came to Chicago* was called "The New Journalist" by contemporaries. Like the "new journalists" of the 1960s, he was criticized by some other journalists, but he also received praise. His style was similar to that of the modern "new journalists."

1170. Fuess, Claude M. *Carl Schurz, Reformer (1820-1906)*. New York: Dodd, 1932. Schurz, the liberal Chicago editor, was the "self-constituted incarnation of the national conscience" from the 1860s until his death in 1906. One of his main concerns was civil service reform. Generally independent in politics, he nevertheless was active in the Liberal Republican movement.

1171. Goodrich, Lloyd. "Thomas Nast." *AGR* 1 (March 1935): 12-16, 55.

1172. Hall, Mark W. "The San Francisco *Chronicle*: Its Fight for the 1879 Constitution." *JQ* 46 (1969): 505-10. With the adoption of the California constitution, "[t]he final victory in the ten-year struggle of California's working classes against the corrupt practices of the state's industrial, agricultural and transportation giants can be directly attributed to the vigorous efforts of California's leading 19th century newspaper -- the San Francisco *Chronicle*." (505)

1173. Harrison, John M. "David Ross Locke and the Fight on Reconstruction." *JQ* 39 (1962): 491-99. In the Republican debate over Reconstruction policies, Locke -- in the guise of "Petroleum V. Nasby" -- sided with the moderate approach of President Andrew Johnson. It was not until later, after 1866, that he became an outspoken radical.

1174. Harrison, John M. *The Man Who Made Nasby, David Ross Locke*. Chapel Hill: University of North Carolina Press, 1969. Locke created the "Petroleum V. Nasby" character and column in 1860. They reached maturity during Locke's editorship of the Toledo *Blade* after 1865. Nasby was a staunch opponent of slavery, alcohol, and Democrats. He advocated "the rights of man," public education, and Reconstruction policies. Locke was a "significant American writer, editor and publisher."

1175. Hart, Jack R. "Horatio Alger in the Newsroom: Social Origins of American Editors." *JQ* 53 (1976): 14-20. Editors of the largest newspapers during 1875-1900 were comparable in origin to executives in other major industries; they were from the business class, forming a socio-economic elite. The trend toward these types of individuals increased over the period.

1176. Holbo, Paul S. *Tarnished Expansion: The Alaska Scandal, the Press and Congress, 1867-1871*. Knoxville: University of Tennessee Press, 1983. Newspapers published sensational reports, dubious allegations, and details of investigations during the controversy over the United States' acquisition of Alaska.

1177. Hower, Ralph M. *The History of an Advertising Agency: N.W. Ayer & Sons at Work 1869-1939*. Cambridge, Mass.: Harvard University Press, 1939. Institutional, business history of a company, whose founder, Francis Wayand Ayer, typified the 19th-century success story: beginning with no money, he worked hard and used good judgment to build an enterprise.

1178. Kaplan, Sidney. "Harvard and the Influence of Godkin's *Nation*." *JQ* 40 (1963): 599-602. Educators made up a large part of the *Nation's* readership, including those at Harvard. Much of the *Nation's* content was contributed by or influenced by

Harvard professors. It generally was liberal, but Godkin believed the *Nation* had less influence on America (despite the fact that more Americans were becoming college graduates) than did millionaires. The Harvard connection was largely responsible for the *Nation's* influence.

1179. Keller, Morton. *The Art and Politics of Thomas Nast.* New York: Oxford University Press, 1968. Nast was a liberal/radical social reform thinker. However, his attacks on Tammany Hall and Tweed may have been spurred also by his anti-Catholicism. His great theme was the "interplay of men and issues that make up the flow of party controversy."

1180. Kielbowicz, Richard B. "Growing Interaction of the Federal Bureaucracy and the Press: The Case of a Postal Rule, 1879-1917." *AJ* 4 (1987): 5-18. In the last quarter of the 19th century, the Post Office Department began to impinge on the newspaper business through its various regulations concerning the second-class mail category.

1181. Kielbowicz, Richard Burket. "Origins of the Second-Class Mail Category and the Business of Policymaking, 1863-1879." *JM* 96 (1986). "The 1879 law was the product of certain concerns about public policy, especially the role of the government in fostering the dissemination of information....[Some of its features] also reflected some of the currents shaping the modern publishing industry, notably the growing importance of magazines and an increasing competition for advertising. There were inklings of...'political capitalism' -- business interests promoting selected federal regulations to cripple rising competition. The law, too, represented a growing autonomy on the part of the federal bureaucracy, in this case the biggest unit of all, the U.S. Post Office Department. Between 1863 and 1879, professional post office administrators steadily insinuated themselves into the policymaking process that had once been the realm of Congress." (2)

1182. Knaufft, Ernest. "Thomas Nast." *ARR* 27 (January 1903): 31-35. Memorial essay on the occasion of Nast's death relates the details of his career and artistic techniques.

1183. Knights, Peter R. "'Competition' in the U.S. Daily Newspaper Industry, 1865-68." *JQ* 45 (1968): 473-80. "Within the framework of a changing economy, the daily newspaper industry also changed. Among the trends...were a marked western growth of dailies (following population shifts), tendencies toward political 'independence,' evening publication, and changed competitive conditions....[T]he trend toward political 'independence,' through its effects on local competitive situations, may well have contributed substantially to the decline of daily competition with us today." (473)

1184. Knights, Peter R. "The Press Association War of 1866-1867." *JM* 6 (1967). Dissatisfied with the New York Press Association's control of telegraph news, Midwest publishers established a new agency. The two agencies "fought one another until an overburdened telegraph company forced peace upon them." (2) Study of the economic and technological factors involved in the competition.

1185. Kocher, Douglas J. "Temporary Vilification: The Chicago Press and Chester Arthur, 1881." *JH* 9 (1982): 53-55, 60. In the wake of President James Garfield's assassination, Chicago newspapers for a brief time ridiculed his successor, Arthur. Soon, however, he had turned around public and press opinion and received editorial support.

1186. Krieling, Albert. "The Rise of the Black Press in Chicago." *JH* 4 (1977): 132-36, 156. From 1874 to the late 1890s, "in the tumultuous currents of an industrializing society, blacks like other Americans were forging modern patterns of life and thought which received expression in new publiations." The black newspapers that "appeared to serve the small but growing middle-class populations of urban black communities...served as organs of news and commentary for the growing fabric of middle-class social and political life." (132)

1187. Krock, Arthur, ed. *The Editorials of Henry Watterson*. New York: Doran, 1923. Anthology of editorials by the editor of the Louisville *Courier-Journal*.

1188. Leiter, Kelly. "A President and One Newspaper: U.S. Grant and the Chicago *Tribune*." *JQ* 47 (1970): 71-80. The *Tribune* had been an enthusiastic supporter of Grant since his Civil War exploits. As President, however, Grant displayed his limited experience in dealing with other people, sometimes ignoring the *Tribune's* advice and making mistakes which incensed the *Tribune*. The paper viewed Grant as an incapable President and withdrew its support from him.

1189. Locke, David Ross. *The Nasby Letters*. Toledo, Ohio: Toledo Blade, 1893. Collection of the Locke's writings as "Petroleum V. Nasby."

1190. Locke, David Ross. *The Struggles of Petroleum V. Nasby*. Boston: I.N. Richardson, 1872. Collection of columns by the humorist.

1191. Logan, Lena. "Henry Watterson, the Border Nationalist." Ph.D. dissertation, Indiana University, 1942. Study of Watterson's role during Reconstruction.

1192. Logsdon, Joseph. *Horace White, Nineteenth Century Liberal*. Westport, Conn.: Greenwood, 1971.

    White (of the Chicago *Tribune*, New York *Evening Post, Nation*) was a reform-minded, liberal Republican, but by the 1890s he could not change with the times. Primarily interested in monetary policy, he was not an original thinker. His liberal views had become outmolded and even conservative by 1900.

1194. Lynn, Kenneth S. *William Dean Howells: An American Life*. New York: Harcourt Brace Jovanovich, 1971. Literary biography of the magazine editor and novelist whose earliest career was briefly in newspapers.

1195. Marcosson, Isaac. *Marse Henry: A Biography of Henry Watterson*. New York: Dodd, Mead, 1951. Detailed chronological biography of the Louisville editor and noted editorial writer. Watterson was a colorful "personal" editor.

1196. Masel-Walters, Lynne. "A Burning Cloud by Day: The History and Content of the 'Women's Journal.'" *JH* 3 (1977): 103-10. Favorable feminist history of the publication (1870-1914) aimed at elevating the status of women. It had "a high purpose, filled with a sense of moral duty and a devotion to the cause of feminine advancement. It was a purpose one would expect of a newspaper published by two such committed moralists and feminists as Henry B. Blackwell and his wife, Lucy Stone." (103)

1197. Masel-Walters, Lynne. "Their Rights and Nothing More: A History of *The*

Revolution, 1868-70." *JQ* 53 (1976): 242-51. "The first major national publication concerned with feminine equality, *The Revolution* championed not only voting rights but women's rights in general. It was also the most loyal to the cause." (242) It "set down for the first time in a major national forum arguments for women's equality that are still being used." (251)

1198. Mathews, Joseph F. *George Washburn Smalley: Forty Years a Foreign Correspondent*. Chapel Hill: University of North Carolina Press, 1973. Smalley, a New York *Tribune* correspondent (1867-1895) and London *Times* correspondent (1895-1906), was esteemed highly as a journalist and had access to many people in high places. He was closely involved with his subjects, wrote epistles primarily rather than straight reports, believed he should make his own editorial judgments, and prided himself in not conforming with the viewpoints of his papers.

1199. Maurice, Arthur B. "Thomas Nast and His Cartoons." *Bookman* 15 (1902): 19-25. Nast was America's preeminent caricaturist. On public issues, he had keen sympathies and antagonisms.

1200. Maushart, Susan. "Self-reflexiveness and the Institution of Journalism." *Et cetera* 43 (1986): 272-78. In the 1860s and 1870s, the American press, as evidenced by the New York *Times*, began to reflect on its own behavior, marking the "birthday of the modern newspaper." (273) Such self-awareness "reveals both the restlessness and the idealism of an adolescent institution: an increasingly unwieldy content in search of a form, a fledgling philosophy in search of worthy adherents, an expanding consciousness in search of ethical behavior." (278)

1201. McJimsey, George. *Genteel Partisan: Manton Marble, 1834-1917*. Ames: Iowa State University Press, 1971. Biography based on the theme of the conflicts between a man's principles, the ways he finds to implement those principles, and his personal ambitions. Marble went into politics because of the opportunities it offered for ambitious, native born, old stock Americans. He approached it with relish. An advocate of Spencerian social ideas, he characterized himself as a "merchant of news" and changed the *World's* orientation from religion to sensationalism. As the American press moved in its transition to the modern press, Marble found himself being moved toward the masses despite himself.

1202. McKerns, Joseph Patrick. "Benjamin Perley Poore of the *Boston Journal*: His Life and Times as a Washington Correspondent, 1850-1887." Ph.D. dissertation, University of Minnesota, 1979. Poore's "career embraced a period in which Washington reporting evolved from an informal system of letter-writers to the beginning of the formal, institutionalized system of today. Therefore, this study also examines the changing press-government relationship during his career." Despite the growth of the penny press, "the press remained close ideologically to political parties."

1203. Miller, Aaron. "The Paradoxical Godkin, Founder of *The Nation*." JQ 42 (1965): 198-202. Liberal-progressive interpretation of Godkin: although Godkin was a reform-minded liberal in the industrial age, the times caught up with him and he could not change as new conditions demanded liberal answers. He became a reactionary. His politcal-economic views proved unrealistic and unworkable as conditions changed.

1204. Mitchell, Edward P. "Mr. Dana of 'The Sun.'" *McClure's Magazine* 3 (October

1894): 374-94. Personalized essay by Dana's associate describing the attitudes and work habits of "the most famous, if not the greatest, editor that English journalism has known." (374)

1205. Mitchell, Edward P. "The Newspaper Man's Newspaper." *Scribner's* (August 1924): 149-62. Memoirs of a former New York *Sun* editor giving a laudatory picture of the paper and Dana.

1206. Munday, Eugene. "Historical Sketch of the Public Ledger of Philadelphia." Supplement to the Philadelphia *Public Ledger* (July 1870).

1207. Murray, James G. "Edwin Lawrence Godkin and *The Nation*: A Study in Political, Economic and Social Morality." Ph.D. dissertation, New York University, 1954.

1208. Murray, Randall L. "Edwin Lawrence Godkin: Unbending Editor in Times of Change." *JH* 1 (1974): 77-81, 89.

1209. Murrell, William. "Nast, Gladiator of the Political Pencil." *ASc* 5 (1936): 472-85. Nast was the "most outstanding figure in American graphic history...the only American artist who has made himself a political force solely through his drawings....He was a born crusader" during a period when political effectiveness derived from "his driving power, his capacity for indignation and hate, and the bitterness and savagery of his attack." (472) He "was at his best amid turmoil and conflict, in times when men's passions were aroused over political and moral issues." (484)

1210. Nelson, William Rockhill. *The Story of a Man, a Newspaper, and a City*. Kansas City, 1915. Autobiography of the founder of the Kansas City *Star*.

1211. Neuman, Fred G. *Irvin S. Cobb: His Life and Achievements*. Paducah, Ky.: Young, 1934. Admiring biography of the newspaper humor columnist written by a friend.

1212. Nevins, Allan. "E. L. Godkin: Victorian Liberal." *Nation* (July 22, 1950): 76-79. In post-Civil War America, the editor of the *Nation* was a decisive influence on public affairs. "His object was to apply...broad reform principles to American affairs....He seized his opportunity as no other man in the country could have done." (76)

1213. O'Connor, Richard. *The Scandalous Mr. Bennett*. New York: Doubleday, 1962. Popularized, colorful biography of James Gordon Bennett, Jr., owner of the New York *Herald*. Its purpose is not "to assess his contributions to the American newspaper" or any professional accomplishments, but instead to focus on his eccentric behavior.

1214. O'Dell, DeForest. *The History of Journalism Education in the United States*. New York: Teachers College, Columbia University, 1935. Error-filled book which provides weak evidence for its thesis. "Professional education in journalism came into being in the United States in 1869 as the result of the thrity-nine year conflict between the American social order and the Penny Press. Journalism came into being in response to a social need."

1215. Ogden, Rollo, ed. *Life and Letters of Edwin Lawrence Godkin*, 2 vols. New York: Macmillan, 1907. Biography and collection of correspondence. Godkin loved justice and honesty and wrote with acumen and forceful expression. He was intelligent and scholarly, but also could be irritable, extremely individualistic, and overly proud of his British background and culture. Volume two deals with his editorship of the *Nation* and New York *Evening Post*.

1216. Olasky, Marvin. "Opposing Abortion Clinics: A New York *Times* 1871 Crusade." *JQ* 63 (1986): 305-10, 321. The *Times'* successful crusade against abortion "probably had greater long-range social consequence" than its crusade against the Tweed ring. Against illegal abortion practices, the *Times* used "similar elements of sensation, detective work, and courage in the face of opposition from wealth and power" (305) as it had used in the Tweed crusade.

1217. Oliphant, Charles Ashur. "Seventh-day Adventist Publishing and Ellen G. White's Journalistic Principles." Ph.D. dissertation, University of Iowa, 1968. "As co-founder of the Seventh-day Adventist denomination in 1863, Ellen G. White (1827-1915) exerted...a powerful influence, largely through her writings, on the development of many of the church's institutions, among them its system of 44 publishing houses now producing publications in 378 languages throughout the world....[However, her] philosophy of journalism has little impact on Seventh-Day Adventist publishing today."

1218. Paine, Albert Bigelow. *Thomas Nast, His Period and His Pictures*. New York: Macmillan, 1904. Nast was the "father of American caricature." He possessed true artistic ability along with a conviction that his primary goal should be the moral and political advancement of America and her people. "There is a divine heritage which rises above class drill and curriculum -- a God-given impulse which will seek instinctively and find surely the means to enter and the way to conquer and possess the foreordained kingdom. Such a genius was that of Thomas Nast."

1219. Pauly, John J. "The Great Chicago Fire as a National Event." *AQ* 36 (1984): 668-83. Through press accounts, Americans learned about the fire of 1871, and it came to serve as a symbolic rallying point, assuring them that national unity was possible even in an industrialized society.

1220. Peterson, Paul V. "The Chicago Daily Herald: Righting the Historical Record." *JQ* (1970): 697-701, 710. Despite Melville Stone's contention (in *Fifty Years A Journalist*), the *Daily Herald* was founded in 1873 (not 1874) and was committed to permanency.

1221. Phelan, Mary Cortona. *Manton Marble of the New York World*. Washington: Catholic University of America Press, 1957. Brief biography and narrative of Marble's ownership of the *World* from 1862 to 1874, written originally as a doctoral dissertation. During the Civil War, he was the intellectual leader of the northern Democrats and influenced their thinking on moderate Reconstruction policies.

1222. Plummer, Leonard N. "The Political Leadership of Henry Watterson." Ph.D. dissertation, University of Wisconsin, 1940. Applies political science concepts in surveying Watterson's political activities.

1223. Rammelkamp, Julian S. *Pulitzer's Post-Dispatch, 1878-1883*. Princeton, N.J.: Princeton University Press, 1967. The St. Louis newspaper was both an innovator in journalistic methods and a profit-oriented business. It provided the medium through which Pulitzer experimented with the methods, the "new journalism," that he later took so successfully to the New York *World*. Although the *Post-Dispatch's* policies typified the period's "middle class reformism" -- appealing to the professional class's desire to improve civic and industrial conditions -- Pulitzer was "pre-eminently a businessman who happened to be in the business of journalism." While he was dedicated to crusading for reform, he also found that crusading, by attracting circulation, was good for his newspaper's business.

1224. Range, Jane, and Maris A Vinouskis. "Images of Elderly in Popular Magazines: A Content Analysis of Little's Living Age, 1845-1882." *SSH* 5 (Spring 1981): 123-70.

1225. Rogers, Charles E. "William Rockhill Nelson and His Editors of the Star." *JQ* 26 (1949): 15-19, 60. "The largest part of...Nelson's success with the Kansas City *Star* must be attributed to the *Star's* editorial appeal, and this reflected the exceptional ability of Nelson's editors and the editorial staff Nelson's policies attracted to his newspaper. What attracted able men to the *Star* and contributed to their growth on the staff...was the encouragement every man received from Nelson...to write with absolute freedom, unhampered save by the truth as he saw it." (15)

1226. Rogers, Charles Elkins. "William Rockhill Nelson: Independent Editor and Crusading Liberal." Ph.D. dissertation, University of Missouri, 1948.

1227. Rosebault, Charles J. *When Dana was the Sun; A Story of Personal Journalism*. Freeport, N.Y.: Books for Libraries Press/McBride, 1931. Idealized personal reminiscences of a member of the New York *Sun* staff telling the story of Dana's life both before and after he bought the newspaper.

1228. Ruegamer, Lana. *The Paradise of Exceptional Women: Chicago Women Reformers, 1863-1893*. Ann Arbor, Mich.: University Microfilms, 1985. Includes Mary Livermore, a newspaper editor; and Myra Bradwell, publisher of the Chicago *Legal News*.

1229. Schaaf, Barbara C. *Mr. Dooley's America*. New York: Anchor Press/Doubleday, 1977. In the 1890s, Finley Peter Dunne was a perceptive social critic with a rare talent for humor. He was "[f]irmly fixed in the urban environment and influenced by it. More than a quintessential Chicagoan, Dooley was a quintessential urbanite, who drew his examples, ancedotes, and knowledge from city surroundings." Unlike earlier humorists who expressed a rural point of view, Dunne appealed to an audience in an urbanized, industrialized America. Emphasizes Dooley's relationships to the development of Chicago, which was representative of the urban development of America.

1230. Schmidt, Royal J. "The Chicago Daily News and Illinois Politics, 1876-1920." Ph.D. dissertation, University of Chicago, 1957.

1231. Schwartz, Michael. "Did Stanley Really Find Livingstone?" *MHD* 1, 2 (1981): 2-11, 36. "Stanley found Livingstone, but before receiving honors for his efforts, he became embroiled in a humiliating debate. He was branded a liar, an opportunist, and a thief." (2) The fact that an American found Livingstone wounded British pride.

1232. Sim, John Cameron. "19th Century Applications of Suburban Newspaper Concepts." *JQ* (1975): 627-31. "[T]he concepts of central plant publishing, of a group of newspapers all substantially the same except for one or more local news pages, and of promotion of the special merits of a suburb as an audience for advertising, now so

closely identified with the suburban press,...came into extensive use in the 1870s."
(627)

1233. Smith, David C. "Wood Pulp and Newspapers, 1867-1900." *BHR* 38 (Autumn
1964): 328-45.

1234. Smith, Henry Justin. *A Gallery of Chicago Editors*. Chicago: Daily News, 1930.
Twenty-page pamphlet with brief biographies of Chicago journalists.

1235. Smythe, Ted Curtis. "The Advertisers' War to Verify Newspaper Circulation, 1870-
1914." *AJ* 3 (1986): 167-180. Beginning in the 1870s, advertisers and advertising
agencies "worked together to force publishers to provide circulation figures, then to
provide *accurate* and *meaningful* circulation figures....[They] also sought equitable
advertising rates." (167) Their efforts culminated in the founding of the Audit Bureau
of Circulations in 1914.

1236. Steiner, Linda. "Finding Community in Nineteenth Century Suffrage Periodicals." *AJ*
1, 1 (1983): 1-15. In the 1850s to early 1870s, "suffrage papers persuasively illustrated alternative versions of a satisfying life style for women and brought suffragists
into a new and exhilarating world in which their lives had special purpose and meaning." (12)

1237. Steiner, Linda. "The Woman's Suffrage Press, 1850-1900: A Cultural Analysis."
Ph.D. dissertation, University of Illinois, 1979.

Suffrage periodicals were "the arenas in which groups of middle class women created
and celebrated new definitions of womanhood and new styles of life for themselves
which would be appropriate for the new world in which they found themselves and
which would restore to their lives a sense of dignity and significance."

1238. Stevens, Walter B. "Joseph B. McCullagh." *MHR* 25-28 (October 1930-April 1934).
Fifteen-article biography of the "cabin boy, printer, reporter, war correspondent,
Washington journalist" who served for twenty-five years (1872-1897) as the managing editor of the St. Louis *Globe-Democrat*. While he ran the paper free from all outside influence, his policy and methods did more than build a great newspaper. They
helped build the prestige and regional commerical influence of St. Louis.

1239. Stevenson, Elizabeth. *Lafcadio Hearn*. New York: Macmillan, 1961. Detailed, well
documented literary biography of the editorial writer who became famous as a fiction
writer after moving to Japan.

1240. Stevenson, Robert L. "Readability of Conservative and Sensational Papers Since
1872." *JQ* 41 (1964): 201-06. Newspapers in 1960 were not much more readable
than they were in 1872.

1241. Stone, Candace. *Dana and the Sun*. New York: Dodd, Mead: 1938. Biography emphasizing Dana's editorial comment and his role in politics and public affairs. He was
brilliant but inconsistent, his writing fresh, witty, and pungent.

1242. Taft, William H. "David Ross Locke: Forgotten Editor." *JQ* 34 (1957): 202-07.
Chronological, narrative biography whose goal is to bring to light the journalistic career, primarily in Ohio from the 1850s to 1888, of the editor better known for his

literary efforts as "Petroleum V. Nasby."

1243. Thorn, William J. "Hudson's History of Journalism Criticized by His Contemporaries." *JQ* 57 (1980): 99-106. Based on an analysis of newspaper reaction to Frederic Hudson's 1873 journalism history book, Thorn concludes that newspapers' role in promoting democracy was more important than its function of providing news, as Hudson claimed.

1244. Thorn, William J. "Montgomery Schuyler: The Newspaper Architectural Articles of a Protomodern Critic (1868-1907)." Ph.D. dissertation, University of Minnesota, 1976. Schuyler, who worked for the New York *World*, 1865-1883, was an outspoken and perceptive critic of architecture.

1245. Thorp, Robert K. "Marse Henry and the Negro: A New Perspective." *JQ* 46 (1969): 467-74. Although Watterson considered himself an advocate of the rights and equality of blacks, his editorials of 1868-1872 indicate that he was paternalistic and believed the black was inferior. Although, compared to other southern Democrats, he was a friend to the Negro, he actually fought Negro suffrage, civil rights, and the idea of blacks holding office.

1246. Vinson, J. Chal. *Thomas Nast: Political Cartoonist*. Athens: University of Georgia Press, 1967. Mechanical biography of America's first major though intensely partisan newspaper cartoonist, well illustrated with Nast's drawings.

1247. Wall, Joseph F. *Henry Watterson: Reconstructed Rebel* New York: Oxford University Press, 1956. Watterson was influential, well-known, and colorful. He enjoyed editorial wars for causes. He believed in personal journalism and was deeply interested in politics.

1248. Watterson, Henry. *Marse Henry*. New York: Doran, 1919. Autobiography of the editor of the Louisville *Courier-Journal*.

1249. Weitenkampf, Frank. "Thomas Nast -- Artist in Caricature." *NYPLB* 37 (1933): 770-74. Nast's ability indicated he was more than a political caricaturist; he was also a creative, accomplished artist.

1250. "What Made 'Marse Henry' Watterson Great." (Anonymous; reprinted from *The Ohio Newspaper*, May 1927); *JQ* 3 (1926): 69-72. Watterson practiced personal journalism. "The newspaper is not a commodity....It should be...a keeper of the public conscience, its rating professional, like the ministry and the law, not commercial, like the department store and the bucketshop. Its workers should be gentlemen, not eavesdroppers and scavengers." (72)

1251. White, William. "Whitman on Newspaper Practices in the 1870s." *JQ* 37 (1960): 438-39. Short comment by Whitman on fabricated quotes.

1252. Williams, Gilbert Anthony. "The *A.M.E. Christian Recorder*: A Forum for the Social Ideas of Black Americans, 1854-1902." Ph.D. dissertation, University of Illinois, 1979. History of the oldest continuously published black newspaper in the United States, focusing on the Reconstruction era, when "economic forces were the main causal factors in determining the course of events."

9

The Age of New Journalism, 1883–1900

1253. Abrams, Jeanne. "Remembering the Maine: The Jewish Attitude Toward the Spanish-American War as Reflected in the *American Israelite*." *AJH* 76 (1987): 439-55. Along with the arguments for the war which most American newspapers made, the *American Israelite*. added issues that were of special interest to Jews. The war also offered editor Isaac Wise an opportunity to emphasize American Jews' patriotism and integration into American society.

1254. Allen, Douglas. *Frederic Remington and the Spanish-American War*. New York: Crown, 1971. Lavishly illustrated picture-book biography of the illustrator for Hearst.

1255. Annenberg, Maurice, comp. *A Typographical Journey Through the Inland Printer 1839-1900*. Baltimore: Maran, 1977. Collection of articles on typography and printing reprinted from the trade journal *Inland Printer*.

1256. Ashley, Perry J., ed. *American Newspaper Journalists 1873-1900*. Detroit: Gale Research Company, 1983. Collection of biographies by various authors.

1257. Auxier, G.W. "Middle Western Newspapers and the Spanish-American War, 1895-1898." *MVHR* 26 (1940): 523-34. Analysis questions historians' claim that yellow journalism precipitated the war, for that claim relies on the assumption that yellow journalism was "universally imitated by the newspapers throughout the 'entire' United States." (523) Middlewestern newspapers did not all adopt the jingoistic journalism of Pulitzer and Hearst.

1258. Barrett, James W. *Joseph Pulitzer and His World.* New York: Vanguard, 1941. Barrett, last city editor of the *World*, viewed the paper idealistically. Pulitzer's heart was in the editorial page, and he commanded that it lead public opinion. His passion was politics "in the sense of liberty and freedom and ideals of justice." He tried to make the *World* into an agent for fighting the enemies of society.

1259. Batlin, Robert. "San Francisco Newspapers' Campaign Coverage: 1896, 1952." *JQ* 31 (1954): 297-303. Content analysis shows that in 1952 newspapers gave more nearly equal news coverage to the main presidential candidates than in 1896, but still gave editorial preference to the candidate they supported.

1260. Beisner, Robert L. *Twelve Against Empire: The Anti-Imperialists, 1898-1900.* New York: McGraw-Hill, 1968. An analysis, sometimes contradictory, of the "ideas, sentiments and prejudices" of prominent Americans who were opposed to expansion. Journalists E.L. Godkin and Carl Schurz were among them.

1261. Bennion, Sherilyn. "Fremont Older: Advocate for Women." *JH* 3 (1976): 124-27. Older treated women as equals and employed them as reporters.

1262. Berg, Meredith, and David Berg. "The Rhetoric of War Preparation: The New York Press in 1898." *JQ* 45 (1968): 653-60. In the "process of psychological preparation for war...the mass media, and particularly the newspaper, have assumed a major role." Although it is impossible to determine the exact influence that the New York press had in preparing the public for the Spanish-American War (or bringing about the war), there was "a powerful linkage between the press and the people."

1263. Bierce, Ambrose. *Skepticism and Dissent: Selected Journalism from 1898-1901.* Lawrence I. Berkove, ed. Ann Arbor: UMI Research Press, 1980. Collection of 70 articles, many dealing with the Spanish-American War, which Bierce wrote for Hearst's San Francisco *Examiner* and New York *Journal.*

1264. Birkhead, Douglas. "The Power in the Image: Professionalism and the Communications Revolution." *AJ* 1, 2 (1984): 1-14. "The professionalization of journalism [1890-1911] was more than a movement among journalists for occupational identity and prestige. It was a comprehensive social project of reinterpretation, in large part an ideological solution to a crisis of image for the press in the wake of industrialization." (1-2)

1265. Bond, F. Fraser. *Mr. Miller of "The Times," The Story of an Editor.* New York: Scribner's, 1931. Charles R. Miller, editor-in-chief of the New York *Times* from 1883 to 1922, was a man of ideals, ability, and character who exercised a great influence on the *Times* despite the fact that it was a business run by a corporation.

1266. Bradshaw, James Stanford. "The 'Detroit Free Press' in England." *JH* 5 (1978): 4-7. From 1881 to 1899 the *Free Press* published a successful weekly humor/feature paper in London, the first time an American paper had published a British edition.

1267. Bradshaw, James Stanford. "Mrs. Rayne's School of Journalism." *JQ* 60 (1983): 513-17, 579. In 1886 in Detroit, Martha Louise Rayne began giving instruction in journalism for women, the "first 'school' of journalism in the country." (513)

1268. Brooker-Gross, Susan R. "Timeliness: Interpretations from a Sample of 19th

Century Newspapers." *JQ* 58 (1981): 594-98. Analysis of newspaper news content in 1839 and 1899 shows that coverage of foreign news became more timely, while timeliness of local news coverage increased only slightly.

1269. Brown, Charles B. "A Woman's Odyssey: The War Correspondence of Anna Benjamin." *JQ* 46 (1969): 522-30. Benjamin, who covered the Spanish-American War, was an "extraordinary young woman--one of the first of a not very long line of notable women war and foreign correspondents." (530)

1270. Brown, Charles H. *The Correspondents' War* . New York: Scribner's, 1967. The Spanish-American War was a convenient one for reporters to cover. Reporters were a self-important bunch and sometimes fought in battles as well as reported them. The war was not produced by Hearst, as some contemporaries and historians claimed, since the press did not have enough power to start a war.

1271. Brown, Charles H. "Press Censorship in the Spanish-American War." *JQ* 42 (1965): 581-90. Censorship was more extensive and effective than historians have assumed, but the press was careless in reporting troop and ship movements. Although the system of censorship was bumbling, censorship was applied. In a major war, uncensored information could have been dangerous.

1272. Carlisle, Rodney P. "William Randolph Hearst: A Fascist Reputation Reconsidered. *JQ* 50 (1973): 125-33. Over time, from the 1890s to the mid-20th century, there was little change in Hearst's "views, which continued to reflect turn-of-the-century Progressivism." In the 1930s he seemed reactionary because the early "Progressivism was based on values and ideas in some respects directly contradictory to those of the New Deal." (125)

1273. Carlson, Oliver. *Brisbane: A Candid Biography*. New York: Stackpole, 1937. Although his father was an idealist, Arthur Brisbane saw the realities of the world; and he preferred the esteem of businessmen and material acquisitions to inner satisfaction. He was mediocre as a journalist, although important in his time. He wrote his own but usually Hearst's opinion. He was erudite and well educated, but his reading was limited to 17th and 18th century writers and it reflected outmoded concepts in science, history, and philosophy. He also had tremendous energy and was dominating and aggressive.

1274. Carlson, Oliver, and Ernest Bates. *Hearst, Lord of Sam Simeon*. New York: Viking, 1936. Analysis of the social and personal impulses behind Hearst's journalism career. He was a megalomaniac (whose inferiority complex caused him to search for personal powers) and an opportunist. His family background was an important influence in his own life. His relentless ambitions caused inconsistencies in his thinking and action.

1275. Chambers, Henry Kellett, with an introduction by Lawrence Pratt. "A Park Row Interlude: Memoirs of Albert Pulitzer." *JQ* 40 (1963): 539-47. Albert, Joseph Pulitzer's brother, founded the *New York Morning Journal* and made it successful with sensational techniques. This article is an edited version of an account written by one of the *Morning Journal's* reporters.

1276. Churchill, Allen. *Park Row*. New York: Rinehart, 1958. Entertaining, popular history of the colorful era of personal journalism from the 1880s to the 1930s, beginning with Pulitzer through the demise of the *New York World.* Emphasis is on individuals and the yellow journalism competition between Pulitzer and Hearst.

1277. Cline, H.F. "Benjamin Orange Flower and the *Arena, 1889-1909.*" *JQ* 17 (1940): 139-50. Flower, the editor of the magazine, resisted "conventions in all fields" and disregarded "stricture and taboo." (139)

1278. Cline, H.F. "Flower and the *Arena*:: Purpose and Content." *JQ* 17 (1940): 247-57. Flower wanted to make the *Arena* (1889-) a quality magazine to serve as a vehicle for his progressive and radical views. He believed in liberty, justice, and happiness, although his ideas sometimes were sketchy.

1279. Coblentz, Edmond D., ed. *William Randolph Hearst, A Portrait in His Own Words.* New York: Simon & Schuster, 1952. Sympathetic biography based on Hearst's columns, letters, memoranda, and telegrams.

1280. Connery, Thomas. "Julian Ralph: Forgotten Master of Descriptive Detail." *AJ* 2 (1985): 165-73. The New York *Journal* reporter, although not as well known as some other reporters of the time, was an accomplished writer. Of particular note was his technique of providing "illustration to illuminate acts through...masterful use of descriptive detail." (172)

1281. Creelman, James. "Joseph Pulitzer--Master Journalist." *PeM* 21 (March 1909): 229-56. Tribute written by one of Pulitzer's reporters.

1282. Cudlipp, Hugh. *The Prerogative of the Harlot: Press Barons and Power.* London: Bodley Head, 1980. Focuses mainly on British publishers but is critical also of Hearst, who had a "predilection for evil....[Historians] still differ over whether he was a better character assassin than warmonger."

1283. Davis, Richard Harding. *Adventures and Letters of Richard Harding Davis.* Charles Belmont Davis, ed. New York: Scribner's, 1917. Collection of correspondence recounting the war reporter's adventures woven around a personal running narrative by his brother, C.B. Davis.

1284. Davis, Richard Harding. *The Notes of a War Correspondent..* New York: Scribner's, 1910. Sketches of military activities, 1890s-1910.

1285. Dickerson, Donna. "William Cowper Brann: Nineteenth Century Press Critic." *JH* 5 (1978): 42-45. Editor of the *Iconoclast* in Waco, Texas, Brann "emerged during the earliest years of the Yellow Press to challenge the changes being brought about by editors such as Joseph Pulitzer and William Randolph Hearst." (42)

1286. Doherty, Amy S. "Frances Benjamin Johnston, 1864-1952." *HP* 4, 2 (1980): 97-111. Johnston was a pioneer photojournalist in the 1890s.

1287. Dorwart, Jeffery M. "James Creelman, the *New York World* and the Port Arthur Massacre." *JQ* 50 (1973): 697-701. Creelman's coverage of the Sino-Japanese War foreshadowed the methods of sensational journalism used four years later in the Spanish-American War. His reports were gruesome and sensational. (Creelman was the only American correspondent able to cover the war.)

1288. Downey, Fairfax M. *Richard Harding Davis: His Day*. New York: Scribner's, 1933. Admiring narrative of the adventures of the colorful Davis as a reporter, war correspondent, and author until his death in 1916.

1289. Eberhard, Wallace B. "Clark Howell and the *Atlanta Constitution*: A Preliminary Assessment." *Resources in Education* 15 (October 1980).

1290. Emery, Edwin. "William Randolph Hearst: A Tentative Appraisal." *JQ* 28 (1951): 429-39. Considers pro and con arguments on Hearst's journalistic greatness. The tentative conclusion: little of excellence came from Hearst.

1291. Endres, Fred F. "The Pre-Muckraking Days of *McClure's* Magazine, 1893-1901." *JQ* 55 (1978): 154-57. Most of the magazine's articles dealt with "success," not reform.

1292. Erickson, John Edward. "Newspapers and Social Values: Chicago Journalism, 1890-1910." Ph.D. dissertation, University of Illinois, 1973. The press "was undergoing the same industrial growth and expansion characteristic of most of American life and earned a right to the title big business." With America undergoing vast social change, the press "both reported about and embraced a perspective involving value shifts in the areas of social identification, social change and social control."

1293. Everett, George. "The Linotype and U.S. Daily Newspaper Journalism in the 1890s: Analysis of a Relationship." Ph.D. dissertation, University of Iowa, 1972. Rather than determining how newspapers would operate, the Linotype machine permitted them to do things differently. It "(a) tended to neutralize the effects of the 1893 depression on newspapers..., (b) helped destandardize newspaper content, (c) cut composing costs sharply while bringing no great change in the per-hour rate of total composing room output, and (d) was not significantly more beneficial to evening than to morning papers."

1294. Fanning, Charles. *Finley Peter Dunne and Mr. Dooley: The Chicago Years*. Lexington: University Press of Kentucky, 1978. Biography covers the humorist prior to 1898, emphasizing the literary aspects of his writing.

1295. Flinn, Eugene C. "Ambrose Bierce and the Journalization of the American Short Story." Ph.D. dissertation, St. John's University-Brooklyn, 1954.

1296. Folkerts, Jean Lange. "William Allen White's Anti-Populist Rhetoric as an Agenda Setting Technique." *JQ* 60 (1983): 28-34. An attempt to examine the influence of the press by applying the theory of agenda setting historically.

1297. Francke, Warren. "An Argument in Defense of Sensationalism: Probing the Popular and Historiographical Concept." *JH* 5 (1978): 70-73. An attempt to define "sensationalism" for purposes of more accurate historical definition.

1298. Gatewood, Willard B., Jr. "Edward E. Cooper, Black Journalist." *JQ* 55 (1978): 269-75, 324. Narrative biography of the prominent, controversial editor of the *Colored American* from 1881 to 1908.

1299. Gatewood, Willard B., Jr. "A Negro Editor on Imperialism: John Mitchell, 1898-1901." *JQ* 49 (1972): 43-50, 60. Mitchell of the Richmond *Planet* opposed the

Spanish-American War, even though some blacks thought their support of the American effort would gain more respect for their race, because he believed support of the war was not an effective way to benefit blacks.

1300. Gilbert, David A. "Lucius C. Paddock: Voice Against the Thunder." *JQ* 49 (1972): 585-87. The publisher of the Boulder (Colo.) *Daily Camera*, a small-town newspaper, was a responsible, professional journalist and a voice of "idealism and purpose" during the age of sensationalism.

1301. Glass, William D. "Ignatius Donnelly: Populist Bigwig--Writer of the Weird." *MHD* 3, 1 (1983): 15-19. The spokesman of the Populist party in the 1890s was an editor, a humorist, and a book author.

1302. Goldman, Ralph M. "Stumping the Country: 'Rules of the Road' 1896." *JQ* 29 (1952): 303-06. Reprint of the text of a tongue-in-cheek statement of principles used by newspaper reporters covering the presidential campaign of William Jennings Bryan.

1303. Gordon, David. "The 1896 Maryland Shield Law: The American Roots of Evidentiary Privilege for Newsmen." *JM* 22 (1972). Antiquarian attempt to determine the events that led to passage of the law. Newspapers at the time showed little concern about or interest in the law.

1304. Gould, Lewis L., and Richard Greffe. *Photojournalist: The Career of Jimmy Hare*. Austin: University of Texas Press, 1978. Hare was one of the earliest photojournalists, beginning his career in the 1890s and the Spanish-American War and lasting through World War I. His photographs appeared primarily in *Leslie's Illustrated Newspaper* and *Collier's*. His approach was to show the harsh conditions of soldiers. This book includes about 100 of his photographs along with a short biography.

1305. Graham, Thomas S. "Charles H. Jones, 1848-1913: Editor and Progressive Democrat." Ph.D. dissertation, University of Florida, 1973. See following entries.

1306. Graham, Thomas. "Charles H. Jones: Florida's Gilded Age Editor-Politician." *FHQ* 59 (July 1980): 1-23. Jones was the preeminent Democratic editor in Florida in the 1880s and played a leading role in the party and state politics.

1306.1. Graham, Thomas. "Charles H. Jones of the *Post-Dispatch*: Pulitzer's Prize Headache." *JQ* 56 (1979): 788-93, 802. For two years, the volatile, opinionated, ambitious Jones maintained editorial control of the St. Louis newspaper despite the opposition of Pulitzer, its owner.

1306.2. Graham, Thomas. "Charles H. Jones: Spokesman for the Western Idea." *MHR* 75 (April 1981): 294-315. In St. Louis in the 1890s, Jones, editor of the *Republic* and *Post-Dispatch*, was a leading spokesman for the Populist movement, a Democratic party leader, and a "vigorous political operator." (295)

1307. Grenander, Mary Elizabeth. *Ambrose Bierce*. New York: Twayne, 1971.

1308. Halstead, Murat. "Early Editorial Experiences." *LMM* (June 1892): 710-15. Personal account by the energetic Cincinnati reporter-editor.

1309. Harris, Frank. *Presentation of Crime in Newspapers: A Study of Methods in Newspaper Research.*. Hanover, N.H.: Sociological Press, 1932. Study of three Minneapolis papers from 1890 to 1921 reveals that "[f]or approximately half a century, competing newspapers have relinquished the task of being moral guardians of the reading public. Among newspaper publishers the printing of crime news has been taken for granted."

1310. Heaton, John L. *The Story of a Page.* New York: Harper, 1913. Collection of editorials from the New York *World.*

1311. Henry, Susan. "'Dear Companion, Ever-Ready Co-Worker': A Woman's Role in a Media Dynasty." *JQ* 64 (1987): 301-12. Eliza Otis, wife of the owner of the Los Angeles *Times*, Harrison Gray Otis, was important in the family's operation of the paper because of the "family context" she provided and her work "behind-the-scenes." "[N]ewspaper dynasties...should not be examined simply as newspapers and businesses, but also most be studied as families." (312)

1311.1. Henry, Susan. "Reporting 'Deeply and at First Hand': Helen Campbell in the 19th-Century Slums." *JH* 11 (1984): 18-25. The author of an 1886 New York *Tribune* series entitled "Prisoners of Poverty" concerning the plight of women in the slums, Campbell was an accomplished writer and journalist who "became increasingly concerned with--and radicalized by--the problems of poor working women." (19)

1312. Holton, Milne. *Cylinder of Vision: The Fiction and Journalistic Writing of Stephen Crane.* Baton Rouge: Louisiana State University Press, 1972. Examines the approaches literary critics have taken to Crane's work. Focus primarily is on his fiction writing. Crane's characters are best understood as limited by their understanding of the incomprehensible universe.

1313. Howard-Pitney, David. "Calvin Chase's *Washington Bee* and Black Middle-Class Ideology, 1882-1900." *JQ* 63 (1986): 89-97. Chase's treatment of Booker T. Washington indicated that the *Bee's* black editor "was neither exclusively accommodationist nor protest-oriented, but a pragmatic blend of the two." Chase "exemplified the ideological flexibility and commitment with which middle-class black leaders pursued a shared goal and vision of Afro-American progress." (8)

1314. Hughes, David Y. "*The War of the Worlds* in the Yellow Press." *JQ* 43 (1966): 639-46. The New York *Journal* and Boston *Post* serialized the "War of the Worlds" in 1898. Running fiction was not far different from their fictionalizing news. The papers were irresponsible in their attitudes toward H.G. Welles' ownership of the work.

1315. Ireland, Alleyne. *An Adventure with a Genius: Recollections of Joseph Pulitzer.* New York: Dutton, 1914. Personal portrait of Pulitzer during his years of blindness written by one of his secretaries. See next entry.

1315.1. Ireland, Alleyne. *Joseph Pulitzer: Reminiscences of a Secretary* . New York: Kennerley/Dutton, 1914. Pulitzer was "one of the most vigorous, picturesque, and original personalities that ever played a part in the interesting drama of American public life....[D]eep affection, keen intelligence, wide sympathy, tireless energy, delicate sensitiveness, tearing impatience, cold tyranny and flaming scorn" dominated his personality.

1316. John, Arthur. *The Best Years of the Century: Richard Watson Gilder, Scribner's Monthly and Century Magazine, 1870-1909* . Urbana: University of Illinois Press, 1981.

1317. Johns, George S. *Joseph Pulitzer: His Early Life in St. Louis and His Founding and Conduct of the Post-Dispatch up to 1883*. Reprint of six articles from *MHR* (1931-1932). St. Louis: 1932. Adulatory biography by a long-time editor of the *Post-Dispatch*. Pulitzer developed a new form of journalism, combining the superior news techniques of James Gordon Bennett with the courageous, crusading, influential, enlightened editorial approach of Horace Greeley.

1318. Johnson, Icie. F. *William Rockhill Nelson and the Kansas City Star*. Kansas City, Mo.: Burton, 1935. As owner-editor of the *Star*, Nelson devoted himself and his paper to the improvement of Kansas City, and he was the premier reason for the town's progress from a small pioneer town to a metropolis. "He found his city in mud, and he left it in marble." Chronological account focuses on 1880-1915.

1319. Juergens, George. *Joseph Pulitzer and the New York World*. Princeton, N.J.: Princeton University Press, 1966. The *World* was the birth of the modern newspaper, including such areas as illustrations, headlines, newspaper appearances, sports, women's news, sensationalized features, crusaders, concern for poor and workers. The sensationalism of the Spanish-American War was just an aberration from normal practice.

1320. Kahan, Robert S. "The Antecedants of American Photojournalism." Ph.D. dissertation, University of Wisconsin, 1969. "[T]he growth of photojournalism [beginning with the daguerreotype in 1839 through its wide use after 1881, when a photograph was first published in an American magazine] was closely related to technological change both in photography and in the mass media....[C]oncepts of photography as a communication medium held by photographers and editorial personnel were formidable factors in influencing the emergence of photojournalism."

1321. King, Homer W. *Pulitzer's Prize Editor: A Biography of John A. Cockerill, 1845-1896*. Durham, N.C.: Duke University Press, 1965. Cockerill, as the managing editor of the New York *World* from 1883 to 1891, was the true originator of Pulitzer's "New Journalism."

1322. Knox, George L. *Slave and Freeman: The Autobiography of George L. Knox*. Willard B. Gatewood, ed. Lexington: University of Kentucky Press, 1979. Sold as a slave at age three, Knox eventually purchased the Indianapolis (Ind.) *Freeman* in 1892.

1323. Kobre, Sidney. *The Yellow Press and Gilded Age Journalism*. Tallahassee: Florida State University Press, 1964. During the Gilded Age, America went through the transition from an agricultural to an industrial society. The press not only mirrored the change but was a part of it. American journalism changed from one of personal journalism to an industry marked by mechanization, urbanization, centralization, and standardization.

1324. Langford, Gerald. *The Richard Harding Davis Years*. New York: Holt, 1961. Intertwined biographies of the great war correspondent and his mother, a novelist to whom the son was closely attached.

1325. Leach, Frank A. *Recollections of a Newspaper Man.* San Francisco: S. Levinson, 1917.

1326. Littlefield, Roy Everette, III. *William Randolph Hearst: His Role in American Progressivism.* Boston: University Press of America 1980.

1327. Lundberg, Ferdinand. *Imperial Hearst: A Social Biography.* New York: Equinox Cooperative Press, 1936. A critical biography analysizing Hearst's financial empire and economic methods. Hearst was unscrupulous in his financial dealings, and his financial interests influenced his journalism and editorial stands.

1328. Mander, Mary. "Pen and Sword: Problems of Reporting the Spanish-American War." *JH* 9 (1982): 2-9, 28. Historical treatment of yellow journalism and reportage of the Spanish-American War has been colored by preconceptions and stereotypes. In reality, war correspondents faced "extensive problems" in trying "to report accurately." (8) They were serious and practical in doing their job and believed in trying to obtain the facts rather than reporting fanciful versions of the war.

1329. Mangelsdorf, Philip. "When William Allen White and Ed Howe Covered the Republicans." *JQ* 44 (1967): 454-60. Anecdotal narrative of White's and Howe's coverage of the 1896 national convention.

1330. Mann, Russell Arthur. "Investigative Journalism in the Gilded Age: A Study of the Detective Journalism of Melville E. Stone and the *Chicago Morning News*, 1881-1888." Ph.D. dissertation, Southern Illinois University, 1977. "Detective journalism" had these features: "1) investigation of wrongdoing; 2) expose`; 3) assistance in prosecution; 4) promotion of efforts aimed at prevention of a repetition of the wrongdoing; and 5) assistance in mitigating sentences of wrongdoers willing to admit their error and express their sorrow."

1331. Marks, George. *The Black Press Views American Imperialism (1898-1900).* New York: 1933. The American black press identified with colored people around the world and protested American imperialistic exploitation of them.

1332. McGlashan, Zena Beth. "The Professor and the Prophet: John Dewey and Franklin Ford." *JH* 6 (1979): 107-11, 123. Ford, a former newspaper editor, proposed in the 1890s a plan for a newspaper which would report on ideas rather than events. His thinking influenced the philosopher Dewey.

1333. Meier, August. "Booker T. Washington and the Negro Press With Special Reference to the *Colored American.*" *JNH* 39 (January 1953): 67-90. Many editors agreed with Washington that the best rational approach for blacks was not protest but accommodation.

1334. Metcalf, Alan. "How the Press Covered Constitutional Centennial." *MHD* 7, 1 (1987): 7-13, 29. Press coverage of the centennial in 1887 clutched "traditional American values," tapped into nostalgia, eased "the adjustment to changing society amid technological expansion," and stirred "a national excitement not known since the Civil War." (29)

1335. Millis, Walter. *The Martial Spirit; a Study of Our War with Spain.* Boston: Houghton Mifflin, 1931. Critical, ideological examination of the reasons (including the imperialistic, propagandistic efforts which Pulitzer and Hearst) which led the United States jingoistically to go to war with Spain.

1336. Moon, Gordon A., II. "George F. Parker: A 'Near Miss' as First White House Press Chief." *JQ* 41 (1964): 183-90. In the 1892 presidential election, Grover Cleveland used Parker as his press liaison. However, no such position as the modern "press secretary" existed, although conditions were ripe for it, and Cleveland "lacked the foresight to realize how desperately he needed a capable buffer between himself and a hostile press." (183) Thus, Parker did not become the first presidential press secretary.

1337. Morgan, Hugh. "Historical Perspectives of the 'Yellow Press' and the Spanish-American War." *Graduate Communication Studies*, Vol. 1, No. 1 (Spring 1977), published by the School of Journalism, Southern Illinois University. This article, which is one of five in this collection by graduate students at Southern Illinois University, contrasts different interpretations of the part played by Hearst and Pulitzer in causing the war.

1338. Mott, Frank Luther. "Fifty Years of *Life*: The Story of a Satirical Weekly." *JQ* 25 (1948): 224-32. Chronicle of the comic weekly magazine, founded in 1883 and published until 1936. Article appears as a chapter in Mott's *A History of American Magazines*, Vol. 4.

1339. Nord, David Paul. *Newspapers and New Politics: Midwestern Municipal Reform, 1890-1900*. Ann Arbor: UMI Research Press, 1981. See next entry.

1340. Nord, David Paul. "Newspapers and New Politics: Municipal Reform in Chicago and St. Louis, 1890-1900." Ph.D. dissertation, University of Wisconsin, 1979. "This...is a study of the role of the mass-circulation newspapers in the emergence...of a new politics of municipal reform...that depended upon the interplay of political organization and mass communication. The new reformers tried to change the urban political system in two ways. They sought to make local politics more issue oriented and...to expand citizen participation in the political process." They succeeded in Chicago because of newspaper support and failed in St. Louis because of newspaper indifference.

1341. Nord, David Paul. "The Paradox of Municipal Reform in the Late Nineteenth Century." *WMH* 66 (1982-1983): 128-42. Like some other reformers, Joseph Medill of the Chicago *Tribune* was suspicious of mass democracy, but he believed that real "reform could come only when the majority of voters willed it." Thus, he primarily attempted to "educate and arouse the masses" rather than to bring about structural reforms such as the initiative and referendum.

1342. Nord, David Paul. "Working-Class Readers: Family, Community, and Reading in Late Nineteenth-Century America." *CR* 13, 2 (1986): 156-81. In 1889-1890 the amount of textile workers' expenditures for newspapers and books was related to their income. "[S]cholars ought to look more carefully at the history of readers and reading as well as the history of literacy and the publishing trade." (157)

1343. Olasky, Marvin N. "Hawks or Doves? Texas Press and Spanish-American War.' *JQ* 64 (1987): 205-08. "[A]s far as Texas newspapers were concerned, Hearst and Pulitzer did not lead the way, and may even have been in the way [because of their use of rumor and sensationalism]." (208) At first, Texas papers were cautious about starting war with Spain. Once they had the facts, they became firm in support of war.

1344. Olasky, Marvin. "Late 19th-Century Texas Sensationalism: Hypocrisy or Biblical Morality?" *JH* 12 (1985): 96-100. While criticizing New York-style yellow journalism, many Texas newspapers during 1880-1900 were publishing the same type of material. Texas editors, however, were trying to use the sensationalism to point out what they considered to be biblical morals. "Consciously or unconsciously--but at least with an awareness of mission--many Texas editors were making biblical points in their newspapers. There is no reason to assume hypocrisy." (99)

1345. Older, Fremont (Mrs). *William Randolph Hearst, American.* New York: Appleton-Century, 1936. Adulatory, incomplete, and prejudiced account views Hearst as a patriot, friend of man and labor, and a supporter of the best ideals.

1346. Perry, Clay. "John P. Mitchell, Virginia's Journalist of Reform." *JH* 4 (1977): 142-47, 156. The editor of the black *Richmond Planet* (1884-1929) "was never content to be a follower or one who could willingly accept second-class treatment of his race. He was a symbol for blacks to keep their pride and to struggle for what they believed. His steadfastness to his convictions is documented in the *Richmond Planet*, which first and last served as his vehicle for advancing the causes of his people." (156)

1347. Peters, Glen W. "The *American Weekly*." *JQ* 48 (1971): 466-71, 479. Hearst's *American Weekly*, founded in 1896 and edited by Morrill Goddard, was "the first of the syndicated Sunday supplements...[and] at one time had a circulation of over 10,000,000 and was read by 25 percent of the adult population in the United States." (467)

1348. Pfennig, Dennis J. "Evan and Clark Howell and the *Atlanta Constitution*: The Partnership (1889-1897)." Ph.D. dissertation, University of Georgia, 1975.

1349. Phillips, George Howard. "An Analysis of 835 Articles in the Leading American Periodicals for the Period 1890-1914 to Determine What Was Said about American Daily Newspapers." Ph.D. dissertation, University of Iowa, 1962. "The principal criticisms were directed against the inaccuracy and untruthfulness of the press, the unworthiness of the contents, a lack of professionalism and ethics, and business and economic characteristics. The comment was generally more favorable than unfavorable when it concerned individual and personal characteristics, intra-professional relations, and social impact."

1350. Pierce, Robert N. "Lord Northcliffe: Trans-Atlantic Influences." *JM* 40 (1975). Alfred Harmsworth, Lord Northcliffe, England's most popular newspaper publisher, influenced sensational American journalism in the late 1800s and early 1900s, but probably American journalism's influence on him was greater than his on it.

1351. Ponder, Stephen E. "Conservation, Community Economics, and Newspapering: The Seattle Press and the Forest Reserves Controversy of 1897." *AJ* 3 (1986): 50-60. The Seattle *Post-Intelligencer's* changing stands on creation of a new national forest indicated that daily newspapers in the late 19th century were "subject to more complex influences on local editorial policy than implied by [their] commercial orientation or partisan affiliation." (59)

1352. Ralph, Julian. *The Making of a Journalist*. New York: Harper, 1906. Autobiography of the reporter for the New York *Sun* and *Journal*.

1353. Reynolds, William Robinson. "Joseph Pulitzer." Ph.D. dissertation, Columbia University, 1950.

1354. Riis, Jacob A. *The Making of an American*. New York: Macmillan, 1901. Autobiography of the police reporter and urban reformer.

1355. Rischin, Moses. *Grandma Never Lived in America: The New Journalism of Abraham Cahan*. Bloomington: Indiana University Press, 1985. Anthology of Cahan's writing about the Lower East Side in the New York *Commercial Advertiser* covering 1897 to 1902. Introduction: "Cahan's people were real human beings with complex lives and feelings."

1356. Salisbury, William. *The Career of a Journalist*. New York: B.W. Dodge, 1908. Autobiography of a staff member of various metropolitan newspapers, including yellow ones.

1357. Schofler, Patricia. "'A Glorious Adventure.'" *AHL* 15 (February 1981): 28-35. Winifred Sweet ("Annie Laurie") "performed as the Hearst empire's human interest specialist, arousing emotions and loyalties through a unique combination of frontier cynicism, sentimentality, and moral idealism....Colleagues and the public referred to her as the greatest sob sister of them all." (28)

1358. Schuneman, R. Smith. "A Question for Newspaper Editors of the 1890s." *JQ* 42 (1965): 43-52. Photographs were not widely used by mass circulation newspapers until 1897 (even though the technology for photoengraving had been available since 1890) because hand-drawn illustrations had been popular and apparently had helped increase circulation. During a time of great newspaper competition, editors were reluctant to experiment with the new technique of photoengraving. Hand engravers had also waged a fairly successful propaganda campaign to show that readers wanted art and not photography. Photojournalism was used as a tool of yellow journalism/sensationalism and got a bad name.

1359. Seitz, Don C. *Joseph Pulitzer: His Life and Letters*. New York: Simon & Schuster, 1924. Biography of Pulitzer, with almost complete emphasis on his newspaper accomplishments. The author was for 30 years a member of the *World* staff and personal acquaintance of Pulitzer.

1360. Sharp, Eugene W. "Cracking the Media Censorship in 1899 and 1900." *JQ* 20 (1943): 281-85. Criticism by 11 correspondents in 1899 of the censorship in the Philippines cracked the censorship which recurred but never again so drastically.

1361. Sims, Norman Howard. "The Chicago Style of Journalism." Ph.D. dissertation, University of Illinois, 1979. "[J]ournalists [George Ade, Opie Read, and Ben Hecht and some 40 other reporters] working in Chicago found a chaotic, industrial, urban world emerging around them and tried to capture and express their feelings about it in their reports....The Chicago style urban reporter in the 1890s was cynical, tough, literate and sentimental."

1362. Sloan, Wm. David. "Historians Butting Heads: Newspaper Editorials and

Presidential Elections in the Gilded Age." *JCI* 4, 1 (1978): 15-34. Study of the influence of editorials on elections from 1880 to 1900 finds that "rarely have editorials been demonstrably responsible for the success or failure of a presidential candidate" and that "journalism historians tend to exaggerate the impact of...editorials...[while] non-journalism historians tend to overlook or underestimate it." (28)

1363. Smythe, Ted Curtis. "Pulitzer's *World* and the Venezuela Boundary Dispute." *JQ* 46 (1969): 807-11. What effect did Pulitzer have in avoiding the possible war with Britain over the Venezuela boundary dispute? Other newspapers had opposed Cleveland's bellicose approach from the beginning, and threats of war seemed to be absent from the press when Pulitzer began his campaign. Thus, to give Pulitzer credit for the U.S. avoiding the war seems unrealistic.

1364. Smythe, Ted Curtis. "The Reporter, 1880-1900. Working Conditions and Their Influence on News." *JH* 7 (1980): 1-10. Study explores the importance of the reporter to the newspaper by examining employee-employer relations, as defined by pay, tenure, and status. Especiallly important during the period was the influence of economics on news concepts and news practices. Reporting was more a way station on the highway to politics, business, literature, or editorial work than a profession itself. The economic inducements to reporters reflected this attitude. Reporters knew they were not worth much to their publishers. Economic conditions resulted in poor reporting and sensationalism.

1365. Stallman, R.W., and E.R. Hagemann, eds. *The War Dispatches of Stephen Crane*. New York: New York University Press, 1964. Collection of Crane's news stories from the Greco-Turkish and Spanish-American wars with the selection based on literary quality.

1366. Stern, Madeleine B. *Purple Passage: The Life of Mrs. Frank Leslie*. Norman: University of Oklahoma Press, 1953. Entertaining biography of Miriam Follin, the colorful, maukish wife who became editor and publisher of the Leslie periodicals.

1367. Stephens, Gary B. "The Media Buildup: 'Gentleman Jim' vs. 'Ruby Rob.'" *MHD* 3, 1 (1983): 6-14, 45, 64. Newspapers gave massive pre-publicity to the "fight of the century" between Jim Corbett and Bob Fitzsimmons.

1368. Stevens, Walter B. "The New Journalism in Missouri." *MHR* 16-19 (October 1922-July 1925). Series of articles dealing with Pulitzer-style journalism, 1870s-1890s, mainly in St. Louis.

1369. Stewart, Walter. "Eugene Field: Pioneer 'Colyumist,' Managing Editor and Poet." *JQ* 43 (1966): 57-66. Field became America's first columnist with his "Sharps and Flats" column in the Chicago *Daily News*.

1370. Swanberg, W.A. *Citizen Hearst*. New York: Scribner's, 1961. Hearst had good and bad prints, but the bad outweighed the good. Hearst was influenced by his mother's attachment to him, he was driven by a desire to have things his way, and he was a "riot of incongruity." This biography, one of the most highly acclaimed on Hearst, gives considerable emphasis to politics, in which Hearst was disappointed in his aspirations. He was responsible for the Spanish-American War.

1371. Swanberg, W.A. *Pulitzer*. New York: Scribner's, 1967. Pulitzer focused his attention on politics, and his heart was in the editorial page. He "was the most earnest, powerful, and efficient social conscience yet seen in journalism." He was also concerned about the well-being of his newspaper property, especially during its fight with Hearst. Pulitzer was a sensational journalist who was concerned about the welfare of the masses, who probably rarely read his editorial page.

1372. Tebbel, John. *The Life and Good Times of William Randolph Hearst..* New York: Dutton, 1952. The story of how Hearst ran his newspapers and his involvement in politics is "about as sordid a tale as could be related." He was a master newspaper salesman but less a seller of ideas. He comes across as an ideological paradox (changing from liberal to conservative) because he was unable to change with the times and with changing political tides.

1373. Tree, Robert L. "Victor Fremont Lawson and His Newspapers, 1890-1900: A Study of the *Chicago Daily News* and the *Chicago Record*." Ph.D. dissertation, Northwestern University, 1959.

1374. Vanderburg, Ray. "The Paradox That Was Arthur Brisbane." *JQ* 47 (1970): 281-86. The tragedy of Brisbane's life is that he never fulfilled his potential; he never used the fullness of his mental powers. The inconsistency of his stands on issues is partially explained by the fact that, although he had great ability and knowledge, "he lacked the courage of his convictions...[and] feared ridicule, poverty, or some unknown which prevented him from utilizing his powers to the optimum."(286)

1375. Ware, Louise. *Jacob A. Riis. Police Reporter, Reformer, Useful Citizen..* New York: Appleton-Century, 1938. In his career as a police reporter on the New York *Evening Sun*, Riis helped reform housing conditions because he believed that such conditions as those found in the slums were the true cause of people's troubles and wrongdoing.

1376. Watters, Robert. "Chasing Goddard: Episodes in the Genesis of Biography." *JQ* 43 (1966): 231-38. The author chronicles his efforts to write a biography of Morrill Goddard, the editor of Hearst's *American Weekly* Sunday-supplement magazine.

1377. Weber, Herbert Y. "The *St. Paul Globe*, 1878-1905." *JQ* 42 (1965): 279-81. Chronological, descriptive account of an important Democratic newspaper that died during a period of newspaper consolidation.

1378. Wells, Evelyn. *Fremont Older*. New York: Appleton-Century, 1936. Adulatory biography of the crusading San Francisco editor written by a close friend and admirer.

1379. Welter, Mark M. "The 1895-98 Cuban Crisis in Minnesota Newspapers: Testing the 'Yellow Journalism' Theory." *JQ* 47 (1970): 719-24. A representative sample of Minnesota newspapers shows little reflection of New York dailies' sensationalism during the events leading to the Spanish-American War. "Yellow Journalism" did not cause the war. Disagrees with Millis, Wilkerson, and Wisan on yellow journalism's influence on bringing about the war.

1380. Welter, Mark W. "Minnesota Newspapers and the Cuban Crisis, 1895-1898: Minnesota as a Test Case for the 'Yellow Journalism' Theory." Ph.D. dissertation, University of Minnesota, 1970. See previous entry.

1381. Wilkerson, Marcus M. "The Press and the Spanish-American War." *JQ* 9 (1932): 129-48. The press was not the only cause in starting the war, but it was a major influence. The New York papers influenced the news syndicates and wires, which determined the content of papers nationwide.

1382. Wilkerson, Marcus M. *Public Opinion and the Spanish-American War: A Study of War Propaganda.*. Baton Rouge: Louisiana State University Press, 1932. The *World* and *Journal*, along with other newspapers that published material from the two New York City newspapers, exerted a strong influence on America's decision to go to war.

1383. Winkler, John K. *W.R. Hearst: An American Phenomenon*. New York: Simon & Schuster, 1928. Biography offers a favorable assessment of Hearst's life and journalism career.

1384. Winkler, John K. *William Randolph Hearst: A New Appraisal*. New York: Hastings House, 1955. Biography provides nothing original, drawing heavily upon other secondary sources and upon Winkler's own 1928 biography of Hearst, updating it to Hearst's death in 1951. Providing a generally favorable of view of Hearst, it excuses or justifies his faults.

1385. Wisan, Joseph E. *The Cuban Crisis as Reflected in the New York Press.*. New York: Columbia University Press, 1934. The mass of evidence tends to show that the press was influential in creating pro-Cuban sympathy among Americans. Whether or not the press was solely to blame, papers did lead the American people to expect the conflict, which--after the sinking of the *Maine*--seemed inevitable. Papers throughout the country followed the lead of New York papers. Of editors, Hearst was most to blame.

1386. Zabrist, Benedict Karl. "How Victor Lawson's Newspapers Covered the Cuban War of 1898." *JQ* 38 (1961): 323-31. The Chicago *Record* and Chicago *Daily News* were not sensational in their news coverage. They were innovative but responsible. Their news coverage was reliable and thorough.

10

Frontier and Regional Journalism, 1800–1900

1387. Agee, Warren K. "A Study of Small-Town Life in the Texas Cattle Country, 1880-1890, as Reflected in the Press of the Area and Period." Ph.D. dissertation, University of Minnesota, 1955.

1388. Alisky, Marvin. "Arizona's First Newspaper, *The Weekly Arizonian*, 1859." *NMHR* 34 (April 1959): 134-43. The *Arizonian* was founded in Tubac to provide news of mining camps and provide an outlet for advertising. During its life, which expired in 1871, it was courageous in speaking out on issues and problems.

1389. Allen, Eric W. "Oregon Journalism in 1887." *OHQ* 38 (September 1937): 251-64.

1390. Allsop, Fred W. *History of the Arkansas Press for a Hundred Years and More*. Little Rock: Parke-Harper, 1922. Chronological history from the founding of the (Little Rock) *Gazette* in 1819. Composed mainly of brief sketches of the state's papers.

1391. Alter, J. Cecil. *Early Utah Journalism: A Half Century of Forensic Warfare, Waged by the West's Most Militant Press*. Salt Lake City: Utah State Historical Society, 1938. Encyclopedic account of 585 publications. Pioneer Utah journalists were colorful, served as promoters of their communities, and engaged in personal, vituperative clashes.

1392. Armstrong, Robert D. *Nevada Printing History: A Bibliography of Imprints and Publications, 1858-1880*. Reno: University of Nevada Press, 1981. It was in "1858 that a printing press was hauled over the Sierra Nevada to publish the *Territorial Enterprise*," beginning the history of Nevada printing. This is a catalog of imprints and publications.

1393. Ashton, Wendell J. "Voice in the West: Biography of a Pioneer Newspaper." New York: Duell, Sloan & Pearce, 1950. The Salt Lake City *Deseret News*, founded in 1850, is an organ of the Mormon Church and has chronicled the struggle of the church in Utah. This centennial history chronicles the difficulties of frontier publishing in the early years. The paper was "the organ of a well-organized, peaceful, agricultural people who had settled in the mountains for religious freedom" and was the "voice of a people struggling in a desolate desert for their lives and for the church."

1394. Atwood, Roy Alden. "Handwritten Newspapers on the Iowa Frontier." *JH* 7 (1980): 56-59, 66-67. Description of four papers in the small town of Washington. They contained news, editorials, and features for the local audience. They "represent something of a bridge between two cultural forms: written correspondence and printed news...[suggesting] that journalism on the frontier was shaped by a variety of cultural forces and environmental conditions, and that it took on a diversity of forms." (67)

1395. Baltensperger, B. H. "Newspaper Images of the Central Great Plains in the Late Nineteenth Century." *JW* 19 (April 1980): 64-70. Compares the image of the Great Plains in three newspapers between 1867 and 1895, showing that readers in the Plains states often were less likely to read about their own severe weather and agricultural problems than were midwestern and eastern readers.

1396. Barney, Libeus. *Letters of the Pike's Peak Gold Rush: Early Day Letters of Libeus Barney, Reprinted from the Bennington Banner, Vermont, 1859-1860.* San Jose, Calif.: Talisman Press, 1959. (Originally published as *Early-Day Letters from Auraria, 1907.*) Collection of nine letters which a Colorado miner sent to his hometown newspaper in Vermont chronicling the early growth of Denver.

1397. Barton, Albert O. "The Beginnings of the Norwegian Press in America." *WHSP* (1916): 210-11.

1398. Bass, Althea. *Cherokee Messenger.* Norman: University of Oklahoma Press, 1936. Samuel Worcester, a Christian missionary from New England, established the *Cherokee Phoenix* in the 1820s to help convert and Americanize Indians in Oklahoma.

1399. Bauer, Marvin G. "Henry W. Grady, Spokesman of the New South." Ph.D. dissertation, University of Wisconsin, 1936. A "rhetorical and analytical" study of Grady as an orator.

1400. Beebe, Lucius. *Comstock Commotion: The Story of the Territorial Enterprise.* Stanford: Stanford University Press, 1954. The *Territorial Enterprise* of Virginia City, Nev., in the 1860s-1870s was "the pattern and archetype of all western newspapers in pioneer times....[It had] gunfighting editors, celebrated news beats, authority and power in affairs of state, and its hilarious and uninhibited way of life." The paper was prosperous and boisterous. Beebe was the owner of the paper in 1954. This history is written for the popular audience.

1401. Belknap, George N. "*Oregon Sentinel* Extras -- 1858-1864." *PNQ* 70 (October 1979): 178-80. The Jacksonville paper, which was willing to print special editions to accommodate big news, "habitually scooped all the other Oregon newspapers in reporting news from California and the East." Printing these "extras" presented various problems, especially after the telegraph began to serve the area.

1402. Bennion, Sherilyn Cox. Following entries. Sherilyn Bennion has been the most prolific historian of the female frontier journalist. In numerous articles she has pointed out the importance of this topic for historical study. The following entries are not intended to provide an exhaustive bibliography of her work, but merely to illustrate it.

1403. Bennion, Sherilyn Cox. "Early Western Publications Expose Women's Suffrage Cries." *Matrix* 64 (Summer 1979): 6-9. The newspapers and magazines which were published for women have received little historical attention. A study of 30 publications reveals that they were "not only well read but were also recognized as shapers of community opinion." Editors generally were "articulate, self-sufficient and committed, occasionally slightly eccentric, but very rarely dull."

1404. Bennion, Sherilyn Cox. "*The New Northwest* and *Woman's Exponent*: Early Voices of Suffrage." *JQ* 54 (1977): 286-92. The papers, in Portland, Ore., and Salt Lake City, respectively, "were ardent voices in favor of women obtaining the right to vote...[demonstrating] that women's concerns found published expression in the West, as well as in the East, very early in the struggle for suffrage." (286)

1405. Bennion, Sherilyn Cox. "The Pioneer: The First Voice of Women's Suffrage in the West." *PHi* 25 (1981): 15-21.

1406. Bennion, Sherilyn Cox. "The Woman's Exponent: Forty-two Years of Speaking for Women." *UHQ* 44, 3 (1976): 222-39.

1407. Bennion, Sherilyn Cox. "Woman Suffrage Papers of the West, 1869-1914." *AJ* 3 (1986): 125-41. Twelve suffrage papers articulated the ideas of the movement, helped win adherents to the cause, and "enabled suffragists to solidify a base from which to extend their efforts....The papers led the way in the campaigns for suffrage wherever they were published. They helped develop ideas and organization. They provided a forum for a cause which had time -- and justice -- on its side." (140)

1408. Bennion, Sherilyn Cox. "A Working List of Women Editors of the 19th Century West." *JH* 7 (1980): 60-65. Catalog of journalists in Arizona, California, Colorado, Hawaii, Idaho, Nevada, New Mexico, Oregon, Utah, Washington, and Wyoming.

1409. Beshoar, Barron. "The Strife and Struggle of a Newspaper in the Old West." *AmW* 10 (September 1973): 45-63. Narrative of the obstacles that Dr. Michael Beshoar, a physician, faced in founding the *Chieftan*, the first newspaper in Pueblo, Colo., in 1868. He believed that Pueblo and the surrounding area had to have a newspaper "if they were to move ahead. A newspaper would provide the region with a political voice; by making known the potential of the area it would lure settlers; and finally it would act as a civilizing influence to insure law and order....[But] times were hard, money was difficult to come by, the weather was extremely bad, and hostile Indian bands were raising such hob along the trails that the military had held up traffic between...Kansas and...Colorado." (45)

1410. Blake, Henry N. "The First Newspaper in Montana." *Contributions to the Historical Society of Montana* 5 (1904): 253-64.

1411. Blankenburg, William B. "The Role of the Press in an Indian Massacre, 1871." *JQ* 46 (1969): 61-70. Although not encouraging the massacre, the Tucson *Citizen* and *Arizonan* did little to discourage the slaughter of 100 Apaches, mainly women and children, at Camp Grant. "Too many years of hatred, anguish, and villainy had driven the Apaches and the pioneers to virtual war....The editors -- like many other Tucsonans -- could have prevented this attack had they really wished to." (70)

1412. "The 'Blizzard' Press of Dakota." *WMH* 2 (1919): 331-32. South Dakota suffered a paper shortage in the severe winter of 1880-1881.

1413. Blumberg, Nathan B., and Warren J. Brier, eds. *A Century of Montana Journalism*. Missoula: Montain Press, 1971.

1414. Brann, William Cowper. *The Complete Works of Brann the Iconoclast*. New York: Brann, 1919. Collection of the writings of the quarrelsome editor from Waco, Tex., in the 1890s.

1415. Brier, Warren J. "The 'Flumgudgeon Gazette and Bumble Bee Budget.'" *JQ* 36 (1959): 317-20. The *Gazette*, which Charles Pickett started in 1845 and "which was written in longhand...was, in a sense, the first news publication founded on the Pacific Coast and the first English-language news journal" in the far west. (317) It was especially significant in publicizing activities of Oregon's first government.

1416. Bryan, Ferald J. "Thomas E. Watson versus Henry W. Grady: The Rhetorical Struggle for the Mind of the South." Ph.D. dissertation, University of Missouri, 1985.

1417. Burd, Gene. "The Ghost Town Newspaper: An Autopsy Approach to the Frontier Press." *JH* 8 (1981): 99-103. Suggests various approaches historians might take in studying newspapers in mining towns in order to help define the nature of frontier journalism.

1418. Byars, William Vincent. "A Century of Journalism in Missouri." *MHR* 15 (October 1920): 53-73. Centennial history. In the 1820s, Missouri pioneers "looked to the church, the school and the press...for enlightenment, to save them and their posterity from calamities....The county newspaper was thought of as not less necessary than the county courthouse." (53) Throughout the century, the best Missouri newspapers kept the people enlightened so that they could maintain their excellent characteristics.

1419. Carey, Arthur C. "Effects of the Pony Express and the Transcontinental Telegraph Upon Selected California Newspapers." *JQ* 51 (1974): 320-22. Newspapers used more national news with the advent of the pony express and telegraph.

1420. Carmony, Donald F. "The Pioneer Press in Indiana." *IHB* 31 (1954): 187-232. Sesquicentennial overview of the history of the Indiana press, "an honorable institution," since the founding of the territory's first newspaper in 1804.

1421. Carter, C.E. *The Territorial Papers of the United States: The Territory of Louisiana-Missouri, 1815-1821*. Washington: 1951.

1422. Chaplin, W.E. "Some of the Early Newspapers of Wyoming," 7-24 in *Wyoming Historical Society Miscellanies*. Laramie: Laramie Republican, 1919.

1423. Chaplin, W.E. "Wyoming Scrapbook: Some Wyoming Editors I Have Known." *AWy* 18 (January 1946): 79-85. Collection of brief, anecdotal biographies.

1424. Clark, E. Culpepper. *Francis Warrington Dawson and the Politics of Restoration: South Carolina, 1874-1889.* Tuscaloosa: University of Alabama Press, 1980. Political biography of the editor of the Charleston *News* and *Courier*, focusing on his state, regional, and national influence.

1425. Clark, E. Culpepper. "Francis Warrington Dawson: The New South Revisited." *AJ* 3 (1986): 5-23. The editor of the Charleston *News* and *Courier* was a dominant force in South Carolina politics and a leader in the New South movement. Study describes the main features of the New South leaders.

1426. Clayton, Wallace E. "The Editor Who Captured Geronimo." *MHD* 1, 1 (1981): 56-61. Narrative of the western exploits of John Clum, founder of the Tombstone (Ariz.) *Epitaph.*

1427. Cloud, Barbara. "Establishing the Frontier Newspaper: A Study of Eight Western Territories." *JQ* 61 (1984): 805-11. To support a newspaper, a community needed to have a minimum stable population and per capita income, profitable agriculture in the surrounding area, some manufacturing, and a formal government.

1428. Cloud, Barbara L. "A Party Press? Not Just Yet! Political Publishing on the Frontier." *JH* 7 (1980): 54-55, 72-73. See next entry.

1429. Cloud, Barbara Lee. "Start the Presses: The Birth of Journalism in Washington Territory." Ph.D. dissertation, University of Washington, 1979. In most towns from 1852 to 1882, the first newspaper was started primarily for economic reasons. "Subsequent newspapers in each town, however, sometimes were started in order to disseminate a message. In the 1850s and 1860s this message tended to be political; in the later period it varied from religious to theatrical." In most towns, the pattern of development was non-partisan first newspaper, emerging partisanship, competing partisan papers.

1430. Clymer, Rolla A. "A Golden Era of Kansas Journalism." *KHQ* 24 (Spring 1958): 97-111. Commemorative centennial history. Frontier Kansas in the 1850s required sturdy settlers to break the land and preserve liberty. "[I]n those dark and confused years, the printed word helped to keep alight the power of the spirit in Kansas....The early-day editors were both rugged and valiant. The times called for boldness and plain speech -- and they responded in kind." (97)

1431. Coleman, J. Winston, Jr. *John Bradford, Esq.: Pioneer Kentucky Printer and Historian* . Lexington: Winburn, 1950. A brief biography (24-page pamphlet) of the publisher of the *Kentucke Gazette* . He "deserves remembrance not only as the founder of Kentucky's first newssheet, and as a pioneer printer and publisher, but also as a useful, public-spirited and trustworthy citizen."

1432. Connelly, William E. *History of the Newspapers and Magazines Published in Kansas from the Organization of the Kansas Territory, 1854, to January, 1916, Together with Brief Statistical Information of Counties, Cities and Towns of the State* . Topeka: Kansas State Printing Plant, 1916.

1433.   Dane, G. Ezra, ed. *Mark Twain's Letters From the Sandwich Islands*. Palo Alto, Calif.: Stanford University Press, 1938. Collection of letters written from Hawaii for the Sacramento *Union*.

1434.   Davidson, Levette Jay. "O.J. Goldrick, Pioneer Journalist." *CM* 8 (January 1936): 26-37. Biography of one of Colorado's earliest newspaper editors.

1435.   Davis, Harold E. "'A Brave and Beautiful City': Henry Grady and the New South." *AJ* 5 (1988): 131-44. In this re-interpretation of Grady's role in the New South movement, the author explains Grady's primary motivation as gaining political power for himself and Atlanta.

1436.   Davis, Harold E. "Henry Grady, the Atlanta *Constitution*, and the Politics of Farming in the 1880s." *GHQ* 71 (1987): 571-600. As part of the New South movement, Grady, managing editor of the *Constitution*, advocated the improvement of southern agriculture. His plan, however, though sincere originally, eventually served Grady's own political interests and the interests of Atlanta more than the interests of farmers.

1437.   Davis, Harold E. "Henry Grady, Master of the Atlanta Ring -- 1880-1886." *GHQ* 69 (1985), 1-38. Although recognized as the leading spokesman for the New South movement, Grady "made his most intense commitment to and spent the better part of his energies in promoting the city of Atlanta, not the whole South." (1) He went to great lengths "to manipulate politics for the benefit of Atlanta, manipulations which worked to the great disadvantage of other cities" (2); and through a group of politicians known as the Atlanta Ring he was able to keep political power in Georgia concentrated in Atlanta.

1438.   Davis, Horance G., Jr. "Pensacola Newspapers, 1821-1900." *FHQ* 37 (1959): 419-45. Descriptive, antiquarian account of the 23 newspapers published in the 19th century in the Florida city, beginning with the first, *The Floridian*.

1439.   De Loney, Burton. "Press on Wheels." *AWy* 14 (October 1942): 299-314. Biography of Legh Freeman, who carried his press with him from town to town publishing various newspapers.

1440.   Demaree, Albert Lowther. *The American Agricultural Press, 1819-1860*. New York: Columbia University Press, 1941. Description and narrative of agricultural magazines, along with the texts of 28 articles from them.

1441.   Doll, Louis W. *A History of the Newspapers of Ann Arbor, 1829-1920*. Detroit: Wayne State University Press, 1959. Traces the development of Ann Arbor papers from small, short-lived weeklies to monopoly dailies -- similar to trends in other Midwest towns, with the Ann Arbor papers having no unique characteristics.

1442.   Drury, Wells. *An Editor on the Comstock Lode*. Reno: University of Nevada Press, 1984. Reprint of a personal historical account of frontier life in Nevada originally published in 1936. Drury was a newspaper editor and politician.

1443.   Dugat, Gentry. *Life of Henry W. Grady*. Edinburg, Tex.: 1927. Sketch based on secondary sources.

1444.   Dwyer, Richard A., and Richard E. Lingenfelter. *Lying on the Eastern Slope: James*

Townsend's Comic Journalism on the Mining Frontier. Miami: University Presses of Florida, 1984. Editors in the Sierra Nevada, as exemplified by the roving editor "Lying Jim" Townsend, fabricated much of the content in their newspapers, including wild tales, details of mining prosperity, comic episodes, etc., mostly in good humor in the nature of Mark Twain.

1445. Dyer, Oliver. "A Character Sketch of Henry Woodfin Grady," in H. W. Grady, *The New South.* New York: 1890. Admiring tribute written by a member of the New York *Sun* staff.

1446. Dyer, Carolyn Stewart. "The Business History of the Antebellum Wisconsin Newspaper, 1833-1860: A Study of Concentration of Ownership and Diversity of Views." Ph.D. dissertation, University of Wisconsin, 1978. Newspapers generally were not capitalized exclusively by their operators, and the forms of capitalization posed threats to the operators' independence. Approximately one-fourth of newspapers were parts of chains or groups, which reduced the amount of content diversity. The historian's picture of the tramp printer and the movable press is myth.

1447. Dyer, Carolyn Stewart. "Economic Dependence and Concentration of Ownership Among Antebellum Wisconsin Newspapers." *JH* 7 (1980): 42-46. See previous entry.

1448. Ellis, Richard N. "The Apache Chronicle." *NMHR* 47 (1972): 257-83.

1449. Ellison, Rhoda C. *History and Bibliography of Alabama Newspapers in the Nineteenth Century.* Tuscaloosa, Ala.: University of Alabama Press, 1954. Primarily bibliographical listing of newspapers with brief notes on personnel, policy, and ownership.

1450. Ellison, Rhoda C. "Newspaper Publishing in Frontier Alabama." *JQ* 23 (1946): 289-301. What the life of editors was like from 1807 to 1835. The newspaper was the prime means of information, literature, etc.; but it faced many problems, such as non-paying subscribers, difficulty finding printers, maintaining proper relations with contributors and other members of the community, etc. Political and personal feuds were expected as a natural part of newspapering and society. "Yet, under such conditions imposed by the frontier, newspapers were established and continued to spread and flourish." (301)

1451. Endres, Fred F. "Frontier Obituaries as Cultural Reflectors: Toward 'Operationalizing' Carey's Thesis." *JH* 11 (1984): 54-60. Theorizing that obituaries can reveal cultural characteristics, author finds that obituaries in four Ohio newspapers from 1811 to 1850 were male-oriented, revealing a male-dominated society.

1452. Endres, Fred F. "'We Want Money and Must Have It': Profile of an Ohio Weekly." *JH* 7 (1980): 68-71. Study of one newspaper finds that financial problems were severe, as were difficulties in collecting payments from subscribers, although the paper apparently made a modest profit.

1453. Endres, Kathleen. "Jane Grey Swisshelm: 19th Century Journalist and Feminist." *JH* 2 (1975): 128-32. A reporter for the New York *Tribune* in the 1850s, Swisshelm advocated equal treatment of women. She took strong stands on several public issues.

1454. Evans, Herndon J. *The Newspaper Press in Kentucky*. Lexington: University Press of Kentucky, 1976. Superficial history of newspapers, consisting mainly of a catalogue of the first newspapers in many communities and general statements about the press. Its information is, for the most part, compiled from other historical works.

1455. Firebaugh, Dorothy Gile. "The Sacramento *Union*: Voice of California, 1851-75." *JQ* 30 (1953): 321-30. The *Union* "occupied a strategic position. It was a giant of the press in an isolated new state, fabulously rich but undeveloped, where news was at a premium, subscribers were many, and newspapers were the sole medium of mass communication....In the role of the 'miner's bible'...[it] exerted profound influence upon state development...achieved national stature...helped materially to preserve the nation's integrity during the Civil War...pioneered as a leader of California's independent press...[and] was a firm advocate of non-personal journalism in an era when vilification was common." (321)

1456. Fisher, Paul. "A Forgotten Gentry of the Fourth Estate." *JQ* 33 (1956): 167-74. Tramp printers provided a mobile working force for country newspapers. The printer "was a colorful figure and the subject of many a backshop yarn. But he also played a vital role in the expansion of newspapers after the Civil War, until modern efficiency spelled his doom." (167)

1457. Flanagan, John T. *James Hall, Literary Pioneer of the Ohio Valley*. Minneapolis: University of Minnesota Press, 1941. Hall played a leading role in the cultural life of the frontier communities for half a century (1816-1868) as a newspaper editor, literary figure, and political office holder. He edited the *Illinois Gazette* (1820-22) and *Illinois Intelligencer* (1829-32).

1458. Folkerts, Jean. "Functions of the Reform Press." *JH* 12 (1985): 22-25. The Farmers' Alliance press of the 1880s in Texas "provided information that mainstream newspapers either neglected or chose to ignore; it formed the core of a communication network that helped Alliance men and women to develop a sense of community; and it presentd the Alliance movement as a legitimate effort to oppose the dominant political and economic structure." (22)

1459. Folkes, John G. *Nevada's Newspapers: A Bibliography. A Compilation of Nevada History, 1854-1964*. Reno: University of Nevada Press, 1964.

1460. Follett, Frederick. *History of the Press of Western New York*. Rochester: 1847. The first important book on the history of rural weekly newspapers, providing details and anecdotes about them and their printer-editors.

1461. Foreman, Carolyn Thomas. *Oklahoma Imprints, 1835-1907: A History of Printing in Oklahoma Before Statehood*. Norman: University of Oklahoma Press, 1936. Antiquarian notes and sketches of newspapers and other publications arranged chronologically and geographically, including some biographical and descriptive material.

1462. Foster, George E. "Journalism Among the Cherokee Indians. *MAH* 17 (July-December 1887): 65-70.

1463. Gabriel, Ralph Henry. *Elias Boudinot, Cherokee, and His America*. Norman: University of Oklahoma Press, 1941. Indian by birth, Boudinot (the founder of the first American Indian newspaper, the *Cherokee Phoenix*) was educated in theology in

New England and then worked as a Christian missionary among the Cherokees in Georgia and as an instructor in New England Puritan ideas. Most of this biography focuses on his New England influence.

1464. Garcia, Hazel Faye. "Communication in the Migration to Kentucky, 1769-1792." Ph.D. dissertation, University of Wisconsin, 1977. Letters contained more information than newspapers did about the early migration to and settlement of Kentucky.

1465. Garcia, Hazel. "'What a Buzzel is This...about Kentuck?' New Approaches and an Application." *JH* 3 (1976): 11-15, 19. See previous study. Attempts to define conceptual requirements, define the discipline of communications history, and suggest a model for a research approach to the cultural history of journalism.

1466. Giffin, Joseph. *History of the Press of Maine.* 1872.

1467. Gonzales, Juan. "Forgotten Pages: Spanish-Language Newspapers in the Southwest." *JH* 4 (1977): 50-51. Brief overview of several newspapers. The Spanish-language press has been overlooked by most historians.

1468. Gower, Calvin W. "Kansas 'Border Town' Newspapers and the Pike's Peak Gold Rush." *JQ* 44 (1967): 281-88. Historians have unjustly criticized newspapers for inciting gold fever by publishing exaggerated, reckless, and false claims. "Excitement about gold discoveries was not an uncommon occurrence in the mid-point of the 1800s in the United States, and newspaper editors were probably just as susceptible to it as other people in the population." (281)

1469. Graves, John Temple, II. "Sketch of Henry W. Grady." *AHB* 5 (January 1940): 23-31. Essay based on a memorial lecture evaluating Grady's importance on the verge of World War II: "In him was the spirit of America at its healthiest, bravest and best, and beyond all the limitations of regional competition....[His] spirit would have been tonic to us today against the sickness of democracies, talisman in the task of proving and holding America against hateful philosophies across the sea." (30)

1470. Gregory, John G. "Early Wisconsin Editors: Harrison Reed." *WMH* 7 (June 1924): 459-72. Reed, the publisher and editor of the Milwaukee *Sentinel* in the mid-1800s, "was skilled in many things, lent his hand at need to humble tasks, labored unremittingly, and...received...but scant reward." (459)

1471. Griffith, Louis Turner, and John Erwin Talmadge. *Georgia Journalism, 1703-1950.* Athens: University of Georgia Press, 1951. Weekly and daily editors "were inevitably motivated by their Southern heritage and surroundings." The Georgia press provided little real leadership of public opinion.

1472. Gurian, Jay. "Sweetwater Journalism and Western Myth." *AWy* 36 (April 1964): 79-88.

1473. Hafen, Le Roy, and Ann W. Hafen, eds. *Reports from Colorado: The Wildman Letters, 1859-1865, With Other Related Letters and Newspaper Reports.* Glendale, Calif.: Arthur H. Clark, 1961.

1474. Hage, George S. *Newspapers on the Minnesota Frontier, 1849-1860.* St. Paul: Minnesota Historical Society, 1967. Minnesota pioneer editors were colorful activists who performed great services but who nevertheless sometimes were guilty of the excesses of the frontier, which occasionally resulted in donnybrooks caused by harsh invective. Frontier newspapers promoted their local communities and had to work industriously for political and economic survival.

1475. Halaas, David Fridtjof. *Boom Town Newspapers: Journalism on the Rocky Mountain Mining Frontier, 1859-1881*. Albuquerque: University of New Mexico Press, 1981. Newspapers, acting as town boosters and critics, attempted to bring a "semblance of order and permanency" to their towns, attract settlers from the East, and "encourage the introduction of those economic, social and political institutions" that would help the towns grow.

1476. Hall, Mark W. "1831-49: The Pioneer Period for Newspapers in California." *JQ* 49 (1972): 648-55. California's first two newspapers, produced very crudely during the American army's occupation during the Mexican War, were similar to eastern papers of the colonial period. They were begun as a means of a printer's supplementing his meager income and carried little local news, relying primarily on news clipped from other papers. Most were vitriolic.

1477. Hamilton, Milton W. *The Country Printer: New York State, 1785-1830*. New York: Columbia University Press, 1936. This sympathetic study covers such topics as problems of publishing, apprenticeships, freedom of the press, early development of newspaper ethics, sometimes harsh language used against political opponents, how publishers financed their papers, shortage of capital, meager public support, the inadequacy of printers' education, newspaper content (including inadequate news), the fierce independence of pioneer printers, circulation, newspaper influence, and finally the encroachment of city papers. The printer was usually a newspaper publisher as well and was tied (often subservient) to political parties.

1478. Hamilton, Milton W. "The Spread of the Newspaper Press in New York Before 1830." *NYH* 14 (April 1933): 142-51. Like civilization at the edge of the frontier, newspapers gradually moved westward, "a natural development, following trade and population." (143)

1479. Harris, Joel Chandler. *Life of Henry W. Grady, Including His Writings and Speeches*. New York: 1890. Admiring, hastily-written tribute by Grady's fellow editor.

1480. Harris, Julia Collier, ed. *Joel Chandler Harris, Editor and Essayist*. Chapel Hill: University of North Carolina Press, 1931. Collection of "miscellaneous literary, political, and social writings" by Harris, Henry Grady's associate on the Atlanta *Constitution* and author of the "Uncle Remus" tales. As a journalist and publicist, he attempted to explain the South to the North from the perspective of a proud Southerner. In explaining the South's cultural and political situation, the conditions of Reconstruction, and the status of southern blacks, he wrote so reasonably that he influenced northern thinking and relations between the two sections.

1481. Hart, Jerome A. *In Our Second Century*. San Francisco: Pioneer Press, 1931. Anecdotal recollections of journalism in San Francisco, especially of the *Argonaut*, which was founded in 1877.

1482. Haskins, William A. "Rhetorical Vision of Equality: An Analysis of the Rhetoric of the Southern Black Press during Reconstruction." *CQ* 29, 2 (1982): 116-22. While white newspapers continued to stereotype freed slaves and treat them as inferior, black newspapers emphasized the need for equal rights and racial unity.

1483. Heinl, Frank J. "Newspapers and Periodicals in the Lincoln-Douglas Country, 1831-1832." *JISHS* 23 (October 1930): 411-20. Most of the publications received through the Jacksonville, Ill., post office were from outside the area, and many were religious.

1484. Heuterman, Thomas H. "Assessing the 'Press on Wheels': Individualism in Frontier Journalism." *JQ* 53 (1976): 423-28. Because of the western characteristic of "individualism," the *Frontier Index* cannot be considered necessarily typical of western papers or to have mirrored western society. It was, however, partisan, boosterish, and financially successful and carried colorful tales from the west. Its editor (Legh Freeman) was important socially and politically on the local level and believed in rugged individualism.

1485. Heuterman, Thomas H. *Movable Type: Biography of Legh R. Freeman*. Ames: Iowa State University Press, 1979. Realistic, unglamorized picture of the roving frontier editor. "[F]rontier newspapers by their mere existence are said to have raised the educational level of society, civilized the West and been an agent of literacy. Frontiersmen were avid readers, but whether racist, anti-Grant editorials or land promotion schemes achieved such enlightenment is questionable....Freeman hardly helped to civilize the West [through] his inflammatory vigilante or political editorials." Publishing in various states, he left a legacy of "tall tales, boosterism, and even racism."

1486. Heuterman, Thomas. "Racism in Frontier Journalism: A Case Study." *JW* 19 (April 1980): 46-50. Describes the racist writings of Legh Freeman in the *Frontier Index* between 1866-1888. The articles "met an enthusiastic reception on the inherently violent railroad frontier."

1487. Hicks, John Edward. *Adventures of a Tramp Printer, 1880-1890*. Kansas City, Mo.: Midamerica Press, 1950. Composite biography of the printer who moved from one newspaper to another.

1488. Higgins, Frances. "Sniktau: Pioneer Journalist. *CM* 5 (June 1928): 102-08.

1489. Hirsh, Jeffrey L. "Tocqueville and the Frontier Press." *JQ* 51 (1974): 116-19. Between 1835 and 1840s, in the papers of Ann Arbor, Mich., "[p]olitical struggles, violent and seemingly tasteless personal attacks, and promotion of schemes they considered beneficial to the people, were all prominent." (119) They exhibited the features of American democracy which Tocqueville had described.

1490. Holland, C. Joe "The Cherokee Indian Newspapers, 1828-1906: The Tribal Voice of a People in Transition. Ph.D. dissertation, University of Minnesota, 1956.

1491. Holman, Alfred. "Harvey W. Scott, Editor -- Review of His Half-Century Career and Estimate of His Work." *OHQ* 14 (June 1913): 95ff. Summary biography of the editor of the Portland *Oregonian*.

1492. Hooper, Osman Castle. *History of Ohio Journalism 1793-1933*. Columbus: Spahr and Glenn, 1933. The history of Ohio newspapers is one of journalistic development and progress.

1493. Robert L. Housman. Following entries. Housman was the first person to receive a doctoral degree in journalism (University of Missouri, 1934) and was one of the most prolific historians of the frontier press. His dissertation was on Montana journalism, from which he published a number of articles. See following entries.

1494. Housman, Robert L. "The Beginnings of Journalism in Frontier Montana." *FM* 15 (Summer 1935): 3-10.

1495. Housman, Robert L. "Boy Editors of Frontier Montana." *PNQ* 27 (July 1936): 219-26. "If there was one characteristic which the frontier newspapermen shared in common, it was youth. They were not only young in spirit -- venturesome, enthusiastic, vivid -- but young in years as well. They needed youth, of mind and body, to face the hardships of pioneer newspaper making: the long hours, the irregular routines, the work with inadequate equipment." (219) These characteristics are demonstrated in the biographies of two boys, Lee Travis and Allen Hosmer, who became editors in Montana at the ages of 14 and 16, respectively.

1496. Housman, Robert L. "Early Montana Territorial Journalism as a Reflection of the American Frontier in the New Northwest." Ph.D. dissertation, University of Missouri, 1934.

1497. Housman, Robert L. "The End of Frontier Journalism in Montana." *JQ* 12 (1935): 133-45. Frontier journalism was a mirror of the political, social, and economic frontier. Editors brought with them the "tradition of personal journalism characteristic of the general newspaper work of the period." (133) In regard to politics, racial problems, law and order, etc., the frontier press was a reflection of its period; papers emphasized agriculture and frontier conditions. (1870s)

1498. Housman, Robert L. "The Frontier Journalist in Montana. *MJR* 16 (1973): 56ff. The frontier journalist possessed "a restless, nervous energy and a dominant individualism."

1499. Housman, Robert L. "The Frontier Journals of Western Montana." *PNQ* 29 (July 1938): 269-76. Antiquarian account of the first three Montana newspapers on the west slope of the Rocky Mountains.

1500. Housman, Robert L. "Pioneer Montana's Journalistic 'Ghost' Camp -- Virginia City." *PNQ* 29 (January 1938): 53-59. Antiquarian account of newspapers in Montana's leading journalism city. "The first newspapers...on the Montana frontier were in Virginia City. They were rich claims. They were established at the height of the first gold rush. They prospered. It was the sight of their prosperity which stimulated other pioneers of journalism to establish and sustain claims in other sections of the Territory." (53)

1501. Hufford, Kenneth. "*The Arizona Gazette*, a Forgotten Voice in Arizona Journalism." *JAH* 7 (Winter 1966): 182-87.

1502. Hufford, Kenneth. "P.W. Dooner: Pioneer Editor of Tucson." *AW* 10 (Spring 1968): 25-42. Dooner "was not a great editor. He had no national influence, and apparently very little local influence. However, he was articulate, perceptive, sincere in his own beliefs, and vitally interested in the development of Arizona." (42) He was a journalist, however, not a politician; and in combatting the Arizona Territorial Delegate to Congress, he was no match for the politician and eventually had to stop publishing his newspaper, the Tucson *Arizonan*.

1503. Huntzicker, William E. "Historians and the American Frontier Press." *AJ* 5 (1988): 28-45. This historiographical essay provides an excellent summary of the historical study that has been done of the frontier press. For the researcher wishing to gain an overview of historical work, this essay is the best place to start.

1504. Jillson, Willard R. *First Printing in Kentucky*. Louisville: C.T. Dearing, 1936. Thomas Parvin, not John Bradford, founded the *Kentucke Gazette* in Lexington in 1787.

1505. Jillson, Willard R. "The Role of Thomas Parvin." *FCHQ* 11 (July 1937). Responds to Samuel Wilson's claim that Jillson erred in crediting Parvin, not Bradford, with being Kentucky's first printer.

1506. Jones, Douglas C. "Teresa Dean: Lady Correspondent Among the Sioux Indians." *JQ* 49 (1972): 656-62. While writing about Indians for Chicago newspapers, before she had met any, Dean deplored "the state of Sioux existence, brought on, she indicated, primarily through a native laziness and indolence." (657) After getting to know the Sioux, however, she blamed the American government's Indian affairs policies for the problems.

1507. Jordan, Philip D. "The Portrait of a Pioneer Printer." *JISHS* 23 (April 1930): 175-82. James G. Edwards, a printer in Illinois in the 1830s, "has few claims to prominence and practically all the claims to obscurity. He is of interest only because of his supreme normality. A typical frontier newspaperman who set his type by hand, pulled the galley proofs, ran off the edition, delivered it, and then attempted to collect from his subscribers -- this was Edwards and in these chores he was no different from other printers who were hoping to build up a publishing business on the frontier." (175)

1508. "Journalism of the West." *JW* 19 (April 1980). Published in book form as *Journalism in the West*, William H. Lyon, ed. Manhattan, Kan.: Sunflower University Press, 1980. Nine articles in a special issue of *Journal of the West* cover a variety of topics related to western frontier journalism, including religious newspapers, the farm press, and individual western papers and publishers. The best are those by Lyon, "The Significance of Newspapers on the American Frontier"; Heuterman, "Racism in Frontier Journalism"; and Baltensperger, "Newspaper Images of the Central Great Plains in the Late Nineteenth Century."

1509. Karolevitz, Robert F. *Newspapering in the Old West: A Pictorial History of Journalism and Printing on the Frontier*. Seattle: Superior Publishing, 1965. Anecdotal, illustrated treatment of newspapers from 1840 to the latter part of the 1800s. Frontier journalism was rough and tumble; and newspapermen were individualists, not fitting any common characeristics or stereotype.

1510. Karolevitz, Robert. *With a Shirt Tail Full of Type: The Story of Newspapering in South Dakota*. Brookings: South Dakota Press Association, 1982. Chronological narrative from 1859 to the present, illustrated profusely. The discovery of gold in the

Black Hills led a newspaper boom, and editors' boisterous approach to running their newspapers mirrored the conditions on the frontier.

1511. Katz, William A. "Tracing Western Territorial Imprints Through the National Archives." *PBSA* (1965): 1-11. Examines the First Comptroller's records of newspapers and the possible use the records have for bibliographers.

1512. Katz, William A. "The Western Printer and His Publications, 1850-90." *JQ* 44 (1967): 708-14. Publications printed in Washington territory indicate "a level of banality matched only by lack of individuality." (709) Most were printed as official government records and laws and minutes of meetings. Printers relied on government work for most of their income.

1513. Keen, Elizabeth. "The Frontier Press." *University of Wyoming Publications* 20 (July 1956): 75-100.

1514. Kelley, William Dayton. "L.A. Hine: Pioneer Journalist." Ph.D. dissertation, University of Texas, 1958.

1515. Kemble, Edward C. *A History of California Newspapers 1846-1858*, Helen Harding Bretnor, ed. Los Gatos, Calif.: Talisman, 1962. Kemble's history originally appeared in the Sacramento *Union* in 1858, providing an antiquarian record of the early press, names, dates, and places.

1516. Kindig, Everett W. "'I am in purgatory now': Journalist Hooper Warren Survives the Illinois Frontier." *IHJ* 79 (Autumn 1986): 185-96. Narrative of the trials and tribulations of an editor who began one of Illinois' earliest newspapers.

1517. King, C. Richard. "Carey Wentworth Styles: The Texas Years, 1881-1897." *JH* 1 (1974): 52-53, 55. After founding the Atlanta *Constitution*, Styles moved to Texas, where he worked on newspapers in Galveston and Fort Worth and founded two newspapers in small towns.

1518. King, R. Robert. "Media and the Murder of Joseph Smith." *MHD* 6, 1 (1986): 17-25, 53. The relationship between the press and the founder of Mormonism was bitter.

1519. Klassen, Teresa C., and Owen V. Johnson. "Sharpening of the *Blade*: Black Consciousness in Kansas, 1892-97." *JQ* 63 (1986): 298-304. The relationship between an activist black press and the growth of black consciousness and identity developed at the local level in the 1890s, as indicated by the brief history of the weekly newspaper in Parsons, Kan. The *Blade* failed, however, because there had not developed adequate socioeconomic support or a national communications network for the black press.

1520. Knauss, James Owen. *Territorial Florida Journalism*. Deland, Fla.: Florida State Historical Society, 1926. Account of 45 newspapers, beginning with the *Florida Gazette* in 1821, the territory's first; brief biographies of editors; and a checklist of extant copies of newspapers.

1521. Knight, Oliver A. *Following the Indian Wars: The Story of the Newspaper Correspondents Among the Indian Campaigners, 1866-1891*. Norman: University of Oklahoma Press, 1960. Twenty accredited newspaper correspondents covered the army's fight against the Indians. Conditions required that they sometimes had to fight along with the soldiers. Their coverage reflected their personal experiences but in general provided accurate information about campaigns and the American west.

1522. Knight, Oliver. "Mark Kellogg Telegraphed for Custer's Rescue." *NDH* 27 (Spring 1960): 95-99. Kellogg worked as a newspaper correspondent covering Gen. Custer.

1523. Knight, Oliver. "*The Owyhee Avalanche*: The Frontier Newspaper as a Catalyst in Social Change." *PNQ* 58 (April 1967): 74-81. "Although there is a question whether the mass media generally are dynamic elements or simply transmission belts for ideas, it appears likely that the frontier newspaper was an active agent in Western urbanization....[It] was a catalyst in social change in the Trans-Mississippi West. Through the cumulative impact of its frequent and regular appearance, its dissemination of timely information, and its advocacy in controversy, it accelerated the transformation of a chance grouping of individuals into a community similar to communities in the metropolis." (74) Uses the Ruby City (Idaho Territory) newspaper as a case study.

1524. Knight, Oliver. "Reporting a Gold Rush." *JQ* 38 (1961): 43-51. Reporters were on the scene when gold was discovered in the Black Hills in 1874 and when the government verified the finding in 1875, the only such instance in American journalism history of journalists having witnessed the discovery of gold. Their reporting helped fan the flames of the subsequent gold rush, which saw many miners disappointed.

1525. Korn, Anna Lee Brosius. "Major Benjamin Holliday, 1786-1859." *MHR* 14 (October 1919): 16-28. Antiquarian biography of the founder of the *Missouri Intelligencer* and Boone's Lick *Advertiser*. He was a "typical gentleman of the 'Old South' of Democratic politics" who "encouraged all matters pertaining to the public good." (28)

1526. Lacourse, Richard. "An Indian Perspective -- Native American Journalism: An Overview." *JH* 6 (1979): 34-38. Broad, brief survey by an Indian author covering from 1828 into the 20th century. "The general trend of 150 years of media development among Indian people I would capsulize in one phrase: acculturation without assimilation." (34)

1527. Larsen, Arthur J., ed. *Crusader and Feminist. Letters of Jane Grey Swisshelm, 1858-1865*. St. Paul: Minnesota Historical Society, 1934. Collection of letters preceeded by an introductory biographical essay. Swisshelm was an aggressive pioneering woman who founded the Pittsburgh *Saturday Visitor* in 1847. In the 1850s in Minnesota, she edited the St. Cloud *Visiter*, writing caustic editorial attacks on local opposition politicians.

1528. Lee, James W. "Henry W. Grady, Editor, Orator, Man." *Arena* 2 (June 1890): 9-23. See next entry.

1529. Lee, James W. *Henry W. Grady, The Editor, The Orator, The Man*. St. Louis: 1896. Eulogistic character sketch of Grady, an artist and idealist who helped the North and South dissolve their political differences and rejoin into one nation.

1530. Lent, John A. "The Press on Wheels: A History of *The Frontier Index*." *JW* 10 (1971): 662-99. "[I]t was newspapers such as the *Index* and newspapermen such as [brothers Legh and Fred Freeman, publishers of the *Index*] who had a big hand in promoting, developing, and, in the *Index's* unique situation, laying out Western cities and towns. They truly opened up the West as much as did the buffalo hunter, Indian fighter or railroader." (699)

1531. Lingenfelter, Richard E., and Karen Rix Gash. *The Newspapers of Nevada, A History and Bibliography, 1854-1979.* Reno: University of Nevada Press, 1984. (Originally published in 1964 covering the years 1858-1958). Lists 800 newspapers, with a brief historical sketch of each.

1532. Lorenz, Alfred Lawrence. "Harrison Reed: an Editor's Trials on the Wisconsin Frontier." *JQ* 53 (1976): 417-22, 462. As exemplified by Harrison Reed, editor of the *Wisconsin Enquirer*, nearly all printer-editors of Wisconsin Territory in the 1830s and 1840s faces financial, social, and political pressures. Reed left journalism because "he had endured more financial deprivation, political double-dealing and personal abuse...than he could any longer bear....Men like Reed usually established their presses with the financial support of town speculators and promoters who wanted to use the newspapers to attract immigrants to Wisconsin or by politicians who wanted a platform from which to advance their political ambitions. In neither case, however, was the support generous, and the printer-editor's position was nearly always insecure. In the one instance, his ability to stay in business depended on whether his backer held to his vision of the community's future, his enthusiasm for the project, and his money. In the other, the editor who supported a political party or leader could at almost any time find himself a casualty of the treacherous, anything-goes inter-party and intra-party battles which were part and parcel of frontier politics."(417)

1533. Lorenz, A. L. "'Out of Sorts and Out of Cash': Problems of Publishing in Wisconsin Territory, 1833-1848." *JH* 3 (1976): 34-39, 63. Frontier newspapers were founded and maintained under difficult circumstances. Many editors, however, overcame the difficulties.

1534. Luebke, Barbara F. "Elias Boudinot, Cherokee Editor: The Father of American Indian Journalism." Ph.D. dissertation, University of Missouri, 1981. Boudinot edited the first American Indian newspaper, the *Cherokee Phoenix*, for four-and-one-half years. The paper became increasingly politicized. Frustrated with Cherokee difficulties, Boudinot resigned as editor "in a 'free press' dispute with the principal chief....He deserves to be remembered...as a journalist who, to the end, fought for what he believed in."

1535. Luebke, Barbara F. "Elias Boudinot, Indian Editor: Editorial Columns from the *Cherokee Phoenix*." *JH* 6 (1979): 48-51. See previous entry.

1536. Lutrell, Estelle. "Arizona's Frontier Press." *ArHR* 6 (January 1935): 15ff. See next entry.

1537. Lutrell, Estelle. *Newspapers and Periodicals of Arizona, 1859-1911.* Tucson: University of Arizona Press, 1950. Antiquarian account of the 200 papers published in 60 towns.

1538. Lyon, William H. "Joseph Charless, The Father of Missouri Journalism." *MHSB* 17 (January 1961): 133-45. Biography of Missouri's first newpaper publisher. See next entry.

1539. Lyon, William H. *The Pioneer Editor in Missouri, 1808-1860*. Columbia: University of Missouri Press, 1965. This analysis of frontier journalism in Missouri takes into consideration outside factors such as the environment, newspaper purposes, economics, content, news values, freedom, and professional relationships among journalists. Four agents fostered the founding of pioneer papers: government, politicians, the literate citizenry who wanted reading matter, and the editor-printer himself. (Local businessmen are not included as an agent, since such an agent apparently did not appear until after the Civil War.) Frontier editors proclaimed their independence from parties rather consistently, although some of their writings were marked by rabid partisanship and editors apparently seldom equated independence with neutrality. Editors also were concerned that they fulfill their obligation to social responsibility (although their ideas of such responsibility were not the same as ours), but press performance did not always live up to the editors' avowed goals.

1540. Lyon, William H. "The Significance of Newspapers on the American Frontier." *JW* 19 (April 1980): 3-13. Suggests approaches to examining this subject and criticizes journalism historians who have "concentrated on the bizarre or the bland, on the poison pens or the place of publication." One of the essays in a special issue of *Journal of the West* (see earlier entry), challenging historians to upgrade the study of frontier journalism. "Newspapers were so prevalent, yet we know so little about them." (5)

1541. Majors, William R. *Editorial Wild Oats: Edward Ward Carmack and Tennessee Politics*. Macon, Ga.: Mercer University Press, 1984. The vituperative editor, "typical of the dynamic and aggressive editors" of the time, was a major political figure in the 1890s and early 1900s, a U.S. congressman and senator who personalized and "so polarized...issues...that compromise or consensus in public policy was difficult."

1542. Malone, Henry T. "The Cherokee Phoenix: Supreme Expression of Cherokee Nationalism." *GHQ* 34 (September 1950): 163-88. The first American Indian newspaper, founded in 1828, advocated the rights and autonomy of the Cherokees in Georgia, leading "a precariously gallant six-year existence as a defiant and intellectual champion of Indian nationalism" and helping spread "the new literary culture which had been made possible by the recent introduction of a written language." (163)

1543. Marshall, Lawrence W. "Early Denver History as Told by Contemporary Newspaper Advertisements." *CM* 8 (September 1931): 161-73.

1544. Martin, Douglas D. *Tombstone Epitaph*. Albuquerque: University of New Mexico Press, 1959. Reprints excerpts from the Arizona newspaper.

1545. McGinty, Brian. "Hung be the Heavens with Black." *AHL* 17, 10 (1983): 31-39. James King, editor of the San Francisco *Bulletin*, was killed in 1856 opposing corrupt politicians.

1546. McIntyre, Jerilyn. "Communication on a Western Frontier -- Some Questions About Context." *JH* 3 (1976): 53-55, 63. In the 1850s in California and Oregon, the conditions of the frontier exercised a major influence on the methods of communication. See next entry.

1547. McIntyre, Jerilyn Sue. "The Structure of Communication in an Emerging Frontier

Community: Jacksonville, Oregon, 1852-56." Ph.D. dissertation, University of Washington, 1973. Because of geographic isolation and the absence of newspapers, "news and information were literally carried...over the local road system by such individual carriers as express riders, postal agents, packers, travelers, and immigrants....[T]he information...was...used as the basis for action and opinion formation."

1548. McLaws, Monte B. "Early Mormon Journalism and the *Deseret News*, 1850-1898." Ph.D. dissertation, University of Missouri, 1970. The *News* overcame difficulties that could have been fatal to independent newspapers "because of the rigidly prescribed cooperative efforts directed by an all-powerful Church." It served as an organ of information, apologist, and defender for the Mormon church.

1549. McMurtrie, Douglas C. Following entries. McMurtrie was the most prolific historian of the frontier press, with more than 200 books, articles, and pamphlets to his credit. His primary interest was printing, and he documented the westward movement of the press. He took an antiquarian approach to documenting the "firsts" and other details on printing and newspapers in numerous territories and states. The following entries are intended merely to illustrate his work rather than to provide an exhaustive bibliography. A complete list of his works can be found in *McMurtrie Imprints* (Hattiesburg, Miss., 1942) and *McMurtrie Imprints -- Supplement* (Biloxi, Miss., 1946).

1550. McMurtrie, Douglas C. *The Beginning of Printing in New Mexico*. Chicago: 1932.

1551. McMurtrie, Douglas C. "The Beginnings of the Press in South Dakota." *JQ* 10 (1933): 125-31.

1552. McMurtrie, Douglas C. *The Beginnings of Printing in Arizona*. Chicago: Black Cat Press, 1937.

1553. McMurtrie, Douglas C. *A Bibliography of Nevada Newspapers, 1858 to 1875 Inclusive*. Mainz, Germany: Gutenberg-Jahrbuch, 1935.

1554. McMurtrie, Douglas C. *An Early Newspaper of Wyoming: the "Daily Telegraph" of Fort Bridger*. Chicago: Black Cat Press, 1933.

1555. McMurtrie, Douglas C. *Early Printing in Michigan, With a Bibliography of the Michigan Press, 1796-1850*. Chicago: 1931.

1556. McMurtrie, Douglas C. *Early Printing in Milwaukee*. Milwaukee: 1930.

1557. McMurtrie, Douglas C. *Early Printing in Wisconsin, With a Bibliography of the Issues of the Press, 1833-1850*. Seattle, Wash.: 1931.

1558. McMurtrie, Douglas C. *The First Printers of Chicago, With a Bibliography of the Issues of the Chicago Press, 1836-1850*. Chicago: 1927.

1559. McMurtrie, Douglas C. *A History of California Newspapers*. New York: 1927.

1560. McMurtrie, Douglas C. *John Bradford, Pioneer Printer of Kentucky*. Springfield, Ill.: Privately printed, 1931.

1561. McMurtrie, Douglas C. *Joseph Charless, Pioneer Printer of St. Louis.* Chicago: 1931.

1562. McMurtrie, Douglas C. "The Pioneer Press in Montana." *JQ* 9 (1932): 170-81.

1563. McMurtrie, Douglas C. "Pioneer Printing in Wyoming." *AWy* 9 (1933): 729-42.

1564. McMurtrie, Douglas C. "The Public Printig of the First Territorial Legislature of Colorado." *CM* 13 (March 1936): 72-78.

1565. McMurtrie, Douglas C. "The *Shawnee Sun*: The First Indian Language Periodical Published in the United States." *KHQ* 9 (1933): 339-42.

1566. McMurtrie, Douglas C. "The *Sweetwater Mines*, A Pioneer Wyoming Newspaper." *JQ* 12 (1935): 164-65.

1567. McMurtrie, Douglas C. *The Third Historical Record of Printing in California.* San Pedro, Calif.: 1935.

1568. McMurtrie, Douglas C. *The Westward Migration of the Printing Press, 1786-1836.* Mainz, Germany: Gutenberg-Jahrbuch, 1930.

1569. McMurtrie, Douglas C., and Albert H. Allen. *Early Printing in Colorado.* Denver: Hirschfeld Press, 1935. This is McMurtrie's most substantial history, containing a 136-page history along with a listing of imprints and newspapers.

1570. Mellen, George Frederick. "Southern Editors," 470-483 in *The South in the Building of the Nation*, Vol. 7. Richmond: Southern Historical Publications Society, 1909. Compilation of the main southern editors during the 19th century with special emphasis on the changes they brought about.

1571. Mikkelson, Dwight. "'Kentucky Gazette,' 1787-1848: The Herald of a Noisy World." Ph.D. dissertation, University of Kentucky, 1963.

1572. Morford, Lee. "Newspapers of the Black Hills." *BHE* 18 (January 1930): 61-66.

1573. Morgan, Lael. *History of the Tundra Times.* Fairbanks, Alaska: Eskimo, Indian, Aleut Printing Co., 1972.

1574. Murphy, James E., and Sharon M. Murphy. *Let My People Know: American Indian Journalism.* Norman: University of Oklahoma Press, 1981. Survey history and reference work, covering 1828 to 1978, of a subject previously given little attention by historians. Indian journalism developed in response to stereotypes presented in the white press and as an attempt to provide communication channels for Indians themselves. Chapters cover various topics, followed by a directory of Indian media in each state.

1575. Murphy, Sharon. "American Indians and the Media: Neglect and Stereotype." *JH* 6 (1979): 39-43. "Long before television and films, the print media of the 19th Century did their part to foster inaccurate images of Indians. In fact, much of news reporting about Indians was done in advocacy fashion, encouraging or at least condoning the savage treatment of Indians." (39) Such stereotyping continues today.

1576. Murphy, Sharon. "Neglected Pioneers: 19th Century Native American Newspapers."
JH 4 (1977): 79-82, 98-100. Overview of various American Indian newspapers since
their start in 1828. They "have served as watchdog, teacher and advocate, promoting
literacy, reporting on encroachments by white civilizations and commending the heritage and accomplishments of the Indians." (79)

1577. Myers, John M. *Print in a Wild Land*. New York: Doubleday, 1967. Anecdotal history of creative, personalized frontier journalism and its relationship to boisterous
frontier society. This study is composed mainly of writings from newspapers.

1578. Nash, Lee M. "Scott and the *Oregonian*: The Editor as Historian." *OHQ* 70
(September 1969): 197-232. Harvey Scott served as first president of the Oregon
Historical Society and had a special interest in Oregon history.

1579. Nelson, Jack A. "The Comic Frontier." *MHD* 6, 1 (1986): 46-49. "Those enduring
the isolation [of the western frontier] often had little enough to laugh about, and most
editors...saw it as part of their function to offer a laugh now and then." The best humor "sprang from local experience and from the wry scrutiny of the editor of what
was taking place around him." (46)

1580. Nelson, Jack A. "Roommates: Mark Twain and Dan De Quille: Partners in Hoaxes in
Old West." *MHD* 6, 1 (1986): 2-7. The two reporter-humorists were unmatched in
their ability to tell bogus stories. They "brought life and international attention to the
[*Territorial Enterprise*] -- due in no little part to the casual way they viewed the truth,
helped along by the free reign given them by their editors." (2)

1581. Nelson, Jack A. "The Pioneer Press of the Great Basin." Ph.D. dissertation, University of Missouri, 1971. "The portrait of the frontier editor that emerges [from this
study] is far different from that of the crusading editor usually depicted in most accounts. In Nevada...most of the early journals forgot public responsibility and offered their allegiances for sale to the highest bidder....[T]hey seldom crusaded for
unpopular causes."

1582. "Newspapers of South Dakota." *SDHC* 11 (1922): 411-519. Special issue of *South
Dakota Historical Collections* including a tabular survey of newspapers through 1883
and reprints of the front pages of several early papers.

1583. Nichols, Roger L. "Printers' Ink and Red Skins: Western Newspapermen and the
Indians." *KQ* 3 (Fall 1971): 82-88. In recommending how to deal with Indians,
journalists "viewed aborigines through glasses tinted by attitudes of racial or cultural
superiority. As a result, harsh and violent action received open support....[Their
views] usually followed the majority opinion held by their frontier readers." (87)

1584. Nixon, Raymond B. "Henry W. Grady, Reporter: A Reinterpretation." *JQ*
(December 1935): 341-56. Grady was primarily a reporter, rather than an orator, editorial writer, or politician.

1585. Nixon, Raymond B. *Henry W. Grady, Spokesman of the New South*. New York:
Knopf, 1943. The press was part of the renaissance of economic and social forces in
the South. Grady was a passionate and persuasive advocate of the view that the South
was as much a part of the Union as New England and that economic and spritual re-
building had to go hand in hand. Places much emphasis on Grady as an excellent

reporter.

1586. Norris, Wendell W. "The Transient Frontier Weekly as a Stimulant to Home-steading." *JQ* 30 (1953): 44-48. The increase in the number of weekly newspapers in the last third of the 19th century did not result directly from an increase in western settlement and populaton. Many newspapers "were founded only to stimulate prof-itable frontier land booms and to print the legal notices required by the filing of more than a million homestead claims. Such papers were largely scaffolding in the building of the West, and they were discarded once settlement was completed." (44)

1587. Norton, Wesley. *Religious Newspapers in the Old Northwest to 1861: A History, Bibliography, and Record of Opinion.* Athens: Ohio University Press, 1977. News-papers helped shape public opinion and thought on morals, mores, and issues. They were especially concerned about the slavery issue. In an area with young or non-ex-istent institutions, the press could play a comparatively important role. The editors persevered despite personal and financial difficulties.

1588. Nye, Bill. "Wyoming Scrapbook: Bill Nye's Experience." *AWy* 16 (January 1944): 65-70. The humor columnist's recollections of his life in Wyoming newspapering.

1589. Oczon, Annabelle M. "Bilingual and Spanish-Language Newspapers in Territorial New Mexico." *NMHR* 54 (January 1979): 45-52. This winning essay in a New Mexico contest for high school students describes the work of Spanish-American journalists in the last half of the 19th century. Despite the difficulties of publishing, they played important political roles and helped preserve the Hispanic culture.

1590. Oehlerts, Donald E., comp. *Guide to Colorado Newspapers, 1859-1963.* Denver: Bibliographical Center for Research, 1964. Reference guide lists publication dates of all Colorado newspapers and library locations of extant copies.

1591. O'Reilly, Henry. "The First Daily Newspaper in the West, and the First Telegraph Line between the Atlantic and the Mississippi Valley." *HM* 1 (January 1867).: 22-24. Commemorative article marking the 40th anniversary of the founding of the Rochester (N.Y.) *Daily Advertiser*, an "epoch in the history of our Continent." (22)

1592. Perrin, William Henry. *The Pioneer Press of Kentucky: From the Printing of the First Paper West of the Alleghenies, August 11, 1787, to the Establishment of the Daily Press in 1830.* Louisville: John P. Morton, 1888. Commemorative, centennial history describes the operation and content of the first paper in the area, the *Kentucke Gazette*. Backers proposed starting the paper to support their plan to separate Ken-tucky (then a county) from its mother state, Virginia. John Bradford offered to pub-lish the paper if he received adequate patronage.

1593. Pickett, Calder M. *Ed Howe: Country Town Philosopher.* Lawrence: University of Kansas Press, 1968. Biography of the perversely humorous editor of the Atchison (Kan.) *Globe* who was noted for his pithy editorial statements and known as the "Sage of Potato Hill." Howe, who founded the *Globe* in 1877 and served as its stub-born editor into the 20th century, gained a national reputation for his witty editorial comments. He also was a booster of small-town life, a realist philosopher, a preju-diced cynic, and an accomplished journalist.

1594. Purcell, George W. "A Survey of Early Newspapers in the Middle Western States."

IMH 20 (December 1924): 347-63. Summary "of the early history of newspapers in this vast territory," dating from 1787, which "reads like a novel of heroic characters, and brave men -- the torchbearers of the gospel of liberty to light civilization's path over the prairies and in the fertile valleys of the Ohio, Mississippi and Missouri rivers." (347)

1595. Quebral, Nora Cruz. *"Farm Journal* and American Agriculture, 1877-1965." Ph.D. dissertation, University of Illinois, 1966. "Sociological" explanation of the growth, policies, attitudes, organization, and life of the magazine as a result of developments in agriculture and farm magazine publishing.

1596. Quebral, Nora C. "Wilmer Atkinson and the Early *Farm Journal.*" *JQ* 47 (1970): 65-70, 80. The *Farm Journal*, an agriculture magazine, succeeded because it "met the current need of a specific class of readers for a low-priced source of information tailored to their frame of interest." (80)

1597. Raitz, Karl B., and Stanley D. Brunn. "Geographic Patterns in the Historical Development of Farm Publications." *JH* 6 (1979): 14-15, 31-32. "[F]arming and farm journalism [1790s to 1950s] were so intimately interrelated that the locational and technological vagaries of agriculture had a direct effect on the geography of farm journal publication....As the farmer moved west, the farm journal publisher followed. The earliest journals printed little more than general information on plant and animal husbandry, but as agricultural science developed and specialized farming regions evolved, the farm magazine gradually became less descriptive and more analytic and demonstrative of scientific farming techniques." (14)

1598. Ray, Grace E. "Early Oklahoma Newspapers." University of Oklahoma *Bulletin* 28 (1936).

1599. Reed, T.W. *Henry W. Grady -- A Sketch Based Upon Personal Recollections.* Athens: University of Georgia Press, 1935. Anecdotal biography of "one of the greatest men in the history of our country." Despite his other activities, Grady considered himself primarily a journalist.

1600. Reilly, Tom. "A Spanish-Language Voice of Dissent in Antebellum New Orleans." *LaH* 23 (1983): 325-39. *La Patria* and *La Union* "attempted to fulfill their self-appointed role as 'vigilent watchdog for the interests of Spanish nationals'....They continually debated and rebutted the expansionist views of their larger English-language contemporaries, while also serving the business and literary needs of their readership. [They] were activist, outspoken and often reflected political sentiment in their community." (338)

1601. Rice, William B. *Southern California's First Newspaper: The Founding of the Los Angeles Star.* Los Angeles: Glen Dawson, 1941. Brief account of the early financial basis of the *Star*, editorial stands, politics, and difficulties in getting news from the outside because of geography and the slowness of transportation and communication. During the Civil War, it was pro-Democratic and anti-emancipation and encountered difficulties with the government.

1602. Riley, Sam G. "Alex Posey: Creek Indian Editor/Humorist/Poet." *AJ* 1, 2 (1984): 67-76. Posey, the colorful and talented editor of the *Indian Journal* in Oklahoma Indian Territory from 1902-1908, "asserted himself as a forceful spokesman for what he considered to be his people's best interest." (67-68)

1603. Riley, Sam G. *"The Cherokee Phoenix*: The Short Unhappy Life of the First American Indian Newspaper." *JQ* 53 (1976): 666-71. Narrative of the difficulties of editor Elias Boudinot and the *Cherokee Phoenix* and *Indian Advocate*, which "for six troubled years argued the cause of Indian rights" (667) until it suspended publication in 1834.

1604. Riley, Sam G. *"Indian Journal*, Voice of Creek Tribe, Now Oklahoma's Oldest Newspaper." *JQ* 59 (1982): 46-51, 183. Founded in 1876, the newspaper gave its tribe "a chance to write and read about [Indians' own]...accomplishments and problems." (46) Today, it is a small-town weekly and no longer considered an "Indian paper."

1605. Riley, Sam G. "A Note of Caution -- The Indian's Own Prejudice, as Mirrored in the First Native American Newspaper." *JH* 6 (1979): 44-47. Although recent white journalism historians have tended to be sympathetic toward American Indians and critical of Anglo-American treatment of them, they need to recognize that "the Indian was and is no more inherently egalitarian than the whites who engulfed him....Though Cherokees were themselves the victims of intense racial discrimination, an examination of the *Phoenix* [edited by Elias Boudinott] reveals that the tribe had prejudices of its own." (14-15)

1606. Rivers, William L. "William Cowper Brann and His *Iconoclast*." *JQ* 35 (1958): 433-38. Although in the 1890s "Texas had become accustomed to wild-swinging newspapers...Brann's new magazine was different, its iconoclasm overwhelming. The editor slashed at preachers...Texas church-goers...and even postal employes." (433) He angered many people in Waco with his extreme criticism and insults and finally was killed by a lawyer.

1607. Robbins, William G. "Some Perspectives on Law and Order in Frontier Newspapers." *JW* 17 (January 1978): 53-61. Like other Oregonians between 1850 and 1890, editors advocated law and order "in the name of community building and economic progress." Yet, many newspapers advocated extra-legal measures to obtain "justice." Members of minority groups were frequently the targets.

1608. Ross, Mrs. W.P. *The Life and Times of Hon. William P. Ross*. Fort Smith, Ark.: Weldon & Williams, 1893. Ross, former principal chief of the Cherokee Nation, served as editor of the *Cherokee Advocate*, the official newspaper of the Cherokee tribe, and *Indian Journal*, the official newspaper of the Creek tribe in Oklahoma.

1609. Russell, Charles E. *Pioneer Editor in Early Iowa*. Washington: Ransdell, 1941. Sketch of Russell's father, Edward. The editor of the Davenport *Gazette* was an ardent abolitionist and reformer, a crusading editor. He lost his paper after the Civil War in his battle against the railroads.

1610. Sackett, S.J. *E.W. Howe*. New York: Twayne, 1972. Concentrates on the literary efforts of the editor of the Atchison (Kan.) *Globe*. He was a failure as a novelist and philosopher.

1611. Sageser, A. Bower. *Joseph L. Bristow: Kansas Progressive*. Lawrence: University Press of Kansas, 1968. Bristow, a liberal politician and publisher of the *Irrigation*

Farmer and Salina *Evening Journal*, crusaded for reform and against special interests.

1612. Salisbury, Guy H. "Early History of the Press of Erie County." *BHSP* 2 (1880). New York chronicle written by the son of Smith Salisbury, a pioneer printer in Buffalo.

1613. Savage, William W. "Newspapers and Local History: A Critique of Robert R. Dykstra's *The Cattle Towns.*" *JW* 10 (1971): 572-77. Contrary to Dykstra's explanation, newspapers in the American west were not always merely boosters of communities, providing glowing accounts in order to attract development and receiving in return ample advertising and subscriptions. Some were published by special interest groups and had little connection with their towns.

1614. Scheiber, Thomas J. "The Newspaper Chain of W.B. Harris." *JQ* 28 (1951): 219-24. After taking over the weekly newspaper in Ellettsville, Ind., in 1872, Harris eventually publsihed 138 newspapers, maintaining about 15 at any one time.

1615. Schellie, Don. *The Tucson Citizen: A Century of Arizona Journalism*. Tucson: Tucson Daily Citizen, 1970. In-house centennial history sponsored by the newspaper.

1616. Schmitt, Jo Ann. *Fighting Editors: The Story of Editors Who Faced Six-Shooters with Pens and Won*. San Antonio, Tex.: Naylor, 1958. Colorful popular account of Texas editors.

1617. Scott, Frank W. *Newspapers and Periodicals of Illinois, 1814-1879*. Springfield: State Historical Library, 1910. Introductory essay emphasizes political history and methods. Remainder of book is primarily a listing of publications.

1618. Scroggins, Albert Taylor, Jr. "Nathaniel Patten, Jr., and the *Missouri Intelligencer* and *Boone's Lick Advertiser*." Ph.D. dissertation, University of Missouri, 1962. The *Intelligencer* was the first country newspaper in Missouri and the first newspaper west of St. Louis. Patten, its resourceful and enterprising editor, persevered despite the inherent problems of publishing on the frontier

1619. Sibley, Marilyn McAdams. *Lone Stars and State Gazettes: Texas Newspapers before the Civil War*. College Station: Texas A&M University Press, 1983. Comprehensive chronicle (and annotated checklist) of newspapers and editors from 1813 to 1860. The main purpose of most newspapers was to support or oppose politicians, political causes, or religious ideas. When financial support ended, most papers ceased publication.

1620. Simpson, Roger Allan. "The Functions of Communication Activities in Frontier Warfare in Washington Territory, 1855-56." Ph.D. dissertation, University of Washington, 1973. Theoretical approach to a historical situation examines how, during a war between whites and Indians, newspapers performed the functions of "surveillance" and "correlation."

1621. Smith, Henry Nash, ed. *Mark Twain of the Enterprise*. Berkeley: University of California Press, 1957. Collection of 30 articles written by Twain for the *Territorial Enterprise* of Virginia City, Nev. Introductory essay describes Twain's daily work as a reporter and editorial writer and the benefit that the "discipline of a professional journalist" added to his literary writing.

1622. Smith, Robert W. *"The People's Party Paper* and Georgia's Tom Watson." *JQ* 42 (1975): 110-11. Watson, the agrarian reform politician, ran the newspaper on a shoestring.

1623. Spell, Lota M. *Pioneer Printer -- Samuel Bangs in Mexico and Texas.* Austin: University of Texas Press, 1963.

1624. Stewart, Paul R. "The *Prairie Schooner*: A Little Magazine's First 25 Years." Ph.D. dissertation, University of Illinois, 1954.

1625. Stone, William Jesse, Jr. "A Historical Survey of Leading Texas Denominational Newspapers: 1846-1861." Ph.D. dissertation, University of Texas, 1974. "[M]ost papers tended to establish printing headquarters which overran sources of supply, necessitating a 'retreat' eastward to new headquarters; editors generally received so little church compensation that they were forced to preach to provide income; parallel business ventures into job printing, book sales, and book printing were attempted; and the 'news hole' content was often as much secular as sacred. All papers...[were] 'of the world' in that they...[were] defenders of the social, economic, and political status quo."

1626. Stratton, Porter A. *The Territorial Press of New Mexico 1834-1912.* Albuquerque: University of New Mexico Press, 1969. Newspapers in the New Mexico Territory were involved in the political and social debates, including conflicts between the United States and Mexico and fights with Indians.

1627. Stroupe, Henry S. "The Beginning of Religious Journalism in North Carolina, 1823-1865." *NCHR* 30 (January 1953): 1-22. Religious journalism was made possible by religious reawakening in America beginning in the early 19th century. Article contains an historical overview and a checklist of publications and where extant copies can be located.

1628. Stroupe, Henry Smith. *The Religious Press in the South Atlantic States, 1802-1865. An Annotated Bibliography with Historical Introduction and Notes.* Durham, N.C.: Duke University Press, 1956. Profiles of 159 publications.

1629. Summerville, James. "Albert Roberts: Journalist of the New South." *THQ* 42 (1983): 18-38, part I; 179-202, part II. Editor of the Nashville *Republican Banner*, Roberts is not so well known as some of his contemporaries, but he played a leading role in the post-Civil War development of Nashville and foreshadowed the more famous work of Henry Watterson and Henry Grady in the New South movement.

1630. Taeuber, Irene B. "Changes in the Content and Presentation of Reading Material in Minnesota Weekly Newspapers." *JQ* 9 (1932): 281-89. Early newspapers served as newspapers, magazines, and sales media. In 1860-1870, there was greater emphasis on non-local news; by 1890, a greater emphasis on local news. The character of papers was influenced by culture and competing dailies. After 1910, magazine content decreased from 40 per cent to 25 per cent. Advertising throughout the period took up 50 per cent of space. Early papers were political/civic and editorializing organs. Later papers placed more emphasis on cultural, economic, sports, and personal news.

1631. Taft, William H. *Missouri Newspapers.* Columbia: University of Missouri Press, 1964. This chronicle of the rise and development of certain papers, editors, and publishers provides many facts, figures, dates, etc., but little overall analysis or thematic structure. It is more a record than incisive history. The pioneer period had ended by 1850.

1632. Terrell, Russell F. *A Study of the Early Journalistic Writings of Henry W. Grady*. Nashville, Tenn.: George Peabody College, 1927. Analyzes the literary style of selected writings from 1869-1883.

1633. Thrapp, Dan L., ed. *Dateline Fort Bowie: Charles Fletcher Lummis Reports on an Apaches War*. Norman: University of Oklahoma Press, 1979. Collection of Lummis' dispatches to the Los Angeles *Times* on the final Apache uprisings in the 1880s.

1634. Thwaites, R. G. "The Ohio Valley Press before the War of 1812-1815." *AASP* 19 (April 1909): 309-68. Frontier publishers from 1786 to 1820 faced unfavorable conditions and problems. But they were optimistic, innovative, hardworking, and enterprising -- though not prudent or conservative. While politically trenchant, the partisanship and vituperation were "quite in line with prevailing tastes." (352) The pioneer editors "reflected credit on the profession of journalism, and did admirable service in the early development of the Middle West." (353)

1635. Towne, Jackson E. "Printing in New Mexico Beyond Santa Fe and Taos, 1848-1875." *NMHR* 35 (April 1960): 109-17. Antiquarian account of the earliest newspaper publishing in Santa Fe, Taos, Mesilla, and Albuquerque.

1636. Trever, Karl. "Wisconsin Newspapers as Publishers of the Federal Laws, 1836-1874." *WMH* 31 (March 1948): 305-25. Politicians awarded newspaper publishers contracts to print federal laws as a means of dispensing patronage. Narrative history of how the system operated and reasons for its demise.

1637. Turk, Eleanor L. "The German Newspapers of Kansas." *KH* 6 (Spring 1983): 46-64. In the last half of the 19th century, the "German-language press...represented a major German cultural heritage which was deliberately perpetuated despite the strong competition from local American papers....By focusing on materials which would support...readers' pride in being both German and American...the weekly German-language press reinforced that unique quality of being a 'hyphenated-American.'" (64)

1638. Turnbull, George. *History of Oregon Newspapers*. Portland: Binfords and Mort, 1939. This chronicle describes the history with details of individual papers by counties, beginning with the first one established in 1846. Pioneer journalism was personal.

1639. Turnbull, George. "The Schoolmaster of the Oregon Press." *JQ* 13 (1938): 359-69, 382. Laudatory account of the achievements of the Portland *Oregonian's* editor, Harvey Scott. He gave intellectual leadership to his state and its journalism.

1640. Turner, Wallace R. "Frank Hall: Colorado Journalist, Public Servant, and Historian." *CM* 53 (1976): 328-51. Romantic biography of the Denver *Post* editor who was also "a territorial delegate, and a stellar citizen, whose involvement in and concern for the welfare of the region spanned almost six decades" (1860-1917). (328) He "was modest but expectantly ambitious...romantic but not impractical...scrupulously honest and exceedingly stubborn when principles were involved." (351)

1641. van Ravenswaay, Charles. "Pioneer Presses in Missouri." *MHSB* 7 (1951): 296-301.

1642. Wade, John Donald. "Henry W. Grady." *SR* 3 (1938): 479-509. Cynical evalution of Grady's New South philosophy.

1643. Wagner, Henry R. "New Mexico Spanish Press." *NMHR* 12 (January 1937): 1-40. Chronological description of early Spanish-language newspapers, including excerpts of their content and a guide to extant copies.

1644. Watson, Elmo S. "The Indian Wars and the Press, 1866-1867." *JQ* 17 (1940): 301-10. "The kind of news from the 'Wild West' which the newspapers east of the Mississippi began publishing in 1866 reflects little credit upon American journalism. Depending mainly upon volunteer correspondents more gifted in imaginative writing than in accurate reporting, they spread before their readers the kind of highly-colored accounts of Indian raids and 'massacres' that the most sensational yellow journals of a later period might have envied." (302)

1645. Watson, Elmo S. "The Last Indian War, 1890-91 -- A Study of Newspaper Jingoism." *JQ* 20 (1943): 205-19. Newspapers exaggerated, distorted, and faked news stories about the peaceful activities of the Sioux Indians in North and South Dakota, making it appear as if the Indians were beginning an uprising. The misunderstanding of the Sioux actions led to war.

1646. Watson, Helen R. "A Journalistic Medley: Newspapers and Periodicals in a Small North Carolina Community, 1859-1860." *NCHR* 60 (1983): 457-83. Newspapers and magazines played a central role in the lives of the Rocky Mount community and its residents.

1647. Weigle, Clifford F. *The Pioneer Press in California, 1846-1869*. Stanford, Calif.: Stanford University Library, 1937. Chronological narrative of California's earliest newspapers, whose editors were drawn there, along with other miners, by the lure of gold. Most newspapers had short lives, and few editors prospered.

1648. Weigle, Clifford F. "San Francisco Journalism, 1847-1851." *JQ* 14 (1937): 151-57. Chapter in previous entry.

1649. Wentz, Roby. *Eleven Western Presses: An Account of How the First Printing Press Came to Each of the Eleven States*. Los Angeles: Privately Printed, 1956.

1650. Whisenhunt, Donald W. "The Frontier Newspaper: A Guide to Society and Culture." *JQ* 45 (1968): 726-28. Study of newspapers in west and central Texas in the 1860s indicates that small frontier papers served as a barometer of society and of cultural development. The frontier newspaper "played an important role in shaping the thoughts of the average person who usually lived in extreme isolation...[from] the outside world....[It also] reflects trends and thoughts that are often ignored or overlooked in general histories of the frontier." (726) The study provides little documentation of its thesis, concentrating on the histories of a handful of crude, small papers published by the same editor.

1651. Whitaker, John R. "The Influence of the West on the Evolution of Personal Journalism in the United States since the Civil War." Ph.D. dissertation, University of

Texas, 1947.

1652. White, Karl T. "Frontier Journalist Stakes Early Claim." *Matrix* 65 (Spring 1980): 24-27. Naunita Daisey was a frontier journalist who moved to Oklahoma in 1889 after Oklahoma land was first opened to settlement. She worked as a newspaper correspondent for several papers and founded two all-women settlements.

1653. White, Z.L. "Western Journalism." *HNMM* 77 (1888): 678-99. In the 1830s west of the Alleghany Mountains, many "restless, erratic geniuses drifted into journalism, and the frontier newspapers they made, often written and printed under great difficulties, possessed the merit of having at least a positive and unmistakable individuality. They were crude in style and in moral tone as well as in mechanical construction...but the papers were made for a constituency that was as peculiar in its tastes as it was independent in its habits and thought, and cared less for the form than for the substance of what it had to read." (678) The later successful newspapers, such as the Cincinnati *Commercial* and San Francisco *Daily Examiner* throughout the later 1800s, are a legacy from the pioneer press.

1654. Wiley, Bonnie. "History of *The Portland Oregonian* with Emphasis on Early Years." Ph.D. dissertation, Southern Illinois University, 1965. Admiring survey history from the newspaper's founding in 1850 to 1965, with emphasis on Harvey Scott, its editor, and Henry Pittock, its "publisher-businessman," from the 1860s to 1880s. Of concern to them were financial affairs, the editorial page, journalistic quality, the railroads, political issues, and the community.

1655. Willard, James F. "Spreading the News of the Early Discoveries of Gold in Colorado." *CM* 6 (May 1929): 98-104.

1656. Williams, Leonard, ed. *Cavorting on the Devil's Fork: The Pete Whetstone Letters of C.F.M. Noland*. Memphis: Memphis State University Press, 1979. Collection of Noland's humorous newspaper writings from 1837 to 1856.

1657. Williams, Nudie. "The Black Press in Oklahoma: The Formative Years, 1889-1907." *CO* 61 (1983): 308-19. "[W]hile...black newspapers defended blacks almost to the point of losing objectivity, most were true newspapers in every respect....The black press was, for the most part, protesting against the denial of the very basic human and civil rights that were guaranteed to former slaves as citizens of the United States - - rights that were withheld because they were blacks. The attack was not against the principles and ideals of America, but rather against the gross inequities in the application and the distribution of these principles and ideals." (318)

1658. Wilson Quintus C. "A Study and Evaluation of the Editorial Writing and Work of Joseph Wheelock, St. Paul Editor from 1850 to 1906." Ph.D. dissertation, University of Minnesota, 1952.

1659. Wilson, Samuel M. "John Bradford, Kentucky's First Printer." *FCHQ* 11 (October 1937): 260-69. Provides another round in the Jillson-Wilson dispute. See next entry.

1660. Wilson, Samuel M. "John Bradford, Not Thomas Parvin, First Printer in Kentucky." *FCHQ* 11 (April 1937): 145-51. Disputes Jillson's claim that Parvin, not Bradford, was Kentucky's first printer.

1661. Wilson, Samuel M. "The 'Kentucky Gazette' and John Bradford Its Founder." *PBSA* 31, part 2 (1937): 102-32. Laudatory account of Bradford as a talented printer and a public-spirited citizen.

1662. Working, D.W. "Some Forgotten Pioneer Newspapers." *CM* 4 (May 1927): 93-100.

1663. Wright, Donald K. "Hiram Brundage and Wyoming's First Newspaper." *JH* 2 (1975): 15, 32. Brief antiquarian account of the army post telegraph operator who founded the Fort Bridger *Daily Telegraph* in 1863.

1664. Wrone, David R. "John Sterling Harper, Founder of 160 Papers." *JQ* 45 (1968): 538-41. "'The Father of Western Journalism'...[who] founded more newspapers than any other man...followed a pattern....He would found a newspaper in a promising community, it would fail or he would sell out at a good offer, and he then would...start anew." (538) He averaged founding nearly three newspapers a year from 1852 to 1911, mainly in Illinois and the northern Mississippi Valley.

1665. Yates, Norris W. *William T. Porter and the Spirit of the Times: A Study of the Big Bear School of Humor.* Baton Rouge: Louisiana State University Press, 1957. Literary study of the development of southwestern humor from poorly constructed anecdotes to well structured short stories.

1666. Young, John P. *Journalism in California.* San Francisco: Chronicle Publishing Co., 1915.

11

The Emergence of Modern Journalism, 1900–1945

1667. Acheson, Sam Hanna. *35, 000 Days In Texas*. New York: Macmillan, 1938. The history of the Galveston *News* and Dallas *News* and their progress since 1842 shows how to build a successful newspaper. Editors campaigned for local and regional economic improvement: railroads, city parks, government reforms, etc. The Dallas *News* helped transform a hamlet into a metropolis.

1668. Achterkirchen, John. "Prior Restraint Before Near: Was It Sanctioned?" *Graduate Communication Studies*, Vol. 1, No. 1 (Spring 1977), published by the School of Journalism, Southern Illinois University. This article, in a collection of five historical studies by Southern Illinois University graduate students, studies 14 state cases involving prior restraint before the 1931 *Near v. Minnesota* decision. The courts sanctioned prior restraint in four of the cases.

1669. Adams, Samuel Hopkins. *Alexander Wollcott: His Life and His World*. New York: Reynal and Hitchcock, 1945. Wollcott was an outstanding theatrical critic, essayist, war reporter, and observer of human affairs although he was arrogant, egocentric, and cutting in his remarks and sometimes petty and bickering. Yet he also could be sociable and sympathetic. He was so successful as a newspaper journalist and broadcaster that his beginning salary of $15 a week on the New York *Times* reached $100,000 a year at the peak of his radio and writing career.

1670. Adamson, June. "Nellie Kenyon and the Scopes 'Monkey Trial.'" *JH* 2 (1975): 88-89, 97. Interesting group of "tales" concerning Nellie Kenyon's persistence in getting a story and her genius of coverage, using the Scopes' trial as the prime example.

1671. Adler, Betty, and Jane Wilhelm. *H.L.M.: The Mencken Bibliography*. Baltimore: Johns Hopkins Press, 1961. Citations to Mencken's writing, including his newspaper articles.

1672. Allen, Charles L. "Is the (Kansas City) *Star*, a Waning Luminary?" *JQ* 5, 3 (1928): 1-14. Study of the *Star's* influence on municipal affairs after Nelson's death in 1915. "The Star has been very successful" (13) and has kept up Nelson's standards.

1673. Alpern, Sara. *Freda Kirchwey: A Woman of The Nation*. Cambridge, Mass.: Harvard University Press, 1987. Alpern worked as an editor on the liberal *Nation* from 1918 to 1937, when she bought it, and operated it until 1955. She championed such causes as political liberalism, birth control, social welfare, and freedom of expression.

1674. Anderson, Fenwick. "Hail to the Editor-in-Chief: Harding vs. Cox, 1920." *JH* 1 (1974): 46-49. Deals with the presidential race between Harding and Cox, both of whom had ties to the journalism profession. This study explores how the journalistic backgrounds of both candidates affected the campaign and how biased the coverage of it was in their own papers.

1675. Anderson, Fenwick. "Parker as *The Commoner* Depicted Him." *JQ* 49 (1972): 296-305. The *Commoner* (1901-23) was founded by William Jennings Bryan as a political organ. Its stand on the candidacy of Judge Alton B. Parker reflected Bryan's shift in position during the 1904 presidential campaign.

1676. Ashley, Perry J., ed. *American Newspaper Journalists, 1901-1925*. Detroit: Gale Research Co., 1984. Collection of biographies of prominent journalists.

1677. Atwood, Roy Alden. "The Rural Press and the Electronic Mythos: Images and Interlocking Interests in Southeastern Iowa, 1900-1917." *JH* 10 (1983): 18-24. The rural press helped create the "mythical realities" of electricity.

1678. Baker, Richard T. *A History of the Graduate School of Journalism, Columbia University*. New York: Columbia University Press, 1954. Narrative of the school endowed by Joseph Pulitzer and brought to fruition by Columbia president Nicholas Butler. Baker was a member of the school's journalism faculty.

1679. Barrett, James Wyman, ed. *The End of the World*. New York: Harper, 1931. A collection of reminiscences by staff members describing the final days of the New York *World*.

1680. Barrett, James Wyman. *The World, The Flesh and the Messrs. Pulitzer*. New York: Vanguard, 1931. Barrett was a staff member of the *World* who, like other staff members, felt miserable about its sale. Poignant book reveals Barrett's personal bias and blames Pulitzer's sons, who were poor businessmen, for the sale.

1681. Bartness, Harold L. "Hearst in Milwaukee." Ph.D. dissertation, University of Minnesota, 1969. The *Wisconsin News* "was the real Hearst -- the embodiment of the type of journalism for which he is remembered. It wore the typically flashy Hearst typographical dress, shouted news of crime and scandal, and pushed with Hearstian vigor its owner's political ideas."

1682. Beasley, Maurine. "Lorena A. Hickok: Journalistic Influence on Eleanor Roosevelt." *JQ* 57 (1980): 281-86. As a close personal friend of the First Lady, Hickok, an AP reporter, through her extensive coverage helped Mrs. Roosevelt become a public figure and advised her on how to work effectively with the other women reporters assigned to cover her.

1683. Beasley, Maurine. "Women in Journalism Education: The Formative Period, 1908-1930." *JH* 13 (1986): 10-18. In the early 1900s, "journalism education was an inhospitable, if not actually hostile, field for women. Yet despite prejudice in hiring and widespread fears by men and some women that women would lose their femininity by emulating male journalists, women enrolled in journalism schools." (10) "Journalism education conveyed a different message to women students than to men....[T]he two sexes were not treated equally. Women faced a set of expectations and barriers not presented to men. But they persevered in getting an education in journalism even though they often were unable to make the same use of it as men." (17)

1684. Becker, Stephen. *Marshall Field III: a Biography*. New York: Simon & Schuster, 1964. Field was a millionaire with liberal, even leftist, leanings and a philanthropist. He changed from being a playboy because he developed a social consciousness. He operated the newspaper *PM*, 1940-49, and Chicago *Sun*, 1941. He did his good deeds not because of desires for personal gain but because he truly believed that the benefit and security of all classes would be assured only if no class were overlooked. He championed a number of liberal social causes.

1685. Beiswinger, George L. "FDR and the National Daily That Never Was." *MHD* 7, 1 (1987): 2-6, 28. Roosevelt's plans to publish a national newspaper after retiring from the presidency were ended by his death. He long had had an interest in newspaper publishing.

1686. Bell, William Jackson. "A Historical Study of the Kansas City Star Since the Death of William Rockhill Nelson, 1915-1949." Ph.D. dissertation, University of Missouri, 1949.

1687. Bennion, Sherilyn Cox. "Reform Agitation in the American Periodical Press, 1920-29." *JQ* 48 (1971): 692-59, 713. The mass magazines of the 1920s did not talk about reform because their readers did not want to hear about reform. (713) Changes in society had occurred since before World War I, and magazines simply reflected the interests of the public; they were reflectors rather than molders of opinion.

1688. Bethune, Beverly M. "A Case of Overkill: The FBI and the New York City Photo League." JH 7 (1980) 87-91, 108. In the 1930s-1940s, the FBI, as it has been accused in the 1970s of doing, used illegal, improper, and high-handed methods against the Photo League, a social documentary photo group, which in 1947 was listed as a subversive organization and in 1949 was accused of being a Communist front organization. This article, which is anti-FBI, examines the FBI's procedures in general and its posture toward the political left.

1689. Bessie, Simon M. *Jazz Journalism*. New York: Dutton, 1938. Tabloid practices were the offspring of many legitimate traditional journalism practices. The New York *News* was a "vital social instrument, one of the few newspapers in America which can be counted among the liberal supporters of an embattled democracy struggling against the onslaught of economic collapse and reactionary pressure." This study, which seems to have been done hastily and superficially, places most emphasis on the sensational aspects of the New York *News, Mirror,* and *Graphic* and examines only one issue every five years from 1920-1935.

1690. Blanchard, Margaret A. "The Fifth-Amendment Privilege of Newsman George Burdick." *JQ* 55 (1978): 39-46, 67. When Burdick, using an unknown source within the government bureaucracy, wrote stories about Woodrow Wilson's "well-calculated plans for gaining ascendancy over his party," (39) Wilson had the Justice Department try to force Burdick to reveal his source. Burdick refused, citing the Fifth Amendment; and the Supreme Court upheld him.

1691. Blum, John Morton, ed. *Public Philosopher: Selected Letters of Walter Lippmann.* New York: Ticknor & Fields, 1985. These letters, written between 1906 and 1974, are about politics, domestic and international affairs, etc. They were written to such people as Felix Frankfurter, Alfred E. Smith, Herbert Hoover, and Ralph Pulitzer.

1692. Bode, Carl. *Mencken.* Carbondale: Southern Illinois University Press, 1969; rev., Baltimore, Md.: John Hopkins University Press, 1986. The writer for the Baltimore *Sun* and co-founder of the *American Mercury* was the most interesting, critical columnist and leading newspaperman of his day. This book attempts to "analyze Mencken's writing in relation to his life" and "describe the relation between his life and times." Mencken was witty, impertinent, and galling; and he influenced not only Baltimore journalism but American life and letters. Although he was pig-headed and often faulty in his ideas, he helped America face her problems in the 1920-1940s.

1693. Bowers, Thomas A. "The Bankhead Bill: How a Threatened Press Subsidy Was Defeated." *JQ* 53 (1976): 21-27. The proposed legislation would have subsidized some newspapers during World War I through the purchase of War Bond advertising; it was a "thinly-disguised subsidy to the nation's smaller newspapers." (21) It created a controversy among journalists, advertising professionals, and legislators; "the bill might have been a blatant attempt to seek the favor of editors and publishers of small newspapers." It would have set a "dangerous precedent. (27)

1694. Brazil, John R. "Murder Trials, Murder and Twenties America." *AQ* 33, 2 (1981): 163-184. The 1920s tabloids competed with cheap literature and movies to appeal to masses. They gave extensive coverage to trials. This study examines the tabloids' coverage in the context of cultural changes in American attitudes in 1920s, specifically attitudes about individualism.

1695. Bridges, Lamar W. "The Fight Against Boss Crump: Editor C.P.J. Mooney of Memphis." *JQ* 44 (1967): 245-49. Mooney, editor of the *Commercial Appeal,* waged an unsuccessful battle against political boss Ed Crump but was unable to arouse the public against governmental corruption.

1696. Britt, George. *Forty years, Forty Millions.* New York: Farrar & Rinehart, 1935. Critical biography of Frank Munsey as a man who executed papers and made journalism into a business with a primary concern for money. In most instances his editorial stands were determined by their potential to make him money or increase his personal standing. He never was accepted even by those people and leaders whom he admired.

1697. Brod, Donald F. "The Scopes Trial: A Look at Press Coverage after Forty Years." *JQ* 42 (1965): 219-26. Conflict among characters rather than suspense over the outcome of the case was the main element of reader interest in coverage of the Scopes trial. Comparisons can be made with the coverage of similar social conflicts in the contemporary press. This study examines the coverage by the Atlanta *Constitution,* Chicago *Tribune,* and Cleveland *Press.* Most of their comment was unfavorable to the fundamentalists; it considered the South to be backward. In fact, the press was anti-South. The *Tribune* claimed William Jennings Bryan was trying to establish a state-supported religion. The *Constitution* was more interested in harmony than justice.

1698. Bullock, Penelope L. "Profile of a Periodical: The 'Voice of the Negro.'" *AHB* 21 (Spring 1977): 95-114. The establishment of the *Voice of the Negro* in 1904 "marked the substantive beginnings of the commercially published magazine in Atlanta." (95) It reflected black life and provided a black interpretation of events, but it ceased publication after only two years.

1699. Bussel, Alan. "The Fight Against Boss Crump: Editor Meeman's Turn." *JQ* 44 (1967): 250-57. Following the death of C.P.J. Mooney, editor of the Memphis *Commericial Appeal*, the new editor, Edward John Meeman, vigorously continued the battle with city political boss Ed Crump from 1932 to 1948, when Crump's machine finally was defeated in city elections. Meeman's fight was in support of the "small people," city residents who were slow, nevertheless, to be aroused by Crump's corruption.

1700. Cain, James M. *60 Years of Journalism.* Edited and with an introduction by Roy Hoopes. Bowling Green, Ohio: Bowling Green State University Press, 1986. Anthology of Cain's journalistic writing. The author of *The Postman Always Rings Twice* and *Double Indemnity* began his newspaper career in 1917 on the Baltimore *American.*

1701. Carpenter, Reed L. "John L. Morrison and the Origins of the Minnesota Gag Law." *JH* 9 (1982): 16-17, 25-28. Although the *Saturday Press* normally has been recognized as the publication which provoked the legislation proscribing "malicious, scandalous and defamatory" newspapers, the legislation really was initiated in response to the "editorial excesses" of Duluth publisher Morrison.

1702. Casey, Ralph D. "Scripps-Howard Newspapers in the 1928 Presidential Campaign." *JQ* 7 (1930): 207-31. The liberal newspapers of Scripps-Howard permitted, "to the great credit of the group of dailies,...varied expressions of opinion in an election which stirred men so deeply and roused such heated partisanships." (231)

1703. Caswell, Lucy Shelton, and George Loomis, Jr. *Billy Ireland.* Columbus: Ohio State University Library Publications Committee, 1980. Ireland, a cartoonist for the Columbus (Ohio) Dispatch, provided a picture of life as he saw it in Columbus and middle America. Like other cartoonists of the time, he had an understanding of daily, ordinary events and the people of his time.

1704. Cebula, James E. *James M. Cox: Journalist and Politician.* New York: Garland, 1985. Cox, owner of newspapers in Ohio, Florida, and Georgia, served in Congress and as governor of Ohio and was the Democratic candidate for the U.S. presidency in 1920. He was a Progressive, urban leader whose interest was in adjusting "the values of middle class democracy...[to] the pace and rhythm of urban life."

1705. Cebula, James E. "The New City and the New Journalism: The Case of Dayton, Ohio." *OH* 33 (1979): 277-90. See previous entry. With the Dayton *Daily News*, Cox used his newspaper as "a principal communications vehicle for prompting corporate action during a time of social disorganization" when Dayton was changing into a metropolitan city. He used "crusades, promotions, more news, editorial independence, advertising innovations, [and] a professional staff" to influence business and political decisions that were important to the city's growth.

1706. Chacon, Ramon D. "The Chicano Immigrant Press in Los Angeles: The Case of 'El Heraldo de Mexico,' 1916-1920." *JH* 4 (1977): 48-50, 62-4. The Spanish-language newspaper was a product of Mexican immigration. It expressed the political, economic, and social milieu of the Chicano people.

1707. Chapman, John. *Tell It to Sweeney: The Informal History of the New York Daily News*. New York: Doubleday, 1961. The key to the success of the *Daily News* was appealing to the average person, the man on the street, through a lively and condensed style with pictures. In the beginning it emphasized sensationalism and comics and developed into the nation's leading circulation paper. "Sweeney" was the embodiment of the average person, resembling 75 per cent of Americans.

1708. Childs, Marquis, and James B. Reston, eds. *Walter Lippmann and His Times*. New York: Harcourt, Brace, 1959. Collection of 12 essays by various authors. Lippmann was an outstanding critic of politics, morals, and manners who maintained a high level of public philosophy. He had a liberal and humane view, but avoided partisanship. He was a thinking man who had a major impact on his times.

1709. Chivira, Ricardo. "A Case Study: Reporting of Mexican Emigration and Deportation." *JH* 4 (1977): 59-61. Since the 1930s, *La Opinion* has been more compassionate than the L.A. *Times* in covering Mexican immigrant laborers in California.

1710. Christians, Clifford G. "Fifty Years of Scholarship in Media Ethics." *JC* 27 (Autumn 1977): 19-29. Ethics have changed since the 1920s. In the 1920s, ethics took a "nonfunctional approach" emphasizing "moral responsibility to one's professional community." In the 1930s ethics was synonomous with objectivity. After World War II, ethics became more concerned with social responsibility and thorough reporting. In the hectic 1970s, a new ethical framework is needed.

1711. Chu, Chi-ying. "Henry Justin Smith (1875-1936), Managing Editor of the Chicago *Daily News*." Ph.D. dissertation, Southern Illinois University, 1970. "Few managing editors have equaled Smith's ability to sense news. No editor in the country developed so many first-class writers. He was a vigorous crusader. The record of Henry Justin Smith has made him a symbol of responsible editors whose integrity, courage, honesty, and intelligence advance the ideals of journalism."

1712. Clough, Frank C. *William Allen White of Emporia*. New York: Whittlesey, 1941. Personalized biography by the managing editor of the Emporia *Gazette*, emphasizing White as a family man and small-town editor.

1713. Cochran, Negley. *E. W. Scripps*. New York: Harcourt, Brace, 1933. Details the organization and history of the Scripps-Howard chain. Not as racy as Gardner's work, this biography sentimentalizes Scripps' "lustiness." It is intended as a study of "the mind of a great journalist, a profound philosopher, and at once a great master and a great public servant." Scripps deserves credit for America's development of a politically independent press. He was interested in content and the business aspects of papers.

1714. Cohen, Jeremy. "Absence of the First Amendment in Schenck vs. United States: A Reexamination." *AJ* 2 (1985): 49-64. Although Justice Oliver Wendell Holmes formulated the "clear and present danger" doctrine in *Schenck*, his decision "dealt far more with procedural matters and statutory interpretation than with the First Amendment." (62)

1715. Cohen, Lester. *The New York Graphic: The World's Zaniest Newspaper.* Philadelphia: Chilton, 1964. In the 1920s journalism was livelier and more fun than it became shortly afterwards. The press was very competitive, and reporters believed in their freedom to do things as they wanted. Newspaper work was interesting, and it was intended to be so rather than sober and socially responsible. The tabloid's approach to news was irrational as measured by mainstream journalism and even emphasized the insane. Cohen was contest editor for the *Graphic*, but his book does an inadequate job of capturing the essence of the *Graphic* or the journalism of the 1920s.

1716. Collins, Jean E. *She Was There: Stories of Pioneering Women Journalists.* New York: J. Messner, 1980. Fifteen women tell the stories of their careers through interviews and oral history. They had vitality and dedication. (This book is intended for young adults and teenagers, not serious historians.)

1717. Connery, Thomas B. "Hutchins Hapgood and the Search for a 'New Form of Literature.'" *JH* 13 (1986): 2-9. Hapgood's book *The Spirit of Labor* was based on extensive gathering of factual information about workers and the labor movement. In his approach to reporting and writing style, he "was a rough precursor of today's literary journalist." (2)

1718. Conrad, Will C., Kathleen F. Wilson, and Dale Wilson. *The Milwaukee Journal: The First Eighty Years.* Madison: University of Wisconsin Press, 1964. This history was written by three members of the *Journal* staff. Lucius W. Nieman and Harry J. Grant, starting in 1882, built the paper from virtually nothing into an outstanding paper by integrity, tolerance, and awareness. The paper crusaded for the public good and against official corruption. It took strong positions on democracy and freedom and made a number of contributions to newspaper practices such as photo printing and journalism education. The *Journal* was and is an outstanding newspaper because of courage, talent, energy, and desire for public betterment.

1719. Cooney, John. *The Annenbergs: The Salvaging of a Tainted Dynasty.* New York: Simon & Schuster, 1982. Biography of the Annenberg family and the rise, fall, and rise again of their media empire. Full of information, history, and colorful characters, this work deals mainly with the struggles and successes of Moses Annenberg, the father, and Walter Annenberg, the son.

1720. Cooper, Anne Messerly. "Suffrage as News: Ten Dailies' Coverage of the Nineteenth Amendment. *AJ* 1, 1 (1983): 75-91. Author uses content analysis of the newspaper treatment of the Nineteenth Amendment to make hypothetical suggestions about why newspapers approach issues as they do.

1721. Cornwell, Elmer E., Jr. "The Press Conferences of Woodrow Wilson." *JQ* 39

(1962): 292-300. In his relations with White House reporters, Wilson had a number of innovations, including a semi-weekly press conference open to all accredited correspondents.

1722. Covert, Cathy. "A View of the Press in the Twenties." *JH* 2 (1975): 66-67, 92-96. Considers the structure, function, and intellectual aspects of newspapers in the 1920s by examining their coverage of the philosopher and psychologist Sigmund Freud. The press helped to shape people's attitudes and values.

1723. Cowles, Gardner. *Mike Looks Back: The Memoirs of Gardner Cowles.* New York: Gardner Cowles, 1985. Autobiography of a newspaper journalist and founder of *Look* magazine.

1724. Cuthbert, Marlene. "Reaction to International News Agencies: 1930s and 1970s Compared." *Gazette* 26, 2 (1980): 99-110. Similar to Third World protests in the 1970s against "world domination of international news flow channels" by developed countries, in the 1920s and 1930s America protested against Europe's dominance of the news which the Associated Press carried. With both protests, "those who had only limited news outlets felt that they were stereotyped by those who controlled those outlets." Changes in international news flow were demanded in both instances.

1725. Dam, Hari N. *The Intellectual Odyssey of Walter Lippmann.* New York: Gordon, 1973. Lippmann's philosophies were elitist. He "has never been a believer in participative democracy. He has always held the view that the masses are incapable of governing themselves in a complex society. They need to be guided by a trained elite."

1726. Darden, Robert F. *Drawing Power: Knott, Ficklen, and McClanahan, Editorial Cartoonists of the Dallas Morning News.* Waco, Tex.: Markham Press Fund, 1983. Biographies of three cartoonists who worked for one of Texas' largest newspapers, including reproductions of some of their cartoons.

1727. Davenport, Robert W. "Fremont Older in San Francisco Journalism." Ph.D. dissertation, University of California-Los Angeles, 1969.

1728. Delman, Marty. "Holocaust and the Presses: They Day They Blew Up the LA Times." *MHD* 3, 2 (1983): 36-47. The *Times* was in the middle of political turmoil involving organized labor and socialists. In 1910, dynamite blew up its building; union members were convicted.

1729. Desmond, Robert W. *Windows on the World: World News Reporting 1900-1920.* Ames: Iowa State University Press, 1981. This history of foreign correspondence covers the role of the Associated Press in world news coverage, dominance of French and British and German agencies prior to World War I, the appearance of United Press and International News Service, rise of broadcasting, development of the news magazine, importance of photojournalism, censorship, fighting between agencies, problems with desk-bound editors, problems with transmissions, concepts of reporting, interpretive reporting, and syndicated columns.

1730. Diggs, Irene. "Du Bois -- Revolutionary Journalist Then and Now." *CBAA* 4 (March 1971): 95-117.

1731. Drewry, John E., ed. *More Post Biographies of Famous Journalists.* Athens:

University of Georgia Press, 1947. Anthology of 22 articles from *Saturday Evening Post* on notable journalists and newspapers: Hugh Baillie, Helen Bonfils, Mary Coyle Chase, Raymond Clapper, Ding Darling, Gene Howe, John S. Knight, Arthur Krock, Bill Mauldin, Eugene Meyer, Drew Pearson, Emily Post, Ernie Pyle, Mrs. Ogden Reid, *Christian Science Monitor*, Philadelphia *Bulletin*, *Sporting News*, *Who's Who in America*, *Encyclopedia Britannica*, "News Reels," "Paper Dolls," and "Sports Editors."

1732. Drewry, John E., ed. *Post Biographies of Famous Journalists*. Athens: University of Georgia Press, 1942. Twenty-two articles which first appeared in *Saturday Evening Post*: provide the biographies of Arthur Brisbane, Dorothy Dix, Silliman Evans, Clifton Fadiman, Marshall Field III, George Gallup, Edgar Guest, William Randolph Hearst, Roy Howard, Ed Howe, Robert McCormick, Bernarr Macfadden, O.O. McIntyre, Don Marquis, Eleanor Patterson, Westbrook Pegler, Joseph Pulitzer II, Herbert Bayard Swope, Dorothy Thompson, Henry Watterson, and Walter Winchell.

1733. Dryfoos, Susan W. *Iphigene: Memories of Iphigene Ochs Sulzberger of the New York Times Family*. New York: Dodd, Mead, 1981. Iphigene was the daughter, widow, and mother of three New York *Times* publishers.

1734. Du Bois, W.E.B. *The Autobiography of W.E.B. Du Bois*. New York: International Publishers, 1968.

1735. Duffus, Robert L. "Mr. Munsey." *AmM* (July 1924). This critical narrative of Frank Munsey's career was written by a practicing newspaperman. Munsey's papers had no "general or permanent significance. They merely reflect Mr. Munsey, and when he is dead they will reflect someone else. He has acquired no following in daily journalism. He has demonstrated that newspapers are not institutions, like schools and churches, but commodities, like motor cars. He has legitimized journalistic murder. He has invented a new and effective method of doing away with free speech. Perhaps this consoles him for his inability to own and edit one thousand 'independent, fearless and honest' American newspapers."

1736. Eberhard, Wallace B. "Clark Howell and The Atlanta Constitution." *JQ* 60 (1983): 118-22. Howell was the "editor and guiding light" of the *Constitution* . This biography covers 1897-1936, his journalistic career, and his political involvement in Georgia. "Howell has been largely ignored by historians." He was a "dedicated, enthusiastic, and committed journalist, able to attract a superior editorial staff and stimulate it to carry out the day-to-day work."

1737. Elder, Donald. *Ring Lardner*. Garden City, N.Y.: Doubleday, 1956. Emphasizes the non-journalism career of Lardner, who as a journalist was an interesting writer, especially of sports.

1738. Ellis, Elmer. *Mr. Dooley's America*. New York: Knopf, 1941. A favorable biography of Finley Peter Dunne as a valuable and incisive interpreter of the politics and society of his times. He was widely read, and his opinions were considered important. He was fearless in directing his barbs toward anyone, no matter how important or admired. Unlike other muckrakers, Dunne used ridicule (rather than expose) to correct evils.

1739. Emery, Edwin. *History of the American Newspaper Publishers Association.*

Minneapolis: University of Minnesota Press, 1950. Organized in 1887, the ANPA often revealed a self-serving attitude on the part of publishers. As the large newspapers became big businesses, the power of the press was something to be reckoned with when its interests were threatened. This history emphasizes the controversial issues in which the ANPA was involved, including dealings with government and labor.

1740. Emery, Edwin, and Joseph P. McKerns. "AEJMC: 75 Years in the Making: A History of Organizing for Journalism and Mass Communication Education in the United States.." *JM* 104 (1987). Favorable antiquarian chronology of the highlights in the history of the Association for Education in Journalism and Mass Communication, sponsored by the AEJMC on its anniversary. Includes brief biographies of prominent AEJMC leaders.

1741. Emery, Michael C. "The American Mass Media and the Coverage of Five Major Foreign Events, 1900-1950: The Russo-Japanese War, Outbreak of World War I, Rise of Stalin, Munich Crisis, Invasion of South Korea." Ph.D. dissertation, University of Minnesota, 1969. Study of "the newspaper, wire service, magazine and radio reporters at the scene, those Americans who faced both human and mechanical barriers in reporting the developments."

1742. Endres, Kathleen L. "The Symbiotic Relationship of Eleanor Roosevelt and the Press: The Pre-War Years." *MCRJ* 2 (1979): 57-65. The First Lady brought female reporters "through journalistic adolescence and up to an established professional plateau." Both she and the reporters benefitted from their relationship. Through her press conferences, Mrs. Roosevelt was able to present her opinions to the public and the female reporters gained access to national events and received bylines on major stories.

1743. Evans, James Forrest. "B.D. Butler and the Crusading Years of *Prairie Farmer-WLS*." Ph.D. dissertation, University of Illinois, 1968. "The most prominent characteristic of *Prairie Farmer* [a farm paper serving Illinois] under Butler's ownership was its crusading spirit, its active concern for the underdog."

1744. Evans, James F. "Clover Leaf: The Good Luck Chain, 1899-1933." *JQ* 46 (1969): 482-91. One of the 10 earliest chains of dailies in the U.S., Clover Leaf (which included paprs in St. Paul, Omaha, Des Moines, and Kansas City) grew with the help of Scripps and the expansion of rural free delivery. Ironically, it declined in the period of greatest chain newspaper growth, probably because it emphasized rural circulation at a time when urban areas were growing and because in reaching the rural readership it de-emphasized its editorial function and tied itself so closely to the patent medicine business.

1745. Farr, Finis. *Fair Enough: The Life of Westbrook Pegler*. New Rochelle, N.Y.: Arlington House, 1975. Pegler, a conservative national columnist after World War I, would have been regarded more highly by historians if he had been on the left rather than the right.

1746. Farrar, Ronald Truman. "Charles G. Ross: His Life and Times." Ph.D. dissertation, University of Missouri, 1965. Ross was a professor at the first school of journalism (Missouri), an editor for the St. Louis *Post-Dispatch*, and Harry Truman's press secretary.

1747. Fecher, Charles A. *Mencken: A Study of His Thought*. New York: Knopf, 1978. Mencken was very learned but little appreciated in his own time. However, he has now gained a place among the "giants of our cultural history." Mencken was first a newspaperman and a journalist above all else: police reporter, editor, literary critic, political commentator, gadfly, wordsmith, and controversialist.

1748. Fine, Barnett. *A Giant of the Press*. New York: Editor & Publisher Library, 1933. Carr V. Van Anda, managing editor of the New York *Times*, was a genius in journalism. He had great talent, a broad background, and a sound conscience. This short biography is narrative rather than interpretive.

1749. Fisher, Charles. *The Columnists*. New York: Howell, Soskin, 1944. Pro-liberal interpretation of columnists of the 1940s: Thompson, Winchell, Mallon, Kent, Lippmann, Clapper, Pyle. Columnists are successors of the personal journalists of the 19th century, but they have not performed well.

1750. Fleener, Nickieann. "'Breaking Down Buyer Resistance': Marketing the 1935 Pittsburgh *Courier* to Mississippi Blacks." *JH* 13 (1976): 78-85. In a successful effort to build the circulation of the *Courier* among Mississippi blacks, its publisher, George S. Schuyler, "applied principles of newspaper marketing that, when viewed in retrospect, seem to fit more closely within the contemporary newspaper marketing model than they do within the intuitive model more commonly ascribed to this time period. Schuyler believed in producing what the market wanted rather than expecting newspaper agents to simply sell whatever was produced." (84)

1751. Fowler, Gene. *Timber Line*. New York: Covici-Friede, 1933. Well-told adventure story of Harry Tammen and Fred Bonfils, the colorful, crooked owners of the sensational Denver *Post*.

1752. Frazier, P. Jean, and Cecilie Gaziano. "Robert Ezra Park's Theory of News, Public Opinion and Social Control." *JM* 64 (1979). Park, a journalist and sociologist, "must be considered a founder of the sociological study of mass communication and public opinion and the field's first theorist." (1) His theory was concerned with "how social change takes place through successive stages involving the reporting of news and the initiation of public opinion." (37)

1753. Friendly, Fred W. *Minnesota Rag: The Dramatic Story of the Landmark Supreme Court Case that Gave New Meaning to Freedom of the Press*. New York: Random House, 1981. This is the story of the Supreme Court case Near v. Minnesota (1931). Authorities attempted to close the *Saturday Press* in Minneapolis under the Minnesota Public Nuisance Law of 1925. *Saturday Press* was an anti-semitic, tasteless paper. Most respectable Minnesota papers did not oppose the state legislation that was designed to shut down scandal sheets. However, Robert McCormick of the Chicago *Tribune* championed the *Saturday Press'* freedom of the press and became the main figure in the case. Overall, the journalists in the case and the state were not crusading idealists, and many may have been taking bribes and extorting advertising in exchange for favorable stories or squelching expose`s. Friendly lauds the Supreme Court's landmark decision in the case as support of an important principle, freedom of the press.

1754. Gardner, Gilson. *Lusty Scripps: The Life of E.W. Scripps (1854-1926)*. New York: Vanguard, 1932. This is a racy and unawed picture of Scripps, the newspaper chain owner. In operating his chain, he believed in singleness of control, independence from banks and advertisers, sharing profits with newspaper managers, starting his sons at the top, long-distance management, and publishing newspapers for the underdog.

1755. Gatewood, Worth, ed. *Fifty Years in Pictures: The New York Daily News 1919-1969*. Garden City, N.Y.: Doubleday, 1979. Collection of photos from the *Daily News*. The paper made many contributions to newspaper photography.

1756. Gies, Joseph. *The Colonel of Chicago*. New York: Dutton, 1979. Favorable biography of Robert McCormick, owner of the Chicago *Tribune*, who has been criticized by many historians for his conservative reactionarism. Although he was intensely partisan, he was an "original thinker" who contributed much to the practice of journalism and played an important role in American public thinking.

1757. Gleason, Timothy W. "Legal Advocacy and the First Amendment: Elisha Hanson's Attempt to Create First Amendment Protection for the Business of the Press." *AJ* 3 (1986): 195-206. In the 1930s and 1940s, the general counsel of the American Newspaper Publishers Association "aggressively used the First Amendment as part of efforts to shield the newspaper industry from government regulation of labor practices and from taxation." (203) Although Hanson lost all but one First Amendment case he argued before the Supreme Case, jurists did accept some of his rationale.

1758. Gobbel, Alfred Roger. "The Christian Century: Its Editorial Policies and Positions, 1908-1966." Ph.D. dissertation, University of Illinois, 1967. "As an independent religious paper, *The Christian Century* has been one of the leading liberal social and theological religious voices in America. It has insisted that Christian principles should be applied to and made operative in all realms of society. Out of that conviction, it spoke with a courageous and vigorous voice on a multiplicity of concerns and issues."

1759. Good, Howard. *Acquainted with the Night: The Image of Journalists in American Fiction, 1890-1930*. Metuchen, N. J.: Scarecrow, 1986. Novels portrayed journalists in ambivalent and contradictory, in negative and positive, ways: "Journalism invited college men into its ranks; it knocked the college clean out of them. Journalism nurtured aspiring young writers; it destroyed their talent."

1760. Gothberg, John A. "The Local Influence of J. R. Knowland's Oakland Tribune." *JQ* 45 (1968): 487-95. Joseph Knowland became publisher of the *Tribune* in 1915 and for half a century played a major role in the East Bay area, which his son William continued. Knowland, who had been involved in politics, may have bought the *Tribune* as a forum after he lost a race for the U.S. Senate. He declared that he would be a champion of his area and of the Republican Party. The *Tribune* was an expression of Knowland's personality. He was in close touch with area politicians.

1761. Grant, Harry J. *Lucius W. Nieman, Newspaperman*. Cambridge, Mass.: Nieman Foundation, Harvard University, 1941.

1762. Green, Dan S. "W.E.B. Du Bois: His Journalistic Career," *NHB* 40 (1977): 672-77. Du Bois, the black educator and writer, aimed his main efforts at resolving social problems. He founded and edited five periodicals: the *Moon, Crisis, Horizon, Brownies Book*, and *Phylon*, all of which he established because of his need for outlets for his own writings on social problems because other editors were not particularly interested in problems such as race, colonialism, and peace, especially from an outspoken black man; "in a sense...he really had little alternative but to initiate his own journals." (672)

1763. Greene, Lawrence. *The Era of Wonderful Nonsense*. Indianapolis: Bobbs-Merrill, 1939. This entertaining popular history describes what the world and America were like in 1918-1933, with chapters based on newspaper and magazine reporting. Theme: How often does the press manufacture "inconsequential bunk for the sake of very consequential profit"?

1764. Griswold Del Castillo, Richard. "The Mexican Revolution and the Spanish-Language Press in the Borderlands." *JH* 4 (1977): 42-47. Spanish-language editors and newspapers in the U.S. "interpreted the Mexican revolution according to diverse local conditions and philosophies. Their degree of involvement with revolutionary events and issues varied with localities....These editors were, in many ways, the forerunners of a contemporary intellectual and political movement which has sympathetically identified with and championed the cause of the non-white peoples of the Third World." (47)

1765. Halverson, Guy, and William E. Ames. "The Butte *Bulletin*: Beginnings of a Labor Daily." *JQ* 46 (1969): 260-66. Mine workers began the *Bulletin* as a strike newspaper. Despite a short life (1917-1924), it crusaded for better conditions, political reform, and other progressive measures. It failed to survive, however, because its strident tone alienated business.

1766. Haney, John A. "History of Nationally-Syndicated Sunday Magazine Supplements." Ph.D. dissertation, University of Missouri, 1954.

1767. Harlan, Louis R. "Booker T. Washington and the Voice of the Negro, 1904-1907." *JSH* 45 (February 1979): 45-62. Booker T. Washington considered the *Voice of the Negro* and its editor, Jesse Max Barber, a radical threat to his social and political beliefs. He used his influence with blacks to pressure the paper to change its stance, offering "fresh evidence of the totality of his power and the lengths he would go to hound a critic." (45)

1768. Hausman, Linda Weiner. "Criticism of the Press in U.S. Periodicals, 1900-1939: An Annotated Bibliography." *JM* 4 (1967). Bibliography of magazine articles critical of the press.

1769. Healy, Paul F. *Cissy*. New York: Doubleday, 1966. This favorable, ordinary biography was written by an "insider" of the McCormick-Patterson business. It focuses most attention on Eleanor "Cissy" Patterson before she became publisher of the Washington *Times-Herald*, when she was a reporter and Hearst editor.

1770. Heath, S. Burton. *Yankee Reporter*. New York: Wilfred Funk, 1940. Autobiography of a Pulitzer-Prize winning reporter for the New York *World-Telegram* who covered New York City public affairs and corruption.

1771. Heaton, John L., ed. *Cobb of "The World": A Leader in Liberalism*. New York: Dutton, 1924. Frank Cobb was a liberal, honest, sincere, talented editorial who made the New York *World* the leading advocate of liberal causes aimed at improving political, judicial, economic, and social conditions. He was courageous and had a vigorous mind. He was influential, having an impact on a number of conditions. He was a talented journalist, a characteristic American, and a believer in democratic government.

1772. Hendrick, Burton J. *The Life and Letters of Walter Hines Page.* New York: Double-day, 1922. Page, after an early career as a reporter and editor, was appointed ambassador to Great Britain in 1913 by Woodrow Wilson.

1773. Hensher, Alan. "Penny Papers: The Vanderbilt Newspaper Crusade." *CHQ* 55 (Summer 1976): 162-69. The Los Angeles *Daily Illustrated News*, a tabloid founded in 1923 by Cornelius Vanderbilt Jr., was "the flagship of a newspaper chain which championed the virtues of good, wholesome news and pictures." Its attempt at crusading journalism, however, was unsuccessful, and in 1927 its format and editorial approach were popularized to attract readership.

1774. Hiebert, Ray Eldon. "Ivy Lee and Roosevelt Press Relations." *JQ* 43 (1966): 327-31. Lee was an effective public relations agent working with the press and helped Franklin Roosevelt establish good relations with it.

1775. Hilderbrand, Robert C., ed. *The Papers of Woodrow Wilson. Volume 50: The Complete Press Conferences, 1913-1919.* Princeton, N.J.: Princeton University Press, 1985. Wilson was the first president to hold regularly scheduled press conferences. This book is the authoritative record of them.

1776. Himebaugh, Glenn A. "The American Press Views Don Mellet's Murder." *Graduate Communication Studies,* Vol. 1, No. 1 (Spring 1977), published by the School of Journalism, Southern Illinois University. This article, one of five in the a collection of historical studies by Southern Illinois University graduate students, examines newspaper and magazine response to the assassination of Mellet. See next entry.

1777. Himebaugh, Glenn A. "Donald Ring Mellett, Journalist: The Shaping of a Martyr." Ph.D. dissertation, Southern Illinois University, 1978. Mellet, an Ohio editor and publisher, was assassinated in 1926 while exposing a corrupt city police administration and the underworld. His determination reflected "multiple influences accumulated throughout...his lifetime," including "his journalistic family heritage and his training in journalism at Indiana University, both of which contributed to his strong sense of idealism and deep-seated faith in the public service role of the press; his modest professional success in earlier work...; his moralism and deep religious commitment; his competitive spirit; and his record of community involvement."

1778. Hobson, Fred C. Jr. *Serpent In Eden: H.L. Mencken and the South.* Chapel Hill: University of North Carolina Press, 1974. Study of the relationship between Mencken and the South beginning in 1920, including an intellectual examination of Mencken's sarcastic barbs as a reflection of literature and culture. Mencken was one of the founders of a "modern renaissance in Southern literature and thought."

1779. Hochberger, Simon. "Fifty Years of Journalism Education." *JE* 13, 2 (1958): 2-5, 24. "In a half-century journalism education in this country has grown from the fumblings of infancy and the uncertainties of childhood into an adolescence marked by a surprised recognition of increasing power. Now it is entering a period of maturity, a maturity notable, thus far, for introspective self-criticism and self-conscious striving toward improvement." (2) Journalism education has contributed to professional journalism by turning out graduates to work in the field and by research and criticism. It has won a place with both professional journalists and academicians.

1780. Hodges, Lawrence Kaye. *Twenty Eventful Years*. New York: Wilson-Erickson, 1937. Collection of editorials written by Hodges for the Portland *Oregonian* from the inauguration of Woodrow Wilson to that of Franklin Roosevelt.

1781. Hogan, Lawrence D. *A Black National News Service: The Associated Negro Press and Claude Barnett, 1919-1945*. Rutherford, N.J.: Farleigh Dickinson University Press, 1984. Barnett launched the ANP to provide information for black newspapers. Member papers, not wishing to share their news with competitors, did not, however, fully cooperate in providing news for the service; and some publishers failed to pay their fees. Barnett therefore returned to Republican politics and partisanship, thereby compromising the ANP's objectivity and weakening the support from client newspapers.

1782. Hoge, Alice Albright. *Cissy Patterson*. New York: Random House, 1966. This biography is similar in material to Healy's but of lower quality.

1783. Hollis, Daniel Webster. *An Alabama Newspaper Tradition: Grover C. Hall and the Hall Family*. Tuscaloosa: University of Alabama Press, 1983. Grover Cleveland Hall and his son were editors of the Montgomery *Advertiser* from the 1920s to the 1960s and were involved in state politics, civil rights, opposition to the Ku Klux Klan, and other public issues.

1784. Hoopes, Roy. "Birth of a Great Magazine." *AHL* 20, 5 (1986): 34-41. *Life* pioneered a new form of journalism and became "one of the great American magazines of the twentieth century." (35) Ralph Ingersoll was a key figure in its creation.

1785. Hoopes, Roy. *Ralph Ingersoll: A Biography*. New York: Atheneum, 1985. Ingersoll founded the idealistic, adless *PM* newspaper in New York City in 1940. He wanted it to be free of the influence of wealth and to serve mankind. The paper quickly fell into debt, and Ingersoll had to relinquish control to Marshall Field, who had bought out the other stockholders. It failed because of mismanagement and because Ingersoll, who thought of himself as a crusader against social ills, was an egotist and showed little concern in his personal relationships with the staff.

1786. Hosakawa, Bill. *Thunder in the Rockies: The Incredible Denver Post*. New York: William Morrow, 1976. Authorized history written by member of the *Post's* staff. "The Denver Post was, and is, unusual because it was the product of two very unusual men, Frederick Gilmer Bonfils and Harry Heyes Tammen. They in turn were the products of an unusual era in American and Western history. They responded and reacted to these times with a peculiar intensity....Bonfils and Tammen were shrewd businessmen who understood that newspapers must change, just as times and people change, if they are to remain vital." (7)

1787. Hull, Gloria T. "Alice Dunbar-Nelson: Delaware Writer and Woman of Affairs." *DH* 17 (Fall-Winter 1976): 87-103. Although Alice Dunbar-Nelson primarily wrote poetry and fiction (which this biography concentrates on), she edited the Wilmington *Advocate*, a black Delaware newspaper, from 1920 to 1924 and also wrote a syndicated newspaper column for the Associated Negro Press.

1788. Hynes, Terry. "Magazine Portrayal of Women, 1911-1930." *JM* 72 (1981). In contrast to some observers' statements that these two decades witnessed the emergence of the liberated American woman, four popular magazines did not "portray the flapper or the politically, economically and socially liberated woman in the twenties as typical of American women or even as an ideal." (48)

1789. Hynes, Terry. "Media Manipulation and Political Campaigns: Bruce Barton and the Presidential Elections of the Jazz Age." *JH* 4 (1977): 93-98. Barton attempted to package Calvin Coolidge and Herbert Hoover as candidates in ways similar to those of television advertising today.

1790. Ignasias, C. Dennis. "Propaganda and Public Opinion in Harding's Foreign Affairs: The Case for Mexican Recognition." *JQ* 48 (1971): 41-52. To a considerable extent, U.S. recognition of the Obregon government of Mexico in the 1920s reflected the effects of a propaganda campaign directed at the American public and its congressional representatives.

1791. Innis, H.A. *The Press: A Neglected Factor in the Economic History of the Twentieth Century*. London: Oxford University Press, 1949. This survey history covers the period from the penny press to the first half of 20th century and is punctuated with unsupported ideas about the press. The means of communication became industrialized through the change in the manufacture of newsprint from rags to woodpulp and the use by the newspaper of type-casting machines and fast presses. Cheap newsprint made possible large circulations. The advertiser needed a mass medium and forced newspapers to become more popularized.

1792. Johnson, Abby Arthur, and Ronald M. Johnson. "Away from Accommodation: Radical Editors and Protest Journalism, 1900-1910." *JNH* 62 (October 1977): 325-38. "The rivalry between accommodationist and radical approaches to race relations, between Booker T. Washington and W.E.B. Du Bois, climaxed in the first decade of the twentieth century. Nowhere did the controversy appear more clearly and dramatically than in...Afro-American journals." (325) Leading the fight for the Du Bois approach were the *Colored American Magazine, Voice of the Negro, Moon*, and *Horizon*.

1793. Johnson, Gerald W. *An Honorable Titan*. New York: Harper, 1946. Adolph Ochs of the New York *Times* was one of the financial titans who had so much to do with making America what it is; and although many of those titans were materialists and rogues, Ochs was honorable. He represented the ideal of a newspaper as a public institution, impersonal, reliable and responsible, devoted primarily to serving the public with news. His career was an exemplification of principle. This biography is the story of poor boy makes good and of advancing journalism. Like entrepreneurs, he was a product of the industrial times; but unlike many robber barons, he was honorable.

1794. Johnson, Paul W. "The Journalist as Diplomat: E. J. Dillon and the Portsmouth Peace Conference." *JQ* 53 (1976): 689-93. Making use of the increased potential of the press to sway public opinion (as a result of the growth of newspapers in the late 1800s), Dillon attempted to swing American sentiment behind the Russian delegation to the Portsmouth (N.H.) Peace Conference to end the Russo-Japanese War (1904-05). His successful and "assiduous cultivation of the press during the conference...demonstrated the importance of supporting foreign policy objectives with a carefully coordinated public relations campaign." (693)

1795. Johnson, Walter. *William Allen White's America.* New York: Henry Holt, 1947. With age, the Kansas editor's horizons broadened; he accepted more new ideas with time. He was interested in making democratic institutions more suited to changed conditions in technology. His life was set against the background of a social-economic change that took place during his lifetime (1875-1947): the significance of the small town and village in the Midwest was being increasingly overshadowed and frustrated by predatory, urban economic power. White was the symbol of the greatness of small-town America and was the guardian of its democratic culture; he was also the Midwest's leading muckraker and liberal publicist.

1796. Johnson, Walter C., and Arthur T. Robb. *The South and Its Newspapers.* Chattanooga: Southern Newspaper Publishers Association, 1954. Excerpts from the meetings of the SNPA since its founding in 1903 to 1953 chronicling its growth and including such topics as circulation, postal rates, advertising, production costs, etc., of particular interest to publishers.

1797. Kahn, E. J., Jr. *The World of Swope.* New York: Simon & Schuster, 1965. Bayard Swope, executive editor of the New York *World,* believed in Pulitzer's policy of crusading for the masses. He was a rugged individualist who crusaded against the Ku Klux Klan, misuse of convict labor, poor working conditions, etc. He won the Pulitzer Prize and created the op. ed. (opposite editorial) page. He was devoted to important timely causes and to high ethics.

1798. Kane, Harnett T., with Ella Bentley Arthur. *Dear Dorothy Dix: The Story of a Compassionate Woman.* New York: Doubleday, 1952. Sympathetic biography of Dix, who for half a century was a reporter and "sob sister" syndicated advice columnist.

1799. Kemler, Edgar. *The Irreverent Mr. Mencken.* New York: Knopf, 1950. Mencken was a master of style who dealt with ideas. Early in his writing career, it became apparent that "[t]he world of ideas would be his bowling alley, and he would topple the pins of men's faith as he pleased with his clattering verbiage....[As] a journalist, he had the power to reshape the minds of a whole generation of Americans," but his place in literature and scholarship "is a skeptic of the first rank...who has somehow abased his gifts....[H]e devoted himself almost wholly to the [p]assing scene, and...has produced no works likely to endure."

1800. Kennedy, Jean L. "William Allen White: A Study of the Interrelationship of Press, Power and Party Politics." Ph.D. dissertation, University of Kansas, 1981.

1801. Kimbrough, Marvin Gordon. "W.E.B. DuBois as Editor of the *Crisis.*" Ph.D. dissertation, University of Texas, 1974. As editor from 1910 to 1934, "DuBois used the *Crisis* as a podium for his changing ideas,...[but] deviations from the [sponsoring] association's goals and magazine policy caused conflict between the editor and the organization."

1802. Klucsik, David M. "Hello, Halley, Goodbye." *MHD* 6, 1 (1986): 62-64. In 1910 newspapers gave colorful, sensational coverage to the appearance of Halley's comet.

1803. Klurfield, Herman. *Winchell: His Life and Times.* New York: Praeger, 1976. Walter Winchell was insecure, with little concern for the feelings of others. He mistrusted those who disagreed with him. Yet he made some contributions, such as adding some words to the vocabulary. "As a newspaperman, Winchell was representative of that most endangered journalistic species, the nonacademic wise man."

1804. Kneebone, John T. *Southern Liberal Journalists and the Issue of Race, 1920-1944.* Chapel Hill: University of North Carolina Press, 1985. Five leading Southern journalists who supported civil rights for blacks -- Gerald W. Johnson, George Fort Milton, Ralph McGill, Virginius Dabney, and Hodding Carter -- were ideologically unprepared for the emerging civil rights movement after World War II and could not accept a racially integrated society. They thus became members of the conservative, segregationist status quo.

1805. Knight, Oliver. "Scripps and His Adless Newspaper, *The Day Book." JQ* 41 (1964): 51-64. In his efforts to create a successful adless newspaper, Scripps had a dream "of establishing a genuinely free press. To him this meant elimination of reliance upon advertising revenue, and in finding the key to successful and profitable operation of a newspaper whose only income would come from circulation. He had no fear of an advertiser dictating to him personally, but he was convinced that many editors and publishers of his time kow-towed to big advertisers. In his view then, assuming the basic honesty and integrity of the editor, the only obstacle to freedom of the press was advertising, and the obstacle must be removed." Scripps was an incisive thinker far ahead of his contemporaries. Yet he was tied to journalistic traditions in areas other than adlessness and tried no things really new in the *Day Book.*

1806. Kobre, Sidney. *Modern American Journalism.* Tallahassee: Florida State University Press, 1959. This ambitious history, focusing on 1900 to the 1950s, attempts to chronicle and explain the growth of communications in the 20th century through telling the histories of individual newspapers by regions. Emphasis is on the sociological interaction of the newspaper with its environment and on internal editorial, mechanical, advertising, and business changes. The development of chains and syndicates, monopolies, columnists, interpretive journalism, advertising, journalism schools, influential or typical newspapers in all regions are discussed with regard to their environment, personnel, news coverage, and editorial policies. "Gigantic forces" such as population, industrialization, labor organization, and a reform spirit transformed America in the first half of 20th century. "The newspaper mirrored the dramatic events and helped shape the national and social destiny. The press continued many of the traditions forged in the previous century": the art of news writing, dramatic display, new forms of explanatory writing, backgrounding the news, and columnists of interpretation and comment. Syndicates, technology, consolidations and mergers because of rising costs in labor and newsprint, chains to save money and buy material on a large scale mirrored similar developments in grocery chains, etc. Along with all these topics, this book also addresses others such as tabloids, war coverage, press associations, broadcasting, magazines, press clubs and unions, and professionalism (education and trade publications).

1807. Kobre, Sidney. "New York Newspapers and the Case of Celia Cooney." *JQ* 14 (1937): 133-43. Follow-up to Kobre's study of the Zangara case (see next entry). Newspapers sensationalized and failed to see the sociological significance of the details in Cooney's background and to look more deeply than the superficial recital of her criminal escapades. In reporting the news, journalists are too stuck to tradition and do not have an understanding of such areas as sociology needed to do better jobs.

1808. Kobre, Sidney. "The Newspapers and the Zangara Case: A Study of American Crime Reporting." *JQ* 13 (1936): 253-71. This is a narrative of the man who attempted to assassinate Franklin Roosevelt 1933 and the press' inadequate handling of the case. He suffered from a physical illness which may have affected his mentality. "[M]ost American editors, handling this story, chose stereotypes and superficialities rather than the more subtle but certainly more fundamental implications" and emphasized the sensational aspects of the case. Newspapers failed "to present the important news behind the surface facts." (270-71)

1809. Koehler, Mary A. "Facsimile Newspapers: Foolishness or Foresight?" *JQ* 46 (1969): 29-36. This winner of the AEJMC History Division student paper award describes the technological development of fascimile through the mid-1940s. Broadcasting "newspapers" into homes (producing papers through a radio attachment in the home) was an innovation met with enthusiasm in late 1930s. The idea was ahead of its day and thus never succeeded.

1810. Kramer, Dale. *Ross and The New Yorker*. New York: Doubleday, 1951. Ross was "probably the greatest editor of his time." He was a roving newspaperman who wanted to be a hobo but became the genius behind the *New Yorker*, which he founded in 1925. It was exceptional for its talented writers. It emphasized wit and enlightenment.

1811. Kreiling, Albert Lee. "The Making of Racial Identities in the Black Press: A Cultural Analysis of Race Journalism in Chicago, 1878-1929." Ph.D. dissertation, University of Illinois, 1973. Providing "a comprehensive historical account of the rise of black journalism in Chicago...[this] dissertation pictures the black press as a reflection of developing cultural styles and clashes among contending cultural groups within the black community."

1812. Krompak, Frank. "A Wider Niche for Westbrook Pegler." *AJ* 1, 1 (1983): 31-45. Pegler was not just an ascerbic political columnist. He also was a humorist comparable in talent to H. L. Mencken, Damon Runyon, and Ring Lardner.

1813. Kuczun, Sam. "History of the American Newspaper Guild." Ph.D. dissertation, University of Minnesota, 1970. Narrative history from 1933 to 1969, with emphasis on the Guild's founding and early years.

1814. Kulik, Brian. "Socialist Editor Eugene Debs: One Million Votes in Jail." *MHD* 5, 2 (2985): 18-27, 50. Debs helped found the American Socialist party in 1901; edited its paper, the *Appeal to Reason*; was jailed under the Espionage Act of 1917; and received 912,000 votes in the 1920 presidential election. He ran the newspaper as an impassioned voice for the rights of organized labor.

1815. Lawson, Linda. "Advertisements Masquerading as News in Turn-of-the-Century American Periodicals." *AJ* 5 (1988): 81-96. Advertisers used the technique of "reading notices" -- ads printed to look as if they were news stories -- beginning in the 1870s. By the early 1900s, many journalists and Progressive reformers opposed them, resulting in their elimination.

1816. Lendt, David L. *DING: The Life of Jay Norwood Darling*. Ames: Iowa State University Press, 1979. The Pulitzer-Prize winning conservatlve cartoonist worked for the Des Moines *Register and Leader* and was a leading conservationist.

1817. Lendt, David. "J.N. 'Ding' Darling: The Formative Years." *AI* 45 (1979): 123-34. Narrative of Darling's early career in Iowa. See previous entry.

1818. Linn, James Weber. *James Keeley, Newspaperman*. Indianapolis: Bobbs-Merrill, 1937. The managing editor of the Chicago *Tribune* was a colorful, courageous journalist who crusaded against abuses by government and business.

1819. Lisby, Gregory C. "Julian Harris and the *Columbus Enquirer-Sun*: The Consequences of Winning the Pulitzer Prize." *JM* 105 (1988). Although the Georgia newspaper won the 1926 Pulitzer for its liberal stands on racial, social, and political issues, those same stands were unpopular with local readers and caused the loss of numerous subscribers.

1820. Lisenby, Foy. "American Women in Magazine Cartoons." *AJ* 2 (1985): 130-34. In cartoons from 1930 to 1960, women were presented stereotypically as gossips, emotional and indecisive, incompetent drivers, politically uninformed, and spendthrifts.

1821. Lofton, John. *The Press as Guardian of the First Amendment*. Columbia: University of South Carolina, 1980. "[E]xcept when their own freedom was discernibly at stake, established general circulation newspapers have tended to go along with efforts to suppress deviations from the prevailing political and social orthodoxies of their time and place rather than to support the right to dissent." After providing a survey history from the American Revolution to the present, this study places an emphasis on the period after the Schenck case of 1917. Before Schenck, there were no clear standards for assessing First Amendment issues, and this study treats most early episodes in traditional terms.

1822. Luby, James. *James Luby, Journalist*. Washington: Ransdell, 1930. Autobiography of an "old time newspaperman."

1823. Luskin, John. *Lippmann, Liberty and the Press*. Tuscaloosa: University of Alabama Press, 1972. Lippmann was not a great champion of freedom of the press; he wavered on it. "Civility" was the unifying feature of his career; he was an elitist who didn't trust the common people.

1824. Maddox, Lynda M., and Eric J. Zanot. "The Image of the Advertising Practitioner as Presented in the Mass Media, 1900-1972." *AJ* 2 (1985): 117-29. As the emphasis on consumerism increased, the image of advertising professionals as presented in books, popular magazines, and professional journals declined. The professional was often depicted in stereotypical terms as a huckster.

1825. Mahin, Helen Ogden. *The Editor and His People*. New York: Macmillan, 1924. Biography of William Allen White, the Emporia (Kan.) editor.

1826. Manchester, William. *Disturber of the Peace: The Life of H. L. Mencken*. New York: Harper, 1950 (2nd. ed., Amherst, Mass.: University of Massachusetts Press, 1986). Mencken was important as a student of language and as a master at using the language. The author of this biography was a friend of Mencken's, "the last of Mencken's proteges," who had his help in getting the information for the book.

1827. Markham, James W. *Bovard of the Post-Dispatch*. Baton Rouge: Louisiana State University Press, 1954. Oliver K. Bovard, who worked for Joseph Pulitzer on the

St. Louis *Post-Dispatch* and New York *World*, was the "greatest managing editor of all time." After returning from the *World* to the *Post-Dispatch*, he was responsible for building the St. Louis newspaper into one of the world's great newspapers at a time when the *World*, in other editors' hands, was in decline.

1828. Marshall, Max Lawrence. "Frank Luther Mott: Journalism Educator." Ph.D. dissertation, University of Missouri, 1968. Dean of the journalism programs at the Universities of Iowa and Missouri, Mott "figured...importantly in...[the] growth and development" of journalism education. Through his scholarship, he was instrumental in journalism education's "winning acceptance from the academic community."

1829. Martin, Ralph G. *Cissy: The Extraordinary Life of Eleanor Medill Patterson*. New York: Simon & Schuster, 1979. Cissy ran a sensationalist paper with a dose of social concern (along the lines of Hearst and Pulitzer). She was tyrannical and ran the staff according to her whims. At age 50 she began newspaper work as editor of Hearst's Washington *Times and Herald* (1930s). She eventually bought the papers, combined them into the *Times-Herald*, and made them profitable. The emphasis in this biography is on non-journalism life, with her sharp editorial criticisms, power over her staff, and confrontations with public figures providing the journalistic background to the story.

1830. Marzolf, Marion. "The Woman Journalist: Colonial Printer to City Desk, Part II." *JH* 2 (1975): 24-27, 32. From the 1920s to the 1970s, women held more and more jobs in journalism, including editing and reporting rather than just society writing, although there still was discrimination in promotions and salaries.

1831. Mayfield, Sara. *The Constant Circle: H. L. Mencken and His Friends*. New York: Delacorte, 1968. This biography of Mencken -- a sentimental and pleasant memoir by an acquaintance who admired him -- emphasizes his private, rather than public, life. He was not, as some critics claimed, a "bad boy."

1832. McGivena, Leo E. *The News: The First 50 Years of New York's Picture Newspaper*. New York: News Syndicate Co., 1969. A sponsored, authorized history of the New York *Daily News*.

1833. McGlashan, Zena Beth. "Club 'Ladies' and Working 'Girls': Rheta Childe Dorr and the New York *Evening Post*." *JH* 8 (1981): 7-13. Dorr, woman's editor of the New York *Evening Post*, was one of the women responsible for getting the federal government to investigate the number of women in the work force and the conditions under which they worked in 1906. This article is pro-women's rights, dealing with a study of the problems women had to surmount in facing the social perceptions of "woman's place."

1834. McKee, John D. *William Allen White: Maverick on Mainstreet*. Westport, Conn.: Greenwood, 1975. This biography of the Kansas editor attempts to make him seem even more human than he has commonly been depicted. He believed Kansas was to be the nation's conscience and example. He was a good writer and influential journalist who changed from conservative to liberal, typifying the growth of American liberalism in the 20th century. His career reflected America's change from small-town agrarianism to an urban society. White made his private sentiments public opinion and thus had a lasting impact. He was a master craftsman of writing, a leader of various causes (free press, working man, etc.), and a leader in public opinion and political affairs.

1835. McRae, Milton A. *Forty Years in Newspaperdom.*. New York: Bretano, 1924. Autobiography of E.W. Scripps' partner in the Scripps-McRae chain and his reminiscenses of the America's most prominent newspaper owners.

1836. McReynolds, William. "Gene Howe's Promotional Style." *JQ* 51 (1974): 710-12. The Amarillo, Tex., editor used a humorous column to promote his city, a national "Mother-in-Law Day," and conservation.

1837. Meier, August. "Booker T. Washington and the Negro Press, with Special Reference to the Colored American Magazine." *JNH* 38 (January 1953): 67-90. Washington used a variety of means of influence "over the Negro press to squelch movements opposed to him...[yet] most of the leading journals in his orbit did not adopt his accommodating phraseology. *The Colored American Magazine* and other journals undoubtedly expressed the outlook of the militant rising Negro bourgeoisie....[T]he editors of the journals in the Washington orbit, and indeed, Washington himself, shared in the basic desire of American Negroes throughout their history -- the goal of assimilation and the rights of citizenship." (89-90)

1838. Meyers, W. Cameron. "The Chicago Newspaper Hoax in the '36 Election Campaign." *JQ* 37 (1960): 356-64. A battle raged between the Chicago *Tribune* and the *Daily Times* after the *Tribune* claimed that Russia's Communist party had ordered U.S. Communists to support Roosevelt. Actually, the claim was based on a Chicago speech by Earl Browder, quoted out of context from a Society journal. The campaign battle between the *Daily Times* and Chicago's anti-Roosevelt papers often was bitter.

1839. Meyers, W. Cameron. "Chicago's Mr. Finnegan: A Gentle Man of the Press." Ph.D. dissertation, Norhtwestern University, 1959. Richard Finnegan was the first editor the Chicago *Daily News*, founded in 1929.

1840. Midrua, Edmund M. "A.J. Liebling: The Wayward Pressman as Critic." *JM* 33 (1974). Liebling's column "The Wayward Press" in the *New Yorker* (1925-63) was "one of the most sustained -- although irregular and uneven -- series of magazine articles on press performance." Through the articles and three books, Liebling "became the leading press critic of his day." (2)

1841. Mills, George. *Harvey Ingham and Gardner Cowles, Sr.: Things Don't Just Happen.* Ames: Iowa State University Press, 1977. The Des Moines *Register* gained its its news and editorial quality as a result of the foresighted business practices of the elder Cowles, which were continued by his sons John and Gardner Jr. Through effective use of Iowa's railroad system, Cowles gained statewide circulation for the paper. He advocated improved roads and highways with the paper's circulation in mind. Concurrently, he used innovative circulation techniques. He increased advertising by wooing advertisers with imaginative ideas; and even though he was concerned about increasing advertising, he rejected some advertising because of his high principles. At the same time, the liberal internationalist Ingham was director of the news-editorial operation and developed a superior news and editorial operation.

1842. Mills, Todd. "Pencil Pushers and Ink Slingers: The Globe Newspaper War of 1911." *JAH* 21 (Summer 1980): 147-70. After the 1910 Enabling Act was passed, allowing Arizona territory to draft a tentative state constitution, newspapers played a major part in the political battle. The town of Globe had a fierce newspaper war during which "a dozen fly-by-night journalists' passed through Globe, leaving two daily newspapers on the fourth estate's scrapheap along with a thick trail of absurd and inflamatory rhetoric."

1843. Moreau, John Adam. "The Often Enraged Heywood Broun: His Career and Thought Revisited." *JQ* 44 (1967): 497-507. The newspaper columnist's words were bitter, but he never hated anyone, except those who helped put Sacco and Vanzetti in the electric chair. He was a hero of the liberals of the 1920s and 1930s. He was pro-liberty and pro-labor and tried to help mankind. "He took and gave much joy in life." (507)

1844. Morgan, Gwen, and Arthur Veysey. *Poor Little Rich Boy: (And How He Made Good)*. Carpentersville, Ill.: Crossroads Communications, 1985. Narrative biography of Robert R. McCormick, owner of the Chicago *Tribune* written by two *Tribune* staff members and close McCormick acquaintances.

1845. Morris, Edmund. "Publicity, Publicity, Publicity." *WJR* 2 (May 1980): 45. Theodore Roosevelt was "the first president to use the press as an arm of government" for through it he "demolish[ed] his opposition." A group of reporters and cartoonists loyal to Roosevelt gave him favorable treatment. In return, he cooperated as a news source and gave them opportunities for interesting stories.

1846. Morris, Joe Alex. *Deadline Every Minute: The Story of the United Press*. Garden City, N.Y.: Doubleday, 1957. This adulatory history, written on the 50th anniversary of United Press, provides virtually a handbook on the art of the enterprising reporter who works in a competitive situation. It details the performance of United Press in reporting major news events of the first half of the 20th century, its news techniques and coverage, and its contributions to journalism. United Press beat the Associated Press through alertness, ingenuity, improvisation, extemporization, inventiveness, foresight, and hard work. Its overriding goal was to reach every newsroom ahead of its deadline. Besides its emphasis on reporting, this book has an underlying theme of the UP's leaders' concern about the threat of monopoly in the syndicated news business. E.W. Scripps, who was opposed to monopoly, set up UP to compete with the Associated Press.

1847. Morris, Loverne. "When a journalistic giant is the man across the street." *CCJ* 13, 1 (Winter): 6-7. A retired journalist's recollections of William Allen White.

1848. Morrison, Joseph L. "Josephus Daniels and the Bassett Academic Freedom Case." *JQ* 39 (1962): 187-95. After Daniels and white North Carolinians criticized Prof. John Bassett for remarks involving race and called for his removal from Trinity College, the school's trustees supported Bassett on the grounds of academic freedom. While historians have criticized Daniels for failing to support academic freedom, Daniels himself actually never considered the issue one of academic freedom but a predominantly political incident.

1849. Morrison, Joseph L. "Josephus Daniels as 'Tar Heel Editor,' 1894-1913." Ph.D. dissertation, Duke University, 1961. See next entry.

1849.1. Morrison, Joseph L. *Josephus Daniels Says....* Chapel Hill: University of North Carolina Press, 1962. Sympathetic political biography of the publisher of the Raleigh

(N.C.) *News and Observer* covering 1894 to 1913. See next entry.

1850. Morrison, Joseph L. *Josephus Daniels: The Small-d Democrat*. Chapel Hill: University of North Carolina Press, 1966. Although Daniels was a Democratic politician, he was a democrat in the larger sense of campaigning for social reform, public education, rights of labor unions, women's rights, and other policies of benefit to the mass public.

1851. Morrison, Joseph L. *W.J. Cash: Southern Prophet*. New York: Knopf, 1967. Cash, the author of the book *The Mind of the South*, was a writer for the Charlotte (N.C.) *News* in the 1930s and 1940s who argued that the romanticized former South had never existed except in later imagination and that Southerners needed to come to grips with the reality of modern life.

1852. Moscowitz, Raymond. *Stuffy: The Life of Newspaper Pioneer Basil "Snuffy" Walters*. Ames: Iowa State University Press, 1982.

1853. Mott, Frank Luther. *Time Enough*. Chapel Hill: University of North Carolina Press, 1962. Autobiography of the journalism historian.

1854. Murphy, Bill. "The Unforgettable 'Anything for a Story' Ben Hecht." *MHD* 5, 2 (1985): 32-39. The Chicago reporter used extraordinary, sometimes questionable tactics to get information; and at times he fabricated stories.

1855. Murphy, Mary Pat. "The United States vs. the AP." *MJR* 17 (1974): 40-46. Details of the antitrust case.

1856. *"The Nation*: The McWilliams Years." *The Nation* (Dec. 2, 1978). This special issue of the weekly journal of opinion "celebrates the mind, character and accomplishments of Carey McWilliams," who served as editor of the *Nation* from 1926 to 1976. Writing from a liberal viewpoint, he addressed various national issues, such as McCarthyism and America's reliance on military stances in its foreign policy.

1857. Neuman, Fred G. *Irvin S. Cobb: His Life and Achievements*. Paducah, Ky.: Young, 1934. This admiring biography paints Cobb as an amiable and talented journalist. He was a reporter, editor, and war correspondent who never was content with less than a prodigious amount of work. His pride was in being a good reporter.

1858. Neurath, Paul. "One-Publisher Communities: Factors Influencing Trend." *JQ* 21 (1944): 230-42. There has been an increasing trend toward newspaper monopoly since 1890. The factors have been the increasing size and growth of cities and geographic location.

1859. Nixon, Raymond B. "Concentration and Absenteeism in Daily Newspaper Ownership." *JQ* 22 (1945): 97-114. This quasi-historical study was motivated primarily about conditions in 1945. In every state the historical trend had been toward monopoly. Economic forces were the cause. "Above all, the American press must find ways of adopting itself to changing ['inexorable'] economic conditions without losing its editorial vitality and independence. As a result of suspensions and consolidations, the daily newspaper admittedly has gained greater economic stability than ever before. We must make certain that this stability does not bring with it editorial rigidity and sterility." (114)

1860. Nolte, William H. "The Literary Criticism of H.L. Mencken." Ph.D. dissertation, University of Illinois, 1959.

1861. Noon, Robert. "Vaudeville with a Vengeance -- Starring the Not-So-Kind Critics." *MHD* 3, 2 (1983): 2-7, 18-19. In the early 1900s, newspaper critics were merciless, the most notable of whom was Epes W. Sargent. Although he wrote caustically, however, he helped improve the quality of vaudeville.

1862. Olasky, Marvin N. "When World Views Collide: Journalists and the Great Monkey Trial." *AJ* 4 (1987): 133-46. Reporters covering the Scopes trial in 1925 considered themselves open-minded, but they were opposed to fundamental Christianity and thus interpreted the trial and its participants to fit their prejudices, giving biased and inaccurate accounts. "Ironically, reporters who praised 'open-mindedness'...showed great closed-mindedness when confronted with a world view opposed in many ways to their own." (142)

1863. Olson, McKinley C. *J. W. Gitt's Sweet Land of Liberty*. New York: Jerome S. Ozer, 1975. This biography was written by a member of Gitt's newspaper staff who viewed Gitt favorably as the epitome of what a journalist should be. Gitt was editor/publisher of the York *Gazette and Daily* from 1915 to 1970 and "incurred the wrath of those who feared and hated truthful reporting and insightful editorials." He aggressively opposed racism, the wealthy elite, and militarism.

1864. O'Shea, Nancy. "A Rude Dude: Reporter, Critic Alexander Woollcott." *MHD* 3, 2 (198): 11-15, 29. Woollcott, the theater critic for the New York *Times* and *Herald*, was insulting and outrageous, but he was the nation's best critic.

1865. Partington, Paul G. "The Moon Illustrated Weekly -- The Precursor of the *Crisis*." *JNH* 48 (July 1963): 206-16. Narrative of one of the magazines founded by the black activist W.E.B. Du Bois.

1866. Peel, Robert. *Mary Baker Eddy: The Years of Authority*. New York: Holt, Rinehart, Winston, 1977. Eddy, the founder of the *Christian Science Monitor*, tried to bridge the widening gap between science and religion. She stood "at the crossroads between Christianity and science, between faith based on revelation and authority based on demonstration." Pulitzer's *World* and *McClure's* attempted to outdo each other with sensational attacks on her in 1906-1907, each disregarding facts and using primarily slander and gossip. The launching of the *Christian Science Monitor* was, in part, a response to yellow journalism which had attacked her. She believed a wholesome publication was needed to give balanced and objective news, while also serving a religious function.

1867. Perry, J. Douglas. "Philadelphia Newspapers and the O'Conner Case." *JQ* 15 (1938): 349-58, 378. Newspapers were not "uniformly judicious" in presenting the 1937-1938 story of the murder of a five-year-old girl and the trial of the accused, who claimed the death was by accident.

1868. Peterson, Theodore B. "Magazines in the United States, 1900-1950: A Social and Economic History." Ph.D. dissertation, University of Illinois, 1954.

1869. Peterson, Theodore. "Mass Media and Their Environments: A Journey into the Past," 13-32 in Elie Abel, ed. *What's News: The Media in American Society*. San

Francisco: Institute for Contemporary Studies, 1981. In the last two decades of the 1800s, America changed from an agricultural to an industrial society. The change had a major impact on the media. By the 1890s metropolitan dailies had evolved into the large institutions they are today. In the 20th century, as the media grew in mass circulation, advertising (which needed big circulation media to promote mass-produced goods) became the primary means of support of media. "[T]he press took on the characteristics of the other mass-production industries its advertising served. It took advantage of new technology in gathering its raw materials and in manufacturing its final product. It specialized and standardized the tasks of its workers. It standardized not only the steps in the manufacture of its product, but also the product itself. By doing so, it was about to turn out, with great efficiency, a low-cost product that found ready acceptance in the mass market. Like many other industries, it underwent consolidation and concentration of ownership." (22) Thus survey includes such topics in advances in communication and production, newspaper standardization, the nature of freedom of the press (classical liberalism vs. responsibility to society), and the effect of the cultural, economic, and political environment on press.

1870. Peterson, Wilbur. "Is Daily Circulation Keeping Pace with the Nation's Growth?" *JQ* 36 (1959): 12-22. In the 1930s and 1950s the ratio of newspaper circulation to population decreased, although in the 1940s it increased. The author explains these changes by non-journalism factors (such as depression, war, and personal income).

1871. Pfaff, Daniel W. "Joseph Pulitzer II and Advertising Censorship, 1929-1939." *JM* 77 (1982). Despite the conventional wisdom about honesty in advertising, that "'purely voluntary efforts at self-regulation are not likely to be successful'...the self-imposed censorship of advertising copy at the St. Louis *Post-Dispatch*...is an exception to that rule -- and the paper's high standards of advertising acceptability begun a half century ago are still being followed." (1)

1872. Pfaff, Daniel W. "The Letters of H.L. Mencken and Fred Lewis Pattee, 1922-1948." *JH* 3 (1976): 80-84. Collection of letters which Mencken wrote to a professor of literature. They are friendly, warm letters to a man who represented many things Mencken professed to oppose: formal education, Christianity, teetotalism, etc.

1873. Pierce, Robert N. "Lord Northcliffe: Trans-Atlantic Influences." *JM* 40 (August 1975). Northcliffe, from the 1890s to the 1920s, influenced American journalism and was influenced by it. This study is an attempt to examine "the internationalization of journalism history." (i)

1874. Pilat, Oliver. *Angry Man of the Press*. Boston: Beacon, 1963. Westbrook Pegler was a shallow, egotistical, reactionary columnist.

1875. Pusey, Merlo J. *Eugene Meyer*. New York: Knopf, 1974. This biography deals primarily with Eugene Meyer's life after he purchased the Washington *Post*. Under his leadership, the *Post* developed as an excellent newspaper.

1876. Ray, Royal H. "Economic Forces as Factors in Daily Newspaper Concentration." *JQ* 29 (1952): 31-42. Maintaining competition in the daily newspaper industry under the economic conditions in the first half of the 20th century was difficult. There is a need for self-discipline by "monopoly" papers to stave off governmental intervention.

1877. Reed, John David. "Lindbergh Meets the Chicago Press: Fact or Fiction? or Both?" *MCRJ* 2 (1979): 47-56. This study concludes that two anecdotal stories of a 1925 incident dealing with Charles Lindbergh's actions in delivering photographic plates to a Chicago newspaper are apocryphal.

1878. Reed, Perley I. "The Rise of ASJSA." *JE* 3, 1 (1958): 10-18. Reed, the first president of the American Society of Journalism School Administrators, first became aware "of the growth of a professional consciousness among journalism educators" in 1922 (10). Prior to the ASJSA the leading journalism school directors were becoming elitist and attempting to limit the number of schools and membership of the American Association of Schools and Department of Journalism (AASDJ). The outschools then organized the ASJSA in response to the attitude of monopoly and arbitrary limitations in the AASDJ in 1944. This account details the struggle between the ASJSA and AASDJ and then discusses the growth of the ASJSA after 1954.

1879. Rich, Everett. *William Allen White, The Man from Emporia.* New York: Tarrar & Rinehart, 1941. This favorable biography relies primarily on direct quotations from White to tell the story.

1880. Ropel, Timothy. "Walter Winchell: The Thirteenth Juror." *MHD* 5, 4 (1985): 56-61. In reporting on criminals, the tabloid gossip columnist disregarded accuracy, fairness, and justice; but he exercised great influence. This article emphasizes Winchell's coverage of Bruno Hauptmann, the kidnaper of the Lindbergh baby.

1881. Ross, Ishbel. *Ladies of the Press.* New York: Harper, 1936. Narrative of the adventures of hundreds of female journalists, including pioneers but with emphasis on the 20th century.

1882. Rucker, Frank W. *Walter Williams.* Columbia: Missourian Publishing Association, 1964. Williams founded the University of Missouri journalism school in 1908 and served as its first dean. This favorable biography, written by a University of Missouri faculty member, details his accomplishments in education and journalism..

1883. Rudner, Lawrence S., ed. "Communications in America." *JPC* 15, 2 (1981): 1-129. This special issue of the *Journal of Popular Culture* contains 15 articles, several of which deal with history, including biographies of Ambrose Bierce, Walter Lippmann, Edward R. Murrow, and Lincoln Steffens.

1884. Rush, Ramona R. "Patterson, Grindstead and Hostetter: Pioneer Journalism Educators." *JH* 1 (1974): 129-32. This account briefly tells the stories of three women who paved the way for women in journalism education and became educator models for males and females in the field.

1885. Saalberg, Harvey. "Don Mellett, Editor of the Canton *News*, was Slain While Exposing Underworld." *JQ* 58 (1981): 88-93. Mellet was killed by criminal bosses in league with corrupt police because of his investigations. He was a "martyr to the press."

1886. Sanders, Marion K. *Dorothy Thompson: A Legend in Her Time.* Boston: Houghton Mifflin, 1973. From the 1920s to 1950s Thompson was a major figure in journalism and world events. Because of her ability to get interviews with leading political figures and to uncover hidden facts, she was an outstanding journalist. She believed strongly in the causes she supported (for example, anti-Nazis), and usually she was right in her beliefs. She placed her professional life above her tempestuous private life, for her real love was the profession of journalism. Her maxim was, "Get the news accurately. If possible get it first."

1887. Schapsmeir, Edward L., and Frederick N. Schapsmeir. *Walter Lippmann: Philosopher-Journalist*. Washington: Public Affairs Press, 1969. Lippmann was at the forefront of American political thought as a journalist, philosopher, and analyst of government. "Always probing deeper aspects of contemporary occurrences as the disinterested observer, he stimulated many to think seriously about mankind's predicament."

1888. Schuneman, R. Smith. "The Photograph in Print: An Examination of New York Daily Newspapers 1890-1937." Ph.D. dissertation, University of Minnesota, 1966. Qauntitative pictoral analysis examines changes in newspaper use of photographs and concludes that "utilization of the photograph in the daily newspaper has been an important development in 20th century mass communication."

1889. Seldes, George. *Lords of the Press*. New York: Julian Messner, 1938. Seldes was a trenchant liberal critic of the press. This book primarily was a criticism of the contemporary press, but its structure was built around historical biographies of leading newspaper publishers. Big newspapers in the 1930s had come under the control in most instances of wealthy money-makers who were over-conservative and typically failed to ensure fair news treatment for labor or social and economic reforms. The press of the 1930s was wanting in comparison with the press of the past.

1890. Sharpe, Ernest. *G. B. Dealey of the Dallas News*. New York: Henry Holt, 1955. Dealey founded the *News* in 1887. He died in 1946. He and the paper played a significant role in the building of a great city. Through numerous campaigns oriented toward city planning and improvement, Dealey fought for a better Dallas and a better Texas. He fought the Ku Klux Klan in the 1920s, even though the fight and a business depression almost bankrupted the paper. He refused oil-promotion advertising (because it carried swindle schemes) worth $500,000. He believed "a newspaper always has a moral responsibility to help its readers to higher standards."

1891. Shaub, Earl L. *All in a Day's Work*. New York: G.S. Rand, 1961. Personal account of several major news stories (such as the Sacco-Vanzetti trial and the first demonstration of television) which Shaub covered.

1892. Shepard, Bernard A. "C.K. McClatchy and the Sacramento Bee." Ph.D. dissertation, Syracuse University, 1960.

1893. Shields, Art. *My Shaping-Up Years: The Early Life of Labor's Great Reporter*. New York: International, 1982. This autobiographical account details Shields' early adventures and journalistic experiences through World War I.

1894. Simmons, George E. "Crusading Newspapers in Louisiana." *JQ* 16 (1939): 325-33. New Orleans newspapers helped bring to light charges of corruption against Louisiana officials in the late 1930s.

1895. Singh, Harnam. "American Press Opinion on Indian Government and Politics, 1918-1935." Ph.D. dissertation, Georgetown University, 1949.

1896. Sloan, Wm. David. "Historians and the American Press, 1900-1945: Working Profession or Big Business?" *AJ* 3 (1986): 154-66. Historiographical essay examines how historians have explained the press of the first half of the 20th century. This essay is a good place to start for researchers interested in understanding historical treatment of this period.

1897. Smith, C. Zoe. "Black Star Picture Agency: *Life's* European Connection." *JH* 13 (1986): 19-25. In the 1930s, "Black Star became a conduit through which American publishers and editors [led by Henry Luce] in need of talented, trained European photographers could hire those emigres who were forced to leave their jobs and their homeland because of the Nazis." (19) "Black Star owners were well acquainted with the operation of the German mass circulation picture magazines," (25) and their photographers brought their ideas to American magazines.

1898. Smith, Donald L. "Zechariah Chafee Jr. and the Positive View of Press Freedom." *JH* 5 (1978): 86-92. With publication of *Freedom of Speech* (1920) Chafee "became the nation's first great scholar of free speech." (88) He was the primary advocate of the concept of "balancing" constitutional rights, defining the nature of personal liberty and the permissible scope of governmental power to restrict it. This article contains a biography of Chafee and a brief history of his concept.

1899. Smith, Edward J. "The Normative Characteristics of the Cumulative News Story: A Descriptive Analysis." Ph.D. dissertation, Southern Illinois University, 1978. "The purpose of this content analytic study is to describe the characteristics of the cumulative news story [the type of story that reappears intermittently, expanding or adding new information to subjects reported in earlier stories] as it has been produced by the press in the U.S. during the period 1925-1975."

1900. Smith, Hampton Sidney, Jr. *Tramp Reporter*. Caldwell, Idaho: Caxton Printers, 1937. Autobiography (intended for general readers, not historians) of a reporter who worked for a number of papers.

1901. Sokolov, Raymond. *The Wayward Reporter: The Life of A. J. Liebling*. New York: Harper & Row, 1980.. Liebling wrote for the *New Yorker* about people on the fringe of society from 1935 to 1963. He was an excellent writer during a time of changing social and journalistic conditions. He was a critic of the giant publishers and was something of a "new journalist" with his personal involvement in the telling of his stories. He identified more with the lowlife characters of society than with the media owners.

1902. Steele, Ronald. *Walter Lippmann and the American Century*. Boston: Little, Brown, 1980. Lippmann was the greatest journalist of his time and one of the most influential of any time. He was closely involved in politics and world affairs. He possessed rare intellect, was from a cultured background, and received his education at Harvard. Often thought of as a leader of liberal thought, he really often was reactionary.

1903. Stenerson, Douglas C. *H. L. Mencken: Iconoclast from Baltimore*. Chicago: University of Chicago Press, 1971. Study of the interrelationships between what Mencken wrote and some of the principal strands in American thought and criticism in the late 19th and early 20th centuries. His writing was influenced by realism and naturalism. He was adviser to the young American rebels of the 1920s. He had a healthy influence on American affairs without establishing a consistent and convincing set of critical standards. He backed the right people and causes at the right time; yet his thinking was shallow, sometimes inconsistent and contradictory. Yet it was love of his country that was at the root of his criticism of so many of its institutions. The two aspects of his work that are most durable are his libertarianism and the gusto and artistry with which he expressed it.

1904. Stenerson, Douglas C. "Mencken's Early Newspaper Experience: The Genesis of a Style." *AL* 37 (May 1965): 153-66. Part of research conducted for previous entry.

1905. Stevens, George E. "Scripps' Cincinnati *Post*: Liberalism at Home." *JQ* 48 (1971): 231-34. As the first newspaper in which E.W. Scripps owned a controlling interest, the *Post* was the base from which he started his chain. It was also a proving ground for many of his most talented people. "Scripps was respected by many Cincinnatians because the Post emphasized local political reform....As the city's most liberal daily, the Post vigorously fought political corruption and bossism. The newspaper became regionally and even nationally famous for its good government crusades." (231)

1906. Stevens, George E. "Winning the Pulitzer Prize: The Indianapolis *Times* Battles Political Corruption, 1926-27." *JH* 2 (1975): 80-83. The narrative of the Indianapolis *Times'* state-wide campaign against the Ku Klux Klan, how the battle was fought, and the results.

1907. Stevens, John D. "The Black Press Looks at 1920's Journalism." *JH* 7 (1980): 109-13. The black press "had always been a 'fighting press,'" and while it did not abandon that opinion-leader role, it turned more and more to news as its staple" in the 1920s. During that time, "black newspapers became viable businesses." (109) They were sensational because such material sold papers. Black editors were defensive about their papers, but they saw little to admire in white papers. Major criticisms were racial identifications in stories and negative news.

1908. Stevens, John D. "Reflections in a Dark Mirror: Comic Strips in Black Newspapers." *JPC* 10 (Summer 1976): 239-48. Two of the most popular comic strips in black newspapers reflected black life. The changes in "Bungleton Green" and "Sunny Boy Sam" that had taken place since 1925 paralleled changes in both the opportunities available to blacks in America and the editorial content of black newspapers.

1909. Stolberg, Benjamin. "The Man Behind the *Times*." *AM* (December 1926): 721-31. Adolph Ochs, publisher of the New York *Times*, had an "absolute faith in the 'ordinary virtues'" (hard work, common sense, self-reliance, honesty), and these were responsible for his success with the *Times*. "He is the living norm of the median culture of American life." He was courageous, daring, honorable. The *Times* adapted to conditions. Ochs "caught the idea of mass production at just the right time in the New York newspaper field." (364) The *Times*, emphasized *news*, Ochs emphasized high-quality advertising, he never was influenced by advertisers, and he maintained a low editorial profile.

1910. Strong, Tracy B., and Helene Keyssar. *Right in Her Soul: :The Life of Anna Louise Strong*. New York: Random House, 1983. Do-goodism and an affinity for Communism marked the career of Anna Louise Strong, the brash, imperious foreign correspondent, from the early 1900s to 1970. Originally concerned about improving humanity, she became a Communist propagandist, kicked out of Russia but buried with honor in China.

1911. Suggs, Henry Lewis. "Black Strategy and Ideology in the Segregation Era: P. B. Young and the Norfolk *Journal and Guide*, 1910-1954." *VMHB* 91 (1983): 161-90. "Ever a cautious and practical man...Young's...accommodationism troubled his participation in the [black] protests of the late 1930s and 1940s. Although he was among the founders of an organization [NAACP] which ultimately attacked segregation outright, Young and his generation were bypassed by younger men and women in the new age of protest in the 1950s." (161)

1912. Suggs, Henry Lewis. "P. B. Young of the Norfolk Journal and Guide: A Booker T. Washington Militant, 1904-1928." *JNH* 64 (Fall 1979): 365-76. Young, a leading black journalist who supported Booker T. Washington, was, like Washington, an economic conservative who appealed to whites. Yet after Washington's death, he increasingly realized that "Washington's philosophy did not fit well with many of the realities of life" in the changing social conditions and times after World War I. He therefore broke with the Republican party and spoke out against segregation.

1913. Swanberg, W. A. *Whitney Father, Whitney Heiress*. New York: Scribner's, 1980. Combined biography of William Collins Whitney; his wife, Flora Payne Whitney; their daughter Dorothy Whitney Straight; and her husband, William Straight. The last two founded the *New Republic* .

1914. Swanson, Walter S. J. *The Thin Gold Watch, A Personal History of the Newspaper Copleys*. New York: Macmillan, 1964. The author of this biography was a Copley executive and paints a favorable picture of Ira Copley, who was one of the first of 20th-century businessmen to see that the newspaper was a business that could make a profit. Before entering the newspaper field, Copley previously had made money in gas and electric utilities.

1915. Taft, William H. "Bernarr Macfadden: One of a Kind." *JQ* 45 (1968): 627-33. Macfadden, the publisher of health and romance publications, was more significant in his contributions to journalism than historians have recognized.

1916. Tait, Samuel W., Jr. "The St. Louis *Post-Dispatch. AM* 22 (April 1931): 403-12. After Pulitzer's death, the *Post-Dispatch*, under the direction of Joseph Pulitzer Jr., "completely realized the Pulitzer ideal of a newspaper which should be absolutely independent of all party and financial interests, should be constantly fighting vigorous and interesting battles, and should at the same time make a lot of money." (403)

1917. Tebbel, John. *The Marshall Fields: A Study in Wealth*. New York: Dutton, 1947. Marshall Field III was motivated by a social conscience and attempted to use his wealth as a liberalizing influence through *PM* and the Chicago *Sun* and philanthropies. The difficult economic conditions which many people faced in the Great Depression caused Field to change from a conservative playboy. He believed in freedom of expression.

1918. Thornburgh, Emma L. *T. Thomas Fortune: Militant Journalist*. Chicago: University of Chicago Press, 1972. With the New York *Age*, Fortune was a black activist and spokesman for the national black movement.

1919. Toole, Robert C. "Mass Communications: Norristown, Pa., 1900-1950." Ph.D. dissertation, University of Pennsylvania, 1954.

1920. Towers, Wayne M. "World Series Coverage in New York City in the 1920s." *JM* 73 (August 1981). Coverage of the World Series established sports coverage, especially of baseball, as an important part of the news media.

1921. Turnbull, George S. *An Oregon Crusader*. Portland: Binfords & Mort, 1955. George Putnam, editor of the Salem *Capital Journal* in the 1920s, had editorial courage. He fought powerful political groups and reactionary forces, even though the electorate sometimes was indifferent. He believed in fair and uncensored news and in the need for an editorial page that attacked evils. He was a "fighting editor" who opposed legal, political, and judicial corruption, and racial and religious bigotry, while other editors looked the other way. He was an influential force in standing up for what was right.

1922. Turnbull, George S. *An Oregon Editor's Battle for Freedom of the Press*. Portland: Binford & Mort, 1952. Putnam fought the local judicial system when he was charged with criminal libel for editorializing that a grand jury had been corrupt in not indicting a railroad president for throwing an ax at the city mayor in Roseburg, Ore., in 1907.

1923. Villard, Oswald Garrison, *The Disappearing Daily: Chapters in American Newspaper Evolution*. New York: Knopf, 1944. This critical history is written from a liberal viewpoint that fighting crusades is more important for newspapers than providing news. Villard was one of the most strident Progressive critics of the press among journalism historians. He deplored the trend toward pictures and features and argued that the role of journalism was to "educate and illuminate": newspapers should watch the government to protect the people. A pacifist, Villard praised isolationists and criticized interventionists. This book scorns the "crass materialism of the bulk of the American press." The newspaper that doesn't champion enough causes is the "disappearing daily."

1924. Villard, Oswald Garrison. *Some Newspapers and Newspaper-Men*. New York: Knopf, 1923. In this book, Villard criticized conservative newspapers and praised liberal ones in the context of biographies of journalists such as Adolph Ochs, Frank Munsey, Fremont Older, and Henry Watterson. The New York *Times*, for example, was racist and encouraged a discriminatory separation of views between blacks and whites. Concerned with newspapers as social forces, this account evaluates newspapers as organs of opinion, molders of public thought, and crusaders for social improvement. Newspapers too often gave up leadership and appealed to public tastes in scandal, racial antipathies, and social hatred because they tried to make profit by appealing to public passions, rather than basing their approach on principle.

1925. Vito, Stephen. "Hollywood Versus the Press." *AF* 3 (May 1978): 30-32, 49-54, 69. In covering Hollywood in the 1920s, "reporters with the enterprise of forty-niners and the ethics of barn-burners treated movie stars with undisguised contempt." The press was set on its "muckraking rampage" by a combination of "reckless yellow journalism in America" (led by the Hearst press) and a large number of Hollywood "scandals of love and death."

1926. Vivian, John H. "Spelling an End to Orthographical Reforms: Newspaper Response to the 1906 Roosevelt Simplifications." *AmSp* 54, 3 (1979): 163-74. Newspaper reporting and commentary helped kill the president's order to simplify spellings used in government documents.

1927. Waldrop, Frank C. *McCormick of Chicago*. Englewood Cliffs, N.J.: Prentice-Hall, 1966. This non-thematic biography views Col. Robert McCormick of the Chicago *Tribune* as a product of a conservative family and social environment.

1928. Watson, Elmo Scott. *A History of Newspaper Syndicates in the U.S., 1865-1935*. Chicago: Western Newspaper Union, 1936. Factual history of the organization and development of feature syndicates and press associations. In the wholesaling of news, the same trend is noticeable that is found in other commodities: it is handled by a few companies that do an enormous business and can outbid smaller competitors, although (because of the nature of the situation) the monopolistic tendency is stronger in the providing of news than of features.

1929. Weigle, Clifford F. "The Young Scripps Editor: Keystone of E. W.'s 'System.'" *JQ* 41 (1964): 360-66. Scripps got promising young men to start new papers by directing them to a city, advancing them capital, and then leaving them alone and allowing them to buy a 10-20 per cent share of the paper. Many were so inspired by these principles that they worked tirelessly on starvation budgets.

1930. Weinfeld, William. "The Growth of Daily Newspaper Chains in the U.S.: 1923, 1926-1935." *JQ* 13 (1936): 357-80. Chains grew rapidly. By 1923 they "had become established as a formidable factor in the cultural pattern of American journalism." (362)

1931. Weingast, David E. *Walter Lippmann*. New Brunswick, N.J.: Rutgers University Press, 1949. Study of Lippmann's syndicated column, especially his views on domestic issues during the first seven years of Franklin Roosevelt's administration. Weingast provides a liberal/progressive and pro-New Deal perspective. Lippmann had a "high degree of literary excellence"; his writing was "disinterested and reasonable, the product of a sober, responsible thinker." But he drew too many of his ideas from "important figures in politics, diplomacy and business" and not enough from "labor and farm people, and from leaders of minority groups." His "support of liberal theories of social reform" was largely offset by "frequent disapproval of the actual legislation" to implement that reform.

1932. Wellborn, Charles. *Twentieth Century Pilgrimage: Walter Lippmann and the Public Philosophy*. Baton Rouge: Louisiana State University Press, 1969. This analysis of Lippmann's writing is based on the thesis that the attempt to link earthly structures with some ultimate, spiritual reality is a productive approach to a true understanding of contemporary society. It traces the development of Lippmann's thought on the nature of man, the maladies of democracy, the meaning and function of law, and the relevance of religion.

1933. Wells, George Y. "Patterson and the *Daily News*." *AM* 50 (December 1944): 671-79. The New York *Daily News* gained its circulation, the largest in the United States despite its erratic editorial policy, through its sensationalism and comics.

1934. Whitaker, Wayne Richard. "Warren G. Harding and the Press." Ph.D. dissertation, Ohio University, 1972. Harding had "excellent press relations....[H]e was frank and candid with newsmen...and made it a point to speak before gatherings of journalists....Of most importance...[he] advanced the status of the White House correspondent to the point that newsmen could no longer be ignored by a president."

1935.   Whitaker, W. Richard. "The Working Press and the Harding Myth." *JH* 2 (1975): 90-91. The press uncovered corruption in the Harding administration, particularly after his death.

1936.   White, William. "Hemingway as Reporter: An Unknown News Story." *JQ* 3 (1926): 538-42. Reprints the text of an article on the Yokohama Quake which Hemingway wrote for the Toronto *Daily Star* in 1923.

1937.   White, William Allen. *The Autobiography of William Allen White.* New York: Macmillan, 1946. A marvelously written life story of the Emporia (Kan.) *Gazette* editor.

1938.   White, William Allen. *Forty Years on Main Street.* Russell H. Fitzgibbon, comp. New York: Farrar & Rinehart, 1937. Collection of White's editorials from 1896 to 1937.

1939.   White, William S. *The Making of a Journalist.* Lexington: University Press of Kentucky, 1986. Autobiography of a New York *Times* reporter and syndicated columnist.

1940.   Wilcox, Walter. "Historical Trends in Journalism Education." *JE* 14, 3 (1959): 2-7, 32.

1941.   Williams, Sara Lockwood. *Twenty Years of Journalism: A History of the School of Journalism of the University of Missouri, Columbia, Missouri, U.S.A..* Columbia: Missourian Publishing Co., 1929.

1942.   Williamson, Samuel T. *Imprint of a Publisher: The Story of Frank Gannett and His Newspapers.* New York: McBride, 1948. In this authorized biography, parts of which were written as part of Gannett's campaign for the 1940 presidential nomination, the life of Gannett is told as a success story of a poor boy who rises to riches and power. Gannett was a businessman, and nothing so inspired him as a business opportunity. He bought, merged, operated, and controlled newspapers with an ideal of editorial independence. He allowed his local editors to determine editorial policy. His newspapers were good ones. Although generally conservative, he had a record of responsible stands on issues.

1943.   Wood, Barry Robert. "Denver Newspaper Publishers and Teapot Dome." *EMCH* 1, 1 (1983): 25-37. Bonfils and Shaffer blackmailed a senator involved in the Teapot Dome scandal. Their unsavory actions inspired the American Society of Newspaper Editors to adopt a code of ethics.

1944.   Woodruff, Olive. "A Quarter-Century of Advice to Parents of Young Children in Selected Newspapers and Magazines, 1921-1945." Ph.D. dissertation, Ohio State University, 1947.

1945.   Wright, Benjamin F. *Five Public Philosophies of Walter Lippmann.* Austin: University of Texas Press, 1973. Lippmann was the most important journalist of the century. This study analyzes nine of his books on social and political philosophy.

1946.   Yardley, Jonathan. *A Biography of Ring Lardner.* New York: Random House, 1978. Lardner was a successful and talented sports writer and fiction writer during a career from 1906 to 1933.

1947. Yates, Norris W. *The American Humorist: Conscience of the Twentieth Century.* Ames: Iowa State University Press, 1964. Yates' intention is to "set forth what humorists in the first half of this century believed concerning such important phenomena as man, society, and the cosmos." He examines the careers of 16 humorists, all of whom but Will Rogers were journalists. The most typical American humorist changed from the 19th-century rustic philosopher to a harassed "Little Man" in a complex urban environment.

1948. Zobrist, Benedict K. "Edward Price Bell and the Development of the Foreign News Service of the Chicago Daily News." Ph.D. dissertation, Northwestern University, 1953.

1949. Zynda, Thomas H. "The Hollywood Version: Movie Portrayals of the Press." *JH* 6 (1979): 16-25, 32. Since the 1930s, movies have portrayed (1) the character of the reporter, (2) the nature of the press organization, (3) the social role of the press (4) and the character of the society in which the press functions. Films generally are unfavorable, critical, and cynical. "Hollywood's journalists are often intent less on truth than on advancing their own careers by writing whatever the editors or owners want. In the movies, successful journalists are often less than admirable characters....The movies often depict the press as the most ruthless of businesses, aimed solely at profit and taking that profit by exploiting innocent people." (17) In the "real world," the press has a little loftier goal than the movies portray. Yet, "as the press serves as a watch-dog on government, so Hollywood, likewise on behalf of the public and with a like commercial basis, keeps an eye on the press." (32)

12

The Press and the Age of Reform, 1900–1917

1950. Baker, Ray Stannard. *American Chronicle*. New York: Scribner's, 1945. Autobiography of the muckraker.

1951. Bannister, Robert C., Jr. *Ray Stannard Baker: The Mind and Thought of a Progressive*. New Haven: Yale University Press, 1966. Intellectual history of Baker, an influential muckraker. An "important minor figure in American history," he had a deep concern for social problems but preferred moderate reform measures rather than radical ones. Typical of Progressives, Baker was concerned about problems of the 20th century but had a 19th century philosophy about what conditions should be. From a rural, middle-class, Protestant background, he reacted with anguish to the urban problems confronting America.

1952. Beasley, Maurine. "The Muckrakers and Lynching: A Case Study." *JH* 9 (1982): 86-91. Muckrakers showed little concern about the problem of lynching of black people. Ray Stannard Baker was the only one to do major study of it.

1953. Bok, Edward. *The Americanization of Edward Bok*. New York: Scribner's, 1920. Autobiography of the founder and editor of *Ladies' Home Journal*, a reform magazine in its early years.

1954. Bradshaw, James Stanford. "The Journalist as Pariah: Three Muckraking Newspaper Novels by Samuel Hopkins Adams." *JH* 10 (1983): 10-13. In the three novels, "each with a newspaper background and with a strong muckraking flavor," Adams "explored, in a fictionalized form, the state of American journalism, what it was, and what, as a liberal, he felt it should be....A central point in each was the...well-documented influence of advertisers upon newspapers. But a new theme was that newsmen were 'pariahs' in American society, prostituted by the greed of their publishers to the malign service of business and politics, as well as to the prurient curiosity of the public." (10)

1955.   Brady, Kathleen. *Ida Tarbell: Portrait of a Muckraker*. New York: Seaview/Putnam, 1984. Tarbell, an intelligent and determined muckraker, was one of the most respected and feared journalists of her day; yet she was an anti-suffragist. She investigated the injustices of factory conditions, Standard Oil, and the tariff system.

1956.   Britt, Albert. *Ellen Browning Scripps: Journalist and Idealist*. London: Oxford University Press, 1960. Admiring biography of a woman who distinguished herself in journalism, education, and philosophy.

1957.   Cassedy, James H. "Muckraking and Medicine, Samuel Hopkins Adams." *AQ* 16 (1964): 85-99. Adams progressed from a muckraker exposing problems in medicine to a medical writer. In 1920s he left medical writing because medicine had advanced and more knowledgeable writers were available. As a muckraker, he was not an expert on medicine. However, he did serve an important function by educating the public and helping bring about reform. Also, he was more positive than most muckrakers.

1958.   Chalmers, David M., ed. *The Muckrake Years*. New York: Van Nostrand-Reinhold, 1974. "The prime...achievement of the muckrakers was to point out the conflict between the growth of large scale private economic power and the needs of the new national American society." They failed, however, to follow-up adequately on their articles and to truly understand the fundamental causes of problems. This book provides an introductory essay, followed by muckrakers' writings.

1959.   Chalmers, David. "The Muckrakers and the Growth of Corporate Power: A Study in Constructive Journalism." *AJES* 18 (1959): 295-311. Muckrakers were important because of their critical attitude toward big business. This analysis challenges Hofstadter's, et.al., critiques of the Progressive ideology. Although muckrakers occasionally used questionable tactics (such as sensationalism), they were important. The reason some historians have misunderstood them (saying they were not sincere) is that they were journalists, not philosophers. "Their work was adopted to the nature of the popular magazines and tended to develop in installment fashion. Few writers began with a broad analysis of the national ills." (299) But they wound up realizing that the small chapters were part of a greater national problem. By informing the public, they laid "the popular groundwork of public concern which resulted in many reforms of the next half century. The fact that they presented no innovations to the world of social theory and that their functions were often crude and unsophisticated does not detract from the importance of the role that they played as educators of the public. If the picture they painted was rough and a little overdrawn, it was because they were describing a new business dynamo at the period of its greatest and most unabashed power."The significance of the muckrakers is they had positive views to express and were able to do so over a decade in the popular magazines of the nation. These journalists made the public aware of the degree to which corruption had become general in the national life. They explained that it resulted from the privileges sought and obtained by the giant business enterprises that had emerged in the United States after the Civil War. The muckrakers did not reject the new industrialism and the dominant corporate form but rather insisted that both be consciously directed to the public good." (310-11)

1960. Chalmers, David M. *The Social and Political Ideas of the Muckrakers*. New York: Citadel Press, 1964. This is a positive interpretation of muckrakers which is intended as a response to the revisionist interpretation of the Progressive movement. It argues that they did attempt to gain worthy achievements and perform worthwhile service, that they were interested in more than commercial sensationalism and moral indignation, and that they did offer specific solutions for the cure of social ills. This book analyzes the economic philosophies of 13 writers. Some journalists believed that all ills could be solved if businessmen were given control, while others (such as Charles Russell) were socialists and others were in the political middle. In general, they were moderates who concluded that society's problems were caused by the failure of businessmen to accept their social responsibility.

1961. Chamberlain, John. *Farewell to Reform*. New York: John Day, 1932. Chamberlain, a Marxist, was critical of Progressivism because of its superficial approach to solving deep-seated problems, when radical solutions were needed. The Progressive movement was a terrible failure, its followers motivated by a desire to return to a golden past, when virtue had vanquished evil. Such was not the situation in the early 1900s, when capitalists were motivated by self-interest. Some muckrakers were sincere and effective, while others (such as David Graham Phillips and William Randolph Hearst) were in it for money. Muckrakers "swarmed all over the land, doing some harm, but an incalculable amount of good in the way of educating the American people to realities. Muck-raking, indeed, provided the basis for the entire movement toward Social Democracy that came to its head in the first Wilson Administration." (127-128) Muckrakers accomplished many reforms, but they were powerless to solve the underlying problems of the system (such as the rising cost of living, the fundamental nature of business, etc.). "They could no nothing, ultimately, to right any of the fundamental wrongs." (142)

1962. Cook, Fred J. *The Muckrakers: Crusading Journalists Who Changed America*. New York: Doubleday, 1972. Biographies of crusading writers whose expose`s forced major changes by arousing public contempt: (1) Ida Tarbell forced Standard Oil to back down from its attempt to monopolize the industry, (2) Upton Sinclair persuaded the government to regulate food and drug industries, (3) David Graham Phillips forced the Senate to reform, (4) Josiah "Cigarette" Flint brought public scrutiny to the underworld, (5) Charles Edward Russell revealed the slum holdings of New York City's prosperous Trinity Church. (This book is intended for high-school-age readers.)

1963. Filler, Louis. *Appointment at Armageddon: Muckraking and Progressivism in the American Tradition*. Westport, Conn.: Greenwood, 1966. This survey history of reformers throughout American history serves as a basis for Filler's criticism of modern historians who have dismissed the Progressive movement as unimportant or nonexistent.

1964. Filler, Louis. *The Muckrakers: Crusaders for American Liberalism*. New York: Harcourt, Brace, 1939. This is the standard work on the muckrakers, providing a liberal, anti-big business, pro-muckraker interpretation. Written from a classic Progressive, conflict interpretation of the muckrakers, it argues that business "deliberately planned and accomplished" the destruction of muckraking magazines by an advertising boycott. The 1976 edition is prefaced with an introduction reacting to historians who have criticized the muckraking movement. It states Filler's argument succinctly: The muckrakers were "neither radical nor conservative, but "fed" the several social sectors of society with knowledge and understanding." (viii) Dealing with "facts and not theory," they were tough-minded, non-ideological investigators who "wrote because there was a demand for their work, and because they wanted more reform and more democracy." (5, 217) Muckraking was the logical response to the abuses that accompanied industrialization and urbanization. After reaching its zenith in 1906, muckraking's emphasis shifted from "exposure to reform -- and the reforms aimed at were so broad, so interrelated, that they predicted a full change in American life and thought." (260) The outcome of the Progressive movement was that "these crusaders did not transform the nation; they modernized it. No other band of social workers in any country or time ever accomplished more." (170)

1965. Filler, Louis. "The Muckrakers in Flower and in Failure," pp. 251-70 in Donald Sheehan and Harold C. Syrett, *Essays in American Historiography*. New York: Columbia University Press, 1960. "In rousing common citizens to their own interests and duties, the muckrakers reaffirmed the reality of democracy." (261) Since muckrakers' decline, liberal intellectuals have lost direct, sympathetic contact with the people.

1966. Filler, Louis. *Progressivism and Muckraking*. New York: R. R. Bowker, 1976. A bibliography of works on muckraking.

1967. Francke, Warren Theodore. "Investigative Exposure in the Nineteenth Century: The Journalistic Heritage of the Muckrakers." Ph.D. dissertation, University of Minnesota, 1974. Investigative, expose' journalism began in the 1800s. Muckraking was not a new kind of journalism but a continuation of such reporting methods.

1968. Geiger, Louis G. "Muckrakers -- Then and Now." *JQ* 43 (1966): 469-76. This is a pro-muckraking article that praises muckrakers' idealism and positive influence on American attitudes toward reform. The muckrakers, who set out to create a general climate of reform, did not succeed, but the failure was as much a limitation of the media and the audience as it was a fault of the writers. Yet the "muckrakers typified their own times in their enthusiasm about the possibilities of solving their problems." (473-74) Muckrakers believed in hope and personal involvement. Although they may not have achieved everything they wanted, they were sincerely dedicated to their causes and wanted to improve society.

1969. Gibson, William M. *Theodore Roosevelt Among the Humorists: W. D. Howells, Mark Twain, and Mr. Dooley*. Knoxville: University of Tennessee Press, 1980. During the Progressive era, Roosevelt had a notable relationship with literary figures, who freely recorded their impressions of him: Twain, Howells, and Finley Peter Dunne. All three loved him as a man but were critical of him as a statesman and politician.

1970. Goldman, Eric F. "Public Relations and the Progressive Surge, 1898-1917." *PRR* (Fall 1978): 52-62. Reformers tried to use the press to bring about political reform. Some muckrakers "seized hold of the general Progressive awareness of publicity and discovered conscious, controlled publicity as a major instrument of modern America."

1971. Grenier, Judson A. "Muckraking and Muckrakers: An Historical Definition." *JQ* 37 (1960): 552-58. This is primarily an attempt to define the term "muckraking" and to identify muckrakers. "Wealthy and widely-read [magazines]...became journalistic empires by the process of unveiling the problems of nineteenth century society. From 1902-1912 these writers led the nation in the systematic uncovering of the strands of a giant web of control, linking politics, education, the press, religion, health and high finance." (554) "One conviction common to all Progressive journalists was their faith in Truth, in facts" and the good of mankind. (556)

1972. Harris, Leon. *Upton Sinclair: American Rebel.* New York: Crowell, 1975. Sinclair was "the most important writer in the history of the United States" because of the effect he had. He believed the death of muckraking magazines was the result of a capitalist plot. In *The Brass Check* he saw no hope in a capitalist press and argued that the best remedies were a reporters' union and a national newspaper to publish nothing but the truth. He was concerned about how various institutions were strangling American liberties. Harris paints a favorable, simplistic picture of Sinclair, including his fictionalized *The Jungle* which brought about changes in the meatpacking industry. This study is optimistic about Progressive reform and liberal progress, but it views American history in simplistic one-sided terms, sometimes crediting Sinclair with reform rather than realizing the full background of the change that took place.

1973. Harrison, John M. "Finley Peter Dunne and the Progressive Movement." *JQ* 41, (1967): 475-81. Dunne was a philosophical anarchist and effective critic and reformer. He can be considered an early muckraker because he "had in him all the indignation, all the outrage against the false values of the Gilded Age, all the compassion for the worsening plight of the individual in his relationship with the civilization in which he lived." (476)

1974. Harrison, John M., and Harry Stein, eds. *Muckraking: Past, Present and Future.* University Park: Pennsylvania State University Press, 1973. Collection of essays by Filler, Chalmers, Bannister, etc.

1975. Hofstadter, Richard. *The Age of Reform.* New York: Knopf, 1955. Hofstadter developed the "status anxiety" evaluation of Progressive reformers as members of a class who had seen their leading position in society endangered by big-business and industrialists. They therefore attacked business' abuses in order to try to regain their position. Despite this critical evaluation of the Progressive movement in general, Hofstadter nevertheless commends muckrakers, for "to an extraordinary degree the work of the Progressive movement rested upon journalism."

1976. Horton, Russell M. *Lincoln Steffens.* New York: Twayne, 1974. Steffens was liberal and influential. However, his "success as a muckraker, indeed the success of muckrakers in general, was based on a direct appeal to the moral and civic pride of the mass middle class rather than any intellectual challenge. With a few notable exceptions, the expose` journalists of the Progressive era scrupulously avoided even the suggestion of any radical changes in the basic arrangement of society. Rather, they emphasized the need for a rejuvenation of traditional Protestant values." (69) Horton, unlike Chamberlain, finds such values and the muckrakers' approach worthy. This biography offers a favorable view of Steffens not as a radical but as a person concerned with improving conditions in the best of American values and traditions.

1977. Hudson, Robert Vernon. "Journeyman Journalist: An Analytical Biography of Will

Irwin." Ph.D. dissertation, University of Minnesota, 1970. Biography of the reporter and muckraking free-lancer who wrote "The American Newspaper" series for *Collier's*, covered World War I, crusaded for international cooperation and against propaganda, and was a close friend of Herbert Hoover.

1978. Hudson, Robert V. "Will Irwin's Articles on 'The American Newspaper' Which Appeared in *Collier's*." *JH* 2 (1975): 84-85, 97. See next entry.

1979. Hudson, Robert V. "Will Irwin's Pioneering Criticism of the Press." *JQ* 47 (1970): 263-71. Summarizes Irwin's articles on "The American Newspaper" which *Collier's* published. "The distinguishing characteristics of Irwin's...series are careful documentation and fairness....[He drew] the lines for much modern criticism of the press." (271)

1980. Hudson, Robert V. *The Writing Game: A Biography of Will Irwin*. Ames: Iowa State University Press, 1982. Irwin was a serious, versatile writer who worked for the San Francisco *Chronicle*, New York *Sun*, and *McClure's* and as a free-lancer and book author. He had a deep concern for public issues.

1981. Irwin, Will. *The American Newspaper*. Ames: Iowa State University Press, 1969. Reprint of the articles in the 1911 *Collier's* series.

1982. Jernigan, E. Jay. *William Allen White*. Boston: Twayne, 1983. Evaluates White's work in Midwestern Progressivism and reform.

1983. Juergens, George. *News From The White House: The Presidential-Press Relationship in the Progressive Era*. Chicago: University of Chicago Press, 1981. Study of Theodore Roosevelt's and Woodrow Wilson's use of publicity and the press, including the functions of press bulletins used by the White House, news conferences, reporters' visits to the White House, other innovations, and the adversary relationship.

1984. Kaplan, Justin. *Lincoln Steffens: A Biography*. New York: Simon & Schuster, 1974. Favorable account of Steffens as a Horatio Alger who was important to the evolution of the Progressive Democratic movement from the 1890s to the New Deal. Steffens was intent on revealing the sins of a corrupt system. He was a radical who believed that the ownership and distribution of property were as important in creating the "shame of the cities" and other shortcomings of the American democracy as were personal dishonesty, lack of patriotism, and contempt of the law. Progressives were moderate as compared to Steffens. He believed strongly in the welfare of the person as an individual rather than in people as units. He was not Communist, however, but liberal.

1985. Kielbowicz, Richard B. "The Limits of the Press as an Agent of Reform." *JQ* 59 (1982): 21-27. This thoughtful article examines historians' method. Historians should be cautious in ascribing influence to the press. They tend to exaggerate the effect exposure has on bringing about reform. The reasons are that (1) historians tend to "select obtrusive incidents of change for their study," and (2) they do not adequately specify their standards. This case study of the impact of reform publications finds that Minneapolis newspapers were not as successful in bringing about reform in city government as historians believe.

1986. Larsen, Robin. "Ida: the mouse that roared." *MHD* 2, 1 (1982): 2-6. "Tarbell helped to create a new American conscience. She forced citizens to ask themselves whether materialism was a cardinal sin, and whether corporate capitalism was able to correct its illegal and corrupt practices. She also helped to develop a new form of journalism that has again become popular, a writing form with a flexible structure that exposes patterns within the political, social and economic order which are in opposition to the perceived public interest." (6) This article doesn't provide adequate evidence to support the conclusions.

1987. Levy, David W. *Herbert Croly of the New Republic: The Life and Thought of an American Progressive.* Princeton, N.J.: Princeton University Press, 1985. Croly founded the *New Republic* (1914) and was a political philosopher.

1988. Littlefield, Roy Everett, III. *William Randolph Hearst: His Role in American Progressivism.* Lanham, Md.: University Press of America, 1980. Hearst should deserve a better reputation as a Progressive publisher and reform politician. His role in the Spanish-American war was reformist, since the war was viewed by Americans as one to free Cuba from Spanish tyranny. In the early 1900s he waged a number of laudable social campaigns, including support of labor.

1989. Lyon, Peter. *Success Story: The Life and Times of S. S. McClure.* New York: Scribner's, 1963. McClure "revolutionized American journalism," editing "the best general magazine ever published anywhere." His exposure of political corruption, monopoly trusts, unscrupulous meat packers, etc., had a tremendous influence on legislation. He channeled creative writing into a more meaningful field.

1990. Maddox, Lynda M. "Muckrakers Attack the Advertising-Patent Medicine Liaison," in *Graduate Communication Studies.* Carbondale: School of Journalism, Southern Illinois University, 1977. This article, one in a collection of five historical studies by Southern Illinois University graduate students, details the muckrakers' crusades against the patent medicine industry.

1991. Marcosson, Isaac F. *David Graham Phillips and His Times.* New York: Dodd, Mead, 1932. This narrative biography (emphasizing anecdotes and written in a mechanic style) provides a favorable account of Phillips as a talented muckraking journalist.

1992. Marmarelli, Ron. "William Hard as Progressive Journalist." *AJ* 3 (1986): 142-53. In his magazine writing of 1900-1920, Hard was "a kind of model of the progressive journalist," involving "himself directly...with a range of ideas and issues among the many on the progressive agenda." (143) He was "a champion of order and efficiency, of social justice and social control" who, like the Progressives as a group, nevertheless were unable to mold "the kind of 'democratic and cooperative world' he sought." (150)

1993. Maxwell, Robert S. "A Note on the Muckrakers." *Mid-America* 43 (1961): 55-60.

Careless reporting by Ray Stannard Baker provoked a libel suit against *McClure's* magazine and helped hasten the end of muckraking.

1994. McClure, S. S. *My Autobiography.* New York: Stokes, 1914. The founder of *McClure's* magazine tells his story.

1995. Miraldi, Robert. "Fictional Techniques in the Journalism of David Graham Phillips." *AJ* 4 (1987): 181-90. By using fictional techniques in his muckraking journalism, Phillips lost much of the effectiveness he might have had if he had adhered to factual reporting. Such fictionalizing was one factor that led to public distrust and the decline of muckraking.

1996. Mott, Frank Luther. "The Magazine Called 'Success.'" *JQ* 34 (1957): 46-50. "The signficance of the magazine *Success* [1897-1911] lies mainly in its embodiment of the cult of success which was so prominent an element of the national spirit at the beginning of the 20th century, but it was also important as a popular general magazine and as a participant in the last phase of the muckraking movement." (50)

1997. Mowry, George E. *Theodore Roosevelt and the Progressive Movement.* Madison, Wis.: 1946. Mowry, along with Hofstadter, was one of the first historians to consider the Progressive movement as an attempt by a particular socio-economic class of people to regain their lost position of leadership. They believed in individualistic values and opposed the concentration of power in large industry and business. While trying to restore the traditional values and social system, they failed to provide any answers or solutions to the fundamental problems of the times. Muckrakers, however, were important. "Perhaps no other single force was more responsible for the success of the progressive movement than the group of popular writers that emerged to write for the fast-flourishing muckrake magazines. Nothing was too holy for their prying eyes, no institution too sacred for their debunking pens. If at times they bordered on the sensational they at least exposed a picture of American politics and social conditions that had never before been revealed. The American public gasped with consternation and anger at what they saw." (20) For a fuller view of Mowry's approach to the Progressive movement and the muckrakers, see his *The Progressive Era, 1900-20: The Reform Persuasion* (Washington: American History Association, 1972) and the next entry.

1998. Mowry, George E., and Judson A. Grenier, eds. *The Treason of the Senate*, Chicago: Quadrangle, 1964. See previous entry. The editors provide an anaylitic introduction preceding David Graham Phillips' muckraking series.

1999. Parmenter, William. "*The Jungle* and Its Effects." *JH* 10 (1983): 14-17, 33-34. With *The Jungle*, Upton Sinclair contributed to passage of the Pure Food and Drug Act, but the book did not succeed at Sinclair's "larger purpose of contributing to the creation of a socialist state in America....That leaves as *The Jungle's* chief legacy its contribution to social justice literature. People of the period sensitive to social conditions shuddered when they saw the portrait of American society Sinclair had outlined, and they reacted to it." (33)

2000. Piott, Stephen L. "The Lesson of the Immigrant: Views of Immigrants in Muckraking Magazines 1900-1909." *AS* 19 (Spring 1978): 21-23. Fiction writers, as contrasted with muckraking journalists, in muckraking magazines characterized immigrants as innocent victims of industrialist capitalism. They "not only recognized the contributions of immigrants to American culture," but "sought to regain lost values: to establish moral responsibility, and to rediscover the idea of community by uniting producers and consumers."

2001. Ponder, Stephen. "Federal News Management in the Progressive Era: Gifford Pinchot and the Conservation Crusade." *JH* 13 (1986): 42-48. Pinchot, the chief of the

U.S. Forest Service from 1898 to 1910, provided newspapers with news of federal conservation efforts, thus contributing to the government management of news. During Theodore Roosevelt's administration, the Progressive desire to enlighten the public about issues to gain support added impetus to the efforts of the government to provide news. "This engineering of public support by government use of information, however idealistic the motivation, formed an important precedent for stronger government direction of the press to support the American cause in World War I." (47)

2002. Rabitz, Abe C. *David Graham Phillips*. New York: Twayne, 1966.

2003. Regier, C. C. *The Era of the Muckrakers*. Chapel Hill: University of North Carolina Press, 1932. Steffens, Baker, Samuel Hopkins Adams, Tarbell, Sinclair, Mark Sullivan, William Allen White, Benjamin O. Flower and others exposed many social, economic, and political evils. This study examines the conditions which stimulated muckraking, the rise of popular-priced magazines which provided a medium, the subjects of exposure, the results, and the reasons for the decline of muckraking. Muckraking was "the inevitable result of decades of indifference to the illegalities and immoralities attendant upon the industrial development of America." The cheap magazines (*McClure's, Arena, Cosmopolitan*, etc.) made muckraking "a paying business enlisting the most skillful pens the nation could boast." As for determining the results of muckraking, "it is impossible to prove that business methods were bettered in such and such a way by such and such an attack, but it is quite possible to argue that the whole tone of business in the United States was raised because of the persistent exposures of corruption and injustice." The achievements of "the liberal movement" were in the numerous reforms between 1900 and 1915. Muckraking declined because reforms had been accomplished, increasing sensationalism discredited the genuine investigative efforts, and finally the impatient public which wanted reform as well as exposure grew tired of muckraking. The achievement of the Progressive movement was largely due to muckrakers. Muckrakers played an important part in forming public opinion. Americans were in a crusading mood, recognizing that the chief culprits were the selfish and privileged business interests. Yet muckraking was to a considerable extent "little more than a fad" and "essentially a superficial attack upon fundamental problems."

2004. Reynolds, Robert D. "The 1906 Campaign to Sway Muckraking Periodicals." *JQ* 56 (1979): 513-20, 589. Some magazines were more interested in economic survival than journalistic integrity. U.S. Senator John Dryden was able to "squelch an unflattering profile of him in *Cosmopolitan*...and substitute material complimentary to him and to his company" through advertising pressure from Prudential Insurance Company. "There is a great deal of circumstantial evidence to indicate that in 1906 [earlier than most historians have suggested] economic expediency took precedence over journalistic integrity not only at *Cosmopolitan* but throughout the periodical industry when dealing with Prudential....Dryden enlisted the help out only of the editorial and advertising departments of magazines but the writing ability and reputations of a number of well-known muckrakers." (513) "Even before 1910 business did at times try to sway the content of muckraking periodicals using unethical and conspiratorial tactics" (589) and sometimes was successful.

2005. Robinson, Phyllis C. "Mr. McClure and Willa." *AH* 34, 5 (1983): 26-31. Study of the working relationship between Willa Cather and the owner of *McClure's* magazine.

2006. Rosenberg, Vivian Graff. *Turn of the Century American Journalist, Home-Spun Philosopher, Ray Stannard Baker.* New York: published by the author, 1977. This is a highly favorable biography of the muckraker, as the author confesses: "It is no exaggeration to say that I have come to love him as one does a dearest friend."

2007. Sarasohn, David. "Power Without Glory: Hearst in the Progressive Era." *JQ* 53 (1976): 474-82. Between 1900 and 1912 Hearst was a major political power in both the Demoratic party and the nation. He received support from organized labor and the lower class. Although he personally was ambitious, he played an important role in liberalizing the Democratic party. He opposed party bossism and trusts and was hated by conservatives. He was unsuccessful in politics, however, because he changed directions too often, was blatantly self-promoting, and used vitriolic personal attacks on opponents. Still, he "was a major radical politician with labor and urban support," and "his newspapers helped keep the party on a progressive, pro-labor course." (482)

2008. Schapsmeier, Edward L., and Frederick H. Schapsmeier. "The Wallaces and Their Farm Paper: A Story of Agrarian Leadership." *JQ* 44 (1967): 289-96. Henry Wallace, who founded *Wallace's Farmer & Editor* in 1895 and ran it until 1916, "was a crusading editor. He was fearless in his attacks upon trusts, railroads or monopolistic conditions harmful to farmers." He "sympathized with them [agricultural political movements such as Populists] and agitated for legislation to alleviate the plight of the rural sector of the population." (289) He was primarily concerned with doing "the greatest service to humanity." (296)

2009. Schultz, Stanley K. "The Morality of Politics: The Muckrakers' Vision of Democracy" *JAH* 52 (1965): 527-47. Muckrakers believed in the American tradition of democracy: they "claimed to be the American democrats seeking to preserve the legacy of the national dream....[They] mounted a concentrated attack against the citadels of evil which they believed dominated the republican landscape...[and] posed as democrats trying to turn into success the failures of a democratic society." (527)

2010. Schwantes, Carlos A. "Washington State's Pioneer Labor-Reform Press," *PNQ* 71 (July 1980): 112-26. Annotated checklist and bibliographical essay on publications of Washington's labor movement, 1885-1917. The publications "constituted a veritable fount of information for militant, reform-minded, producer-conscious workers." The labor movement progressed from "youthful fascination with class consciousness and utopian radicalism to the sober maturity that results from success, social acceptance and bureaucratization."

2011. Semonche, John E. "The American Magazine of 1906-15: Principle vs. Profit." *JQ* 40 (1963): 36-44, 86. Muckraking staffers from *McClure's* magazine, discontented with S.S. McClure's plans for a corporate speculative venture with the magazine, bought the *American Magazine* in 1906 and tried to make it a reform publication. Financially, however, *American Magazine* had difficulties, and by 1915 "it had discarded all vestiges of its early idealism and concept of public service in an all-out drive to make money. The life-blood of the popular magazine was its advertising, and [Ray Stannard] Baker was sure that he discerned a drift toward greater control of the *American* by its advertisers." (44) In 1915 most of the staff resigned. "John M. Siddall, now in full charge of the *American*, had never been hindered by ideas of reform and public service. During his editorship from 1915 to 1923, the journal made an unabashed, sentimental appeal to the family audience...with the astounding result that its circulation soared to 1,700,000. The noble adventure had at last become a great financial success -- too late to profit the original crusaders and too clearly a different magazine from the one envisioned in 1906." (86)

2012. Semonche, John E. *Ray Stannard Baker: A Quest for Democracy in Modern America*. Chapel Hill: University of North Carolina Press, 1969. This sympathetic biography challenges the arguments of Hofstadter, et.al., that Progressive reformers were not motivated fundamentally by the desire to solve problems and improve society. The reformers primarily called for government action and wanted America to subordinate "self-interest to a sense of social responsibility." Progressives should not be discounted for their failure to solve problems that still resist solution. Baker, one of the reformers, was ultimately a reporter who was "a sensitive barometer of his times."

2013. Shapiro, Herbert, ed. *Muckraking and American Society*. Boston: D. C. Heath, 1968. Collection of muckraking articles and historical essays.

2014. Sinclair, Upton. *The Autobiography of Upton Sinclair*. New York: Harcourt, Brace, World, 1962. The muckraking journalist and book author's main concern was social justice. This book provides a mellowed retrospective of his ideas, work, and writing style.

2015. Steffens, Joseph Lincoln. *Autobiography of Lincoln Steffens*. New York: Harcourt, Brace, 1931. Steffens' goal was to find a "scientific" basis for ethics and moral order; finally he wound up adopting Christian forgiveness of those against whom he had muckraked. This narrative gently recounts the causes he espoused, the corruption he opposed, and the various other deeds of his career.

2016. Steffens, Pete. "The Identity Struggle of Lincoln Steffens -- Writer or Reporter?" *JH* 2 (1975): 16-18, 32. Steffens had difficulty deciding whether to be a fiction writer or a reporter. This article focuses on his fiction writing that preceded his reporting.

2017. Stein, Harry H. "American Muckrakers and Muckraking: The 50-Year Scholarship." *JQ* 56 (1979): 9-17. Historiographical essay on the various explanations historians have given of muckrakers. The scholarship has been marked by "vagueness."

2018. Stein, Harry. "Lincoln Steffens: Interviewer." *JQ* 46 (1969): 727-36. Steffens was able to induce people to tell him many things which were almost confidential. "The traditional reportorial interview became in his hands a finely-precisioned instrument." (727) He thus was able to get reliable inside information and extensive material which contributed to reader credibility of *McClure's*.

2019. Stinson, Robert. "Ida M. Tarbell and the Ambiguities of Feminism." *PMHB* 101 (April 1977): 217-39. In 1909 the muckraker wrote a series of articles for *McClure's* magazine attacking feminism, "urging women to recover their 'female nature,' refrain from direct participation in political affairs, and embrace their true role as wives, mothers, and homemakers." Her opposition to feminism was a result of both her own values and the social norms of the day, and the articles were "a fresh articulation, a public statement of those views with which she had lived in uneasy tension for thirty-five years."

2020. Stinson, Robert. "McClure's Road to *McClure's*: How Revolutionary Were 1890s Magazines?" *JQ* 47 (1970): 256-62. A narrative of the background of the founding of

McClure's in 1893. S.S. McClure took what he considered to be a popular formula for magazines and aimed it at a mass audience through low price.

2021. Stinson, Robert. "S.S. McClure's *My Autobiography*: The Progressive as Self-Made Man." *AQ* 22 (1970): 203-12. McClure rose from rags to riches through persistence.

2022. Tarbell, Ida M. *All in a Day's Work*. New York: Macmillan, 1939. Autobiography of the muckraker.

2023. Tomkins, Mary E. *Ida M. Tarbell*. New York: Twayne, 1974. Tarbell was an effective magazine journalist, but her attempts at biography and fiction were failures. Philosophically, she was primarily a defender of traditional, puritan New England values. She was concerned for morals, democracy, justice, and individual independence, and thus in her Standard-Oil expose` attacked Rockefeller because of his lack of concern for morality and his ruthless methods, similar to those that had been used to drive her father and middle-class oil producers out of business.

2024. Uselding, Paul, ed. "In Dispraise of Muckrakers: United States Occupational Mortality, 1890-1910," 334-71 in *Research in Economic History I*. Greenwich, Conn.: JAI Press, 1976. This is a conservative, pro-business interpretation of muckraking. Muckrakers served "admirably as the press agents of reform." (351) However, in their attacks on industry for its danger to mortality, they exaggerated, or at least statistically it is difficult to say that mortality in industry was inordinately high.

2025. Weinberg, Arthur, and Lila Weinberg. *The Muckrakers*. New York: Simon & Schuster, 1961. Anthology of articles written by muckrakers, 1902-1912.

2026. Wells, Evelyn. *Fremont Older*. New York: Appleton-Century, 1936. This narrative biography, written by a close friend of Older, provides a favorable account of a righteous man who crusaded for principle.

2027. Wilson, Harold S. *McClure's Magazine and the Muckrakers*. Princeton, N.J.: Princeton University Press, 1970. This neo-liberal interpretation of muckrakers, along the lines of Filler and Chalmers, claims that muckrakers were interested in reform, and that S.S. McClure's motivation was not primarily monetary; nor was muckraking marked by excessive sensationalism. *McClure's* instead was fairly sedate.

13

The Media and National Crises,
1917–1945

NOTE: The works in this section deal with World Wars I and II, the Great Depression, and issues associated with those crises.

2028. Adamson, June. "From Bulletin to Broadside: A History of By-Authority Journalism in Oak Ridge, Tennessee." *THQ* 38 (1979): 479-93. Oak Ridge was "a war-time city created almost overnight for the purpose of developing the atomic bomb." Military authorities, therefore, controlled its journalism. This study examines the Oak Ridge *Journal* and includes interviews with some of its staff members from 1943 to 1948 to examine the type of information the paper carried, what it omitted, and how the censorship system worked.

2029. Alsbrook, James E. "Historic Color Bias in Print: Career Aid to Three 'Black Officials.'" *JQ* 48 (1971): 480-85. The *Afro-American* (Washington, D.C.) discriminated against darker Negroes in favor of lighter-skinned Negroes. Thus, it practiced the discriminatory attitude which it criticized in white publications. Lighter skin was an advantage for "so-called 'blacks' who had 'white' kinfolk or 'white' physical features," including Robert C. Weaver, Edward H. Brooke, Thurgood Marshall.

2030. Ames, William E., and Roger A. Simpson. *Unionism or Hearst: The Seattle Post-Intelligencer Strike of 1936*. Seattle: Pacific Northwest Labor History Assoc., 1978. Pro-labor account of the American Newspaper Guild's first victory. The strike was encouraged by "undesirable working conditions" which were the result of Hearst newspaper policies.

2031. Beasley, Maurine H. *Eleanor Roosevelt and the Media: A Public Quest for Self-Ful-fillment*. Urbana: University of Illinois Press, 1987. Mrs. Roosevelt had a psychological need to be recognized as a successful professional woman. She developed from a shy young bride of a politician to a confident, skilled manager of the press.

2032. Beasley, Maurine. "A 'Front Page Girl' Covers the Lindbergh Kidnaping: An Ethical Dilemma." *AJ* 1, 1 (1983): 63-74. Lorena Hickok's "reportorial conduct" in covering the kidnaping raised ethical questions about journalistic practices in the 1930s. Newspapers were more concerned with beating the competition than with serving the public interest or respecting individual privacy.

2033. Beasley, Maurine. "Lorena A. Hickok: Woman Journalist." *JH* 7 (1980): 92-5, 113. Article based on Lowitt and Beasley's book. Hickok was an outstanding journalist of the 1930s who became important as a publicist in the Roosevelt administration. She reported on the economic problems faced by millions of Americans.

2034. Beasley, Maurine, ed. *The White House Conferences of Eleanor Roosevelt*. New York: Garland, 1983. From the transcripts of 87 press conferences Mrs. Roosevelt held during her husband's presidency, she emerges as a public speaker, mother, and public servant.

2035. Beck, Elmer A. "Autopsy of a Labor Daily: The Milwaukee *Leader*." *JM* 16 (1970). This history of the most successful labor daily ever published in the U.S. (1911-1942) examines why it succeeded and the factors in its eventual failure. A Socialist supporter in the beginning, it opposed the "capitalist press and particularly. The Milwaukee *Journal*."(2) In its decline it reflected labor's changing attitude toward ideology: the disappearance of socialism into unionism. In its later years it was owned and managed by labor rather than socialists. It was doomed by the ever-increasing costs of big business journalism and the fact that it lost its social cause. However, "in the final analysis, who is to say the Milwaukee *Leader* failed because it failed to survive as a daily newspaper? Indeed, it may be held that the *Leader* succeeded because it succeeded in achieving the purposes for which it was founded and some of the objectives for which it fought, such as bringing news and comment to its subscribers which they wanted to read but which the other papers did not print; preaching the gospel of class consciousness that its believers wanted to hear; promoting the political morality that the voters of Milwaukee preferred; and in being the daily medium of Education that would light the way to the future."(40)

2036. Behr, Edward. *Bearings: A Foreign Correspondent's Life Behind the Lines*. New York: Viking, 1978. Autobiography.

2037. Bennett, Ira E. *Editorials from The Washington Post, 1917-20*. Washington: Washington Post, 1921. Anthology.

2038. Berres, Jean L. "Local Aspects of the Campaign for Americanism: The *Milwaukee Journal* in World War I." Ph.D. dissertation, Southern Illinois University, 1977. "The Campaign...was the persistent effort of the...*Journal*...to instill total Wilsonian Americanism into Milwaukee and Wisconsin citizens, and to combat the activities of any person or group who seemed in opposition to the cause." Readers and the country adopted many of the attitudes and actions which the *Journal* advocated.

2039. Bishop, Robert Lee. "The Overseas Branch of the Office of War Information." Ph.D.

dissertation, University of Wisconsin, 1966. The OWI "pointed out the dangers in allowing distorted ideas of the United States to exist throughout the world and...gained initial acceptance of the role of government in correcting these stereotypes."

2040. Bishop, Robert L., and LeMar S. MacKay. "Mysterious Silence, Lyrical Scream: Government Information in World War II." *JM* 19 (1971). This study outlines the "main problems encountered in setting up U.S. information agencies for World War II." Its concern is about "how we may protect the historic right of the people to know about the politics and programs of their government while maintaining the security of the nation." Because of the complexity of government and the largeness of propaganda operations, the information agency (OWI) can no longer be the leader in forming policy but must work with both government and the media and in effect serve as an auxiliary weapon for the nation, rather than as a leader setting policy, as it had been able to do during World War II.

2041. Blanchard, Margaret A. "Press Criticism and National Reform Movements: The Progressive Era and the New Deal." *JH* 5 (1978): 33-37, 54-55. Press critics during the Progressive era believed that press owners should be using their money to help other people, the less fortunate members of society, but that owners instead "had sold [their] soul to the devil incarnate, the capitalist class. News, according to these critics, was suppressed, manufactured or distorted in order to increase circulation. Pressures for increased circulation mounted as it became harder to obtain advertising dollars. Soon, press critics claimed, the emphasis was on the role of the counting room, distorting the watchwords of 'freedom of the press' into 'freedom of the press to make money.' The press had forfeited its sacred charge to serve the people; liberty of the press had become license. By the end of the two reform periods under study, press critics had moved from the Progressive ideal of having the press reform itself from within to the New Deal view of having the press reformed from without--by the federal government."(33)

2042. Bloomfield, Douglas M. "Joe Tumulty and the Press." *JQ* 42 (1965): 413-21. Woodrow Wilson's only press secretary, volatile Joseph Tumulty, began practices which are now considered traditional. A student of public opinion, Tumulty gave advice often invaluable to a president who didn't trust the press. It was to Tumulty's credit that contact with the press was maintained during World War I and that there was no news blackout after the war began and Wilson stopped meeting regularly with the press.

2043. Blum, Steven. *Walter Lippmann: Cosmopolitanism in the Century of Total War.* Ithaca: Cornell University Press, 1984. Lippmann opposed American isolationism and believed that liberalism required that Americans adopt a cosmopolitan, international view. The modern world, in the "century of total war," required "international interdependence in politics, commerce, thought, and culture."

2044. Boston *Globe. World War II: From D-Day to V-J Day, 40 Years Later.* Boston: Boston Globe, 1986. Collection of articles and photographs which the *Globe* published during the war.

2045.1. Bow, James. "The *Times's* Financial Markets Column in the Period Around the 1929 Crash." *JQ* 57 (1980): 447-50, 497. Reporters had difficulty understanding the full implications and significance of the stock market crash.

2045.2. Bowles, Dorothy. "Newspaper Support for Free Expression in Times of Alarm, 1920 and 1940." *JQ* 54 (1977): 271-79. "A content analysis of editorials in 16 large-city newspapers reveals a pattern of support for free expression." (271)

2046. Boyle, Hal. "Reminiscences of a Columnist." *MJR* 16 (1973): 37-38. The Associated Press writer nostalgically remembers such people as Ernie Pyle.

2047. Braestrup, Peter. "Battle Lines." *NR* 39 (1985): 43-56. Journalists in World War II and the Korean War accepted censorship, for it did not prevent criticism of the military or inhibit news analysis. This article is an excerpt from the 180-page report, "Battle Lines," issued by the Twentieth Century Fund in 1984 following the American invasion of Grenada.

2048. Bridges, Lamar W. "The Zimmerman Telegram: Reaction of Southern, Southwestern Newspapers." *JQ* 46 (1969): 81-86. The proposal of a Mexican-Japanese-German alliance against the U.S. in 1917 was not viewed as a serious threat to American Territory by 13 newspapers directly affected. But they did consider the telegram an act of war. Although the Southwest was not as pro-war as the Northeast, it did favor entering the war on the side of the Allies.

2049. Britton, John A. "In Defense of Revolution: American Journalists in Mexico, 1920-1929." *JH* 5 (1978): 124-30. "Journalists Carleton Beals, Ernest Gruening and Frank Tannenbaum were sympathetic to the revolutionary changes underway in Mexico and condemned the State Department's preoccupation with American property rights there." (124) But there was a negative response in America to the journalists' writing. This article is critical of the conservative, imperialistic role of America in Mexican affairs. The three journalists were leftist and "were the first reporters from the United States to explain in depth the social significance of the revolution." They discredited the conservative views of other journalists and the U.S. government. "Their independent journalism provided an antidote to the image of a hopelessly chaotic Mexico that emerged in the U.S. government and press in the 1910s and 1920s." (136)

2050. Burd, Gene. "The Newspaper Critic and His Critics: George Seldes and Press Criticism." *SWMCJ* 1 (1985).

2051. Carlisle, Rodney P. "The Foreign Policy Views of an Isolationist Press Lord: W.R. Hearst and the International Crisis, 1936-1941." *JCH* 9 (July 1974): 217-27. Hearst was the "most prominent American isolationist" in the 1930s. His "opposition to Roosevelt's domestic policies coupled with a readership of six million had turned him into a kind of symbolic arch-enemy of New Deal Liberalism and Rooseveltian Foreign Policy." (217) His positions, however, "were not based on simple opposition to war, nor on a simple desire that the United States stay out of foreign affairs. Rather, he worked from a militant nationalism, from anti-communism, and a long-held suspicion of the British, French, Japanese, and Russians." (226)

2052. Carlisle, Rodney P. *Hearst and the New Deal: The Progressive as Reactionary.* New York: Garland, 1979. Hearst was a major newspaper owner without much power; he was an old-line Progressive but not a respected reformer. By 1935, although he earlier had supported the New Deal, he broke with Roosevelt. He changed from a Progressive to a reactionary. He stopped supporting New Deal reform in 1935 because

75 per cent. Hearst claimed the tax was communistic and had the potential to create class antagonism. As Hearst more and more was attacked by liberals, the more popular he came to be; yet his influence was limited because his circulation primarily was among the urban working class, a group which supported Roosevelt.

2053. Carlisle, Rodney P. "William Randolph Hearst's Reaction to the American Newspaper Guild: A Challenge to New Deal Labor Legislation." *LH* 10 (Winter 1969): 74-99. Hearst resisted the Guild's efforts to unionize newspapers under the National Industrial Recovery Act of 1933. Confronted with his opposition, the Guild began to use aggressive tactics, finally winning in the Supreme Court's decision that unionization was not a violation of freedom of the press.

2054. Carroll, Wallace. *Persuade or Perish.* Boston: Houghton Mifflin, 1948. This story of the Office of War Information's work in World War II was written by the OWI's director. It focuses on psychological warfare in Italy and Europe.

2055. Chaffee, Zechariah Jr. *Free Speech in the United States.* Cambridge, Mass.: Harvard University Press, 1941 (originally published as *Freedom of Speech* in 1920). In the face of the approaching World War II, this classic work examines civil liberty from colonial times to cases up to 1940. It argues for a libertarian approach to freedom of expression.

2056. Clardy, Andrea, ed.. *Gordon Gammack: Columns From Three Wars.* Ames: Iowa State University Press, 1979. Anthology of works by the Des Moines columnist.

2057. Cobb, Irvin S. *Exit Laughing.* Indianapolis: Bobbs-Merrill, 1941. Autobiography of the journalist, war correspondent, short-story writer, and novelist.

2058. Coggeshall, Reginald. "Paris Peace Conference Sources of News, 1919." *JQ* 17 (1940): 1-10. Coggeshall had been a member of the staff of the Paris edition of New York *Herald* covering the conference to work out the peace treaty for World War I. The conference was one of the most difficult news-gathering assignments in history. Correspondents were faced with secrecy from conference organizers and delegates from the very opening of the preliminary session. They had to rely on brief, official communique`s, statements from individual, and a "flood of propaganda."

2059. Coggeshall, Reginald. "Peace Conference Publicity: Lessons of 1919." *JQ* 19 (1942): 1-11. Negotiators failed to come up with a workable and lasting peace plan because they did not pay attention to public opinion, which emerged in 1914-1918 as a major national (hence world) force. The press was important as a vehicle of information. This essay attempts to point out what negotiators after World War II should learn from World War I.

2060. Coggeshall, Reginald. "Was There Censorship at the Paris Peace Conference?" *JQ* 16 (1939): 125-35. This study argues against the historical view and conclusions by some contemporary journalists that there was impermissible censorship by American officials. Military officers considered the conference to be part of a continuing war, thus justifying control of information, while the censorship or control of the news that did exist usually was unintentional.

2061. Cogswell, Andrew C. "The Montana Press and War: 1914 to 1917." *JQ* 21 (1944): 137-47. As early as 1914 Montana newspapers favored the Allied cause in World

War I. (The findings of this article resemble those of Costrell's study [below]. Cogswell selected Montana newspapers to study because northeastern papers were more truculent.) As Costrell found with Maine, Montana newspapers were pro-ally by July 1914. "On the whole, the Montana press went to war, step by step, with Wilson."(147) Historians err in claiming that Woodrow Wilson's war attitude (for intervention of war on the side of the Allies) was not shared by American citizens. "[T]hrough the pre-war Montana newspapers of 1913 and 1914 ran discernible threads of traditional American concepts of right and wrong. Upon these concepts Montana newspapers judged the Central Powers. It is hard to believe that these concepts were those of newspapers alone." (147)

2062. Corbalis, Kathy J. "'Atomic Bill' Laurence: He Reported the Birth of the A-Bomb." *MHD* 5, 3 (1985): 9-11, 28-30. William Laurence of the New York *Times* reported more comprehensively on the development of the atomic bomb than any other journalist. He witnessed the bombing of Nagasaki.

2063. Cornebise, Alfred E. *The Amaroc News: The Daily Newspaper of the American Forces in Germany, 1919-1923*. Carbondale: Southern Illinois University Press, 1981. The *Amaroc News* was the main newspaper published by the American occupation army in the Rhineland after World War I, 1919-1923. This account examines its content, price, editors, etc.

2064. Cornebise, Alfred E. *The Stars and Stripes: Doughboy Journalism in World War I*. Contribution in Military History #37. Westport, Conn.: Greenwood, 1984. The military newspaper covered the war (during U.S. involvement in 1918-1919) from the common soldier's perspective, rather than that of the brass; it was a true newspaper rather than a pubic relations organ, subject to little interference from military authorities. By including much content from the paper and arranging it thematically, this study provides "glimpses and insights...of Americans soldiering in Europe."

2065. Costrell, Edwin. "Newspapers' Attitudes Toward War in Maine 1914-17." *JQ* 16 (1939): 334-44. This study of American attitudes toward participation in World War I as reflected by six Maine newspapers attempts to answer the question of whether U.S. leaders got American into war contrary to popular desire. "Gone [by 1917] was all opposition to jingoism, all desire for neutrality, all talk of isolation. Although, then, as many writers contend, public opinion may not have been the primary cause of America's involvement in the World War and its citizens may not even have desired to engage in hostilities, the people of Maine may safely be said to have definitely committed themselves in favor of a belligerent course. War headline after war headline over a period of more than two years at last had infected Yankee blood, aided by Germany's renewed disregard for the rights of American nationals; and a restless belligerency which had been held in abeyance by stronger peace forces broke all bounds. War sentiment had grown slowly; it had not come to full flower during the crisis, nor during the crisis which shortly followed; but by February of 1917 it had undoubtedly come into its own, not reversing itself once in the two months which intervened before war actually was declared. Whatever the rest of the nation may have thought, Maine advanced to battle when it most fervently desired to go."(344)

2066. Covert, Catherine L., and John D. Stevens, eds. *Mass Media between the Wars: Perceptions of Cultural Tension, 1918-1941*. Syracuse, N.Y.: Syracuse University Press, 1984. Collection of fourteen essays, including a bibliography, by various authors dealing primarily with the relationship between the media and American culture.

2067. Crozier, Emmet. *American Reporters on the Western Front, 1914-1918*. New York: Oxford University Press, 1959. Popular, anecdotal account of the reporters' heroism and the conditions in which they worked: "I have dealt mainly with those personalities and events that interested me as a working journalist rather than the broader aspects which might engage the professional scholar." Journalists faced great hazards to get the news but usually were successful. The research sources for this narrative primarily are secondary ones, biographies and autobiographies.

2068. Desmond, Robert W. *Crisis and Conflict: World News Reporting Between Two Wars, 1920-1940*. Iowa City: University of Iowa Press, 1982. The third volume in Desmond's series on international reporting examines "world press patterns," the character of the press as evidenced by its content and format, with the purpose of bringing together "diverse elements in the reporting of public affairs, internationally, and of history-in-the-making." (xii)

2069. Desmond, Robert W. *Tides of War: World News Reporting, 1931-1945*. Iowa City: University of Iowa Press, 1984. A continuation of Desmond's series, this volumes focuses on events leading to World War II and the war itself.

2070. Edwards, Jerome. *The Foreign Policy of Col. McCormick's Tribune, 1929-1941*. Reno: University of Nevada Press, 1971.

Robert McCormick was reactionary, believing, for example, that Franklin Roosevelt wanted to join the Allied cause in order to achieve his great dream of complete dictatorship. McCormick was slow to oppose Hitler and believed that England was already fascist in the 1930s. News and opinion in the *Tribune* were one-sided, giving readers a view that was isolationist and ethnocentric and giving news that often was very good in its foreign reporting but at other times was dishonest.

2071. Farrar, Ronald T., ed. "Report to the President." *JM* 7. Collection of the documents compiled by Elmer Davis in working with Franklin Roosevelt during World War II.

2072. Farson, Negley. *The Way of a Transgressor*. New York: Carroll & Graf, 1984. Autobiography of a foreign correspondent (originally published in 1936).

2073. Fielding, Raymond. *The March of Time, 1935-1951*. New York: Oxford University Press, 1978. "March of Time," a newsreel on current events, was not, as some critics have charged, a politically conservative product.

2074. Finkle, Lee. "Forum for Protest: The Black Press During World War II." Ph.D. dissertation, New York University, 1971. Black editors were more conservative than their readers. While they favored elimination of discrimination, they believed a world crisis was no time to demand a complete change in racial practices. They argued that blacks should support the American war effort because such support should result in equal treatment of blacks after the war. The wartime protest against discrimination was a last effort of the older generation's approach rather than a harbinger of the militant efforts used by the succeeding generation.

2075. Finkle, Lee. *Forum for Protest: The Black Press During World War II*. Cranbury, N.J.: Farleigh Dickinson University Press, 1975. See previous entry.

2076. Gerald, James Edward, Jr. "The Press and the Constitution, 1932-1944." Ph.D.

dissertation, University of Minnesota, 1947.

2077. Gilbert, Douglas. *Floyd Gibbons, Knight of the Air*. New York: McBride, 1930. Biography focusing on Gibbons' thrilling adventures during World War I as a newspaper correspondent.

2078. Goren, Dina. "Communication, Intelligence and Freedom of the Press: The Chicago *Tribune's* Battle of Midway Dispatch and the Breaking of the Japanese Naval Code." *JCH* 16 (1981): 663-90. In June 1942 the Chicago's *Tribune* published a detailed, front-page article describing U.S. knowledge of Japanese war operations. The article has been used as an illustration of the problems of press restraint in wartime, but the circumstances of its publication never have been fully examined. This study examines published and unpublished documents in an attempt to explain the circumstances surrounding the story and why the government could not prosecute the *Tribune*.

2079. Gothberg, John G. "Press Reaction to Japanese Land Ownership in California." *JQ* 47 (1970): 667-72, 724. Of 60 papers studied, only four opposed the 1920 initiative that sought to prohibit Japanese ownership or leasing of California land. Politicians used news columns to exploit the issue. An anti-Oriental attitude persisted in California and was reflected in the press. This article deals primarily with how the press stood on an issue and concludes that the press shared the general views of public.

2080. Gray, L. C. "McCormick of the 'Times.'" *CuH* 50 (July 1939): 27, 64. Brief profile of Anne O'Hare McCormick, winner of a Pulitzer Prize for her international reporting, who was a great journalist on a newspaper, the New York *Times*, which was known as "a man's preserve." (27)

2081. Grierson, Don. "Battling Censors, Chiding Home Office: Harrison Salisbury's Russian Assignment." *JQ* 64 (1987): 313-16, 375. In the period following World War II, the New York *Times'* correspondent had difficulty reporting on the Soviet Union because of Russian censorship. American critics misunderstood his reports and believed he was biased toward Russia.

2082. Grobman, Alex. "What Did They Know? The American Jewish Press and the Holocaust, 1 September 1939-17 December 1942." *AJH* 68 (1979): 327-52. Some Jews have claimed that they had little knowledge of the Holocaust because the American press inadequately reported it. This study of more than 20 Jewish publications reveals that not only did they thoroughly report many atrocities, but that from the beginning "segments of the Jewish press attacked American Jewry for its lack of protest or moral outrage at the atrocities.... [I]mplicit in the calls for action was the fact that American Jewry understood what was happening in Europe, but for some inexplicable reason chose not to react in any forceful manner."

2083. Groth, Michael. *The Road to New York: The Emigration of Berlin Journalists, 1933-1945*. Munchen: Miverva-Fachserie Geisteswissenschaften, 1984. "German emigre journalists...who were persecuted and expatriated" by the Nazi regime found their way to New York City, where many of them took up journalism again.

2084. Hamilton, John Maxwell. "China Reporter Edgar Snow: Forty-Five Years on Back of a Tiger." *MHD* 7, 1 (1987): 55-64. Snow was the leading American reporter explaining the fight over communism in China. He covered China and wrote books about it from 1927 to 1972.

2085. Hamilton, John Maxwell. "The Missouri News Monopoly and American Altruism in China: Thomas F.F. Millard, J.B. Powell, and Edgar Snow." *PHR* 55 (1986): 27-48. Journalists trained at the University of Missouri and who served as correpondents covering pre-World War II China "consistently and honestly sought to help the Chinese." They extended the influence of Missouri and the United States not through physical or military force but "'through the force of ideals and by means of faithful, efficient and self-forgetful service.'" (48)

2086. Hohenberg, John. *Foreign Correspondence: The Great Reporters and Their Times.* New York: Columbia University Press, 1964. This narrative of the development of the reporting of foreign affairs and the conflicts between old and new breeds of reporters emphasizes reporters' dramatic adventures. It is the story of derring-do, especially during wartime and the continuing struggle for access to information. The successful correspondents were those concerned with speed in transmitting news. This account provides a survey from the French Revolution to the Vietnam war.

2087. Hudson, Robert V. "Will Irwin's Crusade for the League of Nations." *JH* 2 (1975): 84-85, 97. Appalled at the killing of World War I, Irwin preached "permanent peace through international cooperation." He actively crusaded for the League. He supported "true morals and...democracy" in human and international relations, (84) but he became disillusioned because of America's unconcern or lack of support for an international organization.

2088. Humes, D. Joy. *Oswald Garrison Villard: Liberal of the 1920's.* Syracuse, N.Y.: Syracuse University Press, 1960. Villard was a true liberal. Along with being a pacifist, he battled for human rights and dignity and for the extension of democracy to more groups and people. Even in the 1920s, there were many liberal causes, and Villard was a leader. Despite conservatism in America, he supported liberalism and passed it to the New Deal. His was a modern liberalism which was willing to experiment with methods to protect the underprivileged and which required "an effort on the part of the privileged class to have their privileges extended to others."

2089. Hutton, Bud, and Andy Rooney. *The Story of the Stars and Stripes.* New York: Little and Ives, 1946. The paper had a mission: written primarily for the G.I., it was first intended as a paper for the average soldier, then as a newspaper, then a trade journal for soldiers, and not as an outlet for brass propaganda. It was proud and free, crusading for the common soldier.

2090. Hutton, Bud, and T. A. MacMahon. "Brass Hats and Blue Pencils: How *Stars and Stripes* Became an Organ of Propaganda." *Collier's* 117 (May 18, 1946): 24, 67-71. The paper, originally a soldiers' newspaper, eventually became dominated by the brass.

2091. Ickes, Harold L. *America's House of Lords.* New York: Harcourt, Brace, 1939. This is a trenchant attack on newspaper publishers who opposed the New Deal, written by one of Roosevelt's cabinet members. The shortcomings of the press were the result of modern publishers being businessmen and running their newspapers as business enterprises. Such motives gave to metropolitan newspapers an "upper stratum interest and outlook" and caused them to be private profit-seeking businesses rather than public-spirited agencies concerned about social welfare. The emphasis on business endangered the free press required by a democracy. Editorial direction should have been left to reporters and editors. They would have produced good newspapers if publishers had allowed them to do so.

2092. Irwin, William Henry. *Propaganda and the News, or What Makes You Think So?*. Westport, Conn.: Greenwood, 1936. Although this book is primarily a study of propaganda in the contemporary society, Irwin gives an overview history of daily newspapers and brings an historical perspective to his explanation of propaganda, begining with George Creel's Committee on Public Information in World War I.

2093. Johnson, Carl E. "A Twentieth Century Seeker: A Biography of James Vincent Sheean." Ph.D. dissertation, University of Wisconsin, 1974. Reporting for the Chicago *Tribune* since 1922, Sheean "may be ranked as one of the most important foreign correspondents of the century as his work influenced a generation of newsmen to speak out interpretively in assessing America's role in world events."

2094. Johnson, Charles S. "The Montana Council of Defense." *MJR* 16 (1973): 2-16. Two Montana newspapers questioned the procedures and purposes of the council, which was created to support the World War I war effort.

2095. Johnson, Gerald W. "Freedom of the Newspaper Press." *AAAPS* 200 (1938): 60-75. The press must behave responsibly to merit freedom. Restrictions during wartime, as were applied during World War I, are not real abridgements of press freedom and do not indicate an abandonment of the concept of freedom in democratic philosophy. Publishers seem irresponsible when they use freedom of the press to argue against such things as unionization of journalists.

2096. Jones, Lester. "The Editorial Policy of Negro Newspapers of 1917-1918 as Compared with That of 1941-1942." *JNH* 29 (January 1944): 24-31. Editorials exhibited "the fundamental national loyalty and patriotism of the editors." (24)

2097. Kelley, William G. "Heywood Broun Before and After Sacco-Vanzetti." *JQ* 50 (1973): 567-69. Broun, a liberal columnist, wrote columns for the New York *World* that were less liberal after the Sacco-Vanzetti case because he feared Ralph Pulitzer might fire him for his liberal defense of the two. After joining the staff of the *Nation*, a liberal magazine, his writing became more liberal than it had before the case, probably because the *Nation* gave him free rein.

2098. Kenney, Anne R. "'She Got to Berlin': Virginia Irwin, *St. Louis Post-Dispatch* War Correspondent." *MHR* 79 (1985): 456-79. Irwin was a great reporter who covered World War II, including the German surrender.

2099. Knightley, Philip. *The First Casualty*. New York: Harcourt, Brace, Jovanovich, 1975. (rev. ed., London: Quartet, 1982.) The "first casualty" in war is truth. War correspondents (from the Crimean War to the Vietnam war) have trampled on truth and have served more often as "hero, propagandist and mythmaker" than as objective reporters. The fault of bad reporting does not lie primarily with government but with reporters. In wartime, correspondents forgot they were journalists and became instead part liar, part hero, part soldier, and part diplomat. If the press had reported truthfully, the course of history would have been different, for the press was influential in starting wars.

2100. Koop, Theodore F. *Weapon of Silence*. Chicago: University of Chicago Press, 1946. This study of civilian censorship (primarily the Office of Censorship under

Byron Price) during World War II concludes that although at times censorship was a little overdone, all in all it served a very useful purpose and prohibited little non-dangerous material from being distributed. Price was responsible in his policies and concerned both about public information and national welfare.

2101. Kornweibel, Theodore, Jr. *No Crystal Stair: Black Life and the Messenger, 1917-1928*. Westport, Conn.: Greenwood, 1975. History of the radical magazine published in the 1920s by A. Phillip Randolph and others and of black experience from World War I to the end of the 1920s. The black experience was a sobering one, and the era one of disillusionment. Neither the right nor the left, government, industry, nor labor was any help to blacks. The magazine was founded as a socialist organ, but once it became clear that the Socialist Party offered no promise for blacks, Randolph moved the magazine to a pro-business position and toward the center of American mainstream politics. Randolph's pragmatism allowed the magazine to survive as long as it did.

2102. Kramer, Dale. *Heywood Broun: A Biographical Portrait*. New York: Current Books--A. A. Wynn, 1949. Broun made a number of achievements in sports writing, drama criticism, column writing, establishment of the Newspaper Guild, and literature. People who knew him held him in deep affection.

2103. Krome, Frederic. "From Liberal Philosophy to Conservative Ideology? Walter Lippmann's Opposition to the New Deal." *JAC* 10 (Spring 1987).

2104. Krompak, Frank John. "Socio-Economic Influences Affecting the Texas Press in the Great Depression." Ph.D. dissertation, University of Texas, 1975. Advertising and circulation declined modestly through 1933 but then rebounded. "The crisis demonstrated the resiliency and durability of the state's press....[F]ew...newspapers went bankrupt, in contrast to widespread business failures across Texas."

2105. Lancaster, Paul. "Ernie Pyle: Chronicler of 'The Men Who Do the Dying.'" *AH* 32, 2 (1981): 30-40. Popular biography of the war reporter.

2106. Larson, Bruce L. "A Kansas Newspaper and the Nonpartisan League, 1919-20." *JQ* 49 (1972): 98-106. "More than any other single influence, the *Ellsworth County Leader* made the Nonpartisan League a reality to the farmers of Kansas." Its emphasis on political items contrasted sharply with other state weeklies. Founded by farmers, the paper had as its purpose the advocacy of the League. It was an effective propaganda force. It and other such papers were a critical factor in the success of the League and an integral part of the movement.

2107. Larson, Cedric. "Censorship of Army News During the World War, 1917-1918." *JQ* 17 (1940): 313-323. The censorship operations of the Military Intelligence Section were necessary for control of information during wartime.

2108. Lawrence, Thomas A. "Eclipse of Liberty: Civil Liberties in the United States During the First World War." *WLR* 22 (November 1974): 33-112. The courts joined with others, all politically motivated, in suppressing foreigners' and radicals' freedom of the press and speech during a time of national hysteria.

2109. Lawson, Anita. *Irvin S. Cobb*. Bowling Green, Ohio: Bowling Green State University Popular Press, 1984. Cobb, a newspaperman, war correspondent, and radio personality, was "an authority on every aspect of American life."

2110. Libbey, James K. "Liberal Journals and the Moscow Trials of 1936-38." *JQ* 52 (1975): 85-92, 137. The totalitarian nature of the political trials resulted in disenchantment among American publications that were sympathetic to Communist Russia. "Not only did the trials illuminate a callous disregard for civil liberties, but Russian methods of dictatorial control blurred with those of her fascist-militarist enemies, Germany, Italy and Japan." (85)

2111. Lipstadt, Deborah. *Beyond Belief: The American Press and the Coming of the Holocaust 1933-1945*. New York: Free Press, 1986. Although newspapers and magazines carried many stories about the Nazi extermination of Jews, they did not recognize it as a central part of the Nazi program. Sometimes doubting the credibility of their own stories, journalists failed to generate public pressure for efforts to help the Jews.

2112. Lowitt, Richard, and Maurine Beasley, eds. *One Third of a Nation: Lorena Hickok Reports the Great Depression*. Urbana: University of Illinois Press, 1981. Hickok toured the country in the 1930s to report to Franklin Roosevelt on economic conditions. After interviewing the unemployed, she provided insight into the human conditions associated with the statistics involved in the Federal Emergency Relief Administration in 1933-1934. This collection of letters she wrote to the administration has little historical narrative by the editors.

2113. MacKay, Lamar Seal. "Domestic Operations of the Office of War Information in World War II." Ph.D. dissertation, University of Wisconsin, 1966. Citizens of a democracy distrusted propaganda, and Congress limited the OWI to non-domestic activities; but the OWI did an effective job of supporting the war effort.

2114. MacKinnon, Stephen R., and Oris Friesen. *China Reporting: An Oral History of American Journalism in the 1930s and 1940s*. Berkeley: University of California Press, 1987. Proceedings of a 1982 conference composed of journalists who covered China and historians, including reminiscenses and explanations of the coverage. Topics include language difficulties, living conditions, censorship, editorial policies, journalistic bias primarily in favor of the Communists, and propaganda. The general conclusion is that correspondents did a good job of getting the story of wartime China.

2115. Maddux, Thomas R. "American News Media and Soviet Diplomacy, 1934-41." *JQ* 58 (1981): 29-37. "Neither isolationism nor the partisan political orientation of the newspapers influenced their assessments [of Stalin's motives] as much as their degree of interest in foreign affairs. The editors with the strongest interest believed that Stalin had pretty much abandoned hopes for a world revolution, whereas newspapers with the weakest interest never abandoned the image of Stalin as a disciple of Marx and Lenin." (37)

2116. Mader, Joseph H. "The North Dakota Press and the Non-partisan League." *JQ* 14 (1937): 321-22. The quick growth of the League, an agrarian protest movement founded in 1915, was a result of its leaders' organizing genius and "mastery of propaganda techniques." (323) However, their careless financial management and political bickering ultimately caused their papers to fail.

2117. Mander, Mary S. "American Correspondents During World War II: Common Sense as a View of the World." *AJ* 1, 1 (1983): 17-30. "The hallmark of the imagination and manners of the journalist reporting World War II...was *common sense*....Gone were the days of the flamboyant romantic of the nineteenth century; in his place stood the down-to-earth, realistic reporter of modern times." (17)

2118.   Mander, Mary S. "The Journalist as Cynic." *AR* 38, 1 (1980): 91-107. During World War I, journalists changed into cynics. See next entry.

2119.   Mander, Mary Sue. "Pen and Sword: A Cultural History of the American War Correspondent, 1895-1945." Ph.D. dissertation, University of Illinois, 1979. "The predominant sentiment of reporters of the Spanish-American War was display...a habit of arranging one's self in an eye-catching manner against the background of battle. The Great War [World War I] transformed the romantic into the modern day stereotype of the journalist [a cynic]....It was through the frame of irony that he viewed reality. Finally, during World War II the predominant sentiment was common sense....[C]ommon sense means more than sound judgment. It means being down-to-earth and realistic."

2120.   Martinson, David L. "Coverage of La Follette Offers Insights for 1972 Campaign." *JQ* 52 (1975): 539-42. Newspapers provided superficial treatment of La Follette's stands on issues and presented a negative stereotype.

2121.   Matthews, Joseph J. *Reporting the Wars*. Minneapolis: University of Minnesota Press, 1957. This survey overview blends journalism history with military history from the 1700s to World War II. While war reporting was often colored and incomplete, correspondents' primary motivation was to provide immediate information for the public. Correspondents sometimes had an influence on shaping events. The truly professional war reporter emerged in the late 19th and early 20th centuries.

2122.   May, Antoinette. *Witness to War: A Biography of Marguerite Higgins*. New York: Beaufort, 1983. Higgins covered World War II, the Korean war, and the Vietnam war. A leading female journalist, she won the Pulitzer Prize for her Korean reporting.

2123.   McClure, Leslie. "An Analysis of Advertising Volume in World War I." *JQ* 19 (1942): 262-67. "The volume of newspaper and magazine advertising...from 1914 to 1923 was definitely influenced by World War I, but the marked trend toward more and more use of advertising by American business, although interrupted, was not stopped by the war." (262)

2124.   Miller, Lee G. *The Story of Ernie Pyle*. New York: Viking, 1950. Pyle did not succeed as a journalist by accident. He had university training and had worked as a reporter and copy editor. As a journalist, he was concerned about preparing for his career, human interest, and accuracy. He was a man of integrity, sympathy, and ability.

2125.   Mock, James R. *Censorship, 1917*. Princeton, N.J.: Princeton University Press, 1941. Examines America's experience with censorship in World War I and its relevance to 1941. Although there were occasional excesses, censorship during the war generally was done acceptably. The danger was the threat to American democratic government resulting from carrying over into peacetime the repressive measures used during the war.

2126.   Moffett, Albert E. "Hometown Radio in 1942: The Role of Local Stations During the

First Year of Total War." *AJ* 3 (1986): 87-98. Local radio stations "preached national unity, sought and got unrestrained community participation, and showered listeners with unabashed patriotism--all helping to create a national consensus on the World War II home front." (88)

2127. Morrison, Joseph L. "Editor for Sale--A World War II Case History." *JQ* 43 (1966): 34-42. The magazine *The Living Age* fell into the hands of an editor financed by the Japanese from 1938 to 1941. It ran propaganda in the guise of objective articles by mainly American authors, many of whom were actually Japanese authors. The magazine failed, and the editor went to jail; but the law should have acted sooner to shut down the magazine.

2128. Mould, David H. *American Newsfilm: 1914-1919, the Underexposed War*. New York: Garland, 1983. Newsfilm, only a few years old, became a serious method of recording events during World War I. It evolved from a business into journalism.

2129. Mowrer, Edgar Ansel. *Triumph and Turmoil: A Personal History of Our Times*. New York: Weybright and Talley, 1968. Autobiography and recollections of the Chicago *Daily News* correspondent who covered World War II and Europe.

2130. Nelson, Harold L. "The Political Reform Press: A Case Study." *JQ* 29 (1952): 294-302. The Minnesota *Daily Star* (1920-24), a paper founded and operated by the pro-labor, pro-farmer Nonpartisan League, failed because it could not attract business support and (even though it was intended as a complete newspaper) because potential subscribers viewed it as subject to the views of labor and the League.

2131. Neuman, Fred G. *Irvin S. Cobb: His Life and Letters*. Emmaus, Pa.: Rodale, 1938. Cobb was a humorist who rose from beginning reporter to prominent war correspondent. This biography focuses on his humor and fiction.

2132. Nicholas, David, ed. *Ernie's War: The Best of Ernie Pyle's World War II Dispatches*. New York: Random House, 1986. Anthology of Pyle's news stories, with a brief biography.

2133. Nichols, John E. "Publishers and Drug Advertising: 1933-38." *JQ* 49 (1972): 144-47. "It is a truism that advertisers sometimes influence editorial content. Between 1933 and 1938, when publishers were faced with a major loss in advertising revenue that would come if Congress approved a bill strengthening the Pure Food and Drug Act of 1906, they fought the bill with inaccurate and distorted reporting, lobbying and testimony before congress. They were successful; it was generally conceded that the bill as passed was ineffective." (144) Drug advertising was a substantial part of national advertising, and "very few newspapers and magazines came out in favor of the bill." (145) Newspapers were pro-business and anti-consumer.

2134. O'Connor, Richard. *Heywood Broun: A Biography*. New York: Putnam's, 1975. Similar to Kramer's biography: strongly sympathetic, popularized book. Broun was a "boozy, amiable baseball writer" who became "one of the most eloquent and revered totems of the liberalism of his time." He was a courageous crusader who was indignant over injustice and who as a writer had a wonderful sense of realism.

2135. O'Neill, William L. *The Last Romantic, a Life of Max Eastman*. New York: Oxford University Press, 1978. Study of Eastman's role in political journalism in relation to the "social history of ideas." He was best at serious journalism, but he measured his own success by the critical acclaim of his poetry and his literary criticism. He had been a radical before World War I and a Trotskyite in the 1920s before becoming an anti-Stalinist in the 1930s and an anti-Communist in the 1940s and '50s.

2136. O'Rourke, James S. "The San Francisco *Chronicle* and the Air Mail Emergency of 1934." *JH* 6 (1979): 8-13. George T. Cameron, publisher of the *Chronicle*, attempted to influence the emergency because of his "fears of nationalization of the airline industry by Roosevelt's 'rubber stamp' Congress, solid financial ties to the air carriers and a strong affiliation with California-based aircraft manufacturers." (13) He had financially selfish reasons for wanting to influence a decision to return the air mail job to private airlines. For the press in general, "motives other than public service and the common good appear to have played a dominant role in their actions." (8)

2137. Ostrow, Michael S., and Thomas J. Piscitello. "Richard Harding Davis: Dandy of the Battlefield." *MHD* 2, 1 (1982): 29-33, 39. Brief summary of the war correspondent's career

2138. Peterson, H. C. *Propaganda for War: The Campaign Against American Neutrality 1914-1917*. Norman: University of Oklahoma Press, 1939. British propaganda was a major factor in persuading America to enter World War I. It gulled Americans, and British influence permeated the American press. (Peterson was pro-German, or at least non-interventionist, and opposed America's siding with Great Britain.)

2139. Pfaff, Daniel W. "The Press and the Scottsboro Rape Cases, 1931-32." *JH* 1 (1974): 72-76. "The sensational Scottsboro rape cases of 1931 were an interesting challenge to the press to exercise its function as interpreter in the struggle between truth and falsehood and as watchdog in the interests of fair and equal justice. They served to demonstrate the viscissitudes of dealing evenhandedly in print with a story that involved both inflammatory racial attitudes and international ideological controversy." (72) The press was prejudiced, and the information and editorial opinion it carried failed to provide the public with a fair or accurate story.

2140. Phillips, John. *It Happened in Our Lifetime: A Memoir in Words and Pictures*. Boston: Little, Brown, 1985. Narrative and photographs by a *Life* magazine photographer who covered Nazism and World War II.

2141. Pilat, Oliver. *Pegler: Angry Man of the Press*. Boston: Beacon, 1963. This biography deprecates its subject. Pegler was idiosyncratic, inconsistent, and colorful in his writing. He was savage toward liberal journalists, politicians, and issues, including labor. He supported conservative and reactionary causes and people such as Joseph McCarthy. On political and social issues, his thinking was shallow; and as a political writer he was unable to convince "important" people that he had anything significant to say.

2142. Pratte, Alf. "The Honolulu *Star-Bulletin* and the 'Day of Infamy.'" *AJ* 5 (1988): 5-13. The work of the *Star-Bulletin* on the day the Japanese bombed Pearl Harbor "provides one of the more dramatic illustrations in American history of the press' performance in a major, fast-breaking crisis....[W]ith events moving at a frenzied pace, the newspaper had to gather facts about a surprise military attack and rapidly disseminate raw information throughout an island community, while at the same time it also contributed as a cooperative source in getting facts sent to the mainland United States." The story of the performance of the newspaper and its editor, Riley Allen, "provides a picture of the fragile task that many newspapers during World War II had in combining concern for serving their communities, their country, and military operations with their ideals of professional journalism." (5-6)

2143. Reuss, Carol. "The *Ladies' Home Journal* and Hoover's Food Program." *JQ* 49 (1972): 740-42. The press sometimes can serve best by distributing government information to the public rather than by being a watchdog over government. During World War I, *Ladies' Home Journal* assisted by "sharing wartime food problems and suggestions with readers." (740)

2144. Reynolds, Quentin. *By Quentin Reynolds*. New York: McGraw-Hill, 1963. Autobiography of *Collier's* correspondent who served longer than any other reporter in covering World War II. This book is aimed at a general audience rather than historians.

2145. Richstad, Jim Andrew. "The Press and the Courts Under Martial Rule in Hawaii During World War II--from Pearl Harbor to *Duncan v. Kahanamoku*." Ph.D. dissertation, University of Minnesota, 1967. The press was first censored by the military; later, staff members exercised self-censorship. The control of civil liberties was harsh.

2146. Richstad, Jim Andrew. "The Press Under Martial Law: The Hawaiian Experience." *JM* 17 (1970). See previous entry.

2147. Roberts, Nancy L. *Dorothy Day and the Catholic Worker*. Albany: State University of New York Press, 1984. Adulatory biography of Day, the founder and editor of the *Catholic Worker*, a religious and social-reform periodical which united Christian teachings with radical-left values.

2148. Robinson, Michael J. "Fifty Years in the Doghouse: Blaming the Press is Nothing New." *WJR* (March 1986): 44-45. Polls from the 1930s show that the public criticized newspapers then, just as it does now.

2149. Ross, Robert W. *So It Was True: The American Protestant Press and the Nazi Persecution of the Jews*. Minneapolis: University of Minnesota Press, 1980. Did the Protestant press make a creditable attempt to inform Americans of the Nazis' plan to exterminate Jews? It did report the news, although often perhaps in disbelief.

2150. Ryant, Carl G. "From Isolation to Intervention: *The Saturday Evening Post* 1939-42." *JQ* 48 (1971): 79-87. From an absolute denial of the relevance of the European war for America and an unwillingness to brand Germany or Italy as America's enemies, the magazine came to take American intervention in the war as a crusade. At first, it was isolationist, but by 1942 it changed its position enough "to permit acceptance if not approval of the war." (680) It opposed Roosevelt; but as the middle class came to depend on the New Deal program of the government, the magazine, which mirrored middle-class views, accepted the program. Financial policy and "material as well as ideological considerations" accounted for its editorial policy.

2151. Schaleban, Joy. "Getting the Story Out of Nazi Germany: Louis P. Lochner." *JM* 11 (1969). Narrative of the exploits of the Associated Press' bureau chief in Berlin. To obtain information for his news reports, he relied on social contacts.

2152. Schreiner, George A. *Cables and Wireless*. 1924. The author, a war correspondent, tells of his World War I experiences, but more as a reporter than as an historian.

2153. Seller, Maxine S. "Defining Socialist Womanhood: The Women's Page of the *Jewish Daily Forward* in 1919." *AJH* 76 (1987): 416-38. Although the *Forward* was "the voice of a vibrant left-wing working class Yiddish culture" (416), its women's page "did not urge readers to make radical changes in their values or lifestyles. Nor did it emphasize conflict between either the classes or the sexes. Rather, it reinforced the democratic, progressive approach to public affairs already held by many of its readers and educated others in that approach." (438)

2154. Shaber, Sarah R. "Hemingway's Literary Journalism: The Spanish Civil War Dispatches." *JQ* 57 (1980): 420-24, 535. Hemingway "used literary techniques usually absent from mainstream reporting" (420), and his approach can serve as a good model for journalists today.

2155. Sheean, Vincent. *Personal History*. Secaucus, N.J.: Citadel Press, 1935; reprinted 1986). Memoirs of the Chicago *Tribune* correspondent emphasizing the period surrounding World War I.

2156. Shirer, William L. *20th Century Journey. A Memoir of a Life and the Times, the Start: 1904-1930*. New York: Simon & Schuster, 1976. Autobiography: how Shirer developed as a journalist.

2157. Shirer, William L. *20th Century Journey: A Memoir of a Life and the Times. Vol. II: The Nightmare Years, 1930-1940*. Boston: Little, Brown, 1984. Continuation of Shirer's autobiography, focusing on Germany before World War II.

2158. Short, K.R.M., ed. *Film and Radio Propaganda in World War II*. Knoxville: University of Tennessee Press, 1983. Governments used movies and radio on a massive scale. Essays by various authors examine the use of propaganda by the Allies, Germany, Italy, and Japan. The essays are on such topics as Thomas Cripps' "The Idea of Racial Integration in Wartime Propaganda and Peacetime 'Message Movies' in the USA" and David Culbert's "The American 'Why We Fight' Series: Social Engineering for a Democratic Society at War."

2159. Simmons, Earl W. "The Labor Dailies." *AmM* 15 (September 1928): 85-93. History of various labor newspapers, most of which had short lives, from 1886 to 1924. "The American labor movement has not made much progress in the field of daily journalism....With few exceptions the American editors have been first-rate fighters, but they have lacked the cultural breadth necessary for a clear perspective on national and international problems....The average American working man is not class conscious enough to support a labor press." (93)

2160. Smith, C. Calvin. "Arkansas, 1940-1945: Public and Press Reaction to War and Wartime Pressures." Ph.D. dissertation, University of Arkansas, 1978.

2161. Smith, C. Zoe. "Fritz Goro: Emigre Photojournalist." *AJ* 3 (1986): 206-21. Goro fled to the United States from Nazi Germany and, along with other German emigre photographers, greatly influenced *Life*, America's first picture magazine.

2162. Snorgrass, J. William. "The Baltimore *Afro-American* and the Election Campaigns of FDR." *AJ* 1, 2 (1984): 35-50. The *Afro-American* supported Roosevelt in 1932 and 1936 but opposed him in 1940 and 1944, each time because of racial issues.

2163. Sorenson, Thomas C. *The Word War: The Story of American Propaganda.* New York: Harper & Row, 1968. An inside story of the United States Information Agency by a USIA official. This personal account often is bitter.

2164. Startt, James D. "Early Press Reaction to Wilson's League Proposal." *JQ* 39 (1962): 301-08. The majority of American dailies supported the League of Nations concept in early 1919. Later Woodrow Wilson encountered hostility from the press, but still it treated him fairly. The arguments used by the anti-Wilson, anti-League press were practical and realistic, while the pro-Wilson press arguments were idealistic and abstract. Wilson had assumed that the support for the League would be absolute rather than simply favorable. It was this weakness that led to his defeat on the League issue.

2165. Startt, James D. *Journalism's Unofficial Ambassador: A Biography of Edward Price Bell, 1869-1943.* Athens: Ohio University Press, 1979. Bell worked as director of the foreign news service of Victor Lawson's Chicago *Daily News.* Lawson believed that peace and international understanding could be attained through intelligent, in-depth reporting of foreign affairs. Bell believed wholeheartedly in Lawson's concept. He directed the paper's European operation from 1900 to 1922 and acquired an international reputation as a spokesman for peace, understanding, and American foreign policy. He provides an example of the fact that a professional journalist can back a cause such as international peace.

2166. Steele, Richard W. *Propaganda in an Open Society: The Roosevelt Administration and the Media, 1933-1941.* Westport, Conn.: Greenwood, 1985. Roosevelt used public relations, including radio and film, to gain public support for his policies aimed at combating economic problems and the international aggression of the Axis powers.

2167. Stein, M. L. *Under Fire: The Story of American War Correspondence.* New York: Julian Messner, 1968. History of war reporters from the American Revolution to Vietnam, with an emphasis on the 20th century: events, personalities, photographers, women, soldier reporters, broadcasters, heroism, humor, and tragedy. Reporters have performed with determination and gallantry in the performance of their professional duty.

2168. Stern, David J. *Memoirs of a Maverick Publisher.* New York: Simon & Schuster, 1962. Autobiography of the owner of the New York *Post* in the 1930s. A liberal, he was the first publisher to sign a contract with the American Newspaper Guild. Although idealistic, he had to wrestle with running a big business.

2169. Stevens, John D. "From the Back of the Foxhole: Black Correspondents in World War II." *JM* 27 (1973). The 27 black reporters who covered World War II did an admirable job despite the problems they faced because of their race. "Although they suffered little discrimination themselves...they saw it and reported it. They accepted the unenviable extra task of being ombudsmen for the GIs with their largely white officers....They didn't win any journalistic prizes, mostly because they were writing for blacks about blacks....[T]hey did the tough, thankless job of writing about support troops who were doing tough, thankless jobs." (60)

2170. Stevens, John D. "Press and Community Toleration: Wisconsin in World War I." *JQ* 46 (1969): 255-59. See next entry.

2171. Stevens, John D. "Suppression of Expression in Wisconsin during World War I." Ph.D. dissertation, University of Wisconsin, 1967. "In Wisconsin, the state with the nation's heaviest German population, federal, state and local officials cooperated with state and county defense councils and 'patriotic' organizations and individuals to silence dissenters....The state's press did not champion minority rights."

2172. Sullivan, Paul W. "G. D. Crain Jr. and the Founding of *Advertising Age*." *JH* 1 (1974): 94-95. Favorable biography covering 1930 to World War II. Crain, a consumer advocate, referred to *Advertising Age* as "a real newspaper" based on hard news, investigative reporting, and informative columns. His "tenacity in insisting on editorial excellence and in refusing to let depression economics force him to quit carved a unique position in the field of business publications." (95)

2173. Summers, Robert E. *Wartime Censorship of Press and Radio*. New York: H.W. Wilson, 1942. Collection of documents and articles about censorship in the United States between 1940 and 1942.

2174. Taylor, Sally. "The Life, Work and Times of Walter Duranty, Moscow Correspondent for the *New York Times*, 1921-1941." Ph.D. dissertation, Southern Illinois University, 1979. "In spite of his personal flamboyance and amorality, and in spite of his position as a symbol of the antagonism between the Soviet Union and the West, Duranty's contributions to the field of foreign correspondence make him one of the most important figures in journalism during the first half of the twentieth century."

2175. Tebbel, John. *George Horace Lorimer and the Saturday Evening Post*. Garden City, N.Y.: Doubleday, 1948. Lorimer was a great editor, an outstanding example of a success story, building the *Post* from a run-down publication when bought by Curtis in 1898 into one of the most profitable magazines in America. He succeeded because he had a genius for knowing what the ordinary American wanted. The magazine romanticized rugged Americanism. Despite its success with fiction, its heart was the editorial page.

2176. Teel, Leonard Ray. "The Shaping of a Southern Opinion Leader: Ralph McGill and Freedom of Information." *AJ* 5 (1988): 14-27. Near the end of World War II, McGill was part of a three-member mission of the American Society of Newspaper Editors which visited various countries to try to lay plans for assuring freedom of the press. American idealism, however, was not acceptable to non-democratic nations, and the mission failed to win universal agreement on any aspect of press freedom.

2177. Villard, Oswald Garrison. *Fighting Years: Memoirs of a Liberal Editor*. New York: Harcourt, Brace, 1939. Autobiography, beginning in the 1890s, of the New York *Evening Post* owner and *Nation* editor who opposed American imperialism and participation in World War I.

2178. Ward, Hiley H. "50 Years Ago: What They Said When Hitler Became Chancellor." *MHD* 3, 2 (1983): 8-10. Collection of quotes from American newspapers in 1933.

2179. Washburn, Patrick S. "J. Edgar Hoover and the Black Press in World War II." *JH* 13 (1986): 26-33. The FBI director had little symphathy for dissidents and government critics. Attorney General Francis Biddle and other Justice Department officials, however, prevented his efforts "to obtain a sedition indictment of the emerging and highly critical black press." (26)

2180. Washburn, Patrick S. "The *Pittsburgh Courier's* Double V Campaign in 1942." *AJ* 3 (1986): 73-86. The *Courier*, a black newspaper, adopted an editorial policy aimed at gaining civil rights advances for black Americans by supporting American victory in World War II.

2181. Washburn, Patrick S. *A Question of Sedition: The Federal Government's Investigation of the Black Press During World War II*. New York: Oxford University Press, 1986. Concern about national security and wartime morale led to federal attempts to muzzle the black press. However, Francis Biddle, the U.S. attorney general, believed strongly in freedom of expression and blocked the efforts.

2182. Waters, Marilyn. "Will Rogers: The Not Always Humorous Columnist." *MHD* 6, 1 (1986): 54-59. Rogers, writing as a New York *Times* columnist from 1926 to 1935, "at times took a serious bent, and when he went beyond harmless humor, Rogers stirred up some hornets' nests." (54)

2183. Weaver, Bill, and Oscar C. Page. "The Black Press and the Drive for Integrated Graduate and Professional Schools." *Phylon* 43 (Spring 1982), 15ff. Analysis of how 11 black newspapers responded to the efforts of the NAACP to attack segregation in the 1930s.

2184. Wreszin, Michael. *Oswald Garrison Villard: Pacifist at War*. Bloomington: Indiana University Press, 1965. Study of the effect that Villard's devotion to pacifism and other causes had on his editorial judgment. He involved *The Nation* in the pacifist movement at the time of World War I and supported disarmament and neutrality prior to World War II. Wreszin disputes critics who claim that Villard's idealism kept him from being realistic and pragmatic and that he was either a naive dogmatist or was in the anti-war movement just for sport. Villard's liberalism "was genuine and compatible with the mainstream of liberal thought in the early thirties."

2185. Yamaguchi, Mayumi, and John Lent. "40 Years Ago: How Big Papers Covered Bombs That Ended War." *MHD* 5, 3 (1985): 2-5, 30-31, 38-41. Collection of stories from the New York *Times* and Asahi *Shimbun* on the dropping of the atomic bomb.

2186. Zagano, Phyllis. "The Arguments of the Thirties: Of Politics, Journalism and Art." *BF* 6, 2 (1982): 257-62. Such journals as *The Nation* and *The New Republic* espoused liberal belief and "shaped public policy and opinion in a way perhaps previously unequalled by journalism." Their type of liberalism "often found voice through fiction and poetry and literary criticism." (262)

2187. Zoak, Mervin D. "How U. S. Magazines Covered Objectors in World War II." *JQ* 48 (1971): 550-54. This study of magazine attitudes toward conscientious objectors, 1939-1947, finds that national consumer magazines with substantial circulation tended to support objectors, while religious magazines treated them no more favorably than many secular magazines did.

14

Broadcasting,
1920–Present

2188. Archer, Gleason L. *Big Business and Radio*. New York: American Historical Society, 1939. In the war for control of radio from 1922 to 1939, businessmen owners used cut-throat practices. Then, sensing threats by government to establish rules and regulations, the more brilliant leaders relied on arbitration, mediation, investigation, litigation, and discussions, finally resulting in a set of legal documents. This study includes such topics as the FTC's investigation of RCA; the anti-trust suit against the Radio Group; rise of NBC, CBS, and Mutual Broadcasting System; development of television and radio facsimile; and the conquests of radio by business interests, led by David Sarnoff, president of RCA.

2189. Archer, Gleason L. *History of Radio to 1926*. New York: American Historical Society, 1938. This chronological discussion of radio (the founding of RCA, regulation, rivalry, networks, "firsts," etc.) attempts to peg down incidents and dates. It gives special attention to technology: experiments with electricity, telegraphy, trans-oceanic cable, telephone, alternators, vacuum tubes, etc.

2190. Ashdown, Paul G. "WTVJ's Miami Crime War: A Television Crusade." *FHQ* 28 (1980): 427-437. Miami television station WTVJ's 1966 campaign against Dade County crime was possibly "television's first and most significant editorial crusade." Following its 65 consecutive daily editorials, supported by documentary reports and interviews, crime decreased in the Miami area while the station's ratings increased. The campaign demonstrated that "a television crusade was different than a newspaper crusade and that it required intensity and a dramatic element to attract public interest."

2191. Avery, Robert K., and Robert Pepper. "Balancing the Equation: Public Radio Comes of Age." *PTR* 7 (March-April 1980): 19-30. The growth of noncommercial radio from pre-World War I college experimental stations to the present has been influenced by such factors as technological developments, opposition from commercial stations and networks, changes in government regulations, competition from television, and disagreement among public radio leaders.

2192. Avery, Robert K., and Robert Pepper. *The Politics of Interconnection: A History of Public Television at the National Level*. Washington: National Association of Educational Broadcasters, 1979. Account of the internal politics of public television from 1968 to 1976.

2193. Bailey, George A. "Interpretive Reporting of the Vietnam War by Anchormen 1965-1970." *JQ* 53 (1976): 319-24. Anchormen generally read straight reports rather than giving "challenging, adversary interpretation." Their approaches were simplistic and accepted the surface details rather than probing in a critical way.

2194. Bailey, George A. "Television War: Trends in Network Coverage of Vietnam 1965-1970." *JOB* 20 (1976): 147-58. This content analysis (which addresses the topics of anchormen, quantity of coverage, and subject matter) calls for scholars to do more insightful, data-based history of the war.

2195. Bailey, George A., and Lawrence Lichty. "Rough Justice on a Saigon Street: A Gatekeeper Study of NBC's Tet Execution Film." *JQ* 49 (1972): 221-29, 238. Most questions about whether to show the film of South Vietnamese army officer shooting a member of the Viet Cong were related to taste.

2196. Baker, John C. *Farm Broadcasting: The First Sixty Years*. Ames: Iowa State University Press, 1981. Radio programs for farmers covered education, extension, farming, ranching, rodeos, and entertainment. Radio and television were vital in bringing information to farmers and helped in more efficient production and wiser marketing. Agriculture broadcasting began with weather reports to farmers in 1921 and expanded to market reports and finally educators, extension agents, government representatives, and industry spokesmen talking to farmers. This history covers the development of agriculture programming, regional and national farm networks and wire services, the National Association of Farm Broadcasters, the importance of farm advertising, and advice for college students thinking about a career in agriculture broadcasting.

2197. Barkin, Steve M. "Eisenhower's Television Planning Board: An Unwritten Chapter in the History of Political Broadcasting." *JOB* 27 (1983): 319-31. During the 1952 presidential campaign, Eisenhower had a secret board which advised him on the use of television.

2198. Barnouw, Erik. *The Golden Web: A History of Broadcasting in the United States, 1933-1953*. New York: Oxford University Press, 1968. This second volume in Barnouw's three-volume history covers Father Coughlin, the broadcast of Orson Welles' radio drama about Mars' invasion of Earth, FDR's fireside chats, Eddie Cantor, Kaltenborn, Murrow, Elmer Davis, World War II, the press-radio conflict of the 1930s, government investigation of monopoly, and broadcasting ownership. It is critical of the influence of advertising on programming.

2199. Barnouw, Erik. *The Image Empire: A History of Broadcasting in the United States from 1953.* New York: Oxford University Press, 1970. The military-industrial complex, big business, and the eastern establishment took control of the media in both the U.S. and the world during the 1950s. By 1953 American television had permeated other countries, reflecting the "growing United States involvement in the lives of other nations -- an involvement of imperial scope." That effect was accomplished through such activities as the Voice of America, Radio Free Europe, and television network news. American broadcasting became the tool of government and industry. Management of events, and therefore management of the news, became common. Public broadcasting as an alternative to commercial television might be a solution to the entertainment-oriented commercial television.

2200. Barnouw, Erik. *A Tower in Babel: A History of Broadcasting in the United States, to 1933..* New York: Oxford University Press, 1966. The second volume in Barnouw's history covers early experimenters, the origin and rise of RCA, the conflict between AT&T and the Radio Group in the mid-1920s, the establishment and eventual domination of broadcasting by networks, government regulation (anti-trust suits, Radio Act of 1927), the needs and desires of advertisers, local stations, educational broadcasting, roles of advertising and business, social role of radio, fairness doctrine, etc.

2201. Barnouw, Erik. *Tube of Plenty: Evolution of American Television.* New York: Oxford University Press, 1975. This book is a condensation and updating of *The Image Empire*, which ended in 1970. It provides a chronological narrative, beginning with the technological background preceding television. Television's experimental years from 1920-1945 were marked by experimentation in technology. During the 1945-1953 period, television emerged as a national medium, and it made advances in technology and development of programming. In 1953-1963 the prominent television items included crime shows, westerns, quiz shows, and news. ("In one decade -- the Eisenhower and Kennedy years -- American television had reached fabulous proportions. It had developed its technology and skills to a degree that earned astonishment. It had become not only a national but an international institution."). In 1964-1975 television grew and matured in programming and journalistic capabilities; it became "the voice and image of an era" and also "a thoughtful observer, an elder statesman, an ombudsman" for society.

2202. Baughman, James L. "The Strange Birth of CBS Reports' Revisited." *HJFRT* 2, 1: 27-38.

2203. Baughman, James L. *Television's Guardians: The FCC and the Politics of Programming, 1958-1967.* Knoxville: University of Tennessee Press, 1985. The Federal Communications Commission was unsuccessful at regulating television because it could not get cooperation from either the legislative, executive, or judicial branch of the federal government.

2204. Benjamin, Louise M. "Broadcast Campaign Precedents from the 1924 Presidential Election." *JOB* 31 (1987): 449-60. The campaign began the practices of treating candidates fairly and of covering conventions.

2205. Berkman, Dave. "The 'Blue Book' and Charles Siepmann as Reported in *Broadcasting* Magazine." *AJ* 2 (1985): 37-48. *Broadcasting* magazine in 1945-1947 attacked the FCC license-renewal policy (which was authored by Siepmann) of comparing radio stations' performance with the promises they had given at the time they had applied for their original licenses. The magazine did a "hatchet job" (46) by charging inaccurately that Siepmann favored censorship.

2206. Berkman, Dave. "Let's Sightsee Radiovision -- TV Terms That Didn't Last." *JQ* 63 (1986): 626-27. Slight article listing the words applied to television during its early years.

2207. Berkman, Dave. "Politics and Radio in the 1924 Campaign." *JQ* 64 (1987): 422-33. Newspapers and magazines in 1924 believed that radio would have a lasting effect on politics.

2208. Blackman, David. "Radio's Popular Jerry Buckley: Unsolved Detroit Murder." *MHD* 5, 2 (1985): 57-59, 64. The broadcaster was murdered during his efforts to stamp out corruption in Detroit's city government.

2209. Bliss, Edward, Jr. "Lowell Thomas." *Quill* (August 1974): 14-18. Thomas was a great journalist and broadcaster. This is a popular biography, not a serious historical study.

2210. Bliss, Edward, Jr. "Remembering Edward R. Murrow." *Saturday Review* (May 31, 1975): 17-21. Murrow had a fierce dedication to free speech and free debate. He reacted with a sense of outrage and a sense of history whenever a citizen was denied his basic rights. Bliss was a former CBS news editor.

2211. Bluem, A. William. *Documentary in American Television*. New York: Hastings House, 1965. This account covers the development, use, and potential of television documentary from pre-television still photography and films to 1965 television documentaries. Documentary television is "the only logical instrument" for achieving social progress, reducing society's tensions, and solving "the political and economic complexities of a world faced by threats of atomic horror."

2212. Bohn, Thomas W. "Broadcasting National Election Returns: 1916-1948." *JOB* 12 (1968): 267-86. This brief summary of each election covers the development of radio reporting of returns, including studio facilities and equipment, personnel, program formats, coverage, audience, innovations, and differences. Election night coverage often has provided a testing ground for many major developments in broadcasting. Coverage developed slowly because of the inability of broadcasting to collect and assemble data and because broadcasters thought the audience would not enjoy intense information and news coverage from broadcasting. As full-time coverage occurred, however, stations and networks found they couldn't fill the entire time with statistics; so analysis and interpretation were given more attention.

2213. Brown, James A. "Selling Airtime for Controversy: NAB Self-Regulation and Father Coughlin." *JOB* 24 (1980): 199-224. Rev. Charles Coughlin's controversial broadcasts in the 1930s caused CBS to make policy changes, the National Association of Broadcasters Code to modify its code, and the FCC to consider intervention into program guidelines. His departure from national radio resulted not primarily because of pressure from his religious superiors but from actions of broadcasters "under implied pressure from the FCC -- and indirectly the White House."

2214. Burlingame, Roger. *Don't Let Them Scare You: The Life and Times of Elmer Davis*. Philadelphia: Lippincott, 1961. Davis was a talented and courageous journalist who stood up for those ideas (usually liberal) in which he believed. This adulatory biography emphasizes the courageous spirit of a great journalist and American who could clearly see the truth and transmit it to others.

2215. Carroll, Raymond L. "The 1948 Truman Campaign: The Threshold of the Modern Era." *JOB* 24 (1980): 173-88. Harry Truman used not only the "traditional tools" of radio and personal appearances in his 1948 presidential campaign but televison and newsreel as well. With most newspapers Republican and therefore hostile to him, he used radio to provide him direct access to the voters.

2216. Chamberlin, Bill F. "The FCC and the First Principle of the Fairness Doctrine: A History of Neglect and Distortion." *FCL* 31 (1979): 361-411. In 1949 the FCC required broadcasters to run programs on public issues.

2217. Chase, Francis, Jr. *Sound and Fury.* New York: Harper, 1942. This is an "informal history" of the growth of radio in the U.S., told in terms of people and anecdotes: Marconi, DeForest, Sarnoff, early history, the chaos of the early 1920s, the development of networks, FTC, technology, entertainers, etc. This is not a book intended for the serious historian.

2218. Chester, Giraud. "The Radio Commentaries of H.V. Kaltenborn: A Case Study in Persuasion." Ph.D. dissertation, University of Wisconsin, 1947.

2219. Clark, David Gillis. "The Dean of Commentators: A Biography of H.V. Kaltenborn." Ph.D. dissertation, University of Wisconsin, 1966. "Kaltenborn's major contributions to American life included his educating of the American public to its new role as world leader and helping to alert it to dangers from abroad. His...fight for freedom to express his views...stands as a model for libertarians..., and his effort to professionalize news analysis and commentary must be counted, though perhaps a failure, a noble one."

2220. Clark, David G. "H.V. Kaltenborn and His Sponsors: Controversial Broadcasting and the Sponsor's Role." *JOB* 12 (1968): 309-21. Kaltenborn's experiences indicate that "successful airing of controversial public issues depends not so much on commentator or network willingness to speak out, as on sponsor willingness to stand the gaff. For as the price of admission to the marketplace of ideas has increased, the precepts of Milton and Mill regarding the speaker's commitment to the search for truth have been expanded to include a man seldom heard from in the public dialogue: the businessman-sponsor." (309) Commitment to principle by the sponsor appears to be the determining factor in whether a company will sponsor a controversial program in the face of critics and opponents and the resulting economic pressure.

2221. Clark, David G. "H.V. Kaltenborn's First Year on the Air." *JQ* 42 (1965): 373-81. Kaltenborn set the patterns for 35 years of news analysis and commentary. This account tells the story of his first year, with WEAF in 1923. Because of his views on issues, he angered many people and groups, and his station declined to renew his contract. "The significance of that year in Kaltenborn's career lies in the facts of his personal courage in refusing to yield to pressure, the [Brooklyn] *Eagle's* courage in backing him, WEAF's weakness in succumbing to fear of possible consequences, and the public's demonstration that it was, indeed, composed of many parts. Kaltenborn that year was a pathfinder for freedom of expression on the air, and his controversies show that personal and institutional courage were prerequisites for the journey." (373)

2222. Clark, David G. "Radio in Presidential Campaigns: The Early Years (1924-1932)." *JOB* 6 (1961-1962): 229-38. The election of 1928 "saw the emergence of radio as a full grown campaign device...and from the first, the special requirements of broadcasting have made themselves felt in political campaigns." (230) Focusing on candidates' use of radio, rather than news coverage, this article describes some of the early problems connected with radio campaigns, some solutions found, and the development of radio's use as a campaign instrument.

2223. Clift, Charles E., III. "The WLBT-TV Case, 1964-1969: An Historical Analysis." Ph.D. dissertation, Indiana University, 1974. WLBT lost its license for failing to adquately serve the black population in Jackson, Miss. The case indicated the "bureaucratic inertia" in the FCC.

2224. Cochran, Thomas C. "Media as Business: A Brief History." *JC* 25 (1975): 155-65. Technological advances and rising costs placed control of American media in the hands of large centralized organizations whose values are those of the marketplace. "The history of the mass media in the last 150 years is an unusually interesting example of the interrelations of business, technology, and general culture. In the course of this history, business has become an even more dominant influence in American culture, and technology has continuously vested greater control of the media in the hands of large private companies." (155) Of particular importance in this history have been industrial printing technology, large press associations, electronic media technology developments, and the effect of management and advertising on content and freedom of expression. In television, the profit motive determines practices (programming, etc.) although all large companies must compete for public favor, making them responsive to broad shifts in public attitudes.

2225. Cole, Barry G., and Al Paul Klose. "A Selected Bibliography on the History of Broadcasting." *JOB* 7 (1962-1963): 247-68. Reference work.

2226. Cole, Jeffery Ian. "Born to the New Art: CBS Correspondents and the Emergence of Broadcast News, 1930-1941." Ph.D. dissertation, University of California, Los Angeles, 1985.

2227. Cook, David A., ed. "The Economic and Political Structure of American Television." *QRFS* 8, 3 (1983): 1-55. This special issue of *QRFS* contains two historical articles: David A. Cook, "The Birth of the Network: How Westinghouse, GE, AT&T, and RCA Invented the Concept of Advertiser-Supported Broadcasting," pp. 3-8, providing an economic explanation of the motives of the founders of the NBC radio network; and Gary Edgerton and Cathy Pratt, "The Influence of the Paramount Decision on Network Television in America," pp. 9-24, a discussion of the 1948 antitrust decision against Paramount.

2228. Crabb, Richard. *Radio's Beautiful Day*. Aberdeen, S.D.: North Plains Press, 1983. Narrative of Everett Mitchell, the "Voice of American Agriculture" and originator of the "Beautiful Day" Christian outlook, and his 50 years in broadcasting.

2229. Craig, R. Stephen. "The American Forces Network, Europe: A Case Study in Military Broadcasting." *JOB* 30 (1986): 33-46. Since 1946 not only has the network provided the military heirarchy with "instant communication with off-duty American soldiers and their families," but has helped "maintain morale and reduce disciplinary problems." (33) It has been able "to overcome the image of military control" of its programming because of its "close imitation of American commercial broadcasting in both form and content." (42)

2230. Cranston, Pat. "Political Convention Broadcasts: Their History and Influence." *JQ* 37 (1960): 186-94. Radio reporting of national conventions began in 1924 and the first telecasts in 1940. The electronic media have helped shape the way in which sessions are conducted and have influenced the behavior of delegates. Also the "speed and technical skill of broadcast coverage has affected journalism as a whole." (183) "From the history of political convention broadcasting it is evident that the presence of the electronic media has induced changes in the national conventions. The convention time schedule and location, use of visual material in the hall, the behavior of delegates and the pacing of proceedings all now bear the mark of planning for electronic coverage. To brighten the package in hopes of pleasing the audience, convention planners have added entertainers....The printed media have re-evaluated their convention reporting role. A new depth in convention reporting in print seems evident." (192)

2231. Cranston, Pat. "Some Historical Newscasts of the American Forces Network." *JQ* 41 (1964): 395-98. AFN reported the death of President John Kennedy with as much speed as domestic networks reported it. Its coverage demonstrated "how American forces overseas are kept continually and accurately informed of news events at home and abroad" (396) by a network formed in 1942.

2232. Crotts, Gail. "'A Spectacular Coup': Television and the 1948 Conventions." *JH* 1 (1974): 90-93. This is an account of the precedents set by and the lessons learned from the first presidential conventions covered by television.

2233. Culbert, David Holbrook. *News for Everyman: Radio and Foreign Affairs in Thirties America*. Westport, Conn.: Greenwood, 1976.. This history recounts the development of commentary in the 1930s and the relationship between radio's coverage of foreign affairs and the making of foreign policy by the Roosevelt administration. It focuses on the style and impact of Boake Carter, Kaltenborn, Swing, E. Davis, Fulton Lewis Jr., and Murrow. Radio news created a mass audience for foreign affairs after the 1938 Munich crisis. Commentators' broadcasts, although differing widely in their political beliefs, changed public opinion on American involvement in World War II from isolationist to interventionist, thus greatly influencing the foreign affairs process. Davis, Swing, Kaltenborn, and Murrow "came to believe in one course of action [intervention] so fervently that they lost the capacity for objectivity...[and] ceased offering even constructive criticism of administration foreign policy." The most serious shortcoming of the six commentators was their neglect of news about the Far East before Pearl Harbor. In common, all six were pioneers who developed a reputation in a new field and who developed a large personal following. "Radio news came to serve as an integrating force in America by helping to create a national foreign policy consensus."

2234. Cusack, Mary Ann. "The Emergence of Political Editorializing in Broadcasting." *JOB* 8 (1963-1964): 53-62. History perhaps can teach broadcasters "what we must do to advance our responsibilities to inform the public, to air interpretation as well as fact." (53) Editorializing has not always been accepted by critics, but it is an important aspect of broadcast journalism.

2235. Danna, Sammy R. "The Press-Radio War." *Freedom of Information Center Report No. 213*. School of Journalism, University of Missouri (December 1968): 1-7. This is a sketchy treatment of numerous episodes in the development of the history of news services available to radio to 1941.

2236. Danna, Sammy R. "The Rise of Radio News." *Freedom of Information Center Report No. 211*. School of Journalism, University of Missouri (November 1968): 1-7. Brief history of radio news and the reaction of newspapers. "For several hundred years, newspapers have worked hard for their freedom, their prestige and their general accomplishments. When radio, a new and generally faster means of disseminating news to the public, evolved, it was only natural that the press would react violently. After all, before radio emerged, the newspapers were virtually the sole means of daily mass news dissemination. During the time covered in this paper (1921-1933) the newspapers' reactions to radio news were often unsure, hasty, panicky, unfair, and without precedent. The radio stations who 'lifted' newspaper and press service news stories without paying for them were far from guiltless. (7)

2237. Diamond, Edwin. *The Tin Kazoo: Television, Politics, and The News*. Cambridge, Mass.: MIT Press, 1975. Television no longer has such awesome power as it had in the 1960s to persuade people's political views. Television has become "blunted and tinny by overuse or misuses." In covering such episodes and the Vietnam war, Pentagon Papers, civil rights, Richard Nixon, and Watergate, broadcast did a poor job, lacking "completeness, accuracy and originality."

2238. Edelman, Murray. *The Licensing of Radio Services in the United States, 1927 to 1947*. Urbana: University of Illinois Press, 1950. Analysis of the policies and actions of the regulatory agencies in licensing radio services 1927-1947.

2239. Emery, Michael C. "The Munich Crisis Broadcasts: Radio News Comes of Age." *JQ* 42 (1965): 576-80, 590. Radio's reporting of Hitler's challenge to Czechoslovakia in 1938 demonstrated the power of broadcasting to inform the world. "The important thing was that the networks now were cognizant of their potentialities and were ready to continue foreign broadcasts in depth....America responded to [the correspondents'] descriptions with a vast and deep interest. When World War II finally came the networks had matured greatly and so had the United States. This was the contribution of more than 200 radio men of all types to America's growth as a world power." (590)

2240. Fang, Irving. *Those Radio Commentators*. Ames: Iowa State University Press, 1977. Examines 15 commentators (similar to Culbert including Kaltenborn, Swing, Thomas, Carter, Dorothy Thompson, Lewis, Winchell, Davis, and Murrow) and the influence they had on America from 1929 to 1948. "For whatever reason, Americans came to trust radio commentators more than they did newspapers....These were troubled times. The commentators brought explanations, sometimes along with delivering the day's news....The radio commentators helped to clarify it all, letting others see matters as they saw matters, talking to their fellow Americans....[O]ur favorite radio commentator was there to sort it all out." (3-4)

2241. Fant, Charles H. "Televising Presidential Conventions, 1952-1980." *JC* 30, 4 (1980): 130-39. By cooperating with political parties, television helped them manipulate the public.

2242. Fellows, Harold E. "The Expanding Sphere of Journalism." *JOB* 1 (1965): 211-19. Many parallels exist between the development of newspaper journalism and broadcast journalism, including the development of technology, early government regulation, and advertising support. Broadcasting should be thought of and treated as print journalism is.

2243. Fielding, Raymond. *The American Newsreel 1911-1967*. Norman: University of Oklahoma, 1972. Newsreel: its role, production, etc.

2244. "The First 60 Years of NBC." *Broadcasting* 110 (June 9, 1986): 49-104. Special issue on NBC's 60th anniversary, focusing on its accomplishments since the late 1970s.

2245. Friendly, Fred. *Due to Circumstances Beyond Our Control*. New York: Random House, 1967. Personal account of Friendly's professional relationship with Edward R. Murrow, their controversial CBS documentaries, and Friendly's break with CBS. Friendly wanted aggressive journalism; CBS wanted to make money, which it was not doing with documentaries. CBS was too concerned with economic success and profits.

2246. Gans, Herbert J. *Deciding What's News: A Study of CBS Evening News, NBC Nightly News, Newsweek and Time*. New York: Pantheon, 1979. How national news organizations since 1965 have worked in deciding what is news: the need for dramatic stories, constraints of formats, journalists' insistence on "professionalism," and the balancing of audience, government, and economic interests. The news has an "upper-middle-class content and tone," and the public has accepted this version as a correct picture of reality. That picture includes individualism, beneficient capitalism, democracy, moderate politics, nationalism, etc. Such views began with the Progressive era and have not been seriously challenged. Progressive reformers and professional journalists share the same view on the dominant American culture, politics, and economics.

2247. Garay, Ronald. *Congressional Television: A Legislative History*. Westport, Conn.: Greenwood, 1984. For 60 years, Congress has debated the establishment and management of broadcast coverage of its proceedings. This straightforward narrative covers the discussions.

2248. Garay, Ron. "Television and the 1951 Senate Crime Committee Hearings." *JOB* 22 (1978): 469-90. The 1951 Kefauver Committee hearings on organized crime "captured the attention of millions, transformed obscure politicians into national figures, and promoted television during the industry's formative years." Television not only gave viewers a first-hand view of the hearings, but transformed news and information into entertainment and drama, and members of the committee into performers.

2249. Garvey, Daniel E. "Secretary Hoover and the Quest for Broadcast Regulation." *JH* 3 (1976): 66-70, 85. Herbert Hoover, as U.S. Secretary of Commerce, 1921-1928, "was a staunch and unceasing advocate of strong federal regulation of broadcasting." (66).

2250. Gates, Gary. *Air Time: The Inside Story of CBS News*. New York: Harper and Row, 1978. This gossipy, behind-the-scenes look at what makes CBS's news operation tick deals with personalities and small controversies rather than significant aspects of operation. CBS anchormen and correspondents influence the news. Murrow had a limited view of how important television could be as an information medium and underestimated its power. CBS was marked by egos and infighting. Gates was a CBS news writer from 1969 to 1973. This book is not a meaningful history.

2251. Godfrey, Donald G. "The 1927 Radio Act: People and Politics." *JH* 4 (1977): 74-78. An account of the people and political dealing that lay behind passage of the act, which led to a number of important actions, including the creation of the Federal Radio Commission and the establishment of standards for broadcasting to operate in the public interest, convenience, and necessity.

2252. Godfrey, Donald G. "Senator Dill and the 1927 Radio Act." *JOB* 23 (1979): 477-89. The actions of Sen. Clarence Dill, co-author of the Radio Act of 1927, "had a permanent impact on radio legislation." This article examines his role in the fight for passage of the act. Confronted by questions of censorship, freedom of speech, and monopoly ownership his Senate committee developed solutions which "set the traditional concepts which are still valid today."

2253. Greb, Gordon B. "The Golden Anniversary of Broadcasting." *JOB* 3 (1958-1959): 3-13. Herrold's Station (begun in 1909) of the Garden City Bank Building in San Jose, Calif., is the world's oldest radio station.

2254. Hammargren, Russell J. "The Origin of Press-Radio Conflict." *JQ* 13 (1936): 91-93. The war between press and radio began "with the formation of chain broadcasting, competition for the national advertising dollar, and sharp focusing of national attention upon the Dodge advertising program of 1928 and the national election of the same year." (91) In 1925-1928 radio began to gain more advertising through radio chain hook-ups. In 1928 the Associated Press paid $250,000 to gather the election news, while national radio networks contracted with more than 125 stations to carry at little cost the results of AP coverage. "Only the national advertiser, under our system of private enterprise, really had the power to finance broadcasting, and when radio began to compete on a national scale for the attention and for the dollar that had previously belonged exclusively to the printed message, the period of press-radio conflict can be said to have begun." (93)

2255. Hammond, Charles Montgomery, Jr. *The Image Decade: Television Documentary, 1965-1975*. New York: Heatings House, 1981. The documentary has made a serious artistic and cultural impact on America. This study, which consider the period since Murrow and Friendly did their work and updates Bluem's study, examines (1) style, context, method, (2) producers, their craft, and their product, (3) problems and accomplishments of the documentary reporter, and (4) events covered by documentary, including Vietnam, urban disorder, and Watergate.

2256. Hayes, Marcus R. "The Influence of Lar Daly in the Congressional Amendments to and the FCC Interpretations of the Communications Act of 1934." Ph.D. dissertation, University of Mississippi, 1986.

2257. Hazard, Patrick D. *Radio Before Television. (Documentary) History of Broadcasting: 1920-1950, Vol. I*. Folkways Records, 1965. Recording of radio broadcasts.

2258. Hemenway, Paul. "Philadelphia Commercial Radio Before and After Deregulation: A Time-Series Case Study of Non-Entertainment Programming in the Nation's Fourth Market." Ph.D. dissertation, Temple University, 1986. After government deregulation of programming in 1985, most radio stations' amount of news and non-entertainment programming declined from levels of 1969-1981.

2259. Hosley, David H. *As Good As Any: Foreign Correspondence on American Radio, 1930-1940*. Westport, Conn.: Greenwood, 1984. This is a history of the origins and development of American radio correspondence in Europe. American correspondents performed well in covering the events leading to and including the early years of World War II despite the fact that they were working under technical constraints.

2260. Howard, Herbert H. "Broadcast Station Group Ownership: A 20th Century Phenomenon." *JH* 2 (1975): 68-71, 83. Multi-station ownership began in the 1920s, shortly after radio moved from amateur status to commercial. "Clearly the group owners are in the best position to lead the broadcasting industry into positive areas of economic productivity and public service. It behooves them to do so in their own self interest as well as for public interest considerations." (83)

2261. Johnson, Glenn A. "Secretary of Commerce Herbert C. Hoover: The First Regulator of American Broadcasting, 1921-1928." Ph.D. dissertation, University of Iowa, 1970. Hoover used several "innovations to achieve stability in a volatile industry. For enforcement, he principally relied on public opinion and industry self-regulation.... Many principles Hoover enunciated were encompassed in the Radio Act of 1927 and later in the Communication Act of 1934."

2262. Kahn, Frank J. *Documents of American Broadcasting*, 4th ed. Englewood Cliffs, N.J.: Prentice-Hall, 1984. Collection of primary source material dealing with public policy and other legal aspects of broadcasting.

2263. Kendrick, Alexander. *Prime Time: The Life of Edward R. Murrow*. Boston: Little, Brown, 1969. Murrow was an outstanding broadcast journalist. He would have made the news even better had it not been for pressure from advertisers and CBS management. Although he was an outstanding war correspondent, he was even more important in building up CBS' stable of correspondents and providing a model for other networks. Indicts contemporary television. By the 1950s, however, the medium Murrow had worked so hard to make great was dying to the ratings race, and even the news documentary was losing its boldness, in contrast to Murrow's works. He grew disillusioned with the commercialization of broadcasting, with its emphasis on meaningless entertainment rather than news in the late 1950s.

2264. Kittross, John M. *A Bibliography of Theses and Dissertations in Broadcasting: 1920-1973*. Washington, D.C.: Broadcast Education Association, 1978. Reference work citing 4,334 theses and dissertations.

2265. Krasnow, Erwin G., Lawrence D. Longley, and Herbert A. Terry. *The Politics of Broadcast Regulation*, 3rd ed. New York: St. Martin's, 1982. Uses five case studies to analyze broadcasting regulation, its origins, Congress' role in regulation, and the factors that influence it.

2266. Lashner, Marilyn A. *The Chilling Effect in TV News: Intimidation by the Nixon White House*. New York: Praeger, 1984. The Nixon administration used a wide range of tactics to intimidate television journalism, diminishing its freedom and willingness to report.

2267. LeShay, Steven V. "So Long Until Tomorrow, Lowell." *MHD* 3, 1 (1983): 60-63. Biography and adventures of Lowell Thomas.

2268. Levin, Harvey J. *Broadcast Regulation and Joint Ownership of Media.* New York: New York University Press, 1960. Historical survey of the inter-relationship of the mass media's economic structure, emphasizing radio's impact on the newspaper industry and resulting joint ownership. There has been a steady trend toward monopoly ownership (group- and newspaper-owned broadcast media) and control of the mass media. Newspapers often buy broadcast media to protect their newspapers (with their great financial investment) from competition. The FCC shows favoritism to media owners or has lost control in regulating ownership.

2269. Lichty, Lawrence W. "The Night at the End of the Tunnel: How Television Reported the End of the Indochina War." *FC* 11, 4 (1975): 32ff. Television gave strong images and straight information but little needed interpretation as the Vietnam war drew to a close.

2270. Lichty, Lawrence W., and Thomas W. Bohn. "Radio's 'March of Time': Dramatized News." *JQ* 51 (1974): 458-62. "March of Time" (1930s) was "the prototype of many broadcast programs -- dramatic and documentary, fact and fiction -- that followed." This narrative is told within the context of the developmental history of radio news programs.

2271. Lichty, Lawrence W., and David J. Leroy. "Missing the Newscaster: Reactions to the 1967 AFTRA Strike." *JOB* 16 (1972): 175-84. The strike of network anchormen, who were replaced by substitutes, had little effect on viewing habits.

2272. Lichty, Lawrence W., and Malachi C. Topping. *American Broadcasting: A Source Book on the History of Radio and Television.* New York: Hastings House, 1975. This collection of articles includes works on the following topics: (1) technical (wireless, Marconi, 1876-1920, wireless telephone, super-heterodyne, television to 1930s, magnetic recording, color television), (2) stations (KDKA, oldest, first, pioneer, FM development, etc.), (3) networks (programming, 1923-1926, first CBS program, CBS, chain broadcasting, Mutual, Liberty, Dumont), (4) economics (radio and advertising, who is to pay for broadcasting, costs, broadcast economics, competition), (5) employment (careers), (6) programming (opera, radio drama, "March of Time," entertainment, World War II, soap operas, radio mystery theatre, television programming, Top 40, game shows, news), (7) audiences (interests and attitudes), and (8) regulation (Radio Act of 1927, censorship, Brinkley, FCC, FRC, etc.).

2273. Liebovich, Louis. "H.V. Kaltenborn and the Origins of the Cold War: A Study in Personal Expression in Radio." *JH* 14 (1987).

2274. Long, Stewart L. "A Fourth Television Network and Diversity: Some Historical Evidence." *JQ* 56 (1979): 341-45. The demise of the DuMont network in the 1950s decreased the diversity of programming.

2275. Lorenz, Lawrence. "Truman and the Broadcaster." *JOB* 13 (1968-1969): 17-22. The origin of the presidential broadcast news conference dates to Harry Truman.

Although the news conference had been used by Theodore Roosevelt, conferences were not broadcast until Truman. This article looks at the developments of the conference during Truman's administrations. By 1952 the conference had become established, to the benefit of both the president and the public.

2276. Lott, George E. "The Press-Radio War of the 1930s." *JOB* 14 (1970): 275-86. The cause of the war was the "finite number of dollars being spent on advertising in all media." (276) Because of the concern for getting advertising, little attention was paid to the public interest and welfare. "[R]adio's challenge in the area of news represented the first serious challenge made against the printed media. They had not met such a challenge before, and they were not prepared for it when it came. That radio was delivering the news faster than newspapers, that radio was making money doing this, and that the public obviously wanted radio to perform this service, were all bitter pills for the publishers to swallow. In the end, however, positions of social usefulness for both parties were carved out, and the press and the radio may well have become stronger as a result." (285) Broadcast journalism emerged as a result of the war. While radio was not entirely blameless, the primary fault lay with newspapers for the problems and for the war itself.

2277. Lyons, Eugene. *David Sarnoff: A Biography*. New York: Harper and Row, 1966. Sarnoff played a leading role in the major developments in wireless communications and broadcasting. He was central to the growth of RCA and the technological and commercial development of broadcasting. "From the very beginning Sarnoff's expectations for broadcasting were high pitched and idealist; perhaps romantic. His first sketch of the Music Box, years before its advent, listed sports and other popular titillations among the gifts it would bring into simple homes. But his emphasis was on education, good music, fine theatre, the improved functioning of democracy," and on broadcasting as helping creative talents.

2278. MacDonald, J. Fred. *Don't Touch That Dial: Radio Programming in American Life From 1920 to 1960*. Chicago: Nelson-Hall, 1979. Radio in the "Golden Age" reflected a "commercial democracy and the character of the people who made it work." Network radio "bound together the American people as had no single commercial medium since the printing press." In popular culture, broadcasting was important in the lives of most Americans and was a reflector and creator of popular values, attitudes, fantasies and realities. Radio started "the most important development in 20th Century reporting, broadcast journalism." By the mid-1950s radio news achievements had laid the foundation for greater accomplishments in television, and broadcast news became one of the most critical factors in modern American freedom and democracy. The American social-cultural environment has determined the nature of radio programming. Some critics might call the commercial nature of radio programming a shortcoming, and radio programming was indeed geared to business' advertising needs. But programming simply reflected the capitalistic nature of the American economy and society. In the absence of workable alternative methods of financing, "the development of American radio as a commercialized medium was inevitable." Most radio programming was aimed at the lowest common cultural denominator, but in a nation dominated by middle class and democratic values, such an approach to programming was understandable. "The nature of popular culture in American society" is such that "it functions to improve and stabilize society, not to undermine its operative value system."

2279. MacDonald, J. Fred. *Television and the Red Menace: The Video Road to Vietnam*.

New York: Praeger, 1985. "[Y]ears of misrepresentation on television actually led the American public toward" the Vietnam war. Beginning in the 1940s, American television "fed the nation a powerful menu of propagandized, persuasive programming" and "heightened militaristic values and lavished praise on the American military establishment." Therefore, when the United States made its early military commitments in Vietnam, the American public accepted them.

2280. Mander, Mary S. "The Public Debate About Broadcasting in the Twenties: An Interpretive History." *JOB* 28 (1984): 167-85. In the debates over the Radio Act of 1927, "a market model prevailed....Thus, the habits of industrial capitalism, a form of government in which commerce takes precedence over the social well-being of the community, made it unavoidable that economics [would] determine the future use and social development of broadcasting in the United States." (184-85)

2281. Matusow, Barbara. *The Evening Stars: The Rise of the Network News Anchors.* Houghton Mifflin, 1983. This is primarily a criticism of the superficiality of television news, but it does provide some historical background. "What of the anchor who turns out to be lacking in personal integrity? What is to stop him if, in the quest for higher ratings or personal aggrandizement, he sensationalizes the news or ignores dull but vital stories for fear of driving viewers away? The sobering reality is that very little can be done?" Anchors have become too powerful, with too much control over news content. Selection of anchors is based too much on appeal rather than journalistic ability.

2282. McCombs, Maxwell E. "Negro Use of Television and Newspapers for Political Information, 1952-1964." *JOB* 12 (1968): 261-66. From 1952 to 1964 Negro participation in the political process increased. One reason might be increased Negro use of media as a result of the development of television.

2283. McKerns, Joseph P. "Industry Skeptics and Radio Regulation in the 1920s." *JH* 3 (1976): 128-131, 136. The radio industry withheld its support of the Federal Radio Act of 1927 "until a bill was offered which guaranteed its interests." However, without the legal security the act gave to broadcasting, broadcasting might "not have survived its formative years in the 1920s." (136).

2284. McMahon, Robert Sears. *Federal Regulation of the Radio and Television Broadcast Industry in the United States, 1927-1959.* New York: Arno, 1979. The FCC failed to become an effective guardian of the public's interest, as it was charged to do by requiring radio and television to operate in the public interest, convenience, and necessity in its first 25 years. One problem was that after Congress initially gave the FCC broad powers, Congress consistently refused to give it adequate support in setting more specific standards. On the other hand, the FCC did not wish to battle the giants and therefore failed to adequately oversee the industry.

2285. Meehan, Eileen R. "Critical Theorizing on Broadcast History." *JOB* 30 (1986): 393-411. Historians have used structuralism, institutionalism, and instrumentalism in explaining broadcasting history. By combining various perspectives, "the resulting theoretical synthesis should generate more adequate accounts of and more sufficient causal explanations for the events that shaped and continue to shape broadcasting." (409)

2286. Metz, Robert. *CBS, Reflections in a Bloodshot Eye.* New York: Playboy, 1975.

Popular, sketchily researched narrative covers trivial and well-known stories, emphasizing personalities, money, power, intrigue, censorship, corporate success. The heroes are Murrow, Cronkite, Archie Bunker, Tommy Smothers; the enemies, McCarthy, CBS censors, prejudiced viewers, and occasionally William S. Paley and Frank Stanton. This account provides an inside look at programming, pressures that Nixon applied to CBS, payola scandals, etc. The main character is Paley, a genius in television programming who made CBS very successful. He was almost ruthless in building CBS and thought no one indispensable. News programming succeeded only against opposition from some executives and finally through the personal efforts of Murrow and Friendly.

2287. Metz, Robert. *The Today Show: An Inside Look at 25 Tumultuous Years...and the Colorful and Controversial People Behind the Scenes*. Chicago: Playboy, 1977. Gossipy anecdotes about the people involved with network television's longest-running program.

2288. Michael, Rudolph D. "History and Criticism of Press-Radio Relationships." *JQ* 15 (1938): 178-184, 220. Narrative history of newspaper attitudes toward radio from 1922 to 1938, including competition, use of news, AP regulations, newspaper ownership of stations, etc.

2289. Murray, Michael. "Research in Broadcasting: An Overview of Major Resource Centers." *AJ* 1, 2 (1984): 77-80. Reference guide to collections of broadcasting material useful to the historian.

2290. Murray, Michael D. "Television's Desperate Moment: A Conversation with Fred W. Friendly." *JH* 1 (1974): 68-71. Interview.

2291. Nielsen, Ted. "A History of Network News," in Lichty and Topping (see above), 421-44. "In the development of network television news [1937-1974], most of the advances have been brought about by the necessity of providing daily, visual reports of what is happening." (421)

2292. O'Connor, John E., ed. *American History/American Television: Interpreting the Video Past*. New York: Ungar, 1983. Collection of 15 essays, including an introduction, on news and entertainment by political, social, and cultural historians viewing "television both as a force in recent history and as a medium for scholarly research." (ix) "[I]n a very real sense, *television is American Culture*....At least for the vast majority of Americans -- people who may never attend a play or a concert, visit a museum, or read a book -- TV is all there is." (xiv)

2293. Orbison, Charley. "'Fighting Bob' Shuler: Early Radio Crusader." *JOB* 21 (1977): 459-72. In the 1920s, California minister Bob Shuler "considered it his responsibility to expose sin and corruption in the wicked city of Los Angeles." He used his broadcasts to do so, and the FCC revoked his radio license.

2294. Osgood, Dick. *Wyxie Wonderland: An Unauthorized 50-year Diary of WXYZ Detroit*. Bowling Green, Ohio: Bowling Green University Popular Press, 1981. History of the rise and decline of various aspects of radio, written by a staff member who had worked for WXYZ for 36 years.

2295. Paley, William S. *As it Happened*. Garden City, N.J.: Doubleday, 1979. Personal account of the achievements of CBS, with Paley as the hero.

2296. Powers, Ron. *The Newscasters: The News Business as Show Business*. New York: St. Martin's, 1977. To get higher ratings, television executives from the 1960s to 1977 steadily debased their local newscasts by using marketing principles to determine what viewers wanted to see, thus pushing news in the direction of show business. This was contrary to the best approach that American journalism normally has used: "mining areas that the public did not know even existed" (such as Watergate, Pentagon Papers, Tweed Ring, etc.). The role of the journalist is to decide what the audience needs, rather than what it wants.

2297. Price, Tom. *Radio Program Timelines, 1920-1980*. Salinas, Calif.: Author, 1980. Reference work.

2298. Pusateri, C. Joseph. "FDR, Huey Long and the Politics of Radio." *JOB* 21 (1977): 85-95. Politics played an important role in the case of the Federal Radio Commission's 1934 decision allocating a highly desirable channel to one of two competing Louisiana radio stations, thus showing that the FRC was susceptible to political pressure.

2299. Rader, Benjamin G. *In Its Own Image: How Television Has Transformed Sports*. New York: Free Press, 1984. Television has had a major impact on the nature of sports since the late 1940s.

2300. Reinsch, J. Leonard. "Broadcasting the Political Conventions." *JOB* 12 (1968): 219-23. Reinsch was a network employee who worked with convention coverage. This article defends television against the charge that it changed conventions. It was only one of a number of factors which historically have affected conventions (such as the railroad and telegraph).

2301. Riggs, Frank L. "The Changing Role of Radio." *JOB* 8 (1964): 331-40. The story of how how radio content developed from 1948 to what it was in 1964. The trend was toward talk shows and away from complete domination by music. The trend was a result of radio's environment: primarily, television providing entertainment and the audience's need for information.

2302. Robinson, Thomas Porter. *Radio Networks and the Federal Government*. New York: Columbia University Press, 1943. History of the legal relationship of the government and broadcasting with particular emphasis on network broadcasting.

2303. Rollins, Peter C. "Television's Vietnam: The Visual Language of Television News." *JAC* 4 (1981): 114-35. Describes the research behind the documentary "Television's Vietnam."

2304. Rose, Ernest D. "How the U.S. Heard about Pearl Harbor." *JOB* 5 (1961): 285-98. Americans heard on radio that they were at war. Although imperfect, the reports helped shape the nation's attitude and world events. "[W]ords which are uttered at the very outset of any cataclysmic event...not only reveal much about the speaker but they frequently mold an impression which remains in an audience's memory even after the initial pattern of communication changes. What kinds of things happened to our news communication under conditions of extreme surprise, complete emotional involvement, and little first hand information?" (285) The reporting of Pearl Harbor was often inaccurate, there was confusion about what should be withheld for the common good, there was misinterpretation and even deliberate falsification, and there was a preference for "what could be" over the reality of "what is." For a better job of reporting under such circumstances, there needs to be more "responsibility" and more "wisdom." "[H]ow to update the democratic handling of communications in a modern world is an inseparable part of our battle for survival." (298)

2305. Rosen, Philip T. *The Modern Stentors: Radio Broadcasters and the Federal Government, 1920-1934*. Westport, Conn.: Greenwood, 1980. This is an examination of the developing years of broadcasting, especially the formulation of radio regulation, emergence of broadcasting as a significant communications medium, and growth as solid business enterprise. "But for the particular interplay during the crucial years 1920 to 1934 among businessmen in the nascent industry, the prospective market, politics, and bureaucrats" the broadcasting system might have been very different. Broadcasting might have developed into a state-run system like the BBC, or without the Navy's input, it might not have developed at all. Although radio had perhaps as great consequences as any technical development in modern America, it at first lacked the regulation and standardization needed for development in an orderly manner. The regulation has served to benefit radio for half a century.

2306. Rowland, John A. "A Sociological Analysis of Radio as a Form of Mass Communication in American Life." Ph.D. dissertation, University of Pittsburgh, 1948.

2307. Rowland, Willard D., Jr. "The Illusion of Fulfillment: The Broadcast Reform Movement." *JM* 79 (1982). The attempts of citizen groups to reform and gain greater access to broadcasting from the 1950s to the 1970s met with mixed results.

2308. Rubin, Richard L. *Press, Party, and Presidency*. New York: Norton, 1981. Television has had a major impact on the political system, including helping erode the party structure and making presidents and candidates become more concerned about popularity than about long-term policy. A familiar overview (based on secondary sources) of the history of the press and politics precedes the discussion of television.

2309. Schement, Jorge Reina, and Ricardo Hores. "The Origins of Spanish-Language Radio: The Case of San Antonio, Texas." *JH* 4 (1977): 56-58, 61. This story of the development and growth of KCOR is an attempt "to partially describe some of the unique factors contributing to the growth of Spanish-language radio stations in the United States." Those factors include problems with advertising because advertisers were reluctant to invest in Spanish advertising because they weren't convinced Chicanos had enough income, the search for effective programming, obtaining trained personnel, and gathering news (a problem which was solved by reading the newspaper).

2310. Schroeder, Morton Richard. "The History of WBAP-TV, The First Ten Years, 1948-1957." Ed.D. dissertation, East Texas State University, 1983. Narrative history of the Fort Worth station, which in 1948 originated the first local television news program.

2311. Schubert, Paul. *The Electric Word: The Rise of Radio*. New York: Macmillan, 1928. Survey of American governmental and technical developments and the importance of economic factors before 1928.

2312. Scroggins, Donald. "The Origins and Development of Public Radio in Tennessee, 1949-1980." Ph.D. dissertation, University of Tennessee, 1981. "[H]istorical account of the development of the six public radio stations in the state," some of which had a serious commitment to news and public affairs.

2313. Severin, Werner J. "Commercial vs. Non-Commercial Radio During Broadcasting's Early Years." *JOB* 22 (1978): 491-504. Radio was primarily an educational medium before World War I, when agricultural schools broadcast useful information over experimental stations. These stations were forced off the spectrum of frequencies, however, beginning in 1920 with the growth of commercial broadcasting. The number of educational stations was cut in half (from 94 to 47) from 1927 to 1931. Commercial broadcasters wanted and got their frequencies.

2314. Sharp, Harry, Jr.. "Live from Washington: The Telecasting of President Kennedy's News Conferences." *JOB* 13 (1968-1969): 23-32. Kennedy's opening his news conferences in 1960 to simultaneous coverage by radio and television was an "historic decision." This article describes the making of the decision and how government and the press reacted to it.

2315. Shaw, Charles. "A CBS War Correspondent Remembers: Death in the Afternoon." *MHD* 1, 2 (1981): 16-21. First-person recollection of the death of Tom Treanor, the only broadcast correspondent killed in World War II.

2316. Shelby, Maurice E. "John R. Brinkley and the *Kansas City Star*." *JOB* 22 (1978): 33-45. The *Star* waged "one of the most intense newspaper attacks ever...against a single individual in the history of American journalism." Most historians have claimed the attack was motivated by the *Star's* financial desire to get rid of competition. "The *Star* waged a highly emotional, often irrational campaign against Brinkley. Although the *Star* has been accused of non-altruism by some of its critics, no documentary evidence has been uncovered to substantiate claims that the newspaper engaged in the campaign more for its own private gain rather than the public interest. The high-handed tactics used by the *Star*, however, contributed little towards quelling suspicions." (43) What impact the *Star* had is difficult to determine.

2317. Skiers, George. "Television 50 Years Ago." *JOB* 19 (1975): 387-400. This article recounts the developments, technology, and personalities involved in experiments with television 1926. John Logie Baird, an Englishman, developed a system of "whirling disks and spinning mirror drums and other electro-mechanical methods" which allowed him to produce "real television" in 1925.

2318. Slate, Sam J., and Joe Cook. *It Sounds Impossible*. Macmillan, 1963. Informal account of the early days of radio, with an emphasis on "firsts," personalities, and anecdotes.

2319. Smith, F. Leslie. "Education for Broadcasting: 1929-1963." *JOB* 8 (1964): 383-98. The growth of education has coincided with the growth of broadcasting as a profession. "[B]roadcasting education has generally managed to follow the trends and needs of the industry. The first radio course was offered within a decade of the beginnings of that industry. And as the infant radio/broadcasting industry grew to great and influential proportions, Radio Speech grew into a major in Radio. When commercial broadcasters criticized the products sent them by the colleges, the colleges responded by gradually upgrading their level of instruction, quality of equipment, and competence of instructors. As the network broadcasting industry concentrated on television and the nature of radio changed markedly, the major became Radio and Television or simply Broadcasting. Education and industry now work together....The future of the major and its curriculum can, therefore, best be predicted in terms of the future of the broadcasting industry. (394-95)

2320. Smith, F. Leslie. "'Selling of the Pentagon' and the First Amendment." *JH* 2 (1975): 2-5, 14. Although an effort to have Congress cite CBS for contempt for not providing outtakes of film for the program, press freedom suffered because CBS delayed in resisting government efforts; and precedents for government investigation and efforts were set.

2321. Smith, F. Leslie. *Perspectives on Radio and Television: Telecommunication in the United States*, 2nd ed. New York: Harper & Row, 1985. This textbook offers some historical interpretation.

2322. Smith, R. Franklin. *Edward R. Murrow -- The War Years*. Kalamazoo: New Issues Press, 1978. This biography covers Murrow's role as a war correspondent and his development as a novice, young reporter and analyst into a seasoned and leading newsman. While he had good presentation, he was primarily interested in content and had a natural instinct for news.

2323. Smith, R. Franklin. "'Oldest Station in the Nation'?." *JOB* 4 (1959-1960): 40-55. This study proposes criteria by which to judge claims that particular radio stations are the oldest or were the first, attempting to formulate a workable definition of the term "broadcasting station." WHA, which sometimes has been cited as the first, was not the first.

2324. Smith, Ralph Lewis. *A Study of Professional Criticism of Broadcasting in the United States 1920-1955*. New York: Arno, 1979. A study of the ideas and perspectives of selected broadcasting critics, including the background and nature of criticism, program genres, advertising, and the effects of criticisms.

2325. Smith, Robert. "The Origins of Radio Network News Commentary." *JOB* 9 (1965): 113-22. News commentary began in the 1930s, not during World War II as most historians have argued. The development of news commentary was related to social and political developments of the 1930s. Commentary was encouraged by the emergence of early radio news personalities such as Kaltenborn, the press-radio war of the 1930s, political and gossip columns in newspapers, and the advent of World War II. This article considers the various factors producing the development of commentary.

2326. Spaulding, John W. "1928: Radio Becomes a Mass Advertising Medium." *JOB* 8 (1963-1964): 31-44. In the late 1920s broadcast facilities, audiences, programs, and station owner attitudes were right for the national advertiser to enter radio sponsorship in a serious way. Radio had not done much to service advertisers until 1928, although the first commercials were run in 1922. To serve effectively as an advertising medium, radio had to have the technical facilities for broadcasting and receiving, an audience of considerable size was needed, broadcasters had to accept advertisers as partners in producing programs, and radio stations had to provide programs as appropriate formats. These were accomplished in 1928.

2327. Sperber, Ann M. *Murrow: His Life and Times*. New York: Freundlich, 1986. This biography, which won the Kappa Tau Alpha research award, emphasizes Murrow's professional career, from the development of radio news in the 1930s, through World War II, into television news in the 1950s, the documentaries of the 1960s, and the various controversies about broadcast journalism in which Murrow was involved.

2328. Stelzner, Sara L. "A Qualitative Content Analysis of Regional and Nationally Broadcast Speeches of Eisenhower and Stevenson in the 1952 Presidential Campaign." Ph.D. dissertation, University of Illinois, 1958.

2329. Sterling, Christopher H. "Newspaper Ownership of Broadcast Stations, 1920-1968." *JQ* 46 (1969): 227-236, 254. A straightforward account of the legal challenges to newspaper publishers holding broadcast licenses, along with the arguments for and against such cross-ownership.

2330. Sterling, Christopher, and John Kittross. *Stay Tuned: A Concise History of American Broadcasting*. Belmont, Calif.: Wadsworth, 1978. This narrative history of the development of broadcasting (1920 to 1977) covers broadcasting's origins (1920-1926), commercialization (1926-1933), technology, stations, networks, educational broadcasting, advertising, programming, audiences, regulation, foreign developments. The emphasis is on basic events and developments, and the purpose is to show how broadcasting reached the present.

2331. Straight, Michael. *Trial By Television*. New York: Devon Press, 1979. Essays on events observed by the author from the 1930s to the 1950s, including the 1954 Army-McCarthy Hearings, during which television emerged as a resource for democracy.

2332. Swing, Raymond. *Good Evening: A Professional Memoir*. Harcourt, Brace, World, 1964. Autobiography of one of the first radio commentators.

2333. Tebbel, John. *David Sarnoff: Putting Electrons to Work*. Encyclopedia Britannica, 1964. This biography of the RCA founder is aimed at a youthful audience.

2334. Tenney, Craig. "The 1943 Debate on Opinionated Broadcast News." *JH* 7 (1980): 11-15. The evolution of broadcast news philosophy began with the CBS news rule that stories carry no personal opinions or editorial comment. In the dispute between news director Paul W. White and Cecil B. Brown, nationally-known news analyst, White contended that Brown had editorialized in a 1943 broadcast, contrary to the CBS rule and the 1941 "Mayflower" decision. He argued that "a limited spectrum imposed non-editorializing responsibilities on broadcasters." Sponsors exerted pressure on CBS, and Brown was forced to resign. The episode provided no solution to the central questions of the nature of news analysis and opinion. However, today personal opinions are labeled as commentary, and newscasters on straight news shows are not to express their opinions.

2335. Thomas, Lowell. *Good Evening, Everybody*. New York: Morrow, 1976. Light, entertaining autobiography detailing Thomas' adventures covering news around the world.

2336. Thomson, Charles A.H. *Television and Presidential Politics: The Experience in 1952 and the Problems Ahead*. Washington: Brookings Institute, 1956. This study summarizes the relationship between television and politics in 1952 and provids a detailed analysis of the 1952 campaign. However, it offers no conclusions, thesis, generalization, or answers.

2337. Udelson, Joseph. *The Great Television Race: A History of the American Television Industry, 1925-1941*. Tuscaloosa: University of Alabama Press, 1982. This study focuses on the history of television technology: survey of research, experiments, and telecasting prior to 1941, when commercial television was authorized. Commercial television constitutes a unified system, composed of interconnected engineering, programming, and marketing.

2338. Ward, Hiley H. "Radio's Father Coughlin: A Last Interview." MHD 1, 1 (1981): 32-35, 62. Brief collection of Coughlin's reflections, taken from a 1978 interview, on various political topics.

2339. Weeks, Lewis Elton. "Order Out of Chaos: The Formative Years of American Broadcasting, 1920-1927." Ph.D. dissertation, Michigan State University, 1962. "The formative years of American broadcasting were 1920 to 1927. Events which occurred in those years from the lifting of the ban imposed on radio during World War I until the Radio Act was passed in 1927 set the pattern for American broadcasting for the future." Events included coast-to-coast broadcasting, political convention broadcasts, multi-station hookups, network broadcasting, the emergence of advertising as the means to finance broadcasting, the formation of NBC, and government regulation.

2340. Weeks, Lewis E. "The Radio Election of 1924." *JOB* 8 (1964): 233-43. Radio "grew up" during the 1924 campaign. "The radio campaign of 1924 was of significance because it introduced new techniques in political campaigning, and because it served as a proving ground for the interconnection of radio stations by wire and short wave for the purpose of nation-wide broadcasting. By 1928, when the Hoover-Smith contest took place, the major parties had accepted radio as a major campaigning tool. AT&T and Westinghouse made use of the broadcasting of political talks of the 1924 campaign to perfect techniques for coast-to-coast radio transmission. AT&T did outstanding work in the interconnection of stations by long distance telephone wires; Westinghouse linked the East to the Pacific coast by short wave. Certainly these accomplishments would have come about in time, but the stimulus of using radio as a medium of political campaigning in 1924 probably brought about the advances sooner than could have been expected without the radio election." (242-43) The campaign probably benefited radio more than it did politics.

2341. Wesolowski, James Walter. "Before Canon 35: WGN Broadcasts the Monkey Trial." *JH* 2 (1975): 76-79, 86. Radio coverage had an impact on the Scopes trial. Since this was the first time radio had covered a trial, participants and officials had no precedents by which to determine their practices.

2342. White, Melvin R. "History of Radio Regulation Affecting Program Policy." Ph.D. dissertation, University of Wisconsin, 1949.

2343. Wiebe, Gerhart D. "An Historical Setting for Television Journalism." *JOB* 1 (1956): 33-38. Television has operated in a "pattern" that "might be described as the continuing competition and compromise between the idea of simple democracy and the practical necessity of republican delegation of authority." (33) Since television is important in the context of political democracy, key considerations are citizen participation and the question of whether officials who have power over broadcasting can be trusted to use it for the common good. Television seems to be a means by which officials can present their ideas to the public, who have clamored to participate in making political decisions but who prefer only to be spectators.

2344. Wik, Reynold. "The Radio in Rural America during the 1920s." *AgH* 55 (October 1981): 339-50. Radio influenced rural culture. "The radio was of profound importance for the American people because it opened their ears to the sounds of the world and provided a medium which became an instrument for social change....Rural Americans may have benefited the most from radio because they were the most isolated and had the most to gain from an improved communication system....[T]he farmer's main interests were practical [such as needing] the daily weather forecasts to help protect his property and to help in the management of his affairs." (340-41) Stations early on began broadcasting weather reports and commodity market reports and running advertising.

2345. Wilam, Lorenzo Wilson. *The Radio Papers From RAB to KCHU.* San Diego: Mho & Mho Works, 1986. Wilam established listener-supported radio stations in the 1960s and 1970s. His purpose was to provide a "voice of reason in a broadcast band otherwise garish and ugly with commercialism and rank anti-intellectualism." This book is a collection of essays he broadcast over his stations.

2346. Wilbur, Susan K. "The History of Television in Los Angeles, 1931-1952." *SCQ* 60 (1978): 59-76, 183-205, 255-85. This three-part series details the major episodes in the development of L.A. television, including television's relationship with other media in the area, "the boom years" of 1947-1952, programs, audiences, the FCC "freeze" on the construction of new stations from 1948 to 1952, industry growth, competition among the city's seven stations in the early 1950s, and the impact on network programming, especially the decline in the importance of local programming.

2347. Will, Thomas E. *Telecommunications Structure and Management in the Executive Branch of Government, 1900-1970.* Boulder, Colo: Westview, 1978. The U.S. government played an important role in the formulation of broadcast regulation. This study includes major items such as the Radio Act of 1927, Communications Act of 1934, technological advances, telecommunications advisors to U.S. presidents from 1951 to 1967, the creation of President's Task Force in 1967 to deal with problems stemming from the limited radio spectrum, and the motives behind the telecommunications policy of the Nixon administration.

2348. Williams, Robert. "The Politics of American Broadcasting: Public Purposes and Private Interests." *JAS* 10 (1976): 329-40. In the history of government regulation, a "gulf...has developed between the 'theory' and the practice of broadcast regulation." Since regulation began in the 1920s the theory (that "the airwaves are assumed to be in the public domain and to be used for the public interest") has differed from reality. In practice, "broadcasters are pretty much free to pursue their private interests without fear of government controls." During the half-century of regulation, the actions of Congress have been largely responsible for this situation.

2349. Williamson, Mary E. "Judith Cary Waller: Chicago Broadcasting Pioneer." *JH* 3 (1976): 111-15. Biographical narrative of Waller's success as manager of WMAQ since 1922.

2350. Winfield, Betty Houchin, and Lois B. DeFleur, eds. *The Edward R. Murrow Heritage: Challenge for the Future*. Ames: Iowa State University Press, 1986. Collection of essays and abstracts of proceedings of a 1983 Murrow Symposium at Washington State University looking at Murrow's career and contributions.

2351. Wollert, James A., and Michael O. Wirth. "UHF Television Program Performance: Continuing Questions on Spectrum Use." *JH* 56 (1979): 346-52. UHF stations have less news and public affairs programming than VHF stations. Because of the problems confronting UHF, it has not been successful.

2352. Wuliger, Gregory Tod. "The Fairness Doctrine in Its Historical Context: A Symbolic Approach." Ph.D. dissertation, University of Illinois, 1987. The Fairness Doctrine is a "symbol closely related to such broad general myths as 'freedom of expression,' 'free enterprise,' and 'the marketplace of ideas.'" Such symbols have no objective reality. The Fairness Doctrine has been ineffective.

2353. Yaeger, Murray R. "The Evolution of See It Now." *JOB* 1 (1956): 337-44. Narrative of the development and history of the "See It Now" television program: where the idea came from, its radio background, changes, etc.

15

The Contemporary Media, 1945–Present

2354. Adler, Renate. *Reckless Disregard: Westmoreland v. CBS et al.; Sharon v. Time*. New York: Knopf, 1986. The two libel cases brought by Gen. Westmoreland and Ariel Sharon demonstrated the excesses and irresponsiblity of the media. They turned into "legal...shams" because of the provocative, dishonest, and intimidating tactics employed by CBS' and *Time's* legal counsel.

2355. Agee, Warren K. "Cross-Channel Ownership of Communication Media." *JQ* 26 (1949): 410-16. Chains which link newspapers, radio, and television are replacing newspaper chains. The proportion of radio stations owned by newspapers has dropped, while newspaper ownership of television stations has increased. This study provides no explanation, just a straightforward listing of figures.

2356. Alexander, Holmes. *Never Lose a War: Memoirs and Observations of a National Columnist.*. Greenwich, Conn.: Devin-Adair, 1984. Memoirs of the "Dean of Conservative Columnists."

2357. Altschull, J. Herbert. "Khrushchev and the Berlin 'Ultimatum': The Jackal Syndrome and the Cold War." *JQ* 54 (1977): 545-51. This article questions the reliability of newspapers as sources of historical data. The New York *Times* incorrectly interpreted the motive and events surrounding the 1958 ultimatum. Historians, relying on the *Times* as an accurate source of information, also have misinterpreted the situation.

2358. Anderson, Douglas A. "The Muckraking Books of Pearson, Allen, and Anderson." *AJ* 2 (1985): 5-21. The muckraking spirit of the Progressive reformers was rekindled in the books of Drew Pearson, Robert S. Allen, and Jack Anderson. The three authors of the "Washington Merry-Go-Round" column used books written from the 1930s to the 1960s "to air their concerns and philosophies about the governmental, societal, and business issues that permeate American life." (17)

2359. Anderson, Fenwick. "Bricks Without Straw: The Mirage of Competition in the Desert of Phoenix Daily Journalism Since 1947." Ph.D. Dissertation, University of Illinois, 1980.

2359.1. Anderson, Fenwick. "Inadequate to Prevent the Present: *The American Mercury* at 50." *JQ* 51 (1974): 297-302, 382. Founded by H.L. Mencken and George Jean Nathan in 1924 to ridicule the attitudes and values of the middle class, the magazine was sold a number of times to publishers who tried to make it succeed financially. By the 1950s it had sunk "into the quicksand of right-wing extremism." (297)

2359.2. Anderson, Fenwick. "Last Flight of the Phoenix: The Short Life of *The Atlanta Times.*" *Atlanta History* 31 (1987).

2360. Anderson, Jack, and James Boyd. *Confessions of a Muckraker: The Inside Story of Life in Washington during the Truman, Eisenhower, Kennedy and Johnson Years.* New York: Random House, 1980. Autobiography of Anderson covering 1947 to 1969 and emphasizing his investigative and muckraking techniques, with much material on Drew Pearson, for whom "nothing produce[d] so much exhilaration, zest for daily life, and all-around gratification as protracted, ugly, bitter-end vendetta that rages for years and exhausts both sides, often bringing one to ruin." Although this book is favorable of Anderson, it reveals his frequently questionable practices.

2361. Aronson, James. *The Press and the Cold War.* Indianapolis. Bobbs-Merrill, 1970. A liberal, anti-conservative, anti-establishment, anti-government critique of what has happened to American media since World War II. The press helped to lead the nation into accepting a quarter century of the Cold War, with the awfulness that ensued. "An alternative press can help dismantle the Cold War and lead the nation into accepting its place in the family of man." This study recounts how American newspapers have treated various episodes in some of America's most critical periods since the Russian Bolsheviks' withdrawal from World War I in 1918. Growing military, private, and government bureaucracies have inserted themselves into the information transmission process. The press has played a major supporting and sometimes initiating role in accepting or promoting without seriously questioning government actions such as McCarthyism, the imperialistic role of the U.S., internal attacks on socialists, liberals, and Marxists, the Bay of Pigs, the CIA's influence, and the Vietnam debacle. The government manages news. The press aids reactionary efforts by the government. The government, in league with giant economic interests, attempts to promote the status quo. People who control the press have the same interests as the establishment. The press has given up its role of independent analysis and criticism. "Despite my grave doubt that the press of the country is willing to reform itself, I believe that there is in the United States a company of honest journalists of all ages, conscious of the potential power of an informed people, who will never give up the effort to establish an honorable communications network."

2362. Atwater, Tony. "Editorial Policy of *Ebony* Before and After the Civil Rights Act of 1964." *JQ* 59 (1982): 87-91. *Ebony's* coverage of civil rights increased after passage of the 1964 law. The photo-editorial was its main means of advocacy. "The civil rights era of the 1960s shook the American conscience. Accompanying the racial conflict of this period was a revolutionary growth in black consciousness -- from a state of self-pity to a state of self-pride. Expansion of the black middle class resulted in what some historians have called a black 'mass culture.' The black press of the 1960s mirrored this phenomenon. One publication, in particular, was aimed at raising black consciousness in America. *Ebony* mirrored the development of the black community; its drawing cards were 'success' and 'black pride.'" (87) This study of *Ebony* content in two years preceding the Civil Rights Act and two years after analyzes whether its editorial content reflected greater emphasis on civil rights after and whether *Ebony* served as an advocate during the civil rights era of the 1960s. The answer is yes to both questions.

2363. Bagdikian, Ben. *The Media Monopoly.* Boston: Beacon, 1983. Since 1960, corporations have gained such large ownership in the media that 50 of them "control what America sees, hears and reads....For the first time in the history of American journalism, news and public information have been integrated formally into the highest levels of financial and nonjournalistic corporate control." Because of the concern about profits, mass advertising exercises a profound influence on the media, and the media have less concern about the underprivileged and other social problems.

2364. Baker, Richard. "Games Others Play." *Forbes* 7 (May 19, 1986): 144-51. Donald Reynolds, owner of the Donrey Media Group, is the last sole owner of a major newspaper chain.

2365. Baldasty, Gerald J., and Betty Houchin Winfield. "Institutional Paralysis in the Press: The Cold War in Washington State." *JQ* 58 (1981): 273-78, 285. This study examines the press in the late 1940s in its coverage of the Washington State Committee on Un-American Activities' investigation of alleged Communist infiltration at the University of Washington. The press, during a period of societal stress, failed to meet its responsibilities to provide a truthful and comprehensive account. The press showed little sympathy for faculty members accused of being Communists; it was predominantly negative, emphasizing unfavorable stories and playing down stories supportive of faculty and relying primarily on sources hostile to the faculty. "In those times of political stress, the press did not provide a sympathetic or even a neutral hearing for the accused faculty member. Balanced reports may have been victims of the very real and widespread fears of the Cold War. But more importantly, the institutional, systematic method of collecting news from sources -- and particularly from institutional sources -- may be the antithesis of a full meaningful account of the day's events without some consideration for rebuttal of clarification." (285) The press should help make the society free and should protect freedom of the individual and of speech.

2366. Balk, Alfred, and James Boylan. *Our Troubled Press: Ten Years of the Columbia Journalism Review.* Boston: Little, Brown, 1971. This anthology of articles that appeared in *CJR* shows that it has served as a critic of the press on such issues as coverage of presidential campaigns, the press' uncritical support of the government line in Vietnam, white bias (because reporters were white) in covering race relations, monopoly, and media as business. It has examined press councils, freedom of the press, reporter power, access to media, etc.

2367. Barkin, Steve M. "Changes in Business Sections, 1931-1979." *JQ* 59 (1982): 435-39. The Washington *Post*, Baltimore *Sun*, and New York *Times* now emphasize the stock market less and international business more. However, consumer news improved little during the consumer movement of 1960s. "Other types of news have fared better since 1931. International economy news has steadily grown as a percentage of all business news. Multinational corporations, increased international trade, and the rise of OPEC are factors that have made the world economy difficult to overlook. With an apparent increase in news of the professional business community, newspapers also are devoting more space to the businessmen and businesswomen in their communities. Although the relative coverage of individual firms has not significantly increased in the past five decades, today's business sections appear less dominated by Wall Street and Washington. If diversity of subject matter can be considered an index of improvement, business coverage has improved." (439)

2368. Barkin, Steve M. "The Journalist as Storyteller: An Interdisciplinary Perspective." *AJ* 1, 2 (1984): 27-34. When journalists "tell stories" personalized in terms of the people involved, rather than provide information in the traditional structure of news stories, they "make sense of the world" in personal terms and perform an important socializing function. This article is a summary overview of a stylistic and structural device rather than substantial history.

2369. Bayley, Edwin R. *Joe McCarthy and the Press.* Madison: University of Wisconsin Press, 1981. McCarthy used the press between 1950 and 1954 because the press reported only the routine, deadline news and because newspapers did not want to run news counter to their Republican, centrist politics. Even though McCarthy was a buffoon and schemer, the press treated him seriously. Still, he had some critics in the press, and it was their opposition which made it possible for the centrist politicians who dominated the Senate and the Eisenhower administration to act against him. McCarthy exploited the press' commitment to objectivity and impartiality, but journalists at the same time were subjected to professional and public scrutiny, and the press in the end behaved very responsibly. Wire service reporting was "inadequate, flat, unimaginative, devoid of interpretation or analysis, lacking even description." By 1954, however, significant and lasting changes had taken place in newspaper practices: "interpretive reporting and news analysis had become standard practice," with the recognition that "objectivity" was not always useful or best.

2370. Beasley, Maurine, and Paul Belgrade. "Media Coverage of a Silent Partner: Mamie Eisenhower as First Lady." *AJ* 3 (1986): 39-49. "Mamie Eisenhower's kid-glove treatment by the media represented a throwback to a previous era. The press delicately avoided any mention of the gossip that surrounded her [rumors of her drinking]....By focusing only on Mrs. Eisenhower as a hostess and self-effacing wife, the media failed to present her as an actual individual. The fact that the portrayal was rarely questioned demonstrated that journalists of the era tended to reinforce patriarchal stereotypes concerning suitable social roles for women." (47-48)

2371. Beasley, Maurine Hoffman, and Richard R. Harlow. *Voices of Change: Southern Pulitzer Winners.* Washington: University Press of America, 1979. Pulitzer winners were vitally concerned about human rights. The brief introduction to each of seven winners, followed by an interview, emphasizes their journalistic achievements.

2372. Bell, Lillian Smith. "The Role and Performance of Black and Metro Newspapers in Relation to Political Campaigns in Selected, Racially-Mixed Congressional Elections: 1960-1970." Ph.D. dissertation, Northwestern University, 1973. A study of "the relationship between the emerging black politician and the press."

2373. Berner, R. Thomas. "Unitypo: The ITU's Editor and Publisher." *AJ* 2 (1985): 144-64. The International Typographical Union created its "Unitypo" newspapers to promote its labor union point of view and published them in competition with existing newspapers which had been struck by ITU members. The papers, however, lost money and were ineffective.

2374. Bigman, Stanley. "Public Reaction to the Death of a Daily." *JQ* 32 (1955): 267-76. There was little public concern over the social implications of the purchase in 1954 of the Washington *Times-Herald* by the *Post* and their merger into one paper. *Times-Herald* readers were won over to the combined daily by inclusion of their favorite comics, sports news, and columnists. Readers were more attached to their sports and comics than to the *Times-Herald* editorials.

2375. Blanchard, Margaret A. "The Associated Press Antitrust Suit: A Philosophical Clash Over Ownership of First Amendment Rights." *BHR* 61 (1987).

2376. Blanchard, Margaret A. *Exporting the First Amendment: The Press Government Crusade of 1945-1952.* New York: Longman, 1986. American news organizations believed that if freedom of the press were assured -- if journalists throughout the world were free to gather and disseminate information -- freedom would assure world peace. The American government agreed that world press freedom would help and therefore joined the press in attempting to get the rest of the world to adopt the American concept of press freedom. The effort was doomed to failure, however, because of differing political and social conditions in other countries.

2377. Blanchard, Margaret A. "The Hutchins Commission, the Press, and the Responsibility Concept." *JM* 49 (1977). The press, contrary to what historians have assumed, gradually although sometimes grudgingly accepted the concept of responsiblity, as the Hutchins Commission on Freedom of the Press had recommended, because it "needed to rebuild its public image and revive its credibility." (2)

2378. Bliss, Robert M. "Development of Fair Comment as a Defense to Libel." *JQ* 44 (1967): 627-37. Analysis of the *Times v. Sullivan* case tracing the historical development of the doctrine of fair comment. This is primarily a legal analysis, attempting to explain legal philosophies and precedents behind the decision and to predict what direction libel law might take.

2379. Braestrap, Peter. *Big Story: How the American Press and Television Reported and Interpreted the Crisis of Tet 1968 in Vietnam and Washington.* Boulder, Colo.: Westview, 1977. The media performed poorly in covering the Tet offensive, for Tet was a defeat for North Vietnam and the Viet Cong (because it did not achieve their objectives), but the media wrongly concluded that it was a victory. This eventually caused President Johnson to change his commitment to the war and led to the withdrawal of American troops and the defeat of South Vietnam. The national press misrepresented most aspects of Tet, which failed to achieve most of North Vietnam and the Viet Cong's objectives. The press, however, pictured it as a major disaster of U.S. policy and as an indication that North Vietnam and the Viet Cong could mount a major offensive. The press emphasized the future futility of U.S. policy. Its misinterpretation was based on and led to factual errors. The press emphasized the U.S.'s supposed shortcomings and North Vietnam/Viet Cong's superiority (the press falsely claimed) in ethics, support from people, military discipline, will to win, etc. The press not only distorted the real situation; it falsified. The press' shortcomings were caused by logistical and structural problems in press operation (not by ideology except at the New York *Times*) and by the press' negative reactions to Johnson's assurances that everything was going well in Vietnam.

2380. Bramlett, Sharon A. "Southern vs. Northern Newspaper Coverrage of a Race Crisis -- The Lunch Counter Sit-in Movement, 1960-1964." Ph.D. dissertation, Indiana University, 1987.

2381. Bray, Howard. *The Pillars of the Post: The Making of a News Empire in Washington.* New York: Norton, 1980. History of the Washington *Post* from Eugene Meyer's purchase of the paper in 1933 to Donald Graham's becoming chairman of the board in 1979, including financing in the early years, Vietnam, racism on the paper's staff, and Watergate. Katharine Graham became publisher upon her husband's suicide in 1963. This non-analytical, favorable treatment of her as a publisher and businesswoman glosses over the internal difficulties on the *Post*: her injustices and bitterness were justified by her triumphs. She believed in journalistic excellence. Likewise, editor Ben Bradlee receives favorable treatment. He made the *Post* perhaps the most interesting paper in the world. The paper also grew into a very successful financial venture.

2382. Brewin, Bob, and Sydney Shaw. *Vietnam on Trial: Westmoreland vs. CBS.* New York: Atheneum, 1987. Even-handed account of Gen. Westmoreland's libel suit against CBS.

2383. Brogan, Patrick. *Spiked: The Short Life of the National News Council.* New York: Priority Press, 1984. This history covering 1973 to 1984 attempts to explain why the council failed.

2384. Brown, Lee. *The Reluctant Reformation: On Criticizing the Press in America.* New York: David McKay, 1974. Outlines the major themes, patterns, and concerns of media criticism of the past. "The press often has been slow to heed its critics, reluctant to adopt the reforms that society constantly requires of its press. Even so, few of our institutions have improved so much in the past two decades. Time has not produced solutions to the perceived failings of the press. In three hundred years the criticism has changed more in expression than in kind, and the basic criticisms have endured and grown through elaboration and repetition."

2385. Brown, Robert DePue. "Curtis: Philadelphia's Best Known Publisher." *DLQ* 12 (July 1976): 45-58. Cyrus H. K. Curtis founded *Ladies' Home Journal* in the early 1900s. It was the beginning of the huge Curtis Publishing Co. Curtis' success came from his advertising policies, marketing techniques, editorial policies, and technical accomplishments. The company failed in 1969 because of the weaknesses in Curtis' successors -- "men whose concern was with the status quo and not with visions of the future."

2386. Buckley, James Homer. "Suburban Evangel: Trade Associations and the Emergence of the Suburban Newspaper Industry, 1945-1970." Ph.D. dissertation, University of Washington, 1986. Faced with major soical and economic changes, suburban newspapers banded together in associations. The associations "played a crucial role in helping the suburban newspaper industry set its goals, identify its priorities, establish its legitimacy, promote its values, defines its products and markets, and identify its most strategic issues."

2387. Burd, Gene Arnold. "The Role of the Chicago Daily Newspapers in the Selection of the Chicago Campus for the University of Illinois." Ph.d. dissertation, Northwestern University, 1964. This study "contains a record of otherwise unreported 'behind the scenes' activity in one of Chicago's most controversial and biggest news stories with sociological significance in the last decade."

2388. Busha, Charles H. "Censorship and Intellectual Freedom: A Bibliography, 1970-1981." *DLQ* 18, 1 (1982): 101-08. Contains references to 94 books and dissertations, dealing mostly with recent issues.

2389. Canham, Erwin D. *Commitment to Freedom: The Story of the Christian Science Monitor*. Boston: Houghton Mifflin, 1958. Canham was editor of the paper from 1941 to 1958. It was intended to be a "real newspaper," not a narrow denominational one, but its sectarian foundation has affected its news coverage. While the paper acquired an international reputation for its quality, its religious views did affect its treatment of even such subjects as weather and sports.

2390. Casey, William E., Jr. "The Press and the 1952 New Hampshire Primary: A Perception of Significance." *JH* 5 (1978): 115-19. One reason Truman decided not to run for re-election was that he had lost the primary to Kefauver. The primary was thus an important national event, and the "press played an integral role in the development." Because the primary became a national media event, much attention of the public was focused on it, making it seem to be of great consequence in the presidential nominating process. This study draws parallels between 1952 and 1976: television and other news media influenced the latter campaign by how they treated the results of the New York primary.

2391. Chaffee, Steven H., ed., with Godwin C. Chu, Jack Lyle, and Wayne Danielson. "Contributions of Wilbur Schramm to Mass Communication Research." *JM* 36 (1974). Collection of three admiring essays on the educator-theorist who "towers above our field." (preface)

2392. Chamberlain, John. *A Life with the Printed Word*. Chicago: Regnery, 1982. Autobiography of the writer for the New York *Times, Life, Fortune*, and *National Review*.

2393. Chambless, Timothy M. "Muckraker at Work: Columnist Jack Anderson and the Watergate Scandal, 1972-74." Ph.D. dissertation, University of Utah, 1987.

2394. Chaney, Lindsay, and Michael Cieply. *The Hearsts: Family and Empire -- The Later Years*. New York: Simon & Schuster, 1981. The Hearst media empire declined after Hearst's death in 1951. Under uninspired corporate leadership, the newspapers began to fold. In recent years, however, concern for journalism leadership and quality has been shown with *Cosmopolitan* magazine, the San Franciso *Examiner*, and Los Angeles *Herald Examiner*.

2395. Christians, Clifford G. "Fifty Years of Scholarship in Media Ethics." *JC* 27 (Autumn 1977): 19-29. Ethics have changed since the 1920s. In the 1920s, ethics took a "nonfunctional approach" emphasizing "moral responsibility to one's professional community." In the 1930s ethics was synonomous with objectivity. After World War II, ethics became more concerned with social responsibility and thorough reporting. In the hectic 1970s, a new ethical framework is needed.

2396. Clarke, Peter, and Susan H. Evans. *Covering Campaigns: Journalism in Congressional Elections*. Stanford, Calif.: Stanford University Press, 1983. Study of newspaper coverage of 82 campaigns in 1978, including paper content and interviews with journalists.

2397. Cobbs, Nicholas H., Jr. "Hamner Cobbs as Editor of the Greensboro *Watchman*." *AIR* 39: 261-70. As editor of the Alabama newspaper from 1940 to 1968, Hamner emphasized editorial opinion and served as the "conscience of the Black Belt." (270)

2398. Conn, Earl Lewis. "The American Council of Education for Journalism: An Accrediting History." Ed.D. dissertation, Indiana University, 1970. A study of the council since 1953 notes issues it faced.

2399. Coulson, David C. "Nelson Poynter of the *St. Petersburg Times*: An Independent Publisher with Unique Ownership Standards." *MCR* 12 (Winter-Spring-Fall, 1985): 11-17.

2400. Cronin, Walter. "Four American Columnists: A Study in the Partisan Ideology of David Lawrence, Walter Lippmann, Drew Pearson, and George Sokolsky." Ph.D. dissertation, University of Minnesota, 1953.

2401. Dalton, Joseph. "The Legend of Hank Greenspan." *HM* (June 1982): 32-43. Popular, featurized profile of the controversial publisher of the Las Vegas *Sun*.

2402. Dan, Uri. *Blood Libel: The Inside Story of General Ariel Sharon's History-Making Suit Against Time Magazine*. New York: Simon & Schuster, 1987. Sharon, an Israeli military general who sued *Time* for libel, was a victim of journalistic partisanship. Although the magazine was absolved of the charge of actual malice, the jury findings of defamation and falsity constituted a legal victory for Sharon.

2403. Daniel, Clifton. *Lords, Ladies and Gentlemen: A Memoir*. New York: Arbor House, 1984. Autobiography of the New York *Times* managing editor which focused on interesting people he met.

2404. Davis, Deborah. *Katharine the Great: Katharine Graham and the Washington Post*. New York: Harcourt Brace Jovanovich, 1980. Critical study of the *Post* as a newspaper committed primarily to preserving the establishment and the government in power. Its history provides a good example of "mediapolitics."

2405. Demaitre, Edmund. *Eyewitness: A Journalist Covers the 20th Century*. New York: Ungar, 1981. Autobiographical memoir.

2406. Dennis, Everett E., Donald Gillman, and David L. Grey, eds. *Justice Hugo Black and the First Amendment*. Ames: Iowa State University Press, 1978. Collection of essays by various authors. Black held an absolutist interpretation of the First Amendment.

2407. Devol, Kenneth S., ed. *Mass Media and the Supreme Court: The Legacy of the Warren Years*, 3rd. ed. New York: Hastings House, 1982. Collection of Supreme Court cases and reprints of articles.

2408. Donovan, Hedley. *Roosevelt to Reagan: A Reporter's Encounters with Nine*

Presidents. New York: Harper & Row, 1985. The author gives his personal observations of the presidents' performance.

2409. Donovan, Robert. "White Tie and Hallowed Nonsense: The Gridiron Club Turns 100." *WJR* (April 1985): 43-47. Anecdotal account of the history of the Washington press club, with emphasis on a first-person account of meetings since 1958.

2410. Doudna, Martin K. *Concern About the Planet: The Reporter Magazine and American Liberalism, 1949-1968*. Westport, Conn.: Greenwood, 1977. *Reporter's* founder and editor, Max Acsoli, was a liberal on civil liberties, civil rights, nuclear testing, and foreign policy.

2411. Douglas, Sara U. *Labor's New Voice: Unions and Mass Media*. Norwood, N.J.: Ablex, 1986. Survey history from 1828, when the first labor newspaper was founded, with emphasis on recent events. Organized labor has resorted to public relations and planned events in an attempt to get favorable media coverage.

2412. Dunne, Gerald T.. *Hugo Black and the Judicial Revolution*. New York: Simon & Schuster, Touchstone Books, 1977.

2413. Eagles, Charles W. *Jonathan Daniels and Race Relations: The Evolution of a Southern Liberal*. Knoxville: University of Tennessee Press, 1982. Daniels edited the Raleigh (N.C.) *News and Observer* from 1933 to 1942 and 1948 to the mid-1960s. In his views on race, he moved slowly toward liberalism, careful not to get too far ahead of his readers. He advocated racial justice and helped to bring about an integrated South.

2414. Eberhard, Wallace B. "Circulation and Population: Comparison of 1940 and 1970." 51 (1974): 503-07. "There was no significant difference in overall circulation penetration (a ratio of newspapers over occupied housing units) for dailies" (505) between 1940 and 1970. However, there was a decline in circulation penetration in large urban areas.

2415. Eberhard, Wallace B. "Daily Newspaper Starts and Suspensions, 1960-69." *JQ* 52 (1975): 117-20. Despite the fact that the total number of papers remained about constant, there actually were a large number of starts and suspensions.

2416. Elwood, Virginia. "A Preliminary Bibliography: Images of Women in the Media, 1971-76." *JH* 3 (1976): 121-23.

2417. Emery, Edwin. "The Press in the Vietnam Quagmire." *JQ* 48: 619-26. This article is an excerpt from the 1972 edition of *The Press and America*. Journalists' coverage of the war may have helped change American attitudes from the Cold War mentality and the Manifest Destiny approach.

2418. Farrar, Ronald. "Harry Truman and the Press: A View from Inside." *JH* 2 (1981): 56-62, 70. Notes from a just-released diary kept by one of Truman's staff members show that Truman did not have much respect for publishers or columnists. Most newspapers had opposed his re-election, and he thought they and columnists had inflated ideas of their importance. He also felt they unfairly slanted their material.

2419. Faulk, John Henry. *Fear on Trial*. Austin: University of Texas Press, 1983.

Autobiography of Faulk's experiences during the McCarthy era when he was blacklisted.

2420. Ferrell, Robert H., ed. *The Diary of James C. Hagerty: Eisenhower in Mid-Course, 1954-1955*. Bloomington: Indiana University Press, 1983. Diary entries of the president's press secretary, including details on such items as use of television and press conferences.

2421. Fischer, Heinz-Dietrich, ed. *Outstanding International Press Reporting: Pulitzer Prize Winning Articles in Foreign Correspondence; Volume 2: 1946-1962*. Berlin and New York: Walter de Gruyter, 1985. Anthology of stories by each winner of the Pulitzer foreign-correspondence categories.

2422. Fonzi, Gaeton. *Annenberg: A Biography of Power*. New York: Weybright & Talley, 1970. Walter Annenberg was vindictive and interested primarily in making money. His father, Moe Annenberg, came from poverty and thought money was the way to become respectable and influential. He failed at both. Walter Annenberg, the son, apparently felt the same way. Despite the fact that he made a success out of the Philadelphia *Inquirer* and Philadelphia *Bulletin, Television Guide, Seventeen,* six television and nine radio stations, contributed generously to charities and institutions (such as the Annenberg School of Communications), and was appointed U.S. ambassador to England, he is still a failure because he never showed any concern for truth (which should be the highest motive of a journalist). He was always willing to twist the truth for the benefit of friends and himself (including Nixon). He especially used his news media to benefit his conservative political friends such as Nixon and Reagan. Even the *Inquirer*, which was sold to Knight in 1970, was a failure and had no respect from its staff, other journalists, or readers. Even its top investigative reporter received bribes from the underworld. The reporter was able to do so because Annenberg had used his newspaper to get even with people with whom he had problems, and people assumed the reporter had the support of Annenberg in extorting money from the criminals.

2423. Friedman, Monroe. "Brand-Name Use in News Columns of American Newspapers Since 1964." *JQ* 63 (1986): 161-66. The use of commercial brand names increased and has had an impact on culture and language.

2424. Garrigues, George L. "The Great Conspiracy Against the UCLA *Daily Bruin*." *SCQ* 59, 2 (1977): 217-30. During the Cold War the college newspaper was harrassed because of its liberal editorial opinion.

2425. Garrison, Bruce M. "William Hodding Carter Jr: A Different Perspective of the Crusading Editor." *JH* 3 (1976): 90-93, 96. Carter, the editor of the *Delta Democrat Times* in Greenville, Miss., "fought against corrupt and unfair government as strongly as he did against racial injustice, and with as much energy." (90)

2426. Geyer, Georgie Anne. *Buying the Night Flight: The Autobiography of a Woman Foreign Correspondent*. New York: Delacorte/Seymour Lawrence, 1983. First person account of the adventures of a foreign reporter for the Chicago *Daily News* from 1960 to the mid-1970s.

2427. Ghiglione, Loren, ed. *Gentlemen of the Press: Profiles of American Newspaper Editors*. Indianapolis: Berg, 1984. Brief biographies, selected from the *Bulletin* of the

American Society of Newspaper Editors, of more than one hundred editors.

2428. Gittlin, Todd. *The Whole World Is Watching: Mass Media in the Making and Un-making of the New Left.* Berkley and Los Angeles: University of California Press, 1980. This political, polemical study provides a Marxist interpretation of the relationship of the New Left to the mass media in the 1960s, "hegemony" (domination by a ruling class), and stereotyping of news. Mainstream journalism tends to stereotype challenges to the established order and to attempt to make them look ridiculous. The media characterized the New Left as violent, deviant, and silly.

2429. Gordon, Douglas E. *"The Great Speckled Bird*: Harassment of an Underground Newspaper." *JQ* 56 (1979): 289-95. Atlanta's "premier underground newspaper" from 1968 to 1976 "met hostility from both the private and the public sectors." The "result, and probable intent, of this harassment was the suppression of *The Speckled Bird's* editorial content as well as of the newspaper staff....The public harassment -- obscenity suits, frequent building inspections, police intimidation -- were reflections of the political community's hostility toward the liberal politics and life-style of the hippy community *The Speckled Bird* represented." (289)

2430. Gould, Lewis. "First Ladies and the Press: Bess Truman to Lady Bird Johnson." *AJ* 1, 1 (1983): 47-62. Summary of the relations between the press and First Ladies after Eleanor Roosevelt. After Mrs. Roosevelt's active, "non-traditional" performance as First Lady, later presidents "have pursued a defensive strategy in which they made the most of having a wife by insuring that these women did not become political or cultural liabilities. Since the press would likely reveal when such negative results had taken place, the ability to manage journalists emerged as the first essential of a successful First Lady." (57-58)

2431. Graber, Doris A. "Press Coverage and Voter Reaction in the 1968 Presidential Election." *PSQ* 89, 1 (1974): 68-100. Newspapers focused on candidates' personal characteristics rather than on issues.

2432. Grauer, Neil A. *Wits & Sages.* Baltimore: Johns Hopkins University Press, 1984. Profiles of 12 newspaper columnists, including material from their columns and interviews.

2433. Griggs, Harry H. "Coverage of National Economic Conditions by Five Mass Circulation Daily Newspapers during Three Crucial Months of the 1957-58 Recession." Ph.D. dissertation, University of Iowa, 1962. Newspapers lagged in reporting the declining phase of the recession because they did not rely sufficiently on statistical indicators.

2434. Grimes, Millard B. *The Last Linotype: : The Story of Georgia and Its Newspapers Since World War II.* Macon: Mercer University Press, 1985. Collection of narratives of newspapers based on information provided by each and written by a long-time member of the state press.

2435. Grotta, Gerald L. "Changes in the Ownership Structure of Daily Newspapers and Selected Performance Characteristics, 1950-1968." Ph.D. dissertation, Southern Illinois University, 1970. "[W]hen newspapers changed from two-newspaper competition to one-newspaper monopoly, consumers paid significantly higher prices without compensating increases in quality." When chains bought newspapers, "consumers received none of the assumed benefits from this form of concentration of ownership."

2436. Guimary, Donald. "The Decline and Death of Portland's Daily Reporter." *JQ* 45 (1968): 91-94. During a 1961 strike, the Portland *Reporter* was started on a shoestring. It lasted until 1964, when it died because it was "unable to overcome its identification with the unions and the strike, the reluctance of key retail advertisers who refused to support the paper, and its chronic lack of finances." (91) It had internal problems, but the primary difficulty was in its financing and management.

2437. Hachten, William A. "The Metropolitan Sunday Newspaper in the United States: A Study of Trends in Content and Practices." Ph.D. dissertation, University of Minnesota, 1961. Content analysis measures the changes and trends from 1939 to 1959.

2438. Halberstam, David. *The Powers That Be.* New York: Knopf, 1979. The press has great influence; great journalists and media shape history. Recent media history has been marked by a philosophical debate over a private enterprise media system versus one supporting and supported by the government. The huge media often shape U.S. politics and society, relishing their status and the profits they acquire along the way. Since the 1930s the big media have acquired more and more importance. Although the Los Angeles *Times* had a history of being biased against people who opposed the *Times'* interests financially, in general the media have responded well to their power and prestige. The Washington *Post* used its profits to improve its news coverage, and the Los Angeles *Times* under Otis Chandler opened its columns to both liberals and conservatives. At CBS, however, William S. Paley let highly profitable entertainment supersede news, commentary, and documentary. Big money is extremely important to media owners, although making money is no crime, for money is necessary for a medium to continue operation. "It was a curious irony of capitalism that among the only outlets rich enough and powerful enough to stand up to an overblown, occasionally reckless, otherwise unchallenged central government were journalistic institutions that had very, very secure financial bases."

2439. Hall, William E. "An Analysis of Post-World War II Efforts to Expand Press Freedom Internationally." Ph.D. dissertation, University of Iowa, 1954.

2440. Halverson, Roy Kenneth. "Trends in Daily Newspaper Circulation." Ph.D. dissertation, University of Illinois, 1970. Circulation "grew and fell among the adult population according to economic conditions between 1920 and 1940. It rose sharply with the rise in per capita expenditures through World War II. But after the war, several factors appeared to impinge on circulation." The primary reason for the decline probably was the availability of other media, such as television.

2441. Hamilton, Mary Allienne. "J.W. Gitt: The Cold War's 'Voice in the Wilderness.'" *JM* 91 (1985). The "Progressive" publisher of the York (Pa.) *Gazette and Daily* served as a voice for the "ideals of...democracy" and as a "conscience for the community." (31)

2442. Harkey, Ira. *The Smell of Burning Crosses: An Autobiography of a Mississippi Newspaperman.* Jacksonville, Ill.: Harris-Wolfe, 1967. Harkey won the 1963 Pulitzer Prize for editorial writing for his opposition for segregation.

2443. Harrison, John M., and Harry H. Stein, eds. *Muckraking -- Past, Present and Future.* University Park: Pennsylvania State Univesity Press, 1973. Collection of essays, with an emphasis on muckrakers' ideas rather than muckraking's journalistic nature.

2444. Hart, Roderick P., Kathleen Turner, and Ralph Knupp. "A Rhetorical Profile of Religious News: *Time,* 1947-1976." *JC* 31, 3 (1981): 58-68. *Time* magazine gave most attention to Episcopalians, Catholics, and Jews, the religious groups with greatest participation on the East Coast.

2445. Hathaway, William L. "Interest in Politics: Measured by the Readership of News about Politics in a Metropolitan Daily Newspaper, 1950-59." Ph.D. dissertation, University of Minnesota, 1962. The political content of the Minneapolis *Star* and *Tribune* suggests useful "models of man as a political creature [and] of mass media as political institutions."

2446. Havard, William C. "The Journalist as Interpreter of the South." *VQR* 59, 1 (1983): 1-21. Essay on James Kilpatrick, Hodding Carter II, and P.D. East.

2447. Hensher, Alan. "No News Today: How Los Angeles Lost a Daily." *JQ* 47 (1970): 684-88. The *Daily News,* Los Angeles' only independently owned daily from 1923 to 1954, died not so much because of television or suburban press competition but because of debilitating union demands and its lack of the immense capital required in a metropolis. The Los Angeles Newspaper Guild refused to make any concessions which would have made it possible for the paper's new owner in 1954 to eliminate the paper's losses. Facing the difficulty of meeting "the debilitating, long-term demands of the union," Clinton McKinnon finally had to sell the paper to the Times-Mirror Company.

2448. Highton, Jake. "Why Do Newspapers All Sing the Same (Establishment) Song?" *Masthead* 34, 2 (1982): 8-11. "The nation's press has historically allied itself with the status quo and against the interests of most people in America and abroad....'Country Club' editorials almost always back the more conservative presidential candidate." (8) The press also slants its news coverage because editors "lean the way their publishers lean" and "often tailor the product -- consciously or unconsciously -- to their bosses' wishes. And those bosses are almost invariably conservative business people." (9) "The sad truth is that the nation's newspapers and magazines have not lent essential radical critiques and perspectives on local, state, national and world affairs." (10) The "honorable exceptions" are publications such as *The Nation, the Village Voice,* and *Progressive.*

2449. Hixson, Richard F. "A Brief Look at New Jersey's Prosperous Daily Press." *JQ* 43 (1966): 765-69. Brief, faborable history and assessment of the present conditions of New Jersey's 29 dailies, all of which were prosperous and enjoying rapid expansion.

2450. Hofstetter, C. Richard. "News Bias in the 1972 Campaign: A Cross-Media Comparison." *JM* 58 (November 1978). Network television, the wire services, and two papers biased coverage because of their structure, although they exhibited no partisan bias. The structural bias was caused by the nature of media.

2451. Hollstein, Milton. "The Noble Experiment that was the *National Observer.*" *Quill* (September 1977): 27-29.

2452. Howland, William S. "Unforgettable Ralph McGill." *NR* 26, 3 (1972): 1, 26-7.

Reprint from *Readers Digest* (August 1971). McGill was a crusader for the rights of blacks.

2453. Huey, Gary L. *Rebel With a Cause: P.D. East, Southern Liberalism, and the Civil Rights Movement, 1953-1971*. Wilmington, Del.: Scholarly Resources, 1985. East started the *Petal Pusher* newspaper in Mississippi primarily to make money. Both courageous and foolhardy, however, he opposed segregation and became popular among northern liberals. He combatted racial injustice ineffectively, though, because he had few readers in his own community and state, he was poorly educated, he had a low social status, and he had inadequate financial support for his paper.

2454. Jensen, Jay. "The New Journalism in Historical Perspective." *JH* 1 (1974): 37, 66. Excerpt from the book edited by Charles C. Flippen, *Liberating the Media: The New Journalism* (Washington: Acropolis Books, 1974). New journalism has its antecedants in journalism history, although it was a break from objective reporting.

2455. Jones, Eugene W. "A Decade of the Country Editor, 1954-1964." *WTHA Yearbook* 62 (1986).

2456. Jordan, Myron K. "Presidential Health Reporting: The Eisehower Watershed." *AJ* 4 (1987): 147-58. The press presented Eisenhower's health problems as a major issue in the 1956 presidential election. Its aggressive coverage marked a turning point in how the press treats American presidents.

2457. Kennedy, Daniel D. "The Bay of Pigs and the New York *Times*: Another View of What Happened." *JQ* 63 (1986): 524-29. The *Times*, unlike what critics have said, did not withhold information about the planned invasion of Cuba.

2458. Kern, Montague, Patricia W. Levering, and Ralph B. Levering. *The Kennedy Crisis: The Press, the Presidency, and Foreign Policy*. Chapel Hill: University North Carolina, 1983. Content analysis of five newspapers shows that they brought issues to the attention of the public and President Kennedy, who then took the initiative. Sometimes the press influenced Kennedy, while at other times he gained uncritical acceptance of his policies. The relationship was not simply one in which a U.S. president manipulated the press.

2459. King, Spencer B. *Sound of Drums: Selected Writings of Spencer B. King from His Civil War Centennial Columns Appearing in the Macon (Georgia) Telegraph-News 1960-1965*. Macon: Mercer University Press, 1984. Anthology of essays written from a Southern perspective.

2460. Klejment, Anne, and Alice Klejment. *Dorothy Day and the Catholic Worker: A Bibliography and Index*. New York: Garland, 1985. Reference work for 1933-1983.

2461. Klempner, John A. "A Newspaper in Dissonance: The *Christian Science Monitor* Election Coverage, 1928 and 1960." Ph.D. dissertation, Michigan State University, 1960.

2462. Klurfield, Herman. *Behind the Lines: The World of Drew Pearson*. Englewood Cliffs, N.J.: Prentice-Hall, 1968. This favorable, but poorly researched biography of the investigative columnist focuses mainly on Washington gossip and Pearson's influence on national affairs.

2463. Knudson, Jerry W. "Herbert L. Matthews and the Cuban Story." *JQ* 54 (1978). This liberal interpreter of Castro and the Cuban revolution was an admirable journalist who exercised "[m]oral courage in reporting the truth as [he saw it]." (22)

2464. Knudson, Jerry W. "Philadelphia Story: The Murder of John S. Knight III." *MCR* 6, 2 (1979): 11-16. The press, in a wave of new sensationalism, has lost its concern for social and human value.

2465. Koerner, Thomas F. "Benjamin C. Willis and the Chicago Press." Ph.D. dissertation, Northwestern University, 1968. As Willis, the superintendent of Chicago's public schools from 1953 to 1966, came under criticism, newspapers failed to inform the public adequately about the controversies or to give unbiased reports. Willis himself was partly responsible because he was insensitive to the need to communicate with the press or public. The general implication is that school officials and journalists, "whose duties in a democratic society are extremely important, must be completely candid and frank with the publics they serve."

2466. Koval, James J. "Beyond the First Amendment: Impact of the Other Amendments on the Press." *MHD* 7, 2 (1987): 54-60. "[T]he right against unreasonable searches and seizures under the Fourth Amendment, the implied right of privacy under the Fourth, Fifth and Ninth Amendments, and the right to fair trial under the Sixth Amendment, have to some extent worked to impede the media in the full exercise of rights many would believe implied under the First Amendment." (54)

2467. Kriegh, Andrew. *Spiked: How Chain Management Corrupted America's Oldest Newspaper*. Old Saybrook, Conn.: Peregrine, 1987. After the Times-Mirror Co. of Los Angeles bought the Hartford (Conn.) *Courant* in 1979, the chain was more concerned about its public image and about winning awards than about publishing a good, public-spirited newspaper. "[H]idden corporate imperatives and taboos thwarted the newspaper's mission of truth-telling. The chain conferred power onto fiercely loyal, ruthlessly ambitious executives brought in from afar. By controlling the region's dominant information source as tightly as they did, the chieftains were free to bungle and lie, and to suppress inconvenient facts and ideas." (14)

2468. Larson, Carl M. "The Struggle of Paddock Publications Versus Field Enterprises, Inc." *JQ* 48 (1971): 700-06, 713. Market research, good management, and new information systems can combat the circulation-gap syndrome and stem the drift to fewer editorial voices. The success of Paddock publications (a group of suburban papers in Chicago) in surviving competition from Field Enterprises, Inc., from 1966 to 1970 "is once again the story of a little David besting a Goliath." (700) This account tells the story of how Paddock did it: "1) suburban communities are assuming a more dominant role in the life-style of the people throughout the country. Consequently metropolitan dailies will attempt, as did Field Enterprises, to take over suburban newspapers either through merger or by driving them out, 2) the circulation-gap-syndrome can be combatted by good management and new information systems, 3) market research is an effective tool to identify readers and suggest methods for improving the newspaper package and 4) a drift to fewer editorial voices is a trend that must be vigilantly fought." (713)

2469. Leapman, Michael. *Arrogant Aussie: The Rupert Murdoch Story*. Secaucus, N.J.: Lyle Stuart, 1985. Murdoch, an Australian media owner, is a controversial publisher who has bought into the American market.

2470. *The Lee Papers: A Saga of Midwestern Journalism.* Kewanee, Ill.: Star-Courier Press, 1947. The newspaper chain has interested primarily in the public good. This favorable narrative account was written by staff members.

2471. Lent, John A. *Newhouse, Newspapers, Nuisances: Highlights in the Growth of a Communications Empire.* New York: Exposition, 1966. The life of S.I. Newhouse is the success story of a boy who went from rags to riches. As a publisher, he has had an "impact on the American scene." A major part of this biography, which is based on little original research, deals with the conflict between Newhouse newspapers and the American Newspaper Guild from 1930 to 1964.

2472. Lentz, Richard. "Resurrection of the Prophet: Dr. Martin Luther King, Jr., and the News Weeklies." *AJ* 4 (1987): 59-81. *Time, Newsweek,* and *U.S. News & World Report,* in the three weeks after King's assassination, falsely but intentionally presented him as a moderate rather than a radical and "resurrected [him] as a gentle prophet from a simpler era." (76)

2473. Lentz, Richard. "Sixty-five Days in Memphis: A Study of Culture, Symbols, and the Press." *JM* 98 (1986). Study of the "symbols" used by Memphis' two newspapers "to make sense" of a 1968 garbage strike "within a cultural framework." (2) The papers told of the strike by black workers in terms of "black anarchy and paternalism." (33)

2474. Leslie, Larry Z. "Newspaper Photo Coverage of the Censure of McCarthy." *JQ* 63 (1986): 850-53. Photographs generally showed Sen. Joseph McCarthy favorably.

2475. Liebovich, Louis William. "The Press and the Origins of the Cold War, 1944-1947." Ph.D. dissertation, University of Wisconsin, 1986. Four publications (New York *Herald Tribune,* Chicago *Tribune,* San Francisco *Chronicle,* and *Time* magazine) "failed to either strongly support peaceful coexistence or influence the changing world order, but...with different editorial approaches they could have had some impact during this uncertain time....[W]hile all but one had favored accommodation with Russia in 1944...all...had rejected hope of friendly relations with the Soviet Union by 1947."

2476. Logue, Calvin M. "Ralph McGill: Convictions of a Southern Editor." *JQ* 45 (1968): 647-52. The Atlanta *Constitution* editor was a crusader for equal rights, justice, education, economic opportunity, and freedom for blacks. He was ahead of thinking in the South, although his views in the 1940s and 1950s now may appear a little less than liberal.

2477. Logue, Calvin McLeod. *Ralph McGill, Editor and Publisher.* Durham, N.C.: Moore, 1969. McGill was a classic liberal who favored freedom, rightness, social and racial equality, etc. This biography, which relies almost solely on what McGill himself said and wrote, deals simplistically with moral truths (e.g., free individuals should oppose moral wrong, education is important, all people should be treated equally).

2478. Long, Howard Rusk, ed. *Main Street Militants: an Anthology from Grassroots Editor.* Carbondale: Southern Illinois University Press, 1977. Editors of small papers are the "legitimate heirs to the American journalistic profession." They faced threats, suppression of information, economic boycotts, office bombings, etc., in their battles against government corruption, racism, etc., and for freedom of the press. This anthology of articles from *Grassroots Editor* tells the stories of 28 independent, crusading journalists' (Hazel Brannon Smith, Penn Jones, Jr., etc.) who faced terrifying experiences in their attempt to make America and their communities better places to live.

2479. Lowery, Shearon A., and Melvin L. De Fleur. *Milestones in Mass Communication Research.* New York: Longman, 1988. Textbook collection of research articles written during the past half century by various scholars dealing primarily with the effects of mass media.

2480. Lyons, Schley R. "The Labor Press and Its Audience: The Case of the Toledo *Union Journal.*" *JQ* 46 (1969): 558-64. The union newspaper was held in high esteem by a large proportion of its membership and provided a competitive political news service to its blue collar audience. This study covers the 1967 non-partisan primary election for city council in Toledo in an attempt to determine if union members relied on and trusted the paper.

2481. Marchese, John. "Saul Bellow: Reluctant War Correspondent." *MHD* 5, 3 (1983): 15-18, 41. In covering hostilities between Israel and its Arab neighbors in the 1960s, Bellows thought of himself as a novelist rather than a journalist.

2482. Marler, Charles H. "Abilene Editor: Frank Grimes and West Texas." Ph.D. dissertation, University of Missouri, 1975. A reporter, editorial writer, and editor of the Abilene (Tex.) *Reporter-News* from 1914 to 1961, Grimes "was a transition newspaperman who reflected the influence of two journalistic eras, personal journalism and objective journalism." In his editorial writing "are the essence of West Texas individualism, sincerity, frankness, persistance, and a peculiar blend of idealism and pragmatism, liberalism and conservatism."

2483. Marler, Charles H. "'Often a Bridesmaid, Never a Bride': Frank Grimes and the Pulitzer Prize for Editorial Writing." *SWMCJ* 1 (1985). Grimes probably would have won the Pulitzer Prize except for questionable approaches used by the Pulitzer committee.

2484. Marsh, Harry D. "Hodding Carter's Newspaper on School Desegregation, 1954-55." *JM* 92 (1985). The editor of the *Delta Democrat-Times* in Greenville, Miss., "was a spokesman of and to the South regarding racial matters." (1) He was able to serve as an effective and responsible editor because of his "ownership of the medium, active participation as a citizen in the community, respect in the wider journalistic community and on the national scene,...ability to write lucidly and in the rhetoric of [his] readers and...capacity for formulating independent views and the desire (perhaps compulsion) to express them." (21)

2485. Martin, Harold H. *Ralph McGill, Reporter.* Boston: Little, Brown, 1973. The Atlanta *Constitution* editor was a southerner who wrote persuasively on equal rights for blacks in education, employment, equal opportunity, etc. He deplored violence and attempted to prick the conscience of southerners. He identified with the poor. Although he was a good observer, he was also a reflective thinker. He was a courageous man who dared to say what he believed was right. (Martin was an Atlanta journalist, not a serious historian.)

2486. Martin, John Bartlow. *It Seems Like Only Yesterday: Memoirs of Writing,*

Presidential Politics, and the Diplomatic Life. New York: Morrow, 1986. Autobiography of a journalist turned political speech writer and ambassador.

2487. Mather, Anne. "A History of Feminist Periodicals," 3 parts. *JH* 1 (1974): 82-85, 108-11; *JH* 2 (1975): 19-23, 31. Antiquarian survey history tracing the founding and lives of recent feminist publications. "They offer an alternative viewpoint of our culture and of women, in particular." (31)

2488. May, Hal, ed. *Contemporary Authors: A Bio-Bibliographical Guide to Current Writers in Fiction, General Nonfiction, Poetry, Journalism, Drama, Motion Pictures, Television, and Other Fields*, Vol. 108. Detroit: Gale Research, 1983. Contains 45 biographies, including quotes by them and about them by contemporaries.

2489. McAuliffe, Kevin Michael. *The Great American Newspaper: The Rise and Fall of the Village Voice.* New York: Scribner's, 1978. Beginning in 1954, the paper's first editor, Dan Wolf, gave writers a free hand (but paid little money for contributions). Under Rupert Murdoch's ownership (1976-) the paper faced the drawbacks of corporate operation. The paper has had an impact on New York and national history and has made waves in journalism.

2490. McGlashan, Zena Beth. "The Evolving Status of Newspaperwomen." Ph.D. dissertation, University of Iowa, 1978. Feminist analysis of women in newspaper management argues that journalism history should be "re-constructed so that the successes of the past may be part of socialization through education" aimed at helping more women move into management.

2491. McIntyre, Jerilyn S. "The Hutchins Commission's Search for a Moral Framework." *JH* 6 (1979): 54-57, 63. The commission (1944-1946) confronted questions on freedom of the press and ethics. Its deliberations show how "the implementation of moral principles is shaped by practical restrictions." (54) Problems stemmed from "the conflict between standards based on individual rights of free expression, and those based on social needs and expectations -- a conflict which still exists, and a problem still in need of solution." (63) The media vigorously opposed the commission's recommendations.

2492. Miller, Allan R. *The History of Current Maine Newspapers.* Libson Falls, Me. Eastland, 1978. This catalogue and description of all existing Maine papers, emphasizing the middle and latter parts of the 20th century, includes biographical sketches of their editors.

2493. Milner, Jay. "Hodding Carter: A Profile in Courage." *NR* 24, 4 (1970): 6-9.

2494. Mollenhoff, Clark R. *Washington Cover-Up.* New York: Doubleday, 1962. The federal government under Truman and Eisenhower concealed of information. The presidents maintained government secrecy by using executive privilege to withhold information from Congress, the press, and the public. Since World War II presidents generally have used executive privilege -- under the excuse of national security -- to avoid giving Congress information about mistakes, corruption, and embarrassing predicaments. (This book deals primarily with Congress and presidents rather than the press.)

2495. Nagorski, Andrew. *Reluctant Farewell..* New York: Holt, Rinehart & Winston,

1985. Nagorski, *Newsweek's* West Germany bureau chief, tells of the difficulties in reporting on Communist life.

2496. Nixon, Raymond B. "Trends in Daily Newspaper Ownership Since 1945." *JQ* 31 (1954): 3-14. With one-daily cities and regional newspaper groups both showing steady gains, and with increases in the total number of daily cities keeping abreast with the nation's growth, the daily newspaper publishing industry in the U.S. appears to have attained the highest degree of stability in its history.

2497. Nixon, Raymond B., and Jean Ward. "Trends in Newspaper Ownership and Inter-Media Competition." *JQ* 28 (1961): 3-14. There should be little concern for the disappearance of newspaper competition. "[T]he last 16 years have brought us very close to the realization of...the possibility that competition from the broadcast media would increase to such an extent that fears as to the consequences of local newspaper 'monopoly' would subside. For newspaper ownership in the United States now has stabilized according to a pattern of only one publisher to a community in all except the larger cities, and the public obviously has accepted the situation with equanimity."(3) Daily papers have continued to prosper. The competition between broadcast and print provides the public with a method of checking the other. More media voices compete for attention than ever before. Continued growth of daily newspapers in the face of a great increase in broadcast competition indicates that each medium has distinctive functions to perform. "In those cities where each medium performs well the distinctive functions that it is best suited to perform, the media seem to supplement and complement each other even more than they compete." (12)

2498. Norrell, R. Jefferson. "Reporters and Reformers: The Story of the *Southern Courier*. *SAQ* 79 1 (1980): 93-104. From 1965 to 1968 liberal northern students published a newspaper to cover the civil rights movement in Alabama.

2499. Nowell, William Robert. "The Evolution of Rock Journalism at the *New York Times* and the *Los Angeles Times*, 1956-1978: A Frame Analysis." Ph.D. dissertation, Indiana University, 1986. The "prevailing frames for [reporting and reviewing] rock music shifted from generally negative to generally positive over time."

2500. O'Brien, Michael. "Robert Fleming, Senator McCarthy and the Myth of the Marine Hero." *JQ* 50 (1973): 48-53. Fleming, a reporter for the Milwaukee *Journal*, debunked the myth of McCarthy as a war hero and exposed his unethical personal conduct. Fleming in 1952 uncovered the story of McCarthy's military background and provided a source of information for foes of McCarthy. The public disapproval McCarthy had reached by 1954 was much a result of Fleming's work. "In the final accounting of this change in sentiment the journalistic efforts of Robert Fleming deserve attention for uncovering damaging facts in the life of the nation's most gifted demagogue." (53)

2501. Ogan, Christine, et. al. "The Changing Front Page of the New York *Times*, 1900-1970." *JQ* 52 (1975): 340-44. "[T]he amount of front page news has remained about the same...but there has been an increase in the number of stories judged to be of long-range, in-depth significance." (342)

2502. Osmer, Harold H. *U.S. Religious Journalism and the Korean War*. Washington: University Press of America, 1980. Because of its circulation (50 million) and increased interest in political, social, and economic events, the religious press was "in a position to serve an educative function by disseminating many viewpoints to many people on the United States' policy of containment during the Korean War years." The religious press generally favored strong U.S. measures against communism, although many journals disagreed with John Foster Dulles' idea of aggressively attempting to liberate all countries from communist control.

2503. O'Kelly, Charlotte G. "Black Newspapers and the Black Protest Movement, 1946-1972." *Phylon* 41 (1980): 313-24. The editorials of four large black regional newspapers "consistently treated and supported the issues, organizations, individuals, and activities current in the movement." Over-whelmingly integrationist and non-violent, they publicized activities and problems.

2504. Payne, Darwin. "The Press Corps and the Kennedy Assassination." *JM* 15 (1970). "This monograph, in examining the activities and influences of the news media in Dallas, consists of a chronological summary of how newsmen covered the story, an examination of the problem created by the sheer numbers of newsmen and a determination of how the press may have influenced events." (vi) The press created "a chaotic atmosphere...primarily at the police station. But a judgment that the press disrupted events and opened the way for [Lee Harvey] Oswald's murder is not supported by the evidence." (53)

2505. Peck, Abe. *Uncovering the Sixties: The Life and Times of the Underground Press.* New York: Pantheon, 1985. The underground press not only chronicled but also helped shape the cultural and political rebellion of the 1960s. Various factors -- such as the diversity of goals of the movement, violence, and declining popular support -- led, however, to its rapid decline.

2506. Peterson, Wilbur. "Loss in Country Weekly Newspapers Heavy in 1950s." *JQ* 38 (1961): 15-24. Suspensions of weeklies occurred in 488 towns under 1,000 population in 1950-1959, leaving those towns without local papers. The total of all weeklies dropped 788, with 703 of the decrease in small towns. Only 5 per cent of country weekly towns retain competitive newspapers. The reason for the decline seemed to be a poor economy in small towns, coupled with increasing production costs for papers and the failure of papers to increase their prices for ads and subscriptions to keep pace.

2507. Peterson, Wilbur, and Robert Thorp. "Weeklies' Editorial Effort Less Than 30 Years Ago." *JQ* 30 (1962): 53-56. A study of 215 non-daily Iowa newspapers found only 41 per cent with editorial pages, compared to 63 per cent in a 1930 study. Weeklies under 2,500 circulation had editorial pages in only 27 per cent of the cases. Personal columns were found to be weak substitutes for traditional editorials. This article gives no explanation for the decline.

2508. Pilat, Oliver. *Drew Pearson: An Unauthorized Biography.* New York: Harper's Magazine Press, 1973. Pearson's "Washington Merry-Go-Round" "restored to the capital the pejorative journalism missing since Ann Royal." Pearson uncovered much information critical of individuals, many of whom would have sued had it not been for embarassing details that Pearson's assistant investigators had obtained about their private lives. Despite some of his questionable tactics, he did contribute significantly to journalism, primarily because of his untiring devotion to his work.

2509. Pollard, James E. "Eisenhower and the Press: The Final Phase." *JQ* 38 (1961): 181-

86. President Eisenhower held formal press conferences only a little more than half as often as Truman and only one-third as often as Roosevelt. Although Eisenhower did not especially like to deal with newsmen, his administration closed with an "atmosphere of good feeling with the news media." (186) Television cameras were permitted into press conferences for the first time, and practically unlimited direct quotation was allowed.

2510. Pollard, James E. "The Kennedy Administration and the Press." *JQ* 41 (1964): 3-14. In his relations with the mass media, President Kennedy enjoyed a degree of accessibility and warmth unmatched by a previous administration. Still, criticisms of his news policies reached serious proportions. He used a number of innovations to give reporters better access and to get to know them (luncheons, interviews, etc.). However, journalists thought that Kennedy tried to control the flow of news too much (including in press conferences). Pollard criticizes presidential attempts that placed "the free flow of information...in some danger," when the purpose of the press conference and reporters was to provide accurate information for the public. One solution "is for the news media to stick everlastingly to their function of probing government and those who man it" (14) and to ask probing questions.

2511. Pollard, James E. *The Presidents and the Press: Truman to Johnson*. Washington: Public Affairs Press, 1964. "Because of the tremendous advances in news coverage, particularly through radio and television, the relationship between the executive branch of government...and the news media has taken on added importance since the death of Franklin D. Roosevelt."

2512. Porter, William. E. *Assault on the Media: The Nixon Years*. Ann Arbor: University of Michigan Press, 1976. Nixon waged a deliberate campaign to "intimidate, harass, regulate and damage the news media." As a result of criticism of the press, newspapers now use more conservative material (such as columnists), the media are more willing to correct errors, local stations stood up to networks, local government bodies and officials are more prone to be secretive on meetings and records, and the watchdog role is sometimes viewed suspiciously. All these things help point out the "frailty" of press freedom. Nixon's running battle with the press posed a grave threat to freedom of the press. The relationship between Nixon and the press was one of mutual antagonism. In the long run, freedom of the press was damaged by Nixon.

2513. Powell, Jody. *The Other Side of the Story*. New York: Morrow, 1984. President Jimmy Carter's press secretary criticizes the Washington press for its tactics and techniques.

2514. Pratte, Alf. "Ke Alaka'i: The Leadership Role of the Honolulu *Star-Bulletin* in the Hawaiian Statehood Movement." *AJ* 2 (1985): 65-78. Through "the single-mindedness of the *Star-Bulletin* owners and key editors, and through its status as the major institution disseminating information and opinion and by controlling the...space" (75) for public debate, the newspaper played the key role in Hawaii's attaining statehood.

2515. Prendergast, Curtis, with Geoffrey Colvin and Robert Lubar, eds. *The World of Time Inc.: The Intimate History of a Changing Enterprise, Volume Three, 1960-1980*. New York: Antheneum, 1986. In-house institutional history carries the account of Time Inc. from Henry Luce's last years to the major recent corporate changes, including acquisition of other magazines, broadcasting ventures, paper production, etc. The emphasis is on corporate operations and how Time Inc. publications covered major events.

2516. Pulliam, Russell. *Publisher: Gene Pulliam, Last of the Newspaper Titans.* Ottawa, Ill.: Jameson, 1984. Author tells of his grandfather's crusading career as a personal newspaper owner and editor in Indianapolis and Phoenix.

2517. Rankin, William Rankin. "The Evolution of the Business Management of Selected General Consumer Magazines in the United States from 1900 through 1975." Ph.D. dissertation, New York University, 1979. Examination of five magazines, including *Newsweek.*

2518. Read, William H. *America's Mass Media Merchants.* Baltimore: John Hopkins University Press, 1976. U.S. media have extended their operations far beyond America. Profits, not policy, underline their efforts and content. These "transnational" media include AP, UPI, New York Times News Service, *Time, Reader's Digest,* etc. Since World War II, thye have gained worldwide distribution, sizable financial investments abroad, and major international impact. Their expansion has raised serious questions about U.S. media influence abroad and about other countries' information sovereignty vs. a free flow of information.

2519. Real, Michael Robert. "The National Catholic Reporter: Communications and Change in a Turbulent Era." Ph.D. dissertation, University of Illinois, 1972. The liberal, aggressive *Reporter* "made as well as recorded history during a turbulent period [1964-1971] in American and Catholic life. This dissertation sought to identify the paper's role and to provide a partial history and interpretation of American Catholicism, its press, and especially its liberal movement, during that significant era."

2520. Real, Michael R. "Trends in Structure and Policy in the American Catholic Press." *JQ* 52 (1975): 265-71. The trends have been similar to those of the secular press. "[T]he Cahtolic newspaper press has tended to...[explain] its policy as that of a free press with libertarian roots but...[with] its structure as one of heirarchical economic institutions with authoritarian roots." (271)

2521. Reinhardt, Richard. "Doesn't Everybody Hate the Chronicle?" *C J R* (January/February 1982): 25-32. The San Francisco *Chronicle* began as a sensational newspaper in 1855. Then Michael deYoung "transformed the vituperative little scandal sheet of the 1870s into a member of the trinity of prosperous, family-owned, Republican dailies that dominated California politics for sixty years." In the 20th century, his successors tried first to make it into "the New York Times of the West," then into a newspaper which "would stand on its head while playing the glockenspiele" to gain attention. Since the early 1970s, it has become solid and serious.

2522. Robinson, Michael J., and Margaret A. Sheehan. *Over the Wire and On TV: CBS and UPI in Campaign '80.* New York: Russell Sage Foundation, 1983. This study examines the fairness, completeness, and general nature of CBS's and UPI's 1980 presidential campaign coverage.

2523. Rollins, Peter C. "The Vietnam War: Perceptions Through Literature, Film, and Television." *AQ* 36 (1984): 419-32. Historiographical essay on media treatment of the war.

2524. Rosenberg, Jerry Martin. *Inside the Wall Street Journal.* New York: Macmillan,

1982. History of "America's most influential newspaper" and its parent company (Dow Jones & Company), beginning with their founding by reporters Charles Dow and Edward Jones.

2525. Rosenblum, Mort. *Coups and Earthquakes: Reporting the World for America.* New York: Harper & Row, 1979. This is primarily a contemporary study of foreign correspondence. Before 1945 Europe was considered the center for international news. Since World War II the number of correspondents has declined dramatically, and editors tend to underestimate the public's interest in foreign news.

2526. Rosse, James N. "The Decline of Direct Newspaper Competition." *JC* 30, 2 (1980): 65-71. The newspaper market has been segmented among various media.

2527. Rucker, Bryce. *The First Freedom.* Carbondale. Southern Illinois University Press, 1968. Overwhelming economic concentration transformed the news media into gigantic interconnected conglomerates of news and information gathering, transmitting, and news value judgments. This critical narrative includes a discussion of the economic-industrial structure of American newspapers, news services, broadcasting, magazines, the growth of economic power in the media, chains, corporations, their restraint of trade to eliminate competition, etc.. All these factors present a threat to press freedom and democratic.

2528. Ruetten, Richard T. "Anaconda Journalism: The End of an Era." *JQ* 37 (1960): 3-12, 104. Under the ownership of the Anaconda mining company, eight daily Montana newspapers were characterized by apathy, special interests, favoritism, secretiveness, and mediocrity. After decades of criticism, Anaconda sold them in 1959.

2529. Russonello, John M., and Frank Wolf. "Newspaper Coverage of the 1976 and 1968 Presidential Campaigns." *JQ* 56 (1979): 360-64, 432. Coverage of the 1976 campaign emphasized more substantive news than of 1986. Analysis of New York *Times*, Chicago *Sun-Times* and Chicago *Tribune* revealed that "there was a higher proportion of attention given to campaign issues and to the personal qualities of the candidates than to the campaign understood merely as a dramatic contest." (360) Data emphasize what newspaper coverage was (rather than why it was that way).

2530. Sage, Joseph. *Three to Zero: The Story of the Birth and Death of the World Journal Tribune.* New York: American Newspapers Publishers Association, 1967. History of *WJT's* brief life and death (1967) from the management's point of view. (This book was commissioned by the American Newspaper Publishers Association.) Printers' and other craft unions were to blame for the problems. Unions played each of New York's papers against each other. They attempted to assume management's prerogatives: measures to cut costs, adoption of time-saving devices, etc. As one result, the *WJT* was forced to keep on its payroll 500 employees for whom there was no job. Bert Powers, leader of the union, was ambitious (and reflected his own views more than the rank and file of the union). The ANPA, on the other hand, failed to present a united front against the union. The *WJT* failed becfause the union was reckless in its demands.

2531. Salisbury, Harrison E. *A Journey for Our Times: A Memoir.* New York: Harper & Row, 1983. Observations by the New York *Times* reporter, focusing primarily on international political affairs.

2532. Salisbury, Harrison E. *Without Fear or Favor: An Uncompromising Look at the New York Times*. New York: Times Books, 1980. This favorable account of the *Times*, written by an associate editor, deals with such topics as Adolph Ochs, civil rights in the South in the 1950s, the *Times v. Sullivan* libel case, investigative reporting, the struggle to keep the *Times* independent of the CIA (which wanted to use reporters as agents), *Times'* courage against McCarthy, and the adversarial relationship of the press to government. In defying the federal government on the "Pentagon Papers" (1971), the *Times* became an "independent power with independent rights." It moved from being only a recorder of events to being a participant, the change coming with the Pentagon Papers.

2533. Schoenbrun, David. *America Inside Out*. New York: McGraw-Hill, 1984. Memoirs on domestic and international politics since early the 1930s, written by a broadcast journalist.

2534. Schoenstein, Ralph. *Citizen Paul*. New York: Farrar Strauss Giroux, 1978. Humorous personal recollections of an editor for the New York *Journal-American*.

2535. Schwarzlose, Richard A. "Trends in U.S. Newspapers' Wire Service Resources, 1934-66." *JQ* 43 (1966): 627-38. Only 24 per cent of U.S. dailies receive news from two major press associations, compared to 30 per cent in 1948. Only 16 per cent subscribe to a supplemental service. In a period of declining newspaper competition, such a trend presents a danger of the public not being informed of all sides or given a complete picture. "It can be assumed...that having multiple wire resources indicates a newspaper's awareness of and commitment to its responsibility to its readers and establishes a greater probability of insightful and complete news presentation." (628)

2536. Severin, Werner J. "The Milwaukee *Journal*: Employee-owned Prizewinner." *JQ* 56 (1979): 783-87. In the day of chain newspapers and disappearing family-owned newspapers, the *Journal* is owned by employees. This is a narrative of the plan and process through which employees bought its stock. It provides a favorable treatment of the *Journal* as a good paper in comparison to chain and corporate newspapers, with the implication that they are primarily oriented toward profit and not serving their readers.

2537. Sharp, Sallie Martin. "The Evolution of the Invasion of Privacy Tort and Its Newsworthiness Limitations." Ph.D. dissertation, University of Texas, 1981. Sample cases show that in 1967-1981 the U.S. Supreme Court "held that the First Amendment protects some types of newsworthy speech from invasion of privacy judgments."

2538. Sheed, Wilfrid. *Clare Booth Luce*. New York: Dutton, 1982. Popularized biography of the magazine journalist (managing editor of *Vanity Fair* and originator of the concept for *Life*) who also wrote short stories, satire, and plays. She was a member of Congress, and in the 1950s she was U.S. ambassador to Italy.

2539. Shmanske, Stephen. "News as a Public Good: Cooperative Ownership, Price Commitments, and the Success of the Associated Press." *BHR* 60 (Spring 1986): 55-80. In a competitive, free-market economy, the non-profit AP has succeeded because of its cooperative ownership structure and the inflexible system it uses to determine rates charged to customers and because it is dealing with a commodity (news) which is a "public good."

2540. Sim, John Cameron. "The Daily's Weekly: A Report on the Survivors." *JQ* 56 (1979): 856-61. Whereas most dailies in the mid-1800s also published weeklies, very few do so today. This brief discussion (covering 1876, 1926, and 1976) considers why the 52 remaining weeklies are still publishing, the problems with publishing weekly editions, and suggestions for how new weekly editions might be a benefit to both readers and daily publishers.

2541. Singletary, Michael W. "Newspaper Use of Supplemental Services: 1960-73." *JQ* 52 (1975): 748-51. This study considers data (from 1960, 1970 and 1973) on Copley, NEA, and other services and how many papers use them by paper size.

2542. Smith, C. Calvin. "From 'Separate but Equal' to Desegregation: The Changing Philosophy of L.C. Bates." *AHQ* 42 (1983): 254-70. Bates, publisher of Little Rock's *Arkansas State Press*, favored school desegregation, with his efforts beginning in 1941, but the reaction to desegregation closed down his newspaper in 1959.

2543. Smith, C. Calvin. "L.C. Bates: Newsman and Civil Rights Activist." *NHB* 45 (1982): 99-103. Bates was a strong advocate of civil rights. See previous entry.

2544. Spear, Joseph C. *Presidents and the Press: The Nixon Legacy*. Cambridge, Mass.: MIT Press, 1984. Nixon attempted to manipulate and intimidate the press.

2545. Spragens, William C., with Carole Ann Terwood. *From Spokesman to Press Secretary: White House Media Operations*. Lanham, Md.: University Press of America, 1980. In the 1970s the White House press office became a center of media attention because of the relationships between the presidency and press. The emergence of television as the dominant medium (over print) made the difference as the press office grew in importance from 1960 to 1980. (The accuracy of the historical sources in this book is questionable.)

2546. Stein, Harry H. "The Muckraking Book in America, 1946-1973." *JQ* 52 (1975): 297-303. The authors of 10 muckraking books share many beliefs of the muckraking journalists of the Progressive era.

2547. Stephens, Mitchell, and Naydyne G. Edison. "News Media Coverage of Issues During the Accident at Three-Mile Island." *JQ* 59 (1982): 199-204, 259. How well did the press handle the disaster in 1979? Coverage was neither unbalanced (favoring or opposing one side), alarming, nor negative. "[T]he media...covered these controversial and potentially nightmarish scientific issues and developments with restraint." (259)

2548. Stephens, Y. Jean. "Lucius Morris Beebe, Seeing the Elephant." Ph.D. dissertation, University of Iowa, 1972. The Nevada newspaper owner was a prolific writer and "one of the most widely-read and respected authorities on gourmet dining and railroad history."

2549. Sterling, Christopher H. "Trends in Daily Newspaper and Broadcast Ownership, 1922-70." *JQ* 52 (1975): 247-56, 320. This study examines how much media control has been concentrated in the top 100 markets over the past half century, examining specifically the trends in broadcasting and cross-media (newspaper-broadcast) ownership in those markets. While the number of newspapers decreased, the expansion of broadcasting meant an increase in the total number of outlets and voices. However, the trend is toward increasing concentration. "As long as sufficient channels remain available for expansion of service and diversity of ownership, monopoly within markets should not become a problem....But once the technical or economic limits of existing services have been reached," (256) a problem begins to emerge. "Thus far, the economic marketplace has limited any trend to media monopoly within the largest 100 markets." So far, the "variety of voices and points of view is almost numberless." (320)

2550. Stewart, Walter, and Elma Stewart. *Colorado Newspapers, Editors, Owners, 1935-1977*. Greeley, Colo.: Elmarry, 1978. Lists editors, newspapers, etc.

2551. Strother, T. Ella. "The Black Image in the Chicago *Defender*, 1905-1975." *JH* 4 (1977-1978): 137-41. "The Chicago *Defender* projects a black image that is a collage of individual personalities engaged in a broad range of occupations and activities. Traditionally, blacks have experienced the most success in sports and entertainment, but today they are also making strides in politics, civil rights and education. Anti-social behavior by blacks is still headlined both as an example of inappropriate behavior and as a technique for selling newspapers. However, socially acceptable behavior is reported more frequently throughout more sections of the paper so that the overall image is one of black citizens demonstrating racial pride through their accomplishments and contributions to the betterment of society." (156)

2552. Sullivan, Julie. "Another Voice: The Black Cartoonists." *MHD* 5, 4 (1985): 28-31, 46-48. Brief biographical sketches of several black political cartoonists working for newspapers today.

2553. Swayne, Elizabeth Eames. "The Last Families: A Study of Metropolitan Newspaper Ownership 1950-1967." Ph.D. dissertation, Northwestern University, 1969. "Traditional patterns of family ownership were being seriously challenged by the late 1960s....[G]roup ownership expanded rapidly, especially after 1960....An exodus of single-city metropolitan owners took place....All [but five] attempts to establish new metropolitan newspapers from 1950 through 1967 failed."

2554. Taft, William H. *Encyclopedia of Twentieth-Century Journalists*. New York: Garland, 1986. Brief profiles of 750 journalists, mostly from the post-World War II period.

2555. Talese, Gay. *The Kingdom and the Power*. New York: World, 1969. This "story of the men who influence the institution that influences the world" deals primarily with the dynamics of the New York *Times* itself: there were inter-personal rivalries, but they were dominated by a sense of the greatness and eternal life of the *Times*. Individuals have competed for power in an attempt to determine the nature of the *Times*, but their ambitions and personalities were secondary to the institution itself in determining the direction it took. *Times* staff members (executives, editors, reporters, and publishers) were motivated by a modicum of ambition and by the institution of the *Times*, which like large corporations has a life and continuing daily operation of its own. The struggle for determining the direction and nature the *Times* would take seemed to be among the younger and older staff and the institution itself. Yet, while staff members would fight intensely for the policies they preferred, when the battles were over, they would work together again, a part of the inexorable movement of the paper.

2556. Thomas, Helen. *Dateline: White House*. New York: Macmillan, 1975. This inside view of White House reporting after Vietnam argues that reporters need to be aggressive and vigilant and ask tough questions.

2557. Trayes, Edward John. *"The National Observer*: History and Development." Ph.D. dissertation, University of Iowa, 1967. Analysis of the operations and news content of "America's first serious attempt at a national newspaper," founded in 1960.

2558. Turner, Kathleen J. *Lyndon Johnson's Dual War: Vietnam and the Press*. Chicago: University of Chicago Press, 1985. Media coverage influenced Johnson's Vietnam policy and politics.

2559. Udell, Jon G. *Economic Trends in the Daily Newspaper Business, 1946 to 1970*. Madison, Wis.: American Newspaper Publishers Association, 1970.

2560. Veblen, Eric. *The Manchester Union Leader in New Hampshire Elections*. Hanover, N.J.: University Press of New England, 1975. Publisher William Loeb has considerable influence in statewide races in New Hampshire. The reason is that candidates believe Loeb influences voters, and candidates thus are influenced by Loeb's views. Loeb's paper has 40 per cent of the daily circulation in New Hampshire, and there are few television stations. The paper is also a vigorous advocate of its political views, and its extensive state news coverage gives it widespread readership.

2561. Vincent, Richard C. "The Evolution of Television Criticism in the New York *Times*, 1949-1977." *JQ* 57 (1980): 647-51, 676. "For more than 30 years, the *Times* has served as an organ for some of the most respected critics who write on [television]." (647)

2562. Vivian, John H. "Through with *Thru* at the Chicago *Tribune*: The McCormick Spelling Experiment." *JH* 6 (1980): 84-87, 96. Since 1934 the *Tribune* has tried to simplify spelling.

2563. Wackman, Daniel B., et.al. "Chain Newspaper Autonomy as Reflected in Presidential Campaign Endorsements." *JQ* 52 (1975): 411-20. Chain newspapers during the period of 1960-1972 are more likely to endorse candidates than non-chain papers. However, there seems to be a degree of uniformity in whom the chain newspapers endorse, suggesting that "the insistence of chain spokesman that their endorsement policies are independent from chain direction" may be inaccurate. "At an overt level, in terms of formal structural controls, this may be true, but at an informal level questions should be raised about the degree to which hiring practices, management procedures and peer pressure push chain newspapers toward uniformity of editorial posture." (419-20)

2564. Weaver, Bill L. "The Black Press and the Assault on Professional Baseball's 'Color Line,' October, 1945-April, 1947." *Phylon* 40 (1979): 303-17. In covering the 17-month period during which Jackie Robinson integrated professional baseball, the black press commented on the breakthrough's significance, expressed appreciation to the president of the Brooklyn Dodgers, who signed Robinson, expressed racial hope, pinned on Robinson, analyzed Robinson's difficult situation, and expressed cautious optimism about the outcome of the situation. Black newspapers "played an important part in his successful assault on professional baseball's 'color line.'"

2565. Weaver, David H., and G. Cleveland Wilhoit. "News Media Coverage of U.S. Senators in Four Congresses, 1953-1974." *JM* 67 (1980). Senators, especially Republicans, who occupied important positions in the Senate received fuller national media coverage than less important senators. More critical in determining coverage, however, are the "journalistic values of immediacy, conflict, event-oriented activity and personality-based action." (30)

2566. Webb, Joseph M. "Historical Perspective on the New Journalism." *JH* 1 (1974): 38-42, 60. New Journalism is based on Romanticism, an approach which has been used by journalists for at least two centuries, and is therefore not new.

2567. Wechsler, James A. *The Age of Suspicion*. New York: Don Fine, 1985. Autobiography of a New York *Post* editor who challenged Sen. Joseph McCarthy.

2568. White, William S. *The Making of a Journalist*. Lexington: University Press of Kentucky, 1986. Autobiography of a reporter who covered the New Deal, World War II, and national affairs.

2569. Whitfield, Stephen J. "Dwight Macdonald's *Politics* Magazine." *JH* 3 (1976): 86-88, 96. The magazine was outstanding, and it offered "for the historian an interesting missing link between the old Left and the radicalism of the 1960s." Macdonald was a Marxist. The magazine was never commercially successful, but some of its ideas and contributors played a positive part in the New Left movement of the 1960s.

2570. Whitfield, Stephen J. "From Publick Occurrences to Pseudo-Events: Journalists and Their Critics." *AJH* 72 (1983): 52-81. "American Jews...have found the mass media a hospitable ambience for their...talents and interests." America's political and social systems have placed a special emphasis on openness and information; therefore, "[t]o members of a minority which has long favored an open society and which has come to expect the accessibility of public life, [the role of the press] is unlikely to become less attractive or less problematic." (81)

2571. Williams, Herbert Lee. *The Newspaperman's President: Harry S. Truman*. Chicago: Nelson-Hall, 1984. Truman was forthright with journalists and therefore created controversy.

2572. Williams, Herbert Lee. "Truman and the Press." Ph.D. dissertation, Michigan State University, 1955. See previous entry.

2573. Willis, Gary. *Lead Time: A Journalist's Education*. Garden City, N.Y.: Doubleday, 1983. Memoirs of Willis' work in journalism, beginning with *Esquire* in 1967.

2574. Wilson, Noel Avon. "The Kansas City Call: An Inside View of the Negro Market." Ph.D. dissertation, University of Illinois, 1968. The *Call's* circulation decline beginning in the 1950s suggests that black newspapers, whose "function is to lead a minority group into acceptance by a general society," are in for difficult times.

2575. Windhauser, John W., Will Norton Jr., and Sonny Rhodes. "Editorial Patterns of the Tribune Under Three Editors." *JQ* 60 (1983): 524-28. Under Robert McCormick and his two successors as editor of the Chicago *Tribune*, "significant differences occurred in the editorial patterns of the *Tribune* with each successive change of editor, regardless of the personal philosophy advocated by his predecessor." (527)

2576. Winter, James Patrick. "Differential Media-Public Agenda-Setting Effects for Selected Issues, 1948-1976." Ph.D. dissertation, Syracuse University, 1981. Study of New York *Times* front pages and Gallup surveys "indicated greater agenda-setting effects for unobtrusive issues." Media effects are short-term rather than cumulative.

2577. Winter, Willis Leslie, Jr. "The Metamorphosis of a Newspaper: The San Francisco *Chronicle*, 1935-1965." Ph.D. dissertation, University of Illinois, 1968. A chronicle of the newspaper's change from serious to sensational content, along with reasons for the change.

2578. Wiseman, Diane. "The Underwood Beat." *Westways* 72 (February 1980): 28-32, 84. Agness Underwood, who was a Los Angeles newspaperwoman for 43 years and city editor of the Los Angeles *Herald-Express* from 1947-1964, was "what many believe to be the first woman in the country to be a city editor of a metropolitan daily."

2579. Wolseley, Roland E. *Still in Print: Journey of a Writer, Teacher, Journalist.* Elgin, Ill.: David C. Cook, 1985. Autobiography of the journalism educator who specialized in the history of magazines, religious journaism, and the black press.

2580. Wyatt, Clarence R. "'At the Cannon's Mouth': The American Press and the Vietnam War." *JH* 13 (1986): 104-13. Study of the content of six newspapers shows that "the press was not as independent as popularly conceived....[T]he government and military were able to control the flow of information from its source and the reporter's access to the combat areas, making the press dependent on official sources....Nor was the press as monolithic as [has been suggested]. There was a marked difference in the coverage presented by the papers....There was at least a coincidental connection between a paper's coverage...and its editorial stance." (111)

2581. Zerbinos, Eugenia. "Analysis of the Increase in Weekly Circulation, 1960-1980." *JQ* 59 (1982): 467-71. The 102 per cent increase in circulation can be accounted for best by the fact that there was an increase in free circulation. Free newspapers were located primarily in urban and suburban areas where weeklies are likely to be competing with dailies and other media for advertising revenue. "Free circulation newspapers are also more likely to be part of a chain or group, which is probably one of the most significant findings. Group-owned free circulation newspapers constitute a barrier to entry into the industry. A newspaper group has the benefits of economies of scale that a single, independent firm does not have unless, of course, that firm takes advantage of central printing. Because the chain-owned newspaper can offer an advertiser larger circulation through combination rates, the chain-owned newspaper can make up in advertising revenue what it does not earn in subscription revenue. The fact that only 12.6 per cent of the weeklies had competition from other weekly publications indicates that the barriers to entry into the industry are already very high." (470)

16

Research Guides and
Reference Works

2582. Albaugh, Gordon. "American Presbyterian Periodicals and Newspapers, 1752-1830, With Library Locations." *JPH* 41-42 (September 1963-June 1964). Series of four articles listing reference and research sources.

2583. Altschull, J. Herbert. "The Journalist and Instant History: An Example of the Jackal Syndrome." *JQ* 50 (1973): 389-96. Journalists quickly and superficially analyze contemporary events and create "instant history." Historians later accept the analyses as valid and base their own research and explanations on them.

2584. Atwood, Roy. "New Directions for Journalism Historiography." *JCI* 14, 1 (1978): 3-14. Bibliographical essay on suggestions for how journalism history should be studied. Historians need to be more aware of historical approaches.

2585. Bashin, Bryan Jay. "How TV Stations Are Trashing History." *CJR* (May/June 1985): 51-54. Television stations need to save their film news footage, rather than throwing most of it away or letting it deteriorate, as they now are doing.

2586. Beasley, Maurine, and Richard R. Harlow. "Oral History: Additional Tool for Journalism Historians." *JH* 7 (1980): 38-39. Explains the methods and procedures used in recording oral history.

2587. Blum, Eleanor. *Basic Books in the Mass Media*. Urbana: University of Illinois Press, 1972. Annotated bibliography.

2588. Boyce, D. G. "Public Opinion and Historians." *History, the Journal of the Historical Association* (June 1978): 214-28. Warns historians that the mass media are poor sources for determining public opinion.

2589. Brayer, Herbert O. "Preliminary Guide to Indexed Newspapers in the United States, 1850-1900." *MVHR* 33 (1946): 237-58.

2590. Brown, Warren. *Check List of Negro Newspapers in the United States, 1827-1946.* Jefferson City, Mo.: Lincoln University School of Journalism, 1946.

2591. Campbell, Luce B., comp. *Black Periodicals and Newspapers: Holdings of Seventy-Four Libraries in the State of Virginia.* Hampton, Va.: Hampton Institute, 1973.

2592. Cannon, Carl. *Journalism: A Bibliography.* New York: New York Public Library, 1924. This bibliography contains references to some historical works.

2593. Carey, James W. "The Problem of Journalism History." *JH* 1 (1974): 3-5, 27. The telling of journalism history has been dominated by a "Whig" interpretation. Needed is a "cultural" interpretation which emphasizes the "idea of the report," that is, how the media have shaped people's understanding of reality. (This article has been frequently cited by other historians.)

2594. Casey, Ralph D. "The Scholarship of Frank Luther Mott." *JQ* 42 (1965): 77-81. Tribute written on the occasion of the historian's death. Mott combined an interest in the scholarly and the practical.

2595. *Contributions to Bibliography in Journalism.* Various authors. Lincoln, Neb.: various years. These bibliographies contain references to some historical works.

2596. "A Conversation with Alfred McClung Lee." *JH* 4 (1977): 2-7. Interview with the sociologist-historian.

2597. "A Conversation with Edwin Emery." *JH* 7 (1980): 20-23. Interview with the senior author of *The Press and America.*

2598. Covert, Catherine L. "Journalism History and Women's Experience: A Problem in Conceptual Change." *JH* 8 (1981): 2-6. The writing of journalism history has had certain "value assumptions" because it "has been traditionally written from the male perspective." It could give a truer picture of the past if it incorporated "some new organizing values suggested by the experience of women." (2)

2599. Covert, Cathy. "Some Thoughts on Research." *JH* 1 (1974): 32-33. Journalism historians should not be compared unfavorably to trained historians but should be thought of primarily as professional journalists who now write history.

2600. Dahl, Folke. "On Quoting Newspapers: A Problem and a Solution." *JQ* 25 (1948): 331-38. When using quotes from newspapers, historians must examine the original publication and be meticulous in ascertaining the correctness of the quoted material.

2601. Dahl, Hans Frederick. "The Art of Writing Broadcast History." *Gazette* 24 (1978): 130-37. Overview of the contemporary state of the international study of broadcast history. Broadcast historians must do their research differently from press historians, since "the administrative routine of a broadcasting institution, being far more bureaucratic on all levels than the newspaper, places at the disposal of the historian a mass of data far greater than that of any other mass medium." On the other hand, little background written material remains for news broadcasts -- "the aspect of broadcasting most similar to the newspapers."

2602. Danky, James P., ed. *Index to Wisconsin Native American Periodicals, 1897-1981*. Westport, Conn.: Greenwood, 1983. Contains more than 40,000 entries on items in thirty-one publications. (Microfiche)

2603. Danky, James P., ed. *Native American Periodicals and Newspapers, 1828-1982: Bibliography, Publishing Record, and Holdings*. Westport, Conn.: Greenwood, 1984. Contains information on 1,164 publications by and about American Indians.

2604. Dennis, Everett E., and Claude-Jean Bertrand. "Seldes at 90: They Don't Give Pulitzers for That Kind of Criticism." *JH* 7 (1980): 81-86, 120. Seldes was a liberal, trenchant critic of the conservative press. He was a valuable moral crusader, but he was criticized unfairly for being anti-American.

2605. Dunson, Alvis A. "Checklist of German Newspapers in Missouri up to 1940." Ph.D. dissertation, Ohio State University, 1954.

2606. Eason, David L. "The New Social History of the Newspaper." *CR* 11 (January 1984): 141-51. Reviews Schiller's and Schudson's histories and argues that it is impossible to understand "the newspaper's role in the creation and maintenance of social order without giving sustained attention to the social, economic and cultural circumstances under which the newspaper grew up." Newspapers created symbols which incorporated audiences into a common culture.

2607. Emery, Michael. "The Writing of American Journalism History." *JH* 10 (1983): 38-43. Historiographical essay on "the state of the art," general survey histories, "the debate over historical method," and "the construction of reality" (the application of sociology to journalism history).

2608. Endres, Kitty. "Oral History: Preserving a Multimedia Past." *Matrix* 65 (Spring 1980): 8-10. Brief discussion of oral history methods and techniques.

2609. Farrar, Ronald T. "Journalism history must not be dehumanized." *JE* 27, 1 (1972): 3-5.

2610. Ford, Edwin H. *History of Journalism in the United States, A Bibliography of Books and Annotated Articles*. Minneapolis: University of Minnesota, 1938.

2611. Gavit, Joseph, comp. *American Newspaper Reprints*. (Reprinted from the *Bulletin of the New York Public Library*.) New York: New York Public Library, 1931. Lists reproductions of early or historic American newspapers, including such items as facsimile issues and pages appearing as illustrations in books.

2612. Graham, Robert X. *A Bibliography in the History and Backgrounds of Journalism*. Pittsburgh: University of Pittsburgh, 1940.

2613. Gregory, Winifred, ed. *American Newspapers 1821-1936, A Union List of Files Available in the United States and Canada*. New York: H.W. Wilson, 1937. Lists newspapers geographically.

2614. Gutierrez, Felix, and Jorge Reina Schement. "Chicanos and the Media: A Bibliography of Select Materials." *JH* 4 (1977): 52-55. This bibliography includes approximately 125 works, although most of them are not historical.

2615. Hart, Horace. *A Bibliography of the History of Printing in the Library of Congress*. Springwater: Horace Hart, 1987.

2616. Henry, Susan J. "Private Lives: An Added Dimension for Understanding Journalism History." *JH* 6 (1979): 98-102. Recent studies of women in journalism, with their special emphasis on the women's non-journalism lives, suggest that historians generally should examine journalists' personal circumstances in addition to their journalistic careers.

2617. Hill, George M. *Black Media in America: A Resource Guide*. Boston: G.K. Hall, 1984. Bibliography of books, dissertations, theses, and articles.

2618. *Historical Bibliography of the Press*, Bulletin of the International Committee of Historical Sciences, Vol. 6, part 1, no. 2. Paris: Les Presses Universitaires de France, 1935. A bibliography of bibliographies of works on journalism from various nations, including the United States.

2619. Homsher, Lola. *Guide to Wyoming Newspapers 1867-1967*. Cheyenne: Wyoming State Library, 1971. Reference guide.

2620. Housman, Robert T. "Journalism Research in Relation to Regional History." *JQ* 13 (1936): 402-06. Suggests approaches for using the newspaper as a source in historical research.

2621. Kahan, Robert S. "Historians: Our Critics, Craft and Mental Health." *JH* 6 (1979): 70-72. Journalism historians should be comfortable with what they are and not be unduly alarmed by critics.

2622. Kobre, Sidney. "The Sociological Approach in Research in Newspaper History." *JQ* 22 (1945): 12-22. Emphasis should be on the political, economic, geographical, technological, cultural, and social factors that affected journalism history, rather than just on facts and the chronology of the internal workings of the press. Historians should not treat the press as an isolated institution but should relate it to society. The sociological approach studies the newspaper as a changing, evolving social institution.

2623. Kolar, Carol Koehmstedt. *Union List of North Dakota Newspapers 1867-1967*. Bismarck: North Dakota Institute for Regional Studies, 1976.

2624. Littlefield, Daniel F. Jr., and James W. Parins, eds. *American Indian and Alaska Native Newspapers and Periodicals 1971-1985*. Westport, Conn.: Greenwood, 1986. Reference guide.

2625. Martin, L. John, and Harold L. Nelson. "The Historical Standard in Analyzing Press Performance." *JQ* 33 (1956): 456-66. How to evaluate newspaper reporting of an event in terms of reporting accuracy, selection of facts, and judgment.

2626. Marzolf, Marion. "American Studies -- Ideas for Media Historians." *JH* 5 (1978): cover, 13-16. "The task before communications historians is to study the content of the media in the past, the journalist or media professionals, and the fit between these and the cultural context and society in which they existed." (15)

2627. McKerns, Joseph P. "The Limits of Progressive Journalism History." *JH* 4 (1977): 88-92. A Progressive interpretation -- "good" vs. "evil," liberalism vs. conservatism, etc.-- has dominated the writing of journalism history, as shown by a study of a number of general survey histories. Historians need to discard the Progressive interpretation and "turn to a study of the dominant ideas in society, and to the journalistic purveyors and conveyors of those ideas, within the context of the times." (91) (This article has been frequently cited by other historians.)

2628. McKerns, Joseph P. "Media Ethics: A Bibliographical Essay." *JH* 5 (1978): 50-3, 68. Annotated bibliography.

2629. Mercer, Paul, comp. *Bibliographies and Lists of New York State Newspapers: An Annotated Guide*. Albany: New York State Library, 1981.

2630. Mott, Frank Luther. "Evidences of Reliability in Newspapers and Periodicals in Historical Studies." *JQ* 21 (1944): 304-10. Lists characteristics of newspapers which the historian should consider as indications of how reliable individual papers may be as historical sources.

2631. Nevins, Allan. "American Journalism and Its Historical Treatment." *JQ* 36 (1959): 411-22. Journalism history should be studied in terms of its "relation to the working of democratic government." (p.411) Emphasis should be on news coverage. Historical study has been uncritical and even dishonest.

2632. *Newspapers and Periodicals By and About Black People: Southeastern Library Holdings*. Boston: G.K. Hall, 1978. Checklist that is part of the African American Materials Project.

2633. Pallay, Richard W. *Information Sources in Advertising History*. Westport, Conn.: Greenwood, 1979. Annotated bibliography which includes a number of references to journalism.

2634. Price, Warren C., and Calder Pickett. *An Annotated Journalism Bibliography 1958-1968*. Minneapolis: University of Minnesota Press, 1970. This bibliography contains references to some historical works.

2635. Price, Warren C. *The Literature of Journalism: An Annotated Bibliography*. Minneapolis: University of Minnesota Press, 1959. This bibliography contains references to some historical works.

2636. Pride, Armistead S. "The Black Press to 1968: A Bibliography." *JH* 4 (1977): 148-53. Bibliographical citations to works on various aspects of black journalism, including a number on history.

2637. "'Putting the World at Peril': A Conversation with James W. Carey." *JH* 12 (1985): 38-53. Interview with the originator of a type of "cultural" interpretation of journalism history that emphasizes "the idea of the report."

2638. Rapport, Leonard. "Fakes and Facsimiles: Problems of Identification." *AA* 42 (January 1979): 13-58. How to recognize real and false historical documents, including reproductions of newspapers.

2639. Salmon, Lucy Maynard. *The Newspaper and the Historian.* New York: Oxford University Press, 1923. Offers guidelines that historians should apply when considering the validity and reliability of newspapers as sources. Considers newspapers as invaluable sources for historical research, though of dubious accuracy.

2640. Schmuhl, Robert. "American Communications and American Studies." *CSMC* 2, 2 (June 1985): 183-94. Scholars from American Studies are showing an increasing interest in mass communication.

2641. Schwarzlose, Richard A. "A Conversation with Fredrick S. Siebert." *JH* 5 (1978): 106-09, 123. Interview with the legal scholar and historian.

2642. Schwarzlose, Richard A. "A Plea from Amid the Letter Boxes." *JH* 1 (1974): 50-51. The collected letters and papers of journalists and journalism organizations are meager.

2643. Schwarzlose, Richard A. *Newspapers: A Reference Guide.* Westport, Conn.: Greenwood Press, 1987. Contains bibliographies of books on journalism history, accompanied by several useful bibliographical essays.

2644. "Seeking New Paths in Research." *JH* 2 (1975). This special issue of *Journalism History* contains five essays "dealing with various aspects of the state of research in the field." Three of them struggle with proposals for applying James Carey's "Cultural" interpretation (see entry above) to journalism history: Richard Schwarzlose, "First Things First: A Proposal," 34-37; John E. Erickson, "One Approach to the Cultural History of Reporting," 40-42; and Marion Marzolf, "Operationalizing Carey -- An Approach to the Cultural History of Journalism," 42-43. The other two essays are Garth S. Jowett, "Toward a History of Communication," 34-37; and David H. Weaver, "Frank Luther Mott and the Future of Journalism History," 44-47.

2645. Singerman, Robert. "The American Jewish Press, 1823-1983; A Bibliographic Survey of Research and Study." *AJH* 73 (1986): 422-44. Bibliographical essay calls for more study of the Jewish press in the U.S.

2646. Sloan, Wm. David. "Journalism historians, lost in the past, need direction." *JE* 42 (1987): 4-7, 48. Using Developmental and Progressive interpretations, journalism historians have failed to understand history and have presented superficial explanations.

2647. Snorgrass, J. William, and Gloria T. Woody, eds. *Blacks and Media: A Selected, Annotated Bibliography.* Tallahassee: Florida A&M University Press, 1985. Contains 743 entries, including many on history.

2648. Startt, James D., and Wm. David Sloan. *Historical Methods in Mass Communication.* Hillsdale, N.J.: Lawrence Erlbaum, 1989. The only book-length treatment of the techniques of researching and writing journalism history.

2649. Stempel III, Guido H., and Bruce H. Westley, eds. *Research Methods in Mass Communication.* Englewood Cliffs, N.J.: Prentice-Hall, 1981. Includes two chapters on historical research: David Paul Nord and Harold L. Nelson, "The Logic of Historical Research," Chapter 15, pp. 278-304; and Mary Ann Yodelis Smith, "The Method of History," Chapter 16, pp. 305-19.

2650. Stevens, John D., and Hazel Dicken Garcia. *Communication History.* Beverly Hills, Calif.: Sage, 1980. Series of essays discusses such topics as the inadequacy of traditional approaches to history, the need for new approaches and for appropriate research methods, variables involved in communication history, etc.

2651. Stevens, John D., and Donald L. Shaw. "Research Needs in Communications History: A Survey of Teachers." *JQ* 45 (1968): 547-49. Emphasis should be more on the twentieth century and on economics, labor, and technology, and less on history of newspapers and editors.

2652. Taft, William. "Let's Probe Your State's Newspaper History." *JE* 19: 4 (1964): 115-18.

2653. Taft, William H. *Newspapers as Tools for Historians.* Columbia, Mo.: Lucas Brothers, 1970. Examines various aspects of the newspaper's worth in historical research. Although newspapers are valuable, the historian needs to use them with caution.

2654. Vacha, John E. "The Student Newspaper as a Historical Source." *SE* 43 (January 1979): 35-36. History teachers should use student newspapers to bridge "the gap between the insulation of the classroom and the actual experience of history in its vibrant, raw form."

2655. Ward, Jean. "Interdisciplinary Research and Journalism Historians." *JH* 5 (1978): cover, 17-19. "Our greatest need at the moment is for histories that take mass communication as their subject and include journalism as a part of that larger topic." (17) Interdisciplinary ideas from American Studies and new methods of historians and social scientists "can play a useful part in the development of the field." (19)

2656. Weaver, David H. "Frank Luther Mott and the Future of Journalism History." *JH* 2 (1975): 44-47. Mott's work, like that of most other journalism historians, was primarily descriptive and chronological. Historians need to provide more explanation and to concentrate more on general laws of human behavior.

2657. Wolseley, Roland E. *The Journalist's Bookshelf: An Annotated and Selected Bibliography of United States Print Journalism,* 7th ed. Indianapolis: R.J. Berg: 1986. This bibliography contains references to a number of biographies and historical works.

Index

Abolition. See "Anti-slavery."

Abuse. See "Vilification."

Abortion, 826, 827, 1166, 1216.

Academic freedom, 1848.

Access to information, 669.

Access to the media, 2307.

Acculturation, 1526.

Acsoli, Max, 2410.

Adams, Abijah, 632.

Adams, Henry, 902.

Adams, President John, 532, 600, 731, 750.

Adams, Sam, 370, 393, 412, 451.

Adams, Samuel Hopkins, 1954, 1957.

Adams, Thomas, 632.

Ade, George, 1361.

Advertising, 99, 259, 306, 454, 465, 826, 827, 992, 1166, 1177, 1181, 1235, 1543, 1630, 1693, 1791, 1805, 1815, 1824, 1869, 1871, 1990, 2004, 2011, 2104, 2123, 2133, 2220, 2227, 2278, 2326, 2339, 2344, 2633.

Advertising Age, 2172.

Afro-American. See "Black."

Agenda-setting, 1296, 2576.

Agrarianism, 22, 840, 1622, 2008, 2106, 2116.

Agriculture, 1427, 1440, 1508, 1595, 1597, 1611, 1743, 2196, 2228, 2313.

Air mail, 2136.

Alabama, 1449, 1450, 1783, 2397, 2498.

Alaska, 133, 1176, 1573, 2624.

Alien and Sedition Acts. See "Sedition Act of 1798."

Alexander, James, 645, 655, 695.

Allen, Robert S., 2358.

Alternative press, 114.

Alton, Ill., 67.

A.M.E. Christian Recorder, 1252.

Amarac News, 2063.

American Bible Society, 580.

American Council or Education for Journalism, 2398.

American Forces Network, 2229, 2231.

American Indian press, 52, 133, 162, 1398, 1448, 1462, 1463, 1526, 1565, 1574, 1576, 1605, 2602, 2603, 2624.

American Indians and the press, 42, 346, 1411, 1506, 1521, 1575, 1583, 1620, 1626, 1633, 1644, 1645.

American Israelite, 1253.

American Magazine, 2011.

American Mercury magazine, 2359.

American Mercury newspaper, 274.

American Newspaper, The, 1979, 1981.

American Newspaper Guild, 1813, 2030, 2053, 2102, 2471.

American Newspaper Publishers Association, 1739, 1758.

American Review, 520.

American Society of Journalism School Administrators, 1878.

American Society of Newspaper Editors (ASNE), 2176, 2427.

American Sporting Chronicle, 790.

American studies, 2626, 2640, 2655.

American Tract Society, 580.

American Weekly, 1347.

Ames, Mary Clemmer, 1149.

Anaconda mining company, 2528.

Anarchism, 29, 1973.

Anchors, television, 2193, 2271, 2281.

Anderson, Jack, 2358, 2360, 2393.

Anglo-African Magazine, 899.

Ann Arbor, Mich., 1441, 1489.

Annenberg, Moses, 1719, 2422.

Annenberg, Walter, 1719, 2422.

Anthologies of journalistic writing, 53, 164, 182, 217, 218, 372, 791, 907, 917, 939, 965, 972, 973, 987, 991, 1003, 1122, 1134, 1187, 1189, 1190, 1263, 1365, 1414, 1480, 1621, 1633, 1656, 1700, 1780, 1938, 2013, 2025, 2037, 2044, 2056, 2132, 2345, 2421, 2459.

Antimasonry, 474.

Anti-slavery, 658, 888, 892, 897, 898, 910, 915, 916, 919, 925, 926, 928, 934, 935, 940, 944, 947-949, 951, 952, 962, 966, 968, 970, 991, 1001, 1004, 1121, 1135, 1609.

Antitrust, 1855, 2227, 2375.

Apache Chronicle, 1448.

Apache Indians, 1633.

Arabic press, 62, 2.

Architecture, 1244.

Arena magazine, 1277, 1278.

Argus of Western America, 573.

Arizona, 931, 1388, 1536, 1537, 1552, 1842.

Arizona *Gazette*, 1501.

Arkansas, 1390, 2160.

Armed forces, U.S., 2063, 2064.

Army-McCarthy Hearings, 2331.

Arthur, Chester A., 1185.

Assimilation, 142, 153, 833, 866, 899, 1526, 1837.

Associated Negro Press, 1781.

Associated Press, 85, 198, 851, 852, 1855, 2046, 2151, 2375, 2539.

Association for Education in Journalism and Mass

About the Compiler

WM. DAVID SLOAN is Associate Professor of Journalism at the University of Alabama, Tuscaloosa. He is the editor of *Pulitzer Prize Editorials: America's Best Editorial Writing, 1917-1979* (1980), *The Best of Pulitzer Prize News Writing* (1986), and the history journal *American Journalism* and co-author of *Historical Methods in Mass Communication* (1989).